LOVE FRAUD

How marriage to a sociopath fulfilled my spiritual plan

Donna Andersen

Anderly Publishing

Logo design by Beth Thomson
Cover design by Sheryl Ginsburg
Photography by Bill Horin

Anderly Publishing
3121-D Fire Road, #304
Egg Harbor Township, NJ 08234 USA
www.anderlypublishing.com

Library of Congress Control Number: 2010908311
ISBN: 978-0-9827057-0-4

First hardcover edition August 2010

LOVE FRAUD

To my wonderful husband, Terry Kelly,
without whom this book would not exist.

Introduction

This story is true. Every incident that I relate is as I experienced it. The story, however, includes claims and promises made by my ex-husband, James Alwyn Montgomery, originally from Sydney, Australia. Although I accurately recount what he said to me, his statements may not be true.

That's because, in my opinion, James Alwyn Montgomery is a pathological liar. A sociopath.

Most people do not know what the word "sociopath" means—hardened criminal? Deranged serial killer? These are cultural misconceptions, more Hollywood fiction than fact. In reality, sociopaths are far more likely to cheat on romantic partners, assault their spouses, lie to family members, abuse drugs and alcohol, steal from employers, swindle investors and defraud credit card companies than they are to commit murder.

According to experts, sociopaths make up 1 percent to 4 percent of the population. This is a huge number—of the 309 million people living in the United States, 3 million to 12 million are sociopaths. In a world population of more than 6.8 billion, there may be 68 million to 272 million sociopaths.

Some sociopaths are in jail, but most are not—they live freely among us, and not just in "bad" neighborhoods. Sociopaths roam all communities and all segments of society. They are male, female, rich, poor, all ages, all races, all religions, all education levels, all demographic groups. Their deceptive and manipulative behavior causes confusion and chaos wherever they go. Although the actions of sociopaths are immoral if not criminal, many are never arrested for anything. They may hold long-term careers in every imaginable field—business, entertainment, government, medicine, law enforcement, the military and even the clergy. They occupy many corner offices, although employees would probably describe them not as inspired leaders, but as ruthless, unethical bullies.

Anyone who becomes involved with a sociopath is likely to experience emotional, psychological, physical or financial devastation—or all of the above. In this book, I tell what happened to me and other women that James Montgomery snagged—he was a prolific con artist. Some do not want to be named. Any name in this book followed by an asterisk [*] when it is first mentioned is a pseudonym.

But this is not only our story. The twisted, parasitic behavior James Montgomery exhibited, I have learned, is typical of a sociopath. Because of my website, Lovefraud.com, thousands of other victims of sociopaths have contacted me. Their stories sound a lot like mine.

Many victims are intelligent, caring and upstanding citizens, yet they were unwittingly sucked into devastating dramas. The statement I hear most often is, "I never knew such evil existed." It does, and this book describes what the evil looks like.

The next thing I hear from Lovefraud readers is a question, "Why did this happen to me?"

I asked that question—emphatically, vehemently. I am an honest, forthright and competent person. I didn't deserve to have my hopes and dreams crushed. I didn't deserve to be humiliated. Yet it happened.

Seeking to find out why James Montgomery crashed through my life, I embarked on a journey that took me not only deep within myself, but into my relationship with God and the universe. So, intertwined with this story of betrayal is a parallel story of personal and spiritual growth.

My run-in with James Montgomery, it turned out, had a larger, divine purpose. The experience, in all its affliction, was lifetimes in the making and fulfilled my own spiritual plan.

I didn't know this as it was happening. I didn't know it as I poured my anguish and confusion into my journal, trying to fathom why, in my search for love and happiness, my life was torn to shreds. I prayed for answers and guidance from my higher self, God, anyone who was listening. Sometimes I vociferously demanded answers.

I got them—although they weren't what I expected.

Chapter 1

Keeping the candles lit was difficult. The wind on the deserted beach was more than a breeze, snuffing out the four small flames even though they were sheltered deep inside glass luminaries. Thankfully, the wind wasn't strong enough to whip up the sand, so our summer solstice ceremony could continue.

Five women sat in a circle around the sometimes-burning candles. It was nighttime, but it wasn't truly dark. The moon created a sparkling silver path on the ocean and a gentle glow on land. Much brighter light was generated by Atlantic City's casinos. Although they were more than a mile down the Boardwalk, the towering beachfront structures were totally illuminated by many well-placed floodlights. And the lights never went out in Atlantic City, New Jersey.

Usually, our small group met in the suburban home of one of our members. By June 20, 1996, the night of our solstice ceremony, I had been attending the twice-a-month gatherings for more than a year. What did we do? Good question. We recreated Native American traditions, with altars to honor spirits of the North, South, East and West. We sculpted clay—our version of art therapy. One session was devoted to dealing with anger. Another to soul recognition.

My participation in the circle could be classified under the general heading of New Age Experiences. I was a dilettante, a dabbler in the realm of positive thinking-universal energy-spiritual guidance. Did I have this stuff figured out? No. But every once in awhile it seemed to offer a reasonable explanation for the issues in my life. And it usually made me feel better.

What was the problem? I was alone.

I was a poster girl for the dilemma of successful working women of the '90s. I was professional, talented, organized, hardworking and thorough. I had a closet full of suits, a Rolodex full of contacts and even pitched for my own softball team. Still, I did not consider myself complete.

The question of the decade was, "Sure you can run a business. But can you get a date?"

I came to Atlantic City in June 1978, shortly after graduating summa cum laude from Syracuse University. My degree was in magazine journalism, and I landed a job as the first editor of Atlantic City Magazine.

The job wasn't as big as it sounded. Atlantic City's first casino, Resorts International, had opened a month earlier. Atlantic City Magazine had published only two issues—neither of them pillars of journalism. Along with being the first editor, I was the first employee. The publisher didn't even get an office until I was hired.

Still, excitement charged the salt air as people stood in line to play the slot machines. No one expected gambling to be such a hit in Atlantic City, and when it was, the bandwagon quickly became overloaded. Before long, 42 different companies announced plans to build casinos. Most of the plans evaporated, but the forward momentum kept Atlantic City, population a mere 40,000, constantly in the news.

For a young, idealistic journalist, it was a great opportunity. Atlantic City Magazine was originally a quarterly menu guide; I was given the responsibility of turning it into a monthly city magazine. I attended press conferences and opening nights. I wrote articles about everything from casino construction to juvenile delinquents to the best junk food on the Boardwalk. The publication grew, the staff grew, and I worked. Worked and worked. By June 1982, the magazine was making its mark, and I was thoroughly burned out.

The magazine and I parted company. After a few months of collecting unemployment, I began receiving calls for freelance writing. One project led to another, and by 1983, at the age of 26, I was in business for myself.

My business grew, although I never hired employees and never rented an office. Still, I produced newsletters for casinos like Caesars and Showboat. As a subcontractor to a marketing company, I wrote numerous brochures for AT&T, putting highly technical information into plain features-and-benefits English. By 1996 I was well-established and well-paid.

I was also resentful.

Why? Essentially I worked alone, and I hated how my business ran my life.

There was a difference between being a freelancer and being a businesswoman. A freelancer was a hired gun, brought in to fill a need. A freelancer was responsible to the company that retained her—in my field, usually an advertising agency or marketing firm. She completed the assignment, hopefully she got paid, and she went on her way.

A businesswoman was responsible to the ultimate customer. My customers didn't hire me to write for them; they hired me to produce a brochure or newsletter. I managed the project, kept the customer on schedule, and retained the subcontractors, such as graphic designers and printers. If there was a screw-up, it cost me money.

One of the reasons why I was able to start from nothing and hang in until my business got established was low overhead. Long before telecommuting became a buzzword, I worked from home. I bought my first computer in 1983, my first fax machine when they cost $1,100, and answered the phone professionally by identifying myself, "Donna Andersen."

I tried to stick to a Monday through Friday, nine-to-five schedule. Not because I needed the discipline to get the work done. No—the work was always there, beckoning for my attention. I needed the schedule so I knew when to stop.

To plan vacations, I got out my date book and turned to the pages with the miniature calendars, so I could see all 12 months of the year at once. I drew lines through the dates when my jobs would be in production—a different color for each project. I looked for gaps that were big enough for me to get away. Then I tried to think of something to do.

I blamed my never-ending work for the sorry state of my social life. I was so busy being responsible for Atlantic City Magazine that I missed my early twenties. I was so scared about my new business that I missed my late twenties. Each year of my thirties, I asked the same questions: Will someone send me flowers on Valentine's Day? Will someone take me out for my birthday? Will I have a date for New Year's Eve? At the end of each year, the answer was usually no.

What was wrong? I couldn't figure it out. I was reasonably attractive—not model material, but pretty in a girl-next-door fashion. I was cheerful, considerate and not prone to temper tantrums. I could watch sports on TV without asking stupid questions. I was smart—perhaps that's what scared the guys away.

So I read all the books: *What Every Woman Should Know About Men,* by Dr. Joyce Brothers. *Secrets About Men Every Woman Should Know,* by Barbara DeAngelis, Ph.D. *How to Love a Nice Guy,* by Judy Kuriansky, Ph.D. *Men Are from Mars, Women Are from Venus,* by John Gray, Ph.D. Still, my relationships, with a couple of rare exceptions, never lasted more than two months.

Along the way, a friend introduced me to metaphysical philosophies. The first time I had my palm read—and not by a Boardwalk fortuneteller—I was blown away by the psychic's accuracy and insights. So I looked for answers— browsing the New Age section of bookstores, attending metaphysical health expos, listening to positive-thinking tapes, visiting channelers. This winding path of exploration led me to a truly amazing energy healer, and through her, I connected with the women on the beach.

As was our custom, we began our gathering by chanting the traditional "om." We started simultaneously, but because everyone sustained the sound for different lengths of time, our voices soon blended into continuous tone, with fluctuations but no breaks. This went on for several minutes, and then seemingly of its own accord, the chant ended.

One of the women brought along her new Native American drum, which she beat to release the spirit of her aging cat. The rest of us banged sticks together and shook rattles as we stomped around our little circle in the sand. The objective was to get the energy flowing, and somehow, it always worked.

At that point, the plan was for each of us to go off separately and do whatever we were inspired to do. Exercises like this were always difficult for me, because I was never sure if I were truly receiving spiritual guidance, or simply talking to myself. But I wandered toward the waves breaking on the beach. I waded into the chilly water—it was only June, and in New Jersey, the Atlantic Ocean doesn't warm up until the end of July. I was up to my ankles, then my knees. The voice in my head said, "Jump in! Just jump in!"

Well, even if the spirits were urging me to jump in, I didn't want to—it was nighttime, and the ocean was cold. But I scooped the water up with my hands, and poured it over my head. Another handful, and another. I splashed my arms and my face. Before long, I was soaked.

The exercise turned out to be quite the premonition.

Chapter 2

July 19, 1996 was a hot, dry summer night in Atlantic City—thank goodness. It rained heavily all morning and part of the afternoon, threatening to put a serious damper, literally, on my 40th birthday party.

I believed all birthdays should be celebrated extensively. The big 4-0 was a milestone, of course, and I certainly intended to mark the occasion. I invited my family and all my friends, even people I hadn't seen in years, to help celebrate. I was expecting about 50 guests.

No way could that many people fit in my classic, seashore-style house. I loved the house, bought it on my own and put a lot of time and money into fixing it up, but it was small. Built in 1912, it was two stories tall and only 15 feet wide, so the rooms were narrow. The house had 35 windows and no air conditioning. I counted on seating people on the wraparound porch, with its classic columns, and thanked my lucky stars that the rain stopped.

I liked to say that I lived near the ocean and by the bay, which was true. My house was on Absecon Island, New Jersey—home to Atlantic City, Ventnor, Margate and Longport. The houses across from me were all waterfront. The beach—the Atlantic Ocean—was three blocks down the street.

As guests arrived, my friends from my softball team, the Donna Andersen Copywriting "Erasers," staked out the front porch, sitting on the wicker sofa and chairs, programs in hand. Yes, programs. I had several distinct circles of friends—call them my softball friends, my Philadelphia Folk Festival friends, my business friends—plus my family. I didn't want the party to break up into separate groups of people who already knew each other, which could easily happen. So to encourage everyone to get acquainted, I made a little program called *Who's Who at Donna's Party.* Inside the booklet was a brief introduction to everyone who would be there.

The Erasers anointed themselves the welcoming committee. Every time a new guest walked up the porch steps, the team members opened up their booklets and asked, "Who are you?" The new arrivals, of course, were mystified, until they got their own programs and began asking the question in return.

Before long, the party was well off the ground. Music was playing on the stereo, with speakers at both ends of the house. People were everywhere. The dining room table was heaped with food, so that was a popular spot. Everyone passed through the kitchen on the way to the tiny back deck, which was where the bar was set up. Not surprisingly, my relatives parked themselves on the back deck.

I almost had a date for the night. For a few weeks I had been corresponding with a fascinating man that I met through the America Online personal ads. But a blind date at my own 40th birthday party was a bit daunting, even for a personal ads professional like me.

My first experience with personal ads came back in 1980, when I was editor of Atlantic City Magazine. Our advertising director, seeking an additional sales opportunity, wanted to start a classifieds section. Well, how do you start a classifieds section in a new magazine? Printing two or three tiny ads on a full page would look stupid. So, to fill the page, the three of us on the editorial staff made up personals.

In the November/December 1980 issue, I wrote three personal ads, making them sound like they were placed by three different women. They were all accurate, but reflected different aspects of my personality and interests:

> Good-looking white female (blonde, bottomless blue eyes), age 24, who can cook terrific spaghetti and run long distances, seeks young executive male (age 24-32), with class and talent for sincere company. Respond to Atlantic City Magazine, Box 114.

> Sensitive young female, terrific listener, looking for understanding white male. Emotional satisfaction and professional respect prerequisite to sex. Respond to Atlantic City Magazine, Box 108.

> I'm new in town, and looking for friends. Not necessarily romantic relationship. I'm female, interested in good conversation, athletics, good times. Respond to Atlantic City Magazine, Box 110.

Much to my surprise, letters started arriving at Atlantic City Magazine, addressed to Boxes 114, 108 and 110. This was long before ubiquitous Internet dating sites. These men actually had to write a letter on paper, address an envelope, lick a stamp and put it in the mail. Still, within a few months, 27 men responded to my fictitious ads.

What was I to do with all these letters? The obvious—write a story. In fact, we planned a themed issue of the magazine—"Single in Atlantic City." I began contacting the men as research for my story, with the ulterior motive that perhaps something magical would happen.

It didn't, but I did have fun. I met a business consultant, a construction worker, a professional gambler, a tire salesman and a recent college graduate. I got adept at picking out the man I was supposed to meet from the crowd around a bar. And I found that after some initial discomfort and floundering, there was always something to talk about.

I also discovered a strange truth about meeting someone via personal ads: The fact that both parties took a chance and put themselves on the line immediately stripped away any pretense. I sometimes had deeper and more revealing conversations with these men, who were strangers, than I could with people I saw every day.

The issue came out in March 1981. On the cover was a beautiful blond model, perfectly made-up and coifed, wearing a formal lace dress. She sat at a dinner table set for one, holding a crystal glass of red wine in her manicured hand, toasting to the camera. The table was graced with fresh flowers and a flickering candle. But on the exquisite Lenox plate in front of her was a TV dinner, still in its aluminum foil tray. The photo credit listed meatloaf by Swanson's.

We published six different stories in the special singles section. One of them was my *Get Personal* story, in which I described the experience of meeting men via the classifieds:

> I didn't get letters from any weirdoes. On the contrary, the letters were honest, expressing a genuine interest in company, friendship, "perhaps something more." As time went on, the whole experience of personal advertising became an adventure, filled with the unexpected.

I described some of the encounters, using first names only. One of the men, a 23-year-old casino worker named Mike, made a career of placing and responding to personal ads. Mike studied marketing in college, and applied what he learned to the classifieds. "If you describe the way you see yourself, you'll get people who feel the same way," Mike said. "The most important thing is to be honest, sensitive and straightforward."

I concluded that the personals were harmless enough, and could actually turn out to be interesting. Here's how I ended the story:

> Writing classified ads convinced me of the value of being open-minded. Sometimes, I formed an opinion based on a man's handwriting, grammar or voice—and often I was wrong. Men I expected to find boring were entertaining; men I thought would be dull were brilliant; men I couldn't wait to see turned out to be less than interesting. There were no fail-safe signs, no guarantees. Each person had something different to offer—the trick was finding it.
>
> I might put in another ad. You never know when or where you will find that mysterious chemistry that makes a relationship click. In the meantime, I have the knowledge that writing personals can be rewarding—and fun.

About 10 years later, 900 numbers and voice mail made placing and responding to personal ads easy and fast, and everyone was doing it. Since I was between relationships more than I was in relationships, I thought, why not? My experience at the magazine was all right. So I responded to ads in the local newspaper. Then I got up the nerve to place a couple of ads myself. I even laid out $200 for the regional epitome of personals, Philadelphia Magazine.

By this time I was an advertising writer, which certainly helped when it came to putting the ads together. Mine were always honest, but as a features-and-benefits expert, I knew how to make myself sound alluring. I received plenty of responses, and spent many hours talking on the phone to men I had never met.

The phone calls were intended to screen the men, to find out if we might be compatible. But no matter how many questions I asked over the phone—and I asked a lot—that first meeting was often a surprise. Take the guy who described himself as "6'5," 250 lbs., and into working out." I pictured a muscular Adonis. When we met, the guy was 6 feet, 5 inches tall and 250 pounds because he was significantly overweight, and into working out because he was trying to get in shape. Plus he had a huge wart on the end of his nose. My list of questions did not include one about warts.

Still, he was friendly enough, and even stopped by my house with flowers and a fresh-baked apple pie. His pleasant attitude and willingness to try were typical of personal ad users. I employed the medium on and off over three or four years, and the men I met were normal guys trying to make a connection. Sometimes I knew instantly it wouldn't work; sometimes we went out a few times. Through the personals I met a guy who I actually dated for six months—one of my longest relationships ever.

By the mid-'90s, the Internet became the medium of choice for personal ads. My "between relationships" status often upset me, and during one of those emotional moments, in September 1995, I discovered the America Online "romance" section and posted a personal ad entitled, *SWF, 39, spills guts.*

The ad captured my reflective mood, in which I wondered where the time had gone, and why I was still alone. I shouldn't have been in that situation—I was attractive, accomplished and easy to get along with. But there I was, unaccompanied, and ready for the next phase of my life.

Responses flooded my AOL mailbox.

When posting a personal ad on the Internet, the first week was the most difficult. I always tried to respond to everyone, because it was impossible to tell in the beginning who would continue to correspond, and of that group, who would be worth meeting. Of course, once I responded, that person wrote another e-mail to me, which required another response. So for awhile, the amount of e-mail I received grew geometrically—initial letters from men who just saw the ad, plus continuing correspondence from those who had already responded. It was overwhelming.

Still, it was fun. I liked going online several times a day and hearing that perky greeting, "You've got mail!" And I enjoyed the back-and-forth, the cleverness and mild flirting with each of my potential online suitors. One by one, however, the suitors fell by the wayside.

Many of the matches were doomed from the start. Why? Although what I had written was sensitive and heartfelt, it was also extremely general. An ace truck driver could consider himself to have achieved "professional accomplishment." "Never-ending youthfulness" could be claimed by someone whose musical taste was stuck in '50s doo-wop. The biggest problem, however, was usually distance. Yes, the Internet turned the world into a global village, but it was still mighty inconvenient to meet for a drink when someone lived two or three hours away.

I spent another miserable holiday season alone, and another New Year's Eve dateless. After my last experiment with the personals, I began to think they were a waste of time. Then it occurred to me that posting on the Internet would work better if, to put it in sales terms, I could qualify the leads. So I decided to try again, this time writing an ad that would be much more specific about the type of man I wanted to meet.

Using my best direct mail techniques, I wrote an ad describing my appearance, personality and interests—fairly standard stuff. But along with the ad I developed "Donna's Compatibility Quiz." It consisted of 12 multiple-choice questions written to probe the basics—like whether a guy was single, in the right age bracket, reasonably health-conscious and lived within driving distance. I posted the ad in February 1996.

Do you want a relationship with a fine woman?
Are you sure?
Will you take action to get it?

I'd like to make an observation: Most of the men I've met online are all type and no action. So if you're only interested in virtual romance, if you want to connect from the safety of your den, I suggest you go on to the next posting. I want the real thing.

More than anything in the world, I want a loyal, committed relationship, full of love, respect and fun. I want to share myself, emotionally and physically. Do you? If your answer is yes, let me describe myself. Then, maybe you'll want to take my little compatibility quiz. Really! :)

Appearance (I'm sure that's your first interest): 5'8" tall, with great legs and a trim, athletic figure from years of playing sports. Shoulder-length, wavy blond hair, blue eyes. A Hollywood smile. I'm 39, and look about five years younger. GIF available upon request.

Personality: I'm positive and optimistic, easy to get along with, self-sufficient, sensitive, caring and honest. And sometimes, in case you didn't notice, direct, but never manipulative. I have a great sense of humor, and love to laugh. In fact, I hope you find this letter funny as well as serious.

Profession: I'm a self-employed advertising writer. Well-established and well-paid.

Interests: Many, ranging from softball to language study, travel to business, antiques to zoos. I'm easily entertained, as long as you don't ask me to jump out of airplanes.

You may be wondering: With so many wonderful qualities, why am I still alone? The short answer is I simply haven't been ready to get involved. Now I am.

Are you interested?

If you are, why don't you take my compatibility quiz? Please don't be offended. We both know that there are certain things we truly want in a relationship. My goal is a real romance, with a real man, so I don't want to spin my wheels on situations that won't work.

Of course, there are no right or wrong answers. But there are answers that will help determine if you and I have the potential to be a good match.

Donna's Compatibility Quiz

1. You are: A - single. B - divorced. C - married.
2. Your age is: A - 23 to 33. B - 34 to 44. C - 45 to 55.
3. Your race is: A - Caucasian. B - African American. C - Asian.
   D - Hispanic.
4. You earn your livelihood as: A - Artist/creative. B - Construction
   worker. C - Professional. D - Civil servant. E - Entrepreneur.
   F - Hourly worker.
5. Your working hours are: A - Monday through Friday, more or less 9
   to 5. B - Evenings. C - Weekends.
6. Your height is: A - 5'6" or less. B - 5'7" or taller.
7. Your weight is about where it should be, give or take 10 pounds:
   A - true. B - false.
8. You are a smoker: A - true. B - false.
9. You exercise: A - Three or more times a week. B - At least once a
   week. C - rarely.
10. Driving no faster than 67 mph, you could reach Atlantic City in:
    A - less than 1 hour. B - 1 to 2 hours. C - 2 to 3 hours.
11. Your religious background/beliefs are: A - Christian. B - Jewish.
    C - Muslim. D - Hindu. E - New Age.
12. You want to get married and have children: A - true. B - false.

The characteristics I was looking for were in the answer key—a SWM who was close to my age, my height or taller, had a good career and a healthy lifestyle, lived within a convenient driving distance of Atlantic City, held similar philosophical beliefs and wanted to get married and have children.

The ad worked. I got quite a few responses, but not an overwhelming amount, which meant my qualification process was effective. Those who replied were generally close to what I was looking for—some even sent me their quiz scores. A few of those who didn't "pass" the quiz wrote just to tell me they thought the ad was cool.

One respondent was David Hansen,* who described himself as 6 feet 4 inches tall, 40 years old, with thick gray hair that "made him look distinguished." He worked in his own business. He was divorced and had an eight-year-old son who lived with him. He wanted a whole "boatload" of children. David sent me his 800 number in his first e-mail.

After a few conversations, we agreed to meet for lunch on February 22, 1996. David lived about an hour away, but was willing to make the trip to Atlantic City. I suggested Peking Duck, an upscale Chinese restaurant.

David met me at the restaurant door at noon, wearing dress slacks, a white shirt and a classic olive raincoat. He did, in fact, look distinguished, like a self-confident executive. Yes, his hair was gray, but it was thick and straight, and his clean-shaven face was youthful. He had dark eyes—almost black—and dark eyebrows. Even though I preferred athletic-looking men to distinguished-looking men, I had to admit he was handsome.

At first we were the only customers in the dimly lit restaurant. David spoke to the waiters in Chinese—a skill he learned when he owned a manufacturing company. We had a nice, leisurely lunch, with plenty to talk about.

"When I saw your ad, I said, whoa, let me print this out," David told me.

"What did you think of it?" I asked.

"I thought, here's a woman who really knows what she wants."

"Well, I've been out there long enough. I hope I know what I'm looking for."

"You know, I haven't dated a woman since my divorce two years ago."

"Why not?"

"Mostly because of my son. My son is from my first marriage, but his mother has mental problems, so I have custody. My second wife, I'm embarrassed to say, was what you call a 'trophy wife.' She was young and absolutely gorgeous. While we were married, my son lived with us and got attached to her. Everything was fine, until I started having trouble with my business because my accountant screwed up the taxes. I told Cindy,* my wife, that we'd have to cut back our fun spending—like going out to dinner and to the racetrack–to about $900 per week."

"Cutting *back* to $900 per week!" I exclaimed, incredulous.

"Yeah. Can you imagine? And it wasn't good enough."

"You're kidding."

"No. We started arguing. Then one day, Cindy drives my son to school and me to work, like she always did. When she dropped me off, she asked if I wanted pork chops for dinner.

"Late that afternoon, I got a call from the school—no one had come to pick up my son. So I got an employee to drive me over. We got my son, and then drove home. I walk into the house, and there's nothing there. It's completely empty. All that was left in the house was my one chair and my clothes. Everything else was gone."

"Oh, my God."

"She must have been planning it for a long time—everything was packed and out by the time the school day was over. Plus, she raided my bank account and took cash advances on my American Express platinum card. She took more than a million dollars. And Cindy's leaving really hurt my son—he had grown close to her. So I vowed I wouldn't ever expose my son to something like that again."

I was shocked that anyone could be as ruthless and calculating as David's former wife. I was so genuine and straightforward that I couldn't imagine doing anything like it.

Lunch came to an end, and David got our coats. There was a mirror on the wall near the coatroom, and as he helped me with mine, he touched me gently on the shoulders and turned me so that both our images were reflected, side-by-side.

"Don't we make a good-looking couple?" David asked.

The romance was hot and heavy. On our first date, we went to my favorite restaurant, a little place with eclectic, nouveau cuisine. David brought me a corsage—overkill, I thought, but at least he was trying. One Saturday afternoon he took me to the luxurious health spa at Bally's casino, paying the guest fee and signing me up for an hour-long massage—not a cheap date. Next he took me to dinner at the Knife and Fork Inn, a fine Atlantic City restaurant that first opened in 1927, and presented me with a gold-link bracelet. My jaw dropped—I was lucky I didn't drool on my salad. Another time we went to the Bacchanal at Caesars, a seven-course gourmet dinner with actors creating the ambience of a Roman feast.

A month after we met, I went on a long-planned vacation to Scandinavia with my father, Allan Andersen; his fiancée, Pat Roberts; and my sister, Tracy Andersen. My grandmother had emigrated from Finland when she was 18 years old. Dad wanted to see the old country, so we planned a 15-day visit.

Our itinerary was to spend the first few days in Stockholm, Sweden, and then take an overnight cruise to Helsinki, Finland, where we had family. Looking at a map of the region, I noticed that Helsinki was fairly close to St. Petersburg, Russia. Why not visit Russia too?

As I talked about my family's plans to David, he said, "St. Petersburg is really something. Everything is big. Everything. The buildings, the statues, they're all massive."

"When were you in St. Petersburg?" I asked.

"Oh, I've been there several times."

"Why?"

"I was with the CIA."

Well, that stopped me. "You were with the CIA?" I asked.

"Yes."

"What did you do?"

"I was a case officer. It's the lowest job in the world. You try to get people to tell you things they shouldn't tell you. You're a worm, a piece of scum."

"How long were you with the CIA?"

"A long time. In fact, I still do work for them."

"You do? What?"

"I find things."

David called several times while I was in Finland, just to tell me that he was thinking of me. I bought him souvenirs, like two designer Finnish ties at $100 a pop and an authentic Finnish hand line for ice fishing. I returned to the United States on April 11, 1996, and the next evening David took me to see Tony Bennett at Caesars. At dinner before the show, he pulled a small gift-wrapped box out of his pocket. Any woman can spot a jewelry box from 50 feet, and I knew it was a ring. I opened the box, and found a diamond-shaped ring encrusted with a field of 25 tiny pavé diamonds. It looked like a diamond had been peeled off a playing card, doubled in size and sprinkled with glitter. It was huge and hideous.

What was I to do? He probably paid a small fortune for the clunker. I wore the ring to the Tony Bennett show—David tipped the maitre d' so we were right up front—and the next day somehow managed to tell him that I thought the ring was a bit, well, large.

"Cindy would have worn it," he said, referring to his ex-trophy wife.

"Well, my taste is a little more—artistic," I said, as delicately as possible.

After a bit of joking, David agreed to exchange it for a different one. He did much better on his second attempt. The ring had five small, narrow sapphires arranged in a free-flowing pattern, somewhat like a fan, anchored by a cluster of small diamonds. It was truly unusual, and beautiful. I was stunned.

The opening game for the Erasers' 1996 softball season was scheduled for April 18, a mere week after I returned from my European vacation. Ours was a reasonably serious team—we played hard enough to win, but not hard enough to start fistfights with our opponents. I was one of the pitchers, and pitching, of course, was critical to the game. Having missed all but one of the preseason practices, I felt rusty—not quite ready for prime time.

David was coming to the game, which was to begin at 6:30 p.m. Earlier in the day, he called me.

"Since you're the star pitcher, how about some sex before the game?" he asked.

"Absolutely not," I responded, without even thinking about it. Little did I know that David was highly insulted.

He arrived at 5:30 in a taxi—he always took a train to Atlantic City and then a cab to my house—and we left for the game in my car. On the way, David said he was hungry, and wanted to stop for something to eat. I was more interested in getting as much warm-up time as possible, and suggested that once we got to the field, he could take my car and go back to the highway rest stop that we passed for a hamburger. It would only take a few minutes—he could be back before the game started.

David didn't return to the field until the third inning. I saw him pull up, and since I was not on the mound because my team was at bat, went over to meet him. He got out of the car, glared at me and growled, "I am not pleased with you," drawing out each word for impact.

Huh?

That was just the beginning. Every time I came off the pitcher's mound, he complained. He felt like he was being ignored and mistreated. I was in no mood for his crap—I was trying to concentrate on the game. I finally told David that he was acting like an asshole. He sulked.

Even though I was highly agitated, I threw strikes, and we won convincingly. My teammates, carefully ignoring the scene created by my sullen companion, congratulated me on the win. "Donna wasn't really on vacation in Europe," joked our shortstop. "She was training with the Russian national team."

Instead of going with the team to our favorite bar as I always did, David and I went home. He smoked in the car—a habit I didn't know he had. When we got back to my house, I tried to calmly explain that I needed to focus on the game, and he shouldn't take it personally. It didn't work. Instead of being his usual charming self, David was bitter and sarcastic. He sat on the staircase landing in my living room and said some of the meanest, nastiest and most condescending things to me that I'd ever heard—like putting down my "little business" as if it were a weekend hobby. Angry, I tried to give him his ring back. He refused. He finally left, and I figured our relationship was over.

That night, at 2:30 a.m., David called me. I hung up the phone. He called again, and I let the answering machine pick up. His message said he was coming over. Frightened—and I had never been frightened by a man before—I got up, dressed, put my dog on a leash and the two of us got into the car. But where could I go at 2:30 in the morning? I drove around the corner and parked to see if a taxi arrived.

Suddenly he was there, standing on the corner, illuminated by a streetlight. Eventually I could see that David didn't intend to hurt me, so I drove back to my house and we stood in the street and talked. At first he was angry, but then he started to cry. I held him; he came in; we had sex and he spent the night.

Still, the whole episode was chilling. The next day I was on the phone, telling the story to my sister and girlfriends. They all advised caution.

The following weekend, David came over, and we made up. "I'll never stop loving you, no matter what you do," he said to me. "I'll never leave you."

David had been looking forward to Kentucky Derby Day since I met him. It was the annual occasion upon which he wore his white suit, white shirt and white shoes, drank mint juleps, and talked with his best Colonel Sanders accent—which was pretty good. The famous horse race was slated for Saturday, May 4, 1996, two weeks after the softball game incident, and we had plans to watch it at Bally's Park Place casino.

He arrived at my house smoking and in a bad mood. David had already been to the casino to play baccarat. He started out with $2,000 and kept winning until he had more than $6,000. He wanted to get to $7,000, then he would stop. David never reached his goal. Instead, as often happened in the casino, he lost everything. He had no money to take me to Bally's for the Kentucky Derby.

I was appalled. Although I lived in Atlantic City and earned my living doing work for the casinos, I was not a gambler. Throwing away $2,000 on cards was beyond my comprehension. I wasn't interested in being with a man who was willing to do that, which, in a fit of irritation, I fumed to David.

We had words, and then, somehow, decided to go to Bally's to watch the Kentucky Derby anyway. David put on his white suit and wrote me a check for $500. I put the check in my wallet and gave him $100 in cash. When we got to the casino, I took another $400 out of the ATM, which I also gave him.

The day was tense. I expected to be watching the horse race at a private high-rollers party. Instead, we were sitting on folding chairs at folding tables in the casino's second-floor foyer, drinking cocktails out of plastic cups. The only reason David had mint in his mint juleps was that he brought his own—a drooping bunch he picked up at a produce store on the way to the casino.

I tried to maintain a positive attitude, and actually won $100 with a lucky bet on a horse race. Afterwards, we went to the gourmet steak house, where I had two glasses of wine—later realizing that they were triple-sized glasses. After dinner, David tried to recoup some of his losses at a Let It Ride table, where he was admonished by the pit boss for standing, when casino regulations required that he sit in order to play. He lost more money.

When we got back to my house, my intuition told me to take his $500 check out of my wallet, which I noticed, but did not act upon. With a tongue loosened by alcohol, however, I did act upon my urge to tell David what I thought of his behavior. It was not a pleasant scene. David spent the night in an Atlantic City motel.

The following Monday I had errands to run, including taking David's check to the bank. I opened my wallet and stopped cold—the check wasn't there. I was positive that I had left it in the wallet, but with a sinking feeling in my stomach, I spent a futile half-hour looking around the house for it.

Finally, I got on the phone. "David," I said, "I can't find that check you gave me."

"Where is it?" he asked.

"It should be in my wallet. I didn't take it out, and I haven't been anywhere since you left."

"Are you saying I took it?"

"Well, did you?"

"Do you know how much money I've spent on you?" he bellowed. "How many times have we been out to dinner? Do you think those Tony Bennett tickets were cheap? How about that day at Bally's spa—do you know how much that cost? And you're willing to take a $2,500 ring from me!"

I hung up the phone in fury and disbelief. I paced around the house—stomped would be more accurate—for about an hour. Then I called him back.

"David, I think we should call it quits."

"Why? Because I lost money in the casino?"

"Look, David, I am not happy. This is not what I want. And I am really upset about the fact that you went into my wallet and took out that check." By this point, I was almost screaming into the phone.

"Oh, you're just Miss Perfect, now, aren't you," he said, his voice dripping with sarcasm. "And if someone has a flaw, you just throw them away."

"David, just send me the fucking money."

"Oh, you want your money? Well, you won $100 on the horse race, so I guess you're only out $400."

"Bullshit, David," I screamed. "You send me a check for $500."

"What about that ring? You liked that, didn't you? It's okay for me to buy you an expensive ring. You'll take that."

"I didn't ask you to buy me a fucking ring. You want it back; you can have it."

Suddenly, he changed tactics. "Why don't we get together and talk about this?" David asked, dropping his voice and trying to pacify me.

"David, I never want to see you again."

"Oh, so that's it."

"Yes, it is."

"What shall we do? Send each other packages by Federal Express? Let them pass each other in Memphis?"

"Sounds good to me."

That's what we decided to do—return everything we had that belonged to the other via overnight Fed Ex. I made up a package with his bathrobe, one of his Finnish ties and the ring, in its original box. I sent it out, with a declared value of $2,700.

David's package arrived the next day. Inside was a framed picture of myself and some greeting cards that I had given him. There was no check.

Furious, I picked up the phone.

"David, the package is here," I said, my voice calm and hard. "There's no check."

"Yes, I know," he answered, matter-of-factly.

"Where is it?"

"I spoke to my attorney. He advised me not to send it."

On that, I lost my cool. "You son of a bitch. You owe me $500."

"Look, we can get together, and ..."

"Are you crazy? I never want to see you for the rest of my life."

"Look, Donna, all you're worried about is your $500. I feel like I've had my heart ripped out of me."

"Well, you should have thought about that before you took the $500!" I slammed down the phone.

David, I realized, had serious problems. He had a dark, manipulative and hurtful side that came out when he was angry. I understood why his wife left him the way she did—when David went on the attack, there was no winning, no reasoning and no defense. I almost didn't care if it cost me $500. I was emotionally exhausted, he scared me, and I was glad to be rid of him.

I wish I could have gotten off as easily in my next romantic adventure.

My 40th birthday was approaching and once again, I was between relationships. I felt reasonably recovered from the David Hansen fiasco, so on a slow day, I logged on to the AOL personals—just looking. In the men seeking women section, one headline caught my eye: "Atl City widower seeks mate!"

Well, if this man was in Atlantic City, that solved one of the biggest problems of Internet personals—distance. On that basis alone, the ad was worth reading, so I clicked to see the full text.

From: FUTRON01
Subj: Atl City widower seeks mate!

Finished mourning! Ready to move on! Really!!

Deeply involved in the development of AtlCity of 2000; late 40's Sean Connery lookalike, 6'2". From Hollywood Film & TV scene as writer/prod; now into Entert. Biz in greatest city in USA. Emot. & Fin. secure, Ex-Green Beret; no drugs, don't even drink! Daughter grown up. Hold several advanced degrees but I baby talk to my dog. No hobbies, just threw myself into work; time to change all that! The grieving is complete.

You will be stunning! Let me repeat, you will stop the room when you walk in!! Somewhere between 30 and 45. There are no other parameters. I have traveled the world and fell in love in its many nooks, crevices and corners. Tangoed with a Tongan once, took a Tibettan to the drive-in!

You must be able to host Donald and Marla [you don't have to talk to her!] and finish with a beer with my mates at the Legion Post [Nam!] Order from the menu at Ivana's in French or Italian and cook me scrapple and real scrambled eggs [made with milk and tabasco].

Discuss Dante or Donald Duck. Talk writing with writers, directing with directors, the future with those who shape it, my stockbroker or my gardener ... and baby talk to my dog.

Freeze the doorman with a stare, melt me with a touch.

Shake hands with Christy and charm Pinky [if you don't know, you ain't from here! but that's ok].

You will be my cheerleader, I will be the best confidante/advisor your career ever had.

I will make you laugh, you will make me cry.

You get the picture!!

You will not believe in Rush; that Nixon was persecuted; you can lose 10 lbs in 10 days; he never inhaled; born again equates with an IQ, that white wine only goes with fish; Patek Philippe is a French rapper; a Corvette is a car, that the correct place for a dachshund is the backyard! I am a Republican but voted straight Democrat till I started my first TV network.

Life together must be a two way street ...

Make mine a happier journey and I guarantee you will not feel any of the potholes on that highway.

I am a hopeless romantic; an experienced and regular lover, very few hangups, but not into one night stands ... three little words please, before three times a night!

If you fit the above -please E-mail; this ad is genuine, too easy to check in the AC Press or on WMGM- if you don't [or if you feel your reply should start with the words "I am not really..."] ... don't waste both our time [get a life!].

The standards are high; mine always have been but the rewards match!

I met her online, perhaps, lightning can strike twice? I will always love her, but there is room for another equally fierce, relationship/part-nership/marriage ... whatever ... in my life. I may sound tough but I am also incredibly alone!

James ... by the water in Mays Landing [who would live on the island?]
Harold James ... [he's the mini-dachsie]
Herbert James ... [he's an English hedgehog who lives in the bath, I am a shower person, deeply influenced by Hugh Lofting ... and they make no noise!]

The ad, even though creatively punctuated, was certainly more descriptive and interesting than most online personals. This man—James—said he had big plans in Atlantic City, which was intriguing. Another wave of casino development was hitting the town, and it was starting to get exciting—almost as exciting as when I was at Atlantic City Magazine. I went back and read the ad again.

Being from Atlantic City, I understood the references James made. He was apparently doing business with Donald Trump and New Jersey Governor Christine Todd Whitman. He had media connections—Pinky Kravitz was a local radio and television talk show host. He dined at Ivana's—a gourmet restaurant in the Trump Plaza casino. Although I had corresponded with other successful and creative people that I met through the personals, this James sounded like he was a cut above the rest. But—was I really up for this? Another personal?

For the moment, I decided to do nothing.

A few days later, I looked on AOL again—the personal from James was still there. Another few days passed—the ad was still online. Finally, I broke down and replied.

You'll never know unless you try, I said to myself.

I composed a letter that responded to the statements in James' ad:

From: DONNACOPY
Subj: Greetings from Atlantic City

Dear James,
I was intrigued by your posting ...
Goings-on in Atlantic City have always fascinated me, although I must admit I've gotten out of the loop in recent years. As the original editor of Atlantic City Magazine, I was quite involved with the develop-

ment of Atlantic City 1980. Since I left, I've just been doing business with a few of the casinos, quietly taking my earnings to the bank. But the town is getting exciting again … I may have to start paying attention.

Re: your one parameter—in the right dress, yes, I am stunning. I've been mistaken for a groupie at the Miss America Pageant. Usually, however, I'm just attractive with a casual, girl-next-door look. 5'8" tall. A trim, athletic figure from years of playing sports. Wavy, shoulder-length blond hair—my natural color. Big blue eyes and a Hollywood smile. If an Irish/Scandinavian combination appeals to you, you'll probably find me attractive. Photo available upon request.

I can hold a conversation with all those people you mentioned. The Donald makes time for you? I'm impressed. I'd probably enjoy your buddies at the post, as long as you'd enjoy the folks on my softball team. And I'd be happy to baby talk to your dog. I do it to mine.

My French is coming along—I'm going to Paris in a few months, so yes, I'd better learn how to order. I'm afraid I'm not going to attempt Italian—Spanish will have to do.

I'd be happy to make you scrambled eggs, although I must admit I cringe at the thought of scrapple. It goes against my health-conscious grain. But then, you probably wouldn't like my tofu breakfast. That's okay, I won't make you eat it.

I'll be 40 shortly, have yet to marry, and wonder where the time has gone. I've been wrapped up in being a responsible businesswoman, so it's definitely time to add another dimension to my life. You know what they say about all work and no play.

If you'd like to know more, please drop me a note. I look forward to hearing from you.

By the bay on the island,
(Really, it's not bad)
Donna

I clicked "send" and waited.

A few days later, a reply arrived. It started with magic words, "You sound delightful!" Even more intriguing, the reply came from Australia, where James said he was visiting family and doing business. He sent me his phone number.

A man who lived in Atlantic City and was writing to me from Australia—a foreigner, I assumed, noticing the British spelling of the word, "recognise." I called the local phone number and heard James' voice on his answering machine—he definitely had an English or Australian accent. How exotic! Of course, I wrote back.

I asked questions about his business in Australia, his business in Atlantic City and his family. I learned that James was staying with his daughter in Australia, and that his reason for coming to Atlantic City had something to do with virtual reality simulators and Donald Trump—a weeklong visit turned into two years. This was all very interesting.

Anyone who was ever hopeful about romantic prospects—which probably encompassed the entire human race—knew the fluttery feeling that preceded a prospect becoming reality. Are we going to get along? Could this be a match?

My love life so far had been a parade of disappointment. All I really wanted was a husband and a family, but every time I tried to make a connection, I failed. Every other aspect of my life was successful—business, sports, friendships—which made my failure at romance even more painful. And now, to make matters worse, I was about to turn 40. My biological clock was ticking loudly.

Still, I knew that one success, one good connection, was all I needed. The more James and I corresponded, the more I started to hope that perhaps—finally—my turn had come.

"Donna I like how you write and think," James wrote. "You have made my return home something to look forward to ... and I mean that sincerely!"

James forwarded to me a copy of his resume, which listed several extraordinary accomplishments:

James Montgomery
President of JAG, Inc.
The Jaypat America Group

A specialist in Electronic Entertainment, he has several firsts to his credit:-

• the launch of the highly successful World Wide Web site: Sports-Line in August of 1995

• the development & launch of Hollywood's own "E" basic cable network. -on-air in July '87

• the world's first, fully interactive banking system with hi-tech partners: AT&T/NCR in '86

• won a hotly contested contract from Florida Govt. computerizing tourism marketing in '90

• created what was the world's largest TV buying service for Lever Bros. and Warner Bros.

James believes that every minute of his three decades in commerce has been necessary to enable him to create the CelebAM on the Boardwalk concept; even the three decades spent with the military reserve contributed to his ability to create this unique electronic theme park concept.

After formal training in Sociology, he joined NY's Grey Advertising in product and marketing research; graduating to marketing counsel and, finally, TV buying and production. During this period, he extended his formal training to the law, making his postgraduate specialty - contract law.

Advertising and Marketing schooled him in Communications and Research. In 1970, he founded Jaypat Sales Promotion - a high tech marketing specialist: using the packaged goods techniques he had learned with Grey, NY on clients like Revlon, P&G, Bristol Myers, General Foods to the newly emerging technologies of Wang, Nixdorf, Unisys, Data Technology. He was deeply involved in the development and launch of the Word Processing concept world-wide.

Jaypat SP gave him a very solid grounding in Electronic Data Processing and Computers. A founder of one of the largest TV production facilities in the Southern Hemisphere; he was involved in the early days of interactive laser disc, starting his long association, of nearly 20 years, with interactive multimedia; creating a decade of International Expo exhibits for Commerce & Govt.

Jaypat Productions, Inc. of LA was an Interactive Pioneer. His time in Hollywood as a writer/producer made him many of the personal contacts he has used in creating CelebAM. However, it was combining his creative skills with his interactive knowledge plus his background in TV advertising that led him to co-found the basic cable network now known as 'E' … surprisingly, the first cable network to telecast from Hollywood about Hollywood. After the most successful launch in cable history, it was sold to Time Warner in 1989.

JAG developed and maintains a very strong Studio & Network Film & TV Nexus. Following the disposal of the cable network, NCR asked JAG to bid against some 200 other corporations for a terminal system to dispense tourism information in Florida for their Department of Commerce. The tourism industry chose JAG. That contract was awarded in 1990.

JAG has spent six years deeply involved in every aspect of Florida Theme Park Research. He received a Cable ACE for the launch of the 'E' Network, two CLIO's, and a Hoover Marketing Award. He has a masters degree in Psychology and Sociology and a postgraduate Law degree. Part of JAG is a highly specialized, anti-terrorism consultancy. It was asked to consult on the future roles for Special Operations and played a very small, but strategic, role in the development of SDI. James is a member of several Legion Posts inc. Mays Landing and Somers Point, he has been active in Viet Vet affairs for over a decade. A reserve officer in Special Forces for over two decades inc. Vietnam service. A member of The Special Forces Association, Special Ops. Command, FL. A member of the Veterans Advisory Board and a resident of Atlantic County.

This man launched multiple businesses, spent 30 years in the military and acted as a consultant to Special Forces. I was blown away. But it seemed to me that he had done quite a bit for a man still in his 40s. Perhaps he was actually older than he said. I questioned him on it:

Your resume is quite impressive. You've certainly piled up the accomplishments in your life. So I must ask, are you a child prodigy? Or does "late 40s" reflect your state of mind more than the actual passage of time? Please forgive my asking about this point. It's just that I've recently had a fairly nasty experience with someone who turned out not to be the person he presented himself to be. I never did understand the point of misrepresentation in these affairs. The truth always comes out, and then everything is worse.

"Nup, genuine Boomer," James replied. "License says 1948." He also wrote that although he was born in Australia, he was now an American citizen.

James had obviously looked up my AOL profile, and figured out that the day of his return, July 19, 1996, was my 40th birthday. So he continued, "I assume that you will already be booked on Friday night celebrating your 40th ... so perhaps coffee over the weekend?"

For most of my life, I spent my birthday dateless. Sometimes I was out with my softball team, sometimes I was out with the girls, but I could remember only one time when I had a boyfriend on my birthday, and even then the celebration was a group affair, not a romantic dinner. I wanted a date on my special day, but I hadn't even met this man. Here's what I wrote:

> We could, if you like, get together for lunch on Friday. Then, if we hit it off—after all, you never really know with these things—you might like to come to the party. For mere mortals, I realize this would be a daunting proposition—meeting me, plus all my friends and family, on the same day. But I get the impression you are accustomed to jumping into things with two feet. Or, we could, as you suggest, get together for coffee over the weekend. It would be a bit more relaxed.

Between James' jet lag and my party preparations, we decided it would be best to meet after my soiree. Still, I couldn't help but think how nice it would have been to share an occasion as momentous as my 40th birthday with a special someone.

My Folk Festival friends, as I expected, arrived at the birthday party late. Pam Breyer,* whom I'd known since childhood, came sometime between 9 and 10 p.m. John Cucinotta, who was the spiritual center of the gang—he organized the annual festival pilgrimage—worked a late shift and then drove an hour and a half, arriving after midnight. During his entire trip to Atlantic City, "Cooch," as he was called, looked forward to alcohol, so as soon as he arrived, he downed a row of shots.

A little while later, giggles emanated from behind the closed door of my upstairs office. Then Cooch made a grand entrance down the stairs wearing a flowing blue and white sundress—he'd changed clothes with one of the Folk Festival women. Cooch still looked like he did in his hippie days, so with his flat chest, long black hair and full beard, he failed miserably as a drag queen. But he sure drew a howl of laughter from the rest of the party.

There was another round of giggling from the office, and this time Cooch emerged wearing Pam's skin-tight white Lycra skirt. It left little to the imagination, much to the delight of all the women.

My 62-year-old father, Allan, observed this entire display from an upholstered chair in the living room, probably with one raised eyebrow. Now, although he looked far younger than his age, Dad was a regular guy, a carpenter, whose favorite piece of history was World War II. He was not exactly liberal when it came to bearded, long-haired men, especially when they dressed like women. He was also not exactly accustomed to keeping his mouth shut.

Dad made some snide remarks to Cooch, questioning his masculinity. Cooch thought this was funny, and started egging my father on. Suddenly, the two of them were wrestling in the middle of my living room floor. I watched in amazement from the staircase landing.

After a bit of tussling, Cooch rolled into the bottom step, hitting his head with a loud thud, and the contest was instantly over. Both men stood up, Cooch rubbing his head and laughing. "Man," he said. "I hope I can do that when I'm 62."

The party went on until about 2:30 a.m.—one of my friends, exhausted, couldn't remember the last time she stayed up that late. By the time I went to bed it was 4 a.m. I was still pumped, and couldn't fall asleep. My birthday turned out to be wonderful—but part of my excitement was anticipation about meeting James Montgomery. I was so tired of being alone—would my luck finally change at 40?

Chapter 3

At 8:30 a.m. on Saturday, July 20, 1996, the morning after my birthday party, the phone rang.

"Good morning, Donna," said the voice on the other end of the line. "This is James." He pronounced his name as if it were spelled "Jay-ems." He definitely had an Australian accent, although it wasn't as harsh as listening to Paul Hogan in *Crocodile Dundee*. "Did I wake you?"

"Well, no, but we're not moving too fast around here," I answered. My sister, Tracy, stayed overnight. So did Cooch. He was in no condition to drive home. "We had quite the party last night. People were here until two or three in the morning. Too bad you missed it."

"I wouldn't have made a very good impression," James said. "I was pretty tired after 24 hours of travel."

"I can imagine."

"Would you like to meet for brekkie?"

"For what?"

"Brekkie. That's Australian for breakfast."

I hesitated. I was tired, the house was a mess, and I didn't know how long my overnight guests would stay. "Actually, I think I'd be in better shape tomorrow," I answered.

"All right," James replied. "In the meantime, I'll send you a PCX."

"A what?"

"A PCX. A picture. So you can see what I look like."

"Okay. That would be nice."

"Let's meet at the Courthouse Café in Mays Landing tomorrow. I go there all the time; it's like my second office. I know the cook—he'll take care of us. Is 9 o'clock okay?"

"Can we make it 10?"

"Done. I'll see you tomorrow. I look forward to meeting you, Donna."

I hung up the phone. Well, this one certainly is anxious to get together, I thought to myself.

I had already told my sister, Tracy, about meeting James online. In fact, Tracy knew about all my adventures with the personals.

Tracy was five years younger than me, but as we got older, the age difference disappeared. We had a lot in common, especially personality traits like independence, self-reliance and an impatient, get-it-done attitude.

Still, people often found it hard to believe we were sisters. We were both 5 feet 8 inches tall and about the same weight. We both had blondish hair and blue eyes. But the hair was of different textures and the eyes were different shades of blue. Our facial features and figures had no similarities. In reality, we looked nothing alike.

Tracy didn't look like our brothers, either. Doug Andersen was almost two years younger than me, and Gregory Andersen was 11 years younger. Doug, Greg and I shared a family resemblance. But Tracy—well, we joked that she was the milkman's daughter.

My sister was standing behind me when I downloaded James' picture. It was a horizontal black-and-white shot of him sitting beside a desk in a small office. He was talking to a man seated in a chair near him, their knees almost touching. The other man was the actor Robert Culp.

I studied the photo. James' resemblance to Sean Connery, I discovered, was limited to the fact that they both had male pattern baldness and close-cropped beards. And I distinctly saw the makings of a spare tire around James' gut.

"This is kind of an odd picture to send," I said to Tracy.

"I guess he likes it," she shrugged.

All day long, as I cleaned up after my birthday party, my anticipation about meeting my potential new suitor grew. James and I had been corresponding for two weeks. Even if he didn't look like Sean Connery, his e-mails were clever, well-written and gracious. What he told me about his life and accomplishments was intriguing. Best of all, unlike most of the men I'd met through online personals, he wasn't hedging or waffling. James made it very clear that he wanted to meet me. Right away.

The next morning, getting ready for our rendezvous, I debated what to wear. I settled on teal-blue Jones New York shorts and a teal and green tropical blouse. Bright colors, especially blues, flattered me.

I drove through the morning sunshine a half-hour inland to Mays Landing, and arrived at the Courthouse Café at 10 o'clock, right on time. I walked into the restaurant, where only one table, a maroon vinyl booth by the front window, was occupied. It was James—and his stuff.

I sat down. James looked like a typical Scotsman. His face was somewhat round and broad, and his complexion was ruddy. His eyes were small and pale blue, but his ears were large and protruding. His hair, what there was of it, was brown and straight. So was his beard, which was close-cropped and trimmed to make a little open square around his mouth. He wore a dark green polo shirt with a small, embroidered logo—ABC Sports. The shirt was obviously chosen to impress me. Beside him in the booth was a gray canvas briefcase with an embroidered emblem—"Congressional Medal of Honor Society." In front of him on the table was a pile of photos. They were wedding pictures.

This, I thought to myself, was something I'd never seen.

"Finally, we meet," James said to me, smiling broadly. "I've been wanting to meet you ever since I received your first e-mail while I was in Australia."

"I've been looking forward to meeting you as well," I replied.

After more introductory small talk and placing an order with the waitress, James reached for the pictures. "These are from my wedding to Gale, who passed away," James explained softly, with a touch of sadness in his voice. "She was already 40, and it was her first wedding. So she wanted everything—the long gown, the big cake. We got married in a 200-year-old church in South Carolina. We even had an honor guard, and walked under an archway of swords as we left the church."

I looked at the pictures. Gale was an attractive woman, with short, dark hair and hazel eyes. She wore a champagne colored satin gown cut in a full, traditional style, and a small spray of flowers in her hair. Very classy.

"That's Harold James," James said when I got to a picture of a stubby dog. "He's a black and white dachshund. My friend, Lee Patterson,* walked him down the aisle on a leash. Everyone thought Lee was the best man, but really it was Harold James.

"I got Harold James when I lived in Florida," he continued. "He was born during Hurricane Andrew. That's the one that flattened Homestead Air Force Base. He was the runt of the litter and had buckteeth. It cost me a fortune to get his teeth fixed, and they never were quite right.

"When Gale and I got married, I had only one request: Harold James was mine—everything else we shared. That didn't last very long—Gale became keeper of the dog. She took him for walks every day. When she lay on the chaise in the living room to watch television, Harold James would lay on her stomach. The two of them would fall asleep."

"I have a dog—a coon hound. His name is Beau," I said. "But he's too big to do that."

"I don't have Harold James any more," James continued. "Gale's father, John, recently had a kidney removed. When I went down to South Carolina to visit him, I brought the dog. I left Harold James with John for company, to lift his spirits."

My scrambled eggs arrived—James only ordered coffee. I set the pictures aside and changed the subject. "So you've worked in Hollywood?" I asked.

"Yes, I was one of the founders of the cable channel, Movietime. Later the channel was sold to Time Warner and became E! Entertainment Television. When I was there, our concept was to make Movietime interactive. But this was back in the late '80s—we were ahead of our time.

"I also did some screenwriting—I have credits for *Crocodile Dundee II*. The *Crocodile Dundee* movies were based on skits we wrote for an Australian TV show. You remember the part where Paul Hogan runs into a hood in New York who pulls a switchblade on him? And then Paul Hogan pulls out his big hunting knife, and says, 'No, *this* is a knife.' Well, that was all done before on the TV show."

"It was funny," I said, impressed that he wrote the gag.

"It was old," James said disparagingly. "Nothing new. The whole movie was a typical fish-out-of-water story."

James poured cream and three packages of Sweet 'n' Low into his coffee. Then, stirring the coffee, he continued. "The last big project I did was the bible for *Star Trek Voyager*."

"A bible? What's that?"

"It tells the basic premise of the show, what we call the backstory. It defines the characters, tells their history, establishes the situation they are in. For example, it says that Voyager is lost in an unknown, distant part of the galaxy, and the crew's objective is to find its way home. One of the things they wanted was that the captain would be a woman. So I created Kathryn Janeway. And she *is* the captain, there's nothing to convey she's a token woman in the job."

"That's pretty cool. I like *Star Trek*."

James made a face. "It's not real science fiction—it's *Wagon Train*," he said, with a dismissive gesture. "It's such a formula. Something bad happens, they circle the wagons, and in the last 15 minutes of the show, everything is resolved."

"Well, I still like it. Although I like the new shows better than the old ones. Are you still doing it?"

"No, and my agent—he's one of the best in the business—is mad at me. When I write, he makes money. But now I'm working on theme parks."

"Is that what you're bringing to Atlantic City?"

This was obviously the question James was waiting for. "Yes—I'm developing an LBE—which means location-based entertainment—called CelebAM," he enthusiastically explained. "That's short for Celebrate America. It's a brand-new entertainment concept, targeted toward older demographics—the people who visit Atlantic City. It will be an electronic, interactive museum, mixing virtual reality with live presenters.

"CelebAM will have three wings—the Golden Years of Hollywood, the Medal of Honor Hall of Heroes, and the Atlantic City Hall of Fame, with 'boxing and beauties.' We already have most of the materiel for the museum. We own a collection of original Hollywood costumes, like the dress Julie Andrews wore in *The Sound of Music*. We have exclusive rights to film and video from the Congressional Medal of Honor Society. And we have the rights to the biggest private boxing collection in the world."

After a sip of coffee, James continued. "Another part of CelebAM is called Cyberia. That's where we'll have the virtual reality, but it's not shoot 'em up kids' games; it's geared for adults. We'll have 100 two-person pods. People will be able to sit in them and feel like they're flying a helicopter to Cape May or Philadelphia or New York. They'll see the ground below—except the year may be 1492. That's what you can do with virtual reality software; you can make anything. And when they're finished, they can buy a personalized VHS tape of their ride."

James' concept struck me as truly innovative. "How long have you been working on this?" I asked.

"I put four years into CelebAM down in Tampa," James replied. "We had agreements with simulator companies and architectural renderings for the building. Then last year we lost our land to the Tampa Port Authority—they took it through eminent domain to build a cruise ship terminal."

"What did you do then?"

"About that time I got a call from Trump to look at some electronic simulation. So I came to Atlantic City for 10 days and never left. I realized with Celeb-AM's over-50 market target, Atlantic City was a perfect place for it. Thirty-six million people a year visit Atlantic City. Once they walk out of a casino, there really isn't anything for them to do."

"That's true," I said. "For a long time, the casinos really didn't care if there was anything else here for people to do. In fact, for the first 10 or 15 years, they wanted nothing to do with family entertainment. The thinking was, kids can't gamble, so why attract kids? But now that gambling is legal in other areas of the country, like the riverboats and Indian casinos, people in Atlantic City realize they have to make the town more of a destination resort."

"Exactly," James said. "So I've been talking to the ACCA—the Atlantic City Convention Authority—about the old Convention Hall."

Atlantic City's original Convention Hall opened on the Boardwalk in 1929. At the time, it was the world's first and largest full-service convention facility, and the largest building in the world constructed without roof posts and pillars. The arched ceiling of the main exhibit hall was 137 feet high—I'd seen pictures of helicopters flying around inside it during World War II. But the landmark building did not meet the needs of modern meeting planners. A new, state-of-the-art convention center was under construction at the foot of the Atlantic City Expressway—the highway that linked Atlantic City to Philadelphia and the rest of the world. The local powers-that-be had not yet determined exactly what would become of the old hall—and its valuable 320 feet of Boardwalk frontage—once the new one opened.

"I had a deal to put CelebAM in the front section of the building," James said. "The head guy loved the CelebAM concept. I was ready to start construction, and he was fired. My deal went down the tubes."

"So what are you going to do?" I asked.

"I have to start selling the idea all over again," James said. "The problem is, with the boss gone, no one really knows who is in charge."

James took another sip of his coffee. "Gale was an engineer, you know. She was working with me on the project."

"When did she die?" I asked.

James hesitated. Then he answered, "Four months ago."

I sat back in the booth—this was not the answer I expected. "That's too soon," I said quickly. "You can't be ready to get involved again."

James looked at me, and I could see sadness in his eyes. "I've lost a lot of people," he said quietly. "Many good friends in Vietnam. And those who survived the war are now dying from cancer because of the chemicals. I lost my father last year. I've learned that I have to get over it quickly and move on.

"Gale was young, but there was a history of heart problems in her family, and she smoked. She had a heart attack in our home—I was there when it happened. I called 911. Then I tried to give her CPR. I picked her up—there's a way that a body feels when it's dead; it's heavier than when a person is alive. That's how she felt."

"But four months," I protested. "You can't possibly be over it already."

James paused. "I took some time and went to Australia to be with my daughter and grandchildren," he said. "But now I have to move on. Gale would want me to."

Unconvinced, I looked down and grasped my coffee mug with two hands, making sounds which, roughly translated, meant, I don't think so.

"I'm talking myself out of this, aren't I," James said softly.

Glancing up, I asked almost flippantly, "Why, do you think we have a chance?"

He looked deep into my eyes with a mixture of sincerity and wistfulness. "Yes," was his barely audible answer. "I do."

I was silent, but my mind was racing. Physically, this man was not at all what I wanted. He was out of shape, older than me and probably would have flunked my compatibility quiz. But the words of the first psychic I ever visited echoed in my head: "Love is a choice." The admonition meant that we can spend our entire lives waiting for Mr. or Ms. Right to come along, or we can choose to love the person who stands before us. This man was talking about his hopes for togetherness. It was not something, in my experience, that men usually talked about.

Well, James was intelligent, successful, ambitious and willing to love again. The least I could do was give him a chance.

We finished our coffee, and that awkward moment near the end of first meetings arrived. What was next? In situations like this, there was always ice cream. Right down the street from the Courthouse Café was an ice cream parlor called Scoops. We decided to go there, and James offered to drive—his black Ford Explorer, Eddie Bauer edition, was parked behind the restaurant.

As I surveyed the ice cream flavors, James talked to the proprietor, who was running for a seat on the Hamilton Township Committee. They discussed the upcoming election—James was involved in local politics, and was working on the campaign of Joe Nickles, a Mays Landing resident who was running for county freeholder.

I ordered chocolate peanut butter, and James picked sugar-free vanilla, explaining that he was diabetic and careful about his sugar intake. We took our ice cream outside to the store's back deck, which overlooked the Mays Landing park and the Great Egg Harbor River—beautiful on a sunny day.

"It's great living in a small town," James declared. "I've never done it before. I've lived in New York, Los Angeles, Tampa and Sydney, but this is the best. In a small town, you can know everyone and have access to everyone. I love it!"

"Atlantic City was a lot of fun when the casinos first opened," I agreed. "A really small group of people ran everything, and I knew them all. I went to all the casino groundbreakings and opening nights for the shows. But everything changed. It used to be a big party; now it's just big business."

"I think Atlantic City is a gold mine. It's like southern California was 10 years ago. With all the new casinos coming in, this place is ready to explode. For anyone with imagination, there are so many opportunities. For example, all the new casinos are going to be much more elaborate, with a lot of themed décor. That's the trend in the entertainment and restaurant business. So one of the businesses that I'm working on is a factory that's going to make the materials."

"What do you mean?"

"There's a company in Australia that creates specialty façades out of polyurethane. You can mold polyurethane to make it look like anything—statues, trees, spaceships—whatever you want. They built everything for the Warner Brothers theme park on the Gold Coast of Australia. I'm importing the technology so we can do it here. Originally I wanted to do it for CelebAM, but I think there's going to be a big market with the new casinos. We're going to take over the old Wheaton Plastics factory right by the lake in Mays Landing. It will probably create a couple hundred jobs."

Wow—from movies to factories, James Montgomery had his hand in everything. "Is that why you went to Australia?" I asked.

"It was one reason. Mainly I went to see my daughter, Margaret,* and my new granddaughter. She was born in March. I have two other grandchildren, a 10-year-old boy and eight-year-old girl.

"I never knew Margaret until two years ago," James continued. "I had a relationship with her mother when I was a teenager. She got pregnant. She had the baby and put her up for adoption. When Australia liberalized its adoption laws a few years ago, Margaret decided to look for her birth parents.

"First she contacted my brother, Bob. He's Dr. Bob Montgomery, one of the most well-known psychologists in Australia. Used to have a radio show—he was known as 'Dr. Bob.' At first Bob was hesitant, but then he gave Margaret my address in the States. She wrote me a letter. Of course, I was amazed, but meeting my daughter and her family has turned out to be one of the most wonderful experiences of my life."

We were both getting toward the end of our ice cream. "How about if we get together for dinner later?" James asked. "I have to go now—a friend has asked me to be the navigator on his sailboat in a race in Annapolis."

"Annapolis? Today? How are you going to get there? It's at least a four-hour drive!"

"I'm not driving. He's high up in Special Forces, so he's arranged to chopper me down from the air base in Pomona. They need me—he couldn't navigate his way out of a paper bag. The race will take a couple of hours—I'll probably be back around six. We can go to Lai Lai's in Ventnor around seven. I love authentic Chinese food, and theirs is the best."

Well, I thought, this man certainly packs a lot into a day. Flattered by the attention, and thrilled that he wanted to see me again, I agreed.

James took me to my car. As I drove back to Atlantic City, I was awestruck. James Montgomery was larger than life. I read about men like this, the "masters of the universe" described in Tom Wolfe's *Bonfire of the Vanities,* or on the pages of Fortune Magazine. But I never met such a mover and shaker in person. James lived and traveled all over the world; he had all kinds of interesting business projects in the works; he was smart and entertaining. And, he was interested in *me*.

Later that afternoon, as I pulled weeds from my tiny front garden, James called to change plans. "I must have been crazy," he said. "I'll be getting in from the race tonight covered by salt spray—certainly no way to meet such a charming lady. Can we make it tomorrow night?"

So Monday night, I put on a form-fitting red dress with a low-cut neckline. It was fairly long—hanging to mid-calf, but slit to mid-thigh. Just sexy enough. When I arrived at the restaurant, which was practically around the corner from my house, James was already at a table near the front window, talking on his cell phone. He wore a sport coat of a black and cream hounds-tooth fabric and an open-collared shirt. A paisley silk handkerchief sprouted from his breast pocket.

"I have to go now," James said into the phone as I walked up to the table. "My lovely dinner companion has just arrived." He punched the "end" button.

"Don't you ever leave your phone home?" I teased.

"Well, no," James replied. "I have so many projects going on, and the people I deal with are all over the country. I need to be accessible almost 24 hours a day."

I sat down, and noticed that James had placed a small gift by my plate—a tiny bottle of Caleche perfume, from Hermés of Paris. "What a nice surprise," I said. "Thank you."

"You're quite welcome," James replied. "It's the first of many." His words caused a little flutter in my stomach.

The waiter arrived with our menus. James knew exactly what all the Chinese dishes were, and what he wanted. "I've spent so much time in Asia that I've really come to adore real Asian food," he said. "Most Chinese food in this country is the American version of Chinese, not true Chinese. I prefer the real thing. That's why I like this restaurant."

"I can never remember which Chinese dishes I like," I said. "Although I have learned to ask if a dish has brown sauce or white sauce. I like the brown sauce better."

We had a pleasant evening, and never seemed to be at a loss for words. It turned out that both of us had been rowers. I became involved with crew when I was a freshman at Syracuse University. James told me he rowed at Sydney Boys High School in Australia, where the sport was taken very seriously. He continued to row while attending Sydney University, and went on to participate in several international competitions, including the 1964 Olympics in Mexico.

"Was it fun?" I asked.

"Not really," he said. "Before you compete, you're so nervous that you really can't enjoy anything. And after we competed, we left."

James had so many interesting experiences and projects to talk about—I was fascinated. He told me about starting the Movietime cable channel in Los Angeles on a shoestring budget—filling airtime with public domain footage and using promotional movie trailers as programming. One of the staples of the channel was a program called *Power Breakfast,* in which James interviewed movie company executives.

"I started the show to gain access to the movie studios," James said. "Everyone interviews movie stars and directors, but studio executives don't get nearly as much attention. The show appealed to their egos. It eventually took on a life of its own, and the movie execs wanted to be interviewed. I was able to make a lot of connections. I'll show you a tape of it sometime.

"You know," he continued. "I think the South Jersey area is ripe for additional television programming. I've been talking with the people at Suburban Cable about developing some shows. And I've also been thinking about starting another cable channel here. In fact, I'm going to Wildwood in a couple of days to look at a TV station that I may buy. Would you like to come along?"

The idea that James was buying a TV station—well, television had a way of mesmerizing people. Wildwood wasn't far; it was another beach resort 45 minutes south of Atlantic City. Excited to be included, I accepted.

We finished dinner—and that awkward moment arrived again. What were we to do next?

"You know, I live right around the corner," I said. "And I have a nice porch overlooking the bay. Would you like to stop by?"

"I would love to," James answered graciously. "Thank you for inviting me."

So we both got in our cars and drove the two minutes to my house. The evening was warm, with a slight breeze blowing. Sitting on my porch, we made plans to go to Wildwood on Wednesday—James would pick me up at 10 o'clock in the morning. The attire for the trip, James said, would be casual. He intended to wear what he usually wore—shorts and a polo shirt.

"Well, I have to be going," James said. "My day starts at 4 a.m."

We both stood up—another awkward moment arrived. But James didn't let it stay that way; he took a step toward me to kiss me.

I was expecting him to do it—after all, I spent many years dating, and I knew what happened next. But I did not expect that the first part of his body to touch me would be his protruding stomach. *That* was a new experience, and somewhat disconcerting.

The kiss, however, was nice enough. We said goodbye, and I floated into the house, daring to wonder if my luck had finally changed.

At 10 a.m. Wednesday morning, James' Ford Explorer pulled up in front of my house. I climbed in and we began our adventure. James plugged in a CD and cranked up the volume. "It's the Big O, Roy Orbison," he exclaimed. "I love this stuff, the original rock 'n' roll. When it comes to music, I'm nothing but a big kid."

The Big O was a little before my time. In fact, I couldn't name any of his hits. But at least it was rock 'n' roll, and I was pleased to see James smiling and singing along.

We drove through Ventnor, Margate, Longport and Somers Point, then got on the Garden State Parkway. The Parkway, especially in South Jersey, was a scenic road, traversing wetlands and pine forests. When we reached a rest stop,

James pulled in.

At Burger King, James ordered a cheeseburger and a large Diet Coke. Having already eaten breakfast, I got a decaf coffee. As we stood at the condiments bar—I was putting cream in my coffee, and James was putting mustard on his cheeseburger—he asked me, "Will you help me get back in the shape I was in when I was rowing?"

Right then and there, I decided that there might be possibilities with this relationship. Nutrition and fitness were very important to me. Ever since I got over my allergies and started putting on weight in the fourth grade, I battled that five to 10 pounds which represented the difference between "shapely" and "slim." I counted calories and fat grams, and learned the value of strenuous exercise. For years I ran six to eight miles a day on the Atlantic City Boardwalk, although once I moved to the bay, my level of running dropped dramatically. I did, however, install exercise equipment in my basement, and was devoted to *The Firm* aerobics videotapes.

More importantly, in the current context, I liked athletic men. James carried all of his weight in his belly, as if he were pregnant with twins. But I noticed, since he was wearing shorts, that he had nice long legs, with muscular calves. If he was willing to drop the gut and get in shape, if he was willing to share my healthy lifestyle, well, that made a big difference. James instantly became more attractive.

"Sure," I answered. "I'd be happy to help you."

The "television station" in Wildwood was a joke. I expected to see a studio with lights, cameras and action. Instead, we walked into a closet atop a 10-story condominium building that contained electronics equipment. It also held brooms and mops. James, however, seemed to regard the closet as a potential piece of his South Jersey cable empire.

We left, and on the way home, stopped for a late lunch at a bayfront restaurant in Somers Point. James, it turned out, knew about seafood as well as Chinese food—he could tell by the taste that the shrimp in his salad had been frozen too long. Even though the meal was a disappointment, the company was exciting, as James told me more about his projects.

He talked with great enthusiasm, backed by an incredible depth of knowledge, connections and experience. James described how each of the projects would support the others—the key was that they were all entertainment-related. With James' background and his ability to envision the big picture, secure funding and pull people together—well, his excitement was contagious. I could feel it. And I wanted to be part of it.

We finished lunch late in the afternoon and continued to chat as we drove back to my house.

"So," James said to me. "What are your views on sex?"

I was surprised by the bluntness of the question. "I like sex," I replied.

"Every day?" he asked, in a hopeful voice.

"Well, I like sex," I repeated. "I think it's great fun."

We drove a few more blocks, and James said, "Do you have any questions for me?"

I thought for a moment and then asked, "Have you had an AIDS test?"

"That's a very good question," he said, matter-of-factly. "I don't have a gay bone in my body. I have checkups, including blood tests, all the time because of my work with the government. And Gale had a full autopsy when she died. The AIDS tests were negative."

"You have to be careful these days," I said.

We arrived back at my house, and once again, I invited James in.

"Thank you for accompanying me," he said.

"I was happy to go with you," I replied.

James leaned forward to kiss me. Then, pulling me close, he kissed me again.

"I want you so much, Donna," he whispered, his lips close to my ear. "Ever since we met, you're all I can think about."

The kissing continued, becoming more and more passionate, and before long, we were in bed. Yes, I did like sex, and it had been a couple of months since my last encounter with David, so I was quite the enthusiastic participant. And with James, I felt like the most powerful man in the world was making love to me.

He took me. Not violently, but the confidence of a virile man who knew what he deserved, went after it and claimed his rewards. He kissed me, stroked me, spread my legs—we both climaxed, multiple times. Our loving felt like more than physical expression. It felt like destiny.

An hour or so later, James said he had to leave, and he was gone. I lay in wonder for awhile, savoring his scent upon the sheets. Then I dragged myself out of bed, showered, dressed and sat down at the desk in my home office, which was conveniently located right next to the bedroom. Still a bit wobbly, I reflected with astonishment on the events of the day, the events of the week. I was spellbound.

For the first time in my life, I felt wanted by a man who was truly worthy of me. Oh, I'd dated plenty of guys over the past 20 years, but usually they weren't as smart or as successful as me. But lonely, I dated them anyway. With James, there was no compromise. In fact, his accomplishments made mine look miniscule. He was someone I could admire without reservation, accompany without feeling like I settled.

The phone rang; it was James.

"Donna, I just can't believe my good fortune in meeting you," he said. And then, very crisply and properly, he asked, "Will you do me the great honor of becoming my wife?"

I gasped—this was better than anything I ever dreamed. For so long, I wanted to find someone to marry. And now this man, this *super*man, was proposing to me. My head spun. It didn't take me long to make a decision. In fact, the words came out of my mouth of their own accord.

"Yes," I answered. "Yes, James, I would be happy to."

I hoped that one little word—"yes"—would change the direction of my life. It did, but not in the way I expected.

Chapter 4

Astonishment, excitement and relief—the emotions washed over me when James Montgomery proposed. Astonishment that he wanted to marry me after we had known each other for such a short time. Excitement about becoming part of his big plans and big future. And relief that my long, lonely search for companionship was over.

I reflected upon my romantic history, and it was dismal.

Back when I was young—in high school and college—I always thought I would marry when I was 26 years old. Not that I had any prospects. I was what would charitably be called an "awkward teenager"—a brainy girl with glasses, zits and a few extra pounds. In high school I did manage to get dates for my junior and senior proms, but that was about it. Still, I anticipated that I would do what most women did, and 26 seemed like a reasonable age for marriage—old enough to have my feet on the ground, but young enough to have children.

Instead, at 26 I started my business.

This was not a conscious decision. When I lost my job at Atlantic City Magazine in 1982, the reason, I suppose, was stress. The magazine's publication schedule increased from quarterly to monthly, and even though I had four assistant editors, I felt crushed by an exponentially expanding workload. At the same time, I concluded that my on-again, off-again relationship with a mid-level casino executive was definitely off. Despite my wishful thinking, he had other (female) plans, and I was left behind. My fragile state of mind must have been obvious, because in June 1982, my boss told me to take a month off.

What was I going to do?

Friends involved with the management of Historic Gardner's Basin—a waterfront park that was promoted as Atlantic City's great hope for economic revival before the casinos came—invited me to cruise on its tourist attraction, the tall ship *Young America*. The 130-foot square-rigger was sailing from Atlantic City down to a Portsmouth, Virginia, dry dock for maintenance. A few days after the Young America was due to reach Portsmouth, friends of my parents planned to cruise their 40-foot powerboat from Virginia back to New Jersey. My parents and I were invited to join them.

I wrapped up my responsibilities at the magazine, gave the keys to my company car to a carless assistant, and embarked on my nautical adventure. Onboard, besides *Young America's* captain and crew, were two other passengers. One was Jack Keith, the Gardner's Basin park supervisor—I had interviewed him for a magazine article. The other was Dennis Steelman, an engineer at the nearby Federal Aviation Administration Technical Center, who was a Gardner's Basin volunteer. On the outgoing tide, the tall ship motored through Absecon Inlet to the open ocean, and soon I was seasick. The next day I lay motionless on the roof of the galley, while the other passengers—my new best friends—brought me dry saltine crackers to settle my churning stomach. Eventually I got accustomed to the swells and was able to function as a crewmember, albeit an inexperienced one.

I felt much better on the return trip with my parents and their friends—probably due to the more sedate water in the Chesapeake Bay. We stopped in the Baltimore Inner Harbor, which was recently transformed from a decrepit industrial waterfront to a bustling tourist attraction, where a Scandinavian festival was underway. I took a picture of my father with his arms around two blond girls in bright blue folk costumes, and he took my picture with a guy dressed like a big, hairy Viking, complete with a horned helmet and long sword.

After my delightful seafaring adventure, I returned home, rested, relaxed and looking forward to spending the rest of my vacation on the beach that was just steps from my apartment.

In my mailbox I found a severance check from Atlantic City Magazine.

The letter from my boss said something about, "according to our agreement." My recollection of the agreement was that I was taking a month off, not that I was fired. Suddenly, I was no longer editor of Atlantic City Magazine. Which meant I no longer had a job, a car or an identity.

What was I to do? The only part of my life that remained intact was the company softball team. Everything else was gone. South Jersey was not a big media market, so continuing my career in magazines would require moving. But I had a good reputation in Atlantic City, and it was not the time to leave town.

After only four years of legalized gambling, nine casinos were open, and they raked in almost as much money as all of Las Vegas—with one-fifth the casino floor space. A new mayor had been elected, and hope abounded that the town, which completely underestimated the public's appetite for blackjack, craps and slot machines, would finally get organized.

I wanted to stay in Atlantic City, so I collected unemployment and waited for an opportunity. To pass the time that summer, I helped out at Gardner's Basin, answering the phone and booking day cruises for tourists on the *Young America*. It wasn't demanding work. During many slow hours on the job, I had lively discussions with my officemate, Jack Keith.

Jack and I became buddies. Sometimes I talked about my frustrations in dating, or more precisely, my lack of dating. Jack couldn't understand it. He said I was pleasant company and he liked having me around. This was truly a revelation. I suspected that people associated with me because of my brains and organizational ability. There always seemed to be an agenda—they wanted me to do something for them. With Jack, for the first time in my life, I felt like I had a friend who just liked hanging out with me.

Freelance writing assignments came my way, like magazine articles and commercial newsletters. By January 1983, I realized that I was in business. So I made it official—I formed a one-person corporation and bought my first computer.

Determined to succeed in my business, I became an avid consumer of self-help books. They often contained exercises that I dutifully completed, recording the answers in my journal. I'd been writing down my thoughts, experiences and observations almost as long as I could remember. My journal entries back then were mostly resolutions about goal setting and time management. But I certainly didn't want to work on Friday or Saturday nights. In the 1980s, Friday nights were set aside for happy hour at McGettigan's, Atlantic City's yuppie bar. That was the place to be for everybody who was somebody, or wanted to be somebody, or wanted to meet somebody.

Besides McGettigan's, much of my socializing revolved around sports. I joined the Boardwalk Runners Club and raced distances from five kilometers to 10 miles. I took over the Atlantic City Magazine softball team and we joined a co-ed league. I bought a membership in a health club. Although I had an extensive collection of trophies, medals and certificates, competition was not my prime motivation for the sporting life. My true purpose was meeting men.

In 1987, there was a new game in town—volleyball. I joined a Tuesday night adult league where I met a guy named Lou McNally.* I was 30 years old, and Lou was a year or two older. He was taller than me and muscular from working out, with broad shoulders and a trim waist. I was not accustomed to catching the interest of nice-looking men, so if he had been checking me out, I didn't notice. Then one night in December, when everyone went to a local bar after the games, I realized he was flirting with me. As we leaned against the bar with our beers, Lou said he had to be at work early—like 7 a.m.

"I'm glad I don't have to do that," I said.

"When do you have to go to work?" he asked.

"Whenever I want. I work out of my home."

Lou was intrigued. "What do you do?" he asked.

"I'm a writer."

"Oh," he said, feigning disappointment. "My imagination was running wild for a minute there."

We started spending time together after volleyball games. Then I had comp (short for complimentary) tickets from my client at Caesars to see Gene Kelly, the famous dancer of my parents' generation. I invited my parents—my father loved ballroom dancing and was a huge fan—and asked Lou to join us. He did.

After the casino show, Lou and I went to a nightclub. We had a few drinks and danced. As we put on our coats to leave, Lou wrapped my green wool winter scarf around my neck, gently tied it, and pulled me close. I felt a thrill of excitement and anticipation. We spent the night together, although we weren't exactly compatible. I chalked it up to first-time jitters.

The holidays approached, and I invited Lou over to help decorate my Christmas tree—always a task, I felt, that should be shared with someone special. Lou was diplomatic in his approach to hanging ornaments—he unwrapped them and handed them to me, so I could decide where they belonged. When we got together a few days after Christmas, he gave me a gold chain and a heart-shaped cut crystal dish to keep it in. I was impressed.

New Year's Eve arrived, and we went to a small party. Afterwards, we spent the night together again, although we didn't seem to be getting any more compatible. Now, I'd read plenty of articles in women's magazines that said men weren't mind readers, and women had to communicate what we wanted. So I did. After that, Lou stopped calling me.

I was crushed. But we were still playing volleyball, so when I saw Lou at the bar on the following Tuesday, I tried to talk to him, tried to explain. I touched his arm. He jumped back, repulsed.

Another romance crashed and burned. The only thing to do was fix my makeup, put on my high heels and go out looking again. For that, a girl needs girlfriends.

A few months after my latest fiasco, I was happy houring with friends at the Waterfront Restaurant, a new hot spot overlooking the bay in Somers Point. A woman named Betty Davies joined us. We were both in the advertising business—I was a copywriter, she was a freelance graphic designer. More importantly, she was single, laughed a lot and liked having a good time. She also lived just a few blocks from me. We hit it off right away.

Betty was 5 feet 2 inches tall, with long, straight blond hair and hazel eyes. She was three years older than me and had almost married a couple of times. Betty seemed to have a much better understanding of this male-female business than I did, so when she offered advice about men, I listened. I was learning that there was a downside to my management skills—namely, no matter what the circumstances, I expected to manage them. There were men who—if I got any feedback at all—complained that I "always had to be in control." I suspected they were right.

"It's so hard for me to just let things happen," I admitted to Betty, "and not try to control everything."

"Many people believe we should just let life flow through us," Betty said. The idea was to "trust the universe." Betty said there were no accidents, we manifested everything that happened to us and whatever we sent out came back to us tenfold. These concepts, I learned, were classified as metaphysical or New Age thinking. It certainly wasn't what I learned in Catholic school.

But I noticed similar concepts in different places. The previous Christmas, my brother, Doug, gave everyone in the family a copy of *Think and Grow Rich,* by Napoleon Hill. It was originally published in 1937 and hinted at the secret of success employed by many rich and famous Americans. The first point:

"thoughts are things." "Our brains become magnetized with the dominating thoughts which we hold in our minds," Hill wrote, "and these 'magnets' attract to us the forces, the people, the circumstances of life which harmonize with the nature of our dominating thoughts."

Linda Goodman's Love Signs was a book that predicted the pros and cons of romantic relationships based on astrological signs. I consulted it every time I met a potential love interest. But Goodman also wrote, "Love is far more than an emotion or a feeling. Love is a positive electrical impulse."

The ideas fascinated me. I recorded in my journal the concepts that kept showing up: Everything and everyone in the world were connected, and our lives were governed by our own thoughts and internal realities.

In August 1988, Betty called and asked if I wanted to get a psychic reading. Betty's friend made an appointment to see Terrie Bergman, a palm reader, that afternoon, but cancelled. Did I want the appointment?

I had never been to a psychic. I had never considered going to a psychic. But I felt like I really needed some answers, so I went to a home in Margate where she was doing the readings. While I waited for the psychic to finish with another client, I was so nervous that I was shaking.

Terrie Bergman was a slender, dark-haired woman who appeared to be in her late 40s. She was casually but fashionably dressed in slacks and a top. She led me to a small table, about the size of a card table, with two chairs. Attached to the table was a swing-arm magnifier lamp, like the ones my graphic designers used. There was also a tape recorder—Betty had told me to bring a cassette tape.

"What do I do?" I asked as I sat down. "I never did this before."

"I know. Just give me both hands this way," Terrie said, pulling my palms under the lamp so she could see them through the magnifying lens. "I won't hurt. How did she ever talk you into doing this? You've got this practical, logical mind."

I laughed. Then words spilled out of the psychic, as if someone suddenly turned on a faucet full blast.

"Interesting. You're changing," she said. "So you may not know yourself yet. For somebody that was alone and was strong all her life, and did it by herself, you are going through a major shift. And the major shift is, number one, you won't get used the way you used to, and number two, you're going to surround yourself with people, and be a part of the world and it's going to be fabulous for you.

"You're free; you're independent; nobody can ever tell you what to do. You're very much your own person. You're driving yourself crazy because you don't know what to do. And you think you should know what to do."

The psychic pounded her fist on the table for emphasis. Then the flood of words continued.

"Now, for you, this 'I don't know' is a very high state of enlightenment. So don't make it wrong. You're in the process of healing. You're healing your past of being numb your whole life. So you're going to start being less melancholy; you're going to be less frustrated; you're going to stop worrying about the future so much.

"And so from now on, this sounds like strange words, but I'm seeing you join the human race. And it's going to be wonderful for you. You'll be surrounded by people that really love you, and you'll let them love you. Now, as this is happening, you're also going to be thinking, and thinking, trying to figure things out. But you're hiding your beauty."

The psychic paused, somewhat surprised by what she said. "Now, I don't know what I mean by that; you've got to wait for it to come out of me."

After a moment of consideration, Terrie continued. "You don't allow yourself to feel beautiful, so people don't see you as beautiful. People see us the way we see ourselves. I think you look great. But if you're not satisfied with the way you look, I want you to go get a makeover. Go to a cosmetic shop and learn how to put them on; get your hair fixed; do whatever it takes for you to feel beautiful.

"The message that I'm getting to tell you is to come out of hiding. Because you've been hiding behind how you used to be. It's almost like somebody that was fat and lost weight. That's not you, is it?"

"I used to be heavier," I said.

The psychic turned my hands under the light to look at them further. "What your weight was about in the past was that you stuffed tears. Rather than cry, you'd eat. So what you need to know now is, don't stuff, cry. You stuffed your emotions your whole lifetime. You're tough. You're on top of yourself looking down, judging yourself much too harshly. You are a perfectionist; you're always going to be a perfectionist. You have some anger about the physical level of consciousness. So the physical part of you is not satisfied. The spiritual is pretty good. And the mental—you're going to drive yourself crazy, thinking. I feel like between 29 and 30 you almost had a mental breakdown, or you might have actually had one."

"Twenty-seven," I said, remembering the upheaval of losing a relationship and then my job at Atlantic City Magazine.

"Yeah, 27," Terrie said. "You had to have it. And I'll tell you what happened. There was an emotional disappointment, and you felt it mentally. It's like your brain fried, but it was an emotional disappointment. I want you to look back over the experience. You may need to pound a table and get rid of some anger, resentment, helplessness, and get that out of your system."

Terrie turned my hands again. "You've had your share of emotional disappointment," she said, slowly. "You've been used, but you let it happen. From since you were a little girl. How dare them do it to me, but they didn't do it to you, you let them do it. So no blame on them and no blame on you. I can pinpoint the exact problem. The problem is that there's a you from the past that's showing up in the present. So what has to happen is we've got to get rid of the problems of the past that affect now."

Terrie paused briefly, studied my hand, and then continued. "You're not married," she said.

"No."

"Part of the problem is, you think men are going to deceive you, so you attract deceptive men. I want you to start trusting yourself. You don't want to get married right now, but you do want to fall in love. Were you married?"

"No."

"Were you in love about 26 or 27?"

I remembered the casino executive. "I thought I was."

"And he deceived you? Or you felt deceived?"

"He never deceived me. But I made it out to be more than it was. It was all in my own head."

Terry didn't agree with this. "I think part of it is you sense stuff," she said. "I just have a feeling that this guy was a little deceptive."

"Well maybe he was. He never made any promises."

"But he was dishonest to himself. So you were getting double messages from him. You have some tears about him. Let him go, because he's not going to be your deepest love. And I feel like you'll meet somebody and get to know some-body for a while. Did you date somebody with a couple of children?"

"Yes," I said, remembering another disappointment.

"That's what I thought," Terrie said. "You cut yourself off from children. Let me explain that to you. In a past lifetime you had too many kids that drove you nuts. So you said, 'This lifetime, I'm not going to have any, or I'm not going to have many.' It's okay not to have them if you don't want them. It's almost like buying a pair of shoes. You can either buy them or not buy them. And the energy that's attached is only from you. So I don't want you to feel guilty not having kids."

Having bought into society's plan for women—marriage and family—I was taken aback. "I like kids," I weakly protested. "I think I do."

"Yeah, you do," Terrie agreed. "I think you're going to get involved with somebody that has a couple of kids. But don't love somebody that doesn't want you. I don't want you to have an imaginary love. I want you to get a real person, because within the next few years, you're going to fall in love. I feel like you'll go with somebody to get to know him, which is a good idea. At least don't marry anybody without knowing him a year and a half.

"Well, you know what?" she continued. "Through all the pain that you've been through in your whole lifetime, on an emotional level, you absolutely are learning how to love. You did not know how before. Nobody ever taught you. You have a tendency to be too busy for love. Relationships—are you in one now?"

"No."

"Good. At this point in your life you don't want to be married. You have heal-ing in the stomach about relationships of the past. So you need to get them out. And once they're gone, you'll be able to handle a relationship. I can promise you, you will meet somebody; you will fall madly in love; you will be thrilled that you didn't get married before.

"You will be very into spiritual things later in your life. You have natural abil-ity in psychic or spiritual stuff, even though you have this logical mind. After 40 you'll get into it. It's going to be real good for you; it will get you more peaceful.

"Physically, my vision of you is that, I'm seeing you become alive, and I love it. It's like you're not going to be as sad as you were; you're not going to be as numb as you were; you're not going to be as roboty as you were. You're not going to be as alone as you were. You're going through a tough time right now. And there's a shock. I think there's either a death or a loss around you. And it's not sad. But you're at the crossroads of letting go."

The timer went off. My hour was up.

Terrie Bergman never met me and knew nothing about me—yet she knew everything. She saw my life, with all its pain and promise, in the lines of my hands under her magnifying lamp. She read my story like a newscaster read a teleprompter, scrolling from one point to the next. I felt like she looked deep into my soul, seeing secrets I didn't know I had.

The band's lead singer and guitarist stood at the crowded circular bar, not far from me, with a short tumbler in front of him. He was trying to get my attention.

My friend, Betty, got us invited to a corporate Christmas party in 1988. The bandleader wore a dark suit and tie. I wore a calf-length flared skirt and matching tunic of cream and gray knit, with gray heels. The outfit flattered me.

After glancing over several times—perhaps to see if I was with a date—the singer sent me a drink. I raised my fresh glass of white wine to thank him—the opening he was looking for.

"You have the best energy in the room," he said.

Well, that was an opening line I hadn't heard before.

The guy's name was Courtney Colletti. He had a big smile, sparkling brown eyes and kinky brown hair—what was left of it. Courtney was slight—probably two inches shorter than me when I wasn't wearing heels. Although I preferred men who were tall, blond and blue-eyed, Courtney said he felt my energy from the stage and couldn't wait to talk to me—how could I refuse? We chatted until it was time for him to play again. He made me promise to stay through the next set.

Courtney was a master showman, a front man who knew how to get the crowd rocking. He was once a member of Johnny's Dance Band, which had played big concert venues such as the Spectrum in Philadelphia. Courtney was also an excellent singer, and throughout the set inserted my name into the lyrics. Of course I waited for him.

After 40 minutes, the band took another break and the deejay started spinning tunes. Courtney walked right over to me, and when a slow song came on he asked me to dance. In my high heels I towered above him, and it was odd to see my dance partner smiling up at me. I could tell that he was excited to be close to me, but it was also odd to feel the excitement slightly above my knees.

Courtney lived in New Hope, Pennsylvania, but he often made the almost two-hour trip to Atlantic City for work. Every time he had a gig in town, we got together. It was always an overnight visit.

"When I'm with you, I can't keep my hands off you," Courtney said. "I like that." Courtney was very physical—somehow there was sexual energy even in his voice. He was also psychic. He talked about past lives that he remembered us sharing. In one, we were a married couple living as pioneers in the American West. An image formed in my mind, like remembering a dream while I was awake. I saw myself in a homespun shirt and long skirt, in front of a low, hand-built sod home on the prairie. Courtney remembered another life when we were both men fighting in the trenches of World War I.

I had never before met anyone who remembered me from a past life.

One night, after we had been seeing each other for about a month, Courtney called and said, "I haven't felt connected to you. I didn't get the urge to call you and you didn't call me. What's going on?" I had no idea.

Courtney had a directness, a habit of asking probing questions, that forced me to reveal myself to him. For the first time, I started to open myself emotionally to a man. But as a musician, he didn't keep office hours, and the reality of our different lifestyles turned out to be a problem that simply could not be solved. One night in February 1989, I told Courtney that I wanted a relationship with a man who could take me out on a Saturday night. For him, of course, Saturday nights were prime time for making money.

Courtney was understanding. "You're entitled to what you want," he said, without a trace of rancor. For us to stay together, one of us would have to change our lifestyle radically. Acknowledging that we really didn't have a future, Courtney asked, "What do you want our relationship to be?"

A couple of months later, as we amicably parted ways, I knew the experience had been good for me. I hoped to someday hire Courtney's band to play at my wedding.

Much of my frustration about men, Terrie Bergman, the psychic, told me in my second reading with her, was linked to past disappointments. Each man that I attracted was a karmic lesson. I was so filled with frustration that men walked by me and sensed it. "Before any man comes you have to get cleansed," she said. "Clean up your own energy. Release steam."

I needed, Terrie said, an "emotional roto-rooter."

I had a tight wall around me that was blocking me. "What's holding you back is a deep sentence inside—'I've got to do it all by myself,'" Terrie told me. "You have to decide that you can do it yourself—and share your life with someone else."

I started to share my life with a dog.

I always said I was too busy for a pet, so a canine companion was not planned in advance. But my parents took in a dog, a nine-month-old coonhound mix named Beau, who had belonged to my younger brother, Greg. Greg bought the dog while in college to win the affections of a girl. The dog failed to impress the girl, but did impress his housemates, and two of them went out and got their own puppies. The three dogs grew up in an off-campus equivalent of a frat house.

As a hound, Beau was a natural tracker. When Greg visited the college registrar's office for his last semester of classes, he took his puppy along for a ride. Greg pulled his 1976 Mercury Marquis into a parking lot and told Beau to stay in the car, leaving the windows open far enough for the dog to stick his head out. Greg walked to the administrative building and stood in line with a dozen other students. Fifteen minutes later, Beau was sitting next to him. The puppy had squeezed out of the car window, tracked Greg across a courtyard and up the building steps, through two sets of glass doors—which someone had to open for the pooch—up another flight of stairs, down the hallway and past all the other students to find Greg in line. The dog had a good nose.

Greg graduated from college and got a job as an estimator with a multimillion-dollar New York City construction firm. He went to work early in the morning and returned home at dusk, while Beau was left alone in a small apartment in Queens. My father decided this was a terrible life for a dog, and after two weeks, Dad brought Beau to the family homestead in Vineland, New Jersey. But Dad already had an old mutt named Sarge, who considered the energetic puppy to be a nuisance.

About a month later, in October 1990, I visited Mom and Dad, and the two dogs, in Vineland, which was about an hour from Atlantic City. I honestly didn't know why Beau appealed to me; I guess I thought he was cute. He was a medium-sized, short-haired dog, tan in color, with a white patch on his chest. He had floppy ears and a long, curled tail that never stopped wagging. When I went home—by this time, I'd bought my house—Beau went with me.

My plan was to make the dog stay downstairs at night and put him outside during the day. That didn't work—the very first night he crept into my bedroom. Beau also quickly discovered that he could escape the yard by pushing through the slats of my neighbor's rickety picket fence and head for the beach, where there were birds, shells and, under the Boardwalk, half-eaten hamburgers.

I enrolled us in dog-training school. Beau, distracted by all the other dogs in the class, was not the best student. We left the first lesson early because I was traumatized by his lack of cooperation. During our next lesson, I skipped the doggie bathroom break, as it was another distraction. This turned out to be a bad idea—during the second half of the class, Beau relieved himself on my leg.

We did at least learn how dogs were supposed to behave and settled into a routine: I ate breakfast; Beau got a walk; Beau got breakfast. I ate lunch; Beau got a walk. Beau got a walk; Beau got dinner; I got dinner; Beau got table scraps. The dog always knew when it was his turn for attention.

Beau became protective of me. In fact, he was an excellent chaperone. If after a date I invited a guy in for nookie on the couch, Beau sat on the stair landing and cried. If the nookie continued, he barked. If it still continued, he came over to the couch and put his paw on my knee. This proved to be convenient. If I didn't want the guy to stay, I let Beau discourage him. If I did want the guy to stay, I locked Beau in the basement.

I took Beau with me to return camping equipment to Tim Gravino,* with whom I had been semi-involved. Tim and I hadn't spoken for two months, ever since we fought about the Philadelphia Folk Festival.

For 10 years, I spent the last weekend in August with my friends at the Folk Festival, a three-day party of music, camping, jam sessions, crafts, poker, junk food, crowds, alcohol, spot-a-pots, rain, shine, mud, camaraderie and laughs. Our group of 40 to 50 people was among the 20,000 that descended annually upon the Old Pool Farm in Schwenksville, Pennsylvania, located 35 miles north-west of Philadelphia. More than 5,000 festival attendees were campers like us. Tents and tarps, pitched practically on top of each other, covered a 40-acre field.

I invited Tim to accompany me to the 1990 festival. We had been seeing each other, on and off, for about six months. Tim was a college graduate who became a plumber. I was surprised to learn he was my age—with his sparkling eyes and easy laugh, he struck me as being younger. Tim was about my height and had the physique of an athlete. A former football player, he said he had good hands, and I could vouch for that.

Our relationship was always yes, no or maybe, so I was never sure if we were dating or not. At first he was enthusiastic about the Folk Festival, then he didn't want to go. He finally did go with me and enjoyed himself immensely. Then he stopped talking to me. I was angry—I felt like he hung around long enough to party with my friends and then blew me off. Tim didn't say we were over; he just disappeared again.

Did I want more of this? Well, some romance was better than no romance, so when I returned his camping gear, I brought Beau along as an icebreaker. It worked. Tim asked me about the dog, which enabled us to talk, and he started coming around again. Sort of.

I had my third reading with Terrie Bergman on December 10, 1990. Soon after she started speaking, I realized her words were the same: I needed to come out of hiding. In the past, I had to do it all by myself. I had to stop thinking and start doing. I was going to start studying spiritual stuff; I would embark on a spiritual journey.

"All of this you've said before," I complained. "I guess I'm disappointed because nothing's changed."

"That's not my problem, that's yours," Terrie said. "I can only say what I see. You have not shifted your own consciousness. You're not listening to your higher self. All I can do is provide you with an opportunity to change your life around. It's up to you to take the ball and run with it. So if you feel disappointed that you're hearing the same thing, I say that there's disappointment within you that needs to come out."

"How do I do that?" I asked.

"You actually stop thinking and start feeling. Start feeling the disappointment. Cry your eyes out. See, you're waiting for a man, an authority figure, to come and make it better. Make yourself the authority figure and start putting what you want into action."

"How do I do that?" I asked again.

"The first thing you have to do is recognize that your whole life you've been proving yourself," the psychic explained. "Stop proving yourself and start being yourself, whatever that looks like. There's a difference. Proving yourself you never get to enjoy the experience. Being yourself, you get to do what you want on a daily basis. Get out of obligation. And get into being with the public by choice.

You feel like you have to go with the public; you don't feel like you want to."

"I don't."

"Right, I know. But that's just a decision that you made in your mind. You have to change from a mental point of view, or else everything's going to stay the same, just like it stayed the same for the last two readings.

"You're waiting for it to happen to you. But it doesn't happen unless you change. The best I can explain it is you're an energy. Whatever you are is what you bring to yourself. If your thinking is not clear, then you bring to yourself the same shit that you've already had in the past, over and over again. The only way that a healing can occur is if you actually change the way you're thinking. And how do you do that? You do a soul search. Maybe you write your thoughts down, and see what you're thinking. You feel your disappointments and don't intellectualize them. You actually be in your emotional pain.

"You're like a little antenna for everybody else. But you're not sensitive enough to what's going on inside you, or you would understand this clearly. The fact that you don't understand means that you're not in touch with the real you. So I want you to let me speak to your heart. Get out of your head."

"I have no idea how to do that."

"The answer is to be willing to. You're petrified to get out of your head. Because if you got out of your head, you'd feel. And what you would feel is some emotional pain. You'd go through a cleansing and tears, and you wouldn't be able to stop crying. So allow that to occur. And how do you do that? Be willing to do it. In your willingness, spirit comes to help you."

All of this applied directly to my lackluster love life.

"Do you think a man will love you, yes or no?" Terrie asked.

"I don't know," I replied.

"Because you say, 'I don't know,' you get men who don't know if they'll love you," she said. "You have to get off the fence and stop this 'I don't know.' It's not about them; it's about you. You're waiting for them to change. And they're not going to change unless you're willing to change. There's a thought in your mind bringing you what you've got. So we're going to change you instead of them. And you don't want to hear that."

Terrie paused and looked up at me. "I'm stirring it up a little bit by this reading," she told me. "I'm okay that you're going to be upset walking out of here. I want you to feel your upsetness so much that you release a lot of tears. I promise that will be your healing. It does not have to do with this reading. It has to do with what's inside of you that needs to come out.

"Actually feel your upsetness, and you'll feel better. It will be a relief. But it won't come unless you're willing to go to the deeper part of you. See, you've been dealing on the surface of you. Now it's time to deal with all of you. What will happen is your past will be your past, and your present will be your present, and your point of power will be in the present moment.

"As far as relationships go, you will fall in love with somebody, definitely, absolutely. You have to let go of thinking you're going to get deceived by somebody. Let go of that thought."

Terrie was certainly right about one thing—when I got home, I was upset. "I feel like a failure," I wrote in my journal. "I feel like time is passing me by and I'm not getting anywhere. The only one who loves me, who wants me, is my dog. I'm so alone. I've always been so alone."

Terrie's words were echoed in *You Can Heal Your Life,* by Louise Hay, which my sister gave me for my birthday in 1991. It began:

Life is really very simple. What we give out, we get back.

What we think about ourselves becomes the truth for us. I believe that everyone, myself included, is 100 percent responsible for everything in our lives, the best and the worst. Every thought we think is creating our future. Each one of us creates our experiences by our thoughts and our feelings. The thoughts we think and the words we speak create our experiences.

© 1984, Louise L.Hay, *You Can Heal Your Life,* Hay House, Inc., Carlsbad, CA.

I devoured the book. To me, the ideas Louise Hay wrote about made so much sense—the universe supported whatever we believed, even when our beliefs harmed us. Most of us believed we weren't good enough. Often these hurtful beliefs showed up as physical ailments.

Part of the book was "the list"—a catalogue of aches, pains and diseases, and the beliefs that Louise Hay contended were their root causes. I looked up one of my medical problems—hypoglycemia. According to Louise Hay, the thoughts that caused it were, "Overwhelmed by the burdens of life. What's the use?" I could relate to that. Her suggested affirmation to change the thought pattern was, "I now choose to make my life light and easy and joyful."

A few months later, I wondered if the book could have helped my mother, Marie Andersen, who in November 1991 was diagnosed with cancer.

For six months, the doctors couldn't figure out what was wrong. Mom's voice became more and more hoarse, and she was admitted to Thomas Jefferson Hospital in Philadelphia. Although I was extremely squeamish about all things medical—I often passed out while visiting people in hospitals—I did manage to visit her. I was there the day that the doctors reached a conclusion: lung cancer.

The diagnosis was a terrible shock. Mom was 57 years old. She did not smoke.

But finally we knew what the problem was. The doctors put Mom on a radiation program. I drove from Atlantic City to Vineland to take her for one of the treatments. Mom spent most of her adult life working in offices, and was an efficient and conscientious employee. I was stuck by how she had that same businesslike approach while checking in for her radiation treatment, even though she was wearing a warm-up suit and sneakers.

The treatments didn't work. Mom lost her voice, and sat home in an upholstered chair with a little brass hand bell, which she rang to call Dad when she needed something. Then she couldn't eat solid food, because her epiglottis—the trap door in the throat that closes upon swallowing and prevents food from going into the lungs—was stuck open. She got weaker and weaker.

Christmas arrived. Traditionally, our family opened gifts in my parents' home early on Christmas morning, and we were all there. So many presents spilled from under the Christmas tree that it was difficult to walk. The gifts I brought included a coffee mug for each of us imprinted with *Carpe Diem,* or "Seize the day."

There weren't many days left. On December 26, 1991, Mom was admitted into intensive care. The doctors gave her a tracheotomy and put her on a ventilator. It was awful. Tubes were stuck into her body. Monitors on the machines displayed the pounding of her heart. While I was in the ICU, the doctors tried to disconnect the ventilator, but she couldn't breathe on her own.

I tried to breathe with her, tried to help her slow her breaths and racing heart. I wiped her brow and lips, and touched her arm. Doug and Greg arrived, but Mom sent us all away. Before I left, I kissed her and said, "I love you." I tried to do it without choking. I think she responded, "I know."

It was the last time I spoke to her.

I drove home to Atlantic City and went upstairs to my spare bedroom, which I used mostly for journaling and meditation. The walls were light mauve, and the curtains and daybed cover were white with a rose floral pattern. An antique loveseat was upholstered with rose-colored fabric. I sat on it and started to cry.

Beau came into the room. "Mom's really sick," I told him through my tears. "I don't know if she's going to get better." Beau did his best to comfort me. He stood on his hind legs with his front paws on my knees, licking my face, my eyes, my hands, anything he could reach. The harder I cried, the more frantically he licked me.

Finally we went to bed. Beau had his pillow at the top of the stairs, right outside my bedroom door, which was always open. But he had learned that if he waited until I fell asleep, he could jump on the bed and I wouldn't wake up. That night, it was comforting to feel my dog at my feet.

At 6:20 a.m. Sunday morning, December 29, 1991, the phone rang. It was my sister, Tracy. The doctors called and said Mom was "acute," and we should go to the hospital. I quickly dressed and sped up the Atlantic City Expressway. I was still on the road at 7:20 a.m. when a peaceful feeling overcame me. I arrived at the hospital and learned that Mom was gone. She died at 7:20.

The funeral was scheduled for the morning of New Year's Eve. Hundreds of people paid their respects—friends and family, Mom's co-workers and members of the St. Francis of Assisi Catholic Church, where Mom was active. The funeral mass was uplifting. The pastor, Father Carmen Carlone, knew Mom well, and spoke with eloquence about her. "Marie could get more done on her lunch hour than anyone I ever knew," Father Carmen said. He reminded us that life was short, so we should do what we wanted to do today. "Pray to Marie," he said, "and she'll help you from Heaven—on her lunch hour."

Sometimes I did pray—to Mom or whoever in the universe answered prayers. Mine were endless variations on one single theme: "Please, God, send me a man who will love me." On August 5, 1992, I described in my journal exactly what that man would look like:

1. Youthful—around my age, perhaps a little older. But forever young in attitude.

2. Good physical condition. Nice physique. Takes care of himself, regular exercise program. Non-smoker. Broad shoulders, trim waist. Pleasant features. All-American-Irish-Germanic look. Not ethnic. Hair. Six feet or taller. Nice voice. Masculine.

3. Successful. Good career, hot shot. Makes good money. Knows about investing. House, fancy car. Old money okay. Only workaholic when necessary. Hours—sort of 9-5.

4. Great lover. Healthy sexual appetite. Considerate—knows how to please me. Likes to go slow. Full body massage.

5. Smart. Wide range of interests—can talk about all kinds of things. Knows how the world works. Respects my intelligence.

6. Ethical. Some spiritual belief—willing to listen to New Age ideas. Believes in contributing. Educated. Classy.

7. Fun. Likes to do many things. Has friends, likes my friends. Easy to get along with. Likes dancing, Folk Festival, even museums. Good with people, friendly.

8. Calm. Takes things in stride. Even-tempered. Willing to talk things over. Doesn't get worked up over stupid things. Even big things.

9. Loves me. Thinks I'm beautiful, wonderful, smart, fun. Loves making love to me. Treats me like gold. Wants me.

10. Self-confident. Finds me stimulating, not threatening. Sure of who he is, where he's going. Capable with home-handyman jobs.

11. Likes kids. Willing to have a child with me. Good father.

12. Lives around Atlantic City. Wants to be here. Likes the beach.

A few months later, I had another reading with Terrie Bergman. Maybe my prayers had been heard, because her message was finally turning positive. "On an emotional level, you're doing fabulous," Terrie said. "I think you came into this life to learn how to love completely. And you're actually learning it.

"You're much less idealistic with men than you used to be. You're much more willing to be genuine in a relationship. You're seeing good news and bad news, and you say, 'You know what? I still love him.' And that's fabulous for you. Your lesson is not to be sensitive just to his needs, to also be aware of your own needs. Did you ever get married?"

"No."

"How come?"

"I was afraid."

"Right. So whatever that fear is, you have to confront it now. And then after you confront it ..."

"Well, what am I afraid of?"

Terrie examined my hands under the magnifier. "That it will break up. At some level, relationships to you have been and not been, been and not been."

"That's all the time; that's constant."

"Yeah. So there's a fear that it will break up. But you know what? I'll just tell you this: Love is a choice. You'll attract a man, and you'll have an opportunity to work through whatever you're most afraid of."

The heating system in my home by the bay was 90 years old, and in March 1993, it broke. So I called my plumber, who was, of course, Tim Gravino. I stopped by his apartment to give him a key so he could work on it while I was out. A year earlier, Tim had told me he was seeing another woman, but that relationship fizzled. We visited for a while, and my feelings of love came back, stronger than ever.

My emotions at seeing him surprised me. Maybe we were in love. Maybe someone just needed to say it. I didn't want to spend the rest of my life regretting that I didn't have the courage to open my mouth. So when we next spoke on the phone, I told Tim how I felt.

Not long after that, Tim called me for a date. We went out to dinner and spent the night together. "I know this is a loaded question," I said to him in the morning. "But do you know what you want from me?"

Tim wasn't prepared to give me an answer.

"I understand," I said, "all I want is a relatively quick decision."

Two weeks went by—nothing. Then the old pattern resumed. He'd be enthusiastic on the phone—and nothing. He'd promise to call me right back—and nothing. For months, I alternated between feeling warmth for him and feeling rejected. I was confused again.

On a hot day in July 1993, I sat cross-legged on the floor in the upstairs apartment of an old house outside of Philadelphia. The woman I traveled to see, Debra Taylor, sat on the floor across from me.

Debra was about my age, with short, dark hair. She was a channeler, which was not the same as a psychic. Debra was able to hear the communications of nonphysical beings from the spirit world. A client, like me, asked questions, and she conveyed answers from the spirit guides. I'd never heard of channelers, but if this woman could provide me with answers, I was all ears.

Debra was quiet, tuning into the vibrations from the unseen beings. Then she said, "Okay, Donna go ahead with your first question. I'm ready."

"I want to ask about Tim Gravino," I said. "We've had this on and off relationship. Why is he in my life, and why does he make me feel crazy?"

Debra tapped into Tim's spiritual energy, which she could do even though he wasn't there. Then she spoke in a monotone voice, like she was repeating what the guides dictated to her. "We see Tim has a great many things at his disposal— many opportunities for fulfillment. We see him as a wealth of information, connections. Partially why the two of you have come together is so that you will have a higher sense of need to be involved with someone of a higher caliber. We feel there has been difficulty with previous involvements in terms of caliber of individual. We see although he has created some disturbance between the two of you, that there have been some very fine exchanges and very fine experiences."

"The last time we were together I felt so good and happy about it, and then he blew me off again," I said. "I feel like I can't trust my feelings."

"So he has refused another get-together?" Debra asked. Then she relayed the guides' words. "He is going through a great deal within himself. This has affected his ability to accept his feelings. Your feelings are correct. Your interpretations are correct. He is the one who is not always revealing what is happening for him, or he lets a little bit of himself out, and he quick has to pull it back in because it doesn't fit the boxes that have been designed for him, and that he has bought into."

The guides said that, over time, Tim might be willing to let down his guard, although he would need a lot of space. Debra, the channeler, felt that he did want to develop something with me, but he wasn't sure how to go about it.

But after more than three years, I was tired of waiting. "What do I need to do to attract the relationship that I want?" I asked.

The guides answered. "We see a burning desire in your heart to have comfort, to have companionship, to have compassion, to have loyalty, to have an equal desire. Apply yourself to building stronger friendships; don't be concerned about who is calling whom. If you continue to imagine the type of relationship you desire, and continue to express what you want in terms of your feelings, you will indeed attract this person to you."

Debra echoed the guides' advice. "Just keep putting out exactly what you want someone to be," she said. "Be real specific, even writing it down. The more specific you are, the less room you leave for the universe to fill in the gaps and the more it's going to be exactly what you want."

"You have the sense that there will be other men?" I asked.

The answer was yes. I would continue in my search, the guides said, and many options would come to me. In fact, I hadn't yet met the person who would end up being my partner. Debra intuited that I'd meet someone who had more wealth and influence than the men I'd known in the past.

"That's what I feel I need," I said.

"Yes," Debra agreed. "More willing to go places, do things, more financial resources. That's brighter than anything that's come through this reading—the feeling of you being with someone like that. And life is going to be easy for you with this person. You're not going to have to struggle."

The guides, and Debra, recommended that I go places where I could meet high-caliber individuals informally, such as professional seminars or country clubs.

"I guess I'm kind of worried that I'm running out of time to get married and have children. Is that the case?" I asked.

"You're in your late 30s?" Debra asked.

"I'm 37 next week."

The guides replied. "We see it's difficult to predict this. We do not see any malformations as we search in terms of likelihood of physical situations for childbirth. We see that it's very likely you will have a period of time—perhaps a year or two—beyond the normally considered safe period."

Debra interpreted the prediction. "I thought they meant like beyond 40 you would have a year or two."

"It sounds like all of this is pretty far in the future," I griped, discouraged. "What do I do now, to keep me from going crazy and feeling alone and desolate?"

The guides had suggestions. "We would like to suggest two avenues to help you overcome these feelings that haunt you. One very important primary avenue is to deal with the feelings themselves, without needing to try to satisfy those feelings from something outside of you. We see it's not easy to eliminate them totally, but with some repeated rebirthing experiences, and this is a form of breathing over an extended period of time with someone who coaches you, we feel that you can overcome this within yourself more easily. Then you can go about the business of taking your time in finding the right individual.

"We see it's also important to have as much fun as you possibly can," they continued. "We see that the energies of celebration, fun, joy and gleefulness will help to dismiss some of these feelings, even though you may not be attached to a male primary partner. Know that with these two approaches, you can help to dissolve much of what seems to be incredibly overwhelming and filling you with despair. It will also help reduce much of the feeling of panic or urgency around obtaining a partner.

"So focus on self-healing first, and then see that you will automatically attract through the normal means that you use, plus the ones that we have described, someone who will be very helpful, supportive and satisfying for you."

When the guides finished, Debra gave her impressions. "I keep feeling it's like opening a door, and they're going to be on the other side, guys that are more professional, higher caliber."

I immediately put the guides' advice into action. I signed up for fall classes at the University of Pennsylvania Wharton School—it offered a certificate program in Small Business Management, which would certainly be full of professionals. I went to a conference that required an overnight stay, and although it wasn't exclusively for professionals, I did attract men, seemingly by magic.

Tracy and I attended the Whole Life Expo at the Hotel Pennsylvania in New York City on September 18 and 19, 1993. It was a convention on alternative healing, psychic phenomena and spirituality, and the attendees were more likely to be wearing flowing robes than business suits. At the same time, the Grateful Dead was playing a gig at Madison Square Garden, located directly across the street. The hotel lobby was packed with spacey people in tie-dyed clothing, and I couldn't tell if they were attending the conference or the concert.

One of the seminars was given by John Lee, author of *Facing the Fire: Experiencing and Expressing Anger Appropriately.* Lee told his audience that figuring out why you're angry didn't make it go away—the emotion still needed to be released. The way to do it, he said, was physically, in a way that didn't hurt other people or domestic animals. Lee recommended punching pillows, twisting towels or breaking old cups and saucers into trash cans. The idea was to engage in physical movement until it led to a physical release.

I also went to a seminar on Tantric sex. The message was that sex was sacred, and two consenting adults should feel comfortable doing anything that honored and pleased them both. But I was astounded by what happened after the seminar. A youthful-looking man with wire-rimmed glasses and wavy brown hair that hung just above his shoulders approached me. "I just had to tell you that you had the most dynamic energy in the room," he said. He wasn't trying to pick me up—he paid his compliment and walked away.

Later that afternoon, as Tracy and I were in a hotel elevator going up to our room, two men asked about our VIP badges. "We paid extra for the good seats," Tracy quipped.

One of the guys said, "I have an extra ticket to see the Grateful Dead tonight. Would one of you like to go?"

"Sure!" I said, glancing at Tracy. "I've never seen the Grateful Dead."

Tracy didn't mind entertaining herself for the evening. So that night I enjoyed the sold-out show with 20,000 mellow Deadheads, amazed at the male attention I attracted without even trying.

The guides recommended rebirthing, and my search for someone to help me led to Elaine Anderson.

Elaine was a spiritual counselor. She had a traditional degree in psychology, but all her advanced training was in the metaphysical realm. Her work involved past life regressions, restoring the energetic body through breath and relaxation, and chakra balancing. Chakras, in traditional Indian medicine, were seven wheel-like vortices, located from the top of the head to the groin, which connected every person's physical body to universal energy. Cleaning up her clients' chakras and buried energy blocks, Elaine found, was much more effective than talk therapy. Instead of endless discussion, every time she released a client's energy, something was healed.

Elaine worked in Moorestown, New Jersey, a community of majestic old homes located 75 minutes from Atlantic City. She and three other New Age healers shared one of the homes for their practices. When I arrived for my first appointment, a handwritten note on the door greeted me: "Please come in. We'll be right with you."

I sat down in the living room—no one was there—and waited. My appointment was slated to last two and a half hours, and I had no idea what to expect. After a few minutes, a woman wearing cream-colored knit warm-up pants and a matching turtleneck pullover came down the steps. She was slender and about 5 feet, 4 inches tall, with short brown hair and expressive brown eyes. She appeared to be in her late 40s. It was Elaine.

I followed her upstairs to her office, which was also furnished sparingly. There was a small Federal-style table with fresh flowers and two hardback chairs.

There was a folding massage table with white pillows and a cream-colored blanket on top of it, and a straight line of nine large crystals on the floor beneath it. There was a small CD player. Nothing more.

Elaine asked me what was going on in my life. At the time I was in the midst of a major problem with a business associate, so that was the big issue. But of course, I also bemoaned my romantic failures. Elaine listened quietly, taking in everything I told her, totally without judgment.

After I was talked out, Elaine asked me to lie on the massage table for the energy work. New Age practitioners believed that every person's body was surrounded by an energy field, or aura. The aura comprised seven layers, each a bit further from the body. Traumatic experiences and emotions created disturbances in the auras that could stay trapped with a person, even over multiple lifetimes.

Elaine explained that she would call on spiritual guidance to help her access my underlying feelings and release them. The idea was to get past my mental interpretations to the actual emotional energy attached to my experiences.

I took off my shoes and climbed onto the table as Elaine put on a CD of soothing instrumental music. Then Elaine stood at the foot of the massage table and intoned in a ceremonial voice, "We ask for spiritual guidance as we work with the personality we call Donna. We ask for help in releasing any pain."

As I lay there, emotions percolated to the surface of my awareness. I recognized childhood feelings of needing to be perfect, to get all A's in school, to never make a mistake. I had anger associated with what I interpreted to be the demands of my parents. I found a long-held and deeply buried belief that I had to accomplish in order to be loved, that I was not loved just for being.

My hands clenched. Elaine softly told me that I had inner conflicts with my emotions, and tried to control them mentally. On her massage table, that conflict boiled to the surface and was released as grief. A lot of grief.

At the end of the session we felt the spiritual presence of my father. I sensed his love, and his apology for the misunderstandings of my childhood.

I started seeing Elaine regularly. In subsequent sessions, after we talked about what was going on in my life, Elaine asked for a message from the universe, conveyed via Star+Gate cards. These were like tarot cards, with different pictures and messages, designed to provide spiritual insight.

Elaine would ask me to shuffle the cards. When I gave them back to her, she took cards from the top of the pile and laid them out in specific white rectangles on a small, black felt mat. The rectangles were labeled "Behind You," "You Now," "Ahead of You," "Distracting," "Helping," "Old Focus," "New Focus" and "The Issue." She laid one card on the table above the mat; it represented the overall theme of the message. The images on the cards, their positions on the mat and their relationships to each other all provided information from a higher realm about my past, present and future.

For my appointment on January 28, 1994, I knew I wanted to work on my emotions. I told Elaine I was an expert at squashing them. Although I was aware of the problem, I couldn't correct it—I was in a frustrating holding pattern.

Apparently the universe agreed. When Elaine read my Star+Gate cards, my

"Issue" was powder, which meant tearing down old patterns. The "Ahead of You" cards were fog and morning—conveying a new beginning, which Elaine interpreted to mean trusting the unknown.

I lay on the massage table and Elaine put crystals under my hands. "We ask for guidance for the personality we call Donna," Elaine began. "We ask for assistance in helping her experience her emotions."

At first nothing happened. Gradually, I started to feel internal emptiness, then pain. It turned out to be pain from a past life. I saw an image of myself, like remembering a dream, sitting in a rocking chair, wearing a plain blouse and a long skirt, holding a baby. The baby had died in my arms.

But I never had a chance to grieve—I had too many other children who required my attention. I buried my child and moved on. To avoid facing that pain again, I did not want to have children in this life, and kept men away from me to make sure it didn't happen. But there, on Elaine's table, I cried the tears of long-buried grief.

Then I noticed a sensation of energy traveling slowly from my heart, up my neck, behind my right eye and into the right side of my brain. It was as if my right brain—the feminine side—had been parched, and was being rehydrated.

Elaine saw a spirit stroking my right arm.

"I think it's my mother," I said.

"You're right," Elaine replied. "It is,"

I remembered the day before Mom died, when she was in the ICU. I stood at her side and stroked her arm and face—and she resisted me.

So we talked—Mom, Elaine and me. Mom told me there was much joy in having children. Another type of pain came out—I felt the pain of all the days I didn't make time for my mother, and I was sorry. Mom said she was sorry for the occasions when she didn't make time for me. I cried again—the whimpers of a child who needed to be comforted but felt alone. This time, Mom comforted me. I felt warm, like a soothing balm was soaking into my chest. My heart came alive. Where there had been emptiness for most of my life, there was feeling. I wanted to keep it.

My return on investment in newspaper personal ads was paltry—many frogs, no prince. Among the classifieds in the back of Philadelphia Magazine, a matchmaker advertised "personalized service" to find "elegant romance." I decided to try it. I met the matchmaker in her suburban Philadelphia home. She considered me suitable for her discriminating clientele, and promised to make three introductions—for a fee of $700.

Two weeks later the matchmaker called to tell me she had a man for me—Rainer Braun.* Despite his foreign-sounding name, he was an American born and raised in Pennsylvania. Rainer had just turned 40, so he was two-and-a-half years older than me. Divorced with three children, he earned a good living as a stockbroker.

The matchmaker made him sound wonderful. I had been hoping for a guy with no children, but the rest of the package was appealing so I agreed to meet him. She said Rainer would call me.

He did, although I had to wait six frustrating weeks.

We finally made a date to have dinner at an upscale Atlantic City restaurant on Saturday, March 5, 1994. I wore a funky brown dress that hung just below my knees, with black textured stockings and black ankle boots. My date arrived at my house wearing a sport coat but no tie, and carrying a bottle of champagne. He was a nice-looking man with a fair complexion, dark hair and dark eyes. "So far, so good," I thought.

It got even better. We drove to the restaurant in Rainer's hot red Honda sports car—one of three vehicles that he owned. At dinner we talked, joked and laughed—and romantic sparks flew. Afterwards we went back to my house and I invited Rainer in, which lead to nookie on the couch. I locked Beau in the basement.

I was supposed to be in Philadelphia the following Monday evening for my Wharton class, and we made plans to meet before it at a trendy restaurant nearby. I waited at the bar. Rainer was driving in from the ritzy western suburbs of Philadelphia and hit traffic on the Schuylkill Expressway; he was an hour late. He finally arrived right before I had to leave for class, so it wasn't much of a date. Rainer promised to make it up to me.

I wasn't angry that he was late. I was too busy being giddy that I finally met an accomplished man, who I liked, and who appeared to like me. In fact, I was already in love.

The weekend after our too-short date, Rainer invited me to visit him in Newtown Square, Pennsylvania, a well-to-do community outside of Philadelphia. He gave me directions to his home—it was a typical four-bedroom, two-story suburban. When I walked in, the first thing I noticed was an incredible amount of stuff. The family room was jammed with furniture and the walls were covered with pictures, mementos and knick-knacks. The living room contained, along with a sofa and chairs, a self-playing baby grand piano. Nothing seemed to match.

"Interesting décor," I commented as I looked around.

Rainer laughed. "This isn't my stuff," he said. "I rented the house furnished. But the piano is mine." We then went for a ride in his SUV, and he showed me a secluded property he bought on a side of a wooded hill. He planned to tear down the existing house and build a new one.

We went out to dinner and then to a movie—something violent starring Steven Segal. Rainer admitted he liked action movies, but some scenes were so bloody that I had to cover my eyes.

He also liked shooting clays—which was like quail hunting without the killing—and that's what we did the next morning. Rainer took me to a shooting club. I never before fired any kind of gun and had never seen sporting clays—they looked like dome-shaped orange flowerpots. A throwing machine launched them high into the air, and the idea was to shoot them out of the sky, as if shooting birds flushed by dogs. I got a safety lesson and a shooting lesson, then it was my turn. Soon, I hit a double—two clays launched in rapid succession.

After the shooting club, Rainer brought me by his father's home and introduced me. I interpreted this as a good sign—he must be serious about me. So as

I drove back to Atlantic City later that afternoon, I was ecstatic. I just spent a lovely weekend with a fun, successful man—a high-caliber guy—and he promised me we'd do it again soon.

It never happened.

My romance with Rainer was interrupted by the stock market. On February 4, 1994, shortly before we met, the Federal Reserve Bank decided to raise short-term interest rates to slow the growth of the U.S. economy and prevent inflation. In March, a stock market "correction" began. Over the next two months, the market dropped 10 percent.

I couldn't relate to the correction—I didn't have significant investments. All I knew was that Rainer stopped calling. Weeks went by—no word. When I finally did speak to him, he sounded shell-shocked—that can-do energy was gone. Rainer told me that his personal portfolio took a big hit. "I've lost a third of the money for my new house," he said. Still, we made plans to get together.

He stood me up.

I couldn't believe it. I was smitten. I was abandoned. The descent from love-at-first-date to disappointment, anger and pain was swift and cruel.

I talked about it with a new friend, Roseanne Jenkins.* Roseanne was a graphic designer who I met through business connections. She mirrored the stereotype of an unconventional artist—exotic taste in clothes, sometimes scattered in conversation. Roseanne was about my age, single, slender and a good date-search partner. She had also lived through her share of heartbreaks.

"I decided that I can't wait for Rainer," I said to her. "He may come back in a few months, or he may never come back. I have to move forward."

"That's called acceptance," Roseanne said. "This is the way it is right now."

Her words really struck home. In the past I wasted months, even years, waiting for guys to come around, not wanting to accept that the relationships were going nowhere. Finally, with Rainer—probably the most appealing man I'd ever dated—I moved quickly to let it go and get on with my life. If nothing else, I learned that a man like Rainer—handsome, accomplished and professional—could find me attractive.

As much as I hurt, I felt proud of myself. I finally learned from my mistakes.

The Star+Gate cards during my visit to Elaine Anderson on January 9, 1995, identified the issue of the day as a knight, or more precisely, my missing knight-in-shining armor.

Before even beginning the drive to Elaine's Moorestown office, I knew I needed to unearth an incident of past-life violence. The source of my violent thoughts quickly surfaced as I lay on Elaine's massage table. I remembered a past life in which I was a man who killed the woman I loved.

All I could see of her was golden hair, but I knew she was beautiful. So did she. She flirted with other men, just to make me jealous. It worked—one day, I flew into a rage and killed her. I had been punishing myself ever since by not allowing love into my life.

The woman's spirit joined Elaine and me. We agreed that we were both responsible for the tragedy, and we both let go of the pain. Elaine said the universe celebrated. My message was to live in my heart and stay open, allowing life to happen. I was at a crossroads of my life, about to embark on a journey.

After the session, Elaine invited me to attend the Women's Circle, which would meet the following evening. She and the other healers in her building brought together a small group of women for a few hours of spiritual sharing, like a mini-retreat. A woman who lived near me, Carla Gibbons,* participated, and she was thrilled when I called her about driving to Moorestown together.

The meeting started with a dozen women sitting in a circle on the floor, chanting "om"—the ancient Hindu syllable representing the source of existence. Our voices blended together into a continuous tone, a hymn to the manifest and unmanifest aspects of God. Then we took turns sharing what was happening in our lives. Two hours later, the evening ended with another chant of "om."

Afterwards, I felt like I'd been to church—not the church of obligation from my youth, but a church of meaning, connection and fulfillment. All the next day, I was filled with peace and joy.

I was also filled with anticipation. A guy I knew had rented an entire Somers Point nightclub for a private party—the cavernous main bar, the elevated dance floor, the side bars and the second-story balcony overlooking the main floor, which had even more bars. Everyone on the guest list was age-appropriate—a welcome change. Going to clubs on a date search was becoming difficult—most of the people dancing the night away were 20-somethings. Although I didn't look my 38 years and wanted a youthful guy, I drew the line at cradle-robbing.

For weeks, I knew I was going to meet someone at this party. So what to wear? I bought a black crocheted tank top, held together by black and silver laces in the front, that required going braless. I wore the sexy top with a short black skirt, black stockings and new black high heels.

The night of the party arrived. Even though it was January and cold, the club was packed with the biggest selection of eligible potential dates that I'd seen in a long time. I moved through the crowd, sipping wine, chatting from guy to guy. Eventually I started talking to a good-looking man named Don Clement Jr. He was about my age, taller than me, well built, with thick, reddish-brown hair. He told me he had been a professional ballplayer—a pitcher. That got my attention.

After talking for about a half hour, we arrived at a lull in the conversation. I took the next logical step. "Are you going to ask me to dance?" I asked.

Don slowly put out his cigarette. "Let's go," he said.

We danced for a few songs and chatted some more. Don came to the party with a friend, and they decided to go to a nearby diner. I joined them. At the end of the evening, I gave Don my phone number.

Don told me that he once overindulged in drugs and alcohol, which ended his baseball career. "I had to be able to throw at 90 miles per hour," he said. "You can't do that when you're partying." But he cleaned up his act. He married and had a child, but now his ex-wife was giving him a hard time about seeing the child, which hurt him deeply.

Don Clement Jr. really wasn't my type. His lifestyle was more wild than stable. He didn't appear to be educated. He earned a living buying and selling used cars. Yet I was impressed that he overcame the mistakes of his past—he seemed to have more strength of character than many suit-and-tie types. And I felt a connection that was deeper than passing attraction.

Don and I had a little romance. When he picked me up for our first date, he arrived with fresh flowers. By the end of the date, I intuitively knew why I felt such a strong connection to him. I was certain that we were together in a previous life. In fact, I suspected that we were married.

Every time I saw Don, he had a different car. Don bought cars at the National Auto Dealers Exchange in Bordentown, New Jersey, an auction that moved about 5,000 vehicles per week. With used car dealer tags from a company in Barnegat, New Jersey, Don purchased cars, drove them to the shore, then fixed, cleaned and sold them. He picked me up in whatever vehicle was in transition.

On a Tuesday evening, Don called and said he going to the auto auction the next day, and asked if he could borrow my mobile phone. Don didn't have one, and he had a sale pending—he didn't want to miss the call. I agreed to let him use the phone. He promised to have it back the next day. He did return the phone, although it took him three days.

A few nights later, as we were going out, Don told me he had to stop by a friend's house. The guy was in a bind and needed money—Don was lending him some. He drove to a small house in Somers Point, and I waited in the car while Don went inside.

Shortly after that, Don told me about another friend, a woman, who was nursing a newborn baby. She was arrested for outstanding parking tickets and needed bail money. He asked me if I could help. I said the woman had gotten herself in trouble and it was not my problem.

Then the romance was over—Don made some comments about my "rich blood." But with him I felt feminine and sexy, and we had that strong, subconscious connection. So I figured he disappeared because I hadn't expressed my appreciation. I decided to send him a note to say what I hadn't said in person:

> On the one hand, I hate being blown off. On the other hand, I understand. Something tells me you just can't deal with any more emotion right away.
>
> You're a good man, Donnie. I've always been impressed by the strength of character you've shown—even with your wild lifestyle. You have a lot of courage. Believe in yourself. Things will get better.
>
> Thank you for making me feel so sexy—I've enjoyed it. Take care of yourself.

I was glad that I had extended myself, even belatedly. After receiving the note, Don started showing up again. He talked to me about his car business, and how easy it was to make good money. "Most of the cars at the auto exchange are trade-ins," he explained. "You know how a dealer gives you nothing for a car when you trade it in? I can scoop up the good cars, do a little work on them, and sell them for double or triple what I paid."

One day Don called me in a panic. He was between car sales and in a cash flow jam. He needed $500. A friend had given him $200, and he needed $300 more. Could I lend it to him for a few days?

I was taken aback. No man had ever asked me for money. But we were seeing each other again, of sorts. I had the cash, so it wouldn't cause me any problems. I agreed to do it.

When Don got to my house, he told me that he would rather owe only one person, so he gave his other friend the $200 back, and asked me for the whole amount. I wrote a check for $515.

A few days later he called again, all excited. He had an opportunity to make a big sale—a Corvette. He could get the car for $5,000, and knew of a buyer who was willing to pay $10,000. Don offered me a business proposition: If I gave him $2,000 to help buy the car, he would sell it the next day. He'd pay back all the money he owed me, plus I'd make an additional $1,000 overnight. He also asked to borrow my mobile phone again to help get the deal done.

So I gave him another $2,000 and the phone. Don did buy the car, but the transmission needed repairs, according to the mechanic who called me. I put an additional $985 toward the repairs. When the car was sold, Don promised me, I would get $5,500. That would mean $2,000 profit for me.

The sale went through, and after a week, I got my phone back. But I never saw my money. Don disappeared again. He didn't return calls. Worried, I went to the condo where he was living.

It was empty.

My initial shock quickly turned to anger, hurt and embarrassment. I felt like a complete idiot for giving him all that money. Even lending him the mobile phone was a disaster—in 13 days, he ran up $180 in charges. I found out that one of the guys on my softball team knew him. My friend was incredulous that I believed Don's story. "Didn't you see him coming?" he asked me.

I did not.

Feeling angry and stupid, I meditated on what had happened, trying to figure out what to do and how to react. Often, when I asked for answers while meditating, I received them—words formed in my mind. The message I heard that day was that people don't mean to hurt you, but they do. Long ago I decided that I did not want to be hurt. So I built a wall around my life, preventing myself from engaging people so I could avoid pain. The result? An empty life.

"Should I have stayed away from him?" I asked myself in my journal. "I don't know. It was an experience—a human experience. A human mistake perhaps. I haven't had many human experiences, human failures. If I'm going to be human, I guess it's going to happen."

I still felt that Don was good at heart, and that he never intended to rip me off. He was just facing difficult circumstances.

Two months later I found him. Don moved to a house in Northfield, New Jersey, just a few miles from where he used to live in Somers Point. I went right over to the house the afternoon of April 20, 1995. No one was home. I went back that night—he still wasn't there. I showed up at 8:45 the next morning. The result was not what I expected.

Don was there, and he was visibly upset. He told me that his mother died, and he was on his way to jail. His mother's funeral cost him $7,000, Don said, which was why he didn't pay me. He also said he had violated the restraining order his ex-wife had against him. He just wanted to see his kid. But he was arrested, and had to turn himself in. While I was there, two of his friends showed up to take him to the Atlantic County jail. He left, crying. "I'm not going to fuck you, Donna," he said. He also asked me to write him a letter in jail.

I went home and immediately wrote him a letter. In fact, I sent him a book that had helped me when I faced my crises: *Words That Heal—Affirmations and Meditations for Daily Living,* by Douglas Bloch.

On the morning of June 5, 1995, the phone rang. It was Don Clement Jr. He was out of jail, and called to thank me for the book. "I really liked the poems," he said. Don also said he wanted to get on his feet and take care of his obligations.

I was tremendously relieved. I felt like I hadn't made a mistake, and my faith in him was justified.

On June 7, 1995, before 7 a.m., Don called again. He wanted to start working so he could pay me back. He asked me for $3,200 so he could go to the auction that day and buy a car. I would have the money back in the evening, he promised.

As soon as Don asked for the money, I got a strong hit from my intuition: "DON'T DO IT!"

But I continued talking to him. One of the problems with the first time I gave him money, I realized, was that I had nothing on paper. He did not sign an agreement. I had no proof that he actually owed me the money.

I certainly wouldn't make that mistake again. Plus, I knew that if he were going to pay me back, he'd have to start somewhere. If I gave him the money, I figured that I would be priming the pump so he could pay back everything he owed me.

"You'll have to sign an agreement that you owe me the money and you'll repay it, with interest," I said.

"I'll sign it," Don said.

"And the agreement will cover the money from before," I insisted.

"Of course. I'll pay you back everything that I owe you."

"And you'll pay me back the same day."

"Yes."

With a written agreement, I thought I'd be protected. And, it would be proof of the money I had given him back in February. "All right," I agreed.

I hung up the phone and immediately drafted an agreement. It covered the $5,500 from the sale of the Corvette, the cost of his calls on my mobile phone, and four months of interest. The agreement stated that the $3,200 I was lending him on June 7, 1995, would be returned the evening of June 7, 1995.

When I saw Don, I put two copies of the agreement in front of him, and he signed them—Donald C. Clement Jr. Then I wrote a check for $3,200. Don thanked me, promised to return the money that evening, and left.

A few hours later my bank called. Don presented my check to be cashed, and the cashier thought my signature looked odd, so she wanted to verify it.

"Yes, that's my signature," I confirmed.

The check was cashed, but Don didn't pay me back that night. Or the next day. Or the next night. He strung me along, promising he'd have the cash, but it never materialized.

After a week of excuses, I took action. Early one morning, I went to the house in Northfield where he was living. A car was parked out front with used car dealer license plates on it. The plates were made to be easily removable. I took them, went home and called Don.

He did not answer the phone, so I left a message.

"This is Donna Andersen," I informed the answering machine. "I have your used car dealer tags. You can have them back when I get my money."

Don called me back immediately.

"You bring those plates back right now," he demanded.

"I want my money," I replied.

"You'll get your money. But you better bring those plates back. You can't take them. That's theft!"

I caved.

Wearing a blue business suit—I was already dressed for work—I drove back to his house in Northfield with the plates. Don answered the door wearing nothing but a towel. I ignored his attire—or lack of it.

"When are you going to pay me?" I asked.

"As soon as I can," he said. "I talked to my mom—oh, my mom is dead. I'm all mixed up. I'm doing the best I can." Those were the words that came out of his mouth. But from the expression on his face, it seemed that it was all he could do to keep from laughing out loud.

My feeble attempt to stand up for myself was over.

Within a few weeks, I learned that I wasn't the only person who was kicking myself for believing Don Clement Jr. At least six other people had been duped by him. One of them was the guy who was with Don at the party. He gave Don $1,100, and was hanging around him, hoping to collect. He eventually filed charges, but had no evidence that Don owed him money, so they were dismissed. Don also took $4,500 from a woman in Margate, New Jersey. He took $5,300 from a Margate man. He owed his Northfield landlady, who was supposedly a friend, $2,400 in rent and phone expenses. A woman from Vineland gave Don $3,000 to buy a car for her. She had receipts, but no car. Don took $200 from a woman in Pleasantville. The biggest loser was me—I gave him a total of $6,880.

I couldn't believe how stupid I was. My intuition had clearly, forcefully told me not to give him another $3,200, but I ignored it.

On September 9, 1995, I told Elaine Anderson, my spiritual counselor, the whole miserable story. She confirmed what I felt intuitively—Don and I had once been married. In fact, he helped me out of a bad situation, and I owed him a karmic debt. She said I still needed to repay that debt—by putting him in jail. I should write a letter to him—a blunt and powerful letter. It was the only chance to save his life.

A few days later I filed a report with the Atlantic City police department. I stood before the detective as he read it—when he got to the part describing how I wrote Don the second big check, he shook his head in disbelief.

I sent a letter to the judge who let Don out of jail, outlining everything he did and naming all the other victims. I sent copies of the letter to the Atlantic County prosecutor, the probation department, and the National Auto Dealers Exchange, where Don bought his used cars.

With my signed agreement, I filed a claim against Donald C. Clement Jr. in Small Claims Court. An Atlantic County Grand Jury indicted him for theft by deception. Don failed to appear in court and a warrant was issued for his arrest. I was told that if I received information regarding Don Clement's whereabouts, I should notify the Office of Victim-Witness Advocacy.

I did get a tip that Don Clement was in another state. When I called the sheriff's department to tell them, it was clear that they would make no effort to apprehend him. With that phone call, I learned that law enforcement authorities didn't bother to track down small-time con artists.

I was desperate for my life to change, and it wasn't happening.

My sister made a suggestion. She was involved with Global Relationship Centers, a personal development organization that offered an intensive weekend workshop called Understanding Yourself and Others (UYO). For months, Tracy raved about UYO, and tried to talk me into taking the course. After my most recent fiasco, I finally agreed to do it.

I showed up at the Comfort Inn in Bensalem, Pennsylvania, on November 10, 1995, one of five "students." Two instructors, a man and a woman, taught the class. Plus, there were 12 assistants—including three children—who were members of the organization that had taken the class previously.

The program started Friday evening with presentations by the instructors about setting and reaching goals, how relationships affected our lives, and team-building exercises—fairly typical stuff for self-help seminars. But at 9 a.m. Saturday morning, when the other students and I walked into the hotel's meeting room, music was blaring and the UYO faithful, wearing party hats and pieces of costumes, were jumping around and dancing. I thought it was ridiculous—which was obvious from my body language.

"Do you like it?" one instructor asked me.

"No. This is stupid," I replied, in a tone of disgust.

"Great! That's what I like, an honest woman," she replied.

Fuming, I came very close to going home. But after a heated conference with Tracy in the hallway, I agreed to give the program a chance. It was a good decision.

Each student in the class was asked to act out, with feeling and authenticity, a short poem called *Personal Power*. It sounded easy—but the eight lines of the poem touched on issues that held us back, and for every individual, the process brought fears, inhibitions and bad memories to the surface. There were times when a student said, "I can't," and, with gentle encouragement, broke down to tell why. That was the learning experience, the opportunity for release, forgiveness and healing. Some students took a few hours to get through the poem. Often, when someone hit a nerve, the nerve was connected to another person in the room who shared the trauma. About halfway through Saturday morning, I could see the value of the exercise, and began joining in.

When my turn came to start the poem, I sat alone on a tall stool in the front of the room. The male instructor, who was still wearing a silly patchwork hat, asked me where I was in my life.

I talked about feeling alone and unsupported. "I work by myself," I started. "I'm a writer, and I have this business producing newsletters for casinos. I'm totally responsible for the work—if I have a problem, there's no one to help me. And if one of my subcontractors or suppliers screws up, I'm the one who's liable. There's no one for me to count on in my personal life, either. I'm not married, and I can't seem to meet anyone. Even something stupid like getting my car to the repair shop is a major problem."

"Do you have friends?" the instructor asked.

"Yes, I have friends," I replied.

"Do they help you?"

"Yes, but I feel like I'm imposing on them. It's not like having someone around all the time who you can depend on, so you can say, 'Come on, follow me. I have to take the car to the garage.'

"I don't see any way out," I continued. "I don't know anyone who could do my work if I got sick or went on vacation. What am I going to do, tell the customer I don't feel like doing her newsletter this month? I just really feel trapped."

"Well, there is one thing you can change," he said.

"What?" I asked.

"Your attitude."

I sat on that stool in the front of the room, considering the instructor's words. He was right.

As I worked on presenting the poem, one of my issues was the trouble I had saying three simple words: "I love you." I had very little experience with those words, not only because of my sorry relationship record, but because I never heard them spoken in my house as I was growing up.

My mom and dad loved me, I was positive of that. They were caring and attentive parents, carting us around to Girl Scouts or Little League or whatever we kids joined. Mom was always writing cards and notes, telling us how proud she was of us. And my parents were careful not to show favoritism; I think it would be fair to say that they loved us each equally. But verbal affirmation, saying, "I love you," face to face—well, it just didn't happen.

In one of the UYO exercises, each student wrote down his or her goal and dream, with the goal being something to accomplish in the near term. I wrote:

Goal: Tell Dad that I love him, verbally—face to face.

Dream: Get married and have a family.

Before the seminar weekend, I dropped my dog off with Dad in Vineland. Dad was the consummate dog-sitter, always happy to spoil Beau when I went away—and the dog showed it, usually coming home fatter. Monday morning, mindful of my UYO goal, I waited nervously for Dad and Beau to arrive.

Dad and I had a transfer-of-the-dog routine. I made the coffee, and he brought the donuts. We sat at my kitchen table, drinking coffee and eating donuts, while Beau begged. Beau's persistence was always rewarded—no wonder he got fat.

Dad had been worried about Tracy's involvement in UYO, thinking she may have joined a cult. I reassured him. "It's really a good program," I said.

"What do they do?" Dad asked, still suspicious.

"They help people deal with their issues," I explained. "Everyone has issues in their lives—fears, things that happened to them as kids. If you don't figure out a way to deal with them, bring them to the surface and let them go, they can affect your entire life. I found the course to be helpful."

It was time to take the plunge. "You know, something came up for me over the weekend that I'd like to talk to you about."

"Oh yeah? What?" Dad asked, without much enthusiasm. Heart-to-heart conversations were not high on Dad's list of fun things to do.

"You know, when we were growing up, no one ever said 'I love you' in our house."

"We loved you."

"I know that, Dad. But no one said it. To this day, it's hard for me to say those words. I would like for us to say it."

Dad took this in, admirably, I thought, for a regular guy. "I love you, honey," he said.

"I love you too, Dad."

It was done, and I felt a huge sense of relief, and a new level of connection with my father.

We chatted a bit more, finishing the coffee and donuts, with Beau, as always, getting the last bite. Dad got up to leave, and walked through the kitchen and dining room to the front door in the living room. I followed, happily.

Dad put on his coat. He gave me a hug. "I love you, honey," he said.

"I love you," I said to him. And Dad went out the door. I had accomplished my goal. Maybe, one day, my dream would come true as well.

Five women sat in a circle on the carpeted floor. The former family room was empty, except for small, low altars against each of the four walls, honoring the spirits of the North, South, East and West. Candles burned on the altars, providing the only illumination in the room.

Carla Gibbons, with whom I had traveled to the Women's Circle in Moorestown earlier in the year, organized a similar group in her home for local women. Carla invited me to their winter solstice celebration on December 22, 1995. The evening began with a cleansing smoke bath, called smudging. Carla lit a bundle of sage and other herbs with a match; it burnt slowly and released smoke, like a giant incense stick. She waved the smoking sage in the direction of each of the women and generally around the room. The purpose was to purify and protect our physical and spiritual bodies, and banish negative energies. We chanted "om," inviting the positive energy of the universe to join us.

The theme for the evening was looking into the New Year. To be closer to natural forces, we all went outside. Even though we were only in Carla's suburban backyard, we stood among tall, leafless trees under a cold, clear night sky sprinkled with stars. Quietly and individually, we asked for guidance.

I often asked for guidance when I wrote in my journal, usually about my romantic frustrations. In response to my questions, answers formed in my head, which I wrote down. It was like taking dictation from an unseen entity—perhaps the spirit guides that Debra Taylor, the channeler, spoke to, or perhaps the guides who provided messages to Elaine Anderson. I didn't know if they were the same or different beings, and I didn't know how many spirits were offering suggestions. But I wrote down what they told me, referring to the beings as "Guidance," with a capital "G," and hoping to find answers to my interminable questions.

Sometimes the answers were extensive. Months earlier, when I realized Don Clement Jr. had no intention of ever paying me back, Guidance talked to me about my intuition:

> *You are getting better. You need to practice. Calm yourself. Clear yourself and listen. This is hard for you—your mind is so active. But you are right—it will lead you in the right direction. Listen to your heart. You heart is good.*
>
> *You have shut yourself off from all people because of the wounds. Now you can learn to choose the right people to open yourself to. This is progress. You'll probably make more mistakes in your lifetime—everyone does. But they'll be fewer and less painful.*

After spending time under the stars, we went back inside. Carla prepared a ritual to predict the future—somewhat like reading tea leaves. Each of us had a small bowl containing a milky white liquid. We asked a question, then sprinkled a few drops of a brown liquid on top of the white. A picture was supposed to form to answer our question.

When my turn came, I asked, "Will I meet a man to love me?"

I sprinkled the brown liquid, which floated on top of the white. To me, it looked like a brown swirl of chocolate syrup in a glass of milk.

Carla looked at my bowl. "I see a man with a briefcase," she said.

"You do?" I asked.

"Yes, definitely," she repeated. "A man with a briefcase."

Chapter 5

Trembling with excitement, I hung up the phone after that momentous call from James Montgomery, the man with the briefcase, on July 24, 1996. He proposed. I accepted. Life changed.

Luckily, it was near the end of the workday. I couldn't possibly focus on writing any newsletter stories. I got up from my desk and wandered dazedly around the house. After awhile, feeling like I should accomplish something, I took my dog for a walk.

"James and I are getting married," I told Beau. He wagged his tail. Of course, Beau wagged his tail every time I spoke to him.

All the disappointment and pain from my past melted away. Now I knew why I was still single. I had been waiting, and preparing myself, for the love of a lifetime.

The day after we became engaged, James took me out to dinner for a proper celebration. He picked me up in his SUV. As we drove to a small local restaurant, James held out his right hand, palm up. He wanted me to place my hand in his. I did—and felt a little flutter inside. Finally, my lifetime dream was coming true.

James dressed for the occasion in a sport coat and slacks, with another silk handkerchief in his breast pocket. I wore a casual dress. I also, James noticed as we were waiting for our salads, wore a ring on my right hand. He cleared his throat.

I looked at him. James cleared his throat again and raised his bearded chin in the direction of my hand, which was holding the stem of my wine glass.

"What is that?" he asked.

"What?"

"On your hand."

I turned my hand so he could see the ring—a square-cut aquamarine in a simple gold setting. "It belonged to my mother," I said.

"Well," James harrumphed. "We'll have to do something about that." I felt another flutter.

The waitress arrived with our salads, and we chatted as we ate. James told me about the progress he was making toward his dream of building an electronic theme park for adults on the Boardwalk. "It's a totally new concept," he said.

"I'm going to change the entertainment business like Walt Disney did!" His passion and enthusiasm were contagious.

Then he changed the subject. "Donna, I have some bad news," he said. "It couldn't come at a worse time. But I'm afraid I have to go away for awhile."

"Where are you going?"

"I can't tell you. But there are some issues related to Flight 800."

A few days before James and I met—on July 17, 1996—TWA Flight 800 took off from JFK Airport in New York City, flew for 10 minutes, and then exploded in mid-air. The Boeing 747 broke apart and fell into the Atlantic Ocean off Long Island. All 230 people on board were killed.

No one knew why the plane exploded, but there was rampant speculation in the media that it was a terrorist attack—or a tragic error by the United States military attempting to thwart a terrorist attack. Hundreds of eyewitnesses reported seeing a streak of light flying toward the plane. They thought it could have been a missile. So did James.

"When are you leaving?" I asked.

"Tomorrow."

"How long will you be gone?"

"Not long. Maybe a couple of weeks. But I should be able to break it up and get back here for a few hours at some point. I simply do not want to be away from you that long. You know, Donna, I was never able to remain faithful to a woman. But you're different. You totally captivate me. With you as my wife, I know I'll never need anyone else."

I was having trouble taking everything in. This amazing, accomplished man, James Montgomery, was sitting next to me in a restaurant not far from my little home at the Jersey Shore. Yesterday he asked me to marry him. Then he was telling me about the politics of getting his theme park built. Now he was telling me that he had to go away on a military mission—I assumed it was dangerous—in the service of his country. And in the middle of it, he wanted to make time to see me, the one woman who totally captivated him.

This didn't happen in *my* life.

James, however, took it all in stride. He was accustomed to living a few levels above general humanity. With his extensive experience and obvious intelligence—James confessed that, "between me and Herbie the hedgehog, we know just about everything"—he could talk about anything, accomplish anything. Launch an enterprise? Save the world? Come home to his fiancée? No worries.

After dinner, we drove back to my house. It was a warm summer night, and a cool breeze stirred the leaves of the crabapple tree that grew in my tiny front garden. I always liked the tree. In the spring it bloomed with lovely white flowers. In the summer, its leaves created a natural privacy screen.

"Do you want to sit on the porch?" I asked James.

"Only if I can sit here with you," he replied.

Not long after we settled onto the wicker couch, James' cell phone rang.

"Excuse me, Donna," he said. Then, answering the phone, "This is James."

I heard his half of the conversation: "Hello Archie ... Well, actually, I'm in

Atlantic City, sitting with that lovely lady who I told you will become my wife ...
Yes, she's right here. Would you like to speak to her?"

James handed me his phone. "Say hello to Archie. He's calling from Australia."

James had previously told me about his longtime business associate, Archie
Turner,* who lived in Australia, although he was originally English. A few years
earlier, they prepared a proposal for the Florida Department of Commerce to
develop, install and maintain an interactive information system for tourist centers. They won the contract, but it was never implemented—James didn't say
why. He and Archie also worked together back in Australia to produce a television series called *Strike Swiftly,* about real weekend warriors—Australia's Army
Reserves. James wrote the script and Archie was the cameraman—at one point
hanging out of a C-130 turbo-prop Hercules to get footage of the reservists para-
chuting from the plane.

I took the phone. "Hello Archie," I said.

"Hello, Donna. So you're the woman who has caught James' fancy?" he asked.

"Yes, I suppose you could say that."

"I'm very happy for you. I've known him for a long time. He is quite a man,
you know."

"I'm finding that out."

"Well, if you are as beautiful and charming as James tells me, I look forward
to meeting you someday. Perhaps you'll visit Australia."

"Maybe we will. I'm sure you and James would be excellent tour guides."

I handed the phone back to James. He spoke to Archie for a minute, then
ended the conversation. "I would really much rather talk to the young lady here
with me," he said.

James turned and gave me his full attention. "Would you like to visit Australia?" he asked.

I loved to travel—especially to exotic destinations. "Sure," I replied. "That
would be terrific."

"Then we'll do it. I'd like you to meet my family. And for them to meet you.
I was just there, of course, visiting my daughter and my new granddaughter. But
now I have another reason to go—showing you off." He paused for a moment.
"Donna, I have a confession to make."

I waited for him to continue.

"I just can't keep anything from you. I want you to know who I really am. I
fibbed a bit on my AOL ad."

"About what?" I asked.

"My age. I'm not really 48."

This did not surprise me at all. He certainly looked older than 48, and his
resume was extremely long for someone in his 40s. "How old are you?" I asked.

"Fifty-one," James admitted.

Ugh. "Why did you say you were 48?" I asked.

"You know how it is with those personal ads. Everybody lies."

"I didn't lie," I said. Still, I knew that had he posted his real age, I wouldn't
have replied to the ad, and would have missed the extraordinary experience my

life had become.

We went inside and were sitting in the living room when James' cell phone rang again. "This is James," he answered, as he always did.

Once more, I heard half of the conversation: "Yes, sir ... I understand ... Yes, sir ... General, we really shouldn't be discussing this now. This is not a secure line. It's just a hand-held radio phone ... Yes, sir ... I understand."

The call ended. James stood up and moved toward the front door. "I have to go now," he said.

I got up from the couch and walked toward him to say goodbye. James gently took my face in his hands, and kissed me passionately. Then he stopped, pulled something out of his pocket, and placed it in my hand.

"Maybe you'll wear these for me until I return."

It was a long ball chain with two commemorative dog tags. One side was inscribed with James' name, social security number and blood type. The other side was embossed with a figure of Lady Liberty.

I held them gingerly. "Of course, I'll wear them."

"You give me a reason to hurry home," James said. Then he looked off over my shoulder. "Gale wore them four times," he said, softly, with a touch of sadness in his voice.

The next day, July 26, 1996, James left for his mission. I thought about him a lot during the day. Where was he going? What was he supposed to do? Was he in danger? I checked AOL continuously for a message from him. Finally, at night, an e-mail arrived.

From: FUTRON0I
Subj: my link is looking good

> this comes to you courtesy of my uncles satellites
> ... now, I stand just touching you, inhaling you -it's the girl next door
> ... clean and sweet
> you lean one of those fabulous breasts over my mouth ... look into
> my eyes ... no faking, at that very moment you love me more than any
> other person in your life ... and I taste the rest of my life ... the great
> love I will carry to my grave.
> I taste my future

I read and reread the e-mail, basking in the wonder of the words. "The rest of my life!" "The great love I will carry to my grave!" Those sentiments only appeared in ancient poetry and Hallmark greeting cards. I didn't think it was possible for a living, breathing man to write them.

James included an attachment with the e-mail. It was a treatment he had written—a preliminary description for a movie—called *Technowarrior*. I printed it out and read it slowly, savoring every word. The story line seemed distinctly autobiographical. Here was how James described his protagonist:

> Colonel Michael (Mike) Lucas is a longtime reservist with a highly successful career as a Clancy style novelist. After the initial outrage at the data he so freely sprinkled his thrillers with … the Pentagon now counts on his help to sell the public on their latest techno-wishes; his impact on the Hill is even a little stronger…a true friend of the Complex.
>
> His lawyer advises him to get lost for six months during his upcoming divorce … he asks to go on assignment in a highly secure area. The Pentagon is thrilled at the idea.

The prologue of the story, however, started from the point of view of the soon-to-be ex-wife. The words gave a glimpse of how she felt about Mike Lucas.

> It was the first storm of the season and she stood inhaling the freshness in the air and recalled standing on that balcony in Tampa … naked in the rain at two in the morning, after making love. Candles flickered, dancing light shadows over his face and form. He had fallen asleep. Dreaming of what, she wondered, while she walked the rooms of the apartment.
>
> Sitting at her desk, she glanced at the calendar on the wall and realized with a little jolt it was October 10th. Ten years ago tonight he had made love to her for the first time. What could she write to him that could possibly move him the way he had moved her that evening? In that simple conquest of her body, he had changed her life … and over time had become so much more than her lover. From the beginning she had been double-minded about him … not allowing herself to embrace the future she so clearly saw, reining in her dreams, like riding a spirited horse with a curb bit. Fear of falling, of being thrown and broken … again.

As I read the *Technowarrior* treatment, I couldn't help but wonder about James' reasons for sending it. Was he revealing himself through the Mike Lucas character? Was the woman someone from his past—or someone from his future? The story said they were divorcing, which was unsettling—but then, it was just a movie.

The musings made me giddy with amazement, excited to learn more of the story—possibly my story. I replied to James' e-mail:

From: DONNACOPY
Subj: Missing you, my love

Dear James,
    I feel like I'm living in a novel. Five days ago I met you, and my quiet, responsible little life has been turned completely upside down. I'm in love with the most amazing man I have ever met - a true hero, a creative genius, a powerful entrepreneur and an exciting, imaginative lover - and

he's in love with me.

And then I found that the novel has already been started - "Technowarrior." This Mike Lucas character sounds suspiciously familiar…

Whisper to me, my lover, ask … just ask … take my hand and lead me to where you want to go. I lay next to you, or on top of you, it's hard to tell. I stroke whatever part of you is within reach - your face, your arm, your thigh. I couldn't tell you ahead of time what I will do - instinct takes over, and I hear you moan.

I feel my love, your love, our love. And the novel turns out differently than the author expected. Damn. I have to stop. I'm soaking wet, and you're not here. Only myself tonight.

The next morning I awoke and went directly to my computer, where I found a reply from my fiancé.

From: FUTRON01
Subj: Re: I miss you, my love

In country now …
you are truly the one I have been waiting for all my life
only time to tell you I loved my note … keep Thursday night and Friday morning for both our nipples to meet … I will get there by about 2230 - leave circa 1000 on Friday - am trying to get back again for Sunday nite before back here
am writing you a treat my love -- what a combination we are - I am so proud of you - yet you are every part of my erotic fantasies cum [sic] to life …
your lover learning to be your best friend

The attachment was called *The Bet,* and it came with explicit instructions from James for me to read it naked. But the document wouldn't open. I wrote back in exaggerated frustration: "James! I can't download the file. This is worse than a tease!" I suggested that, if he had open phone lines, he try faxing the document to me.

A few hours later I found a four-page fax in my office. The header at the top of every page identified the sending machine as "USNAVYSPECWAR." It was *The Bet,* and I started to read …

"Do you think he wants to fuck me?"

Their dinner guest had just excused himself to make a call and Donna slipped her hand into her lover's and leaned close to him, whispering the words playfully into his ear. They'd had a lovely meal, it was winter again, her favorite season, and tonight she was just … happy. She felt light and sensual, like the microscopic bubbles spiraling in her glass of Cristal, and James looked so handsome in his not-worn-often suit. Fine tailoring always turned her on; he'd been erudite, funny and charming all evening, which was driving her mad, and suddenly she felt giddy and adventurous.

"Why? Do you want him?" James asked dryly, glancing across the crowded room to see if Burton was still out of earshot.

"No. I want you. But I thought maybe we could have some fun. That is if you think he'd be game ... and if you're in the mood."

The story was erotic, with Donna and James as the main characters. James explained to Burton that he was Donna's lover and she would only have an orgasm when he permitted it, no matter what Burton did. The bet was on, and the story told, in glorious detail, how Burton tried to win, and what James did to make it even more difficult for Donna to obey her lover.

As I read it, I could feel sexual desire building. It was really unfair of James to send such a story while he was out of the country. It ended with a note from James: "Now, my princess, you write Chapter Two."

All day Sunday, I thought about James, hoping that he and his men were safe. Sunday evening, I received an e-mail, "In the midst of all this crap," he wrote, "there is you m'love."

Monday I woke up to another fax from James, this one originating from "USNAVYSPECWAR-CommsCtre." It read:

Hello My Lover!

I am so glad you decided to marry me - you have given me purpose beyond my business ... I want you to understand me a little more ... I wrote this over ten years ago as part of a book three of us published ... closest thing I have to a philosophy.

I embedded this in our computer back at Washington, so its sending doesn't necessarily coincide with my arrival back on US Soil.

I am convinced that I will only love you more, as time progresses - that I already am deeply in love with you for so many different reasons it must be real - please understand me, my love, for then you will come to realize that I do not utter those words easily ... and that I mean them!

James sent me a seven-page document called *The Absolute Warrior*—a discussion of martial arts such as tae kwon do. "Which art one chooses to follow is not as important as gaining a thorough understanding of the physical, mental, and even spiritual aspect of your chosen art," the paper said. "It is the total integration of all these aspects that provides the warrior with a basis for action." The paper explained the universal force called ch'i, "an infinitely available, directable stream of energy that flows out of the body."

I had heard of ch'i, but all I knew about martial arts was that they required tremendous practice, concentration and discipline. According to this document, my fiancé had long been an expert. The last page listed the author as: "Colonel James Montgomery, SASR - Australia, on attachment with US Special Operations Command, June, 1985."

I was incredulous. The more I learned about this man—his experience, his strength, his understanding—the more I was in awe of him, and astounded at my good fortune. James Montgomery was far more than I ever imagined I could have. He was worth the wait.

Later, as I was at my desk attempting to work, the phone rang. It was James. He was back in the country, and said he would be by briefly the next morning. He couldn't wait to see me. I was ecstatic—and relieved. The first part of his mission was over. My fiancé was safe, and would soon be in my arms.

On the morning of July 30, 1996, my fiancé walked through my front door and kissed me passionately. Then, standing in the living room, he ripped my clothes off.

He ripped off his own clothes as well, until the only thing he was wearing was a long, thin ball chain around his neck. Dangling from the end of it was a huge engagement ring. "This is a very special ring," James said, removing it from the chain. "Liza Minnelli wore it on Broadway—I got it from a collector. It's a cubic zirconia with 12 little diamonds."

The stone was at least the size of two carats. James lifted my left hand and placed the ring on my finger. It was way too big. "Hmm ... your fingers are really slender. I'll have to get it sized."

As I stood there wearing nothing but the ring—with my hand in a fist so it didn't fall off—I started to feel lightheaded. "Excuse me for a minute, James," I said.

I walked through the dining room and into the kitchen. I leaned against the wooden-topped counter between the stove and the refrigerator, supporting myself with my hands. The huge ring was on my left ring finger, which had never before sported a diamond. I looked at it again—and my knees buckled. I grabbed the counter to keep from crashing to the floor.

"Thank you, God. Thank you, God. Thank you, God," I said softly, waiting for my vision to clear and my balance to return. In a moment I felt better, and I took my future husband to bed.

James, I was learning, knew how to please a woman. He kissed and sucked all my sensitive places, bringing me to the point of desperately wanting him—then satisfying us both. We spent all morning and the early afternoon together, without leaving the bedroom. Then he left.

Later that afternoon, I received a fax from him—a poem:

The Morning of July 30th ... remembered
The lovers sat entwined in front of the window
Burning hotly, the Kundalini energy rising
Time suspended, the eternal life force contained
And cycled in them. The lingam and the yoni,

Becoming one
Slowly their breathing paced their hearts
Beating as one, all cares of the world gone,
But love remained.

James 07/30/96 for his lover Donna

I recognized the terms in the poem from Tantric sex seminar at the Whole Life Expo that I had attended a few years earlier. In order for lovers to give each other pleasure, the presenter said, it was important for them to communicate. But the proper names of the genitals were just too clinical, and the slang words too crude. He recommended using the Sanskrit words from the *Kama Sutra*—*lingam* for the male, and *yoni* for the female. Kundalini referred to energy that lay dormant at the base of the spine, until activated through intense spiritual practice.

James was showing me his knowledge of Eastern philosophies. I liked it.

I replied by e-mail, thanking him for the poem. The next day—Wednesday— I sent him three e-mails. I expressed my pride in his moral convictions. I told James about my renewed sense of energy—just a week earlier, I was having trouble getting started in the morning, but now I wanted to handle my responsibilities quickly so I could spend time with him. That evening, to my surprise, James called, and we spoke for a few minutes.

Shortly after that, the phone rang again—it was my sister, Tracy. I let her talk about what was going on in her life, and then I told her what was going on in mine: I was getting married.

I gushed about James—his intelligence, military service, business experience. I swooned about his romantic e-mails and faxes—leaving out the erotic details. I told her he gave me an engagement ring that had belonged to Liza Minnelli.

Tracy knew my history of pain and loneliness. She was thrilled to hear that I finally found my prince—even if I acted impulsively in saying, "yes." But I'd meditated on what I'd done—albeit after I agreed to marry James—and the words I heard from the spirit guides were nothing but encouraging:

> *Yes—okay Donna rejoice—you have waited so long and yes, your reward is at hand. Love him. Love him forever. He will never hurt you. He will give you children. He will be a great father—a wonderful man—a force in the community—a force to be reckoned with. You will know great joy and love. A true treasure. You are truly blessed. You are both truly blessed. Ah, my love, my lover, the one you have waited for.*
>
> *The fears are only in your imagination—and you are overcoming them. There is nothing to fear, ever again. You will be happy. You are happy.*
>
> *What a treasure—open yourself. Reveal yourself. Find yourself. You are safe.*

After my conversation with Tracy, I sent James one last e-mail for the day, telling him my sister would support whatever we decided to do.

His reply was waiting when I awoke the next morning, August 1, 1996. James enjoyed the incongruity of reading loving messages from his fiancée while plotting actions against bad guys. He said he was "in the middle of a desert - the glow of the screen masked from satellite surveil. - in a place embarrassing to our govt. if we were found," thinking of me and remembering our rendezvous.

I continued to receive e-mail messages and faxes from my fiancé. James sent poems. He sent a draft of a business proposal, telling me that he valued my opinion. He sent another erotic story—and asked me to marry him soon.

I, in the meantime, remembered my assignment, and wrote an erotic story for him. *The Royal Bedchamber* was set in Neuschwanstein Castle in Germany, which I visited on a trip to Europe back in 1993. With magnificent turrets, spires and arched windows, it was the inspiration for Sleeping Beauty's Castle in Disneyland. The castle was commissioned by the German King Ludwig II, also known as Mad Ludwig. One day the king—and his psychiatrist—were found floating dead in a lake.

In my story, Donna and James were taking the last tour of the day in the castle. The tour took them to the royal bedchamber.

The bed itself wasn't very big, but it had a canopy also made of ornately carved wood, row upon row of pinnacles, like stalagmites. "It took a team of artisans four years to carve this room," the tour guide explained. "The carvings on the canopy represent the spires of all the great cathedrals of Europe."

"Yeah, and you know who Ludwig slept here with?" Donna said to James. "Richard Wagner."

"And that bed hasn't seen any action since the old guy sank to the bottom of the lake," James said. "What a pity. I think we should correct that."

Donna looked up at him quickly—she knew that tone in his voice, and that twinkle in his eye. He was coming up with another outrageous scheme.

"C'mon, love," James said. "Let's go for a ride on that royal bed."

"You're not serious, are you?" Donna asked.

"Now, love, you know I'm always serious when it comes to sex."

"I know," Donna said, smiling. "So how do you propose to do this?"

"We'll just hang back and let all these Japanese tourists with camcorders leave. Then we'll sneak back and have a go on the bed."

"We'll get caught!"

"Darling, you know where I've been. I'm sure I can sneak us around a silly tourist trap without getting caught."

By now, Donna was intrigued. So as the tour group headed toward the exit, she and James drifted toward the back of the line, and then ducked into a stairwell.

As the story continued, James said, "This is going to be easy. All we have to do is be quiet." Then I described what James did to make it impossible to stay quiet.

James loved my story. He also said he would be back Sunday night, and would drive directly to my house.

Excited and nervous, I walked into my younger cousin's wedding shower on August 4, 1996. I wore my engagement ring, even though it had not yet been sized correctly. I intended to tell the family—at least the female half—of my plans. As I described James Montgomery, my new fiancé, to various cousins and family friends, everyone was very happy for me. My news was, of course, quite a surprise, since no one had ever met him. But then, with my sorry love life, no one had met any of the men I'd dated. The guys never hung around long enough.

On that day, I was as happy as my soon-to-be-wed cousin. Maybe even happier, because it had taken me so much longer to find love. James sent me a fax—the message was a combination of verbiage and clip-art: "Are you saying that you want to be by my side until this ... (a cartoon of an elderly couple) ... thru all this (cartoons of a bride, groom and wedding bells) ... to this (picture of stork delivering a baby) and even this ... (another stork with a baby) ... because of this? (cartoon of Cupid shooting an arrow)." I taped the fax to the wall next to my desk.

I was also happy because James was home safe, and was coming to see me that evening. In anticipation, I bought three sets of lingerie at Victoria's Secret. At 11 o'clock that night, I lay in bed wearing my new leopard-print silk babydoll and full makeup. When I heard a car pull up, I pulled on my matching leopard-print silk robe and ran outside, barefoot, into the street.

A black Grand Prix was parked under the streetlight. The door opened and James stiffly got out of the car. He wore an olive drab one-piece jumpsuit with embroidered patches—military insignias—on the shoulders. Another patch with his name—Montgomery—was over the breast pocket. Right there, under the shining streetlight, he gave me a long, deep kiss. Then we spoke. "I just drove up from Florida," he said. "I couldn't wait to see you so I came directly here."

"Whose car is this?" I asked.

"It belongs to one of my mates from MacDill. He needed the car brought up north, and I needed to get home. It worked out well."

James moved a bit slowly as we walked into the house, but quickly limbered up. By the time we got upstairs, it was like he hadn't been on the road at all.

"How do you like my new nightgown?" I asked him.

"It's nice," James said, as he took it off.

After the weeklong exchange of erotic e-mails and faxes, we were both ravenous for each other. We passionately indulged our desires, then drifted off to sleep.

Chapter 6

The sun shone brightly as I drove to Mays Landing, New Jersey, on the afternoon of August 6, 1996. The weather matched my disposition. My fiancé had returned from his mission abroad two days earlier, and I was on my way to visit him in his home for the first time.

James lived in a two-story brick townhouse in a development called Mays Landing Village, about 20 minutes inland from Atlantic City. The complex was less than five years old, and the builders had managed to retain a good deal of the scrub oak forest in which the homes were constructed. As I pulled into the parking lot, I passed a pool and a tennis court. The grounds around the homes were nicely landscaped. It looked like my fiancé lived well.

James was outside, on the patio of his townhouse, wearing what I soon learned was his standard attire—shorts, polo shirt and baseball cap. On the wrought iron umbrella table in front of him was an empty aquarium. The aquarium was the home of his pet African pygmy hedgehog, Herbie, and James was changing its bedding of pine shavings.

Herbie was the first hedgehog I ever met. He was about the size of my fist, and somewhat prickly for a pet, covered with sharp quills, like a porcupine. He had a pointy snout and dark eyes, although I didn't see them right away. When Herbie was afraid, he curled up into a ball of protruding quills. It was enough to deter anyone—man or beast—from attempting to snatch or bite him.

"Let me show you around," James said as he finished with Herbie's home. He opened the sliding glass door for us to go inside.

James had told me that he and Gale, his previous wife who died, purchased the townhouse together just two years earlier. I followed him into the ground-level living room, which was tastefully furnished in a traditional style. James stood in the middle of the floor and raised his arms, encompassing not only the living room, but the entire home. "All this will be yours," he proclaimed.

High ceilings and off-white walls made the living room feel spacious. To the left was a fireplace and built-in shelves filled with books and objects d'art, along with a 36-inch television. On the wall opposite the sliding glass door was a small table, flanked by a blue leather recliner and a wing chair covered in a plaid fabric of blue, green and red. The wall above them was decorated with a collection of four botanical prints of blue flowers, framed in gold. To the right was a blue upholstered sofa, and in the corner was an antique-style chaise, also upholstered in plaid.

James invited me to sit on the chaise. In front of it was a coffee table, where he had lined up a row of small gifts: Scented bath gel. A sample-sized bottle of perfume. An oversized pink plastic cup with a lid and built-in straw. The *Sleeping Beauty* trilogy—a box set of erotic books by Anne Rice. I suspected the gifts were recycled, but at least he was thinking of me.

"Let me show you the rest of your new home," James said.

From the living room we walked up two steps into the dining room, which featured a cathedral ceiling. The circular dining room table was draped with a floor-length ivory tablecloth; it was covered with stacks of papers. To the left was a well-stocked wet bar. Beyond the dining room was a small but serviceable kitchen. To the right was the staircase going up to the second floor, and an extraordinarily tall window on the landing was fitted with custom drapes. On each of the first five steps were more tall piles of papers.

"What are all the papers?" I asked.

"That's my work. I have six different businesses going. That's how I keep everything in order."

I preferred organizing with file cabinets and stack trays, but I kept that to myself.

We stepped by the papers and went upstairs. The expansive wall of the staircase was decorated with two framed prints of shorebirds—a heron and an egret—each about 36 inches tall. "I like the pictures," I commented.

"Well, they really aren't my taste," James said. "Gale and I argued about what to hang there for a long time. I wanted something more modern. Finally we just flipped a coin. She won."

At the top of the stairs was the master bedroom. A four-poster canopy bed of dark, intricately carved wood dominated the room. On either side of it were nightstands, and against the walls were a matching triple dresser and chest of drawers. The room's fabrics were French provincial in style—a blue and white designer comforter, legions of pillows, floor-length matching drapes. An antique armoire in the corner had been converted to a TV cabinet.

A woman's presence still filled the room—the dresser was covered with toiletry bottles and small jewelry boxes. "All of those things are Gale's," James explained. "I haven't had the heart to move them."

The adjoining master bath was spacious, and featured both an oversized stall shower and a separate whirlpool tub. The vanity was covered with toiletries, ranging from shaving cream to travel-size shampoos taken from hotel rooms. It, too, was a bit cluttered for my taste.

Also off the bedroom was a walk-in closet, packed from floor to ceiling with women's clothes, shoes, hats and accessories. "I'd like you to look through this and see if you want anything. Some of them may fit you," James said.

The idea of scavenging a dead woman's wardrobe made me uncomfortable.

"Oh, I don't know," I replied slowly.

"Please," James urged. "Gale loved clothes and had a lot of nice, expensive things. She would want you to have them."

The tour continued. The second floor of the townhouse had another full bath and two more bedrooms. One bedroom was a guest room, furnished in a style similar to the master bedroom. The other room was James' office. His computer, along with a printer and scanner, was set up on a table under the window. Three inexpensive, fake-wood bookcases lined one wall, and all the shelves were completely filled with books. Opposite the bookcases was another table. It, too, was covered with books and papers.

I stopped to look at a framed photo on a credenza outside the office. It was a woman astride a horse, wearing a riding coat, breeches and helmet. Throughout the townhouse, I noticed paintings and prints on the walls related to horses and racing. "Gale really loved horses," James explained. "She owned a few and did some competing." James' deceased wife was still very much in that house.

We headed back toward the staircase, past the door to the master bedroom. James took my hand, led me into the room, and started to kiss me.

I resisted. I told James I was creeped out by the idea of taking a dead woman's place in bed.

"Don't think like that," James said softly, continuing to kiss me. "I loved Gale, but she's gone. I have to move on. I need you to help me."

James talked a lot about his work. He was pursuing three main business ventures—CelebAM on the Boardwalk; Faux Façade, a manufacturer of specialty construction materials; and the Jersey Shore Channel, a local television network. In addition, he was pitching a feature film script he had written to movie studios, trying to put his *Strike Swiftly* TV series on the air, founding a Lions Club in Mays Landing, and involved with the local VFW (Veterans of Foreign Wars) and the VVA (Vietnam Veterans Association). James was also involved with politics.

The biggest project was CelebAM. James had enthusiastically described it in our first meeting—an electronic theme park for adults. He showed me a letter from the president of Trump Hotel and Casino Resorts, expressing interest in the proposal. But CelebAM was on hold while James tried to figure out who would decide what to do with Atlantic City's old Convention Hall.

Faux Façade would capitalize on two converging trends: a fresh wave of casino expansions and the increasing popularity of themed construction. Bally's Atlantic City, for example, planned to build a casino addition with a "Wild West" theme. The exterior would look like the streetscape of an Old West town, and inside would be decorative touches like a two-story mountain, an animatronic miner panning for gold and fake Ponderosa pine trees. James envisioned a new factory to create these decorative items out of polyurethane.

The Jersey Shore Channel would carry television programming about happenings at the Jersey Shore, especially at Atlantic City's casinos. James was confident that he could run it cheaply as he did at Movietime, and was making contacts that could be instrumental in launching the network. He met Pinky Kravitz, a local radio talk show host, regularly for breakfast at IHOP. James knew members of the Lenfest family, owners of Suburban Cable, which had more than a million cable television customers in the region. Suburban Cable sponsored the old-fashioned July 4th picnic he had just organized in Mays Landing. James wanted to parlay his contacts into a role in the local media scene.

He saw a big role in all of the businesses for me.

My background, of course, was media, although more print than broadcast. My copywriting business focused on advertising and promotion. And even though I'd never worked in the construction business, it always interested me. My skills, James said, would be tremendously helpful in running the businesses. We were going to make a great team.

The day after I visited James in Mays Landing, he had a draft proposal for me to review. James was coming into Atlantic City to see his chiropractor, and wanted me to meet him outside the office so he could give me the proposal.

This was not particularly convenient for me. The chiropractor was located in the Medical Arts Building on Pacific Avenue. I knew the building well—it was where Atlantic City Magazine once had offices. There was absolutely no parking.

Pacific Avenue had two busy lanes of traffic going each way, with no shoulder. I'd often seen tourists step off the curb, only to jump back in fear for their lives as jitneys—Atlantic City's mini-busses—came barreling toward them at full speed. But I knew about a small street in front of the Medical Arts building, Mount Vernon Avenue, where parking spaces were sometimes available. That's where I went, and I was in luck—I found a spot. I parked and stood on the sidewalk to watch for my fiancé.

"James!" I called, waving, when I saw him come out of the building.

He crossed the busy street to meet me. After a kiss, he searched his canvas briefcase, with its Congressional Medal of Honor emblem, for the proposal. "Will you please read this over and let me know what you think?" he asked.

"Sure," I said. "I'd be happy to."

"Thank you, Donna. I really value your opinion. And thank you for meeting me here; you really saved me some time. Now I've got to get back to work—still more calls to make."

James turned to leave, then stopped. "You know, since you're going to be part of all these businesses, you really should invest in them."

I had been flipping through the proposal. I looked up at him in surprise.

"What do you mean?" I asked.

"Well, as an investor, you'll be entitled to a share of the profits. You'll be paid for any time that you put into the businesses, of course, but there is so much upside potential for these companies that I'd like to see you gain from that as well."

James had tremendous confidence in the success of the ventures, a confidence that was contagious. I was intrigued. "What would I have to do?" I asked.

"Well, at this early stage of the game, $5,000 will get you a few points."

"Points?"

"Percentage points of ownership. When the companies start making money, you'll be entitled to a percentage of the profits. It would be a strong asset for your portfolio."

My portfolio was pretty slim. I had about $25,000 in my money market savings, which was earning some ridiculously low amount of interest. If $5,000 would buy me a slice of businesses that were bound to generate big profits, it seemed like a good idea. I was flattered that James was willing to give me a percentage of his companies, and pleased that he was looking out for me.

"Okay. What do I do?" I agreed.

"Just write a check made out to me and I'll arrange everything," he said.

"All right. I can do that tomorrow."

Two days later poetry from James arrived on my fax machine. It originated from his computer, which he named Prudence ("Proody" for short). James had nicknames for me as well—they were part Australian, part baby talk. He called me "Bubba," which he said was an Australian term of endearment. He also called me "Mouse," "Darwies"—a version of darling—and "Nuffles." I never learned the etymology of Nuffles—I think James made it up.

The header at the top of the fax read, "from Proody - UnApple of Daddy's eye & my dad's in love again!" It was a poem borrowed from W. B. Yeats:

Where You Walk Is Special
Had I the heavens' embroidered cloths,
Enwrought with golden and silver light,
The blue and the dim and the dark cloths,
Of night and light and half-light,
I would spread the cloths under your feet;
But I, being poor, have only my dreams;
I have spread my dreams under your feet;
Tread softly, My Donna, for you tread on my dreams.

W. B. Yeats & Your Fiancé

It was one of many poems James sent me—some were classics, some he wrote. He also sent another series of stories called *The Treat,* featuring more erotic adventures of Donna and James.

One day a handwritten fax arrived with his signature at the top of the page. It read:

James A. Montgomery
loves
Donna Maria Montgomery
Try it!

Below the message, James scrawled his signature—which after the "J" was completely illegible—two more times. He wanted me to try out my new name.

Long ago—I couldn't even remember when—I decided that when I married, I would keep my own name. After operating my business as "Donna Andersen Copywriting" for 13 years, the decision made even more sense. I enjoyed a good reputation as a talented writer and a competent, reliable businesswoman. I saw no point in starting over with a new name. So although I appreciated my fiancé's enthusiasm, no way was I going to become a Montgomery.

A few hours later James called me. "Did you get my fax?" he asked.

"Yes," I answered slowly.

"Donna Maria Montgomery sounds splendid, doesn't it?"

"Well ..." I began. This might be touchy, and diplomacy was not my strong suit. "My middle name isn't 'Maria;' it's 'Marie.'"

"Oh. Well, I was close."

"And I think I'll be keeping 'Andersen.'"

Silence. Then, "Why? You don't like 'Montgomery?'"

"'Montgomery' is okay," I said. "I just want to keep my name. I don't want to give up my identity."

"You don't want to be identified as my wife?"

"It has nothing to do with you, James," I replied. "It's just a personal decision that I've made."

"Well how about 'Andersen-Montgomery?'"

Ugh. I never liked hyphenated names either, and that one was way too clunky.

"I don't think so," I said. "I'm just going to be 'Donna Andersen.'"

A few days later I got a call from James. "I'm ringing on behalf of Clan Montgomery," he began in his best Scottish brogue. "I understand that you've been given the opportunity to become a member in good standing of our clan, and take the Montgomery name, and have refused?"

I laughed.

"'Montgomery' is a fine Scottish name," he continued. "It has an impressive pedigree."

"That's true, Mr. Clan Montgomery, and I appreciate your call," I replied, "but I think I'll remain an Andersen."

James met the Andersens for the first time on August 11, 1996. My brother, Doug, and his wife, Cathy, invited the immediate family—his and hers—to their home for a poolside barbecue in honor of their son's fourth birthday. Their other son was one-and-a-half years old.

It was a typical Andersen event—jokes, stories and free-flowing alcohol. James did not partake in the alcohol, but he did his share of the talking. He told my family about his projects. He also offered to find Australian software developers for Doug's professional services company, which placed information technology experts on short-term assignments.

As the party came to an end, I felt warm and fulfilled. For the first time in my life, I attended a family event with a man who loved me. James seemed to like everyone. "Your brother has a nice family," he said when we got home.

"The boys are really cute," I agreed.

"You know, I never wanted children. I thought it would be too difficult with my work. But then when my daughter contacted me, and I met my grandchildren—well, that changed everything."

"I always wanted children. I just couldn't seem to make a connection."

I remembered a party at my aunt's house two years earlier for my grandmother's 85th birthday. Doug and Cathy's son was two years old, and she was pregnant with their second child. I couldn't bear to look at them. They had their perfect little family, and I had no husband and no prospects. It was so upsetting that I had to leave the party. I went home and cried. I felt like a total failure.

Now, I felt redeemed. Yes, at age 40, I was late, but I was healthy. James and I would have children. I would have my family.

James wanted me to learn more about him, to understand where he had been in his life. He started faxing me "bits and pieces," as he would say, about his military career. One fax was his "Australian Service History."

JAMES A. MONTGOMERY
2243096
AUSTRALIAN SERVICE HISTORY

I COMMANDO COMPANY: Enlisted 1960 transferring from the Commando Regiment in 1975 after eighteen months of career leave. Attained Majority in 1974, attached GHQ Intelligence after posting as Company Intelligence Officer. Served as Squad & Company Commanders, seconded to Special Air Service Regiment and A.A.T.T.V. during Vietnam tours of duty.

QUALIFICATIONS:

PARACHUTE: PJI qualified, HALO, load following, SCUBA and snow courses satisfactorily completed. USSF Snr. Jumpmaster qualified.

MARINE: SCUBA and Basic Submarine qualified, small craft coxswains, inflatable assault craft and underwater demolitions courses satisfactorily completed. US Navy SEAL qualifying and demolitions course completed. UK small scale raiders training.

AIR: International commercial qualifications with all navigation ratings; multi-engine, turbine, 1st class instrument rating, seaplane & floatplane qualifications. CIA foreign aircraft E&E course. Current aerobatic ticket to 500'.

INTELLIGENCE: Clearances upon request. ASIO & CIA courses in Australia, USA, Vietnam and Honduras. 22 SAS (Herfordshire) G2 course with NATO operations. Counter-terrorist courses: Swanbourne, Herfordshire, Israel, Jordan and Indonesia.

SKILLS: Fluent in German and Pindjari. Knowledge of Mandarin, Nung, Russian and Italian. Full quals. radio and morse. Expert drivers course (ScotYd) SAS Mountaineering leaders course (Wales)

OVERSEAS TOURS OF DUTY:

1966/67 The SASR Liaison officer with the 5th Battalion, RAA at Nui Dat, Phouc Tuy Province. Responsible for Long Range Patrols, Intelligence, Amphibious Support. Part of area Task Force with 173rd Airborne Brigade while tasked to clear area. Mentioned In Dispatches. Infantry Combat Award.

1968/69 Attached to the AATTV, as a member of 5th Special Forces Group (Airborne) based in Pleiku. As part of the 2nd Mobile Strike Force command, he commanded the 212 and 213 Companies of 1st Mike Force Battalion under Major Roland Greenwood USSF with native (Nung) strikers. Unit co-ordinated with CIA on tri-border (Vietnam, Laos and Cambodia) operations, downed pilot extraction and intelligence operations. Reassigned to Special Forces Operation Delta for long range intelligence patrols. Instructor at Special Forces Recondo School. Mentioned In Dispatches. RoV Cross of Gallantry (Silver Star)

1971: A member of AATTV, involved in the winding down of all US/AUST operations from Pleiku base, all USSF personnel were ordered redeployed to Ranger or stateside duty by 1971 as part of "Vietnamization." Seconded to Phoenix program, operated in tri-border area with indigent personnel as PRU units. RoV Cross of Gallantry (Palm).

According to the service history, James served three tours of duty in Vietnam, two of them based in Pleiku. Pleiku was located in the Central Highlands of Vietnam, the ancestral homeland of the indigenous Montagnard tribes. The Montagnards were allies of American and Australian forces during the war— James said he had two Montagnard bodyguards, who were with him constantly. While in the region, James said he always ate the local Montagnard food to change his body chemistry. That way when he went out on patrol, the enemy couldn't smell him.

James previously told me that he was awarded the Victoria Cross, Australia's highest military honor, for his service in Vietnam. He didn't want to elaborate, but he did send me a "Mention in Dispatches" report:

MENTION IN DISPATCHES
2243096 CAPTAIN JAMES MONTGOMERY

Captain Montgomery enlisted in the Australian Army Reserve in 1960 and served with 1 Commando Regt. He was commissioned in 1965 and served with Special Air Service Regiment as a reserve officer. He joined the Australian Army Training Team in May 1968 for his second tour in Vietnam.

Captain Montgomery was two weeks short of the end of his tour with the Training Team when, on the 11th May 1969 he was on an operational visit to the 3rd Mobile Strike Force Battalion of the 5th Special Forces group that was on a search and clear operation in Kontum province. In heavy contact with the enemy, forward of the company in which Captain Montgomery was moving, the commander of the Mobile strike battalion was killed and an Australian Warrant Officer and several indigenous soldiers were wounded. In addition, one other Australian Warrant Officer who had been separated from the majority of his troops was contained in the area by enemy fire. Without hesitation, Captain Montgomery joined a small group under the command of a further Australian Warrant Officer, who was a company commander in the battalion, and went forward to the area of contact. While the remainder of the group were extricating the casualties, Captain Montgomery commenced preparation of an area close by to enable a helicopter to winch out the casualties. Unable to obtain the assistance of the indigenous troops, who had been scattered in the contact and who were reluctant to expose themselves, Captain Montgomery cut and prepared the casualty evacuation point on his own and under enemy fire. The helicopter attempted to extract the serious casualties but was forced away by heavy fire. Captain Montgomery, with complete disregard for his own safety, then, single handed, cleared the enemy from the close proximity of the evacuation point using hand grenades and small arms fire. This action delayed the enemy's movement for sufficient time to allow the remainder of the group and the wounded to move out of the immediate contact area. On the tedious and dangerous movement back to the firm base with the casualties, Captain Montgomery quietly assisted the Warrant officer who was in command of the group and helped carry the wounded over much of the difficult terrain.

Captain Montgomery's personal conduct and steadying influence were major contribution factors in enabling the group to extricate the wounded and others successfully from the contact area. His conduct in this action and on a number of other occasions, when he was serving earlier with the Mobile Strike Force, has been exemplary. His professionalism during his extensive operational service has been a credit to himself and the Australian Army Reserves.

Note: For his role as the company commander in this action, WO2 R. S. Simpson of I CDO RGT was awarded the Victoria Cross; Captain Montgomery was awarded the United States Silver Cross for his role and WO2 K. R. Gill was Mentioned in Dispatches posthumously. [authenticate:DRO(V)262/8/690]

Wow.

After Vietnam, James' military career involved Special Forces, intelligence analysis and counter-terrorism. He said he kept trying to retire, and the military kept calling him back—he showed me the involuntary recall notice he received from the Navy.

James told me he was attached to the Navy SEALs (U.S. Navy Sea, Air and Land forces) during the American invasion of Panama on December 20, 1989. I barely remembered the incident. James said his group was tasked with preventing the Panamanian dictator, General Manuel Noriega, from escaping. Their mission was to blow up Noriega's gunboat and destroy his private jet at the Punta

Paitilla Airport. The airport mission succeeded, but at a high cost—four SEALs dead and eight wounded.

James' voice cracked with bitterness as he talked about the mission. "It was a fuck-all disaster," he said. "Bad planning and bad intelligence, all because of some clown at headquarters. And I lost four guys."

Making matters worse, James said, was his wife at the time. "I'm at the airport as the bodies are coming back, and she's there giving me shit," he said.

"What did you do?" I asked.

"I ordered her off the premises."

Life became a spinning tornado, with James at the center of it. He was working at full speed on all his projects, yet called me many times a day, keeping me apprised of his progress. He told me about his meetings, forwarding reports and faxes. He also asked for my help. James wrote newsletters for American Legion, Vietnam Veterans Association and his new Lions Club. He wanted me to use my vendors to get them printed and mailed.

I was busy as well. My business, Donna Andersen Copywriting, Inc., handled three casino newsletters. The Caesars Premium Player was published five times a year for the casino's customers; I had the account since 1984. The Showboat Crew's News was published monthly for that casino's employees, which I'd done since 1989. Showboat had expanded to three different properties and wanted a newsletter for all its employees, so in 1994 I won a contract to produce a semimonthly newsletter called the Learning Network. For each newsletter, I was responsible for researching and writing all the stories, managing the graphic design and photography, and coordinating printers and mailers. It was a lot of work.

Still, James and I wanted to spend as much time together as we could. He suggested that each week we get out our calendars—"diaries," he called them—to plan our evenings. "We'll call your house our 'bay' house, and my house our 'woods' house," he said. "We'll mark which nights we'll be where."

James kept an early schedule—he was up and on his computer at 4 a.m., and went to bed at 8 p.m. I was still sleeping at 4 a.m., so at first, when we were at our bay house, he used my computer to go on the Internet. But he wanted to use his laptop and have access to his files. So I agreed to set up an office for him in the spare bedroom, and had a phone jack installed so he could get online. The back room was soon filled with piles of papers.

The political campaign season was in full swing, and James was working on the campaign of Joe Nickles, a Republican from Hamilton Township (which included Mays Landing), who was running for Atlantic County freeholder. James wanted me to accompany him to campaign appearances and fundraisers. With him, I attended my very first VFW picnic. It was on a bright, sunny afternoon, so we drove there in James' 1977 MGB convertible, with the top down.

Then James wanted me to go with him to a meeting he arranged at Suburban Cable in West Chester, Pennsylvania on August 16, 1996. He was going to talk to them about the Jersey Shore Channel and other possible television ventures. I was pleased to be included in his business plans, and made time for the meeting in my schedule.

A few days before the meeting, I asked James if I should wear a business suit. He seemed surprised by my question. "You're not going into the meeting," he said.

I was confused. "Then why did you ask me to go?"

"It's an important meeting, and I want you to drive so I can get prepared mentally for it and not be distracted by traffic," he said. "And I want to practice my pitch with you on the way up. Then I'll go into the meeting, and you'll wait in the car."

West Chester was an hour and 45 minutes away. James wanted me to leave early in the morning, drive him there, sit in the car for an hour or two while he had his meeting, and drive another hour and 45 minutes to get home. My day would be shot. I was annoyed.

But, I thought, if it would help my fiancé get his TV network going, I guess I should do it. So I agreed to the trip, and brought work with me to do in the car, although without my computer, I accomplished little.

We got back from West Chester in the afternoon. I dropped James off in Mays Landing and continued on to Atlantic City, hoping to salvage something of the day. Later, James would be coming by—it was a night for our bay house.

Late in the afternoon James called me. "I still have a lot of work to do," he said. "It would be better if you came here tonight."

I did not respond immediately. In fact, I was floored.

I had blown most of the day to drive him to a meeting that he certainly could have driven to himself. I, too, had a lot of work to do. And now he wanted me to drop everything and drive to Mays Landing again?

"You know, James, I'm pretty busy myself," I said. "Tonight was supposed to be a night here, and I'd like to stick with that plan."

"Donna, I have to pull information together based on today's meeting. I have more calls to make and more faxes to send. I'm working very hard to build our future. I don't think it's too much to ask you to come here this evening."

By this point I was angry. "Well, James, I too have a business to run, and quite frankly, I lost a lot of time today. So I think I'll just stay home," I said.

"Is that your decision?" he asked, with an accusatory edge in his voice.

"Yes, it is."

"All right, then. Goodbye, Donna."

I hung up the phone with mixed emotions. On the one hand, I was overworked, and I felt James did not respect my time. My anger was justified. On the other hand, I wanted to be supportive of my fiancé. At least I thought I did. But what was I getting myself into?

The next morning we spoke on the phone. I explained to James that I was angry. "I feel like you expect me to give up my life and become one of your appendages," I said.

James suggested that he take me out to breakfast so we could talk. When he picked me up, the first thing I did was give him his ring back. "Maybe it would be best for you to hold on to this," I said. He put the ring in his pocket and we drove to a small local restaurant.

The place was busy with a summer Saturday breakfast crowd. We were seated in a red vinyl booth along the wall. I ordered scrambled eggs. James ordered scrambled eggs as well—with scrapple.

It was time to talk. I wasn't sure of my feelings, and I wasn't sure where to start. So I just started.

"You know, James, I have to send the Showboat job to the printer next week, and the Caesars job goes out the week after that. Driving you to Westchester yesterday really set me back."

"Then you shouldn't have done it."

"You asked me to go with you, and I want to help you. That's why I went with you. I was okay with that. But I needed to get back and get some work done. When you wanted me to drop everything again and come out to Mays Landing, well, that wasn't in the plan."

"My plans change all the time. I'm working on six businesses. I have to deal with multiple, shifting priorities. If we're going to be together, you're going to have to be flexible."

"James, I know how to juggle. I do it all the time. But I need you to understand that I have responsibilities as well."

The waitress arrived with our breakfast. We ate in silence for a few minutes. I started again. "I feel like things are moving too quickly, James. It hasn't even been a month since we met."

"Donna, I've learned that life is short, and can change drastically in an instant. I was with Gale, and then she was gone. Men who were with me in Vietnam were alive one minute, and dead the next. I am accustomed to making quick decisions and taking action. When I asked you to marry me, I committed to putting everything I've got into our future together. I committed to us, boots and all. It's going to be a lot of work, and that doesn't bother me. Things are going to be difficult for another month or so. But I need to know you're with me 100 percent."

I was quiet, trying to sort out how I felt. Was the relationship moving too fast, or was I just afraid? This man was a dynamo. He accomplished much in the past, and he would accomplish even more in the future. He invited me to join him, to be his partner in what was sure to be an exciting journey.

James told me, over and over, how much he loved me. I was the woman he always wanted. I was the woman who completed him. No man had ever said that to me before—and I'd known a lot of men. Wasn't this what I was waiting for all my life?

"Look, Donna, this is a deal-breaker," James said. "If we're going to be together, it must be completely. To me, that's what a marriage is—two people completely supporting each other. If that's not what you want, then we should stop."

I held my coffee mug with two hands, studying it carefully. I agreed with James—a marriage should be two people totally committed to each other. It's what I wanted for so long, and what James promised.

"What do you want to do?" James asked.

I looked up at him. "I want to get married."

"Boots and all?" he asked.

"Yes."

"I'm glad," he said softly. "That's what I want."

Since I'd given James the ring back, he said he'd take it to his jeweler and get it sized.

Boots and all it was. I accompanied James to a political event at the Atlantic City Race Course. I helped him get the Vietnam Veterans Association list of names and addresses formatted on mailing labels. I put in a call to my casino contacts about another project James was working on—a Christmas concert by the Atlantic Symphony Orchestra.

I learned to bring my calendar whenever we had lunch. A restaurant located a few blocks from me, called Agape, became one of James' favorites. He often met his attorney and other associates there.

One sunny afternoon we returned to my house after lunch at Agape. I was walking up the front steps to the porch, with James behind me. Suddenly he said, "Let's move in together."

I stopped in surprise and turned toward him. "Don't you think it's a bit soon?" I asked.

"Oh, nonsense, Donna. Teenagers do it. We're certainly old enough to make our own decisions."

I didn't reply and continued into the house, not prepared to make a decision.

"I have something for you," James said. He opened his hand—there was the engagement ring, modified to fit me—sort of. Because of how the setting was designed—on either side of the stones, the band was just two narrow strips of gold with a large gap between them—it could not be resized. So the jeweler attached a secondary band to the inside of the ring, like a clip-on piece, to make the ring smaller. Although it looked weird, when the ring was on my hand, the clunky modification wasn't apparent.

"You know, Nuffles, the ring was so happy to be back with you that she had babies," James said. He opened his hand again, and there was a pair of diamond stud earrings—at least one carat each. "The ring is a cubic zirconia, but these are real. You need to keep them in a safe place."

No one had ever given me diamond earrings. After that, I agreed to the idea of moving in together. How could I refuse?

"Where do you want to live—at the bay or in the woods?" James asked. For me, that was a no-brainer. I'd much rather be in a single-family home three blocks from the beach than in a townhouse next to a highway. Although James pointed out that the townhouse was new and my home was almost 100 years old, he was willing to go along with moving to the bay.

We also started talking about going to Australia together. James had a business reason to go—he wanted to visit the factory that made the polyurethane construction materials, and convince them to license their technology to Faux Façade. Plus, James wanted me to meet his family.

If we went to Australia, I could do business as well. Showboat had won the right to build the first casino in Sydney. I'd been writing about the project for months in the Learning Network newsletter with information gleaned from photographs and phone interviews. I always preferred to get a first-hand look at what I was writing about—a trip to Australia would give me the opportunity to do it.

My engagement ring no longer fell off my hand. Still, I hesitated to wear it to the Philadelphia Folk Festival. James had no interest in going to the festival—his idea of camping was a Holiday Inn rather than a Marriott. But I wanted to be with my friends one last time—my life was changing dramatically, and I doubted I'd be able to go again. So I spent the weekend of August 23-25, 1996, at the Old Pool Farm, enjoying the music and the party. And I did wear the ring—admitting to myself that I wanted to show it off.

I returned to the tornado—James' work, my work and a new opportunity. My old friend from the tall ship *Young America,* Dennis Steelman, contacted me about a possible contract with the Federal Aviation Administration. The FAA had just completed writing a *Human Factors Design Guide,* which described best practices for ergonomically designing control systems, consoles and similar equipment, and wanted to promote it as an authoritative resource. Dennis thought I would be good for the job. And I thought, with James' marketing and military background, that he would be good for the job. So I brought my new fiancé to a meeting with my old friend and one of his colleagues at the FAA. The conversation turned to security issues. The other FAA manager had some background in that area, and she referred obliquely to a high-security location in Virginia.

"The Farm?" James asked.

The woman looked at James sharply. "The Farm" referred to Camp Peary, a military reservation near Williamsburg, Virginia, which was widely believed to be a covert CIA training facility. I had no idea what James was talking about, until he explained his comment after the meeting.

The *Human Factors Design Guide* project was too big for me to handle by myself, so I brought in the company my sister worked for, Rittenhouse Communications of Yardley, Pennsylvania. We agreed that Rittenhouse would take the lead—they had more resources for the technical parts of the job. James offered to write the marketing strategy section of the proposal, and with his extensive advertising background, everyone thought that was a good idea.

James quickly produced the marketing strategy and gave it to me to read. I was dismayed.

He identified three target markets—ergonomics professionals, institutions that train ergonomics professionals, and Washington legislators responsible for FAA funding. James had good ideas for reaching the target markets. But the document was poorly written. It was incomplete, disorganized and made unexplained references.

What was I supposed to do now?

I cautiously broached the subject with him—some points needed to be clarified. James said I should send his strategy to Rittenhouse the way it was. So I did. Their feedback: The document was not usable. At that point, James allowed me to edit it. The FAA project wasn't a priority for him anyway. Even though our proposed budget was almost $300,000, James viewed it as mere pin money compared to the earnings he expected from the Jersey Shore Channel, CelebAM and Faux Façade.

At the moment, however, his finances were tight. So as we planned our trip to Australia, James asked me to put the expenses on my credit cards. By the time the charges came in, he promised, he would have his funding and would pay them off.

James also wanted to start planning our wedding. One evening we had dinner at a small restaurant in Gravelly Run, a hamlet near Mays Landing.

"So when do you want to do this?" he asked.

"Do what?" I asked.

"Get married."

I hadn't given it any thought. "I don't know," I replied. "I suppose we should know each other at least six months."

"That will be in January. Shall we plan it for then?"

A January wedding. The weather could be nasty—snow, ice, freezing rain. On the other hand, because January was definitely the off-season for weddings, catering facilities would probably be available—maybe even willing to cut a deal. In my opinion, ludicrous amounts of money were spent on weddings. I certainly wasn't going to do that.

We finished eating, and James gave the waitress his credit card to pay the check. She returned a few minutes later, saying his card had been declined. James gave her a different card.

"I'm not surprised about that," James said. "I'm talking to them about funding, and they're trying to pressure me into a deal. They want a bigger percentage of *Strike Swiftly*."

This struck me as odd—I never heard of investments having anything to do with credit cards. But then again, I never looked for major funding—maybe the company was playing hardball.

Apparently it was. A few days later, James asked me to lend him $5,000 to cover his expenses until the funding came through—which would be in October. At that point, he said, he'd be able to pay me back and pay off the credit cards for the Australia trip. So on August 28, 2006, I wrote him another check from my money market account.

We decided to leave for Australia on September 24, 1996 for a two-week visit. Because the trip required 24 hours of travel each way, and we'd be crossing the International Date Line, we'd actually be gone for 18 days. So now I was trying to get my work done, help James with his projects, get ready for my fiancé to move into my house, plan a wedding and prepare for a trip to Australia. "Busy" was an understatement.

Amid all the planning, I accompanied James to social and business events, which to him were one and the same: A Labor Day party at a high-rise condo-minium—James' friend asked what I was doing there with all the retired people. A Lions Club breakfast meeting, where James, the president, discussed its upcoming black-tie dinner and sponsorship of the Atlantic Symphony Orchestra concert. A fundraising barbecue for Joe Nickles, the political candidate, where I knew Joe's wife, but no one else.

I planned home improvements to accommodate my fiancé. The spare bed-room wouldn't do as permanent office, so I gave up my gym in the basement to build an office there. This meant running electricity, telephone lines and cable television. James insisted that he needed Home Box Office and Cinemax—he was, after all, in the movie business. He also said we should "buy another bath-room," as I only had one. So I planned a small powder room for the basement as well. All the work would be done while we were in Australia. It was going to cost about $6,000, which James promised to reimburse.

James also said he needed furniture and supplies for a proper office. So on September 11, 1996, I drove James' SUV to Staples with a shopping list: A four-piece, U-shaped desk that was advertised in a circular. An executive swivel chair. Two folding banquet tables. A new 8mm video camera. Miscellaneous office sup-plies. The shopping spree totaled $1,300. It was a lot of money, but I was proud that I was in a position to contribute to our future.

James was always planning for the future, and a specific concern arose that he thought we should discuss. He found out that Australia was going to change the rules for the beneficiaries of military pensions—they would no longer be available to military spouses who were not Australian citizens. The change would go into effect in 1997.

"I hesitate to bring this up because I don't want you to feel pressured about our plans," James said to me. "But I've spent almost 35 years in the military and I've built up a good pension. I'll probably die before you do, and I want you to be looked after."

"Don't talk like that," I said.

"Donna, we have to be realistic. I'm older than you and I have diabetes."

"So what are you saying?"

"Well, if we got married this year, you'll be eligible for full benefits."

"You want to move the date up? How can we do that? We can't have a wed-ding during the holidays, and there's not enough time to plan one before then."

"We could get married in Australia."

The suggestion was a complete surprise. "That's in a few weeks!" I said. "How would we arrange that?"

"They have weddings every day at the Registry Office in Sydney," James said. "I can have Archie or Margaret look into it to see what is required."

"What about my family?" I asked.

"We'll have another wedding here," James said. "We won't tell them we're already married so they think they're at the real thing."

I didn't answer.

"Darwies, we know we want to be married. There is no reason to delay. And if we do this, I'll know that you will be secure when I'm gone."

James was right. We were getting married in January—what difference would it make if we did it earlier? And if it meant I would have a pension—well, it all made sense.

"Okay," I said. "Find out what we have to do."

James took me to lunch at Agape on September 12, 1996. I was learning that when James took me out to lunch, there was business to discuss.

Earlier that morning, James met Pinky Kravitz, the local radio talk show host, for breakfast, and learned that Atlantic City was going to legalize slot machines on the city's piers. Four piers jutted out into the ocean from the Atlantic City Boardwalk. Two were owned by casinos—the Steel Pier in front of Trump Taj Mahal, and the Ocean One pier in front of Caesars. The city owned Garden Pier, which was an arts center. Central Pier, an amusement center, was the only one privately owned. It belonged to Abraham and Robert Schiff, brothers who also owned much of the property along the Boardwalk.

"Pinky says this is going to be a really big deal, and there will be slot machines on all the piers," James told me. "This is information that we can take advantage of. We can get a six-month option to buy Central Pier. A casino company is going to want that site, so when they go to buy it, they'll have to deal with us."

"You want to buy an option on Central Pier?" I asked.

"Yes. I've been talking to someone who knows the option is available. But we'd have to do it right away. The story is going to be in the newspaper tomorrow, and then it will be too expensive."

"How much is the option?" I asked.

"It's $20,000."

"I don't have $20,000. Plus, I've been spending a lot of money recently."

"I know you have, and I appreciate everything you've done. You're really doing your part to build our future. But I believe we have an opportunity to make some good money here, which will help us with CelebAM and Faux Façade."

I toyed with my salad. I was not a real estate speculator, and this idea made me nervous.

James pulled out a pen and a small slip of paper. He thought carefully, looking up at the ceiling, and then wrote down some figures. He pushed the paper across the table toward me:

Strike Swiftly	$100,000
Jersey Shore Channel	$200,000
Faux Façade	$400,000
CelebAM	$1,000,000
Total	$1.7 million

"That's what we should have coming in within the next few months," James said. "That's our share of the project funding. With the option, we'll see even more money."

"Well, I still don't have $20,000."

"How much do you have?"

"About $10,000."

"That's fine. I can get the rest from John. You know—the guy whose car I drove back from Florida. He's always looking for an opportunity to make money."

I still wasn't comfortable with the idea.

"Donna, I need you to trust me," James said. "This is a good move."

"How do you know?"

"I have very good sources of information."

I caved. "All right," I said.

We finished lunch and went back to our bay house. But as I sat at my desk trying to work, I was still bothered by the whole plan. Finally I went downstairs to talk to my fiancé. "James, I'm having second thoughts about this option business," I said. "I don't think I want to do it."

"I already told them I would take it," James said.

I was stuck. In my business, I always lived up to my commitments. James had committed to taking the option. He was getting established in Atlantic City— I knew it was important for him to follow through on his promises.

"All right," I said. "I'll give you the money tomorrow."

James' new desk required assembly, which I planned to do the following Saturday morning. Another political fundraiser for Joe Nickles was slated for that day—I told James that I'd put his desk together and then meet him there. Political events were boring; I was happy for an excuse to be late.

I didn't get there at all. The desk included a credenza with two locking drawers and a sliding keyboard tray, a hutch with shelves and two doors, a bridge and a conference table—hundreds of parts and screws. Assembling it took far longer than I expected. But I had fun—it was a three-dimensional puzzle.

Late that afternoon, James arrived at my house and came down to the basement just as the desk was finished. I was pleased—it was upright and stable. The doors and drawers worked. The lock and key worked.

James was furious.

"Where were you?" he demanded.

"I was here putting your desk together," I answered, stunned.

"You were supposed to come to the fundraiser."

"Well, this took longer than I thought it would, and I wanted to finish the job. Besides, I'm sure you didn't need me."

"Being involved with politics means showing up at these things. Joe's wife noticed that you weren't there. She seems to have the opinion that you think you're too good for politics."

By now I was angry and defensive. "James, I was working on *your* desk. I intended to go. This just took a lot longer than I anticipated."

James said nothing about the desk. He turned and walked out of the room.

A few days later, however, he faxed me a poem:

The Woods
... My bedroom, and how
you came
over letting your shorts go
as if it was your room
already! And what I was
doing there is
not clear
to me—now—nor
why I am
standing here dumb
lips shaping amazing words
that fall forth duds.
Breathless, my pulse
is doing a waltz
through this room
and very same
"bachelor apartment" air
where, O, you were

James wrote a note at the end of the poem: "can't work ... I just stare at your distinctive marks on the crumpled blue & white stripes ..."

About the same time James sent me another fax—one with a totally different message. At the top it said, "Keep in a locked box. Bring out if ever anything happened to me." Below that were two names, a Washington, D.C. phone number and the title of the document:

Ruff Workin September
Safety Copy

The three-page fax identified a roster of bad guys—names, addresses, phone numbers, relationships and their nefarious activities. Money launderers in Los Angeles. The jihad connection in New York. Diamond fencing by La Cosa Nostra. Drug dealers from Cali, Columbia. Stock manipulation by a corporate executive. Heroin production in Burma.

I was still attempting to digest the information when the phone rang. It was James. "Did you get the fax?" he asked.

"Yes. What is this all about?"

"It would be better if you don't know. Just hold on to it."

I made several copies of Ruff Workin September and put them in different locations—one of which was a safe.

James' "coronation," as he called it, was September 19, 1996. The Lions Club he founded in Hamilton Township, New Jersey, would receive its charter that evening from Lions Clubs International. As president, James would accept it.

James and the other officers wore tuxedos to the dinner at Chet's Restaurant in Mays Landing. I sat at the head table with my fiancé. James had recruited 30 local businesspeople to join the club. Most of them were at the dinner, along with officials from the Lions organization—one of whom traveled all the way from Georgia.

Every guest received a program. In it, James wrote that he had founded a Lions Club in Australia 25 years earlier. "I have been blessed in finding another group of like-minded citizens—proud of their hometown—and willing to work to improve it—while upholding the grand traditions of the International Association of Lions Clubs."

A newspaper photographer took a standard grip-and-grin shot of the officers accepting the framed charter document. The photo appeared, along with an article, on the front page of the Record Journal, the Hamilton Township weekly, on September 26, 1996.

James was now the Lions king.

Chapter 7

"People with diabetes are at a higher risk of heart disease." I highlighted the statement with my fluorescent pink marker.

Flying from Philadelphia to Los Angeles, and then from Los Angeles to Sydney, meant James and I would be stuck in airplanes for 20 hours. I was determined to pass the time productively. I wanted to help my soon-to-be husband eat properly so he could lose his protruding belly and keep his diabetes under control. So my reading material included a 2.5-pound tome—Prevention Magazine's *Nutrition Advisor*.

James thought it was funny that I lugged the heavy reference book to Australia. He brought pop fiction.

At one point on the first flight I interrupted his reading with a few questions. He answered them impatiently and returned to his book. Then I tried to start a conversation.

"No talking on airplanes," he said.

"What?"

"You're not supposed to talk on a flight; you're supposed to read."

"Says who?"

"U.S. Secret Service flight guidelines."

I knew that was bullshit. But I also knew how to take an obvious hint. James was not interested in conversation.

The Qantas flight to Australia left Los Angeles at 10:30 p.m., and we were in the air for approximately 14 hours. It was 6 a.m. when we arrived at the Sydney Airport. For the first four days of our trip, we would stay in the home of James' daughter, Margaret Riley,* who lived in a suburb north of Sydney. But even after going through customs and retrieving our luggage, it was still an extremely uncivilized hour of the morning, far too early to show up there. To pass the time, James drove our rental car into the city center.

With one hand on the steering wheel, he put his other hand out, palm up. I placed my hand in his. The gesture had become a little habit between us—we did it whenever we were in a car. But this time the gesture meant much more—we were about to embark on an adventure, our new life together.

We drove to the Kings Cross neighborhood, where James said he kept an apartment in the wild days of his youth. The area had a reputation for tawdry nightclubs, but at 8 a.m. on a pleasant, sunny morning, all was quiet. While waiting for a sidewalk café to open, James told me stories of partying the night away in Kings Cross and then going directly to his Australian Army Reserve parade drills in the morning. An adventure with his commando mates in a nearby neighborhood, Rushcutter's Bay, resulted in his daughter.

Margaret and her husband lived with their three children—including the newborn baby—in a nice, middle-class home. Most of the family activity took place in their big eat-in kitchen, which had cheerful yellow walls and a white ceramic tile floor with black accents. A long, pine-plank table, surrounded by 10 ladder-back chairs, dominated the room. It looked homey and lived-in.

Up a short staircase from the kitchen was the TV room, where James and I would stay. My body clock was seriously out of kilter, so while I did my best to be friendly to Margaret and the baby—the rest of the family was not home—what I really wanted was a shower and a nap. I excused myself for a few hours.

When I awoke, James informed me that Archie Turner, his business associate, would soon be picking us up. Archie arrived in his red Porsche Boxster convertible. He was younger than James, probably in his mid-forties. Archie had a full head of curly brown hair and a pleasant smile. James had asked Archie to be his best man at our wedding. He agreed.

As we cruised along the highway with the top down, Archie complained to James about his business situation. He and a partner were embroiled in a financial dispute and Archie's bank account was frozen. He had no money.

"We have money," James volunteered. "We can help you out."

I had US$1,000 in cash with me, along with another US$800 in travelers' checks. James knew this, and asked me to give Archie the cash.

"Thank you," Archie said. "I'll pay you back as soon as I get this mess straightened out."

Archie asked about our plans for our visit to Australia. After a few days in Sydney, James told him, we would fly north to Queensland to visit James' brother. It turned out that Archie's girlfriend—a woman considerably younger than him—was playing in a competitive bridge tournament in Queensland at the same time.

"You'll have to meet us there," James said.

"I don't know if I can afford the flight, with all my assets being frozen," Archie replied.

"Don't let that stop you," James said. "We'll put a ticket for you on our credit card."

That was my credit card, of course. So now I had given Archie $1,000 in cash and bought him a $250 airplane ticket. James had known Archie for a long time, so I assumed he would repay me. But I was disconcerted. It was our very first day in Australia, and I already needed money. When we reached our destination—

Pott's Point, a Sydney waterfront neighborhood not far from Kings Cross—I cashed in $300 in travelers checks.

The next morning, after a good night's sleep, I felt much more adjusted to the time difference. I put a short burgundy robe over my short, teal green nightgown and went down to the kitchen for breakfast. James had already been up and on his computer for hours. He was also playing with his new video camera, and taped me as I ate toast and orange juice.

James handed me the camera. Taking on the role of "talent," in the Hollywood sense, he put on a performance for future home viewing.

"We are now Down Under," he narrated, pointing at the floor with both hands for emphasis. "If you look at the sink over there, the water is going around in the opposite direction.

"That way," he continued, pointing to his left, "is an Australian lady, known as a sheila." I turned the camera to focus on Margaret.

"Say g'day," James said to Margaret.

"G'day," Margaret said.

"What do you think of sheep?" James asked, as if conducting an interview.

This was the wrong question. "New Zealanders like sheep," Margaret corrected, in mock exasperation.

"I have to explain that New Zealand is next door," James said, as I panned the camera back to him. He gestured profusely with his hands. "New Zealand and Australia don't quite really mix. Now you're about to see small Australians that they breed. Quick—to the door!"

I pointed the camera toward the back door, where Margaret's 10-year-old son had appeared. "Do you want to be on TV?" Margaret asked him.

"I dunno," he said, making a quick exit, stage right.

James snapped his fingers, demanding that I focus on him again. "'I dunno' is a great Australian philosophical statement on the quality of life," he said to the camera, with his hands speaking as much as his voice. "I dunno."

Then he pointed at the computer in front of him. "This is a computer," he said. "And ... give me the camera ..."

I gave James the video camera, which he pointed at me.

"This is the love of my life."

I giggled and bent sideways from the hip, so I was looking at the camera from an upside down position.

"See, she's Down Under, so she's having trouble lining up where she really is," James narrated.

I bent sideways in the other direction, and giggled some more.

James and I had an important task planned for Friday, September 27, 1996: finalizing our wedding plans at the Registry of Births, Deaths and Marriages in Sydney. As a foreigner, I had to present my birth certificate and passport. Since this was my first marriage, no other paperwork was necessary.

James, however, had three prior marriages—I found out about them one at a time. He told me about his most recent marriage to Gale Lewis, of course, on the day we met. James' second wife was a woman from the Boston, Massachusetts area, named Kathleen Maloney—she was the wife James said he was arguing with during the invasion of Panama. Patricia Heywood was the first wife—they married in Australia on December 1, 1971, when James was 30 years old. She was also his business partner—the "Pat" in Jaypat Productions. They divorced in 1976. To simplify matters for our visit to the Registry, James only listed the marriage to Patricia Heywood, which was recorded in Sydney, on the government form. "If I put down the American marriages, it will drive the bureaucrats nuts," he said.

Finished with the day's official business, we went to meet more of my future in-laws. James' sister and her husband, Heather and Joe Azzopardi, lived with their two boys in another Sydney suburb. They took care of James' mother, Vera. James' father, who died in 1995, had previously divorced her.

Vera, a 75-year-old pensioner, reminded me of my grandmother. She was a sweet little old lady who sometimes didn't hear what was said, or couldn't follow what was being said—one or the other. We repeated ourselves frequently. I sat next to Vera in the Azzopardis' kitchen while James conducted another video interview.

"What are we going to talk about?" Vera asked.

"Poker machines," James said.

"I don't play the poker machines," Vera said. "I'm on a pension, you know. I only played when I was working."

"When did you get off the poker machines?" James asked.

"Who am I going to play with?" Vera asked.

"You were playing pokies when I was here last time," James said, laughing.

"I was not," Vera denied. "I was not, you lying thing."

Next James turned the camera toward his nephews, aged 14 and 8. The younger boy was setting the table for lunch, and asked his mother if he should put out the Vegemite.

James had told me about Vegemite—a brown paste made from brewers yeast, a rich natural source of B vitamins. Australians had been spreading it on toast and sandwiches since it was invented in the 1920s, and doctors recommended the product for its health benefits. But even though nutrition was important to me, the concoction sounded vile, and I was astounded to find out my future family actually ate it. Not only that, but they could sing the Vegemite jingle.

Lunch was delightful, and I felt welcome and comfortable with James' family. They planned to attend our wedding, and I asked Heather to be my maid of honor. She was pleased to accept. We talked briefly about life with James, and the fact that he had already been married three times. I figured that he was young when he married his first wife, the third wife died, so only the second marriage was contentious, and it had ended five years earlier. I expected to be treated with respect by my soon-to-be husband. "I'm not going to put up with any crap," I said to Heather.

"No, I don't think you will," she replied.

James and I spent two more days with his daughter and her family. Much of the time we just hung around the kitchen table while James regaled everyone with stories and additional pseudo-philosophical statements. Perhaps James stayed around the house because he wanted to make up for lost time. Margaret was born in 1960 and put up for adoption. James had no contact with her until 1994, when she wrote him a letter. Margaret had been raised by a loving family who had arranged for her to get otoplasty as a child—cosmetic surgery for her ears. She had, unfortunately, inherited James' flappers, and the cartilage needed to be shaped in three different locations.

Margaret was now a grown woman, with three children of her own—James' grandchildren. So James talked with Margaret and her husband, played with the older kids, and held the baby. He enjoyed the family he never knew he had, and never knew he wanted.

We said goodbye to Margaret early Monday morning, before flying north to visit James' brother, Bob Montgomery, in Queensland. Our plan was to spend six days there, then return to Sydney for our wedding. I was surprised to find out that Margaret and her family would not be attending. They had plans to go out of town for a holiday, which they didn't change.

Australia's Gold Coast, a subtropical area of Queensland bordering the Pacific Ocean, was the country's largest tourist destination. The hour-long flight from Sydney took us to Coolangatta Airport, and from there it was a half-hour drive to the town where James' brother lived with his wife, Laurel, and their 16-year-old son.

Both Bob and Laurel held doctorates in psychology. Bob was the dean of psychology at Bond University in Queensland, where he developed undergraduate and graduate psychology courses emphasizing practical skills. He was also a media personality, known as Dr. Bob, who at one time had his own radio show about psychological issues. Together, Bob and Laurel were authors of a dozen self-help books, such as: *Your Good Health,* on how to enjoy good food and prevent illness. *Successful Sex,* about improving physical satisfaction. And *Living and Loving Together,* a manual for making and keeping good adult relationships.

Bob and Laurel were at work when we arrived at their home—they left a door open for us. Theirs was a well kept, contemporary-style home in a lagoon community surrounded by palm trees. Behind the one-story home were an in-ground swimming pool, the inland waterway and a dock where their cabin cruiser was moored.

Visiting the Gold Coast was like visiting Florida. In the most popular city, Surfers Paradise, high-rise apartment towers and condominiums lined the oceanfront. People came to enjoy the beaches, fishing, boating and the highest concentration of theme parks in Australia. The big attractions included Sea World, Warner Bros. Movie World, Dreamworld and the Wet 'n' Wild waterpark.

All of the theme parks were among the clients of the Sanderson Group, the company that provided the business reason for our trip to Australia. The Sanderson Group specialized in themed construction, such as sculpting a 36-foot skull for a Tower of Terror ride. James had arranged for us to visit the factory at noon. When we got there, the owner of the company, with whom James scheduled his appointment, was not available. We met with one of his assistants in a small, cramped office for a brief, unproductive conversation. James made an appointment to return later in the week.

After a bit of sightseeing we went back to Bob and Laurel's—by this time, they were home. Bob was four years younger than James. He did not inherit the family's male pattern baldness gene and had a full head of salt-and-pepper hair. Like James, however, he wore a beard, so he looked like a psychology professor direct from central casting. Laurel was only a year older than me. She was an attractive woman with a slender figure and short, dark hair.

Laurel had written a pocket-sized book called the *Good Eating Guide,* which offered nutritional information, eating guidelines for health and weight loss, and a long list of food products with their calorie counts. Of course, I was interested enough in the topic to cart that heavy *Nutrition Advisor* book to Australia. In one of our conversations, I told Laurel how I hoped to help James lose weight.

"He'll never do it," Laurel said.

This surprised me. "But he said he would," I protested.

"James isn't going to change," she said. Then Laurel offered some professional advice for the bride-to-be: "Acceptance is the key to a relationship."

Surfer's Paradise, in the heart of the Gold Coast, was a huge draw for Australian and international tourists, which on October 1, 1996, included James and me. The resort enticed visitors with wide sandy beaches, outdoor cafes, street entertainers, exotic cuisine and nightlife. Our visit, however, consisted mostly of shopping.

One of the stores we visited was T&Ski Originals. The company, based in New Zealand, sold high-quality sportswear. We bought two sweatsuits made of extra-heavy fabric—dark green for James and purple for me. They were on sale— half price—and still cost us $278.

James kept looking around, even in the kids' section, where he pulled out a heavy, bright yellow shirt similar to what the Australian rules football players wore. "We should get this as a present for Joe's son," he said.

He was referring to Joe Nickles, the candidate for county freeholder. I looked at the price tag—it was over $100.

"That's a lot of money for a kid's gift," I said.

"Well, Joe is important to us," James replied.

"Do you even know what size his son is?"

Silence. "No," he admitted.

"So you want to spend $100 on a shirt for a kid and you don't even know if it will fit?"

I put the shirt back on the rack, and the issue died. The shopping, however, continued. In all my previous travels—and I'd been abroad several times—I was judicious about buying mementos. James, however, said we wouldn't be back to these stores for a long time, so we should buy what we wanted. Plus, his project funding would soon come through, and he would pay off all the charges.

The next morning, James went back to the Sanderson Group factory. I saw no reason to go, so I stayed at Bob and Laurel's and read by the pool. Instead of the *Nutrition Advisor*, I picked up *Rogue Warrior II: Red Cell*, which James had given me. Hard-core action started right on the first page:

> I rolled from the culvert like a proper ninja and crabbed my way under the left side of the truck, using the shadows to stay invisible to the surveillance cameras. I slipped between the twin rear axles, pulled myself along the sharp, greasy frame past the trailer hitch, and wedged myself just behind the tractor cab.
>
> Bingo. This was child's play. Hunkered, I checked my watch. It was 0140. I was right on schedule.

This was much more interesting than "People with diabetes are at a higher risk of heart disease."

The author of *Rogue Warrior II: Red Cell* was Richard Marcinko, who in real life was the original commanding officer of SEAL Team Six, the U.S. Navy's premier counter-terrorist unit. Marcinko cast himself in the story, even though it was supposed to be fiction. He and his team of macho SEALs with badass attitudes cussed and shot their way into their own military installations, just to test the defenses. Then they took on real bad guys who were smuggling nuclear weapons. The tension that started on the first page never let up.

This was actually Marcinko's second book. His first, *Rogue Warrior,* was his autobiography. Apparently, after it was published, Marcinko was forbidden to reveal any more secrets about SEALs or other defense activities, but the line between fact and fiction was a matter of debate. James said a lot of the incidents were true. "Marcinko writes about an Australian in the nonfiction book," James told me. "He was referring to me."

I was deep into the blood and guts of *Red Cell* when James returned from his meeting. I rarely read fiction because once I got going on a story, I'd rather read than work, sleep or socialize. But James and I had plans to visit Sea World, so I reluctantly put the book down.

James considered the visit to the theme park to be a business trip. He was primarily interested in checking out the Bermuda Triangle ride, built by the Sanderson Group.

The ride was essentially a roller coaster with an elaborate set designed around it. At the entrance to the ride—the queuing area—we stood amid a faux fishing village, with shacks built on stilts over water, rickety walkways and weathered nets. A World War II era plane plunged nose first into the water, apparently falling out of the sky due to the Bermuda Triangle's mysterious affects. When we got to the front of the line, we were told that we were boarding a "research probe" to explore the interior of an active volcano that suddenly appeared in the Bermuda Triangle. Inside it were indications that something supernatural was going on, an atmosphere created by detailed sculptures, animatronics, fiber optics and other special effects. In the end, the volcano spit out our research probe, and we splashed into the water, getting sufficiently wet.

Sanderson constructed the 60-foot high volcano, which, through the magic of pyrotechnics, erupted periodically. They also fabricated the airplane and the weird creatures in the interior of the mountain. James took a multitude of photos.

When our ride was over, he had seen enough of Sea World.

I didn't want to leave. We were on vacation, and we'd already paid—a lot— to get into the park. Surely, I pleaded, we could go on more rides. I managed to convince him to stay for the dolphin show, but that was it. After the obligatory visit to the gift shop, we left.

We drove into downtown Southport, which wasn't far, and walked around the stores. An estate jeweler, otherwise known as a pawnshop, caught James' attention. I'd never been in a pawnshop—in Atlantic City they were far from inviting—but this one looked more like a retail store than a gambler's last hope. I saw an opal ring that I liked. The stone flashed a nice range of colors, and the 14 karat gold setting featured pretty filigree work. Opals were mined in Australia, and James said I'd get a better deal there than anywhere. The ring fit me and looked nice on my hand. It cost $325. James encouraged me to buy it, and I did.

Stately Wayne Manor—the home of Bruce Wayne, aka Batman—loomed in front of us as we walked through the main gate of the Warner Bros. Movie World theme park the next day. The building had that gothic-deco look of the *Batman* movies, with turreted towers, elongated figures and futuristic gargoyles. What appeared to be stone, of course, was fake. Blocks of high-impact foam had been carved, sprayed with liquid urethane that dried into a hard coat, then scenic painted to look like the real thing.

The manor was the pre-show area of the Batman Adventure ride, which used a military-style flight simulator, the same technology that James wanted to bring to CelebAM in Atlantic City, so he wanted to experience it. We sat among 20 other tourists in a car attached to the motion base, which tilted and shifted to unlikely angles. Through "windows"—actually movie screens—we saw the dark and dangerous Gotham City whizzing by. The on-screen images were synchronized with the simulator motion, making us feel like we really were flying along with Batman.

Next we took the tour of the Warner Bros. production studios and special effects stages, including the Superman Blue Screen Demonstration. There I learned first-hand how actors survived flying like Superman without a wire. As our group of about 30 people stood waiting outside the stage door in the sunshine, a tour guide came looking for a volunteer for the demonstration. She picked me.

Blue screen was a technique that enabled composite filmmaking, in which background images and foreground images were sandwiched together to create one picture. The key requirement was a bright, evenly lit, pure background—usually blue or green. Actors performed in front of the blue screen. The scenery was shot (or computer generated) separately. Then the acting and scenery were combined together into one image.

As the designated volunteer, I stood on the set in front of the blue screen, under bright, hot movie lights. I could see the cameraman as he focused on me, but the tour group was in shadow. Stage directions emanated from a speaker above me. "Donna, imagine you're standing on a narrow ledge on the outside of a building, far above the street. Your back is against the building, your toes are hanging over the edge, and you are being chased. We'd like you to spread your arms and grab the building behind you with your fingers, and slide along the ledge to your left."

As I followed the stage directions, I heard a gasp from the tour group. They were looking at a monitor, and could see the composite image, which showed me clinging to the edge of a building. I couldn't see anything.

"Now Donna, please lean forward as if you're looking at the street below."

I imagined what it would be like to be stuck on a dangerously narrow ledge and cautiously leaned forward. My performance earned a round of applause. When I saw it on instant replay, I was dramatically inching my way across the ledge of a building that wasn't there. "My Darwies is a movie star," James said to me, beaming with pride.

After the studio tour, we walked hand-in-hand down Main Street, eventually ending up at the park's major new attraction—the *Lethal Weapon* roller coaster. As we got close to boarding the ride, we were asked to remove hats, glasses and anything in our pockets. Why? We would spend a good portion of the ride upside down. All contents of our pockets were at risk. In fact, people were known to lose clothing, false teeth and even prosthetic limbs.

The *Lethal Weapon* roller coaster was not a train with wheels attached to a track below. Rather, we were strapped into open chairs suspended from above, like a ski lift. Suddenly we were airborne. *Lethal Weapon* was a blur of drops, dives, bends, rollovers, sidewinders, double spins, loops and plunges, ending in a helix. We were totally upside down five times. We were immobilized by four Gs of force. The ride lasted less than a minute, and that was long enough.

The exit route took us through the *Lethal Weapon* gift shop, where photos of all riders were sold. Of course, we bought ours. When I got a good look at it, I was surprised to see that James, my military hero fiancé, had his eyes closed.

After the ride I felt lightheaded, so we stopped by a café. I ordered orange juice and a carrot muffin; James, as usual, ordered a Diet Coke. We wandered around the amusement park a bit longer, and then it was time for other things. Like shopping.

James had already been shopping before we went to Movie World. He stopped in a bookstore and bought *SAS: Phantoms of the Jungle,* a history of the Australian Special Forces, including their actions in Vietnam. For shopping round two, we drove into Surfers Paradise. There James bought a $235 watch to add to the 20 or so watches already in his collection.

The next day James wanted to visit the shops in a town called Broadbeach. One store, Done Art and Design, brimmed with wearable art—t-shirts, sweaters, ties and more. All the fabrics were bright, colorful prints or knits, with patterns that were either vaguely abstract or simple graphics. A wool sweater of lavender, purple, hot pink, canary yellow and bright green caught my eye. Looking closely, I saw that the colors were actually fish. Like most designer clothing, the sweater was expensive, and I hesitated to buy it. "Nonsense," James said. "Done is an important designer, and you should have some pieces." We bought the sweater, a folding umbrella, a tie, and four small wallets for gifts. We spent $435.

I thought the Done line was creative and original until I walked into the next store of Australian designs—Mambo. These artists were surfer dudes with attitudes. Or maybe they'd spent too much time in the sun and their brains were fried. In any event, the store was full of t-shirts that "tend to offend." One image, for example, was a cartoon critter—perhaps a dog—nailed to a cross. His words, immortalized in a bubble: "Forgive them Father they know not what to wear." The title of the drawing was "Spiritual Adventurewear—For Those Not Planning on Inheriting the Earth."

Mambo's objective was "to take a public stand against every kind of conformism." They did, and I loved it, but I couldn't bring it all home. So I bought a book of Mambo's work and a light blue knapsack-style purse decorated with alien faces or masks—it was hard to decide what they were. I bought t-shirts for my brothers—I knew they'd like the humor. We also bought a full-size duffel bag—we needed extra luggage to carry home everything we were buying.

That evening, James and I accompanied Bob and Laurel to a gourmet dinner sponsored by the Wine Society, which was celebrating its 50th anniversary. My future in-laws were members and had planned to attend the event for a long time. For me, fine food and drink were among the true pleasures of life, so accepting their invitation to go was a no-brainer.

It was an occasion for me to wear the one dress-up outfit I had packed—a pale pink suit that was more feminine than businesslike. The tunic-length jacket had short sleeves and a scoop neck. The skirt was long and flowing, made of an almost sheer chiffon. James wore a sport coat and blue dress shirt, but no tie.

The event took place at the Gold Coast International Hotel in Surfers Paradise. At the opening reception, waiters moved among the guests, offering glasses of Domain Chandon Blanc de Blancs. I had a glass, or possibly two. James didn't drink, which was a waste at a Wine Society dinner. But it did mean that Bob, Laurel and I could consume what we wanted, because James was the designated driver.

The next day we were all sufficiently recovered from the free-flowing wine to go for a cruise on Bob and Laurel's boat. The weather was perfect—plenty of sunshine again—as we cast off from their dock and motored slowly through the lagoon, to the river and finally to the Pacific Ocean. We headed south, passing the resort towns, with their high-rises and thousands of beach-goers, on our starboard side. After a couple of hours, we turned around and cruised back. It was a relaxing ride, and a pleasant ending for our visit to Australia's Gold Coast.

For the final leg of our trip, James booked a room for us at the Radisson Hotel in Manly, a suburb north of Sydney that featured one of the area's most popular beaches. When we arrived on October 6, 1996, we learned that Archie had asked the hotel manager to upgrade our room in honor of our upcoming wedding. The Radisson kindly gave us a one-bedroom suite. Balconies off the living room and bedroom offered a view of the beach and Pacific Ocean. The suite had a bar and refrigerator, which came stocked with a bottle of champagne.

Since we were back in his hometown, James wanted to show me where he lived as a child. We drove to Bellevue Hill, an affluent residential neighborhood, home to many rich and famous families. But James' family wasn't one of them. James told me his father worked as a bus driver, so he grew up as a poor kid in a rich neighborhood. He said it left him with psychological scars.

Adjacent to Bellevue Hill was another ritzy neighborhood called Double Bay. It was filled with designer boutiques, five-star restaurants and alfresco bistros where the upper class came to shop and socialize. We went into a men's store called the Squire Shop, and James looked at sport coats. He liked a particular gray jacket; the fabric was a fine, lightweight wool with a subtle plaid pattern. The salesman asked James his size, and helped him try on the jacket. It was too small. The next size up fit his shoulders, but still wouldn't button across his stomach. He could button the next size up, but it could only be described as taut in front.

"Well, James is trying to lose some weight," I said to the salesman.

"That's good," he replied. "Make him lose a few pounds. I don't want to put him in a larger size. It won't look right in the shoulders."

Next James looked at trousers, and found a dark beige pair that he liked. He wanted to buy both the jacket and the trousers, and asked me to put them on my credit card. Although I had watched him try on the clothes, I hadn't looked at any price tags. When I saw the total, I gulped—it was $1,198. I'd never spent that much money on two items of clothing in my life. But it was too late to argue, so I signed.

Like a typical Australian employee, I went to work on Tuesday, October 8, 1996, which I thought was cool. Dressed in a bright red business suit, I joined the throngs of commuters on the Sydney Ferries. One ferry took me from Manly Wharf to Circular Quay, the main terminal. Another ferry took me from Circular Quay to Darling Harbour, where the Sydney Harbour Casino was located. I toured the property and interviewed several executives.

Toward the end of the day I caught up with Olga Santamaria, the vice president of human resources. I already knew Olga—she had been my Learning Network contact in the United States before she was transferred to Sydney Harbour Casino. After telling Olga that I was in Australia to be married, she invited James and me to be her guests at dinner.

We ate at Jake's Grill, the casino's 24-hour restaurant. Another Showboat executive joined us. Our dinners arrived, but I didn't know how James ate his, because he talked through the entire meal. He talked about his advertising days in Australia. He talked about his TV and movie background. He talked about his plans for a theme park in Atlantic City. The Showboat executives barely had a chance to say a word. Several times I steered the conversation toward them, asking questions about the casino. But before long James cut them off and was back to talking about himself.

At least James liked the restaurant. He decided we should bring our guests there for lunch following our wedding on Thursday.

After dinner, I thanked Olga profusely for her hospitality. But as James and I drove back to our hotel, I was quiet, reviewing the evening in my mind, and getting angry. I wanted to talk about it with James—but how?

"It was really nice of Olga to comp us to dinner," I started once we got to our suite.

"Yes, it was brilliant. That's a good restaurant, not expensive—it's perfect for after the wedding. And the casino will be a real treat for everyone. They haven't seen it."

I sat down on the sofa in the living room. "You know, I was kind of bothered tonight by the dinner conversation," I continued.

No response.

I pressed on. "You kind of monopolized it."

"I did not."

"Yes you did, James. You spent the whole night talking about yourself. Olga couldn't get a word in edgewise."

"She could have talked if she wanted to."

"Well, not really. You didn't give her a chance."

"She doesn't need a chance. All she had to do was open her mouth."

"James, in polite conversation, one person talks and the other one listens. Then that person talks while the first person listens. You did all the talking. These were my clients, and I was embarrassed."

"I've been dealing with clients for 35 years. I think I know what I'm doing."

"Well, that's not how I deal with clients. I let them talk."

I got up and went into the bedroom, aggravated. I closed the curtains and took off my red suit jacket. James came to the bedroom door and stood there, glaring at me. Then he threw a green velvet ring box onto the bed. It was open, and I could see a ladies' wedding band.

"So do you want to call off the wedding?" he asked, his voice brimming with hostility.

I didn't know what to respond to first. I was totally surprised to see the wedding band—the fact that we needed it for the ceremony had never entered my brain. And then James was talking about canceling our wedding because we argued about clients.

"James, I think you're overreacting," I said.

"No, you overreacted. There was nothing wrong with my behavior at dinner. But if you think there was, then you must think there's something wrong with me. So perhaps you don't really want to be married to me."

I was astounded. "Of course I want to marry you."

"But I embarrass you in front of your clients."

"James, that's an easy problem to fix. All you have to do is let other people talk."

"Donna, I've been in business a lot longer than you have, dealing with a lot bigger companies. I don't think I have a problem."

This was going nowhere. "Look, let's just drop it."

"You don't want me to call off the wedding?"

"No, don't call off the wedding."

I also forgot about wedding flowers. Among the shops near the hotel was a florist, so the next day James and I walked around the corner to see about ordering some. It was Wednesday morning, October 9, 1996, and we needed the flowers for Thursday morning. We had to choose from what the florist had in stock, so James suggested a theme of native Australian blooms. We ordered a small bouquet for me, boutonnieres for him and Archie, and corsages for Heather and Vera, James' mother.

The next morning, our wedding day, we had a lot to do. We had to pack and check out of the hotel, because a few hours after the ceremony we would fly back to the United States. We had to pick up the flowers—the florist was opening early just for us. We had to dress for the big occasion.

The wedding would be a civil ceremony in a government office building, so I never considered getting a wedding gown—that would be for our next wedding in January. Instead, I pulled something out of my closet to wear—a tailored white shirtdress made of heavy textured cotton. It hung almost to my ankles and had three-quarter length sleeves. I wore it with a black and white belt, white stockings, and black patent leather heels. James wore his new gray sport coat with a white turtleneck and black trousers.

Our wedding was scheduled for 10:40 a.m.—they were performed every 20 minutes at the Registry of Births, Deaths and Marriages. As we drove downtown, James held out his hand for me to place mine in his, as usual. This time, however, he squeezed my hand tight, then raised it to his lips.

"This is a very special day for me and Bubba," James said, kissing my hand.

Archie Turner, James' best man, was already at the Registry Office, waiting outside in the brilliant sunshine. James' sister, Robin Swann, and her family arrived. But my maid of honor and her family, along with James' mother, had not shown up, and it was getting late.

We all went inside and chatted in the lobby. James handed his video camera to Archie, then stood behind me making faces, which Archie captured on tape. I returned the favor, making devil horns with my fingers behind James' head.

Finally, just as the marriage celebrant called for us, our late arrivals rushed through the door. I pinned the corsages on Heather and Vera. We were ready.

The ceremony room was designed for small, nonreligious weddings. The walls were plain white and the carpet dark gray. The ceiling was standard height for an office building, which made it feel low for a special occasion. A mural—sky and clouds—decorated the back wall, providing a nice backdrop for the guy who ran the wedding video concession. Most of the room was filled by chairs—the first row for the wedding party, then two rows for guests. In the front of the room was a small table where we'd sign our marriage documents.

Our celebrant told us exactly what to do. James and I entered the room first and sat in the middle two chairs of the front row. Heather sat next to me; Archie sat next to James. Then our guests came in.

I couldn't stop smiling. In a few minutes I would be married, and my long, lonely single life would be over. I'd met James' relatives; they welcomed me into the family. I put my arm through James' arm. I was happy.

"Ladies and gentleman," the celebrant began. "We are here today to solemnize the marriage according to the Commonwealth Marriage Act between those here present—James Alwyn Montgomery and Donna Marie Andersen."

James took my hand and squeezed it.

"Before you are joined in marriage in the presence of these witnesses, I am to remind you of the solemn and binding nature of the relationship into which you are about to enter," our celebrant said. "Marriage, according to law in Australia, is the union of a man and a woman, to the exclusion of all others, voluntarily entered into for life."

James and I affirmed that there were no impediments to our marriage. Then we stood and faced each other. My fiancé, soon to be my husband, took both of my hands, gently squeezing them again.

"Now James, do you wish to take this woman in marriage to be your lawful wedded wife?" the celebrant asked.

"I do."

"And do you, Donna, wish to take this man in marriage to be your lawful wedded husband?"

Softly I replied, "I do."

"That being so," the celebrant said, "please repeat after me, James." She recited the marriage vow, which James repeated. "I call upon the persons here present," he said, "to witness that I, James Alwyn Montgomery, take you, Donna Marie Andersen, to be my lawful wedded wife."

Then it was my turn.

"I call upon the persons here present," I said, "to witness that I, Donna Marie Andersen, take you, James Alwyn Montgomery, to be my lawful wedded husband."

We exchanged rings, with each of us saying, "With this ring I wed you and pledge my love and fidelity." That was it.

"By the authority vested in me I now pronounce you husband and wife," the celebrant said. "So now, James, you may kiss the bride." James kissed me, and our guests applauded.

There was one bit of official business left—we all had to sign the marriage certificates. I signed, then stood by as James, Heather and Archie signed them. I smiled broadly. I felt like I was there but not there, watching the completion of events that had been set in motion long before that day.

Afterwards, we had an easy, cheerful luncheon at the Sydney Harbour Casino. Before long it was over, and James and I were on our way to the airport.

During the 18 days that we were in Australia, my contractor friends convert-ed my home's basement into an office for James. When we returned, the base-ment had a new powder room and four new electrical circuits to power his equip-ment. But my softball teammate who handled the carpentry wasn't done painting, so James couldn't move in. He was furious.

"This was supposed to be finished. How am I supposed to work?" my hus-band raged.

"Well, maybe you can work out of Mays Landing until they're done," I said, trying to be calm in the face of his vitriol.

"Tell those clowns I need to get into my office," he demanded. "They've had more than two weeks. This office was supposed to be ready for me to hit the ground running when I got back."

Why was James reacting so violently to what was, at worst, a minor incon-venience? Was the honeymoon over already?

I asked my friend to finish the work—without relaying James' comments—and it only took him another day. Then James began transporting things from Mays Landing to my home in Atlantic City. To make room for his plenteous stuff, I gave up the main room of the basement and most of the storage room, which was my organizational pride and joy. The storage room became James' closet; my stuff had to go elsewhere.

I rented a climate-controlled storage unit from my long-time customer, Bob Rosenthal, who operated Black Horse Self Storage. I'd written marketing materi-als for the storage facility ever since it opened, describing the gated entry, comput-erized security and 24-hour closed-circuit television surveillance. To the storage unit went my summer clothes, since it was going into winter, along with old busi-ness records and anything else that wasn't absolutely critical to have in the house. Transferring my possessions required multiple trips. Every trip took 15 minutes, each way, plus the time to unload and arrange the boxes in the storage unit.

Besides the moving, I was trying to catch up on my business. Right before we left for Australia, I got a call about a big new account. Delaware had recently legalized slot parlors at its three racetracks, and Caesars managed one at Dover Downs. They needed a customer newsletter, and my client at Caesars recom-mended me for the job. But I was already managing three newsletters; I didn't think I could manage a fourth. I gave the account to Sheryl Ginsburg, my friend who was the graphic designer on the other newsletters. Sheryl and I had worked and socialized together for many years—she was shorter than me, with dark hair, a voluptuous figure and an effervescent personality. Sheryl could deal with the clients; I would just do the copywriting. We went to Dover, Delaware to meet them and start the project.

I was also helping James with his businesses. A few years earlier I'd done work for a general contractor that specialized in high-end construction. I thought the company could use the synthetic products that James' new company, Faux Façade, was going to make. Because of my past relationship, the two principles agreed to a meeting.

I introduced James, and he talked about the product—hard-coated expanded polystyrene foam—and its many uses. He talked about planning a factory in Mays Landing. Then he asked them for a $100,000 investment.

"I don't have $100,000 to invest," one of my clients said.

I had no idea that James was going to hit them up for money, and I was mortified. After we left the meeting, I told James that he should not have asked them for an investment, which led to an argument.

"Do you want me to get this business going? Yes or no," James demanded.

"James, if that was your intention ..."

"Yes or no?"

Stunned, I stammered, "Yes, of course ..."

"Then there's nothing wrong with asking them for an investment."

"That's not what I told them the meeting was going to be about," I protested. "I told them that we wanted to show them a product that they might be able to use in their work."

"Donna, you're displaying your inexperience. The ends justify the means. Nothing happens if you don't ask. We were offering them a business opportunity."

My resentment started boiling. I was trying to make connections for James and ended up embarrassed. I was running my business, bringing in our only income and paying all the bills. I was getting the house organized and hauling boxes to the storage unit. I was grocery shopping and cooking dinner.

James was playing entrepreneur.

Did I make a huge mistake?

Many, many times before we went to Australia to get married, I meditated, questioning my higher self, asking for advice from Guidance. It was all so fast. In many ways, this man wasn't what I wanted. He was old and out of shape. He was a total slob. Was marrying James the right thing to do?

I did not hear a "DON'T DO IT," like I did when I stupidly wrote that second big check to the con artist, Don Clemens Jr. Even as I gave James far more money than I ever gave Don—all of my $20,000 in savings, plus $15,000 on my credit cards—I got no warnings. Instead, I kept hearing reassurance: James truly loved me. Everything would be fine.

So I continued to work triple time, trying to convince myself that I was doing what a good wife should do. But then, two weeks into my marriage, James made one demand too many and I erupted in anger. "I really feel like I'm carrying more than my share of the burden around here," I fumed, loudly.

I got no sympathy. "I told you things were going to be bad until Christmas," James retorted. "You knew what you were getting into. Boots and all, remember?"

"Well how come I have to cart everything around? You're the one who's moving in."

"I have six businesses to get running. And you seem to want to put things in certain places."

"It would be nice if you helped."

"I know how we can solve everything, Donna. Do you want me to move out?"

My jaw dropped in shock. "James, we just got married!"

"We'll get unmarried. I won't stay where I'm not wanted."

My emotions were in turmoil. I definitely felt like I was doing far more than my share to keep us going. But I had just wed the man, and pledged my love and fidelity. In my view, marriage was a commitment that was kept. And I'd certainly spent a lot of years and anguish trying to get to where I was now—a married woman.

I changed my tone. "Of course I want you here James. I'm just feeling stressed."

With that, James cooled off. He started kissing me, and before long he led me to bed.

Chapter 8

If I had been a reader of romance novels, perhaps I would have expected life as a newlywed to be full of long walks on the beach with my new husband. We would hold hands, or maybe curl our arms around each other's waists, simply basking in the joy of being close to each other. Luckily, I never read romance novels, because that didn't happen. In fact, I didn't know what it felt like to be a newlywed. I was too busy to think about it.

Work was frantic. All of my casino newsletters—the Showboat Crew's News, the Showboat Learning Network, and the Caesars Premium Player—were in production. I was going to the casinos, conducting interviews, writing stories and arranging photography. Plus, Sheryl and I were in the startup phase of our new account, the newsletter for Dover Downs Slots.

James was proud of the prestigious clients that I "looked after," as he said in Australian. Now that he was around full-time, he also wanted me to look after him. James asked me to make doctor appointments and travel arrangements. He wanted me to review his business proposals. He wanted me to accompany him to political and community events.

In November 1996, James was invited to speak to schoolchildren about the importance of Veterans Day. He went to a sixth-grade classroom in nearby Somers Point, New Jersey. With him were Joe Nickles, who had been an Army drill sergeant, and a local mayor who served in World War II. The three men sat on kid-sized chairs in the front of the room, talking about military life and answering student questions. A teacher in the back operated a video camera, transmitting the presentation to the rest of the school via closed circuit TV.

Each of the men spoke of their experiences in a way the children could understand. They talked about training and commitment. They explained what kept them going under fire—concern for their buddies. A boy asked James a question: "Did you lose any friends in Vietnam?"

James answered slowly. "Yes," he said, stretching out the word, "and I felt very sad when it happened. That's why Veterans Day is so important. It's a time to remember all those who served their country, especially those who gave their lives."

Standing in the back of the room, I was proud of everything James did to protect the rest of us.

"Every Veterans Day I remember five men," James had told me when I first met him. "I make sure that I say their names out loud."

"Who are they?" I'd asked.

James spoke each of the five names, slowly and distinctly.

"What happened to them?" I asked.

He was quiet. "Maybe I'll tell you some other time," he replied.

James planned to attend a Veterans Day ceremony in Mays Landing, New Jersey on November 11, 1996. The previous year, he was the keynote speaker. The Press of Atlantic City reported that James spoke about actions taken in service to the nation by comedienne Martha Raye and retired Major Dick Meadows, who participated in the raid on Son Tay, North Vietnam, to rescue POWs. The local Mays Landing Record Journal ran a photo of him wearing his Special Forces beret and camouflage jacket, standing at a podium in the rain.

I was supposed to meet James at the ceremony. But as I was about to leave, I discovered that James had taken his car keys—and mine as well. After a moment of dismay, I was relieved—work deadlines loomed, and I really didn't have time to drive out to Mays Landing, stand at a ceremony, and drive back. But my efficient and logical thinking didn't go over well with my husband.

"Why didn't you turn up?" James demanded when he arrived home.

"I was going to," I said. "You took my car keys."

"You could have come if you wanted to. You could have called a taxi," he retorted, without acknowledging his own error.

"Are you kidding? That would cost a fortune!" I said. "And I've got a lot of work. I was better off staying home and getting it done."

"It appears that what is important to your husband is not important to you. Gale understood how important this is. She used to iron my uniforms."

James stomped downstairs to his office, and I was left to wonder about being compared to my husband's deceased wife. I felt guilty—temporarily—and then I went back to work.

If I didn't arrive home when expected, I learned, James worried. One day, on my way back from an out-of-town trip, I stopped at the mall. After a couple of hours of looking around—I didn't buy much—I drove home. I arrived to find James pacing the living room.

"Where have you been?" James demanded angrily as I walked in the door.

"At the mall," I replied, surprised.

"Why didn't you call me?"

"I didn't think of it."

"You didn't think your husband would want to know where you are?"

I paused, sheepishly. "No," I said. "I'm sorry."

"Donna, because of my work, I need to be concerned about you, and you need to be careful," he said, turning to go downstairs to his office. "Now I've got to call off everything I put in motion." Apparently, he had reported my disappearance to the police—or perhaps the military.

I interpreted James' concern as a sign of his love for me. He demonstrated his affection in other ways as well. A florist was located where James went to the chiropractor. He usually returned from his treatments with a lavish bouquet of fresh flowers. And even though most days he was working right downstairs, James still sent me romantic e-mails and faxes addressed to Bubba, Mouse, Darwies and Nuffles.

James said in his AOL ad that he baby talked to his dog. That dog wasn't around anymore, but he did baby talk to my dog, and to me. He had his own words for things—blueberries, for example, were "burbleberries." The made-up words were cute when we first met, but they started to annoy me. One day James was standing in the kitchen, looking in the pantry. He wanted cereal and burbleberries.

"James, you can cut the baby talk now," I said.

He slowly closed the pantry door and looked at me sadly. "Donna, for so much of my life I have to be tough and hard," James said. "It's very difficult for me to be soft. One of the ways I do it is with the baby talk."

Berating myself for my lack of sensitivity, I never complained to James about burbleberries, or any of his other idiosyncratic words, again. I did, however, complain about the words he used when we made love. One of the benefits of dual home employment was that we could enjoy each other physically whenever we wanted—that's why answering machines were invented. So practically every day, we made an "appointment" for sex.

James liked to talk dirty. Sometimes he talked about what we were doing; sometimes he described fantasies involving other people. For the first couple of months of our relationship it was titillating. But as time went on, I realized that I just was not comfortable with the pornographic language.

After one bedroom session in which James described what an imaginary woman was doing to me, I'd had enough. James took a shower, and I went downstairs to the kitchen, trying to figure out how to handle my discomfort. When my husband came downstairs, I just blurted it out. "James, I need you to stop talking dirty in bed," I said. "It makes me feel like a whore."

James never used the language again, and I appreciated him for being responsive to my request.

Although I was married, I still had a wedding to plan. I did not want a long line of bridesmaids—only my sister, Tracy, and my childhood friend, Pam Breyer. I did not want hundreds of guests. I did not want a unity candle, wishing well or useless party favors. But I did want a nice venue, good food and live music.

Only a few people knew that James and I had already tied the knot. One was Tracy—James told her of our plans before we left for Australia. The other was Joe Nickles, who won election to the Atlantic County Board of Freeholders. Joe was already a member of the Hamilton Township Committee, which meant we could ask him to perform our pseudo-ceremony and it would look right.

Concerned about the possibility of bad weather in January, I wanted to have the ceremony and reception in one place. At the Ram's Head Inn, a classy, Colonial-themed restaurant in nearby Absecon, I found a banquet facility perfectly suited for weddings. Our ceremony would take place in an elegant, high-ceilinged room called the parlor. Damask-style wallpaper, in cream and pale mauve, created a formal atmosphere. Burgundy drapes hung at the windows, and an intricate Oriental carpet lay before a massive fireplace. Cocktails and hors d'oeuvres would be served on the veranda, an enclosed room with a glass wall overlooking the outdoors—I hoped the view would not include snow. Finally, the reception would take place in the adjacent grand ballroom, which had plenty of space for a band and dancing. I still wanted Courtney Colletti, my former boyfriend, to provide the music for my wedding—I knew he'd turn the reception into a fabulous party. Still, I thought it best not to tell James that Courtney and I had once been romantically involved.

The Ram's Head was available on January 18, 1997. Courtney was available then as well. We set the date. My wedding would actually be the first of three for our family in 1997. My youngest brother, Greg, was getting married in April. Then my father was getting married in May.

I couldn't see spending thousands of dollars on a one-use dress, so I hoped to find an inexpensive gown. November 30, 1996 was set aside for shopping—Tracy and my friend, Sheryl Ginsburg, accompanied me. The discount outlets I targeted were a bust—so many gowns, none worth buying. Finally, I went to a traditional wedding boutique in Marlton, New Jersey, located in a classic, two-story building with shutters at the windows and a portico supported by 20-foot columns. As soon as we pulled up, I pictured it as a place where young brides with rich daddies shopped. "I'm not looking in here," I said dismissively.

But the store did have a sale rack of samples and discontinued gowns—and hanging on it were two that I liked, one white and the other ivory. I swallowed my price-chopper pride and tried them on. Both fit almost perfectly and were absolutely stunning. I really liked the ivory gown—it was a sheath of silk shantung with a beaded lace bodice and a short tulle train. The saleswoman showed me a coordinating bridal veil—more tulle attached to a wreath of white silk flowers. I decided to bite the bullet and buy the gown—and then found out that the dress was less than half-price, only $695.

The rest of our wedding plans came together. I selected orchids for the bouquets and table arrangements. My good friend and longtime photographer, Bill Horin, would take our photos. I started to make a program book, like I did for my 40th birthday party, to introduce all the wedding guests to each other. For our honeymoon, James and I decided to go to Paris—which meant that, along with all the other preparations, I had to brush up on my French.

I was worried about how our wedding—and everything else—would be paid for. James originally told me he would pay back the money I lent him in October. That didn't happen. It didn't happen in November either.

James was working hard, sending faxes and making phone calls. The local Congressman, Frank LoBiondo, returned his call and left a message—James proudly played it for me. He continued to attend VVA and Lions Club meetings, although the Christmas concert he previously announced did not materialize. And he traveled. He spent three days in New York City at the end of October. In November, James traveled to New Orleans for the International Association of Amusement Parks and Attractions (IAAPA) trade show, trolling for connections for CelebAM and Faux Façade. I had to buy his plane ticket, plus, while he was there, he asked me to wire him a $500 cash advance on one of my credit cards. I hated to do it, but felt that I had no choice. A couple of weeks later, right before Thanksgiving, James traveled to Florida, telling me he was visiting a factory that already did what he wanted Faux Façade to do—fabricating themed construction materials out of expanded polystyrene foam. But Christmas was coming, followed by our wedding, and there was no project funding.

James had a solution. "You can get a home equity loan," he said to me.

That scared me. My home was precious. It wasn't extravagant, but it was cozy and I'd bought it on my own. Being self-employed, I'd faced cash flow problems before, but I never missed a mortgage payment. The last thing I wanted to do was put my home in jeopardy.

James assured me the loan would just provide us with temporary breathing room until his funding came through. "I'm working toward our future," he said. "It's just taking longer than I expected. I'm disappointed, but I won't quit. I'll get the funding. I won't let you down."

The cold reality was that we needed cash, and I didn't see any other way to get it. So I went to my bank and applied for a $25,000 home equity line of credit. At least the interest would be tax-deductible.

In mid-December, James went on a trip to South Carolina, where the parents of Gale Lewis lived. He told me there were matters to discuss in regards to her estate. While he was gone, I made myself sit down and add up all the money I'd spent on him:

Cash loans to James	$27,000.00
Office improvements and equipment	$9,727.48
Trip to Australia	$13,694.70
Finance charges	$530.39
Trip to New Orleans	$959.00
Trip to South Carolina	$306.00
Office expenses and maintenance	
Cable	$233.06
Phone installation and calls	$904.69
Mobile phone	$281.33
Medical	$121.48
Electric	$90.00
Total as of 12/14/96	$53,848.13

I looked at the totals with fear in my chest and turmoil in my stomach. A year earlier I had been methodically saving $1,000 a month. It was gone. I always paid off my credit cards. Now I just paid the minimum balance due, waiting for James to take care of the total. In the meantime, debt piled up. I actually put two high-interest cash advances for him on my cards. All the money I was earning—and I was doing well—was being siphoned off by his expenses.

What had I gotten myself into? James said things would be bad until Christmas. Well, it was almost Christmas. When was he going to come through as he promised?

By the time James returned, I was pretty well worked up. I didn't want to jump all over him the minute he walked in the door. But the following morning, as we were both in our robes, eating breakfast at the dining room table, I could keep quiet no longer.

"James, I'd like to talk about our financial situation," I said, trying to maintain my composure while inside, I was shaking.

"All right, Nuffles. What do you want to talk about?"

"I've added up what I've been spending. Between the money I've given you, and the expenses I've paid, and what's on my credit cards, it's almost $54,000."

"So?"

"James, that's a lot of money."

"No it's not. Not when we're looking at millions of dollars in income."

"When is this money supposed to come in?"

"Donna, I tell you everything," James said calmly. "You know what's been going on. No one is making any decisions at the Convention Center, so there's no movement on CelebAM. I'm doing what I can to push the TV stations—that's one reason why Archie is coming for the wedding, so he can come with me to some meetings. We're just getting started on Faux Façade, so that one is going to take awhile. I'm working all of the projects at once because I don't know which will come through first."

"What about the wedding? Can we afford it? Should we call it off?"

James stood up and walked around the table to me. "Give me your hand," he said softly. I complied. "Now follow me," he said, leading me into the living room. We sat on the sofa. He was still holding my hand.

"Is the wedding important to Nuffles?" he asked.

"Yes," I said.

"Then Nuffles will have a wedding. I'm not worried about the money. It won't be much longer."

With that, James kissed me.

"I love you," I said.

"I love you more," he replied.

Before long he took my hand again, and led me up the stairs to bed.

My application for a home equity loan received a positive response, but I was still waiting for final approval. In the meantime, James had another idea for us to get money quickly—selling his SUV.

Although the Ford Explorer was a 1992 model, it was fully loaded and still had value. James said we could trade the car in for immediate cash and get something less expensive to drive. He started researching car models and consumer reports. I was happy that he was taking the initiative to ease our financial problems.

James visited car showrooms. He brought me to look at one car, but when the salesman made an offer, James decided it wasn't good enough and walked out, refusing to negotiate further. On Christmas Eve, while driving down the highway, he saw a pearl white 1996 Ford Thunderbird parked on another dealer's lot. James went into the dealership to ask about the car. It was a two-door model with a V-8 engine, leather seats and an upgraded electronics package.

"It was driven temporarily by the dealer's mother," James told me as I sat working at my desk. "It's practically new. I made a great deal. They'll give us over $9,000 for the Explorer."

"Sounds good," I said.

"I think we should do it."

"Okay." My eyes were on my computer screen.

"Well you have to come sign the papers."

I stopped working and looked at him in surprise. "I thought you were buying the car."

"I'm an entrepreneur," he said, as if stating the obvious. "I don't have any credit."

Stunned, I did not reply.

"We have to go," James pressed. "I told them we're coming over to do the deal."

A half-hour later, in a fog, I sat with James in a tiny office at the dealership, signing papers. They cut a check for the SUV to James—I never saw the money. But now, in addition to everything else, I was committed to paying $376 a month to lease a car for him.

So many of my Christmases were spent alone—without a date, let alone a serious relationship. Sometimes I bought gifts for guys I was semi-seeing, in case they showed up at Christmas with one for me. All those years I pined for connection, wanting to wake up on Christmas day with a man committed to loving me. Finally, on December 25, 1996, when I was 40 years old, it happened.

James and I exchanged gifts—"Chrissy presies," as he called them—in the morning. Weeks before the holidays, thinking that James didn't own a winter coat because he'd been living in Florida, I ordered a warm, weatherproof parka for him from L.L. Bean—size extra large and extra tall. To my surprise, he brought a coat back with him when he returned from Florida on Thanksgiving Day. James said it was stored in his locker at MacDill Air Force base.

James also brought back two painted bronze statues, about 12 inches tall, of Buddhist-style dancers. "They came from a Vietnamese temple in the jungle," he explained. And, he brought me a ring with a huge yellow topaz—it had to be 10 carats. James said the ring was part of his share of the booty for the Manuel Noreiga operation in Panama.

The L. L. Bean coat was better than the one James brought back from Florida, so I decided to go ahead and give it to him for Christmas. James gave me a beautiful opal necklace—the stone flashed with orange, green and blue highlights. It was much larger and prettier than the stone in the ring I bought in Australia. For Beau, James bought a bright yellow collar and leash featuring the Indian-head motif of his favorite college football team, the Florida State Seminoles. James called watching the Florida State games "going to church."

Beau wore his new collar, and I wore my new necklace, later in the day when Tracy, Dad and his fiancée, Pat Roberts, came for Christmas dinner. Tracy arrived first to install the batteries and tape into Dad's gift from us and our brothers—a new video camera. Then she and James—both of them video producers—taught Dad how to use the camera. He taped me opening one of the gifts he brought—a set of light wood tray tables. I asked for them because James sometimes liked to eat dinner in front of the television.

Over the holidays, I introduced James to more of my friends. We took Roseanne Jenkins and her fiancé to dinner. Jean Muchanic, my main contact at Showboat, invited us to visit her new home. Jean and James got talking about television, specifically *Seinfeld*.

"I've written a few episodes of *Seinfeld*," James said.

"No kidding!" Jean exclaimed. "Which ones? I love *Seinfeld*. I watch it all the time."

"Oh, they were early on."

"Really, I've seen all of them. Which did you write?"

"They weren't among the well-known shows," James demurred. "I doubt that you saw them."

Jean looked at him quizzically.

On New Year's Day, James flew to South Carolina again. He told me he wanted to spend at least part of the holidays with Gale Lewis' parents, who were having a hard time coming to terms with the passing of their daughter.

While he was gone I made last-minute wedding arrangements. Courtney Colletti was providing music for both the wedding ceremony (guitar and flute) and the reception (five pieces plus singer). James guessed that Courtney and I had been lovers, which led to a few days of tension. He didn't want to believe the relationship was over long ago. It took a lot of talking, but I finally convinced him. Or maybe he just accepted the situation for practical reasons—it was too late to book a different band.

I gave Courtney instructions for the big day: Play *Waltzing Matilda* as the bride and groom were introduced. Play *The Power of Love* for our first dance. Do not play the *Hokey Pokey* or the *Chicken Dance*.

I still worried about the weather for our wedding day. "It will be fine," Courtney assured me. "Cold but sunny."

James walked into the house carrying a birdcage and two brown bags, which he set on the dining room table. One of the bags was moving.

"What do you have?" I asked him.

"A new member of our family," James answered.

Beau was very interested in the moving bag. He stood up with his front paws on the edge of the table, trying to sniff it, his tail spinning in wild circles. "Get down!" I commanded. The dog reluctantly complied.

James opened the bag, and immediately a small gray animal with a long gray tail scrambled out and climbed up his arm. The critter then jumped from James' shoulder to the top of the glass-doored breakfront. Beau barked excitedly. "Get the dog!" James snapped.

I grabbed Beau by the collar. James caught the animal—which was so small that it disappeared into his hand—and put it in the cage.

"What is it?" I asked.

"A sugar glider."

"A what?"

"Sugar glider. They're native to Australia."

Beau was still barking, and the poor thing clung terrified to the side of the cage. James carried the cage and the other bag, which contained pet supplies, downstairs to his office in the basement. I followed, but shut the door to lock Beau upstairs.

The sugar glider looked like a tiny gray chipmunk—about four inches long, with a tail that was another four inches long. Its cute wedge-shaped face had extraordinarily large black eyes, pointy ears, a pink nose and short whiskers. A black stripe ran from the crown of its head to the base of its tail.

"Is it a boy or a girl?" I asked.

"A boy. We'll name him Donald, after you."

Donald was motionless near the top of the birdcage, which James placed on a table against the wall. The animal had five toes on each foot, although the feet were more like hands with claws, which enabled him to climb and grasp. James scattered pine shavings on the bottom of the cage, and then placed a small, hollow log on top of them. He filled a water bottle and attached it to the side of the cage.

"What does he eat?" I asked.

"Birdseed and Gliderade," James replied. He put birdseed in a plastic feeding tray that came with the cage. Gliderade was a nectar and bee pollen powder that needed to be mixed with water. Sugar gliders liked sweet nectar—that's why "sugar" was part of their name.

In the Australian wild, sugar gliders were arboreal and nocturnal. They lived in the trees of deciduous forests, sleeping during the day and coming out to feed at night—the reason for the big eyes and big ears. They also had fur-covered membranes that stretched from their front foot to their rear foot on each side of their bodies, which enabled them to glide from tree to tree—up to 145 feet—like a flying squirrel.

Donald did not come from Australia, however, he came from a local pet store. "I worked out a deal with the shop," James said. "I agreed to talk about sugar gliders to potential customers on the phone, and they sold me this one for only $40."

So now we had two exotic animals in James' office—the sugar glider and Herbie the hedgehog, who had moved in as well. Herbie was also nocturnal, so, because James went to bed so early, it soon became my job to care for the pets. But I didn't mind. They were cute.

January 18, 1997, dawned cold and sunny, just as Courtney predicted.

Tracy, my maid of honor, spent the night before the wedding with me; I banished James to his Mays Landing townhouse. Archie Turner, who was a groomsman for this ceremony, was there to keep him company. I didn't know if Archie was still having financial problems, but James wanted us—meaning me—to pay for his airfare from Sydney to Philadelphia. He would be staying for several weeks, getting acquainted with James' business plans. I rented a car so he would have something to drive. And, I bought a plane ticket for him to fly to England and visit his family while we were on our honeymoon. "He's an important part of our plans and he's coming here to help us," James told me. "It's the least we can do."

On the morning of my big day, I dressed in my wedding gown for the home-of-the-bride photographs. Dad and Pat arrived, then Pam Breyer and her fiancé. The photographer, Bill Horin, posed me, me with Tracy, me with Tracy and Pam, me with Dad, me with Tracy and Dad, me with Dad and Pat. After going on countless photo shoots with Bill over 20 years, I knew that every time he said, "One more," he was lying.

Finally Bill told the truth, and the at-home pictures were finished. I knew they would turn out great—I was radiating happiness.

From where we waited just outside the parlor room of the Ram's Head Inn, Pam, Tracy, Dad and I heard the chatter of our guests quiet down and the flute and guitar music begin—it was time.

Joe Nickles, as the officiant, took his place at the podium in front of that extraordinary fireplace, with its mantle formed by layer upon layer of deep brown molding. James entered from a door on the right side, followed by Chic Attig, his best man and a Vietnam veteran, and Archie. James rented stylish black vests with small white polka dots for them to wear with their tuxedos—quite spiffy. They all stood at the front next to Joe, waiting for us.

Pam walked out first, slowly and gracefully moving down the center aisle between the chairs filled with our guests. Tracy was next, smiling as she walked. My bridesmaids took their places to the left of the podium. Wearing navy blue velvet gowns and carrying orchid bouquets, they both looked beautiful.

Finally, it was my turn. I was the bride, beautiful in my elegant ivory gown with a tulle train and a tulle veil perched toward the back of my head. On my left hand, I wore my engagement ring, soon to be joined—again—by a wedding band. On my right hand was that exquisite topaz ring James gave me. Together, my hands carried a bouquet of cascading orchids.

I grew up during the years of "women's lib." I never debated the propriety of becoming a professional woman and living on my own; I just did it. But no matter how accomplished I was, no matter how many newsletters I produced or softball games I pitched, as a single woman, I felt unfulfilled. The notion of equal rights did not diminish the tremendous pressure society exerted on women to marry. For all of my adult years I felt deficient. I was lacking a man. The lack was about to disappear.

Dad, looking trim in his tuxedo, took my arm. I began my passage down the aisle, a picture of joy. When we reached the front, Dad kissed me and stepped aside. James took his place.

"Friends, we are gathered here to witness and to celebrate the coming together of two separate lives," Joe began, reading from a script James wrote. "We have come to recognize the union of this man, James, and this woman, Donna, in marriage, to share with them in the importance of this commitment.

"The essence of this commitment is the taking of another person in his or her entirety, as lover, companion and friend. It is therefore a decision which is not to be entered into lightly, but rather undertaken with great consideration and respect for both the other person and oneself. Having made this decision, James and Donna may feel justly proud. Today we give social recognition to the decision James and Donna have made to accept each other totally and permanently, and to celebrate the love that they have for one another. Donna and James have asked James' best man, Chic Attig, the Love Doctor, to read from the Bible."

Our guests, belatedly realizing what Joe said, broke into laughter.

Chic read the ever-present wedding passage from the first letter of Paul to the Corinthians, which begins, "Love is patient and kind." We heard two more readings—one by my sister, and another by Archie. Then Joe returned to the podium.

"James and Donna, come now into the union of marriage," Joe said. "James, repeat after me: I, James, take thee, Donna ..."

James cleared his throat, paused and then joked, "I can do it." Our guests laughed again.

"I, James," he said in a strong, clear voice while looking deep into my eyes, "take thee, Donna, to be my lawful wedded wife, to have and to hold, from this day forth, to love, to honor, and to cherish, to comfort and to respect, in sorrow or in joy, in hardship or in plenty, so long as we both shall live."

I repeated the vow to him.

"James and Donna wish to exchange rings as symbols of their vows," Joe resumed. "James has entrusted, whimsically, the safekeeping of those rings to his best man, Chic." More laughter. "I ask Chic to present the first ring to James."

Joe read the final vows from the script, and James repeated:

"This is my beloved and this is my friend. With this ring I thee wed and join my life with yours."

Then I placed the ring on James' hand and said, "This is my beloved and this is my friend. With this ring I thee wed and join my life with yours." Then, jumping the gun, I kissed James. This sparked yet another round of laughter.

"You've got to wait for my cue," Joe playfully admonished, and then began the final statement. "Before these loved ones and friends, James and Donna have pledged themselves to each other and have symbolized this by giving and receiving rings. I now confirm you as husband and wife.

"Now," Joe directed, with emphasis, "you may kiss the bride."

Our guests broke into applause, and to the sounds of *Scotland the Brave,* James and I walked back down the aisle, husband and wife again.

More photos. James and me in a formal portrait. James and me with the bridal party. James and his groomsmen striking a showbiz pose. Tracy, Pam and me hiking up our gowns to show off our legs. Chic, the Love Doctor, giving James a big smooch.

At 3 p.m., the maitre d' ushered our guests into the grand ballroom. Like the parlor, the room was decorated in a formal style—pale yellow walls, a brass candelabra hanging from the ceiling, built-in china cupboards with dishes on the shelves, and a small alcove, set off by heavy swag drapes, where our three-tier wedding cake was on display. Our relatively small guest list required only eight tables, so there was plenty of room for the dance floor, which I knew would be important.

With a flourish, Courtney Colletti, as master of ceremonies, brought us into the ballroom, pair by pair. Dad and his fiancée, Pat. Pam and Archie. Tracy and Chic. He then asked all the guests to stand and the drum roll started. "Would you give a huge round of applause," he energetically requested, "for Mr. and Mrs. James Montgomery!"

James squeezed my hand as we entered to the tune of *Waltzing Matilda,* both of us smiling broadly. As we reached the center of the dance floor, he took both my hands and pulled me close to him. The female vocalist started singing *The Power of Love,* which James selected for our first dance. He held my hand close to his heart, and I rested my head on his chest, my eyes closed, savoring the moment. After a minute or so, Courtney asked the bridal party, and then the rest of our guests, to join us.

As the song finished, Chic, the best man, took the microphone. "While I have everybody's attention, I'd like to take a couple of minutes to talk about Amway," he deadpanned. Another round of laughter.

"Truly, I would like to thank my wife," Chic continued. "She inscribed in our wedding rings the date we got married. It's been very helpful." More laughter. Then Chic raised his glass for a toast. "James and Donna, you have a lot of nice friends here. Everybody wishes you well. That's unquestionable. The love that's in this room is great. Remember it always. Best wishes."

"Here, here," toasted our guests.

James walked up to the bandstand. He brought with him a bright blue, yellow and purple toy megaphone, which distorted his voice as he spoke into it—another joke, another burst of laughter. He set the toy down and picked up the real microphone.

"Donna and I share one thing in common, and that is a love of words," he began. "We've made our living; it's changed our lives; it's changed my life since my early 20s. Throughout the years words have meant a hell of a lot to me, the words that Donna and I exchanged earlier, and the words that even brought us together. But I'm going to make a toast now that comes down to two very special words, and they are, 'thank you.'

"I never got to meet, one of the sad things of my life, I never got to meet Donna's mother. Those of my friends who got to meet Donna over the last six months or so are absolutely spellbound by this incredible creature that I've married.

"To her parents, and more than her parents, to her complete family, to her two brothers and her sister, somewhere along the line, we all start with the same genes, and they did something so special with this lady, it is absolutely incredible. My heartfelt thanks go out to the people that created my Donna for me. I'd ask you to drink a toast now to the parents, and the family, the Andersens."

Everyone in the room applauded.

As the noise died down, Dad stood up, with his crib notes. "I would like to make this toast to Donna and James," he said. "May they have a long, prosperous, healthy and happy marriage." Dad paused and looked around the room until he saw me. "Donna, on this very special day for you and James, I want to say, for your mother and I," his voice cracked, "we love you."

"Would anyone else care to make a toast who hadn't planned on making one?" Courtney asked.

I did. Our guests cheered as I walked to the front and Courtney handed me the microphone. For a moment I stood at the front of the room, soaking up the affection I could feel from our friends and family. "I'm very, very happy," I began, speaking slowly. "James, I love you. This is a very special day, and I thank all of you for being here to share it with us. Now let's have fun!" With big smile and another round of applause, I stepped lightly back to my table.

The party was on. The band started playing ballroom music, and Dad, an accomplished dancer, dominated the floor. For many numbers, he and his partner—Pat, one of my aunts, or me, during *Daddy's Little Girl*—were the only ones out there. Dad didn't mind a bit—it meant he had plenty of room to put on a show.

In the meantime, the buffet stations opened. We had salads, appetizers and three entrées—pasta, shrimp scampi and copper kettles of beef Wellington and duck. Everyone raved about the food. While we ate, Archie got up on the bandstand to read notes of congratulations that James received from wellwishers who could not be with us. First were a post card from James' sister, Heather, and an e-mail from his daughter, Margaret. Archie then read almost a dozen messages that he retrieved from James' answering machine:

"Sorry I couldn't be with you, but will do this in person in a couple of weeks. All the best to you both on this, your very special day. Lee Patterson, Tampa, Florida." Archie explained that Lee was James' lawyer in Florida.

"Paris will be perfect for you. Have a great day, am keeping your coffee warm. Dan Miller and Gerry Lenfest." Archie added that the message was from executives of Suburban Cable, and James was meeting them in Paris on the upcoming Friday.

Archie read the rest of the messages:

"She sounds really cute, Dad. Woof. Harold James, Dachshund in exile, South Carolina."

"Don't bring her this way if she is anything like her photo, unless you want to take us all on. Seriously, all the best for the future, your friends at Special Operations Command, MacDill Air Force Base, Tampa."

"Sorry you chose to get married where they can gamble legally. But the two of you are due down here soon to party in our sun. Have a great day James and Donna. Dick Grecco, Mayor of Tampa, Florida."

Shortly after dinner, it was time to cut the wedding cake. We posed for yet another photo, and James delicately fed me a bite. I was not so kind, and he ended up with white icing in his beard.

Courtney slowly revved up the music—from ballroom to polka to rock 'n' roll. When the band started the ultimate party tune—*Hot, Hot, Hot* by Buster Poindexter—our wedding guests fell into an impromptu Conga line behind James and me. After parading around the dance floor and among the tables, the line broke into a big circle, with everyone hooting and clapping, as James and I danced in the middle. He retreated to the side, and I kept whirling in the middle of the circle until my brother, Greg, came out and danced with me. The band kept the song going, improvising along the way, and I danced my way around the circle, switching partners—my uncle, Dennis Daly. My brother, Doug. My friend, Jean Muchanic. James jumped in and danced with different guests, including Chic Attig and Joe Nickles. Then anyone who felt the urge grabbed a partner and danced a few bars. It was exhilarating.

Earlier in the evening, as I stopped by the tables to make sure everyone was enjoying themselves, my brother, Greg, said to me, "You are the queen." On that day, at my joyous wedding, I indeed felt like the queen.

"What is the French word for 'honeymoon?'" I asked the flight attendant as we were on our way to Paris.

"Lune de miel," she replied. "It's a literal translation of the English word."

Our USAir flight left Philadelphia at 7:25 p.m. on January 19, 1997. We arrived at Charles de Gaulle Airport in Paris Monday morning at 8:50 a.m. After passing through customs, James and I went to collect our luggage.

"I need to use the restroom," I said when we reached the cavernous baggage hall.

"You shouldn't do that," he admonished.

"Why not?"

"That's what terrorists do—they get off the plane and go directly to the restroom."

I didn't care what the terrorists did. It was important for me to use the restroom.

We were staying at the Hotel Sully Saint-Germain on Rue des Ecoles—School Street—in the Latin Quarter. As we pulled up in a taxi, we found that it was a charming boutique hotel with only 61 rooms. A stone fireplace dominated the lobby, and above it hung a medieval knight's shield and swords. Our room was a pleasant surprise—it was larger than most that I'd seen in European hotels. The bathroom was for baths—there was a handheld shower but no shower curtain. The water closet was a separate room—literally the size of a small broom closet.

James and I set out to explore the neighborhood. The Latin Quarter was an ancient section of Paris with narrow, twisting streets. Five- and six-story buildings followed the contours of the streets, separated from the curb by narrow sidewalks. I truly felt like we were strolling through the Old World.

We walked a few blocks toward the Seine River and found ourselves at one of the icons of Paris, the cathedral of Notre Dame. It dominated a small island in the middle of the river called Ile de la Cité. Construction of the massive gothic church began in 1163 and took 170 years. It was extensively and meticulously decorated, from the gargoyles at the tops of the towers to the intricately carved entryways. I was amazed at the scale of the building and the classic religious paintings and statues inside it. Yet as I walked around, I sensed an energy of turmoil within the stone walls. The cathedral had seen a lot of history in almost a thousand years, and not all of it was good. Stepping from the dim interior of the church back into the daylight, I felt a sense of relief.

Just across the river from Notre Dame we found La Bouteille D'Or, or The Golden Bottle, a four-star restaurant situated in a location that had served food since 1631. That evening, James and I returned there for our first dinner in Paris. The waiter seated us at a window table, and as the sky darkened, we were treated to a stunning view of the illuminated cathedral.

The most economical way to eat in Paris was to order from the *prix fixe* menu, which at La Bouteille D'Or included an entrée (appetizer), main course and dessert. We also ordered two glasses of the house champagne—it was the first time that I saw James consume alcohol.

I felt exquisite. After the wedding of my dreams, my husband and I were in Paris, dining on the Left Bank of the Seine in a restaurant that had been serving lovers for centuries. We savored a delectable meal and then walked back, hand in hand, to our hotel. I slipped into my new, flowing white negligee. James and I had not had a proper wedding night—we were both exhausted after our reception on Saturday, and Sunday night we were in the plane over the Atlantic Ocean. The negligee didn't stay on very long.

Paris in January was not Paris in April. It was winter, and Tuesday dawned cold and damp. That morning, James and I set off in a different direction, and in a commercial section a few blocks away, I bought a brown beret to keep my chilly head warm.

Our neighborhood surrounded the Sorbonne, the seat of the University of Paris. That's why it was called the Latin Quarter—since 1253, when the Sorbonne was founded, the area was filled with students, and during the Middle Ages they spoke Latin. But the Sorbonne was only one of many historic landmarks within a quick walk of our hotel. Two nearby neoclassical masterpieces were the Odéon

Theater, opened in 1782, and the Panthéon, completed in 1790.

We crossed the Seine River over Pont Neuf, or the New Bridge, which was actually the oldest bridge in Paris, dating from 1578. Thirty-two bridges spanned the Seine. These were not utilitarian structures of precast concrete like in the United States. They were pedestrian-friendly works of art; some, like Pont Alexandre III, were adorned with gilded statues.

On the other side of Pont Neuf was La Samaritaine department store, which opened in 1869. Inside the store I found my favorite line of cosmetics, Clarins, on sale. Usually I bought Clarins at Macy's—it was expensive and always full price. In Paris, I stocked up on moisturizer and saved money.

James, however, seemed to be looking for opportunities to spend money. He bought another watch. Back near our hotel he spotted solid gold hoop earrings on display in a jewelry store window.

"Do you want them?" James asked.

"They're $700," I replied, aghast.

"So? It's a presie."

James either didn't have a grasp of our financial situation, or was so confident in his entrepreneurial plans that he wasn't worried about spending before money came in. Not sharing his optimism, I didn't buy the $700 earrings. Instead, I selected a pair coated in gold leaf that cost $25.

Wednesday morning I went to the Louvre Museum alone—James wasn't interested. He said something about visiting the French Foreign Legion to collect military ribbons he had earned. I was disappointed that he didn't want to accompany me, but I was going to see the greatest museum in the world, with or without him. Following the advice in our tour book, I got to the Louvre early and went directly to the Mona Lisa so I could see it before the crowds showed up.

Later that day, after a lunch of sushi, James and I went to the Musée d'Orsay, also recommended in the tour book. I was enthralled. The exhibit was small and manageable—at least compared to the Louvre—and we could see it all in a few hours. The collection included renowned works by artists such as Renoir, Manet, Monet and Van Gogh. All the artwork was created between 1848 and 1914, a period of extreme transition in the art world. Some artists still worked in classic religious motifs, some painted expansive landscapes and others experimented with impressionism, so the styles changed radically from room to room.

After the Orsay we went out to dinner near our hotel. We found a cute little country-style restaurant, with white plaster walls, dark exposed beams and red-and-white checked tablecloths. The matronly waitress—perhaps she was the owner's wife—brought us menus. I ordered a salad and James ordered a cold meat appetizer, which looked like a plate of thin-sliced pepperoni. I had two pieces; James ate the rest. We each then had main courses, dessert and coffee.

Back in our hotel room, we both vomited.

All night long, we took turns in the water closet. It must have been the cold meat, because that was the only dish James and I shared. And James, having eaten more of it, was in far worse shape than I was. Morning arrived, and we still felt terrible. We needed medicine, and it was up to me to find it. James couldn't get out of bed.

This was going to put my limited French to the test. I studied Spanish for many years in high school and college, but I learned French only by listening to audiotapes in the car. If the words weren't on the tapes, I didn't know them. Luckily, my pocket-sized French phrase book had a list of medical problems, including *l'intoxication alimentaire*. Food poisoning.

I dressed, slowly, and made my way downstairs. A pharmacy was located a block away on the other side of Rue des Ecoles—we'd passed it many times already. But I was so dizzy that I had to stop to lean against the wall twice during the one-block trip. Then I had to gather my strength to cross the street.

In France, thankfully, a pharmacist could dispense medicine without a prescription. I asked the two women behind the counter if they had something for food poisoning. They weren't sure what I said.

"*L'intoxication alimentaire?*" one woman asked the other.

"*Oui,*" I answered. Yes.

They gave me a box of little black pills, and James and I both took them. An hour or so later, I was fine. James, however, was not yet better. Still, that afternoon he agreed to accompany me to the Musée de Cluny, which was only a few blocks from the hotel. It was a mansion built before 1500—the finest medieval architecture still standing in Paris. We didn't last the whole tour. I felt lightheaded again, and was amazed that James was standing at all.

Friday morning we both felt much better, and visited another part of Paris, the ritzy Champs-Élysées. We had coupons for a free lunch at Planet Hollywood, which to me was a fine reason to visit. Familiar American songs blasted on the sound system as we ate hamburgers and French fries. It was just like eating at the Planet Hollywood in Caesars Atlantic City.

Directly across the Seine River from Champs-Élysées was the Invalides and Eiffel Tower district, where James and I spent Saturday, our last day in Paris. The Hotel des Invalides opened in 1679 as a home for French war veterans. Nearby was the Dome church, where Napoleon Bonaparte and other military heroes were lavishly entombed. The complex also included the Musée de l'Armée, or army museum. We went inside, but James thought the entire exhibit was ludicrous. "The French never fought," he commented derisively. "They just went around giving each other medals."

From Invalides, we strolled the Champ-de-Mars gardens to the Eiffel Tower and rode the elevator to the second level, which was 377 feet above the ground and offered a stunning view of the city. James didn't want to look—he didn't like being that high without a building around him, so he stayed far away from the railings.

Safely on the ground after our tour, we headed back toward our neighborhood for dinner. I had seen posters for a classical concert at the St. Severin church—the program was Vivaldi and Bach on flute and organ. I wanted to go— it would be exquisite to hear that music surrounded by the beauty of St. Severin.

The church was a fine example of flamboyant Gothic architecture. Construction began in the 13th century and took 300 years; I could understand why. Every aspect of the church was lavishly decorated. Multiple arches, carved from stone, surrounded the exterior entryways and windows. Above the arches were faux rooflines with statues adorning the pinnacles. More statues were housed in nooks and crannies around the exterior of the church, and gargoyles guarded the roof.

The sanctuary interior was equally dramatic. The nave was narrow but astoundingly tall, defined by a colonnade of stone arches. In the two aisles alongside the nave, stone columns were carved to resemble trees, which at the top split into branches to hold up the vaulted ceiling. All the stone was gorgeous, but it was also cold. I didn't take off my coat or my gloves, and I wondered if the flutist wore long underwear under his tuxedo. During the intermission we left, walking back to the warmth of our cozy hotel room for our final night in Paris.

We flew back to the United States on January 26, 1997. A few days later, James wrote a letter to our friends and relatives that we enclosed with our wedding thank you cards:

Hotel Sully Saint-Germain
31 rue des Ecoles, 75005 Paris

We have just returned from investing your gift. Investing it in memories—ones we will treasure for years to come. We spent our honeymoon in the old Latin Quarter and we wanted to share those memories with you…

Our first night in Paris, we set out walking towards the Seine—the road leads past the Sorbonne, the Polytechnique and the Pantheon. We're surrounded by buildings hundreds of years old and chose one for our restaurant, in the Left Bank, under the gothic shadow of Notre Dame itself…

La Bouteille D'Or, the Golden Bottle, has traded continuously at its current location for over 350 years. Our waiter wasn't quite that old; in fact, he was a young Italian who proudly brought out a book to show us the paintings and pictures of the restaurant over each century. Its first photograph was taken in 1858.

We chose a prix fixe menu for 130f [servis compris], $27.50 ea. Donna started with 'Soup Paysanne Corse'…a hearty country style soup [no problem getting the fork to stick up in that lot!] from the island of Corsica.

I strayed from the fixed price menu to indulge in a dozen 'Escargot de Borgnone' and Donna ate [and liked] one of my slimys—as we call them Down Under—heaps of garlic & great!

Between courses, one of the large flat tourist barges that ply the Seine at night lit up the old Cathedral [and everything else for a mile or so] … they are long and flat to fit under the 29 odd bridges, below the height of the bank, so we couldn't see them. The effect was quite eerie and unexpected.

One of my few complaints about my adopted home—the USA—is the quality and paucity of local lamb—so I opted to try 'Agneau de lait corse braise a la menthe.' The lamb was served with a totally pink center and could be cut with a spoon with incredible flavors cooked into it.

Donna dove into grouper—'Gratin de merou farci au brocciu'—deviating again from our price fixed guidelines—but she ate it all—especially the cheese and spinach sauce.

I convinced Donna to try 'Profiteroles au chocolat chaud'…an old favorite of mine back when I ate sweets! I matched her delight [all gone again!] with a plate of cheeses. I was surprised that each of the three was very dry and piquant in taste—exquisitely different from the normal cream cheeses and bries served in French restaurants.

To top it off, the house champagne—Lussac St. Emilion—and at $8 a glass, was equal to the best I have ever tasted. It had a slight golden tint, and was clean to the palate.

We kept a copy of the Golden Bottle's biz card and have attached it for you—just tell them the Aussie who doesn't normally drink and insisted on teaching the waiters 'Waltzing Matilda' sent you. It was the first of many fine restaurant adventures.

We thought you would enjoy knowing how we spent your gift. Our honeymoon was truly special, as was our wedding day! Thank you so much,

James

The day before James and I got married again, I was frantically trying to figure out how to pay for our wedding. The bank approved a home equity line of credit for only $16,500, and the funds were not yet available. We didn't have the money to cover our reception, so I took a $5,500 cash advance on my American Express card.

With James' expenses that I paid before the wedding, I was carrying $25,000 in credit card debt. I tried to cut my interest expenses by playing the balance transfer game. I got a $10,000 personal loan and moved the high-interest balances of two credit cards to it. I moved two other balances to a new Citibank card with an introductory rate of 5.9 percent.

I assumed we'd get money as wedding gifts, and we did. Along with crystal stemware, flatware, towels and kitchen accessories from my wish list at the Macy's Bridal Registry, we received checks adding up to $1,200. Without a word of discussion, James took all the checks and deposited them into his bank account. I was taken aback, especially since most of the money was from my family and friends. But not wanting to start an argument, I rationalized that we were married and pooling our resources, and my husband would use the money to benefit us both.

I don't know what James did with the wedding money, but our honeymoon expenses were added to my credit cards.

Chapter 9

As soon as we returned from Paris, James plunged full speed ahead into his business plans. One evening in late January, James hosted a meeting in our dining room. Attending were Archie Turner, returned from visiting his family in England, Joe Nickles, Chic Attig and Pinky Kravitz, the local radio personality. Joe and Chic had been promised ownership interests in the factory that would make construction materials, which James was now calling the Polytechnique Group. I thought "Polytechnique" was stupid—it sounded like a school—but James decided that was the company name, end of discussion.

I did not participate in the meeting. I did, however, receive the reports James generated afterwards about his "JAG strategy." The reports outlined his next steps: Develop programming concepts for the Jersey Shore Channel to present to Suburban Cable in February. Pitch CelebAM for the Atlantic City Convention Center in response to a request for proposal that he anticipated receiving in March. Secure funding to launch the construction materials company.

There were new items on the reports as well. James learned of an opportunity for themed construction materials at the Foxwoods casino in Connecticut, which could jump-start Polytechnique. He came up with an idea to build a new attraction called "Century Park" at Atlantic City's tiny Bader Field airport, which was expected to be decommissioned. It would feature six geodesic domes surrounded by themed entertainment. James also wanted to launch a television network called the Chance Channel—the first national gaming and casino network.

James was elated after the meeting and kept talking about it. "Everybody likes my strategy, Nuffles," he said to me the next day as I was cleaning up the kitchen. "It's really brilliant, you know, with each component supporting the others. One day I'm going to be famous. You just might be married to the next Walt Disney!"

"That's great," I replied, "but what I want right now is to get my credit cards paid off."

Anger gathered on my husband's face. "Donna, I am working day and night to try and make a life for you," he spat, with barely controlled hostility. "The least you can do is be supportive."

The hard edge in my husband's voice stunned me. "James, I think I'm being plenty supportive," I retorted. "I'm supporting you to the tune of about $50,000—and counting."

"You knew what my plans were when you married me and you wanted to be part of them," he shot back. "That's what a marriage is, you know. Two people supporting each other. But you wouldn't know that because you're not normal. You've never been married before."

That was a low blow.

"Look at you," he continued. "Forty years old and you never got married. I can just imagine how people were wondering what was wrong with you."

I couldn't believe the cruelty of his words. In shock, I turned away and left the kitchen. I went upstairs, into the meditation room, and stood at the window overlooking the big locust tree in my backyard. James followed me into the room. He was still angry, and his presence felt physically menacing. He stood between me and the door, and I was afraid.

"Donna ..." he began.

"Oh, don't worry James," I said, my heart and voice broken. "Do whatever you want. I'll never stand up to you again."

Despite the pain I felt at my husband's withering accusations, I didn't go along with everything he wanted. The six-month option that he bought on Central Pier was about to expire, and he thought we should come up with another $20,000 to renew it. I was not interested in throwing good money after bad. Besides, we didn't have any money.

To bring in some short-term cash, James tried to peddle a movie script he had written about the Vietnam War called *The First Casualty*. The title reflected an adage that "truth is the first casualty of war." The script told the story of a journalist covering the war who fell in love with a young Vietnamese woman, then was forced to become involved with the conflict, rather than just reporting it, as Saigon fell.

First, however, James needed an electronic version of the script. He said he only had a printout because his hard drive on a previous computer crashed, vaporizing the file. My sister, Tracy, and I were pressed into service to retype the manuscript—I took the first half and she took the second half.

"What do you think of it?" James asked me after I finished.

"I like it," I answered. "But since you describe the woman as coming from a strict, traditional Vietnamese family, I think she falls in love with the journalist too quickly. It seems like there should be more courtship."

"That's a good point," James said. "I did have more of that in there, but I cut it out because I thought the script was running too long."

Suddenly, another scriptwriting opportunity appeared—one that was much more immediate. Tracy took a new job at an infomercial company in Media, Pennsylvania called Opus One. The company usually produced infomercials for golf products, but a new client wanted to market sunglasses on television. They needed a freelance infomercial script, and Tracy suggested James and me.

We traveled to Media to meet with Tracy and her boss. James brought Archie along, who had considerable television production experience. As James described his new television ventures during the meeting, I noticed that he implied they were much further along than they actually were. Still, he talked a good game, and Opus One retained us, agreeing to pay $4,000 for the script. I was relieved that James would actually earn some money, even if it wasn't millions.

We fell into a married-couple routine, although the timing was unusual. Every day at 4 a.m., James woke up, went to his office in the basement and started working on his computer. At 6 a.m., he brought a glass of orange juice up to our second-floor bedroom, where I was still asleep, and set it on the nightstand beside me. Then he went downstairs to the living room and got Beau's leash out of the closet. He stood at the bottom of the steps rattling the leash until the dog, who slept on a cushion beside our bed, heard it and ran downstairs for his morning walk. Beau wore his Florida State Seminoles collar, and James wore his Special Forces beret.

I got up and ate my standard breakfast—tofu, sliced mushrooms and chopped green peppers, topped with a pinch of curry powder and cooked in the microwave. I invented the breakfast in my early 20s when I realized that I was hypoglycemic. I needed to eat protein at breakfast to stabilize my blood sugar for the day, but I didn't want to consume bacon and eggs every morning. My tofu breakfast looked and tasted unusual, but it was a low-cholesterol way of keeping me from passing out.

Next, as often as I could, I'd exercise. Sometimes I went for a run on the Boardwalk, but usually I did an aerobics videotape. My tapes, an exercise step and a television were now set up in the meditation room, as my basement gym had become James' office.

He certainly took over the space. James' large, U-shaped desk—the one I assembled—filled a corner of the room. On it were his computer, phone and fax machine, along with papers, folders, books, framed photos and assorted trinkets. Mementos, posted with pushpins, covered the walls around the desk: James' face on the cover of Soldier of Fortune magazine as "Warrior of the Year." A certificate for his membership in the Special Forces Association. A certificate of appreciation from the Advertising Club of Victoria, Australia—he was president in 1979 and 1980. Photos of him, in a gold-braided dress uniform, with cadets of the Royal Volunteer Coastal Patrol in Victoria. A photo of him with his seaplane.

Next to the desk was a swing-arm floor lamp. On the arm James hung several ball chain lanyards with plastic ID holders. They contained his laminated Special Forces and Delta Force ID cards, as well as badges from trade shows he attended.

On a low table within an arm's length of the desk was my 27-inch television, which had been replaced in the living room by James' 36-inch TV. The television was always turned on, even while James was working on the computer and talking on the phone.

"How can you work with the TV on?" I asked him. "I need quiet in order to write."

"You can't handle multi-channel input?" James asked, as if it were something anyone could do.

Behind the television were two 12-foot shelves installed on the walls. One of them quickly began sagging with the weight of James' books. That was not an issue with the shelf above it, which displayed James' collection of more than 50 baseball caps.

The two folding banquet tables that I bought were set up as an "L" in the corner of the room diagonally across from the desk. The pet cages were on the tables, housing the hedgehog and two sugar gliders. James had brought home a female sugar glider to share Donald's cage; she was named Jamie, after my husband. Around the cages were more piles of papers, books, videotape cassettes, office supplies and stereo components. Several mugs were filled with pens and markers. I bought James plastic stack trays to help him organize his papers. They were empty.

There were, however, multiple piles of papers on the floor. In fact, the old green carpet was barely visible, except for a narrow path leading from the door to the desk chair. Periodically James got angry when Beau or I walked on the papers. I didn't have any sympathy—if James didn't want his papers walked on, he should have picked them up.

The overall effect was unending clutter, as if James wanted to see everything he owned. I certainly couldn't work that way, but I decided I was not going to worry about my husband's office. My challenge was to prevent his storage methods from spreading to other parts of the house, because James left a trail of paraphernalia wherever he went.

Still, James seemed happy. "My Nuffles made a nice office for me," he told me on several occasions. The biggest problem was the room's low ceiling—six feet four inches—only an inch taller than him. A basic ceiling light fixture was located in the middle of the room—just a porcelain socket with a light bulb screwed in. I took out the fixture and covered the electrical box with a plate. But the box hung about an inch lower than the rest of the ceiling, so James frequently walked into it, cutting the top of his bald head.

James generally came upstairs, wearing a pink bathrobe, to shower around 10 or 11 a.m. Or sometimes that's when we had our appointment for sex. Beau didn't like being shut out of the bedroom for our rendezvous, and barked outside the door until I came up with a bribery plan. Before our appointment, I threw a dog treat down the steps, which Beau, of course, chased. Then I shut the bedroom door. Beau soon started running down the steps as soon as he saw the treat in my hand.

After sex and a shower, James didn't always bother to dress—he liked to walk around in his briefs and a t-shirt. James had nice, long legs and muscular calves, although the effect was ruined by his massive belly hanging below his shirt. I guess he stripped down because his excess weight made him hot, but as my sister-in-law in Australia predicted, James didn't do much to lose it. I cooked healthy dinners using recipes from my weight-loss and natural foods cookbooks. But every week when I went grocery shopping, James wanted me to buy him four two-liter bottles of Diet Coke and a half-gallon of Edy's sugar-free ice cream.

We ate dinner between six and seven p.m. James sat at the head of the dining room table and I sat on the side, so he was to my left. As he only had an audience of one—me—he didn't bother to say much at dinner. When he did talk, it was about himself. One night he started telling me about his role as a military analysis expert on the Kurds—the people of Kurdistan.

"I never heard of the Kurds," I said.

"I know," James said. "That's exactly why I picked them. We were all supposed to specialize in a particular country or ethnic group. Some guys wanted to be in the thick of things and picked groups that we knew were going to be trouble, like the Chinese or the North Koreans. I didn't want any trouble. I wanted a nice, quiet area where nothing was happening. So I picked the Kurds.

"They're an ethnic group in the Middle East spread over several countries— Iran, Iraq, Turkey and Syria. Some genius after World War I decided to chop up their lands and give them to all these different countries, and they've been rebelling periodically ever since. Still, it was relatively quiet until the first Gulf War. Then between Saddam Hussein and militant Islamists, everything was heating up for the Kurds. A couple of the guys were jealous of me because now my group was where all the action was. I told them I never wanted the action; I wanted to take it easy. They didn't believe me."

James often wanted to eat dinner in the living room, in front of the television, on the TV trays Dad bought us for Christmas. When we did, there was even less conversation.

After dinner, James changed into his bathrobe and plugged in a movie that he had recorded during the day. My husband was pretty good at picking movies that I liked. But he went to bed at 8 p.m., in the middle of the movie, leaving me to watch the end by myself.

I asked James to adjust his schedule. "Why don't you get up a little later, so you don't have to go to bed so early and we can spend more time together?"

"You know my business is all over the world," James replied. "I have to be working when the people I'm dealing with are working."

Well, if the early hours would help him get his deals done, and money coming in, I wasn't going to argue.

James told me he had a meeting in Florida with Disney to pitch his *First Casualty* script. I took him to the Atlantic City airport on February 26, 1997 and picked him up on March 2. Every morning at 6 a.m. he called to wake me up and tell me that he loved me. He also called a few more times each day and sent sexy e-mails.

The infomercial script for Tracy's company, in the meantime, was done. James wrote the video portion, in which actors raved about all the features and benefits of the sunglasses. I wrote the call to action—where the announcer says, "Call the number on the screen right now for your sunglasses, only three easy payments of $19.99!" It was my first infomercial and the script came out well.

But the show was never produced. Shortly after we turned in our script, Opus One collapsed. Tracy lost her job, and it did not look like we would be paid. So James turned our invoice over to a "piranha fish"—a collections attorney.

We wouldn't see that $4,000 anytime soon, which added to the anxiety about our finances that consistently bubbled in my stomach. Plus, it was time to file taxes. I went downstairs to James' office, where the lights were off and the television was on, and asked my husband how he wanted to proceed.

"I don't file taxes," he said.

"What do you mean, you don't file taxes?"

"I haven't filed taxes since I've been in this country. A lot of people don't file taxes—that's what loopholes are for. I don't make the rules, I just use them."

"That's not right," I said.

"You're so naive," James said, condescendingly. He must have seen the shock on my face. "But it's part of your charm," he quickly backpedaled.

Disconcerted, I went to my accountant and asked if I would liable for James not paying taxes. He said if problems arose, I might be able to claim the "innocent spouse" defense.

"That's me," I said. "I'm the innocent spouse."

The best thing for me to do was to make my tax status "married, filing single," and hope that the government was satisfied.

My brother Doug's birthday was in March, and on a Sunday afternoon his wife, Cathy, planned a small celebration in their home. James said he had to work, as usual, so I went alone. Toward the end of the party, Doug cornered me in the family room.

"You know, Donna, Dad is concerned about James," he began.

"What's he concerned about?"

"He thinks James doesn't have any money and you paid for the entire wedding."

I froze inside. This was not a topic I was prepared to discuss.

"Well, things are tight right now until his projects come through," I said. "But when they do, we'll be fine."

"Look, Donna, why don't you let me check him out?"

"What do you mean?"

"I'll run a credit check. We do it all the time when my company hires someone new. All I need is his social security number."

If Doug did a credit check on James it would probably come back with problems. James had already told me he had no credit. But the entire family didn't need to know that.

"I don't think that will be necessary," I said to Doug.

Shortly after that conversation, I left. But on the long drive back to Atlantic City, my stomach churned. What had I gotten myself into? James showered me with affection. He promised that we would soon be "living in the lap of luxury."

He continued to make calls and go to meetings to pitch his plans. He recruited people besides me to become part of those plans. He wasn't at all worried. But I was working my butt off, and everything I earned was consumed by his spending. We were in debt—or more precisely, I was in debt. More debt than I ever had in my life.

I remembered a brief conversation James and I had a month earlier.

"The debts are yours," I'd griped at him. "You're the one spending all the money."

"That doesn't matter," he replied. "We're married. My debts are your debts."

The statement—and the callous tone of his voice—horrified me. I thought about those words as I was driving. The implications were not good.

When I got home almost two hours later, I was angry and upset. I didn't really want to talk to James, so I went directly upstairs. I was in our bedroom when I heard my husband coming up the steps.

"When did you get home?" he asked, standing in the doorway.

"A few minutes ago," I said, without looking at him. I busied myself smoothing out the bedspread.

"You have to take me to the airport on Friday," James said. "I'm going to South Carolina to see the Lewises and then to Florida."

"Why are you going to Florida?"

"I have another meeting with the company in Sanford about working with TPG." That was the Polytechnique Group.

"How much is that going to cost?" I asked.

"Not much. I got a $100 plane ticket on Spirit and I'll be staying at a Days Inn."

At this point James noticed that I still hadn't looked at him and my voice was strained. "What's wrong?" he asked me.

Finally, I looked up. "Well, James, today Doug asked me for your social security number. He wants to run a credit check on you."

James didn't say anything.

"I told him that I didn't want him to do a check," I continued. "But if my family knew what was really going on they would have you out of here immediately." My tone and expression clearly communicated that I thought our problems were James' fault.

James took a few steps into the room. When he spoke, his voice was pained. "Donna, I know this isn't what you expected. It isn't what I expected either. I'm pushing as hard as I can. Everything is just taking a lot longer than I thought it would."

I sat on the edge of the bed, partially turning my back toward him.

"Do you want me to leave?"

I looked up. There were tears in his eyes.

"I don't want you to hate me," he continued. "I made a promise to myself—if it ever gets to the point that you hate me, I will leave."

I was in turmoil. I married this man. I made a commitment to stand by him, boots and all. That was the point of marriage—commitment. He was trying, but the plans weren't working out as quickly as he expected. What was I supposed to do? What kind of wife gets rid of her husband because his business plans aren't working out?

"Everything I'm doing is for you," he continued, as a tear slid down his cheek. "But if you want me to leave, I will."

I was quiet for a moment. Then I said, "No, James, we'll keep going."

James pulled me to my feet and put his arms around me. "I need you to believe in me," he said.

When James came back from his trip, he told me that he signed his interest in the Mays Landing townhouse over to the parents of his deceased wife. They were going to put the townhouse on the market.

"Why did you do that?" I asked, thinking that he was entitled to some of the equity.

"I didn't want to fight with them," he said. "The Lewises are very difficult people. Gale didn't get along with her mother at all. She barely spoke to her."

"Well, I'd like to have the bedroom furniture," I said. My antique dresser was too small, and my bed didn't even have a headboard.

A few days later, James reported that he told the Lewises we wanted the bedroom furniture. Then we had to decide what else we wanted. I had no room for any of the other furniture, but there were some decorator items that I liked. I took a watercolor of flowers and a hummingbird to hang in the kitchen, and a small print of a dog and chicks for the dining room. James put a small, framed photo of Gale, his deceased wife, on my low, antique blanket chest that was also in the dining room. I didn't mind—I felt like they had been married, she was gone, and he was honoring her.

James and Gale had a carved wooden bird and an antique duck decoy; I placed them by the faux fireplace mantle in the living room. I didn't like their good flatware, but extra serving pieces were always handy, so I took them. James brought over an expensive set of Le Creuset saucepans. He found a full-sized clothes steamer. "What's it for?" he asked.

"I've never used one, but it's to get wrinkles out of clothes," I answered.

"Will it work for my uniforms?"

"I suppose so."

"Then we should keep it."

I liked the blue and white duvet and pillow shams that were in the master bedroom. The matching curtains didn't fit my windows, but I thought maybe, when we had more money, I could get new curtains, so I saved the bed ensemble in our storage unit.

Then there were the clothes. Gale obviously liked to dress well. Her walk-in closet was stuffed with coordinated sportswear, business suits, silk blouses, embroidered sweaters and casual dresses. To complete her outfits, she had an incredible amount of accessories—belts, scarves and even hats. And shoes. Many pairs of shoes. James told me that Gale shopped at a local discount shoe store for five years—which confused me, because he also told me that they moved up from Florida together and bought the townhouse just two years ago.

According to James, Gale did prune her wardrobe from time to time—she and her girlfriends brought items they no longer wanted to a local consignment store. James thought I should look through the clothing to see if there was anything I wanted, and then take the rest to the consignment store. Perhaps we'd make some money by selling the clothes.

A few months earlier, James gave me a designer shirt of Gale's—it was dark blue with black stripes and funky fabric-covered buttons. He also brought me a long, brown velvet coat with heavy gold embroidery, very Arabic in style. Looking through the closet, I found that Gale had quite a few sweaters that I liked, and three nice cocktail dresses fit me. Most of the clothes, however, weren't my taste—she wore blacks, browns and neutrals, whereas I preferred bright colors. Much of her clothing went to consignment.

James gave me jewelry he had previously given to Gale: A necklace with nine 18-inch strands of gold and silver chain that he said was worn by Cindy Crawford in a fashion shoot. A pin and coordinating earrings designed by Paloma Picasso. A half-inch bangle bracelet of solid gold, worked in a geometric pattern. The bracelet was beautiful, but I couldn't wear it—it was too big and fell off my wrist. An antique ring with a large opal in an intricate setting was also too big. I didn't want to wear it anyway—it was Gale's wedding ring.

But the topaz ring James gave me, which I wore for our wedding, was missing. I looked for it everywhere. It wasn't in my jewelry chest. It wasn't in my travel case. It wasn't in the bathroom. It wasn't in any of my dresser drawers. It wasn't on the floor under the bed.

With trepidation—I feared another angry outburst—I told James that I couldn't find the topaz. To my complete surprise, he didn't react at all. "It's lost," he said. "Sometimes that happens."

My younger brother, Greg, was getting married on April 4, 1997. It was the second Andersen wedding of the year. James refused to go.

"James, you're my husband," I said. "This is an important family event. You should be there."

"Your family thinks I'm taking your money," he retorted. "Why would I want to associate with them?"

I didn't answer.

"Doug wants to run a credit check on me," he continued. "Do you know what that is? It's called tortious interference with marital relations. In some places you can sue for it."

"They're just concerned about me."

"You're an adult. You made a decision to marry me. They have no business trying to second-guess your decision."

I was torn. James was right—I had made the decision to marry him. But my family was also right—I was paying our expenses. Although I wanted to believe James was working toward our financial stability, so far he was costing me money. A lot of money.

And here I was, a married woman, and I still couldn't get a date for a family wedding.

"James, will you please go with me?" I asked.

He was quiet for a few seconds.

"Donna, you know that I love you, and I want you to be happy," he said, in a conciliatory tone. "So I'll go with you to the church. But I won't go to the reception."

The day of the wedding, we prepared to drive up to the most northern part of the Jersey Shore—in two cars. I wore one of the cocktail dresses that had belonged to Gale Lewis. It was a fitted sheath of black wool knit with black and gold balloon sleeves. The dress was a bit warm for April, but it was dramatic enough for the sister of the groom, and it was free.

"Are you sure you won't stay for the reception?" I asked James.

"No. I'm going to sit in the back of the church, and when the ceremony is over, I'll leave."

I was doing a reading during the wedding ceremony, so I would be in one of the first pews.

"James, I need you to sit with me in the front. If you're not going to do that, you might as well stay home."

James did sit with me during the wedding. Then I went, alone, to the reception. It was a wonderful party. Greg and his new wife, Trish, were friendly with a rock band that played area clubs, and that's who they hired for the reception. Their friends were young, so there was a lot of group dancing that I could comfortably join without a partner. For a few of the ballroom-style songs, Dad came over and asked me to dance.

James came home all excited from a morning meeting on Monday, April 7, 1997. The Foxwoods casino in Ledyard, Connecticut needed themed construction materials, and an hour later he was flying there on a private plane—chartered by a local consultant—to check out the job. It was a real, live opportunity for the Polytechnique Group.

Foxwoods Resort Casino was building a $350 million hotel and conference center called the Grand Pequot Tower. Majestic columns were planned for a main concourse. James showed the consultant photos he had taken of the Wayne Manor library at the Warner Bros. theme park in Australia and said Polytechnique could make fake columns that looked exactly like marble. When he got to Foxwoods, James met with construction managers at the job site. Later that afternoon he called to say they gave him architectural drawings, which were spread out all over his hotel room.

A few days later James and I were in Sanford, Florida, near Orlando, discussing the job with the company that was already fabricating out of foam. They agreed to make some small column sections as samples to show different marble-look finishes that they could produce.

After our meeting, James was in a good mood. "Here we go, Nuffles," he said.

"Polytechnique is going to be a real company!"

When we returned to Atlantic City, the column samples arrived via Federal Express and we forwarded them to Foxwoods. If we were going to get an order, we had to establish Polytechnique as a business. The first step was to incorporate. Setting up a small corporation in New Jersey was no mystery—I'd done it before. All it took is filling out a form and buying a prepackaged corporate records kit from a legal supply company. But James insisted that he wanted everything to be "top-shelf," so he retained his lawyer to establish the corporation, who charged $600 to do what I could have done for free.

Atlantic City casinos were required to do a certain amount of business with women- and minority-owned firms, so being a woman-owned company would help us get work. I became the president of Polytechnique. The initial stock grants totaled 2000 shares—600 to James, 75 to Joe Nickles, 60 to Chic Attig, and 1,275 shares to me.

James was traveling again on April 17, 1997—he told me he had a meeting in Los Angeles with studio executives about his *First Casualty* script. The next morning he called to wake me up, as he always did when he was out of town. "I've been invited to fly to the Bahamas for the Nassau Film Festival," James told me. "They're honoring Australian filmmakers, and they're going to give me an award."

"No kidding!"

"Geoffrey Rush will be there—they want me to talk to him about *The First Casualty.*"

I knew of Geoffrey Rush—he was the Australian actor who had just won an Academy Award. I hoped that meant they were serious about James' script.

"That sounds great!" I said.

"I've got to go—I'm flying with them on a private jet. I'll call you tomorrow."

"Okay. I love you," I said to James.

"I love you more," he replied.

When James returned a few days later, he reported that the film festival was a joke. "Look at this stupid award they gave me," he said. "It looks like a bowling trophy!"

The award had a small marble base, a red and gold-tone column about eight inches tall, and a gold-tone laurel wreath on top. It did look like a bowling trophy, and a short one at that. I had nicer trophies from my softball days.

At least James liked the Queen Elizabeth II commemorative plate that he also received. "Everyone wanted the plates," James said, "but only a few of us got them."

"Did you talk to Geoffrey Rush?" I asked.

"Yes, although he hadn't yet seen the script," James answered. "So I gave him the basics of the story and how he could play it. I think he is interested."

The festival may have been a waste of time, but at least James had a chance to visit the Atlantis on Paradise Island. The resort and casino was heavily themed to look like an ancient nautical world that was lost in time. James shot three rolls of film—it was exactly the type of work that Polytechnique would do.

A few days after he returned, James showed me a fax he received from Ricardo Mestres, president of Hollywood Pictures, which was a division of Walt Disney Pictures. A Mickey Mouse logo was at the top of the fax.

To: James Montgomery
From: Ricardo Mestres
Date: Friday, April 25, 1997
Re: Our Thanks for Nassau

James,
　　Michael Eisner and Dick Cook asked me to thank you again for your help with the Film Festival in Nassau and I understand you have agreed to return in '98 as a presenter with your wife, Donna.
　　It looked as if you hit it off with your compatriot Geoffrey, as he certainly had some compliments for you when he flew back to LA with Michael. I am sorry that my people hadn't got a copy of First Casualty to him before your meeting. However, Jody said you did a great job of selling him and it was probably to our mutual advantage that he didn't read it cold.
　　Business Affairs has been given the tape of your conversation on production with Jody and Tim on Saturday morning. I do hope you can clear your desk to produce this. Michael felt that Geoffrey was hinting that it would be a precondition to his becoming attached. Your comments on directors were passed on to Dick Cook. I know they are still talking with Mel Gibson's agent.
　　Jody told me your summary page on production is due here by tonight and we are scheduled to discuss The First Casualty at our Tuesday pre-production-in-progress meeting. Geoffrey is going into post in Orlando for most of May and it may be possible to schedule a script conference with him, yourself, Jody and Tim in the next couple of weeks and get this on our production schedule. Michael asked for Nung's Mermaid on Friday, our Mr. Rush must have raised it!
　　I will be talking to you in the middle of next week.

Take Care Mate!
Ricardo

The letter gave me hope. James was being considered to produce *The First Casualty,* and Disney was also interested in his script called *Nung's Mermaid,* about a 12-year-old Vietnamese boat refugee trying to save an endangered manatee. This was really good news.

In the third Andersen wedding of the year, Dad married Pat Roberts on Saturday, May 3, 1997. The wedding took place at St. Francis of Assisi Church in

Vineland, and the reception was at a nearby country club. Tracy and I, along with Pat's two daughters, were bridesmaids. Luckily I didn't need a special gown—just a pastel dress, which I put on my Macy's credit card.

James did not attend either the ceremony or the reception. This time his excuse was the grand opening of the new Atlantic City Convention Center, scheduled for the same weekend. To make contacts that might be helpful for CelebAM and his other projects, James volunteered to help during the ribbon-cutting celebration. Three days of festivities for the general public were planned, culminating in a black-tie gala, which we could not afford to attend.

On Saturday afternoon, during my father's wedding, James was directing traffic in the Convention Center's new parking garage. When relatives I hadn't seen in a long time asked about my husband, I put on a brave face, explaining that James was helping out with the opening of the Convention Center because it was important for his future business plans. I didn't know if anyone believed me.

For his efforts, James received a ceremonial pair of gold-handled scissors at a thank you luncheon after the opening. I hoped that meant he had been noticed, and was another good omen for his projects. James put the scissors on display in our dining room, next to the bowling trophy.

For the first time in more than a year, and for the first time since I met James, I had a session with Elaine Anderson, my energy therapist, on May 8, 1997. I told her about my new husband. I met and quickly married a man 15 years older than me. (Even when he said he was 51, he lied. He was actually 55.) James' background was advertising, marketing and television, and now he was an entrepreneur with big ideas for theme parks and construction companies—but no deals. Our finances were a disaster; I was paying our household expenses, his business expenses and carrying far too much debt. I was severely stressed.

As always, Elaine listened quietly, without judgment.

James tried to reassure me, saying everything he was doing was for me. I told Elaine that James was confident his plans would work out—they were just taking longer than he anticipated, which he apologized for. He kept telling me that his efforts—and my support—would pay off, and eventually his dreams would come true and we'd have more money than we would know what to do with. But I was worried about how long it would take. I resented carrying the financial burden, and I was afraid of all the debt on my credit cards.

According to the Star+Gate cards, improvement would take time. The issue at the moment, the cards said, was "Aspiration," and my new focus was "Patience." The two cards indicating what lay ahead of me were "Hope" and "Lover." Elaine and I interpreted the cards to mean that realizing our dreams and aspirations would require patience. Patience was not one of my strong points.

So we worked to relieve my stress energetically. I lay on Elaine's massage table with the nine crystals arranged in a straight line below it. Elaine asked for Guidance to assist us, and before long, I felt fear. But it was not only my fear, it was the fear of my mother, who never knew economic security in her marriage.

My mother's contributions were critical to the family's finances—as soon as she got her paycheck every Friday, she spent it on groceries. Then I felt my own fear—the fear of repeating her experience.

I focused on releasing the fear and pain. As the negative energy dissipated, Elaine and I felt the presence of my husband. James had stayed with me during a difficult period of adjustment. He felt my fear, and although he wasn't supporting me financially, he tried to show support in other ways—through affection and our physical encounters.

In the past, I couldn't always feel the love that my family and friends felt for me. But that day, on Elaine's table, I felt my husband's love.

When I got home I told James that I had talked to Elaine about my fears. I also told him that I felt his energy and love. It must have struck a chord, because a few days later he wrote for me another romantic memoir of our honeymoon in Paris:

> Outside, a dark and drizzly day finishes in Atlantic City, but inside, it is a crisp January evening in Paris. I am walking under the plane trees by the Seine, just after a concert of classical music at a tiny, stony, centuries-old church I had serendipitously stumbled upon a few hours before. I am with my wife of a few days but I am not faithful, because I am drunkenly in love with the river, the trees, the party boats that spotlight the elegant facades that line the bank—I am in love with the city, and wherever I go, it is there.
>
> I walk down a tiny alley past galleries and antique shops and bookstores to a place I know, an eight-table restaurant with real sawdust on the floor and waxy wine bottles bearing candles on white paper tablecloths and the best sausages and French fries in town. There is real romance here, too. Lovers sit at the corner tables, their arms intertwined, staring deeply into each other's lives.
>
> I think of Baudelaire and Hemingway, of the blonde I married the week before with the heart-plucking laugh and the Cote d'Azur eyes. I sigh. "It is good," I write in my Toshiba, "to be alive."
>
> So many years, so many memories…Again the scene shifts, and now I am at Shakespeare and Company, talking with the irascible, irreplaceable George Whitman about Lawrence Ferlinghetti and Sylvia Beach and James Joyce, about the writers and pilgrims who still sweep through, looking for inspiration, camaraderie or just a cheap place to stay. I wander into one of the weekly salons, held up a cramped staircase in a book-lined, third-floor room, and listen to a wispy poet read his latest works to coal-eyed women and chain-smoking men.
>
> And I returned to the hell of the Paris of the Orient. It was 1968's Paris.
>
> What is it about Paris that I fell in love with, that so many people fall in love with? Partly it's the sheer beauty of the place, the quirky cobblestone neighborhoods and the grand boulevards lined by elegant immensi-

ties of symmetrical stone. Partly it's the rich history that seems still to infuse the air—the bells pealing from Notre Dame as they have for centuries, the medieval tapestries enlivening Musée de Cluny, the sacrifices commemorated at the Arc de Triomphe. Partly it's the omnipresence of art and culture—the museums and the theaters, the gardens and the galleries. And partly it's the bistros and the boutiques, the cafes and the theatrical life of the streets.

But it's something else, too, something ineffably romantic about the city: the way the light filters through the trees and reflects off the Seine; the way the leaves glisten on the pavement after a winter rain and the smell of them filling the metro stairway as you ascend to the street; the echo of a flute in an arch at the Louvre; the sudden swish of a child's sailboat at a fountain at the Tuileries; the way the city glimmers at night, a metropolitan Milky Way—oh, City of Light.

It is also where my Donna fell deeply in love and we were both 21 again.

Isn't this true of many cities? Well, somehow not.

There's something about Paris that makes people walk hand in hand and stop to kiss long and deep, and sigh, oblivious to all the people passing by.

Remember?

And so I take memory by the hand, walk a little way, and stop: The air is crackly crisp, a breeze rustles the plane leaves, the moon slivers and shimmers on the Seine. "Everything is possible," memory whispers in my ear. I close my eyes, and we are that young again.

May 13, 1997

I was amassing quite a collection of writings and cards that expressed my husband's affections. Frequently he made cards, for no particular occasion, from clip-art software, for "my dearest love, my greatest love."

Love, however, didn't pay the bills. To try and get some extra cash, we placed ads in the paper to sell James' 1977 MGB roadster. No one called. I also took my wedding dress to the consignment store. A few months earlier, I'd told James I was going to sell it. He got upset.

"That's Darwies' wedding dress," he said, plaintively. "Don't you want to keep it?"

"The wedding's over," I said. "What am I going to do with it?"

"It doesn't matter. It's a memory from our special day."

Well, the gown had been hanging in the storage unit since January. So this time, I didn't say anything to James. I just brought it to the store, hoping to turn it into a few hundred dollars.

At least I was still earning good money through my business, because the spending continued. James decided he wanted a bicycle. This was okay with me—maybe some exercise would help him lose weight. But along with the bike, which cost $270, he wanted a radio, bike computer, rack, seat bag, mirror and lock.

We also spent $100 on tickets to see the Broadway show *Cats* when it came to Atlantic City. Originally James said a friend from the Internet, who was involved with the production, would get us comp tickets. That didn't happen. But the friend did give James a *Cats* poster autographed by the entire cast, which he picked up the morning after the show. He gave it to me, and I hung it in my office.

About the same time James got a new handheld personal computer—the Philips Velo 1. It was small—7 inches long, 4 inches wide and 1 inch tall—with a flip-up grayscale display and a tiny keyboard. James didn't use it very much, but at least I didn't pay for it. James said he traded with a business associate, exchanging one of his small computers for the handheld model.

Given our dire financial situation, I still wondered why James was willing to part with his equity in the Mays Landing townhouse. He never really explained—he just seemed to be going along with anything the parents of his deceased wife wanted. They asked for the return of items we'd brought to our bay house—like the Le Creuset saucepans, the flatware serving pieces and the small painting of a dog and chicks. Then I drove by the townhouse and noticed that the custom drapes hanging in the long window above the staircase landing had been replaced by sheets. I told James about it; he said he'd look into it.

Shortly after that I learned that the townhouse had been emptied and sold. Everything—including the bedroom furniture that I wanted—was gone.

Ten wrapped boxes, all for James, were stacked on the dining room table the morning of June 15, 1997—Father's Day. Each box held one of our wedding pictures in a distinctive frame. I worked on the gift for weeks—ordering the pictures, selecting the frames, trimming the photos to fit the frames, wrapping all the boxes.

Sometimes James acted like a big kid, especially around "presies." That morning he made a fuss over each box, dramatically tearing off the paper, commenting about each photo—"Another beautiful picture of me and my Darwies"—then standing the framed photo up on the table.

After opening the presents, James took me in his arms. "Thank you for all the presies," he said.

"Happy Father's Day," I said to him. "I love you."

"I love you more," James replied.

We settled down to eat breakfast and read the Sunday paper. In honor of Father's Day, the Press of Atlantic City ran a special feature called *Father knows best—a tribute to dads on their day.* Earlier, the newspaper had invited readers to share their fathers' favorites expressions.

My dad had dozens of them, which we'd heard since we were children. At dinner, he'd tell us to "fill up on bread." If we were struggling to build something, he'd say, "Whaddya making, a piano?" If we were slow, he'd say, "Snooze and you lose." Then, just for effect, he'd say, "I'm never wrong. I thought I was wrong once, but I was mistaken." We called the sayings "Allanisms."

I sent a list of "Allanisms" to the newspaper. That morning I searched the

Press to see if any were printed, and they were. "Look, James," I said excitedly, showing him the article. "They printed a bunch of my dad's Allanisms!"

James looked at the story:

"Early to bed, early to rise, makes a man early."
"Pick up everything that's not green or nailed down."
"High blood pressure is better than no blood pressure."
"Quicker than the last Mass at a summer resort."
"A short pencil is better than a long memory."
"Do you think the rain will hurt the rhubarb? Not if it's in cans."

—Allan Andersen, Vineland, submitted by Donna Andersen, Atlantic City.

He finished reading and gave me a disapproving look. "What's the matter, don't you want people to know we are married?" he asked.

I was astounded. "What are you talking about?"

"You gave your name as Andersen, not Montgomery."

"My name *is* Andersen."

"Don't you think, if you're going to be in the newspaper, it would be a good idea to give your husband some publicity? Or do you want to keep the fact that we're married a secret?"

His criticism rattled me. On the one hand, I thought it was stupid. I wasn't trying to hide my marriage—I just gave him 10 framed wedding photos for Father's Day—and my name *was* Andersen. On the other hand, it never occurred to me to submit my name as "Montgomery," and I felt guilty. I resolved that the next time I was interviewed, I'd identify myself as "Donna Andersen Montgomery"—if nothing else, it would avoid another confrontation.

A week later, James and I showed up at the Viking Rowing Club in Ventnor, New Jersey, for the first day of the club's summer rowing season. Having given up my softball team—it didn't fit my new life—I thought rowing would be a great form of exercise that James and I could do together.

Rowing was one of the things I learned in college. During my first week as a freshman at Syracuse University, I went with the women's crew club to the college boathouse on Onondaga Lake, where they put me in a boat. I'd never seen anything like it. The boat, called a racing shell, was more than 50 feet long but less than two feet wide, made of lightweight wood. It had eight seats, one behind the other, with four oars on its port side and four on the starboard side. I became a port rower. I learned how to roll forward on the sliding seat to a crouched position, place the oar in the water and then push with my feet, so the seat rolled back as I pulled the oar. Each pull was called a stroke, and every time we went out on the lake, we took a lot of strokes.

I stayed with the sport and got into the best physical condition of my life. The club trained all winter—it was because of rowing that I started running and lifting weights in the gym. We got back on the water in the spring, and by the end of the school year I rowed my first race. We came in second, but I didn't care—I was thrilled about actually doing what we'd practiced for so long. The following year I again joined crew, improving my skills and stamina. But as a college junior, I dropped the sport to work on the Daily Orange, the university newspaper, which I thought was more important for my future career.

At Sydney Boys High School, James was part of a four-man crew—a boat with four oars and a coxswain. A photo of him in the boat was one of many on display in his office. James told me his crew rowed "Canadian style" and was almost unbeatable. Before his crew's last championship race, James envisioned winning and the honors he would receive. But during the race one of his teammates "caught a crab," which meant his oar got stuck in the water, causing the boat to slow down, and they lost. Although that race was a disappointment, James said he continued to row and participated in the 1964 Olympics in Mexico.

Thirty years later, however, James did not look like an Olympian. On that slightly overcast morning, we stood outside the Viking Rowing Club's metal boathouse in a circle with the other members. They were all around the same ages as James and me, but everyone else was in good physical condition. Only my husband had an XXL-sized gut. Perhaps James saw this and felt that the exploits of his past weren't enough to impress the athletes of the present, because he did not row. In fact, James left and returned to pick me up later.

The coach assigned me to a boat. It was the first time I'd been in a racing eight in 20 years, but rowing was like riding a bike—I hadn't forgotten how to do it. I knew how to hold the oar. I knew how to roll slowly up the slide to a crouched position, drop my oar into the water and pull—in unison with the rowers in front of me. I was excited to be on the water again. My body, however, protested. When I got home after an hour of rowing, I could barely move.

The following weekend James volunteered to be a coach. I went out in a four while he followed in a small launch with an outboard motor. Using his watch, James timed our stroke rate. But the next time James came to coach, he drove the launch a few feet from shore and the motor conked out. Sitting in an eight, I could see him angrily struggling to start it. In the meantime, another club member in a single scull—a one-person boat—came over to coach us, and my eight rowed away. Berating the "clowns" in the rowing club, James never coached again.

I, however, continued rowing. Every Saturday and Sunday morning, and Wednesday evening, the coaches assembled crews from whoever showed up. I also made a few friends for early-morning rowing during the week—I liked being out on the bay while the day was young and quiet. My body got accustomed to the movement, and I started to lose fat and build muscle. Perhaps most important, rowing required a lot of concentration—so it took my mind off of my problems, at least for a little while.

James studied the newspaper travel section on Sunday, June 29, 1997, as we ate lunch in the dining room. "I think we should get away together," he said.

"That's a nice idea," I replied, "but we can't afford it."

"Sure we can," he said. "Look at all these package deals. If we go to the islands, it's the off-season, and it's really cheap." James pushed the newspaper in front of me, open to travel agency ads. They offered airfare plus three to five nights of accommodations for less than $1,000 per person.

Maybe a getaway would be good for us.

"I like Bermuda," I said. "Once I stayed at a place with an efficiency kitchen. Maybe if we get a place with a kitchen, we can save money on food."

James was hot on the idea, and within an hour, we were at the travel agency in the mall. I told the agent I wanted a place with an efficiency kitchen. She told us about several hotels in Bermuda. One was the Palmetto Bay Hotel, located on Harrington Sound. "They have cottages with views of the sound," she said. "You can go snorkeling there."

"That sounds good," I said. "I like snorkeling."

The dates that we wanted at the end of July were available. Airfare and four nights of accommodations totaled $1,700.

"Done," James said.

Time elapsed from James' initial suggestion to a confirmed trip to Bermuda: two hours.

Polytechnique did not get the job of producing decorative columns for the Foxwoods casino. But Caesars, one of my newsletter clients, was planning a major renovation that would give the casino a distinctly Roman theme, like Caesars Palace in Las Vegas. One day while I was at the casino to do interviews, I saw samples of various styles of faux stone blocks spread on the floor outside the contractor's office.

"What is this?" I asked a man who happened to be there.

"Architectural samples that we're looking at for the renovation," he replied.

I was smart enough to recognize a business opportunity when I stepped on it. "I'm part of a company that produces these types of materials," I said to the man. "Is there someone we could see about supplying them?"

"Sure," he replied, and told me whom to call.

I called and sent faxes for several weeks before securing an appointment for James and me on July 3, 1997. The construction manager described the scope of the project. It was big.

When the casino first opened in Atlantic City back in 1979, it was called Caesars Boardwalk Regency. The décor, although pleasant, was nondescript. With this extensive renovation, Caesars would finally take advantage of its thematic heritage and become a microcosm of Roman architecture. Replicas of classic statues would be strategically displayed; columns in the casino would appear to be carved from stone.

The construction manager provided us with a fat roll of architectural drawings showing the themed materials that were required. He also provided an itemized list: 1,499 lineal feet of base molding, 8,336 lineal feet of crown molding,

678 lineal feet of cornice molding, 1,060 square feet of wall panels, and 1,657 other pieces—capitals, columns, posts, keystones, medallions.

I was worried. This was a massive project for Polytechnique, a company that didn't really exist. I certainly had no experience with this type of work, and neither did my husband. But James had no qualms about pursuing it. He figured that we'd just sub the job out to the factory in Florida, mark up the cost and make a lot of money. He signed the required documents given to us by the construction manager without reading them—I was appalled. He'd already signed a contract with the local ironworkers union to install the products, despite the fact that this type of work was generally done by carpenters, and unions were generally protective of their turf. When I asked why he did this, since it would cause problems if Polytechnique actually got going, James replied, "The best defense is a good offense." It was a line I was to hear many times.

A few days after the meeting at Caesars, James sent me, alone, to the Florida factory. I was supposed to go over the drawings with the fabricators so they could quote the job. But they took one look at the plans and said the job was too big for them. It was a wasted trip.

When I returned to New Jersey the next day, James had a new plan. While at a trade show the previous year, he met another fabricator located in Rhode Island called Symmetry Products. He called Symmetry about the Caesars job, and they agreed to quote it.

Before sending the drawings to Symmetry, I spread them out on our dining room table. I found where all the elements were required and double-checked the count provided by the contractor—noticing discrepancies.

"Look at this, James," I said, pointing to a specific location on a drawing. "They've got this listed as 48 feet of molding, but I only see 35 feet."

James looked at where I was pointing, but didn't say anything. I turned the page to another drawing. "And over here they're saying we need 1,584 feet of crown molding," I continued, "but I only see 1,048 feet. They're off by 500 feet. What do you think we should do?"

"We'll let the factory figure it out."

"Don't you think we should verify the quantities?"

"Here's what I want you to do. Just tell me how much material is needed along each wall."

"What?"

"Just give me the length of each wall. When we get the price from Symmetry, we'll just quote it as a fee per foot."

"James, that makes no sense. You can't quote the job that way. You have to count up all the elements and figure out exactly how much of everything you need to make. The length of the walls has nothing to do with it. What about all the columns in the middle of the room?"

"What I want is the length of the walls," James insisted.

Suddenly I realized why James didn't comment when I pointed out problems on the drawings, and why he was making such an idiotic request for the total length of the walls. James couldn't read the blueprints.

July 14, 1997 arrived—James' birthday. It would have been nice to buy my husband an expensive new watch for his collection, but I couldn't afford it. So I went to Burger King. Anyone who bought a Burger King meal could also buy a watch based on one of the big movies of the summer, *The Lost World: Jurassic Park*. I got the Dino Eye version, which had a plastic band that looked like dinosaur skin and an orange glint to the watch face. It might not be the Patek Philippe that James wanted, but it was a clever novelty.

I got the idea from James. When he went away on a business trip, he usually returned with a gift for me, like a t-shirt. But after one trip, he came up to my office with his hands behind his back.

"You know I'm always thinking of my Mouse," he said, rocking back and forth on his heels. "I wish I could always buy you nice presies, but I can't yet, so I got you this." James opened his hand, in which he had an unopened, 2.25-ounce bottle of Heinz ketchup that came with his hotel breakfast. "It's to remind you that your husband loves you, and one day he'll get you real presies." I set the ketchup bottle in a place of honor on my computer, where it was always in view as I worked.

We had an intimate celebration for James' birthday. The next day, however, was bill paying day. Regardless of the message of the ketchup bottle, as I opened the bills, I became more and more upset. The emotion was more than I could contain. I strode down to James' office with a fistful of bills. He was sitting behind his desk, leaning back in his executive chair, talking on the phone. I stood there watching him while he finished his conversation. He hung up and looked at me expectantly.

"James, our phone bills for last month added up to $900."

"So?"

"Well James, that's a lot of money."

"It's a necessary expense."

"The auto insurance company just raised our rate by $800—because of your speeding ticket."

"I don't have a speeding ticket."

"It's listed right here on the bill."

"I am an expert driver," James insisted. "I don't have a speeding ticket."

His denial astounded me. "James, I am really tired of the bullshit. When are you going to bring in some money?"

"You know how hard I'm working," he said.

"No, I don't, James. I know that you run up the phone bills. I know that you're always ready to jump on an airplane. I don't know if you're working."

"Look at the conditions I have to deal with," he countered, waving his arm to encompass his office. "I'm down here in a dark cellar trying to get several multimillion dollar businesses going. This is disgraceful. But I keep going. I don't complain. So I don't know why you're upset. Nothing has changed."

"I'm upset because our financial situation is terrible," I said, my voice rising. "We are more than $37,000 in debt."

"We are $37,000 in debt today, we were $37,000 in debt yesterday. What's the difference?"

"The difference is I don't see any improvement and I'm getting tired of it."

"What about Polytechnique? We just met with Caesars and have an opportunity to bid the job."

"Yeah—our non-existent company, depending on a supplier that I don't know."

"I know them. You don't need to know them."

"Why not? I'm the president of the company."

"That's only a title and you know it. You're not responsible for the business. I am."

"Well, the reason we have the Caesars opportunity is because I found it. I followed up and I got the appointment. And I'm the one studying the drawings."

"I don't know why you're wasting your time with that. It's the fabricator's job."

"And what happens if the fabricator has questions? Or the client has questions?"

"You don't need to worry about that."

"Well, since there's nothing for me to do, how about if I resign?"

"Do what you want."

I stared at James, unable to comprehend his cavalier attitude. I turned and left. Somehow, I went back to my office and wrote the checks to pay the bills. Nothing had been resolved, and I felt more stressed than ever.

I'd recently recorded my feelings in my journal, writing to James what I was afraid to say in person:

> Who do you think you are—running around pursuing your grandiose dreams while I'm stuck with my nose to the grindstone, paying the rent? I am so angry. I hate it. I hate you for making me work so hard. I am tired of carrying the burden. I want to work less, not more. I really don't give a shit about your dreams. I just want the pressure off of me. I want to take days off. I want to coast. I want to relax. I don't want to have to work so hard. I really hate it.

That evening, I lay on the floor in the spare bedroom, my meditation room, in the dark. I wanted to calm down, get centered and ask for spiritual assistance. What should I do about Polytechnique? Should I seriously quit the company? Should I put my decision into writing?

I heard a message from Guidance:

> *Be patient—things are coming to a head—yes, it has been long, but you chose the experience—you did need to learn to think of someone else, give to someone else. All your ideas of helping men were manipulative—this is the real thing. And now you don't want it? You feel betrayed—yes, he did lead you on, but in his mind it was the truth. He was presenting the truth of his past experience—he did not know that the next experience would be the*

opposite. It was a lesson for him as well. He, too, is not accustomed to considering someone else in his plans. A lesson for you both.

It will soon get better, but still it will take time. Another year of financial recovery.

This was not a message that I wanted to hear.

James walked by, on his way to the bathroom. "What are you doing?" he asked.

"I'm trying to calm down."

"Yeah," he replied. "I think it's the beginning of the end."

After predicting the imminent end of our marriage, James behaved as if the words were never spoken and everything was fine. He took out the trash as always, feigning pride in being the garbage collector. He brought in the mail, as he did every day. He joked about being relegated to eating low-cost, generic cereal. He wanted to go to the movies.

A small theater was located less than five minutes away from us in Ventnor. *Men in Black* was another hit movie of the summer, and on a Sunday afternoon, we went to see it. As we were leaving our house, I noticed that James had left his new bicycle in the side yard, easily visible from the street. I got a quick intuitive flash to move the bike, but did nothing.

Men in Black, starring Tommy Lee Jones and Will Smith, was billed as a "science fiction comedy action film," and it was. The script was original, the dialog was clever, the special effects were convincing and there was even a profound message at the end. We both enjoyed it thoroughly. "*Men in Black* is a totally new direction in filmmaking," James enthused. "It's going to change the way movies are made."

When we arrived home after the 98-minute film, our gate was open and James' bike was gone.

"I knew it," I said. "I knew it was going to be stolen."

"Then why didn't you say something?" James asked.

I had no answer. We filed a police report, but not expecting to recover the bike, James wanted to replace it immediately. So we bought exactly the same bike again, along with another radio, bike computer, rack, seat bag and mirror. This time James also wanted a tool kit. The store gave us 10 percent off because the original bike, less than two months old, had been stolen, but it still cost $449.

I resolved to listen to my intuition more closely, hoping it would guide me to make good decisions.

Our menagerie needed to be fed while we were in Bermuda. Dad was always happy to take Beau, and the day before we were to leave, I drove my dog to Dad's summer place outside of Sea Isle City, New Jersey. It was a mobile home in a resort park, but we called it by its less glamorous name—the trailer. Behind it was a forest of scrubby oak and pine trees. Beau liked the woods—it was full of tantalizing scents and critters. He also liked visiting Dad, where every meal meant tasty handouts for the dog.

I sat on the screened-in porch drinking a soda while Dad gave Beau the first of the handouts. Knowing that Dad had negative feelings about my husband, I tried to burnish James' image.

"Dad, did you know that James won the Victoria Cross? It's the Australian equivalent of the Congressional Medal of Honor."

My father continued to play with Beau. Without looking at me, he replied, "I don't think James was ever in the army."

I was shocked. Without a word, I set down my soda, got up and left.

Chapter 10

James and I arrived at the Palmetto Hotel and Cottages in Bermuda on a sunny summer day—July 28, 1997. It was a little bit of paradise. The hotel's main building was a two-story mansion, set back from the road and surrounded by a wide lawn, blooming gardens and tall palmetto trees. The mansion's limestone walls were painted a muted shade of rose, and the roof was bright white limestone slate. The cottages behind the main building, where we were staying, had the same look. When we walked into ours, however, we found that it was nothing more than a hotel room in a freestanding building. There was no sitting area and no efficiency kitchen.

I went back to the front desk and told the clerk that we requested a kitchen. She told me there weren't any.

The travel agent had not reserved what we wanted. But because James was in such a rush to book the trip, we didn't ask enough questions. "Done," he'd proclaimed, ending the discussion of the hotel options without clarifying what we were getting. So now, because we'd have to eat in restaurants, the trip was going to cost extra money.

Although I was aggravated about what our cottage lacked, I made myself enjoy what it offered—an exquisite waterfront location. Our patio overlooked Harrington Sound, an inland saltwater lake. Our stunning daytime view was of calm, turquoise water framed by distant hills and trees; at sunset it became a mirror of gold and pink, reflecting the colors of the sky.

A limestone bulkhead defined the rim of the sound, with steps leading into the water. Twice I went snorkeling in what felt like my own private lake. Carrying my mask and fins, I walked down the steps and 50 yards into the warm, shallow water. Then I put on my snorkel gear and swam over a small reef, where I spotted several varieties of tropical fish.

The snorkeling was much better at Church Bay, which we visited during our few days of tourism. Although the public beach was small and surrounded by rocky hills, underwater rocks and reefs were close to shore and attracted plenty of fish. I saw numerous big parrotfish—more than 12 inches long—in iridescent shades of blue, purple and aqua. They munched on algae growing on the rocks, oblivious to all the humans flopping clumsily in the water. James did not participate in the snorkeling—he sat at a table in the small concession stand, drinking a Diet Coke. He was content that I was enjoying myself. "My Mouse is having fun with the fishies," he said.

At the Hog Penny Restaurant in Hamilton, Bermuda's capital, James shocked me by ordering a beer. I'd never seen my husband drink a beer; the last time I saw him consume any alcohol was the champagne he sipped on our first night in Paris. In a way, I was glad to see him with a beer in his hand—I hoped it meant James would start to socialize like a regular guy.

I always got the impression that not drinking was one of the ways in which James proclaimed his superiority over mere mortals. He never relaxed and had fun with other people; he viewed all social engagements as potential business opportunities and worked the room, searching for someone who might be useful. Perhaps he calculated that the chances of finding a useful person in Bermuda were slim, so he might as well have a beer. In fact, during our one gourmet dinner of the trip at the upscale Fourways Inn, he even drank a glass of wine.

The inn wasn't far from where we were staying—nothing was far in Bermuda. Still, it was tough to get around without a vehicle, and tourists were not allowed to rent cars. Visitors could, however, rent motor scooters, which James did on Wednesday. I'd never been on a scooter, but James knew how to drive one, and it certainly beat waiting for taxis and buses. I nervously climbed onto the scooter behind him, and we zipped along the hilly, winding roads to Bermuda's other town, St. George, which was founded in 1612 and still looked like an old British colony. We ate lunch in a pub and looked around the shops. I bought a delicate scarf—more like a shawl—of airy cashmere lace; with its soft texture and open weave, it felt like a warm, snuggly snowflake. The scarf was my only purchase in Bermuda.

James, however, had a new credit card and acted like he received a windfall of cash. He had been pestering me for months, wanting me to make him an authorized user on one of my credit cards. He kept saying he needed access to a credit card when he traveled, which was true. But I knew he'd spend money and I'd be responsible for the bills. I finally got tired of saying no, and added him to the Bank of Boston Visa account. His card arrived in the mail just before we left for vacation. In Bermuda, James whipped the card out at galleries and gift shops, buying pretty things that we didn't need and couldn't afford. I watched in dismay, vainly hoping he'd show some restraint.

Luckily, most stores were closed because of public holidays on July 31 and August 1, 1997. The entire island of Bermuda shut down for two days of cricket called the Cup Match, which was contested between the rival cricket clubs of Somerset and St. George. James wanted to see the match, so we got on the scooter and headed back to St. George. Cricket had a long history in Bermuda and was the second most-popular sport in the world, but I'd never seen it. I soon figured out why it didn't play well with American audiences—the game was slow and boring; a match could take several days to complete. After an hour, I'd seen enough.

The second day of the Cup Match was the last day of our Bermuda vacation.

All the stores were still closed, but James wanted a pair of Bermuda shorts and knee socks. Concerned about spending more money—and making our flight—I tried to talk him out of it, but James adamantly insisted that he had to have the shorts. The only possible place that a store might be open was in Hamilton, the capital of Bermuda, so that's where we went. In the luxury Princess Hotel, a bored clerk stood behind the cash register in the English Sports Shop, and we were the only customers. James spent $55 on a pair of shorts and knee socks. Finally, he was happy.

James also wanted a new laptop computer. He still used the machine that he had brought over from the Mays Landing townhouse. I didn't know how long he owned it, but he said it was old and slow.

My personal philosophy was to keep computers as long as possible; by the time I traded up, they were practically antique. James, however, considered himself a computer expert, and said he needed to be working with the latest technology. Buying a new computer meant putting another $2,000 on a credit card, which I was not anxious to do. But every time I said no, he'd wait awhile and then bring up the discussion again.

I was severely stressed about our finances. James still wasn't making any money and was ripping through everything I earned. The debt remained high. One day we were both in the backyard when the topic came up. It quickly set me off.

"Our financial problems are your fault," I yelled at James. "You're the one spending all the money!"

"Listen to you," he retorted. "You're screaming like a fishmonger. The neighbors don't need to hear our business."

"I don't care what the neighbors hear," I yelled back. "If it weren't for you, I'd have plenty of money."

"So do you want me to leave?"

"I want you to make some money."

"That's not what I asked you. Do you want me to leave? Answer yes or no."

"James ..."

"Yes or no?"

"James, that's not fair."

"Yes or no?"

I felt like I was cornered. "No James, I just want ..."

"Then stop criticizing me." He turned and stomped into the house.

But our financial problems ate away at me. I kept asking for spiritual guidance on what to do. Every time, the answer I received was, "Don't worry. Everything will be fine. Love and support your husband."

So I gave James the credit card. I started paying for his health insurance, switching my coverage from single to husband and wife. I even started writing him a check for $125 three times a month, every time I paid bills. I thought it would be better for his self-esteem to just provide him with a regular stream of money, rather than make him ask me for it.

On August 13, 1997, James came up to my office with a computer catalog promoting a special deal on a Toshiba Tecra laptop. "Look, Nuffles," he said. "Here's the computer that I want, and they're giving away an additional 16 megs of free memory and free installation."

He put the catalog in front of me. I looked at the pictures, but couldn't focus on anything.

"Do you really need this, James?"

"Yes, I do, especially when I travel. I'm having trouble getting on the Internet with my old one."

I sighed. "All right."

"Thank you, Donna," James said quietly, "Thank you for having faith in me."

It wasn't faith that I felt, it was resignation—I was in so deep that the only thing to do was to keep going, hoping something would work out.

Maybe Polytechnique would be awarded the Caesars job. We'd submitted a quote for around $3 million. James got a bid from the factory in Rhode Island and marked it up 16 percent, which meant there was more than $400,000 in the quote for us.

"That would be great if it comes through," I said, hopefully.

"It would be like winning the lottery," James replied.

I was puzzled by James' cryptic comment. Then I realized he thought Polytechnique had no chance of getting the job.

James wasn't earning any money, but my business was in overdrive. I had six casino newsletters to produce between September 1997 and the end of the year, including the holiday issue of the Caesars Premium Player. The design of the Caesars newsletter had been modified several times since I started the project in 1984, but at this point my client wanted a complete overhaul. I suggested a new, larger format, and provided a sample of the size. If Caesars liked the format, the next step would be to talk to them more fully about what they wanted and then develop comprehensive art for the newsletter's new look.

Instead, the purchasing department put the newsletter out to bid with all of Caesars' printing vendors, and asked everyone to submit design ideas.

Developing the design of a printed piece was the most difficult and time-consuming part of the job. It was what creative professionals were paid to do. Caesars essentially asked me to do that part of the job for free, with no direction on what they wanted, and with no assurance that I would get the business. This was called working on speculation. To advertising agencies with staff artists it could be an acceptable risk. But I did not have a staff artist—Sheryl Ginsburg handled my design work as a freelancer. I didn't have the cash to pay her to develop designs on speculation, and I was not comfortable asking her to work for free.

I was a wreck. I told James what was going on, and I blamed him for my predicament.

"You know, if I wasn't spending all my money on you, I could afford to pay Sheryl to do the comps," I practically yelled at him.

"Just ask her to do them on spec," he replied.

"Maybe you work that way, James, but I don't."

"So what do you want me to do?" he asked coldly.

"Stop spending so much money," I retorted. "You fly around the country and nothing happens. You run up the phone bills and nothing happens. You spent all that money buying an option on Central Pier and nothing happened."

"Well, at least I'm pursuing my passions. What are you doing?"

"I don't have any passions, James. I just want to pay the bills."

After days of obsessing on the newsletter problem, I decided to resign the account. I told Caesars that I was cutting back on my work schedule because I wanted to get pregnant. This was partially true—James and I were trying. But the real reason I dropped the account was because I was tired of carrying the financial burden alone. Maybe if my income dropped, James would get moving to bring in some money.

I told James what I was doing and why I was doing it.

He was quiet for a moment. Then he said, "All right, Nuffles. I'll set a deadline of the end of October. If none of the projects come through by then, I'll stop waiting and do something else."

In the sport of rowing, the cooler, crisper air of fall signaled the start of head racing season. Instead of a 1,000-meter sprint with four or five boats lined up next to each other, a head race was two to three miles long. Boats started one after the other and raced against the clock.

I'd never participated in a head race, but after rowing all summer, I wanted to try. The Viking Rowing Club planned to travel to the King's Head Regatta in King of Prussia, Pennsylvania, on September 28, 1997. I organized a group of eight women, plus a coxswain, to race in the club eights division.

James accompanied me to the regatta. He helped as we unloaded our boat from the trailer and attached the riggers. He also helped the eight of us hold the boat as we stood in line, waiting for our turn to launch. "It's nice that your husband is here," one of my teammates said. "My husband never attends anything that I'm involved in."

At the King's Head Regatta, the launching dock was at the finish line; once we got on the water, we had to row nearly three miles up the river to the start. I was in the stroke seat, which meant that I set the pace and everyone followed me. The closer we got to the starting line, the more my stomach did flipflops. Women's eights from clubs all over the region were there, waiting for the event to begin. Each boat had a number on the bow. We were supposed to enter a "chute," outlined by buoys in the water, in numerical order, and build toward racing speed as we approached the start. Approximately every 10 seconds, a boat crossed the starting line and the race was on.

We got in line and rowed into the chute. "Twenty meters to start," an official advised us through a megaphone as I quickened the stroke rate. "Ten meters to start. Viking, you're on the course."

Our coxswain called a power 10—10 hard strokes—then we settled into racing cadence. If our coxswain felt us starting to flag, she called another power 10 to get us going. Any energy boost had to come from our own adrenalin—only trees lined the river, not cheering throngs of people. But even with eight people in the boat, I discovered that a head race was a solitary endeavor. The battle was against myself.

Did I have the strength and stamina to continue?

Roll to the top of the slide. Drop the oar in the water. Push with the legs, then pull with the arms. Tap the oar out of the water. Do it again. And again. And again.

I looked at the coxswain sitting in front of me, without really seeing her. I consumed incredible amounts of oxygen, taking two deep, fast breaths with every stroke. My legs and arms burned.

"Keep going," I told myself. "Just keep going."

In 15 minutes that seemed like forever, the race was over.

We didn't win, but we finished with a reasonably respectable time, especially considering that several members of our crew were novice rowers. After the race, my muscles tightened and I coughed continuously—I had pushed my body hard and the rapid breathing irritated my lungs.

As we glided up to the dock, James helped us get our boat out of the water. "My Nuffles is the rowing Mouse," he said, with pride in his voice. With my wobbly legs and constant coughing, I was very glad that my husband was there to drive me home.

The day after the regatta, despite my still-sore legs, I drove to Rhode Island for a meeting at Symmetry Products, the manufacturer James had contacted about Polytechnique and the Caesars job. Part of the job had been awarded to a competitor, but part was still up for grabs.

I learned more about Symmetry's products and business, and found it all fascinating. I must be my father's daughter—I liked construction. I liked thinking in terms of three-dimensional products that could be seen and touched. Even though I now understood how ridiculous it was for James to imagine he could build a factory, I wondered about changing my career and pursuing this line of work. A huge opportunity for themed construction still beckoned in Atlantic City, and I was in the middle of it. Perhaps I could be a manufacturer's representative for Symmetry Products and earn a commission on sales.

Ten days later, on October 10, 1997, I was back in Rhode Island, but this time it wasn't for business. My brother, Doug, gave James and me a gift certificate for the Victorian Ladies Bed and Breakfast in Newport as a wedding present. We used it to celebrate the first anniversary of our Australian wedding. I hoped the trip would rekindle my faith in our marriage, which was shaky.

After the 200-mile drive to Rhode Island, we didn't want to get back in the car to find a restaurant, so we walked around our neighborhood. We stumbled upon a craft show, with vendors selling food and gift items. One vendor displayed jewelry made from prehistoric amber, and James encouraged me to buy a pair of dangling earrings. "They're for your collection," he said, having already given me several pieces of amber jewelry.

The next day, Saturday, we visited Hammersmith Farm, the summer home of young Jackie Kennedy. Because of the home's connection to President John Kennedy, James was reasonably interested in the tour. Afterwards we went to the Museum of Yachting in Fort Adams State Park—home of Courageous, the 12-meter yacht that twice won the America's Cup race. As we looked at the boats, photos and models, James told me stories of his own yachting exploits.

On Sunday, I wanted to see The Breakers, the grandest of Newport's "summer cottages." These were the homes in which the rich and famous of the late 19th-century Gilded Age spent their summers. "Cottage" was an obscene understatement. They were all huge and exquisitely decorated mansions. A line of people waited to get in. My husband didn't want to join it.

"James, the place is spectacular. I saw it the last time I was here."

"Then what's the point of seeing it again?"

"I think you'll like it. It's amazing to see how these rich people used to live. Besides, we're here, and the line is moving. If we go someplace else, we'll just have to wait in another line."

James relented and we took the tour. The Breakers, built by Cornelius Vanderbilt II and finished in 1895, was a 70-room Italian Renaissance palazzo. It looked like palaces I'd seen in Europe. In fact, some of the rooms were constructed in Europe, disassembled, shipped to Rhode Island, and then reassembled.

James and I agreed that we liked the billiards room best. The décor was rich—its walls were covered in gray-green marble—but the style was far less flamboyant than the other rooms.

"What do you think, James?" I asked. "Can we get a room as nice as this?"

"We'll get one," he assured me.

The end of October approached—the deadline James set for achieving some kind of success. Polytechnique was not awarded any of the work for the Caesars renovation. There was no movement on CelebAM, the television stations, or any of his other proposals. James kept saying he could pack up at any time and go back to Australia, where he would be able to make loads of money and have us living in the lap of luxury. I wanted James to honor the deadline, even if it meant moving to Australia.

When I prayed for guidance, however, I was told to let him keep trying:

> You are angry—this is not what you expected from marriage
> —you thought you would find security from your greatest fear—
> starvation. This is your opportunity to overcome, to learn faith
> and to heal—it will work out—it's not far now—don't let him leave.
> He needs your faith. It will work out in a big way—it may take
> longer than the deadline—don't let him leave.

James did start exploring other ways of making money. He knew of a Princeton company with specialized electronics technology that he thought had applications for slot machines. I arranged a meeting for James with one of my contacts, the head of the slot department at Caesars. In preparation for the meeting, James spent an hour or two reading about slot machines on the Internet. Then he announced, "I know the slot business."

I'd been writing about slots for 13 years—the machines, the regulations and the players. "There's a lot to it, James," I said. "The business is more complicated than it looks."

"It's not that difficult," he insisted. "I understand it."

It was classic James Montgomery—supreme confidence in his own intelligence. James went to the meeting at Caesars. Nothing came of it, except that he spent $125 in the casino's expensive men's fashion store.

Next James told me he found an organization of government contractors that met regularly in Toms River, which was about 45 minutes north of Atlantic City. With his military experience and marketing expertise, he thought he could help them market their services to the government. In fact, he came up with a name for the business: Strategic Advertising Command. I liked it. I thought the name was good and the business plan was practical—it was based on his experience rather than his grandiose dreams. I encouraged him to pursue marketing accounts with the government contractors, and he drove to Toms River for several more luncheons.

James was still involved with local military organizations as well. On October 22, 1997, he spent all day as a volunteer at Operation Stand Down, an effort to reach out to veterans who were homeless or in need of social services. He felt obligated to help his brothers who did not succeed in making the transition back into civilian society. "So many of them are dual diagnostics," he told me, which meant they had multiple problems, such as mental illness and drug addiction.

Veteran's Day arrived, and once again I accompanied James to the school in Somers Point, where he, along with the two other veterans, talked to the school children about the experience of military service. James also told me he was asked to give a presentation to the students of Pleasantville High School, an urban high school in the town next to Atlantic City. I had to get back to work, so I didn't attend.

"You should have come," James told me when he came home. "I think I really got through to the kids."

"What did you say?"

"I got up stage and said, 'Suppose I called you a bunch of niggers.' The kids all got quiet—I had their attention. Then I said, 'What am I doing to you? I am dehumanizing you. That's exactly what happens when soldiers are preparing to go into battle. Someone gets up and calls the enemy a bunch of gooks. Or chinks. Or krauts. The only way a soldier can kill the enemy is if the enemy is first dehumanized.'

"The kids got the point, and the teachers loved it," James said. "As I was leaving, one of them came running after me and said he wanted me to come back to talk to the school again next year."

James had a flair for showmanship—that was a fact. So I thought maybe he should just do what he did best—television. I arranged another meeting—this one with a friend who worked at a video production company in Philadelphia. I went along to introduce my husband.

Just as we started driving up the Atlantic City Expressway a car flew by us—and we weren't going slowly. James immediately stepped on the gas. He was, I had learned, prone to road rage.

I slid down as far as I could in the passenger seat as James caught up with the car and started gesturing wildly at the driver, waving his cell phone and saying he was calling the police.

"Jesus, James, just let it go," I said.

"That clown has no business driving like that."

"So what?"

"I take action," he retorted. "I'm not a doormat like you, Donna. I don't let everybody walk all over me."

The cruelty of his statement paralyzed me.

The rest of the ride, another hour, passed in silence. When we got to Philadelphia, I spoke to James just enough to tell him where to park. Once in the meeting, I acted like everything was fine. I had to.

James showed samples of the video work he produced—his "reel," as it's called in the business. One segment was an engaging clip of gospel singers in white robes—the camera kept moving and the music was uplifting. I always liked it, and my friend liked it too. He said if he heard of an opportunity for James, he'd be in touch.

James went to Florida again for 10 days in November. He had just spent four days in Florida during September—something about business at MacDill Air Force Base in Tampa. This time his plans were to spend the first part of the trip in Fort Lauderdale, and then go to Orlando for another amusement association convention.

Although I hated driving him to the airport—we always fought on the way—I began to look forward to his trips. I was glad to get him out of my house and out of my hair. When he was around, James wanted me to make appointments for him, or phone calls, or travel reservations. He expected me to cook dinner. He expected me to be available for sex, whether I was in the mood or not.

Yes, it was odd that his business travel always spilled into the weekend. It was also odd that many of his business meetings were extremely early in the morning—like 6 a.m. James explained that he had to be available when his business contacts were available, 24 hours a day, seven days a week. I didn't dwell on it. When he was away, I had peace.

In fact, when he got out of bed at 4 a.m., I started encouraging Beau to jump up on the bed with me. I felt more comfort with my dog next to me than my husband.

One morning I woke up early, before James brought me my orange juice, and went down to his office in the basement. He didn't hear me come down the steps. That's because his focus was elsewhere—he was leaning back in his desk chair, naked, eyes closed, masturbating.

James opened his eyes. I turned around and left.

A minute later, wearing his robe, James followed me up the steps to the kitchen. "You see the effect you have on me, Donna," he said. "I can't wait for you."

I did not reply. I also did not believe his morning stimulation had anything to do with me.

James wanted me to be up and operating a tape recorder at 6 a.m. He was going to be a guest on the *Hurley in the Morning* radio talk show on WFPG-AM, hosted by Harry Hurley. James would talk about the entertainment business, much like he did at the Movietime cable television channel almost 10 years earlier. He wanted the entire 15-minute segment recorded—it might help him market himself and his projects.

The interview went well. Relying on information he gleaned from trade websites, James talked about the latest movies, providing background on actors, directors and producers. He was never at a loss for words, and his Australian accent seemed to lend his voice extra authority. Most of Harry Hurley's show was about Atlantic City politics, so a segment on the entertainment business added welcome variety. Hurley invited my husband to be a regular guest, and James started doing a weekly 6 a.m. interview.

This was good, I thought. James was being positioned as an entertainment industry expert—maybe it would help him get work. Plus, there was a little side benefit—Hurley often had comp tickets to casino shows to give away, and sometimes he gave them to James. We started seeing popular entertainers for free.

Then my friend from the video production company in Philadelphia called about a project that might interest James. SmithKline Beecham, the pharmaceutical giant with offices in Philadelphia, was launching a new cholesterol-lowering drug, Baycol. It was expected to be a blockbuster, so the company didn't want to inform the sales reps by sending out a memo. SmithKline Beecham wanted to rally the troops with a high-powered three-day sales meeting in Washington, D.C., staged like a superstar show and choreographed to grab their attention, keep their interest and inspire them to sell, sell, sell.

SmithKline retained a consultant to manage the sales meeting, and the consultant was looking for Hollywood sizzle. I accompanied James to a meeting with the consultant. James immediately came up with an idea—he suggested that the sales meeting borrow the theme of a new movie that was generating a lot of buzz and would come out about the same time as the new drug: *Lost in Space.*

James quickly described how the show could be produced. He'd create a set that looked like a spaceship. Live actors would play key parts from the movie. A functioning robot would roll through the audience. Once the opening *Lost in Space* sequence grabbed the crowd's attention, Baycol would become the star of the show. The consultant liked the concept, as did his client at SmithKline

Beecham. To my surprise and relief, they hired James for the job.

Time was short—James was retained on December 8, 1997, and the sales meeting was slated for January 22 to 24, 1998. He immediately started planning the production, and asked my sister, Tracy, to help. James visited a set design studio, and came home raving about its work. He had several meetings with the consultant.

The consultant's office was in a western suburb of Philadelphia. Normally, the trip from Atlantic City took about 90 minutes. But during the crawling morning rush hour, travel time was unpredictable. So for his morning meetings, James thought it was better to go up the night before and stay at a motel. That way, he was assured of being on time.

Three times in eight days, on December 8, 11 and 15, 1997, James stayed at a Motel 6 in Norristown. He could not pay for the rooms with his new Bank of Boston credit card. Since I gave him the card at the end of July, he ran up $5,500 in charges, and the card was at its limit. For each stay, I had to fax written permission to the motel to charge his room to my American Express.

Every time I brought up the issue of his flagrant and careless spending, James angrily told me he knew what he was doing and I had nothing to worry about. "One day none of this will matter," he said. "So I don't know why you're getting upset."

Maybe he was right. The entertainment business seemed to be lucrative— James quoted a fee of $52,500 to produce the *Lost in Space* show for SmithKline Beecham. If this became the first of a continuing stream of projects—well, I wouldn't have to worry about his credit cards anymore.

James asked for one-third of his fee up front—a standard practice in creative fields. But how should we handle the money? James was already calling his company Strategic Advertising Command. I didn't want to establish yet another corporation, so I set up Strategic Advertising Command as a division of my existing business, Donna Andersen Copywriting, Inc. All I had to do was file an alternate name application with the state and open a bank account. The consultant paid James' initial retainer of $17,500, which I deposited in the new bank account.

Finally, James brought in some money.

He and Tracy met on December 11, 1997, at the Ruby Tuesday restaurant in the King of Prussia Mall. Then they worked "flat to the boards," as James would say, to get the show moving. James searched for a replica of the clunky *Lost in Space* robot—there weren't any; it would have to be built. He wanted to find a look-alike for the evil Dr. Smith—another tough order. Tracy called around to costume shops looking for 1960s-era astronaut outfits—silver lame jumpsuits were also hard to find. The *Lost in Space* concept was proving difficult to implement.

So James switched gears. He decided to get footage from the original TV show and use blue-screen technology to put new heads speaking new lines on the bodies of the old actors—like when I was spliced onto a precarious building ledge at the Warner Bros. Studio in Australia. Some of this would be done live at the show, with Tracy and James operating the blue-screen equipment. In fact, to make the production seem bigger and more complicated than it actually was,

James told Tracy that he planned to bring extra computer equipment to the sales meeting. James laid out $847 for a digital camera and color printer. The equipment wasn't actually necessary, but it would help him justify his fee.

Then everything stopped. A SmithKline Beecham executive who was higher up the food chain did not like the *Lost in Space* idea and killed it. James was no longer on the project. The consultant asked for his retainer to be returned.

"I'm not giving any money back," James said to me. "I told him the money was spent. The robot was already being manufactured."

Under other circumstances, I would have argued for James to give back the retainer. It would help him build a good relationship with his client, and it was the right thing to do. But I was desperate for financial relief. I said nothing.

For a few days, the prospect of James earning $52,500 was real. Then it was gone.

For a few days, I thought there would be an end to the financial turmoil. I remembered some of our many fights about money. One morning, as James stood naked in the kitchen—I didn't try to figure out why he was naked—I launched into a tirade about our debts. He yelled back. "Fuck-all, Donna. What makes you think you have the right to talk to me like that?"

Another time I was so frustrated that I flung a $700 check on his desk—it was the entire balance of my business checking account. "Here, this is all of it," I yelled. "Take everything I've got. Then there will be nothing left."

"Don't be stupid, Donna," James said dismissively, ignoring the check.

For a few days, I felt a glimmer of hope that our situation would finally turn around. Then James lost the *Lost in Space* job. The hope was gone.

Emotionally, I reeled from the blow.

Fear consumed me. Fear that James would never succeed. Fear that I'd made a huge mistake. Fear that I would lose everything. My stomach churned and tension grabbed my chest. Breathing was difficult. My hands trembled.

But I couldn't stop. I still had work to do and errands to run. One of them was getting my car inspected. New Jersey law demanded that every vehicle be inspected annually, and I was several months late. As I drove to the Motor Vehicle Inspection Station in Mays Landing—right around the corner from where James used to live—I imagined being pulled over by a cop for having an expired inspection sticker. I'd explain that I was on my way, at that very moment, to the inspection station.

And then it happened.

As I drove down Route 40, less than a mile from the inspection station, I looked in my rear-view mirror and saw flashing lights. A cop was behind me, signaling for me to pull over.

I stopped and lowered the window. The officer got out of his patrol car and walked up beside me. "License and registration," he said.

I handed him the documents.

"Your inspection sticker is expired," he said.

"I know," I answered. "I'm on my way to get the car inspected right now."

"Do you know how often I hear that?" the cop asked.

He walked back to his car, checked my records and wrote me a ticket.

Somehow, I drove on and got in line for the car inspection. Luckily, there weren't many vehicles ahead of me, because I barely maintained my composure. The ongoing financial stress was crushing me. And now a ticket. It was an expensive one too—$122.

The inspection completed, I drove home. As I neared Atlantic City, I could contain my emotions no longer. Right in the car, I started crying violently. I yelled and pounded the steering wheel. While stopped at a traffic light on the Albany Avenue Bridge near my house, I was wracked with pain, and the tears ran down my face. I saw the passenger side door of the car in front of me open. A young woman got out and walked around to my car.

"Are you okay?" she asked me.

Still crying, I tried to nod. "Thank you," I choked.

She gave me a troubled look and got back into her car. The light turned green. I kept going.

James continued his 6 a.m. appearances on the *Hurley in the Morning* show, and continued talking about the movie business. One of the most anticipated films of the year was *Titanic*, which debuted in the United States on December 19, 1997. In a radio show shortly after its release, James told the audience his opinion of *Titanic*, even though he had yet to see the movie.

Our screening of the film was postponed by the Christmas holidays. We hosted a small dinner party shortly before Christmas, inviting John and Jane Davis, whom I'd known for about three years, and Chic Attig and his wife. Chic was the joke-cracking best man at our wedding in January.

I planned to serve stuffed Cornish hens—it was an elegant meal that could be prepared in advance. After wine and hors d'oeuvres in the living room, the six of us took our seats for dinner, with James in his customary chair at the head of the table. He took the opportunity to wax lengthily and eloquently about various topics of interest—only to himself. He delivered a non-stop monologue, as if he were on the radio talking to an unseen audience. No one else said a word.

For Christmas, I gave James a bit of his homeland—a big jar of Vegemite, that spreadable brown concoction loaded with B vitamins, which I ordered from an Australian catalog. The rest of the gifts I bought for him were sensible and practical, like a shirt and socks. Several of the gifts James bought for me seemed to be for himself. He bought a model train set and track. He bought a new toilet seat for the downstairs bathroom, of which he was the primary user. He also bought an exotic pet—another animal I'd never seen before—a chinchilla. James named him Chuckie.

"One of the things I love about America is that you can have all these interesting pets," James said. "In Australia, most exotic pets are illegal."

I had to admit the chinchilla was cute. Chuckie looked like a small rabbit with a long, fluffy tail. He was full-grown, but weighed only a pound. The chinchilla's fur was exceptionally soft—it felt like a cotton ball—and was gray on top, white on his belly. There was no fur on his ears—they were big and skin-pink with gray spots. Chuckie's ears were exceptionally expressive—they stood upright when he was interested in something, but lay flat against his head when he was sleeping.

Chinchillas were native to the high Andes Mountains of South America, but at our house Chuckie lived in yet another cage in James' office. So now there were four animals keeping my husband company—Chuckie the chinchilla, Herbie the pygmy hedgehog, and the two sugar gliders, Donald and Jamie. Even though James sat with them all day, it was still my responsibility to care for them.

The sugar gliders had a tray of birdseed hanging inside their cage, and each night I shelled a few peanuts for them and made up a small bowl of Gliderade. Once I accidentally left a door to their cage open, and the gliders escaped. They had a big night out, exploring the unending array of stuff on James' tables and shelves. In the morning, he found them curled up, asleep, among his baseball caps.

I bought Herbie a new wire cage—I thought the aquarium was too small and poorly ventilated. When I first put Herbie in his new home, he looked around with interest—he seemed to like it. Herbie ate cat food—I gave him one-third of a can every night. He was also litter-trained. I put a small tray of kitty litter in his cage, and he used it.

Chuckie was easy to feed—he ate little brown pellets of chinchilla food—available at the pet store—and alfalfa grass. The only other thing he needed was a dust bath a few times a week. I put fine, gray chinchilla bath powder, also purchased from the pet store, into a cardboard box. Chuckie learned to come out of his cage and go into the box, where he rolled around in the dust.

I took care of the pets every night, but I didn't know how to interact with them. The gliders sometimes sat on my hand if I stuck it in their cage. Other times, they bit me. Mostly, the pets were trapped in their cages. I hoped they were happy, but I didn't know.

On the day after Christmas, James and I sat at the dining room table. I had requested a "board meeting." I wanted us to come up with a plan for getting out of our financial hole.

I prepared an agenda, with easy items first on the list. Did he need to return the shirt I got him for Christmas? Did he want to make plans to get together with Joe Nickles and his wife? James' answers were yes and yes.

Next on the agenda was Polytechnique. Although James' idea of building a factory was ludicrous, there was certainly a market for themed construction in Atlantic City—perhaps we could cash in by being a sales organization for a company that was already in the business, such as Symmetry Products in Rhode Island. I was interested in pursuing it—especially since it looked like I was going to lose one or two more newsletters. Just before Christmas, a big casino merger was announced—Harrah's Entertainment bought Showboat. My Learning Network newsletter would certainly bite the dust, and perhaps the Crew's News as well.

"I've got the marketing skills to do it, but I'd need to learn more about the construction field," I said to James. "Perhaps I can find some classes."

"If you want to do that, Donna, go ahead," James said. He obviously had lost interest in the entire venture.

Finally, we moved on to our financial discussion. "I think we have three financial objectives," I said. "Pay our current expenses, get out of debt and avoid tax problems."

"All of those issues will be resolved once one of the theme parks is funded," James said. "There's no real point in discussing them now."

"Well, I think we should discuss them now. For example, how should I record the money I'm giving you on the books? Is it a loan or a fee? And which of your expenses are business and which are personal? It will be a lot easier to deal with all of this later if we set it up right."

"When one of the parks is funded, we'll just pay an accountant to figure it out," James said. "I've been giving more thought to Century Park. Bader Field won't be ready for development for several more years. But there is land next to the Atlantic City Expressway that would make a great location for it."

"That's still a long way off, James. I'm concerned about how we survive between now and then. We're carrying over $40,000 in credit card debt, and your card is maxed out ..."

"Just pay the minimum balance. That's all you have to do."

This was going nowhere. James had agreed to the meeting, I realized, just to placate me. He was not concerned about recordkeeping. He was not concerned about controlling expenses. His solution was to get someone to buy his ideas for a few million dollars, and all these other issues would disappear.

All I could do was pray he succeeded.

James wasn't home and I needed a phone number. He'd written it on a piece of paper—I was in his office and saw him do it. Now I needed to find the paper.

I looked through the piles on James' desk—it wasn't there. Maybe he put it in a drawer. I opened the narrow drawer above the desk's kneehole—nothing. I opened the desk's top right drawer—I didn't see the paper, but a pile of photos caught my eye.

Polaroid photos. Ten photos, of 10 different naked women.

I flipped through the photos without really looking at them. These were original photos, not copies. Who were these women? What did this mean? I was James' wife. What was I supposed to do?

When James came home, I confronted him in the kitchen.

"What did you do with the pictures?" he asked.

"I threw them in the trash," I said, gesturing toward the trash can.

James picked them out of the trash. "These are mine," he said. "You can't take them."

"Why do you have them?"

"They're from my past. They don't mean anything anymore. But if I have the pictures to look at, it helps me stay faithful to you."

Should I believe that? If these women were from the past, before we were married, it seemed that I shouldn't worry. But why would he keep the pictures? And how could I know they were from the past?

I turned away. The easiest thing to do was to believe him and let it go.

With all the holiday excitement, it took us a couple of weeks to see *Titanic*. By this time, the film, directed by James Cameron, was a phenomenon. It became a blockbuster hit on its opening weekend, with $29 million in ticket sales. On its second weekend in theaters, the movie made even more money—$35 million. Theaters sold out as young girls, indulging in the romantic fantasy—or lusting after Leonardo DiCaprio—saw the movie a dozen times.

James rode the Titanic wave for several radio appearances. Searching the Internet, he found societies of dedicated Titanic enthusiasts. These people knew the story from start to finish, knew all the important characters in the tragedy, and had theories about what happened. For a special one-hour show, James asked several of these Titanicphiles to call in from around the country and discuss exactly why the ship sank. Did the iceberg rip such a big gash in the hull that water flooded in? Did the rivets that fastened steel plates to the hull pop out so the superstructure failed? They debated the possibilities.

James went to Florida again and visited a Titanic exhibition at the Florida International Museum in St. Petersburg. The movie generated so much publicity that people flocked to the museum to learn more about the story and see real artifacts recovered from the ocean floor.

The Titanic story was all very interesting, but it wasn't making us any money. With no movement on CelebAM or his television shows, James pushed the Century Park idea. James envisioned an attraction with six virtual theaters—he called them time capsules—that would focus on specific time periods and topics of the last 100 years. "The Sports Capsule could open with the first 20 years of the NFL and change three months later to a century of ice hockey," he wrote in a one-page proposal. "The Entertainment Capsule could start with the Big Band Era and segue 90 days later to the Disco '70s ... and so on!" James also wanted Century Park to include a mini-zoo housing a dozen of the rarest animal species left on earth. And, he wanted to have a giant hot-air balloon in the park emblazoned with the logo of the New Jersey Devils, the local Air National Guard unit, "symbolizing flight at the start and the end of the Century."

The land where James wanted to build his park was located just outside of Atlantic City, in Pleasantville. Pleasantville was designated as an Urban Enterprise Zone (UEZ) by the state New Jersey, which meant the city had economic problems and incentives were available for developers who invested there. I knew the director of Pleasantville's UEZ program, and called him to arrange yet another meeting for us. I thought we were going for an exploratory meeting about Century Park, but when we got there, James not only explained his proposal, but asked for funding. The UEZ program, however, didn't give away money. It made loans and offered tax breaks, which, if James had done his homework, he would have known. I was embarrassed. Again.

James wasn't embarrassed at all; he just changed his approach. He faxed his proposal to a company called A. C. Gateway Associates, which actually owned the 150 acres where James wanted to build his park. A. C. Gateway Associates had its own plans for developing the land, and had already secured preliminary permits for multi-family housing, although that didn't stop James from telling them he had a better idea. But one day in the midst of his flurry of faxes to the owner, I drove by the site where he wanted the park. It was gone.

I called James from my cell phone.

"I'm driving on the Expressway by your land," I told him. "It's all under water."

"What do you mean?" he asked.

"The tide is really high, and there is no land. All I see is water."

By the time I got home, James had made calls and learned that developing the land would require dredging the adjacent bay, which would increase problems and costs significantly. That was the end of Century Park.

This failure seemed to affect James. Instead of his usual bravado, he actually appeared disheartened. "I don't know how many more times I can go to the well," he said.

"What well?" I asked.

"My internal well. My creativity. My source of ideas."

I'd never seen James look so forlorn. "Maybe these projects are too hard," I said. "Maybe you should consider something easier, like getting a job."

James didn't react to that suggestion. But at least one thing seemed to be going well for my husband—he received a military promotion. I stood with James in the living room as he excitedly opened an envelope that arrived in the mail. It contained two pins—silver stars. "I've been promoted to general," James told me.

"That's terrific," I said. "When did you find out?"

"I've known about it for awhile. They just got around to sending my paperwork and my stars."

"So you're a general?"

"Technically, I'm now on the general staff. Several of us got promoted. There's going to be a ceremony at MacDill in a couple of weeks. But I'm not going to go."

"Why not? Let's go. I could meet your friends."

James looked surprised for a moment. "Oh, you wouldn't like it," he quickly replied. "And you wouldn't like them. They can be fairly crude. Why don't we celebrate by going back to Paris instead?"

"Paris! We can't afford that."

"Sure we can," James said. "We can't stop living just because we have debts, Nuffles. It's important to take time for ourselves. And it won't cost much during the off season."

I sat down on the landing. After a few moments of searching for the words, I asked my husband, with pain in my voice, "How can you even think about a vacation when we're so broke?"

"You shouldn't worry," he said to console me. "I'll make something work."

"So you just want me to put my life in your hands and believe that everything will be okay?"

James gently took my hands, which were tightly folded in my lap. "Yes," he replied. "I do."

I debated with myself about the Paris trip for a few days. On the one hand, we were still seriously in debt. On the other hand, James had managed to bring in $17,000 and I had paid down some bills—maybe more was coming. I kept getting spiritual messages to trust him and believe in him. Maybe if I agreed to the vacation it would help. Emotionally, I did feel better after our trip to Bermuda—at least for a little while. Perhaps a nice getaway to Paris would be good for us. And if James wasn't worried about the money, why should I worry? "You're right, James," I finally said to him. "I shouldn't worry so much about the money. We'll go to Paris."

"It will be a nice trip," James promised. "We'll have time to ourselves in the most romantic city in the world."

Romance would be good. Our passion had cooled—which I assumed was normal for a marriage—but with the added stress of financial disarray, our relationship was in a rut. We seemed to have less and less to talk about at dinner. In fact, James increasingly wanted to eat in front of the television. I grew to detest the TV trays that Dad gave us for our first Christmas together. In fact, there were times that I absolutely refused to bring my dinner into the living room. On those occasions, James reluctantly sat at the dining room table with me. There still wasn't any conversation.

I felt off-balance. James continued to tell me that he loved me. In fact, when I said, "I love you" to him, he usually replied, "I love you more."

"Please don't say that, James," I finally asked. "It makes me feel like my love isn't good enough."

"But I do love you more," James said. "I love you more than I've ever loved anyone."

Even when we fought about money, James continued to tell me that he loved me, and everything he did was for me. So why didn't I feel it?

Perhaps the trip to Paris would rekindle the flame, and give me the emotional strength to persevere until our situation turned around.

Looming before us as we emerged from the metro tunnel was the famous Arc de Triomphe. It was early in the morning on February 26, 1998, as James and I arrived for our second visit to Paris.

This time we decided to stay in the ritzy neighborhood near the Champs-Élysées. We selected the Hotel Élysées Ceramic on Avenue de Wagram, a moderately priced, 57-room boutique hotel, built in 1904. But first, we had to find it. In an effort to conserve cash, I wanted to take the train from the airport to a stop near the hotel—it was supposed to be easy. The train ride wasn't bad, but dragging our luggage around was. And when we ascended from the depths of the underground station—well, the Arc de Triomphe is positioned in the middle of a traffic circle with 12 roads feeding into it. One of them—we didn't know which—was Avenue de Wagram.

Luckily, we found the street without delay, and it wasn't far to the hotel. We quickly learned why it was called "Ceramic:" sculpted ceramic art was affixed to the front of the building, like an appliqué on fabric. Twisting ceramic vines—fashioned to resemble ivy without leaves—crept from sculpted urns embedded in either side of the entry alcove to a second-floor window. The hotel was a fine example of art nouveau architecture, but our room was considerably smaller than the one we had for our Paris honeymoon. It contained a double bed, 18-inch wardrobe cabinets on either side of the bed, a small desk, a chair and a television. Nothing more.

After unpacking, I wanted breakfast. First, however, James wanted to make a phone call. Although he had given up on the Century Park idea, he was still pursuing one component of it—bringing a hot air balloon ride to Atlantic City. So the trip to Paris had a business purpose. He had contacted the operator of a balloon ride in Chantilly, France, located 25 miles north of Paris, who agreed to meet him. We were supposed to call him when we arrived, so that was first on his agenda.

The balloon operator spoke English, but when James called he got the answering machine, and the message was in French. He called again and asked me to listen to the message, but the words were spoken too quickly—I couldn't understand it. So I left a message, starting in French and then switching to English, telling James' contact to call us at the hotel.

James hoped for a return call, so he didn't want to stray far. We found a nearby restaurant for brunch and explored our neighborhood, making our way to the Avenue de Champs-Élysées. When we returned to the hotel, James did connect with the balloon operator and arranged for us to visit the next day.

Our trip to Chantilly, a region known for its lush forests and horse farms, took place on a cold, gray winter day. We could have traveled to Chantilly by public transportation, but James didn't want to get lost and be late, so we took an expensive taxi ride. Our destination was the Chateau de Chantilly, an estate that dated to the 16th century. The main building, the Grand Chateau, was rebuilt in the 1870s, after being destroyed during the French Revolution. It looked like a fairytale castle; it was even surrounded by a moat.

The bright yellow balloon was tethered to the ground a mile from the chateau, easy to spot as it towered above the leafless trees. James told me we'd go for a ride, but on that day, the balloon, which had a gondola that could carry 35 passengers, wasn't going anywhere. The season hadn't yet started—in fact, the balloon had just been inflated. So there in the cold, James had his meeting with the balloon operator. It didn't take very long. We bid *adieu*, and, after a quick tour of the chateau, returned to Paris in time for dinner.

Walking on Avenue de Wagram, away from the Arc de Triomphe, we turned a corner and James spied a restaurant that displayed sample dishes in the window. One of them was steak tartare.

"That's what I want," James said.

"Are you crazy?" I exclaimed. "Do you remember what happened the last time you ate uncooked meat in Paris?"

"People order steak tartare all the time. It will be fine."

We went to the restaurant for dinner and James got his steak tartare. That night he was sick—food poisoning again. He wasn't as ill as he was on our honeymoon, but the next morning, James was in no condition to do anything.

So once again, I went to the Louvre museum alone. This time, along with more artwork, I discovered the apartments of Napoleon III, who, from 1848 to 1870, was both the first president and the last emperor of France. The grand salon was a massive room of crimson and gold—crimson velvet fabric for the drapes, upholstery and wall covering, ornate gilt moldings defining the windows, pilasters and walls. Celestial murals decorated the ceiling. Several of Napoleon's rooms were open to the public—each more opulent than the one before.

"You should have seen these apartments," I said to James when I returned later in the day. "They made the Breakers in Rhode Island look like a dog house."

"So you enjoyed your visit to the museum?" James asked.

"Yes. There's a lot to see."

"I'm glad my Nuffles had a nice day."

James felt better the next day, so we went sightseeing, visiting places we hadn't seen on our honeymoon. We went to the Sacré-Coeur Basilica, the landmark Catholic church built on the summit of Montmartre, one of the highest points in Paris. That was the end of the sightseeing. In fact, with the excursion to Chantilly over, the trip felt like it was already winding down. We spent a lot of time in our hotel room, watching game shows on French television. I was astounded at how amateurish they were—even though I couldn't understand much of what was said, I saw people wearing stupid costumes doing stupid things. Eventually, we got sick of it, and turned off the TV to read.

I could have done that in Atlantic City.

On Monday, March 2, 1998, we went shopping in Paris department stores. On Tuesday, the last real day of our trip, I talked James into visiting the Cité des Sciences et de L'Industrie—the science and industry museum—in northern Paris. Emerging from the metro station, we rode an escalator up to the museum—it was an ultra-modern building dominated by a bright, silver Géode—one of the world's largest geodesic domes. The museum's marquee exhibit that day highlighted the ubiquity of computers, and was promoted by a nerdy looking character called "Cyberman."

For James, the best part of the museum was a complete surprise. On display in the main hall was the Nautile, a bright yellow mini-sub owned by Ifremer, the French Research Institute for Exploration of the Sea. In a very small cabin, it could carry a crew of three to a depth of 6,000 meters—3.7 miles. It had six floodlights, video and still cameras, and two mechanical arms that could recover items from the ocean floor. James wanted me to take plenty of pictures of him in front of the Nautile. Back in 1987, the tiny submersible recovered more than 1,500 artifacts in the first salvage of the Titanic wreck. He would soon put those photos to work in a big way.

Chapter 11

All over Paris, James and I saw movie marquees advertising the biggest block-buster of all time: *Titanic.* By March 6, 1998, just after we arrived home, *Titanic* became the first movie in history to earn more than $1 billion in worldwide theatrical ticket sales. The film's biggest weekend, with $36 million in sales, was Valentine's Day weekend, nearly two months after its initial release in the United States.

The James Cameron film was recognized as not only a commercial success, but an artistic one. Titanic was nominated for 14 Academy Awards, tying a record set in 1950. At the glittering Hollywood ceremony on March 23, 1998, *Titanic* won 11 of them, including Best Director and Best Picture. As Cameron took the stage to accept his Best Director award, he quoted the line that Jack Dawson, played by Leonardo DiCaprio, shouted from the bow of the majestic ship: "I'm the king of the world!"

Three days later, my husband and I were in New York City meeting with the man who first made the Titanic story famous—author and historian Walter Lord.

Walter Lord wrote *A Night To Remember,* a nonfiction account of Titanic's final hours as it sank on its maiden voyage. The tragedy occurred on April 15, 1912, and Lord's book was published in 1955. Lord found and interviewed more than 60 survivors, which enabled him to tell the story with incredible eyewitness detail. *A Night To Remember* quickly became a best seller, and in 1958 it was made into a movie. Lord later wrote another book about the Titanic, *The Night Lives On,* which was published in 1986. He was the quintessential Titanic historian.

James secured an introduction to Lord through one of the Titanic history buffs who made a guest appearance on his radio show. So on March 23, 1998, we drove to Lord's apartment in Manhattan. We were met by Lord's personal secretary, a thin, efficient-looking woman who was probably in her 60s. She showed us into the author's study, which was lined with floor-to-ceiling bookshelves. While James spoke with Lord, I looked around at the Titanic memorabilia on display.

Lord was 80 years old, suffering from Parkinson's disease and confined to a wheelchair. James wanted to propose collaborating with Lord on a further update of the Titanic story. He didn't get that far—Lord's secretary made sure that the meeting was brief. It wouldn't have been possible anyway, given Lord's declining health. But James did ask the author to autograph his copy of *A Night to Remember*. Walter Lord complied, slowly and deliberately willing his shaking hand to sign the inside front cover of the paperback.

James received a phone call from John Glassey, an Atlantic City business-man. They met the previous year, at the suggestion of a mutual acquaintance. At that time my husband and John got together for breakfast, and James told John all about his background as an Australian television producer and a founder of the E! Entertainment Television network. In June 1997, James and I attended John's 50th birthday party at the Pleasantville Yacht Club. It was a big party. John knew a lot of people.

John was a trim, blond-haired man who stayed fit by rowing lifeguard boats and playing ice hockey—he was affiliated with the Philadelphia Flyers hockey organization in 1974 and 1975, when they won the Stanley Cup. He had a doc-torate in rehabilitation administration and spent the first 20 years of his career involved with children's hospitals. When casino gambling came to his hometown of Atlantic City, John began working for a gaming supply company. Eventually he became vice president of marketing for Atlantic City's first casino, Resorts International, after it was bought by television mogul Merv Griffin in 1988. In 1991, when the Foxwoods casino in Ledyard, Connecticut received government approval to offer table games, John went there for two years. Then he became a consultant to casino companies.

In March 1998, John received an assignment from the Sands casino in Atlantic City. The Sands had a collection of movie memorabilia that it no longer needed, and John was asked to dispose of it. So he called one of the local people he knew with movie connections—my husband. James went with John to look at the materials, which were stored in an out-of-town warehouse. During the trip, they talked about the Titanic phenomenon.

Like James, John had seen the Titanic exhibit at the Florida International Museum in St. Petersburg, and was amazed at how sterile it was. Yes, there were artifacts from the wreck. Yes, there were panels that told parts of the story. But the exhibit followed a typical, stodgy, art museum formula, with people walking around wearing headsets, listening to a disembodied voice pontificating about the items on display. John and James agreed that if someone brought showbiz sizzle to a Titanic exhibition, it, like the movie, would be a blockbuster.

Then the two men thought, why can't it be us?

James was hot on the idea of a Titanic exhibition. He wanted to work a deal with R.M.S. Titanic Inc., the company that owned the salvage rights to the wreck and recovered thousands of artifacts. He never got through to them. John Glassey had a contact in a Canadian exhibit design company that was planning its own Titanic show. For a time they were going to work with James and John, but that fell through. So John continued to look for investors while James developed a business plan for the show.

As all this was going on, I was working, although I was not as busy as I used to be. The Showboat *Crew's News* was still an active account, but with Harrah's buying the company, my other Showboat newsletter was gone, and my business future looked bleak. Still considering a career change, I completed two construction classes. That meant I was qualified to get a job as a building inspector, which was a joke. Although I sat through the instruction and passed the exam, I didn't know what most of the materials I would have been inspecting looked like.

I lamented my deteriorating financial situation in my journal. By this point, I'd spent more than $100,000 on James, and incurred $50,000 in debt. As I asked for spiritual guidance, the message I got was to stop feeling sorry for myself.

> *You're just indulging yourself. You're looking for an excuse to complain. Yes it is bad, but it will get better soon. James buys you gifts to maintain his sanity and dignity—let him do it. It will be fine soon—or at least better. He will succeed. You will have money.*
>
> *The battle is within yourself, against your own fears and expectations. Take it minute by minute—each minute brings you closer to resolution. You want to prove your superiority—what superiority? You're a wimp. You never risked anything in your life. You never took a chance. You are taking a chance now—that's what living is about. This is an improvement for you. Maintain your composure. Yes, it's okay to be cautious, but not demeaning. You are over the hump. James is over the hump. The better your attitude, the faster things will turn around. Your trust supports him and gives him purpose. Don't take it away—it's all he has left.*

Guidance predicted that James would have success. He certainly believed it—as a good omen, he received a new credit card in the mail. Chase Bank sent him, unsolicited, a credit card in the name of "Estate of Gale Lewis." "They sent it because I paid off Gale's debts," James said. He continued to promise that he would pay back all the money I spent on him.

One afternoon I was sitting at my desk when James came into my office and opened his checkbook. "I want you to have these," James said as he signed six blank checks. "Soon we're going to have money. The Titanic show is going to come through—I just know it. Then you'll be able to use this money to pay our expenses."

I was doubtful.

About that time I got the opportunity to write about *The Strangest Secret.* My sister, Tracy, had a new job, and retained me to do copywriting for a motivational package that included an audiotape of *The Strangest Secret,* by Earl Nightingale.

Nightingale's message included the same universal truths that I'd heard from other motivational speakers and writers: You become what you think about. Set a goal and work toward it every day. Don't be concerned with how your goal will be achieved—the answers will appear at the right time. It was no coincidence that I got this particular copywriting assignment—these were words I needed to hear. I even attempted Nightingale's 30-day plan to put *The Strangest Secret* into action.

The first step was to write on a card the one positive goal that I wanted more than anything else in the world. So what did I want? To get out of debt? I wasn't sure if that qualified as positive. To earn plenty of money? I felt like the more I earned, the more James spent. To live peacefully and happily with my husband? I didn't know if it was possible.

I listened to the tape several times and wrote the promotional copy. But I could not begin the program for myself.

Sex with James became routine. Yes, there was a lot of it, but it was always the same. Kiss here. Stroke there. We both felt physical release, but to me, that's all it was. Physical release.

There was no delight. There was no emotional connection. There was no love.

One time, as we were lying in bed, James started rubbing the top of my head. It was a gesture of tenderness, the type of sweet, innocent, physical contact that I craved. I told James that I liked it, so he did it every once in awhile. But mostly he just continued with the routine.

On another day, after another empty appointment, I went downstairs into the living room. Wearing my bathrobe, I sat on the sofa, agitated. James came down the steps in his bathrobe and was about to turn towards his office.

"You know, James," I said, "I feel like something is missing in our sex life."

"What?" he asked.

"There doesn't seem to be an emotional connection," I said.

"I love you," he said, as if reporting the obvious.

"But I don't feel it. I don't feel anything. Sex is supposed to be the ultimate union between a man and a woman. A true sharing. The sacred conjunction."

"That doesn't exist," James said.

I thought about encounters with men I knew before I was married. "Yes, it does," I replied. "I know because I've had it."

My husband turned and walked away.

I stared at my computer screen. It was blank. The machine had died. Croaked. Perished. The main circuit board was fried; there would be no resurrection. My only solution was to buy a new computer. Just what I needed—another $2,000 expense.

I was upset, but James wasn't. As far as he was concerned, it was money that had to be spent. "Your computer is your primary tool," he said. "You have to get a new one."

James, in the meantime, was buying everything he could find about the Titanic. Books. Videos. He made another trip to St. Petersburg to see the exhibit at the Florida International Museum again. He was on the phone constantly, trying to figure out a way to mount an exhibition.

Actual artifacts from the wreck were not available for his show. They were all controlled by R.M.S. Titanic Inc., and the company had its own plans for them. There were, however, many artifacts related to the tragedy in the hands of private owners. Passengers sent Titanic post cards before embarking on that fateful voyage; post cards that were delivered after the ship sank. The White Star Line, which owned the Titanic, used identical china on other ships in its fleet; over the years, passengers and employees took many pieces as mementos. Debris from the wreck floated in the North Atlantic Ocean; ships sent out to recover the bodies picked up wood and other scraps. All these materials had been bought and sold by collectors for decades. James figured that if he could accumulate enough of these artifacts, and design an interesting, interactive exhibit around them, people would love it.

Then John Glassey found an investment group from Connecticut that was willing to put up a half-million dollars to fund the show. "We're going to build a Titanic show, Nuffles!" James exclaimed with excitement.

It sounded good, but I was afraid to get my hopes up. In the nearly two years that I'd known James, I'd seen all of his plans evaporate.

So I hedged my bets and took steps toward going into the construction business. On April 30, 1998, I rented a table at a lunchtime business exposition sponsored by the Atlantic City Hotel and Motel Association. All of the casinos and hotels in Atlantic City, as well as their suppliers, were members. I displayed the synthetic polyurethane surfaces manufactured by the Symmetry Products Group in Rhode Island. I showed samples of bark, brick and rock that looked and felt like the real things, but weren't. People were amazed at how realistic the fake products looked. I gave away brochures and talked to people. I heard a few nibbles of interest.

That same day, James and John Glassey went to New York to meet with the potential investors. Late in the afternoon, as I sat at my desk after the trade show, James called me from his car. "I think you should plan a parade," he said.

"What?" I asked, confused.

"A parade for your hero. They signed the contract. They're giving us a half-million dollars, and we're going to build the Titanic show."

"They signed it?" I asked, still not sure if I should believe him.

"Yes, they did. The first payment of $100,000 is due tomorrow. We'll have the show up by July 4th weekend."

I hung up the phone and sat back in my chair. Was it true? James had come up with so many plans—was one of them actually going to work? My husband always said he would succeed. Guidance said he would succeed. Were my struggles finally coming to an end? I felt a tiny spark of hope and relief.

"Come on, Beau," I said to my dog. "We're having a parade."

I snapped Beau's leash on his collar and we went outside and stood on the sidewalk. In a few minutes, James' car approached. As he pulled in front of the house, I clapped and cheered. Beau wagged his tail. James got out of the car and walked over to me, carrying his ever-present briefcase.

"So they're actually going to do it?" I asked.

"Yes, we met with two guys from the investment group," James said excitedly, as we walked up the steps and into the house. "They signed the contract. Then we went out to lunch. When the check came, we joked about who should buy."

"This is great," I said. "I'm glad it's working out."

James put down his briefcase and pulled me close to him. "I'm sorry it took so long," he said softly as he kissed me. "But you'll see. You'll have everything you always wanted."

James announced on his radio show that our Titanic exhibition would be open on Atlantic City's Boardwalk for the big July 4th holiday. To meet the opening date, a lot of work had to be done. Quickly.

The venue needed to be leased—James wanted the old Atlantic City Convention Hall on the Boardwalk. Since the new convention center had opened a year earlier, the historic facility wasn't used much. And the cavernous West Hall—a big-box addition built in the 1970s—wasn't used at all. That's where James wanted to mount the show. He started negotiating with the officials who managed the venue.

Converting the massive open space into an entertaining experience would be challenging. James contacted Declan Weir Productions, the Philadelphia set-building studio that he found during his short-lived *Lost in Space* project. James, John Glassey and I met with the owner and his chief designer in the West Hall. The space was a gigantic garage. It had a concrete floor, a flat, industrial ceiling 30 feet above it, rows of ceiling support columns and hanging lights. One feature was a bit frightening—it had recently rained and there were puddles on the floor. Apparently the roof leaked.

At least there was plenty of room, and somehow we had to fill it. The set designers talked about creative ways to divide the space, create interest and channel the expected throngs of visitors. The way to make money, James kept saying, was throughput. The faster we could push people through the exhibit, the more money we'd make.

Of course, there had to be something for them to see, so we needed to secure the artifacts. James found a collectibles dealer in Allentown, Pennsylvania, Charlie Schalebaum, who had some Titanic items, and knew where to get more. James made several trips to Schalebaum's Allentown warehouse to look at items for the show.

A business entity to operate the show needed to be established. I suggested that we use the Polytechnique Group corporation, which was already formalized but had been all but abandoned. All we had to do was give it an alternate name. James wanted to call the new venture "Jersey Shore Productions." I filed the paperwork with the state of New Jersey and opened a new corporate bank account.

We deposited the first check from the investors—$100,000—in our new bank account. With that, my hopes started burning brighter. Maybe the days of desperation were actually coming to an end.

My husband was cheating on me. The letter from the Bank of Boston credit card department, dated May 4, 1998, confirmed it.

This was the credit card I had given to James. He spent the money; I paid the bills. On the March statement was a charge for the Berlin Motor Lodge. I knew exactly where this place was and what it looked like. It was a small highway motel on Route 73 in Berlin, New Jersey, 35 minutes from where we lived in Atlantic City. There was absolutely no reason for James to be there, except to rendezvous with another woman.

When I saw the charge on the statement, I knew in my heart what it meant. But I hoped it was a mistake, that there was some other logical reason for it. So I decided not to think about it until I had proof. I submitted a formal request to the Bank of Boston for an investigation.

The results were in my hand—copies of the registration card and credit card slip. James had indeed filled out the registration card, giving a Florida address. He had scrawled his unmistakable signature on the credit card slip at 9:40 a.m. on Tuesday, February 10—two weeks before we went to Paris.

I had my proof.

I was shaken.

What should I do?

I was alone with my problem—who could I talk to about it? I wasn't sure that I wanted to talk to anybody—then I might have to start talking about everything else that was going on in my marriage. The lies. The financial problems. The frequent business trips on weekends. I didn't know where such a discussion would lead.

So I turned to my library of self-help books. I looked for an answer in *What Every Woman Should Know About Men,* by Dr. Joyce Brothers, who wrote an advice column in Good Housekeeping magazine for almost 40 years. Chapter 25 of her book was about infidelity. She said 60 percent of men were unfaithful at some point in their marriages. Most men cheated not because they wanted to leave their wives, but because they wanted a little excitement. They didn't take the affair seriously. So if a woman found out about an affair, Dr. Joyce Brothers advised her to do absolutely nothing.

"It takes every bit of discipline and pride a woman can muster to do nothing, to go on with her daily routine," Brothers wrote. "But this is by far the wisest course. No ostentatious moping, no nasty remarks. Her energies should go toward being as pleasant and tender as possible. This is a time to make home and home life as appealing as she knows how."

The idea, Brothers said, was to wait it out. Sooner or later, the husband would tire of the affair, and married life would return to normal. A confrontation, however, would require an ultimatum, which could end the relationship.

It seemed so unfair. My husband was cheating, and I was supposed to ignore it? But I didn't know what else to do, so taking the famous psychologist's advice seemed like a reasonable plan. Plus, at this point, I had a lot of money invested in my relationship, and finally, with the Titanic show, a chance to recover it. If I threw James out, I didn't know what would happen to my money. So even though I felt numb with shock, or maybe because of it, I did exactly what Dr. Joyce Brothers recommended.

Nothing.

Luckily, I was again too busy to think about my marriage. Now that the Titanic project was a go, I had a role to play. I became responsible for the details of the exhibition—coordinating exactly how the artifacts would be displayed in the sets. This meant I had to write all the information cards that would be displayed with the artifacts. Plus, I had to write all the signs and posters that told the Titanic story.

When I started, I knew only the broad strokes about what happened to the Titanic: She was the largest and most luxurious ocean liner ever built. She was supposed to be "unsinkable." She hit an iceberg on her maiden voyage, and there weren't enough lifeboats. A lot of people died.

But as I immersed myself in research—all those Titanic books that James bought—I learned that there wasn't one story, there were thousands. Approximately 2,200 people—passengers and crew—were on the ship. Each of these people had a story. Each of them had joyous or grieving family members with a story. There were stories of the magnitude of the ship. Stories of other ships that heard its distress calls. Stories of heroism and cowardice. Many nights I stayed up late reading the accounts. They were heartbreaking—and fascinating.

When Titanic launched, on April 10, 1912, she was the largest manmade moving object ever constructed—882 feet, 9 inches long, weighing 46,329 gross tons. Titanic was the second of three magnificent ships commissioned by the White Star Line of England in an effort to dominate the lucrative market for ocean liner travel between Europe and North America. The ships, built in the giant Harland and Wolff shipyard in Belfast, Ireland, were designed for comfort. First class was exquisite. Second class was as good as first class on other liners, and third class was better than what any other ship offered to steerage passengers, many of whom were immigrants leaving Europe for a new life in the new world.

The White Star Line promoted Titanic's new standards of luxury, comfort, convenience and safety. One of its technical advances was a hull divided into 16 watertight compartments. Should the hull be punctured at any point, automatic doors would shut, preventing water from spilling into adjacent compartments. Although the ship's owners never specifically used the words, a few trade magazines proclaimed that Titanic was "unsinkable."

Still, Titanic was almost involved in a collision at the very beginning of her maiden voyage. As she pulled away from her home dock in Southampton, England, the huge liner created such a disturbance in the water that the lines mooring a much smaller ship, the New York, snapped. The New York swung out in front of the Titanic. Although the Titanic stopped just in time, some passengers thought the near-accident was an ominous sign.

Titanic sailed first to Cherbourg, France, then to Queenstown, Ireland, picking up passengers in both ports. Finally, the voyage across the North Atlantic to New York City was underway. This was to be the final voyage, the crowning achievement, in the 40-year career of Captain Edward J. Smith, commodore of the White Star Line. Smith was known as the "Millionaire's Captain," because he was popular with the wealthy members of society who traveled on his ships. For Titanic's maiden voyage, those prominent socialites included figures such as John Jacob Astor, who had scandalously divorced his wife and married a woman younger than his son. Also on board were Isidore Strauss, founder of Macy's department store, and his wife, Ida; millionaire playboy Benjamin Guggenheim; and the extremely wealthy George Widener of Philadelphia, who was traveling with his wife, Eleanor, and son, Harry.

First class amenities befitted passengers of their stature. The lounge was decorated in a Louis Quinze style, with rich upholstery and carpet, and graceful rounded moldings on the walls and ceiling. The first class dining saloon extended the entire width of the ship—92 feet—and was the largest room afloat. It featured Jacobean-style alcoves, heavy furniture and leaded windows. The most extraordinary feature in first class, however, was the glass-domed grand staircase, with its polished oak paneling and elaborate gilded balustrades. On the landing was a majestic clock with carved figures of Honor and Glory crowning Time. At the base of the staircase was a statue of a winged cherub holding a torch, which was actually a lamp.

Comfort was the ship's emphasis, but J. Bruce Ismay, managing director of the White Star Line, also focused on speed. He was a passenger aboard the Titanic—staying in one of the parlor suites—and he wanted the ship to arrive in New York well ahead of schedule. Titanic's speed steadily increased during the voyage as additional boilers were fired up. The evening of Sunday, April 14, 1912, the ship was traveling at almost top speed.

Earlier in the day, at 1:42 p.m., the two young wireless operators, who were employees of the Marconi Wireless Telegraph Company, not the White Star Line, received an ice warning, which was immediately given to Captain Smith. Rather than posting it for the officers on watch, Smith took it with him as he walked along the promenade. Titanic received six wireless warnings about ice that day. Four were delivered to the bridge, but only one was posted. Another was received at 9:40 p.m. The overworked senior wireless operator, Jack Phillips, was busy sending passenger messages—moneymakers for the Marconi company. He did not think the most recent ice message was important, and did not deliver it. But this one gave the position of a new ice field, and Titanic was steaming directly into it.

At 10:55 p.m. Phillips' transmissions were interrupted by another warning from the nearby steamship Californian, which was stopped and surrounded by ice. The transmission burst loudly into Phillips' headphones as he was trying to catch up on his backlog of passenger messages. Phillips angrily replied, "Shut up!" and did not record it. At 11:30 p.m., the Californian's wireless operator shut down his equipment and went to bed.

Ten minutes later, amid cold, still air and calm seas, Titanic collided with the iceberg.

Titanic's chief designer, Thomas Andrews from Harland and Wolff, was on the maiden voyage to observe the ship's performance. He understood the gravity of the situation. Harland and Wolff's drawings had called for 32 lifeboats, although the davits could hold 64. But Titanic only carried 16 lifeboats and four "collapsibles," which were like rafts with wooden bottoms and canvas sides. Andrews told Captain Smith that the ship was doomed. Smith knew there weren't enough lifeboats.

But no general alarm was raised. At first, neither the crew nor the passengers were informed about the collision. Third-class passengers in the bow of the ship—closest to the impact—knew there was a problem. They were moving aft with their luggage, jamming the corridors.

Eventually some crewmembers heard that Titanic had struck an iceberg. They told passengers to put on their lifebelts and go outside on the boat deck. Other stewards, who didn't know what had happened, told inquiring passengers that everything was fine and to go back to bed.

At approximately 12:10 a.m. on Monday, April 15, 1912, Captain Smith ordered the Marconi wireless operators to send a distress call.

Smith also ordered the crew to uncover the lifeboats, and load women and children first. But passengers hesitated to climb into the lifeboats, which seemed so small—no match for a vast ocean. Many believed the Titanic would not sink and it was safer to remain on the ship. Its lights were still on and the band was still playing. Passengers could see the lights of another ship on the horizon— surely it was heading to their rescue.

As the tragedy unfolded, hundreds of scenes played out aboard the ship. Even though the bow began pitching noticeably into the water, many people continued to believe Titanic would stay afloat. Others were hysterical. At the lifeboats, the ship's officers enforced the "women and children first" policy. Men put their wives into the boats and said goodbye. In the meantime, many people in third class were prevented from reaching the boat decks because of locked gates and crewmembers who ordered them out of first- and second-class areas. Other third-class passengers simply got lost in Titanic's maze of corridors.

Several ships heard Titanic's distress signal. One was the Olympic, Titanic's sister ship, but she was 500 miles away. The closest ship that responded was the Carpathia, which was 58 miles away. She steamed toward Titanic at full speed, but wouldn't arrive for four hours.

Titanic's officers attempted to signal the nearby ship, the one that passengers could see, with rockets. It was the Californian. But because the wireless operator had turned off his equipment, he never heard Titanic's distress call. Crew aboard the Californian saw the rockets, but when they flashed signal lights in Morse code, got no response. Their Morse lamp did not have the range to reach Titanic.

As the big liner began to founder, people panicked. Many rushed to the last boats being launched, the four collapsibles. Two were safely launched, but men were still trying to free the other two when water swamped the bridge. With the ocean flooding the hatches, Titanic's bow plunged swiftly and the stern rose almost vertically into the air. The deck was so steep that people fell into the water.

Suddenly the ship split between its third and fourth funnels. The bow slid into the water, but the stern settled back, almost to an even keel. Then the ocean rushed into the broken end of the stern, and again it rose until it was almost perpendicular to the water. There it paused, with hundreds of people clinging to it, until it disappeared beneath the sea.

Survivors in lifebelts floated in the water, screaming for assistance. Nine of the 16 lifeboats were less than half full. In several of the lifeboats, passengers and crew argued that they should return to pick up survivors, but others overruled them, fearing being swamped. Only one boat returned to find survivors. Another lifeboat later tried to find survivors, but by that time, most people floating in the 28-degree water had died of hypothermia.

More than 1,500 perished in the Titanic disaster. Only 706 were rescued.

John Glassey learned that an old lifeboat, possibly from the Titanic, was parked in the yard of a suburban Atlantic City home. On a sunny afternoon in early May, I went with James to see it. We pulled up to a small ranch-style home. A solid wood fence extended from the side of the house and ran along the perimeter of the backyard. Hidden from view behind the fence, surrounded by grass that desperately needed to be mowed, was the boat.

It was certainly old. Most of the white paint had chipped away, exposing weathered gray wood. Looking at the lifeboat, I felt a chill go down my spine. After all I'd read about the Titanic disaster, seeing a boat that may have been part of it made me appreciate the sometimes thin line, or small craft, between life and untimely death.

The lifeboat was built by Harland and Wolff in 1909. It had the same lines as other White Star Line lifeboats, and matched the dimensions of the cutters described in the official British inquiry report of the Titanic disaster. These were the emergency boats, smaller than the regular lifeboats, which always hung in the ship's davits, ready to be launched if necessary. Titanic carried two of them. Thirteen of Titanic's lifeboats, including the two emergency boats, were recovered along with the survivors. Exactly what happened to the boats was unknown.

In 1930, the Twentieth Century Fox film studio, believing the lifeboat was from the Titanic, purchased it to use as a movie prop. It played roles in Alfred Hitchcock's *Lifeboat* in 1944, the 1953 *Titanic* starring Clifton Webb and Barbara Stanwyck, *The Unsinkable Molly Brown* with Debbie Reynolds in 1964, and other movies. Sotheby's auctioned off a warehouse full of Twentieth Century Fox movie props in 1971, and the lifeboat ended up in a California tourist attraction called "Movie World—Cars of the Stars." In 1984, a man from Egg Harbor Township, New Jersey, purchased the lifeboat and transported it across the country.

James and I agreed that the lifeboat would be a great addition to our show. The price was $25,000. The owner offered to throw in other items from his collection of funky Titanic memorabilia, such as a Titanic-shaped whiskey bottle and period sheet music for songs written about the lost liner. They added an interesting dimension to the story—even in 1912, people were quick to make a buck off of tragedy.

Our show was going to cover not only the Titanic disaster, but also the Titanic phenomenon. We would explain the ship's doomed encounter with an iceberg on the open seas, and then portray how the event became fixed in our cultural memory. James Cameron's movie was the latest, and probably the biggest, installment of the Titanic story. James and I saw the movie again, and after doing so much Titanic research, I appreciated the attention Cameron paid to historical accuracy.

My husband made two trips to Los Angeles to acquire collectibles related to the blockbuster *Titanic* movie. He bought another full-sized lifeboat—one of six constructed as props for the film. That one cost $26,500. He bought miniature props built by the movie's special effects artists and used in filming some scenes.

James also spent a lot of money on artifacts from 1912. At that time, the White Star Line practiced central purchasing for all of its steamers, so most of the ship's amenities simply bore the White Star Line logo—a red and white burgee, or flag. He acquired nine pieces of china with the logo—dishes that were used on other White Star Line ships of the period.

But James also located one of the few items from the ship that actually said "Titanic"—a silver-plated business card case. It was meant to be a souvenir, and would have been sold in Titanic's barbershop. According to legend, a steward on the skeleton crew that brought the just-finished ship from the Harland and Wolff shipyard to her home dock in Southampton pilfered the case. The steward was disappointed at being transferred to the Olympic before Titanic's maiden voyage.

Our collection of memorabilia from the Titanic disaster included one small piece from the actual wreck, which was discovered in 1985. Two years later, a French-American expedition to the wreck, using the French submersible Nautile—which James and I saw in Paris—recovered 1,500 artifacts from the ocean floor. One of the last items brought to the surface in the Nautile's recovery basket was a stained glass window. After the conclusion of the mission, the expedition's photographer accidentally found a small sliver of yellow glass mixed in with sand that was still in the bottom of the recovery basket. It had broken off from that window. He showed the glass to the ship's captain, who told him to keep it as a gift.

The sliver of glass was a half-inch wide and slightly more than three inches long. It was our show's only direct link to the massive wreck of the Titanic lying two-and-a-half miles under the ocean.

Hundreds of items recovered from the wreck were on display at the Florida International Museum in St. Petersburg. James thought I should see the museum's Titanic exhibition, so I flew down—alone—on May 12, 1998.

The collection was impressive. The warning bell from the crow's nest, which the lookout rang when he spotted the iceberg, was on display. Many food service items were retrieved and restored—china plates, coffee cups, silver sauceboats and serving trays, candy dishes, pots and pans. There were even intact bottles of champagne and jars of olives. Hundreds of passenger possessions were recovered—luggage, shoes, smoking pipes, fountain pens, reading glasses, razors; even some clothing survived. And there was exquisite jewelry—a diamond and sapphire ring, a necklace with three gold nuggets, onyx and diamond cuff links, a bracelet with "Amy" spelled in diamonds.

In comparison, our collection was paltry. But James was convinced that interactivity would make our show a crowd-pleaser. Instead of just listening to a taped narrative on headphones—as I did in Florida—we would have live presentations. James lined up a group of Titanic experts to give talks to our audiences. He wanted to have Titanic experts—like docents—stationed in various parts of our show to answer questions. Our show would be a sensory experience, designed so people could imagine themselves on the Titanic that cold, clear night. We'd even create photo opportunities, so visitors could have pictures of themselves against Titanic backdrops. That's why we called our show the "Titanic Experience."

Along with the talks and displays, James wanted to have plenty of Titanic merchandise for visitors to buy. When I commissioned my graphic designer, Sheryl Ginsburg, to create a logo for the show, the most important requirement was that it be suitable for embroidery. We'd put the logo on polo shirts, baseball caps, sweatshirts and anything else our visitors might want to buy. Our retail store would carry other items as well. Since the movie came out, all kinds of novelty manufacturers produced Titanic souvenirs—puzzles, inflatable toys, stuffed polar bears. Just like in 1912, anything to make a buck.

That was, after all, our goal. To reach it, James was constantly on the phone, traveling and spending the investors' money. We gave a $50,000 deposit to Declan Weir Productions to design the sets. The Titanic artifacts would cost somewhere around $150,000 to $175,000—the final price was uncertain, because James kept changing what he wanted to buy. Convinced that the show would be a money machine, James didn't try to negotiate lower prices for the artifacts—which, since the popularity of Cameron's movie, were more expensive than ever. James also bought electronics equipment he said we'd need for the show long before we were ready for it. To him, speed in assembling the Titanic show was more important than vigilance.

It was the same attitude exhibited by Bruce Ismay, managing director of the White Star Line, as the giant ship steamed full speed ahead across the Atlantic Ocean. It was an attitude that led to disaster.

A hand-painted scene of the majestic Titanic at sea, 14 feet tall and nearly 50 feet long, would greet visitors as they entered Convention Hall to buy tickets for our show. Tickets in hand, they would proceed through a dramatic entry, walking under hundreds of nautical signal flags. Greeting them would be a sepia-toned photo of the ship's officers in their dress white uniforms, 13 feet tall and 30 feet wide. It was a massive enlargement of an authentic photo that was taken on Titanic's sister ship, the Olympic. Captain Edward J. Smith was front and center.

As I reviewed the blueprints for our show, I felt my excitement grow. The drawings outlined exactly what needed to be built and how all the elements would fit together. They represented a big step toward making the Titanic Experience a reality.

The first exhibit would be about the Titanic movies. That's where our lifeboat from James Cameron's *Titanic* would be on display, along with costumes and photos. From there, visitors could go into a theater to see clips of Titanic movies and documentaries, or into another theater to hear one of our live guest speakers.

Then visitors would "walk the ship." Our designer planned to recreate, after a fashion, the forward deck of the Titanic. Walking into a darkened enclosure, visitors would see the bridge rising above them, and beyond that, a dark sky with distant stars—twinkling fiber optic lights—but no moon to light the way. From there, visitors would proceed into the Treasure Room, where our artifacts—the White Star Line china, the Titanic business card case, the shard of glass from the wreck—would be on display. In alcoves off the treasure room we'd build a small version of a luxurious Titanic dining room and a replica of the radio room. James was looking for an old Marconi wireless machine.

The next stop in the visitor tour was another darkened room—Memorial Hall. Brilliantly lit on its stage would be our Harland and Wolff lifeboat, the one that may have been on the Titanic. In front of the lifeboat would be a trough of cold water—below freezing, as the water was on the night that Titanic sank. Visitors could dip their hands into it and imagine the iciness all those people felt, bobbing in their lifebelts. From there, visitors would walk past a wall of names— an honor roll of all the people who were lost, listed by first class, second class, third class and crew.

Finally, visitors could get their pictures taken at our photo opportunities. These were three small sets with painted scenery backdrops and physical props in the foreground. One was the bow of the ship, so everyone could pretend to be Leonardo DiCaprio proclaiming, "I'm the king of the world!" Next was Titanic's grand staircase, where visitors could pose on the steps next to a reproduction of the winged cherub lamp. The third was a lifeboat in which visitors could sit while an iceberg loomed on the painted backdrop. The photo opportunities would be fun, and James believed we'd make a fortune selling disposable cameras.

The photo ops were placed along a 160-foot corridor. On the other side of the corridor was a blank wall that needed to be filled. It was the perfect place to tell the countless stories of the Titanic. I researched and wrote 32 informational posters. One series was called "Life and Death on the Titanic," and described what happened to various passengers and crew:

• Isidor Straus, the wealthy and elderly founder of Macy's, refused to leave the Titanic before any other man, and his wife, Ida, refused to leave his side. "Where you go, I go," she said. The couple was last seen going back into the ship.

• William Stead, an English newspaper publisher, wrote editorials complaining that safety laws had not kept up with increased shipping capacity. Ocean liners didn't have enough lifeboats, and if one sank, many lives would be lost. Stead was onboard Titanic when his prediction came true. He never even attempted to escape the sinking vessel.

• Daniel Buckley, a poor, Irish 21-year-old, joined a group of men that jumped into a lifeboat, but officers ordered them out, firing shots over their heads. Buckley was crying, and a woman threw a shawl over him and told him to stay. This sparked rumors of men dressing like women to escape the sinking ship.

Along with the stories of individual passengers and crew, I told other facets of the Titanic tale. Several other ships were trapped in the same ice field, but escaped. Southampton, England, Titanic's port and home to many of its crew, lost 549 residents. Both the British and the American inquiries into the Titanic tragedy found no one to blame.

I spent weeks researching and writing all the stories. As they were finished, I gave them to Sheryl to format into posters. Every one of them looked terrific.

At the same time, I worked with Declan Weir Productions to fine-tune the exhibit layout. On James' last trip to California, he returned with color copies of photos of the Titanic wreck. The photos had been used to plan camera angles for Cameron's movie—some even had notes written on them. I brought the photos to the set designer, and studying them, we both felt the chill of the tragedy. They'd add another dramatic dimension to the show.

Our exhibition was taking shape. I envisioned thousands of people coming through the show, learning more about the Titanic through our entertaining, yet touching, presentation. It would be a suitable tribute to all who were lost. The show might impress people with the morals of the era—rich and famous men put their wives into lifeboats, then stepped back to meet their doom. It might make people think about the dangers of hubris—if the ship had proceeded more cautiously, the tragedy could have been averted. Or perhaps the Titanic story was about fate—for this luxurious ocean liner, considered the epitome of the era's technology, everything that could go wrong, did go wrong.

Titanic had been called the "ship of dreams." Its tragic loss conveyed many lessons for anyone who chose to see them.

James continued to talk about the Titanic Experience on the radio, and he convinced Pinky Kravitz to write about it in Whoot!, Atlantic City's weekly entertainment newspaper. Then on June 2, 1998, James received a fax from the general manager of the Atlantic City Convention Center. "It has come to my attention that over the past couple of days there have been numerous public announcements of the upcoming Titanic Exhibit in the West Hall," the fax stated. "At the present time, we do not have a contractual agreement with your organization to utilize the West Hall. Therefore, the Convention Center's position will continue to be that we are in discussions with an organization that produces the display, but it is not confirmed."

The manager said more information was required to prepare a license agreement—a list of the artifacts from the wreck, documentation of their authenticity, proof of copyright for any items to be sold at the event, and confirmation of the ticketing structure. "It would be inappropriate to put tickets on sale until the license agreement is substantially complete and approved by both parties," the fax concluded.

The point to James was clear: "Not so fast, buddy."

James always said that the best defense was a good offense. He fired back:

> If anyone brought your 'attention' to the story in Whoot [May 7]
> and the continued discussion I make on my own weekly radio program
> —it was me! ... and over a month ago. I gave you a copy of Whoot and
> urged you to listen to my program.

Then James rebutted every point in the fax from the Convention Center: In a previous meeting, James countered, he was told to start promoting and selling tickets early. The Titanic Experience was not focused on artifacts from the wreck, which the Convention Center had been told all along. The pricing structure had been confirmed in a fax sent three weeks earlier and hadn't changed.

In the meantime, James wrote, his one question had not been answered: "Will the roof leak?"

James pointed out that the Titanic Experience was an attraction, not based on gambling, being built by a local company without a penny of government funding:

> We are offering to pay $10,000 a day for 45 days for an otherwise
> unused piece of the old hall in terrible repair [we can't even get the
> walls repainted!] - and pay some 12 percent tax on everything to the
> city. I am sure you can understand a little bit of the frustration we are
> feeling.

Although James' fax was full of righteous indignation, he was throwing up a smokescreen. The real problem was that James had slowed the contract negotiations because our investors weren't coming through with all the funding they promised us.

The investors made the first few payments, totaling $175,000. But the investment group itself was a start-up, and the president, anxious to get a deal going, had exaggerated the Titanic Experience to the men who were actually putting up the money. The primary investor wanted to find out exactly what was going on. The president of the group brought him to Atlantic City, and John Glassey met the two men at a casino.

John was very candid. No, the show was not finished. No, we did not yet have a signed contract to mount the exhibit in any venue. No, they would not make money on the Titanic Experience right away—the plan was to put profits back into the company to develop another show. The investor thanked John for his honesty. After that, despite their signed contract, the investors made no more payments.

Most of the money we'd received from the investors was already spent: $50,000 for the set designers. $26,500 on the Cameron lifeboat. Additional thousands on artifacts, logo development and travel expenses. There wasn't enough money to finish the show.

I was in shock.

A few days earlier I was excited by the progress of the show and the end of my financial problems. Now there was a hole where my stomach should have been and my brain was frozen. All I could think was, "No, not again. Not another disappointment."

James was angry that the investors had reneged, but convinced that funding could be found from another source. "Don't worry, Nuffles," he said. "Our Titanic show is a solid idea. We'll get the money somewhere."

But we had an immediate problem. Expecting the next installment of funding from the investors, James had written a check for $25,000 to purchase the Harland and Wolff lifeboat. Because the investor funds hadn't arrived, the check would bounce. The lifeboat owner, in the meantime, bought a new home. He was counting on the $25,000 for his settlement, which was quickly approaching.

The Harland and Wolff lifeboat was a big part of our exhibit. We couldn't afford to lose it. We had to come up with the money to buy the lifeboat. Fast.

I took action. On June 8, 1998, I wrote three cash advance checks on my credit cards and deposited the money into the Jersey Shore Productions checking account. I got $4,800 from American Express, $8,600 from my USAir credit card, and $2,700 from my AT&T credit card.

A total of $16,100 was added to my debt in one day.

I was convinced it was the right thing to do. James believed in the show. John was contacting new investors. All I had to do, I hoped, was keep the faith a little longer.

We were able to cover the check for the lifeboat. But a week later we had another problem—we owed $90,000 to Charlie Schalebaum for Titanic artifacts. These artifacts were also crucial to the show.

The Titanic Experience was on the verge of collapsing, and so was my life.

I had to do something.

I picked up the phone and called my brother, Doug. He had done well in life. He owned a successful company. When I bought my house, he gave me $5,000 toward my expenses, which I repaid. Perhaps Doug would help me now.

Doug wasn't available—I reached his voice mail. "This is probably the most important call I've ever made to you," I said to the recorder. "Please call me back."

My brother returned my call quickly. I explained what had happened—we were halfway through building the Titanic show, and the investors reneged. We owed $90,000 for artifacts that were critical to the show. Could he help us out?

This was a big request, and Doug wanted more information. He said we should meet in person. He had already invited us to a family barbecue on the upcoming Sunday—Father's Day. He suggested that we arrive early with a proposal to discuss.

The barbecue was set for 2 p.m. I thought James and I should arrive by 1 p.m. to go over the proposal. To do that, we should leave our house by 11:15 a.m. But we got on the road late, and then hit a traffic jam on the Garden State Parkway.

As we crept along well below the speed limit, James was angry with me. "We should have left a lot earlier," he said. I knew arriving late wasn't businesslike. But I thought Doug would help us. After all, he was my brother.

Sitting at an umbrella table by Doug's backyard pool, we had just begun going over the details of the Titanic show when his other guests started arriving. It was no longer possible to discuss business.

"Donna, take a walk with me," Doug said.

We walked around the house out to his expansive front lawn. "What is this all about?" he asked.

"The investors reneged," I said. "James' partner is looking for new investors, but we need to secure the artifacts for the show. That's what the $90,000 is for."

"Donna, I can't make a decision like this. Ninety thousand dollars is a lot of money. You can't show up a half-hour before a party and expect me to make a decision. You should have been here at 10 in the morning."

"I know it and James knows it," I said, sheepishly. "It's my fault. I didn't expect to hit so much traffic."

"And what is it with this guy?" Doug asked. "Why doesn't he have any money?"

"James was planning to build an exhibit in Tampa and lost the land. The city took it to build a cruise ship terminal."

"So? Does he work?"

"He's been working on getting his projects built."

"How many times has he been married?"

"Three times, before me. His most recent wife died, and the first one didn't count."

Doug shook his head. "What do you mean, his marriage didn't count?" he asked incredulously.

My brother paced around the lawn. "Look, Donna, I can't talk about this any more now. People are coming. I'll call you in a few days."

Doug and I walked back to the barbecue. I spent the afternoon trying to be cordial, but inside I was a bundle of nerves. At the end of the afternoon, James and I left and drove back to Atlantic City.

Early the next morning, I woke up with a bad feeling. My stomach was unsettled and I had a sense of impending doom. At 7 a.m., my phone rang. It was Doug.

"I've been all twisted up inside about this $90,000," he said. "I'm not going to do it. I'm sorry."

My intuition was right. Impending doom.

"All right, Doug," I said. "I'll talk to you later."

It was a lie. For the first time in my life, I really needed help, and I felt like I was abandoned. I doubted I'd be talking to my brother any time soon.

Turmoil swirled around me. Still searching for investors, James and John Glassey signed a contract to lease the West Hall of the Atlantic City Convention Hall starting July 21, 1998. John sold some of his personal stock portfolio and put $100,000 into the show, which enabled us to acquire the artifacts, but not build the sets. James kept coming up with new ideas to structure investment opportunities.

My fears of financial collapse, temporarily assuaged by the promise of the Titanic show, gripped me again. I'd learned that talking about my feelings with my husband was useless, so I sent him an e-mail. His reply was brief: "The truth is I love you and things can only hurt us if we let them."

So I continued preparations for the show, although much more slowly than before. What I really wanted was some normalcy in my life.

I signed up for the Viking Rowing Club again, which gave me someplace to go four mornings a week. The strenuous exercise helped me cope with my stress.

My friend, Roseanne Jenkins, was getting married and asked me to be in her wedding—another normal thing to do. She had moved to California, where her fiancé lived, and like me, planned two weddings. The first, for her family, would be in New Jersey. So at 11 a.m. on Monday, July 13, 1998, I walked slowly down the aisle of a nearby Methodist church in front of the bride. Although James was late for the ceremony, he joined me for the reception. It was a low-key luncheon in the church hall, but there was music, and when slow songs came on my husband danced with me.

The closeness didn't last very long. Our financial situation was more precarious than ever, and I blamed him. The next morning, July 14—James' birthday—we were fighting.

"If you hadn't blown so much of the investors' money on travel and restaurants, we might have more to put into the show," I accused.

"The travel was important," James retorted. "How else were we going to get the movie artifacts? It's not my fault that the investors reneged."

Luckily, we couldn't argue for long—I had to leave for a business meeting with Sheryl Ginsburg at Dover Downs Slots in Dover, Delaware. At least I still had some normal work to do.

We drove in her SUV for two and a half hours. At the casino, we had lunch with our clients and then had our meeting. I was calm and businesslike all day—until Sheryl and I headed home. Then, on a highway in Delaware, the stress overwhelmed me. I had a melt down. I told Sheryl that I didn't know if the Titanic Experience would ever open. I told her that I'd spent all my money on James, that I had no more cash and was heavily in debt. I told her that I wasn't happy in my marriage.

My friend didn't know what to say. Her brown eyes filled with worry. Distracted, we both missed the highway exit that we were supposed to take.

"What are you going to do?" she asked.

"I don't know," I lamented. "I guess I'll just wait to see what happens."

When I got home at the end of the day, I went down to James' office in the basement. "I'm sorry I ruined your birthday," I said to him.

James didn't seem to care.

A week later a critical date arrived—July 21, 1998, the day we were supposed to start setting up the Titanic Experience in the West Hall of Atlantic City's Convention Hall. We were in default of our contract with the hall. The show was cancelled.

James went off to huddle with John to decide what to do. I also felt like I needed to decide what to do. Did I keep trying with the show? Did I get a job? Did I leave James? Did I move with him to Australia? I couldn't answer the questions. All I could do was cry.

I'd been crying a lot. This made James angry—he told me to stop crying and stop blaming him. But in my mind, I deserved to be upset and I deserved to be angry. James was the one who took all my money and created the mess we were in.

Two days after the Titanic Experience was cancelled in Atlantic City, James flew down to Florida. He said he had meetings with people about bringing the show there. He was gone for a week. I was glad to see him go.

I took advantage of the quiet to meditate, trying to calm my inner trembling. But every time I asked for spiritual guidance, the message I received was to stand by my husband:

> *He did not take your money—you gave it to him willingly—it is all part of the lesson—the lesson now is to love him—love will give him strength to find a solution. Keep your chin up. Do your part. Let him make the decisions. Go rowing—allow that to be your success for now. It will make you feel better. He will come up with an answer. He feels terrible—he knows how he has let you down, and he hates himself for it. He does not need you to hate him. He will be your answer. And it will be much better. The bravado that you hate will disappear—he will temper his actions. You did need to hit bottom.*

It was not a message that I wanted to hear.

When I couldn't sleep at night—a frequent problem—I went down to James' basement office to visit our nocturnal pets. Herbie, the sharp-quilled hedgehog, was difficult to pick up, but eventually he relaxed in my hand and wasn't so prickly. Chuckie, the chinchilla, would let me pet him, but he didn't want to be picked up at all.

Chuckie had given us a scare earlier in the year. He got out of his cage one morning and James found him lying motionless on the floor. I was in the kitchen when James yelled for me, with panic in his voice. I rushed down the steps and saw James holding the limp little body in one hand. James started chinchilla CPR, pushing on his chest, where he assumed the animal's heart was. To our relief, Chuckie revived. We later discovered what appeared to be blood on the humidifier, and speculated that he had gotten his small foot caught in the grate above the fan, hurt himself and went into shock.

Most of the time, during my late-night visits to the pets, I played with the sugar gliders. When I put my hand into their cage, they'd sit in my palm. I learned that if I took them out of the cage, they'd scamper up my arm and cling to the middle of my back, which made it difficult to catch them and put them back. Taking the sugar gliders out of the cage was a good idea only if I expected an extended bout of insomnia.

Usually James was sleeping when I visited the pets. But one night, as I was standing with my hand in the gliders' cage, I heard him coming down the steps. He opened the door and saw me.

"What are you doing?" he asked.

"I can't sleep," I replied.

"Why not?"

"Well, James, with thousands of dollars in debt and no Titanic show, I've got a lot on my mind."

James gave me a look of annoyance and left.

Despite the admonitions from Guidance, I couldn't help raising questions about our financial situation. Questions quickly escalated into fights over money.

One day in mid-August, as we were standing in the kitchen, I started with the questions. James didn't want to hear them. He turned his back on me and stomped down the stairs to his office.

"I've got a job offer," he threw over his shoulder. "Maybe I should take it."

"A job offer?" I asked, following him. "Take it. Let's go."

"You're not invited."

"Why not? Where is it?"

"Africa."

James went into his office and slammed shut the door.

A week earlier, on August 7, 1997, two powerful car bombs exploded, almost simultaneously, outside the United States embassies in Kenya and Tanzania. In Kenya, 212 people were killed and about 4,000 were wounded. In Tanzania, 11 people were killed and 85 wounded. The explosions appeared to be the work of Islamic terrorists.

I surmised that James had been contacted about another Special Forces mission, but heard nothing more about it. A few days later we were again arguing about money—this time in my office. It was time to pay the bills, I didn't have the cash and my husband didn't care.

"Of course, why should you care?" I asked angrily. "They're all in my name, not yours."

"You don't have to worry about that," James said. "I've always told you that I will pay for everything."

"So will you put that in writing?"

"Yes, I will."

"All right, let's do it right now."

I pulled out a sheet of my letterhead. On it I scrawled, by hand:

8/16/98
James Montgomery agrees to pay Donna Andersen for all the expenses
she has paid on his behalf and agrees that he is responsible for all credit
card debt.

I shoved the paper in front of James and handed him a pen. He signed it.

Four days later, on August 20, 1998, American cruise missiles struck a pharmaceutical plant in Sudan that U.S. intelligence identified as a chemical weapons
facility. Missiles also struck a paramilitary training camp in Afghanistan, operated by groups affiliated with Osama bin Laden. Officials believed al-Qaeda was
responsible for the embassy attacks.

When I heard of the missile strikes, I wondered about James' job offer. He'd
told me that Special Forces operatives sometimes would "paint a target"—focus
a laser beam on it—enabling airborne missiles to home in on the laser signal and
destroy the objective. Did this happen in Africa? Was he supposed to be on the
mission?

The only thing I knew was that James didn't go.

James and John Glassey continued to push the Titanic show—looking for
investors and venues to host it. I had a few copywriting assignments—not
enough to support us—but with the possibility that we might open the exhibit in
some distant city, I didn't want to solicit new accounts. James came up with
$5,000—he said John gave it to us to keep us afloat. We would survive another
month at least, so I spent my days trying to stay calm. That was the advice I kept
getting when I meditated:

> Just wait—everything will be okay—it may not turn out how
> you hoped or expected, and it may take some time, but you will be
> fine. The lesson is to keep your chin up and believe in your man. He
> will get you through. There is nothing for you to do but sit and
> meditate and focus on staying calm. Do not be a burden. Be posi-
> tive. It will turn around eventually. The debt? Don't worry about it.
> No, it is not how you want to live, but it is not a problem. You
> are making the payments. James will figure something out. He
> will never change. He will continue to push to the end—get used to
> the instability. You will never have stability—the only way to get
> stability is to get out—do you want to do that?

Was I hearing this correctly?

> Yes—you do not want to hear this lesson—a lesson in trust—
> trust in your man, trust in the universe, trust in the moment, trust
> in love. Stability does not matter—only love and peace matter.
> You can have love and peace in any moment—if you give up the

*need to control. No, this is not fun. Yes, you hate it. But it is a les-
son and preparation for the future, for the future will be difficult.*

So I rowed four or five mornings a week, and raced in some regattas. My friends from my old softball team invited me to play in a fall league. I hadn't pitched in two years, but I agreed to join the team and was back on the mound. At least after six innings there was an outcome—a win or a loss. It was a welcome change from the rest of my life, in which everything was undecided.

On September 8, 1998, my husband left for Florida again—this time he made the 1,000-mile trip by car. James said he scheduled meetings to talk to people along the way about the Titanic show, and he carried many of our rare and valuable artifacts in his briefcase.

When James got to Orlando, I flew down to join him. He sent faxes back to John with his latest ideas for the Titanic exhibit: Create both large and small versions of the show and place them in different cities simultaneously. Build a "walk the ship" version of the show—with sets even bigger than we planned for Atlantic City—and take it to Australia and Asia. Develop our own line of Titanic merchandise to sell on television shopping channels like QVC.

No business meetings were scheduled in Orlando. James did, however, arrange for us to get together with a former co-worker who lived in the area, Larry Pontius.

James worked with Pontius at Grey Advertising in Sydney, Australia, between 1968 and 1972. Pontius, an American, was the agency's creative director, and James was the research director. That meant James investigated what people thought about products through focus groups and statistical analyses, and Pontius used the information to develop advertising campaigns. Pontius eventually became vice president of marketing for Disney's two theme parks, located in Florida and California. But by 1998, Pontius had health problems and was no longer working.

James arranged for us to have dinner with Pontius and his wife, Harriet, who was an executive at the Universal Studios theme park. We first went to their home, and then drove together to a restaurant called Gina's on the Water in Altamonte Springs, Florida.

Pontius and his wife were very cordial. James and his former co-worker talked about people they knew and incidents they remembered from their agency days. I contributed to the conversation when I could. Our meals were good, and when the check arrived, both men pulled out credit cards to split the cost. A few minutes later the waitress came back to the table—James' card was declined. Embarrassed, I pulled out one of my credit cards to pay for our share of the dinner.

At some point during the evening, James secured an offer from Harriet Pontius to get us into Universal Studios for free. The next morning, she met us at the front gate with complimentary tickets. James and I spent most of the day in the park, going on the movie-themed rides, such as *Twister* and *Jaws*. We toured the Lucille Ball exhibit and went to the Blues Brothers show.

Then, with no real business having been transacted, we left Florida to drive back to New Jersey. It wasn't a pleasant trip.

Our first day of driving took us 280 miles to Savannah, Georgia. I'd read *Midnight in the Garden of Good and Evil,* the quirky book based on a true story of eccentric personalities, voodoo and murder in Savannah, so I was interested to see the city. James and I drove around Savannah, had dinner, and then got back on the highway to find accommodations for the night.

This turned out to be difficult. We pulled into four or five name-brand hotel chains—all of them were booked solid. Finally, after 11 p.m., James pulled off the highway into a no-name motel. The place was less than uninviting—the night clerk barely spoke English and sat behind bulletproof glass—but they had a room and we were tired, so we took it. The room wasn't blatantly dirty, but I didn't want to walk around in bare feet. We got into the queen-sized bed, turned out the lights, and then I had a terrifying thought:

"James!" I exclaimed. "The artifacts! They're still in the car!"

"They'll be fine."

"Are you kidding me? Look at this place! We should get the artifacts and bring them inside!" I had visions of someone breaking into the car, taking James' briefcase, and running off with the Titanic pieces, which cost hundreds of thousands of dollars and were uninsured.

"I'm telling you, Donna, they'll be fine," he retorted.

I lay in the dark, worrying. After a few minutes, it became apparent that James was not going to get out of bed, so I'd have to do it.

"Where are your keys?" I asked. "I'll get them."

"Are you saying I am not capable of protecting the artifacts?"

"I'm saying this is a bad neighborhood and we should be careful." I sat up and started looking for my shoes.

"Donna, get back in bed," James ordered. "Nothing is going to happen to them."

I couldn't believe how he was talking to me. I also couldn't believe his arrogant attitude. So I gave up. Back under the sheets, I worried myself to sleep.

No one broke into the car overnight, which James sneeringly pointed out to me in the morning. The day was not off to a good start, and it only got worse.

We headed north on I-95, but James soon wanted to get off the highway and visit the Patriots Point Naval and Maritime Museum outside of Charleston, South Carolina. He was driving, so that's where we went.

Patriots Point was the home of three retired battle ships that saw action in World War II, and a submarine that was commissioned in 1945. But James and I didn't tour the ships. We didn't look at the museum's collection of military aircraft, either. We went into the gift shop.

Along with Patriots Point souvenirs, the shop had merchandise related to the Around Alone Race, which was about to set sail from Charleston Harbor. In this extraordinary event, sailors would single-handedly navigate sailboats around the world—a distance of 27,000 miles. James picked up a baseball cap with the Around Alone logo on it and headed for the cash register.

Why was he buying that hat?

I couldn't believe it. I was struggling to make the minimum payments on all my credit cards, pay the mortgage and keep the utilities from being turned off. At the grocery store, I was buying only low-cost generic food. I was doing everything I could to keep us afloat. My husband had at least 50 baseball caps. The Around Alone Race was of no importance to us. Why would he waste money buying the hat?

"James, what are you doing?" I asked.

He stopped and looked at me.

"We can't afford to spend any extra money," I admonished.

"It's only $15," he said.

"So what! We're broke! And you have plenty of hats!"

James turned his back on me and bought the hat. I could not believe he squandered our scarce resources on something so stupid.

Then James wanted to see one of the Patriots Point exhibits—a recreation of a Vietnam War firebase that provided artillery support for infantry operations. On display in the encampment were Vietnam-era river patrol boats, Huey and Cobra helicopters and weaponry.

To see them, we'd have to pay the museum entry fee. I was not interested. In fact, I was so overwrought by my husband's callous disregard for our financial predicament, and his refusal to cooperate in responsible money management, that I could barely speak.

"Donna, we're here. The firebase is here."

"We'll see it some other time."

"When are we ever going to come back here?"

"I don't know. But I don't want to see it now."

"So the fact that this represents an important part of my past really doesn't matter to you."

I did not reply. I felt a twinge of guilt, but it was quickly squashed by anger. We got back in the car and onto the highway, and kept driving until we reached Atlantic City near midnight. Most of the ride passed in silence.

John Glassey kept looking for ways to save our sinking Titanic show, and found a potential opportunity to open it on the Queen Mary, the historic ocean liner that was permanently docked in Long Beach, California.

This was a hot lead. The Queen Mary was already hosting a Titanic exhibition that had attracted thousands of visitors. But everything Titanic was still so popular that the ship's management thought another Titanic show would attract thousands of visitors again. James really wanted to do this deal, so in mid-October, 1998, he made plans to fly to California and pitch it personally.

One of the goals of the trip was to figure out how to install our show into the Queen Mary's limited exhibit space. I was more familiar with our exhibit materials than James was, so he wanted me to look at the venue. Worried about spending more money, I hesitated. But the Queen Mary was actually a floating hotel, and the managers offered to put us up for free.

James was also talking to On Stage Entertainment, a Las Vegas company that owned "celebrity tribute" shows called *Legends in Concert*. Productions had been running for years in Las Vegas and Atlantic City—I'd seen a show at Bally's Park Place casino. The company also owned several themed dinner theaters in Orlando. James, who had been flying back and forth to Florida, thought we could put the Titanic show in one of the dinner theaters. After the meetings in California, he wanted to drive to Las Vegas for negotiations with On Stage Entertainment. The company was agreeable, and arranged accommodations for us in Las Vegas.

So James managed to get free rooms in both Long Beach and Las Vegas. I decided to go on the trip, and flew into the Los Angeles airport on October 26, 1998.

When we arrived at the R.M.S. Queen Mary, an English ocean liner that made her maiden voyage in 1936, I was amazed at her size. The ship was 136 feet longer than the Titanic. She weighed 81,237 gross tons, compared with Titanic's 46,329 gross tons. Most significantly, she crossed the Atlantic Ocean 1,001 times—swiftly evading German U-boats while serving as a troop carrier during World War II. After the war, the ship returned to passenger service, which continued until 1967.

Many rich and famous people sailed on the liner—like Winston Churchill, Clark Gable, Gary Cooper, Marlene Dietrich, Walt Disney, Loretta Young, Bob Hope and William Randolf Hearst. When they did, they often stayed in the royalty suite. These same accommodations were provided to James and me.

The bellman led us into a spacious stateroom, paneled in light wood. Art deco-style furniture included a king-sized bed, dresser, desk, dressing table and wardrobes. We could have danced in all the open space in the middle of the room, and the adjoining full bathroom was also large. But there was more—a passageway led to a kitchenette, another king stateroom just as big as the first, another full bathroom and a sitting room. I'd never stayed in such a big suite—on water or land. As I giddily wandered around our sumptuous accommodations, I counted 17 doors.

I just started to unpack when there was a knock on one of the doors that led to the hotel corridor. I opened it to find a uniformed Queen Mary employee who was extremely surprised to see me. With him were four people in casual clothes—they had the look of tourists.

"Is this your room?" the employee asked.

"Yes," I replied. "We just checked in."

The employee apologized for the interruption and left.

A few minutes later the phone rang. It was a woman from the front desk, wanting to confirm the name on the room. "Montgomery," I replied. "We just checked in."

We had dinner that evening with the Queen Mary's vice president at the captain's table in the ship's elegant dining room. During the conversation, we learned that our royalty suite was actually two adjoining suites. We were only supposed to get one of them—the other was on the visitors' tour of the ship. But no one locked the door that connected the two suites, which is why we thought it was all was ours.

We were not asked to vacate one of the suites, which was good. When James and I returned to our rooms, I was tired and crawled into one of the king beds. James, saying he wanted to watch television, lay in the king bed in the other stateroom. He never joined me.

The next morning James and I had our formal meeting with the vice president and members of his staff. James, as usual, did a lot of talking. Not only did he talk about the Titanic Experience, James told our hosts how they should run their business, confident that he was imparting words of wisdom. The Queen Mary executives did not appear to be interested in his advice.

Afterwards, the vice president showed us the Queen Mary's exhibit space, which was indeed small, although we discussed the possibility of incorporating adjoining space that was being used for storage. Getting our full-sized lifeboats in would certainly be a challenge.

James' plan for the second day of our visit included additional meetings with the executives and gathering precise measurements of the available space. The meetings did not materialize, and the measurements didn't take very long. Soon there was nothing left for us to do on the Queen Mary. We checked out, got in our rental car and started driving toward Las Vegas, Nevada.

The Queen Mary executives had not given us a definitive answer about hosting our Titanic exhibition, but James believed they wanted it. As we drove along the highway, he asked me, "So what do you think about being a California Mouse?"

As I considered his question, I realized I was not at all happy about moving from New Jersey across the continent to California. "I don't know," I said hesitantly. "It's a big change."

This was not the answer James wanted to hear, and he became angry. "I'm making something work for us," he snapped. "The least you could do is show some enthusiasm."

It was a long drive to Las Vegas.

Legends in Concert played in the Imperial Palace Hotel and Casino, and that's where we stayed. The casino was small but its location was superb—right in the center of the Las Vegas strip. Across the street was Caesars Palace with its magnificent Forum Shops—a high-end shopping mall that featured Roman décor and heroic-sized animatronic statues. Just down the road was the Mirage Casino, where an artificial volcano at the entrance erupted every hour on the hour, from 7 p.m. to midnight. Next to the Mirage was the Treasure Island casino, where actors staged mock pirate battles daily in "Buccaneer Bay," complete with square-rigged sailing ships and cannon fire.

Although our accommodations at the Imperial Palace weren't nearly as luxurious as the Queen Mary, we did get something the 1930s-era ocean liner lacked— a luv tub. Right next to the king-sized bed was a whirlpool bath big enough for two. And, affixed to the ceiling above the bed, was a huge mirror. I'd heard about such amenities, and that night, for the first time, I experienced them.

First, however, James and I met Johnny Stuart, the chairman of On Stage Entertainment, for cocktails in one of the hotel bars. It was an opportunity to get acquainted, and Stuart arranged for us to see the evening's performance of *Legends in Concert.* Generally I wasn't a fan of impersonator shows—maybe I saw too many fake Elvis Presleys on television—but I thoroughly enjoyed this one. No wonder it ran for 15 years.

The next day, James and I went to the On Stage Entertainment production facility, located close to the Las Vegas strip. James told me that Johnny Stuart was going to invest in the Titanic show by building the sets at his own expense, and he wanted me to meet separately with the construction department manager to go over the details of our exhibit. But while I kept talking about the sets we wanted, the manager kept talking about costs. After the meeting, I asked James to clarify On Stage Entertainment's involvement in our plans—were they paying for the sets or not? I didn't get a direct answer.

We were going to meet with Johnny Stuart again, but not for a couple of days, so James and I had time to kill in Las Vegas. I wanted to see *Mystére,* the Cirque du Soleil show at the Treasure Island casino. Our seats were in the very first row, along the side of the stage. Enormous Japanese taiko drums, with performers pounding them, were lowered from the ceiling to open the show. All of the drummers had chiseled physiques—unlike the man who accompanied me.

I gaped through the entire show. Acrobats vaulted through the air on massive trampolines. They slithered up vertical poles, upside down. And the trapeze act—they were indeed flying. *Mystére* was an inspiring display of human strength, embellished by fantastical costumes and set to exhilarating music. I loved every minute of it.

The next day, James and I went to the Las Vegas Hilton to see *Star Trek: The Experience.* When I first met James, he dismissed *Star Trek* as *Wagon Train* in a space ship, not real science fiction. Perhaps—but legions of Trekkies swore their allegiance, and waited to board the ride.

Actors playing the roles of Starfleet officers instructed us on our responsibilities during our "mission." Suddenly the lights went out. When they came on, all of us tourists had been "beamed" to the bridge of the starship Enterprise. To get back to Las Vegas, the Starfleet officers pushed us into the shuttle bay—actually a motion simulator ride. We sped along the time-space continuum—we could see it passing by our windows—back to the Hilton. Exiting the shuttle, we followed twisting passageways until we found ourselves in Quark's Bar and Grill, a real restaurant modeled after the space hangout on Star Trek.

At some point during the ride, James and I became separated. I found him sitting at the bar in Quark's, drinking something that looked like a piña colada. "They took my idea!" James exclaimed as I approached. "I was going to build a theme park ride with a Quark's bar! They took it!"

"Well, I guess it was a good idea," I said as I ordered a drink. "How did you like the ride? I thought it was great. The actors were fabulous—they really made it seem realistic."

"I was going to build Quark's bar," James repeated. "I knew it would work. I'm always ahead of my time."

Finally, on Sunday, November 1, 1998—our last day in Las Vegas—James and I met again with Johnny Stuart. We sat in his home and discussed Titanic possibilities. James showed him the artifacts and talked about audience throughput and merchandising opportunities. Stuart suggested another dimension to the show—a Celine Dion impersonator singing the hit theme song of the hit *Titanic* movie, *My Heart Will Go On*. James loved the idea.

I was impressed with Stuart. He was creative. He knew the entertainment business and had built a successful company. Although no final decision was made, it sounded like he was interested in working with us to develop some kind of Titanic production.

The tension between James and me, temporarily alleviated by the trip to the West, came back in full force with our return to Atlantic City. We were in debt, no money was coming in, and I was terrified.

James told me that, based on the negotiations with the Queen Mary and On Stage Entertainment, John Glassey was able to arrange another $50,000 investment into our Titanic show.

I didn't believe him.

James was infuriated. "Are you calling me a liar?" he demanded.

I was shocked at his accusation. "John has been talking to those investors since June and they haven't done anything," I reasoned. "Why should they act now?"

"I'm telling you, they are putting $50,000 into the show."

"Yeah, right."

At this point James launched into a full-blown attack, berating me for not believing in him and accusing me of making our life miserable because all I did was cry. I could not withstand his verbal violence. I retreated.

I did, however, send him an e-mail to express how I felt:

From: DONNACOPY
Subj: post card

    I am absolutely paralyzed with fear, and you attack me. I can't eat, I can't do anything constructive, and you criticize me for making myself sick.
    You have asked me to live a life that is totally contrary to my nature. To you a roller coaster ride is no big deal. To me it is a disaster. Yet you expect me to jump on and enjoy the ride. I can't do it. I am not wired for this level of risk.
    I said I didn't believe you when you said the money would be here on Wednesday because the investors haven't acted for six months, why should they change their style now? There was never even any indication of a written agreement until today! You, however, took it personally, and

insisted that I called you a liar. There was no way that I could defend myself.

It seems to me that everything is fine between us as long as I happily agree to anything you want to do. The minute I object, or I get upset, you attack me. And I am not strong enough to survive your attacks. You are the skilled debater. I am not. You are excellent at turning whatever the problem is around so that it is all my fault. The only thing I can do is withdraw and keep my mouth shut.

I feel like eventually, I will be crushed.

I'm so sick to my stomach that I've eaten three antacid tablets and it still hurts. Every time Beau comes to me I scream at him. The heater is leaking and I start to cry. This is too much stress for me. You are breaking my heart.

James replied to my e-mail, essentially putting his verbal attack into writing. I was not surprised, which I told him in another e-mail:

From: DONNACOPY
Subj: post card

Congratulations, James, you have proven my point.

I have raised a number of issues, all of which you dismiss with a simplistic "only because you won't believe in me" - once again attempting to make all of our problems my fault. I don't buy it.

You are incapable of having an adult discussion about any personal issue. I feel very alone in our relationship, because I cannot talk to my husband. You have no true communication skills - you just use your "best defense is to attack" technique to bulldoze your way over people, especially me. In this regard I find our relationship highly disappointing.

The only way we can have a conversation is to talk about our pets. That is truly pathetic. Your baby talk is a poor substitute for communication. I would much rather be able to talk about important issues than say "nuffles nuffles." Your attempts at communication are truly childish.

I'm not even sure you want a mature relationship. I think all you want is a young looking china doll hanging on your arm that you can let everyone know you are fucking.

And you want me to believe in you? I can't even talk to you. For a married couple, that is truly sad.

James, my needs in this relationship are not being met. And I'm not just referring to my need for financial security - which I have doubts will ever be met. We may make money, and you'll just blow it all on some other adventure. But even if the money does stabilize, will we ever establish a mature connection? Not unless you change and learn how to relate. How long am I willing to wait for that? I'm not sure.

The investors actually did come through with $50,000. According to the loan memo, dated November 6, 1998, the money was supposed to be used to secure Titanic artifacts. But James took thousands of dollars to pay our current living expenses and credit card bills. Somehow, in authorizing me to write the checks, he again managed—with great vitriol—to blame the sad state of our marriage on me not having faith in his ability to succeed as an entrepreneur.

James also took some of the investors' money to pay for yet another trip to Florida. The day after he returned, we went to the Great American Pub in Mays Landing. Located in a shopping center, it was nicer than a hole-in-the-wall bar, but not as stylized as a national restaurant chain. As we sat at the bar with our beers and hamburgers, I played a computerized trivia game that was linked to bars around the country. The questions were posted on the wide-screen television, and I answered many of them quickly and correctly, happily racking up points.

"This is the first time I've seen you smile in months," James observed. It was a telling commentary about my state of mind, because before my marriage to James, I was known for my smiles and laughter.

Two days later, on November 13, 1998, I had an appointment with my energy worker, Elaine Anderson. It had been a year and a half since I last saw her, and I desperately felt like I needed therapy.

I told Elaine all that had gone on with the Titanic—how the exhibit was going to open in Atlantic City, and how it collapsed. Even though a deal was supposed to come through any day, I was having trouble being supportive of my husband. I was angry and blamed James for our financial problems.

I lay on the table and Elaine began the energy work. We asked for spiritual guidance, and slowly, we both started to receive messages. Guidance said that James was sorry for how our marriage was, and my anger made him feel like a failure.

"He wants your support," Elaine said.

As I went deeper into the session, images of a past life, like fuzzy memories, floated into my mind. I don't know when or where it was, but I was embroiled in politics, which led to me being stabbed in the back—literally. I was killed by someone I trusted.

Elaine also saw the past life and the past trauma. "It was a deep, deep wound," she said, "the energy of betrayal was all around."

Chapter 12

James excitedly announced to me that he had worked out a deal with Johnny Stuart of On Stage Entertainment. We were going to launch the Titanic Exhibition in one of Stuart's dinner theaters in Orlando, Florida.

On Stage Entertainment owned three dinner theaters, which James visited during his recent trips to Florida. One was King Henry's Feast, staged in a building that looked like a castle. Another show was Blazing Pianos, a high-energy sing-along featuring three piano players pounding out popular American tunes from the '50s through the '90s.

The third dinner theater was Wild Bill's Wild West Extravaganza in nearby Kissimmee. This would be most suitable for our show, James said, because along with the main dining room, it had an exhibit area where we could put the Titanic artifacts on display.

I was eating lunch in our dining room when James showed me the photos he had taken of Wild Bill's. Flipping through the pictures, I became more and more apprehensive. Wild Bill's looked exactly as one would expect for a place called Wild Bill's Wild West Extravaganza. The dinner theater and exhibit area were heavily themed in a cowboys-and-Indians motif.

The exterior looked like a stockade fort of the American Old West, circa 1870. Most of James' photos were of the exhibit hall, in which mannequins dressed as American Indians, cowboys and miners posed in scenes from everyday frontier life, such as cooking around a campfire.

What did cowboys and Indians have to do with the Titanic?

I flipped through the photos again. They didn't look any better. "We can't put a Titanic exhibit in here," I said to my husband. "This entire place looks like a frontier town. It will look stupid."

James was not interested in my opinion. "Stuart wants to do the deal," he said. "This is the space he's got. We'll have to work with it."

"But it doesn't make any sense," I protested. "The Titanic was all about comfort and luxury. You've got walls made out of logs here. What are you going to do with them?"

"Either they'll have to be covered up, or the exhibit will have to be lit so that the walls are not visible."

"But what about the exterior of the building? We can't change it, and that's what people are going to see when they first arrive."

"Do you want to launch the show? Yes or no."

"Of course I want to launch the show, but ..."

"Then you're going to have to make it work. This is our opportunity."

Along with the exhibit hall, James said, we'd use the Wild Bill's restaurant. That's where our Titanic experts would give their talks about the ship and the wreck. And at the end of each presentation, James said, a Celine Dion look-alike, supplied by Johnny Stuart, would sing the Titanic anthem, *My Heart Will Go On.*

I was unconvinced, but James was adamant. We had a chance to launch the show in Orlando, and we were taking it. Further arguing was useless. My only choice was to make the best of it.

To redesign our show to fit the venue, I'd have to see the space. So the morning of November 17, 1998, I flew to Florida. I rented a car at the Orlando airport and, early in the afternoon, drove to Wild Bill's Wild West Extravaganza in Kissimmee. The dinner theater looked just like the pictures. I expected to walk around the corner and meet John Wayne.

He wasn't there. In fact, as it was well before any dinner theater customers would arrive, the place was practically deserted. I found an employee and told her that I wanted to see the exhibit space for the Titanic show that we were bringing in. She didn't know what I was talking about. But after making a few phone calls, she got permission to let me into the exhibit section. Generally it was closed—management had apparently discovered that customers weren't interested in the static cowboy and Indian display.

The exhibit room was long, narrow and dark. Vignettes of life in the Old West, starring the costumed mannequins, occupied platforms raised about four inches above the floor against the two long walls. A split-log rail separated the displays from the central aisle, and log rafters supported the A-frame ceiling. The room looked like a big log cabin. I resigned myself to the fact that I'd never be able to erase its frontier atmosphere.

Displaying our lifeboats would pose another problem—there was no room for them. But two side doors along the exterior wall led out to the parking lot. Perhaps we could put some kind of temporary building outside, adjacent to the exhibit space, for the lifeboats. I got out my tape rule, took measurements and made notes. It was a less-than-ideal solution for the boats. But then, the entire venue was less than ideal.

I returned to Wild Bill's in the evening, buying one ticket for a dinner show that catered to families and tour groups. The hosts for the evening were actors playing the parts of Wild Bill and Miss Kitty. They emceed a variety show with square dancers and can-can girls, Native American dancers, a cowboy who did rope tricks and another cowboy who demonstrated his marksmanship, albeit without real bullets. But during the show I looked around the cavernous theater, with a ceiling that appeared to be more than 20 feet high, trying to figure out how to make it suitable for an intimate discussion of the Titanic disaster. This would pose a challenge—especially since whatever we did would have to be removed every evening so the Wild West Extravaganza could go on.

The only way to manage a show in Orlando was to be there. We'd have to move to Florida.

James told me our show was scheduled to open on February 1, 1999, and we'd be at Wild Bill's for a year. That did not qualify as a permanent move, so I obviously wasn't going to sell my house in Atlantic City. But I also wasn't going to live in a hotel room for a year, especially with five pets. We had to find an apartment.

James insisted that he had to be in Florida by the beginning of December. It was already past mid-November; moving in two weeks was impossible. James' solution was that he would drive his car to Florida on December 1, carrying essentials, and I'd follow in a rental truck, towing my car, a few weeks later.

So I became responsible for the move, including finding an apartment. There was no time to go to Orlando and look at them; I'd have to search over the Internet and rent sight unseen.

The biggest problem, I quickly discovered, was locating a place that would accept my dog, Beau. Cats were allowed, along with yappers—otherwise known as small dogs. At 50 pounds, Beau was a medium-sized dog. After numerous phone calls to apartment complexes, I thought I found one, but the rental agent requested a picture of Beau. My dog was rejected—he was too big. The apartment search was not going well, and that was only one item on my to-do list for the move.

I had to figure out how to make our Titanic show, originally designed for a massive convention center, fit into a 92-foot by 23-foot log cabin. Then all my Titanic stories, which at that point were only computer files, needed to be produced. I wanted to use vendors I knew, rather than chance unknown suppliers in Florida, so everything had to be readied for digital output—quickly.

I had to button up my house in Atlantic City, which would be unoccupied for a year. That meant cleaning the yard, making sure nothing important was sitting on the basement floor in case the bay flooded, and giving keys to the neighbors. I brought in an electrician to look at a couple of wiring problems—the last thing I needed was a fire. I also wanted to install a security system, but James said it would be too expensive.

And of course, I had to pack—clothes, housewares, business equipment, files, pet supplies. I worried about my car—my 1990 Ford Probe had well over 100,000 miles and was showing its age. The car had recently been towed to a transmission shop. I hoped that once the Titanic show got going I could buy a new car, so I packed my car title.

Moving was a massive job, and James was absolutely no help.

On November 20, 1998, James left for Las Vegas to see Johnny Stuart again about launching the show in Orlando. James wanted to stop in Dallas on the way so he could spend a few hours at the amusement association convention. "Everyone in the exhibit business will be there," he said. "I might be able to find another opportunity for our Titanic show." With the extra stop, his airfare was a staggering $2,161.

In the meantime, I found a potential venue for our Titanic show close to home—a shopping mall called Ocean One. It was the pier—once known as the Million Dollar Pier—that stretched out over the Atlantic Ocean in front of the Caesars Atlantic City casino. The pier had space for the show in a third-floor area that overlooked the food court. I made an initial phone call to the pier's marketing manager, and she was interested.

So while my husband flew around the country looking for deals, I found an easier opportunity right in Atlantic City. James was pleased about placing the exhibit in Ocean One, and thought it would be a good second stop for our show. But he said negotiations with Ocean One were just starting, and Orlando was a done deal, so he wanted me to keep preparing for our move.

That's what I did. I reserved a U-Haul truck and trailer to drive down to Florida and kept looking for a place to live. I made trips to the storage unit to get extra dishes and other household items that we could use in our yet-to-be-located apartment. I bought a cheap set of silverware. I bought three blue plastic pet carriers to transport our small animals.

I was doing all the work. Plus, James wanted me to make travel arrangements for him to go to Australia. He told me that he'd been talking to his Australian contacts about bringing the Titanic show there, and if he met with them in person he could finalize a deal. James also wanted to see his mother. He was positive that the upcoming Christmas would be her last.

"How can you know that your mother is going to die?" I asked him.

"I just do," he said, with absolute certainty.

James and I were invited to eat Thanksgiving dinner at the home of my uncle, Dennis Daly. I was grateful and relieved for the invitation—especially because most of my immediate family wouldn't be there. I hadn't spoken to either of my brothers since Father's Day in June, when Doug refused to help with the Titanic show. My father would be spending the holiday with his wife's family. So on Thanksgiving I'd see my sister along with another aunt and uncle, and assorted cousins. I didn't anticipate any awkward confrontations.

On Thanksgiving morning, as usual, James got up long before me and went down to his office in the basement, even though he just flew in from Las Vegas the day before. I was in the kitchen, getting ready to prepare my contribution to the day's feast—a casserole of carrots and apples—when he came upstairs, wearing his bathrobe.

"We should leave around one o'clock for my uncle's house," I said.

"All right," James replied.

"I've been looking for apartments in Orlando," I continued. "I still haven't found one that will take Beau. But it looks like the rent will be about $1,000 to $1,200."

No reply.

"I also reserved a 14-foot U-Haul truck. That's the minimum size needed to tow a car trailer. A five-day rental is going to cost about $1,300. And, I've put the Titanic stories into production. They'll be printed out, mounted and laminated. The shop quoted more than $2,000 for the job."

"All right."

"Well, James, I don't have the money to pay for all this. Do you?"

"I talked to Johnny Stuart about investing in the show."

"Is he going to do it?"

"Yes."

"When?"

"I should know within a few days. He thinks the show will do great. He's going to have someone clear out the exhibit room."

"James, you want to leave for Florida on December first. That's four days from now."

"I know that."

"Well, when are you going to find out about the money? How are we going to pay for the move?"

"Don't worry about it," James said. "You just get ready to go to Florida."

"That's what I'm trying to do," I replied, with barely contained frustration. "I need money to get the exhibit ready. Besides producing the stories, I have to know what we can do to cover those log walls. And we need to rent a temporary building for the lifeboats."

"First of all, forget about the walls. People won't care what they look like."

"Forget about the walls?" I asked, incredulous.

"The draw is Titanic. People will be there to see the artifacts and listen to our speakers."

"You don't think they will notice that the logs look a little odd?"

"They won't figure it out until after they've bought their tickets. Anyway, when they hear our Celine Dion look-alike, they'll be happy."

With that statement, I realized James was perfectly willing to take people's money and give them a crappy experience. I stared at him in disbelief for a few seconds.

"Well, we have another problem, James," I said, trying to hold on to my composure. "I don't have the money to pay the mortgage."

"Donna, I am well aware of our financial situation," James harshly replied. "Why do you think I'm trying to get this show going? Do you think I want to live the way we're living? Do you think I like working out of a cellar?"

"When I built the office for you—with my money—you liked it. So what's the problem now?"

"I suppose that because you paid for it I have no right to my opinion."

"Well, I've paid for everything you've done practically from the day I met you. And what do I have to show for it? I'm broke and in debt. You, in the meantime, come up with grandiose plans and don't give a shit about what they cost me."

"You were very happy to participate in the Titanic plan when we had investors. It's not my fault that they backed out."

"But it is your fault that we have no money. If you hadn't blown through everything I had, and all my credit, we might be able to get somewhere."

"We are getting somewhere. We're opening the show in Orlando."

"If we can afford to make the move."

"You just focus on packing. I'll take care of the money."

"And how are you going to do that?"

"Well, I'm not going to get hysterical like you. Perhaps if you learned to control yourself you'd realize the situation isn't that bad. The Titanic show is going to open on February 1. All we have to do is make it until then. So why don't you stop complaining?"

So now I was the problem.

"Are you through?" James demanded. "I came up to take a shower." Not waiting for an answer, he stomped out of the kitchen.

The carrots and apples for my casserole lay expectantly on the kitchen counter. I picked up a knife to slice them; I was lucky that I didn't cut off my finger, because I had no feeling. Somehow I got the casserole in the oven. Then I dressed and put on my makeup.

At one o'clock, I got in the car with James for the hour-and-a-half trip to Thanksgiving dinner with my relatives. He drove; neither of us spoke. But as the numbness began to lift, my mind started racing.

I was on the verge of losing my home and everything I'd worked for, and my husband didn't care. To make matters worse, I was in business with him, and I hated the way he did business. He had no pride in his work and no standards. Schlock was just fine with him.

James had embarrassed me before, and it looked like he'd embarrass me again. Unfortunately, at the moment I was stuck. I couldn't walk away now, not when there was a chance to get my money back. But once the Titanic show opened in February, we'd finally start earning some cash. When my financial situation stabilized, I could get a divorce.

My own thoughts surprised me. For the first time, I was seriously considering divorce.

At my uncle's house, I pushed all the internal dialog aside to engage in small talk with my relatives. I casually mentioned that we were going to Florida, without a hint of the trauma involved.

"Large pets welcome." Those magic words jumped from the website for Brittany at Waterford Lakes, which I found after days of searching the Internet. This brand-new apartment complex was located in a developing corner of sprawling Orlando, far from Wild Bill's in Kissimmee. But highway entrances were nearby; one-, two- and three-bedroom units were available; and most importantly, Beau was allowed to live there.

We needed three bedrooms—one for sleeping, one for my office and one for James' office. The master bedroom—with its private bath—would be James' suite. My husband's housekeeping had not improved, so I hoped his rubble could be contained there. The apartment had another full bath; I was thrilled by the idea of not sharing.

Brittany at Waterford Lakes offered other amenities, like garages, a pool, a health club and a business center. We didn't have to commit to a full year—a six-month lease was available, although it cost an extra $25 per month. Still, the rent, including a garage, was a reasonable $1,095 per month.

A nice, three-bedroom unit on the second floor was available. I sent a deposit.

We needed furniture—I wasn't about to dismantle my home and drag everything to Florida, especially since James anticipated that we'd return to Atlantic City from time to time for business. Furniture rental would add another $527 per month to our expenses, and the company wanted the first two months paid in advance. I gave them a credit card and authorized delivery for December 2, 1998.

Since James was going to arrive first, he would have to sign the lease and pay the balance of the rent. James said he'd get the money from an advance on his military pension.

Huh? If he could borrow against his military pension, I thought, why didn't he do it before? Why did he let me struggle to pay the bills, run up my credit cards and take out a second mortgage on my home, if he had access to cash?

I wondered, but I did not ask. Questions always turned into arguments, and I had enough stress. He was paying the rent. I let it go at that.

As planned, James left for Florida early on December 1, 1998, with the Ford Thunderbird packed full of clothes, computers and household essentials. James expected to make it to Orlando by the next day. He did, but there was some kind of delay with his pension money. It finally came through on December 3, 1998. James went to Brittany at Waterford Lakes, signed the lease, paid the rent and moved in.

"Nuffles did a good job of finding an apartment," James said when he called me. "You're going to love it here."

"Really? It's nice?"

"It's great. Everything is new. We're the first ones living in this apartment. In fact, only a few buildings are finished. The rest are under construction. And the location is terrific. There's a shopping center right across the street with a nice supermarket. Everything is new here."

"The furniture is okay?"

"Yes. It was all set up. I have a nice desk and credenza. We'll be very comfortable. We're going to have a nice Chrissy—you, me and the dawg. And our other pets too."

James would only be in the apartment for a week. He was leaving for Australia from the Orlando airport on December 10, 1998 and would return on December 20. That was the day that I planned to start driving the U-Haul truck to Florida. I anticipated that the trip would take two to three days, meaning I'd arrive at our new apartment before Christmas.

But I'd miss Christmas with my family—something I'd never done. So I planned my own little Christmas dinner for the Saturday before I left, December

13, 1998. I invited Dad and his wife, Pat, Tracy, and my friend, Sheryl Ginsburg. I did not invite my brothers.

To make my home feel a little bit festive, I bought a small artificial Christmas tree, about two feet tall, and placed it on a table in front of my pseudo-fireplace. I decorated the tree with lights and miniature ornaments—apples, tiny birds and bows. With a two-foot tree, it only took a few minutes.

The party was lovely. We exchanged gifts—Dad and Pat gave me a sparkly gold twin set sweater, along with a check, which was much appreciated. My dinner came out well. Throughout the evening, I could feel the warmth and affection of my family and good friend.

The countdown for departure began the next day.

The Titanic artifacts were bubble-wrapped and packed into individual, labeled boxes. The digital output shop printed my Titanic stories, but they were not mounted and laminated—James didn't come through with the money for that, so I had to tell the vendor not to complete the job. I had wardrobe boxes of clothes for both James and me. I even bought Christmas presents for James. The biggest one was a microwave oven for our apartment, which I charged to my Macy's card.

In the midst of packing, I had a meeting with the manager of Ocean One about our Titanic exhibit. I arrived early and took another look at venue. The shopping pier was approximately 900 feet long—the same size as the Titanic. The seating area where I wanted to install the show was at the very end of the pier, well out over the ocean, and its floor-to-ceiling windows gave the impression of being on a boat, surrounded by water. The view would certainly add to the drama of the exhibit.

My meeting went well and the manager asked for a proposal.

Another opportunity for the Titanic show. I felt a glimmer of hope that perhaps financial stress, my constant companion, would soon start to melt away.

December 20, 1998 arrived—departure day. I'd picked up the rental truck from my long-time customer, Bob Rosenthal, at Black Horse Self Storage, the day before. Dad came and helped me load it. The packing was organized so that items I might need during the trip—such as my suitcase and pet food—were easily accessible near the truck's roll-up back door. I packed refrigerator items into a cooler. I packed a lunch. I packed the little Christmas tree and decorations.

Then I had to round up the pets—none of the little ones had ever been in a pet carrier. Herbie, the hedgehog, was easy. Even though he curled up into a ball with his sharp quills sticking out, I could pick him up. Donald and Jamie, the sugar gliders, were sleeping as they always did during the day, so I grabbed them before they knew what was happening.

Chuckie the chinchilla, however, was a problem. He did not want to be picked up, he was fast, and if I grabbed him, he released his fur. Several attempts left me with a fistful of fluffy gray hairs while he scampered to the other side of his cage. Eventually I got him into his carrier.

Then there was Beau, my excitable coonhound. I'd never taken him on such a long trip and I wanted him to stay calm. I had doggie Valiums, given to me by a substitute veterinarian who was appalled by my dog's lack of cooperation during his annual checkup. He said I should give Beau a pill before the next visit. This seemed like a good time to use it.

Beau climbed into the truck and sat on the passenger side seat—he was always happy to go for a ride. The three pet carriers went on the floor of the truck in front of Beau. He sniffed at them briefly, but the Valium was kicking in. Beau looked at me with confusion on his face, as if to ask, "What's the matter with me?" The dog's eyes were bloodshot, and I worried that I'd made a mistake. Well, there was nothing I could do about it. He'd just have to sleep it off.

I drove the packed rental truck to Black Horse Self Storage, where I'd left my car. On the way there, I noticed that the small pets seemed distressed in the carriers. The heat was blowing directly on them and the floor of the truck was vibrating. So after Bob and his employees attached the trailer to the back of the U-Haul truck and secured my car on it, I put the pet carriers in the car. At least the ride would be smooth and quiet. Finally, a few hours later than I hoped, I was ready to get on the road.

"I've never driven a truck with a trailer," I said to Bob.

"Don't worry. You'll be fine," he reassured me. "You have power steering and power brakes. It's like driving a car. Just take the turns slowly."

We were off.

U.S. Route 40 was known as "America's Golden Highway." During its heyday in the 1950s, the road ran from Atlantic City, New Jersey, across the entire country to San Francisco, California, and carried more automobile traffic than any other transcontinental highway. Route 40 cut through the most rural part of the state, where towns looked like they hadn't changed since the 1950s.

I followed it over the Delaware Memorial Bridge, where I picked up Interstate 95, the highway that hugged the east coast of the United States and would take me 900 miles to Florida. Traffic through the major cities of Wilmington, Delaware; Baltimore, Maryland; and Washington, D.C., was always heavy. Because of my late start, I was stuck on I-95 around Washington, where the highway was known as the Capital Beltway, during rush hour.

Beau was sleeping, but I was anxious. Night fell, traffic was heavy, and because of the trailer, it was difficult for me to change lanes. So I stayed to the right, in the slow lane, with cars lined up bumper-to-bumper ahead of me. As soon as I was beyond Washington, I decided, I'd get off the road.

When I cleared the Beltway and made it to Virginia, I picked an exit at random. It brought me to a highway lined with chain stores and fast food restaurants—a typical American suburb. I pulled into a restaurant to get dinner and find out where I was. My book of pet-friendly motels was organized by state and city, so to use it, I had to know the name of the town where I was staying.

I went into the restaurant and ordered a hamburger, French fries and a chocolate milkshake. When the young cashier brought my order to the counter, I paid and asked her for the information I vitally needed: "What town are we in?"

She was mystified. "What?" she asked.

"Can you tell me the name of the town this restaurant is in?"

"I don't know."

"Well, does somebody else know?"

The girl turned around and called out to her co-workers, "Does anyone know what town we're in?"

"Woodbridge," came a voice from the kitchen.

Back at the truck, Beau was instantly interested in my hamburger. I ate most of it and gave him the last bite, and then checked my pet-friendly motel book. There was only one listing in Woodbridge, Virginia, and it stated, "small pets only." This was not good.

I was tired and didn't want to drive around looking for a place to stay. Just up the street I saw a Quality Inn. I decided to stop in and ask if my pets were allowed. I was in luck. The answer was yes.

Moving in turned into a parade. First I walked through the lobby with two pet carriers, past the front desk and down the hall to my room on the first floor. On my second trip I brought another pet carrier and a bag of pet supplies. On my third trip I carried my overnight bag and walked Beau on his leash. With such a menagerie passing by, I thought the hotel might rescind my welcome, but it didn't.

My plan was to let the small pets stay in the carriers for the entire trip to Florida. The little blue boxes were lined up on the dresser, and I fed the animals through sliding doors. Exhausted, I undressed, shut the lights and climbed under the covers. Beau jumped on the bed and curled up at my feet.

Just as I was drifting off to sleep a horrible racket arose from the direction of the pet carriers. One of the sugar gliders emitted a noise I'd never heard before—it sounded like continuous, high-pitched barking. I was terrified— maybe the glider was sick. Maybe he was dying. Maybe I should put him in his regular cage, which was still in the back of the truck. Maybe I should put all the animals in their regular cages.

I dressed, went out to the truck and resumed the parade. First I brought the glider cage through the hotel lobby, then the hedgehog cage and finally the chinchilla cage. Back in familiar surroundings, everyone settled down and we all went to sleep.

The next morning, I adjusted my travel plans. I put the cages, with the animals inside, directly into the car that was riding on the trailer, so the pets could stay in their homes. For my next motel, I'd look for a room with access directly to the parking lot, so I didn't have to drag all the animals through a hotel lobby. And, I'd look for a place with a driveway that went all the way around the building. As I struggled to leave the Quality Inn parking lot, I learned that I did not have the driving skills to navigate a truck and trailer in reverse.

Somehow I got back on I-95 and our trip continued. As the miles passed by, my only distraction was searching for new radio stations. Beau slept on the seat beside me. At our stops for food and gas, he jumped happily out of the truck, excited to investigate so many new and unusual scents. We were on an adventure.

On the last day of our trip I got on the road early. I was 450 miles from Orlando and determined to finish the journey. A radio station played continuous classical Christmas music. The traditional songs kindled a feeling of hope within me—maybe the New Year would bring me peace.

Late in the afternoon, I reached Daytona Beach in northern Florida. That's where I left I-95 and got onto I-4, which would take me 50 miles to Orlando, in the middle of the state. Darkness fell, and in the Orlando metropolitan area, exits came at me fast and furious. Once again, it was rush hour. I missed my final exit off the East-West Expressway, so I had to get off the highway, turn around, and go back in the opposite direction. This time I found what I was looking for—Alafaya Trail. From there I called James on his cell phone so he could talk me through the final few blocks of the trip.

"Turn left at the shopping center," he said.

"What shopping center?" I asked frantically.

"It's on the left. You can't miss it."

I looked to my left and realized I was driving past it. The shopping center was hidden from the highway by a stand of trees, which James forgot to tell me.

I turned around again and found my way to the apartment complex. The entrance was marked by a large manmade pond with a jet of water shooting up from the center. When I pulled up in front of our building, James was standing on our second-floor balcony, backlit by the lights of our new living room, waiting for me. "Nuffles made it," he warmly welcomed me.

For the first time in my adult life, I lived in someplace new and modern.

The door to our apartment opened into a foyer. James' domain, the master suite, was on the immediate right. I peeked in and saw he was moved in—the floor was cluttered with piles of papers.

Straight ahead was the living room-dining room. The kitchen, on my left, was also part of the main living space, separated only by a bar-height counter. That's where the sink was, so if I were filling a coffee pot with water or cleaning up after dinner, I was still part of any activity in the living room.

A short hallway, directly opposite the foyer, led from the living room to the remaining rooms. On the right was our bedroom. On the left was the other full bathroom. Straight ahead was the smallest bedroom—my office.

Everything was new and white and fresh. The kitchen appliances had never been used. The beige carpet was clean. The blue-and-white striped sofa and love seat looked comfortable. James had already bought a TV and signed up for cable service. Spending a year in this apartment would be easy.

My husband was excited about being back in Florida, and glad that I was there with him. We had been apart for three weeks, and after I had a chance to eat and relax, he showed me how much he missed me. "You'll see, Darwies," James told me. "Everything will get better now."

The next day I unloaded the U-Haul truck myself, making 30 or 40 trips up to our second-floor apartment, carrying boxes. I could have been resentful that James didn't help, but after three days on the road, the physical exercise felt good. As the boxes were emptied, I stacked them neatly in our garage.

While returning the truck and trailer, I discovered a nearby K-Mart. I'd never shopped in a K-Mart, but I needed household basics and we were broke, so I decided the low-cost megadiscounter would do just fine. Braving the Christmas Eve crowd, I bought a shower curtain, cutlery tray and a few more Christmas gifts—dog chews for Beau and a heating pad for James. I thought the heating pad might help my husband's back, which constantly hurt him.

With our apartment organized, I set up the little Christmas tree in the corner of the living room. Around the tree, I ran the model train that James gave me the year before.

"You brought us a tree? And the train?" James asked, sounding almost childlike.

"Sure," I said. "I want us to have a special Christmas."

That evening, Christmas Eve, I cooked a nice chicken dinner. James talked about his visit to Australia the previous week. His family was fine, and his mother was happy to see him. James met with his partner, Archie Turner, who was working on a plan to set up schools for Chinese students in English-speaking countries. "China is joining the international economy, and millions of Chinese want to speak fluent English," James said. "Archie has a good one here. This project looks like it's going to come through."

Most importantly for us, James told me that the Jacobsen Group, one of the biggest entertainment companies in Australia, wanted our Titanic show. "All of Australia is going nuts over anything Titanic," he said. "Jacobsen wants to cash in on it. They're willing to advance us a half-million dollars to purchase more artifacts. I've got a letter expressing their interest in our exhibit."

James showed me the letter:

JACOBSEN

December 18th, 1998

Dear James

Thank you for presenting to us The Titanic Experience and for giving the Jacobsen organization the opportunity to be involved in your project.

I see no way that Titanic can ever lose its enormous public appeal and your wealth of fascinating artifacts would seem to guarantee interest in any part of the world. Close to the Maritime Museum in Darling Harbor in the old Showboat Casino site would be an ideal location. I am meeting with the rental company responsible for leasing the property and will e-mail that data to you.

Let me confirm that we would like to form a joint venture to run The Titanic Experience at this site as soon as you can acquire sufficient artifacts for another show. That you would personally set up and launch the show, run and supervise it and we would aid with all site negotiations and PR and Marketing. I am authorized to tell you that we can advance up to A$500,000 to aid you with your artifact purchase subject to an agreement between us along the lines we discussed yesterday. Further, that stills and video of the Orlando exhibition as well as some financial and statistical information may enable us to increase the size of that offer.

Kind regards
John Lynn
Business Manager
Jacobsen Entertainment Group

Yet another opportunity for the Titanic. That's good, I thought. Maybe we'd get out of the hole. Maybe we'd even have some discretionary income. I went to bed feeling hopeful.

Christmas morning in Florida dawned 63 degrees and humid, unlike New Jersey, where the weather was freezing. I turned on the Christmas tree lights and set the model train in motion. Then James and I exchanged presents. I bought him practical gifts, like slacks, socks and the heating pad.

"Your gift is on the train," James said to me.

I looked at the model train and noticed a small, open jewelry box riding around on it. Inside was a pair of fiery opal earrings that James had purchased in Australia.

"They're beautiful," I said. "Thank you."

James suggested that we eat breakfast at home, and then go out for Christmas dinner in the afternoon. So I made eggs—poached for James, scrambled for me. As I stood at the sink after breakfast, cleaning up, I watched James on the sofa, teasing Beau, who would do anything for his Christmas dog chews. My heart glowed with warmth. I was in Florida with my real family—my husband and my pets. We were about to embark on a new beginning. I had a sense that everything was going to change.

By two o'clock, when James and I went out to find a restaurant for Christmas dinner, the sky turned gray and overcast. We drove by several eateries in our new neighborhood—they were all closed.

We had no choice but to go home and eat leftover chicken.

Right after January 1, 1999, James flew back to Atlantic City for a few days of business meetings.

Beau and I explored our new neighborhood. A water drainage pond right behind our apartment building was convenient for quick dog walks. Small frogs inhabited the pond—they inevitably jumped into the water before Beau noticed them. For our longer walks we could go in several directions right on the grounds of our apartment complex. I even found a dirt road that led to a cow pasture. Beau had never seen cows, and he didn't know what to make of the beasts.

I had plenty of opportunities to get exercise for myself as well. The health club in our apartment complex was small but useful. I found a jogging trail in a nearby housing development.

This was all very nice, but I didn't move to Florida for a warm-weather work-out. I came to set up the Titanic exhibit so James and I could start earning money. After James returned from Atlantic City, I walked into his office, where he was sitting at his computer.

"What's going on with Wild Bill's?" I asked him.

"I met with Johnny Stuart's guy in Atlantic City," he replied, not taking his eyes from his computer monitor.

"When are we supposed to open the show?"

"We're still working out the details," he replied.

I was quiet for a moment.

"So we don't really have a deal," I stated, matter-of -factly.

"Not yet."

I stared at my husband, who continued to look at his monitor. Then, my voice thick with accusation, I questioned him. "Then why the hell did we move to Florida? You said you had to be here the beginning of December. You said the show was opening February 1. We spent money we don't have to get here, and then you went to Australia. What the hell were you thinking?"

"We had an opportunity," James retorted. "We still have an opportunity. We had to be here so that when Johnny Stuart pulls the trigger, we're ready to jump into action."

"So this whole move was one big gamble."

"Yes, I gambled. But if you don't gamble, you don't win."

"Jesus Christ, James. It never occurred to you that it might be better to have a deal in place before moving here?"

James finally looked at me, with sadness in his eyes. "I thought Stuart was coming through," he said, his voice low. "And I knew how upset you were about our financial situation. I wanted to take action right away to get some revenue coming in. I did this for you, Donna."

I looked over James' head and out the window.

"I love you, Donna," he continued, quietly. "Nothing else really matters, you know. Money will come and go. The only thing that lasts is that we love each other."

I was so agitated that I couldn't respond.

James stood up and put his arms around me, pulling me close. "I'm so sorry that things haven't worked out like I thought they would," he whispered to me. "But it will get better. I'll make it up to you. You'll see."

James' admission that he dragged us to Florida on a gamble unnerved me. I tried to keep from crying, although not always successfully. I kept telling myself it was important to remain positive, that positive energy would bring positive results. I decided to make the best of the situation by building a life for myself in Orlando.

First, I'd earn money. Luckily, I had another issue of the Dover Downs Slots newsletter to write, and all my interviews could be done over the phone.

Then, I'd make friends. I contacted the Orlando Rowing Club, which I found on the Internet. A group of women trained at 5:15 a.m., and there was room in the eight for an experienced rower.

The club rowed on Lake Fairview, located in the northwestern part of Orlando. Checking my newly purchased map, I discovered that it was clear across the metropolitan area from Brittany at Waterford Lakes. To be at the boathouse at 5:15 a.m.—45 minutes earlier than my earliest rowing starts in Ventnor—I'd have to get up at 4:15 a.m. Well, I wanted to row, so that's what I'd do.

I arrived at the boathouse for my first row on Thursday, January 14, 1999, in total darkness. A stalwart crew of women assembled, and based on my height, the coach put me in the six seat. Rowers in the five and six seats were the boat's power engines.

I couldn't see where we were going in the darkness, but it felt like we were rowing in a circle. Lake Fairview, it turned out, was only one mile long. We did a couple of laps and returned to the boathouse. My entire workout was done, and the sun had yet to rise.

For his part, James finally took steps to contribute financially. He told me he was asked by the Special Operations Command at MacDill Air Force Base in Tampa, which was just over an hour's drive from Orlando, to work shifts on Friday nights. He would help keep an eye on the world's trouble spots, and in exchange, he'd be able to draw more money from his military pension. James said he would stay over in the bachelor officers' quarters, or BOQ, and return to Orlando on Saturday mornings.

So James was not home when I left for my second row with the Orlando Rowing Club on Saturday, at a much more civilized 6 a.m. By the time I returned home, James was back.

Later that day, January 16, 1999, I flew to Atlantic City. My original reason was a court date for our case against Opus One—they still owed us $4,000 for the infomercial script. Then Ocean One, the shopping mall, requested another meeting about our Titanic show. Negotiations with Ocean One management had been progressing nicely ever since I first made contact. We were now discussing details of launching the show there: We could suspend one of the lifeboats from the ceiling high above the food court as an attention-grabber. We could use a retail store to sell our Titanic merchandise. We could find a Leonardo DiCaprio look-alike to pass out flyers on the Boardwalk promoting the exhibit.

James discussed the Ocean One show, along with the Orlando show, with Johnny Stuart of On Stage Entertainment. He was trying to convince Stuart to invest in our exhibition, and having another venue interested in hosting it made the investment more attractive.

James wanted Ocean One to provide us with a guarantee of revenue. That meant we'd have a revenue target—$50,000 per week—and if we didn't sell enough tickets to meet the target, Ocean One would make up the difference. Ocean One never agreed to a guarantee, which I told James. I also gave James a letter from Ocean One that clearly stated they would not offer a guarantee. But as he talked up the project to Johnny Stuart, James told him Ocean One did indeed promise to guarantee revenue.

Stuart had staff in Atlantic City for his *Legends in Concert* show, so he and James agreed that his manager would accompany me to the meeting with Ocean One on January 18, 1999.

It was my second wedding anniversary. I didn't care.

That morning I received a fax from James with final instructions for the meeting and how I should work with the representative of On Stage Entertainment.

> Nuffles!
>
> Our planned Orlando launch will be Feb 17th.
>
> Johnny's rep has been told that this is a done deal from our POV and not to do anything that would rock the boat—he knows that Johnny has a copy of Ocean One's last letter and I will give Johnny a copy of the signed agreement this week. You can introduce On Stage Entertainment as our landlords and promotional partners in Orlando—and we wanted them to sit in on this meeting to see what they could ADD.
>
> They have been told that we have put in an escape clause for us. If the show doesn't do $50k a week for 3 weeks we can pull out and we have given them the same option—it is better for us to take the materiel to another US site or to Australia. I wouldn't raise it but that is the way it has been put to Johnny.
>
> Now, the rep has been told he is there to just check their level of enthusiasm!!! But use him, he expects to sit in on a discussion of promotion.

The meeting went well. Our discussion covered many issues that needed to be addressed in order to mount the show: The exhibition layout would require approval by Atlantic City's code officials. There was a noise problem in the venue; to dampen it, heavy drapes and carpet would be needed in the theater where our presenters talked about the Titanic. We could fabricate a cherub, matching the one that graced Titanic's grand staircase, and place it on the stairs leading up to the exhibition. This would set the mood for our audience before anyone even reached the show.

"We are 150 percent in favor of making the Titanic Experience happen at Ocean One," the shopping mall's manager stated.

Afterwards, I walked with the representative of On Stage Entertainment to check out our prospective venue. Standing in the area where the show would be, we looked around and discussed its installation. Then he asked about the contract and the guarantee.

"There's no guarantee," I said.

The following day I prepared a detailed report of the meeting and faxed it to James. Then I had nothing to do until our court date on Thursday. On Wednesday, however, I received a $4,000 check from Opus One, so there was no longer any need to go to court. But even with the quick infusion of cash, I didn't have enough money to pay our bills.

Back in Orlando, I recounted the meeting to James.

"Johnny's guy asked about the guarantee," I told him. "I said there wasn't any."

"There is a guarantee," James said.

"No there's not. It's right in Ocean One's last letter, which I gave you. Didn't you read it?"

James had not read the letter. "That's okay, we'll work it out," James said. "Our show will open at Wild Bill's on February 17."

"Who set that date—Johnny Stuart or you?" I asked.

James hesitated. "I did," he admitted.

I knew the date was bogus, and James knew that I knew it was bogus.

How long would we have to hang on in Florida with no revenue? I had no idea, and as each day passed with no deal, I became more and more frightened.

I had to take action, but I was paralyzed. I was filled with anger that James moved me to Florida on a gamble. I was filled with fear that I would lose everything. I was filled with self-loathing for allowing my husband to manipulate me. I was filled with trepidation that, because of all my negative emotions, I would make matters worse.

James said he'd pay $1,400 to my American Express account—the charge for his hotel room in Australia—and surprised me by actually sending a check. James also promised to pay the rent. A Special Forces buddy had agreed to buy one of his computers, he said, and he'd do the deal in a few days.

"What are you waiting for?" I asked. "We need the money now. Can't you sell it right away?"

James thought about it. "Yes, I suppose I can." He came up with more cash—I thought it was a good sign.

I met with two advertising agencies about freelance copywriting—both said they'd have assignments for me. I registered with temp agencies for secretarial work. I continued rowing and expanding my social network, chatting with the woman who lived in the apartment across from us. All of this made me realize that I had the ability to pick up, move to a completely new area and make a life for myself. It gave me a sense of accomplishment.

Still, nagging fear plagued me. Sometimes, as I had in Atlantic City, I sought solace from the pets, who this time, lived in my office. I heard them rustling about as I worked, but often they slept, trusting that everything was fine and I'd feed them in the evening. A few times I shut the office door and let everyone out of their cages. The chinchilla, sugar gliders and hedgehog ran around and climbed on the furniture. They enjoyed exploring their surroundings.

Herbie the hedgehog, however, kept rubbing his face with his paw, where a lump bulged on his cheek. I didn't know what it was. I worried about him.

By the first week of February 1999, James had been in Orlando for more than two months. I'd been there for six weeks. I was still working on plans for the exhibition at Wild Bill's, and needed more information about the facility's dimensions. I called the dinner theater's office.

"We have the Titanic exhibition that's going into Wild Bill's," I said to the manager who answered the phone. "I'd like to stop by and take some more measurements."

"The Titanic exhibition!" exclaimed the manager. "I haven't heard anything about that in ages!"

James' negotiations with Johnny Stuart, I concluded, were not going well.

Even James seemed to believe that the prospects for our show were fading. But we still owned an impressive collection of Titanic artifacts. A year after James Cameron's movie became a blockbuster, public interest in anything Titanic was still high. If we sold the collection, we could clear up our debts and stabilize our financial situation.

To me, that sounded like a great idea.

James told me that he contacted SFX Entertainment, the world's largest promoter, producer and venue operator for live entertainment events. He'd heard that the company was planning a Titanic exhibition. SFX was based in New York City, and James said he could get a meeting with the company, and possibly sell our collection.

I quickly agreed to the plan. "Good," I said. "Go. Let's sell the stuff and call it quits."

"Probably the easiest and cheapest way for me to go would be to fly to Atlantic City," he said. "Then I'll get up to New York."

"Okay."

"Can you book a flight for me?"

All my credit cards were close to being maxed out. But if James went to New York and cut a deal, it would solve our financial problems. Then I could get out of the marriage. I checked the balances and found enough room on my Citibank card to book a $255 flight on Spirit Air. I bought him a ticket to Atlantic City for February 9, 1999, returning February 12, 1999.

A couple of days later, I ran into my neighbor from across the hall as we were both at our front doors. She was an attractive woman, blond, probably in her late 40s. We chatted a bit, and I learned that she was recently divorced. The woman was friendly, and I needed a friend, so knowing James would be leaving for business on February 9, a Tuesday, I invited her over for dinner. She accepted.

On Tuesday morning, James wanted me to drive him to the Orlando airport. We lived less than 20 miles from the airport, so it wasn't a long ride. But it was long enough for a fight.

"When you get to New York, James, I think you should take whatever deal they offer you," I said.

"Our artifacts are worth several hundred thousand dollars," James replied. "If they're not willing to pay that much, then we shouldn't sell."

"The artifacts aren't worth anything if we can't afford to put a show together."

"We'll get investors."

"Are you kidding me? You've been looking for investors for six months."

"They want the show in Australia."

"We already moved to Florida without a deal. Now you want to go to Australia? How the hell are we going to pay for that?"

"Why are you so negative, Donna? We'll get money. We've survived this long."

"Yeah, on my money and my credit. And I'm running out of that. And do you hear that noise in the wheel? This car is dying—but how am I going to get a new one when soon I won't be able to buy groceries?"

"Your complaining doesn't help."

"And your spending doesn't help either. By the way, where are my rings?"

"Why?"

"I want to take them to a pawn shop."

"They're in the lock box in my office."

The rest of the trip passed in silence until we pulled up in front of the terminal. "Take whatever they offer you," I repeated as James opened the passenger side door. He paused for a moment, without looking at me or saying a word. Then he got out of the car and slammed the door.

I watched in the rear-view mirror as James pulled his luggage and briefcase—containing many of our expensive Titanic artifacts—out of the trunk. He slammed the trunk shut. I drove away.

Once again, I was in turmoil. My heart pounded and my stomach churned. I was scared to death that SFX would offer James money for our artifacts and, still believing his grandiose dreams, he'd turn it down.

And the rings—I'd noticed four were missing from my jewelry box. James gave me three of them—they belonged to his deceased wife, Gale Lewis. The fourth belonged to my mother. Why did he take them?

It wasn't the first time James had taken my stuff. A few weeks earlier, when I got into his car with him, I noticed a compass in the cup holder. "I have one just like this," I said, picking it up.

"Uh, it's yours," James admitted.

The compass, which I'd owned since I was a 14-year-old Girl Scout, was kept inside an antique desk in my bedroom back in Atlantic City. Obviously, my husband had gone through my drawers.

When I got back to the apartment, I went directly into James' office. Even though the room was a mess, it didn't take long to find the lock box. Stuck in his closet was a gray metal container about the size of a shoebox, with a handle in the flip-up lid. It was, of course, locked.

So I looked for a key. Opening his top desk drawer, I found a small "I Love NY" key chain, with a key attached, lying right in the front tray. I put the key into the lock. It turned.

The box contained my four rings—but that wasn't all.

It contained a pile of recent photos of my husband with a baby:

• James, cradling the infant over the large expanse of his shirtless gut, feeding her a bottle, grinning.

• James, wearing one of our Titanic Experience polo shirts, showing the baby a picture book.

• James, with the baby riding in a carrier strapped over his shoulders, as he strolled through Walt Disney World in Florida.

• James, cuddling and kissing the baby, in what appeared to be a motel room. In fact, almost all of the photos looked like they were taken in motel rooms.

There was also a photo of a woman holding the baby, who wore a tiny "My First Wildwood" t-shirt. Apparently, the woman was the baby's mother. And apparently, James had driven to Wildwood, 45 minutes south of Atlantic City, to buy the t-shirt.

I trembled in shock.

Then I found a stack of personalized, unsent Christmas cards. The cards showed a photo of the baby seated on a chair in front of a Christmas tree. Printed below the photo was "Seasons' Greetings 1998"—the Christmas we just celebrated. On each card, someone had written in black marker, "James Kim & Janna"—certainly not James, because the writing was legible. It must have been written by "Kim," which was apparently the mother's name.

My husband was having an affair. That fucking bastard.

I found another Christmas card addressed to "my new baby sister, Janna." The card was signed, "Margaret." That would be Margaret Riley, James' daughter, with whom we stayed when we went to Australia to get married. Apparently my daughter-in-law knew all about the child. There was also a birthday card to James—from the baby. "Lucky me to have you for my daddy," it said.

Further into the box, below the photos and cards, was a folded paper, which I pulled out and opened. It was an original birth certificate. Apparently Janna Montgomery* was born in April 1998 in Pinellas County, Florida, which was conveniently close to Tampa. Her mother was listed as Kimberly Goodson.* Her father was listed as James Alwyn Montgomery. She was almost one year old.

My hands shook, but there were more papers in the lock box.

I found a receipt for a new Gateway computer—the computer that was right there in front of me on James' desk. It had been purchased by a woman named Sylvia Banning* on April 15, 1998. James had told me he got it from a business associate who couldn't figure out how to use it. Obviously, he lied.

Below that was another receipt for yet another computer—the miniature Philips Velo that James brought home almost two years earlier. The Velo was purchased by a woman whose address was listed as the *Cats* show in New York City. Maybe that's why James was so hot to see *Cats* when it came to town—and why he went to the hotel the morning after the show.

The lock box was finally empty. So was my brain—it was all too much to absorb. But one clear thought broke through: Now I can leave.

I took my obligation as a wife seriously. I vowed to stand by my husband, for richer or poorer, in sickness and health, till death do us part. Time after time, as I struggled to deal with our deteriorating financial situation, I asked myself, "What kind of a wife leaves her husband because his business plans aren't working?"

This was different. I was leaving my husband because he was an adulterer. James Alwyn Montgomery fathered a child with another woman during our marriage. The inescapable proof was in my hands.

Now I can leave.

But what else had he done? I tore apart James' office. I found his bank statements and spread them out on the floor. Inside were checks James had written to Kimberly Goodson throughout 1998: January 20—$200. May 4—$100. May 13—$1,000. May 19—$650. November 13—$200. November 18—$100. November 20—$135. November 29—$100. December 7—$225.

So while I was desperately trying to pay bills, my husband was giving his mistress our money. That would be my money. In fact, James gave Kimberly Goodson one of his checkbooks. She wrote many of the checks to herself and signed his name.

I stood up, shakily, and walked out of James' office and into the living room. A surprising thought broke through the fog in my brain: Life has just gotten very interesting.

Then I started to pace. My mind was racing so fast that my feet had to move as well.

The marriage was over. But at that moment, my soon-to-be ex-husband was on his way to my home, the home that I paid for, in Atlantic City, New Jersey. I couldn't let him know what I had discovered. I didn't know what he would do, and I didn't want him to trash my house.

I decided that I would leave Florida while he was gone. I also decided that I wouldn't say a word to him until I knew that he was on the plane, flying back to Orlando.

I had three days.

I would take everything that was mine, and all the Titanic artifacts.

I would sell my car and take his car, the Thunderbird, which was leased in my name.

Suddenly, adrenalin flooded my body. From the garage I retrieved the packing boxes that I'd emptied only six weeks earlier. Working like a madwoman, I filled the boxes and taped them shut.

The afternoon flew by. At 5:30 p.m., I knocked on my neighbor's door—she was still expecting to come over for dinner.

"I'm afraid I can't cook for you," I said when she answered the door. "I'm too upset. I just found out that my husband is cheating on me. He had a child with another woman."

"Why don't you come in?" she invited sympathetically.

I did. She gave me a glass of wine, and the name of her lawyer.

I didn't sleep well that night, thinking of all that had to be done so I could leave. It was a long list, and the next morning I started early.

I told the rental agent for Brittany at Waterford Lakes that I was breaking the lease. She said I had to give written notice, and we were still liable for the rent. I didn't argue—rent would be dealt with later.

I called the furniture rental company and told them to come for the furniture. The lease was in my name—I was through paying for James' adventures.

I returned the heating pad I'd bought James for Christmas, which hadn't been used. The refund was a whopping $13. But I wanted to take anything I could back from my husband.

I called U-Haul and rented another truck and trailer. Luckily, because James had paid the American Express bill, I could charge the rental to my Amex card.

I called my neighbor's lawyer and made an appointment for the following day.

Then I had to sell my car. In the few short weeks that I'd been driving around Orlando, I noticed many used car lots offering "Cash for Your Car." I brought my 1990 Ford Probe to two of them.

"How much do you want for it?" the first owner asked.

"Fifteen hundred," I replied.

"I can offer you $1,300," he said.

"I'll think about it," I said.

I drove to another lot.

"How much do you want?" the second owner asked.

"Seventeen hundred," I answered.

He thought about it. "Well, let's take the car for a ride."

The used car dealer drove as I sat in the passenger seat, praying that the wheel wouldn't make its screeching noise. The car behaved perfectly.

The dealer offered me $1,500—the price that I wanted. He said to come back the next day with my car title and he'd have a check for me. As I left, I thanked God for the small miracle of the quiet wheel.

Back at the apartment, I continued packing. I worked quickly, and sealed boxes were piling up. The phone rang. I took a few moments to gather myself, then answered. It was James.

"Hello, Donna," he said.

"Hi," I said, as casually and pleasantly as possible. "How was your flight?"

"It was fine. I got in on time."

"That's good."

"How are you?" James asked.

"Oh, I'm fine," I said, nonchalantly lying through my teeth.

"How are *we*?" James asked, emphasizing the "we."

"Fine," I said, putting a note of surprise in my voice. "When are you going to New York?"

"I'm leaving in the morning," James said.

"That's great. Be careful going up there, and let me know how you make out."

"All right, Nuffles," James replied. "I'll see you on Friday."

No you won't, you bastard, I thought to myself.

As I continued packing, I took anything I had paid for and anything I might be able to sell—such as the new television/VCR James bought. I left everything that belonged to my husband, including the dishes, which he had brought over from the Mays Landing townhouse. I didn't want them.

By Thursday, February 11, 1998, the packing was almost done, but I still faced a dilemma: What should I do about James' computer? I didn't pay for it—that Sylvia Banning woman did, whoever she was. I knew, one way or another, I'd still be dealing with James on the Titanic, and he would need the computer. But maybe it had information that would be important in my upcoming divorce.

I brought up the computer issue when I visited the lawyer, who, upon seeing the baby photos and birth certificate, said I certainly had grounds for divorce. First he said I should leave the computer, then he said I should take it—the information was probably important. When I got home I disassembled the machine, but I was still unsure. The decision was postponed until morning.

The furniture rental people came and took everything away. I was amazed at how quickly they emptied the place. That night, in an apartment containing nothing but boxes, I spread sheets out on the bedroom floor and lay down to sleep, with Beau curled up beside me.

"James—we have a problem," read the note I left on the counter. "Her name is Janna Montgomery. Too bad she has your ears."

It was Friday, February 12, and the U-Haul truck was packed. At the last minute, I'd decided against taking James' computer. I could already hear the tirade if his computer was gone.

When I was certain that James was in the air, flying back to Orlando, I left Brittany at Waterford Lakes, heading for the I-4. About an hour into the trip, I called my husband's cell phone and left a message: "James, I won't be picking you up. I know about the baby and I'm on my way back to Atlantic City. I left cab fare for you on the counter." Then I shut off my cell phone.

We all settled in for the long ride—me and the five pets. Beau curled up on the seat beside me, sleeping. The hedgehog, sugar gliders and chinchilla were all in their cages in the Thunderbird on the trailer. I thought about leaving the small animals—after all, James was the one who brought them home. But I doubted that he would take care of them, and I didn't want the little guys to be abandoned. They were my buddies. So everyone came with me for another long ride. Having done it only six weeks earlier, we all knew what to expect.

Hours and hours on a straight, tree-lined highway required minimal driving focus, which meant the tumultuous thoughts that I shoved aside while repacking for the trip home could take over my mind. Obviously, when James proclaimed he was so in love with me that for the first time in his life he was faithful—he lied. Obviously, my husband's tryst at the Berlin Motor Lodge a year earlier was only one of many. Obviously, James was willing to move us to Florida—with or without a Titanic deal—just to be near his mistress and child. The photos and papers I found in the lock box proved James was involved with at least three other women during our marriage. Were there more? How many? Did I need an AIDS test?

And his lies to get me to move to Florida! Telling me he had a deal with Johnny Stuart. Telling me Stuart was going to invest in our show. And when it finally became apparent that he had no deal, telling me that he gambled on moving us to Florida just for me!

No wonder he made so many trips to Florida—each time telling me it was for business. Yeah, right—so he could carry on his affair. And I'm buying the plane tickets! He's sending the woman my money! And took the kid to Disneyworld!

I'd known for a long time that James lied to me. Still, as I finally had time to absorb the scope of his brazen deceit, it astounded me. The thoughts and questions cycled around and around in my head. What else had he lied about? A few times, I gripped the steering wheel hard and yelled, loudly, as if my lying, cheating husband could hear me. He didn't, of course, but I woke up the dog.

My brain hurt. I had to force myself to retreat from the battle raging in my head. When I focused on my surroundings, I noticed many trucks and trailers on the road decorated with bold colors and NASCAR racing logos. I realized I was traveling in the middle of Speedweek, when 200,000 auto racing fans descended on Daytona Beach. Great. If I wanted to sleep that night, I'd probably have to drive all the way to Georgia.

Hours later I crossed the state line and found a room in the Days Inn in Kingsland, Georgia. When I got settled, I checked my voice mail. James left several messages on both my cell phone and home phone:

"Donna, I really need to talk to you."

"Donna, please call me. It's not what it seems."

"Donna, you know I love you. Please let me explain."

I did not call back.

In the morning, we got on the road again. We traveled 360 miles the second day of the journey, to Fayetteville, North Carolina. Again, I turned off the cell phone as I traveled. After checking into a hotel for the night, I called my voice mail. Again, there were multiple messages from my husband.

On Sunday morning, February 14, 1999, I decided to return James' calls. Sitting on the bed in the motel room, I dialed his cell phone.

James picked up right away. "Where are you?" he asked.

"Somewhere in North Carolina," I replied.

"Donna, listen," James said. "The baby—it's not what you think."

"No? What is it?"

"The mother is a friend of mine. She's a lesbian, and she really wanted a child, so I did her a favor."

Could he come up with anything stupider?

"She means nothing to me, Donna," James continued. "It was just a choice I made to accept paternity. I know I should have told you about it before, and I'm sorry I didn't. You're my wife and I love you. Will you please come home? I want to make everything up to you."

James sounded so plaintive, so desperate to have me return, that for the briefest of nanoseconds, I considered going back to him. But I quickly realized that if I did, I wouldn't be able to leave again, because there was no more room on the credit cards.

"No. I'm not coming back," I replied.

"Donna, please."

"No. I'm going home."

James was silent for a moment. When he spoke, his voice was full of irony. "Happy Valentine's Day," he said.

I hung up. For the first time in my life, I had given absolutely no thought to Valentine's Day.

I sat on the motel room bed for 10 or 15 minutes, planning my next conversation in my mind. Then I placed another call—to my father. "I've left James," I said to Dad. "I'm driving a truck and trailer back to Atlantic City."

"All right, honey," Dad said. "When will you be there?" It was the only question he asked me.

"I hope to get back by tonight."

"Well let me know and I'll help you unload."

I made it as far as Maryland that day; then I could drive no further. I had to spend one more night in a motel. Leaving early in the morning, I arrived in Atlantic City before noon. My sister, Tracy, was already at my house, and Dad pulled up right behind me.

James was gone, I was home and my family was helping me unpack. There were no uncomfortable questions, no heavy conversations, for which I was grateful. I'd start dealing with the wreckage of my life the next day.

Chapter 13

What else did James do? How many women were there? The questions in my mind multiplied exponentially. Maybe my husband's office—his audacious lair right in my home—held answers.

For more than two years, I'd ignored my husband's mounds of paper. Print-outs, letters, envelopes, mail, faxes—to me it was all the clutter of his brilliant but disorganized mind. Now the piles of paper could represent something else—evidence.

I found more bank statements. James had two accounts in the First Union Bank—I'd been vaguely aware of this. One was in his name. The other, an old account that had been transferred to New Jersey from Florida, was a joint account in the name of James A. Montgomery and Cecelia A. Portnoy.* James told me Cecelia Portnoy was his accountant—I assumed that's why her name was on the account. But now I wondered—what exactly was this woman's relationship to my husband?

The Montgomery/Portnoy statement for November 4 through December 4, 1998, showed total deposits of $14,568 for the month. Where did all that money come from? A deposit for $1,000, on November 23, was a wire transfer from me—I remembered his appeal for money while he was in Las Vegas. But there was another deposit of $1,500 five days earlier that I couldn't identify. Then the statement showed two deposits for $6,000 each on December 2 and 3, 1998. One was a funds transfer from Sylvia Banning.

Sylvia Banning—the woman whose name was on the receipt for James' computer. And December 2—that's when James got the money to pay the rent for the Florida apartment, money that he said was an advance from his military pension. Did he actually get the money from that woman?

Another bank statement, from April 1997, showed a wire transfer deposit of $2,000 from Kimberly Goodson. So my husband had been involved with the mother of his child since a few months after our New Jersey wedding—or longer. She also gave him money.

Other statements from 1997 showed two charges, for $300 each, to a local pet store. The purchases were made at the same time that the sugar gliders appeared in our home. That meant James lied about his "deal" in acquiring them—while I was desperately trying to pay for our wedding and the charges on my credit cards, James spent hundreds of dollars on new pets. I also found a receipt from a local trophy store, dated when James told me he went to the Nassau Film Festival. Apparently the award he brought home was, indeed, a bowling trophy, and he bought it himself.

Rooting through more papers, I found letters that James wrote and faxed. In one to Johnny Stuart, dated November 18, 1998, he wrote, "As you know Donna is in Orlando looking at all the properties we have been offered [she believes, with me, we can do quite a job at Wild Bill's]." I was furious. Not only did James ignore the fact that I hated the Wild Bill's location, he told Johnny Stuart I was in favor of it!

I found a sheet of blank stationery from the Jacobsen group. Suddenly, I realized that the letter James showed me, confirming that Jacobsen wanted to form a joint venture with us for the Titanic Experience, was forged. James wrote it himself, and made the reference to "the old Showboat casino site" for my benefit.

I found a letter without an addressee—from the content I deduced that James sent it to the parents of Gale Lewis, his deceased wife, in early 1997. Written after James and I were married but before the Mays Landing townhouse was sold, it was also full of lies:

> Hi Folks!
>
> Well, Disney have optioned the 'First Casualty' script and Lenfest continue to pay me a fee to reorganize their network till we can take it over [a matter of suitable terms] ... I have stabilized my income revenue and can see light at the end of the tunnel for our stock to start moving up!
>
> Poly-T will become viable in the next six months and either Celeb-AM or Century Park will start within twelve months.
>
> It's time for me to start planning the rest of my life.
>
> I have found a place down in AC and will move out of Mays Landing by the end of the month. I will need to take my bedroom furniture, the chaise and sofa, the dining table and the kitchen stuff.

Reading the letter, I became angry again. *The First Casualty* was never optioned. The cable television company never paid him a dime. And James was going to take over the network? What a joke! Furthermore, if James' income stabilized, it was because I was supporting him—although he neglected to mention that he moved to Atlantic City because he married me. And I never saw that bedroom furniture.

Then I found a letter that James received from John Lewis, Gale Lewis' father. As executor of the estate, he demanded the return of his daughter's property. The letter included an itemized list of missing items:

• Hand blender—it was in my kitchen cabinet.

• Stereo receiver, CD player and speakers—the components were on the table in my husband's disheveled office.

• VCR—it, too, was in James' office, connected to my television.

• Watercolor picture of a red tulip vine and blue hummingbird—it was hanging in the kitchen.

• Carved wood bird and duck decoy—they were in my living room.

• Steamer—it was in a closet in the spare bedroom, supposedly so I could steam James' uniforms.

• Duvet, down comforter, pillows and shams—I put the blue and white bed linens in our storage unit, hoping to use them when I could afford to buy matching curtains.

None of this stuff belonged to my husband?

The letter continued:

> Yesterday, May 22, 1997, I received a telephone call from Bell Atlantic Credit Card Center in Millsboro, Del. that the charges on the VISA credit card had not been paid. You said last July, 1996 that you would take care of all the charges on this account, if I would leave the card open. You said they were dual cards in both Gale & your names. Now I find that you have not paid the charges in the amount of $8,223.66 and the card was cancelled by the company last February. I have paid the charges, since Gale was the primary signatory. Please send the $8,223.66 to me ASAP or give a payment schedule to do it within the next six months.

I was sure Gale's father never got his money—I knew how James was with credit cards. In fact, as I continued to search James' office, I found a pile of clothes on the floor. In the middle of the heap was the pair of shorts that James absolutely had to buy before we left Bermuda in August 1997, which he charged to his new credit card. The shorts were never worn. The price tag was still attached.

In the pearl-colored Thunderbird formerly driven by my husband, I pulled up in front of John Glassey's bayfront home. I'd told him that we needed to talk.

John cheerfully invited me in, and we sat in his living room.

"James is cheating on me," I began. "He had a child with another woman."

"Well, that doesn't surprise me," John said.

I gave John the pictures that I found in the lock box. He flipped through the photos as I described how I discovered them and left Florida. When I finished, John handed the pictures back to me. "I guess that means we're partners," he said.

Unfortunately, John and I couldn't simply launch a Titanic show on our own. James still had many of our important artifacts in his possession: The business card case with the Titanic logo. Pieces of White Star Line china. Miniature props from James Cameron's *Titanic* movie. Several Titanic post cards and books. And, he'd made a lot of contacts. We agreed to stay in communication with each other and jointly decide how to proceed with James—John's ex-partner, and my soon-to-be ex-husband.

John was a real businessman with real accomplishments. As he walked me to the door, I knew I could trust him. "You know, James used to cry because he was so afraid of losing me," I said as we stood on his porch. "I can't believe how he lied to me."

"At least we're not him," John observed.

I drove away, with John's words reverberating in my brain. "At least we're not him." No, we were not lying, cheating slimeballs like my husband. But where did my good character get me?

I honored my marriage agreement and stuck by my husband. I persevered as he wasted my money. I did not leave when I found the first clue of his cheating—the photos of naked women. Or the second clue—the receipt for his stay at the Berlin Motor Lodge. Now, as a result of my loyalty, I was the fool. My money and business were gone, and my husband had a child with another woman.

Misery overwhelmed me.

Then I thought, I'm not going to let him win.

And so it went. Every hour, no, every few minutes, my emotions swung between despair and determination. I cursed him and I cried. I crumbled and I pulled myself together.

It was exhausting.

Both of my brothers called me as soon as they heard I was back from Florida.

My younger brother, Greg, was concerned for my physical safety and wanted me to get an alarm system. "Call 1-800-ALARM-ME," he said. "That's Slomin's Security."

"I don't know if I can afford it," I said.

"The installation is free. All you have to do is pay the monthly service, which is about $25."

So much for James' assertion that a security system was too expensive.

My brother Doug asked what I was going to do for work. I hadn't decided. My business wasn't making enough money to support me. I either had to get more work, or throw in the towel and get a job. Even though I'd been self-employed for 17 years, I leaned toward getting a job. I even considered relocating—maybe I should just get out of town and start over.

But finding a job would take time, and I had bills to pay. Doug was expanding his business to capitalize on the dotcom boom, and needed a new website. He retained me to develop the content, and, thankfully, paid me in advance.

James also called—almost every day. He wanted us to get back together. He said he was sorry that he hurt me. He asked me to forgive him. He sounded repentant.

But I was done. Although there had been some good moments in our marriage, there was far too much deceit. I couldn't go back to him.

I began unravelling our financial connections. I cancelled his credit card and his gas card. I stopped payment of his Internet services that were on my other credit cards. James, however, rescinded the apartment lease termination letter that I had submitted to Brittany at Waterford Lakes. He said he'd be able to pay the rent. He also begged me not to shut off his cell phone or cancel his health insurance. James said he'd pay the phone bill, and he asked for one more month of insurance coverage. James needed medication for his diabetes, and although I was angry, I didn't wish him ill. He shouldn't be without coverage.

"All right," I agreed. "I'll keep the coverage until the end of March."

"Thank you," James said, quietly and appreciatively.

James told me he was negotiating with Tampa school district administrators—he sent me copies of their business cards—for a social studies program about the Titanic. James also provided information about his school program to John Glassey.

James then warned me about John. "He will sell you out to preserve his investors," James wrote in an e-mail on March 4, 1999. "He is only interested in taking care of the investor—you share this with him & I won't be able to help you anymore."

Yeah, right.

The school program got nowhere. James gave us revenue projections. Based on those projections, John and I structured a plan in which James would pay the corporation rent for the artifacts he used in the program. Then James told us he couldn't afford the payments.

My husband also had excuses for why the program wasn't yet approved by the school administrators. One of them was that I took his car. "I'm on my way to a meeting," he said, calling from his cell phone. "But it's hard when you have to go by bus." In the background I could hear road noise—and classical music. Since when was classical music played on a bus?

John and I, in the meantime, met with Charlie Schalebaum, the memorabilia dealer. We still owed him $22,000 for Titanic artifacts. We settled the account by returning some of the artifacts. One creditor, at least, was satisfied.

But I had many more creditors, so somehow I had to make money. Every day, I scoured the Internet and newspaper for jobs. I went on an interview at an advertising agency in Trenton, New Jersey. The creative director liked my work. But driving home, I realized that I didn't want to work in Trenton. I didn't want to relocate, and I didn't want to spend four hours a day commuting.

Along with new work, I needed a new social life. In my first outing as a separated woman, I attended a fundraising dinner for the Viking Rowing Club at Bally's Park Place Hotel Casino on March 7, 1999. I dressed up—as did all my friends from the rowing club. Accustomed to seeing each other in sweaty shorts and tank tops, the change was amazing.

One woman had separated from her husband the previous summer in a sudden and nasty break-up. "I just left my husband," I told her. "It's pretty bad."

"Don't worry, it gets better," she replied.

Maybe. But it sure didn't feel that way.

I managed to interact pleasantly throughout the dinner, but when I got home, raw emotion overwhelmed me. Anger at my husband. Fear about money. Pain at the collapse of my dreams.

Why had this happened to me?

What had I done to deserve this?

I got out my journal and reread the entries of the past year. Time and time again, I asked God for help. Knowing my money was being taken, knowing I was being lied to, I asked Guidance to tell me what to do. And every single time, the answer I got was to love my husband, believe in him, support him. Why did I get these messages? Why did they tell me to stay with him? An answer came to me:

It was our way of telling you to hang in because the lessons of the soul are great. Had we told you the truth—that disaster lay ahead—you would have bailed out, and the lessons of the soul would have been lost.

I was astounded.

They *lied* to me. Guidance knew my entire life was going to crash and burn, and they told me to *keep going*. The lesson, they said, was important for the good of my soul.

I looked at the words I just channeled, that I just wrote into my journal, in shock. On that night, alone in my meditation room, terrified about how I was going to survive in this life, I really didn't give a shit about my soul.

Herbie, the African pygmy hedgehog, seemed to have trouble eating, and the side of his face was noticeably swollen. I took him to our family veterinarian, Dr. Leonard Walk, in Ventnor, New Jersey.

Herbie had cancer. Hedgehogs, it turned out, were susceptible to tumors in the mouth. The vet sedated Herbie and pulled a tooth that the tumor had surrounded, hoping it would make the little animal more comfortable. But the prognosis was not good.

In an e-mail, I told James that Herbie was dying. James used the information to make a pitch for our marriage. "I want you," he wrote. "You seem to be a Herbie in my life—I will never see you again."

But the longer I was away from my husband, the less interest I had in reuniting.

The next day, March 12, 1999, James seemed to be resigned to my refusal. "If you believe you will be happier with someone else—as you told me yesterday—I have no right to stop you—I thought we had something special—I will stop—I truly believe you would be most happy if you never saw me again. I have now stopped trying—I believe you. I must find some way to go on."

A few days later James sent a similar message. "I have given up on any hope for us ever," he wrote. "I will try and help you financially. I will never call you again unless you page me first."

James promised to use his contacts to sell the Titanic artifacts. All he wanted in return was for me to "stop the demonizing." "Just concentrate on the good things and don't let anyone take them away from you," he wrote. "Treat me as if I was dead—mourn me by yourself and look for someone to make you happy. You deserve it my love!"

I didn't mourn my husband. I mourned what he took from my life—my financial stability, my pride, my self-esteem. At least he hadn't taken my reputation, which I learned when I had another meeting at the Ocean One shopping mall about launching the Titanic show there. When I explained to the manager that I separated from James, she was pleased to hear it.

"We checked you out," the manager said. "You have a terrific reputation. But your husband apparently has made a lot of statements that he can't back up. He claimed to be doing work for the Claridge casino, but no one over there knows him."

James lied again. What a surprise.

Ocean One was still interested in hosting the exhibition, but we'd have to come up with the money to mount it. John Glassey was still looking for investors. So far he was unsuccessful. Prospects were slim.

In the meantime, I got a call from Jean Muchanic, my former client at Showboat Hotel Casino. A year earlier, Showboat had decided to cut costs by producing the *Crews News* employee newsletter in house. It didn't work out, and the casino president requested that I be brought back to handle the project. That meant regular monthly income for me. I thanked God for my good fortune.

"Do spirit guides fuck with you?" I asked Elaine Anderson, my energy healer, when she called to confirm my upcoming appointment with her.

"Sometimes," she admitted.

I explained the reason for my question—the spirit guides conceded that, in encouraging me to love and trust James, telling me everything would be fine, they lied. Elaine heard the same messages of encouragement during my sessions with her. Yes, the spirit guides told me to stay with James, she confirmed, and they acknowledged not telling me the truth about what would happen.

I was due to see Elaine the following week, on March 31, 1999. In the meantime, she advised me to stay positive. "Keep asking yourself what is the best thing you can do to come out of this situation, to deal with it energetically," she said.

I knew that on March 31 I would be an emotional wreck and unable to work. So I scheduled another appointment on that day, after my session with Elaine. I would take Herbie to be euthanized.

The hedgehog wasn't eating. He rubbed the growing lump on the side of his face with his tiny paw. Sometimes he shook his head, as if he was trying to spit the tumor out. The little guy was suffering, and I couldn't bear to see it continue.

I was Elaine's first appointment, at 10 a.m. She no longer had an office in the big house in Moorestown—she'd left the state, but returned periodically to see her clients, borrowing space in a friend's house. I told her what had happened since my last session in November: The move to Florida. The nonexistent deal for the show at Wild Bill's. The fight on the way to the airport. The lock box filled with evidence of my husband's adultery.

When Elaine laid out the Star+Gate cards, the card that fell in the "You Now" place on the mat was a picture of a hole in the ground. She interpreted it to mean that the bottom had fallen out of my life, but it also meant space was created for something new. The "New Focus" card was a chair, which meant changing structure in my life, and the "Helping" card was a cross, which referred to spiritual direction. The card at the top of the formation, the overall message from the universe, was the Star of Hope.

Almost as soon as I lay on the massage table for the energy work, I began crying. Pain, buried deep in my heart, came flooding out. I felt energy travel through my hands, and then my mouth. Energy was trapped in my mouth because in a past life I'd said too much, and it had gotten James killed.

For the first time, I became aware that James and I were together in a previous life. Hundreds of years ago, in a time of brutal warfare, we knew each other. I wasn't sure of the nature of our relationship—the memories were only fragments. But I was forced by his enemies to tell where he was, and he was caught. I blamed myself and carried the karma into this lifetime.

Then, on Elaine's table, my awareness turned to my current life. This time around, my soul wanted to help him. James wanted what I offered him, but he couldn't reach out to me, couldn't hold on. He blew it. Perhaps he had so many scars in his spirit—he was always a warrior—that he lost his way.

"You did what you could," Elaine said. "But the time comes when you must choose yourself. That's what you did."

We talked about how I would move forward. My family and friends were willing to help me, Elaine said. All I had to do was ask them. Dad already sent me $1,500, which was healing for both of us. He couldn't afford to give me money when I was a child, so to help me as an adult, when I needed it, meant a lot to him. And to me.

My mind drifted to Herbie, the little hedgehog who had a final appointment with the vet that afternoon. I told Elaine that I was taking him to be put down.

"This is no coincidence," Elaine said. "Herbie has a message for you. Can you feel what it is?"

I listened for a message. "I'm just like him," I said. "I've always been all curled up in a ball with spikes sticking out."

"He's offered himself as a symbol of the way you used to live, and that life is coming to an end," Elaine agreed. She paused, and we both considered the imagery. "Herbie is very happy that you heard him," she continued. "He's happy to give himself as a gift to you. He feels special."

When I got home after the session, I tried to make Herbie's last hour pleasant. I took him outside and let him run around in the garden. He sniffed at the new plants sprouting from the earth with the warmth of spring. He burrowed with his snout, looking for bugs. Then it was time to go. I put him in his blue pet carrier and took him to Dr. Walk. I also brought some fabric—a shroud in which to wrap his body.

I followed Dr. Walk into the treatment room, and sat in a chair as the veterinarian took Herbie out of the carrier and placed him on a stainless steel examination table. First he gave Herbie a tranquilizer to put him to sleep before he administered the euthanasia drug.

"This will take a few minutes," he said.

"Can I hold him?" I asked.

"Of course."

I picked up my prickly pet—if his quills hurt my hands, I didn't notice. Holding him close to my chest, I felt Herbie relaxing as I talked to him. "I'm going to miss you, Herbie," I told him. "Thank you for being in my life."

The tiny hedgehog was asleep.

I lay Herbie on that stainless steel table, and Dr. Walk administered the lethal injection. But my one-pound hedgehog was a tough little guy—the vet had to give him far more of the drug than he expected. Then blood spurted from Herbie's nose. Dr. Walk looked up at me and nodded. It was over.

I brought Herbie home and buried him in the garden, where an hour earlier he had been running around, looking for bugs. I cried for him, and for me.

Chapter 14

I was back on the pitcher's mound. In fact, I moved up to the big leagues, at least for co-ed slow-pitch softball.

My objective was networking. I needed to make contacts and get my business going, so I joined the Philadelphia Direct Mail Association and the Philadelphia Advertising Club. On the Ad Club website, I stumbled across information about its softball league. Co-ed softball teams always needed women—this I knew from experience. So I called the league's commissioner, who was director of sales for the WB17 television station. I told him I wanted to get on a team.

"Have you played before?" he asked me.

"Yes—I had my own team for 15 years."

"What position do you play?"

"Pitcher."

"Would you consider yourself an A, B or C player?"

Gee—how should I respond? I could hold my own in a game, but I wasn't a star. "Probably a B," I answered.

"Well, we could use another girl," he said. "Why don't you come to practice?"

On a gray, chilly day in early spring, I traveled to Philadelphia's Fairmount Park for my first practice. The guys liked what they saw, and I was welcomed as a member of the WB17 Frogs—a reference to the station's logo character.

Softball could bring some contacts, but if I was going to resurrect my business, I needed many more. I signed up for representation by recruitment agencies that placed creative professionals on short-term assignments. I made sales calls to advertising agencies and marketing companies that might need copywriting. I contacted publications about doing freelance articles.

I did everything I could think of, because although James still sent me e-mails claiming that he woke up crying for me and wanted to make me whole, I doubted that he would.

James certainly didn't bother to make the family of his deceased wife whole.

Instead, my husband ripped them off.

James told me that Gale Lewis suffered a sudden heart attack. It happened on May 17, 1996, while they were both home—he was upstairs in his office and Gale was downstairs watching television. Gale cried out, and James ran down to find her in pain and struggling to breathe. He called 911, then started CPR. The ambulance arrived within minutes, and emergency medical technicians began treating Gale for cardiac arrest. While speeding to the hospital, James called the Lewises, telling them that their daughter may have suffered a heart attack. James soon called again. Gale was dead on arrival.

Gale was only 43 years old. I would be 43 in a few months.

The Lewis' loss, already unbearable, must have been compounded by the actions of their son-in-law. They felt that James took all they had left of Gale— her belongings. And I was party to it. Even though I didn't know there was a dispute—James certainly acted like he owned everything in the Mays Landing townhouse—I was mortified.

I felt obliged to ameliorate my husband's callous actions. Gathering my courage, I sent a letter to John Lewis, Gale's father, on April 12, 1999, in response to his demand for the return of her possessions:

> Dear Mr. Lewis,
>
> I am the woman who married James Montgomery after the sad passing of your daughter, Gale. Two months ago, I left James, for reasons that I suspect you would understand.
>
> In going through some papers, I came across the enclosed letter from you. I was not aware of the letter in the past. Some of the items you requested are in my home, and I would be happy to return them to you. However, my marriage to James has left me financially devastated. If you would be willing to pay the shipping, I will gladly return them.
>
> I hope this will help you.

A few days later I received a phone call from Loretta Lewis,* Gale's mother. "Thank you very much for contacting us," the woman said. "We're very appreciative."

"I'm very sorry for your loss, Mrs. Lewis," I said. "I had no idea that the things James brought to my home did not belong to him. I'm happy to return them. But as I said in my letter, he's wiped me out financially, so if you will pay the shipping, I will send them to you."

"We'd like to drive up and get everything, if it's all right with you."

"Are you sure? It's a long trip from South Carolina."

"That's okay. We'd like to do it."

We agreed that they would come the following Saturday, April 17, 1999, at noon.

"Do you need directions?" I asked.

"We know where you live," Mrs. Lewis replied.

Promptly at noon on Saturday, a brown conversion van pulled onto my street. The parents of James' deceased wife, who appeared to be in their late 70s, got out and walked up to my front door. John Lewis was tall and thin. He seemed reserved, and had an air of responsibility about him. Loretta Lewis was short and thin. Even though she was now a senior citizen, I could tell that she had always been a glamorous woman. Mrs. Lewis dressed well. Her hair was pulled up into a neat bun and her makeup was artfully applied.

Everything the Lewises wanted was stacked in a pile in my living room. But they arrived with something for me as well—a bottle of luxury bath oil. "Just put a few drops in your bath," Mrs. Lewis said. "The fragrance is wonderful."

I was touched. This poor woman was coming to collect the belongings of her dead daughter, taken by my cheating husband, and she brought me a gift!

Mrs. Lewis also handed me a large manila envelope. "When we were closing down Gale's townhouse, we found these papers in a pile," she explained. "I told John to take them out and get copies made."

I sat on the sofa and looked at the papers. They were printouts of e-mails—initial correspondence between James and women who used the AOL personals. I read letters from three women—they were typical of someone introducing herself to a possible suitor:

> I'm an attractive, college educated 43 year old but look much younger. (Yeah I know they all say that, but really, I do look a lot younger.)

> I'm 39, 5'6", with reddish brown hair and green eyes. I've been married and divorced twice (the first was the stupidity of youth and the second was just plain stupidity).

> I am very professional in my work, extremely successful for a single parent and can hold my own anywhere ... I can change from formal evening wear to jeans and sneakers in a heartbeat.

The e-mails were dated from June 18 to 22, 1996. This must have been shocking to the Lewises—their daughter, James' wife, had died only a month earlier. But it was about the same time that I replied to James' ad. I didn't know how recently he'd become a widower, and I was sure none of the other women did either. I handed the e-mails back to Mrs. Lewis. "I know James was using the personals," I said. "That's how I met him."

We talked a bit more about the person we had in common—James Montgomery. After Gale passed, the Lewises retained a private investigator to look into his background. "He didn't find very much," Loretta said. "It was a waste of money."

A private investigator! Was James doing more than cheating?

Joe Nickles and I had lunch.

When I first met James, he was working on Joe's political campaign for county freeholder. Joe won, and as an elected official, performed our New Jersey wedding. James wanted to involve Joe in his ventures—Joe owned shares in the Polytechnique Group and was on the board of directors. James and I spent time with Joe and his wife socially.

We met in an Atlantic City restaurant that did a brisk lunchtime business. Over sandwiches, I told Joe that James cheated on me with several women. He had a child with one of them. He lied incessantly. He owed me more than $225,000.

Joe was shocked. "I'm usually pretty good at reading people," the politician said. "I knew James was full of shit, but I had no idea that he was so devious."

I told Joe that we used the Polytechnique corporation for the Titanic venture, and the company had assets and debts. John Glassey and I were trying to rescue the show, but I didn't know if we would succeed. I also told Joe that I'd be filing for divorce. "This could get ugly," I said. "It would probably be best for you to resign from the board and relinquish your shares."

Joe agreed. He paid for my lunch and we stood up to leave. "Donna, I'm really sorry this happened to you," Joe said. "If there's anything I can do to help, just let me know."

A Titanic exhibition was coming to Atlantic City, but it wasn't ours. RMS Titanic Inc., the company that salvaged artifacts from the wreck at the bottom of the ocean, made a deal with the Tropicana Hotel and Casino. The Tropicana, located on the Atlantic City Boardwalk, would host an exhibition featuring approximately 200 artifacts for the entire summer. The name of the show, ironically, was "Titanic Experience"—the same name we were using.

"Did you feel like crying last night when the Trop conference was on TV?" John Glassey asked me via e-mail. "I couldn't help but wonder what would have happened for us if we had pulled it off last year. We had all of that set up ... we coulda been contenders!!!!"

There was no longer any point in trying to stage an exhibition at the Ocean One shopping mall. John and I would have to look elsewhere to launch the show—or rely on James. And we couldn't get a straight answer out of James about anything. Concluding that working with my husband was impossible, I asked him to return the Titanic artifacts that he still had in his possession.

On April 20, 1999, war erupted.

James sent three e-mails claiming that I seized the artifacts when I left Orlando, that John and I had cut him out, and therefore we had assumed all the debts. "I would be delighted if John tried to sue me," he wrote. "I would gain my share of ownership of the artifacts—you can't have it both ways, guys!"

James wrote with righteous indignation. He claimed I violated the law. Then he called me and repeated his accusations. "I've already spoken to my lawyer," he said. "According to him, you had no right to seize the artifacts. I created the package that the investors bought and I signed the contract. You two decided to cut me out. You can't do that."

I was on the defensive. "Well, James, when I left you I needed leverage," I replied. "The artifacts gave me leverage."

James changed tactics to conciliation. "Look, Donna, I still love you. I always told you that I would cover all the money you spent helping me, and I'm trying to do that. But you can't take away my tools. I can't do a school program without artifacts. If I'm going to make some money so I can repay you, I need something to work with."

"So do you have any bookings for the school program? How much revenue do you anticipate?"

"Nothing is finalized yet. I don't want to make any commitments that I can't keep. But I should get some feedback soon."

The more James talked, the more my chest tightened. He accused me—had I broken the law? He dropped names and numbers—what was he talking about? He made promises—would he come through? By the time I hung up the phone, I could hardly breathe.

Since I'd left my husband, many people finally told me exactly what they thought of him, and it wasn't good. I decided to let James know in an e-mail:

> You have told too many lies to too many people. Your credibility is pretty well shot. I can't tell you how many people have told me, now that we're separated, that they thought you were essentially full of shit. I don't believe you, and I never will. You have lied to me too often, changed your story too many times.

James ignored my comments about others' opinions of him. Instead, he came back with another offer. He'd keep some of the artifacts in his possession, he'd help liquidate the rest and he'd share the debt if the liquidation failed. "My alternative is to proceed to legally claim my share of the artifacts," he wrote.

His offer was vague, and I had questions: What was his share of the debt? With whom are you negotiating? How will we be kept informed? Will you provide documentation of all discussions and offers?

James kept pressing me, by phone and e-mail, to come to an agreement. He told me I wasn't thinking straight. He said our corporation didn't own any artifacts because it didn't buy them. But the investor money was deposited into the corporation's account, and checks were written from the account to pay for the artifacts. When I pointed this out, James accused me of frustrating his efforts.

Then RMS Titanic Inc. cut a deal with SFX—the big entertainment company with which James claimed to be negotiating. RMS Titanic granted SFX a worldwide license to exhibit its collection. This was not good for us. If SFX had access to genuine artifacts salvaged from the bottom of the ocean, why would they be interested in our post cards?

Prospects for our show were rapidly dimming, and the show was $100,000 in debt. Approximately $20,000 of it was on my credit cards, in addition to all the other charges James ran up.

"The figure of $100k I would accept as real debt as presented," James wrote in an e-mail on April 27, 1999. "My share depends on the actions of you two—but even an idiot should get $100K for those artifacts—and hopefully three or four times more."

"I would like to suggest that your share of the debt is 40 percent—that's the number you picked," I replied two days later. "Do you agree to keeping us in the loop about your negotiations?"

"Do I own 40 percent of the artifacts?" James wrote back. "No ownership—no reliability."

I replied:

> The deal you offered was that you would retain the artifacts that you have and help sell the rest. You would sign a paper saying you have no further claim to the rest of the artifacts. You would shoulder your share of the debt if the artifacts do not sell. I am suggesting that your share of the debt is 40 percent. As part of this deal, I want to know who you are talking to about selling the artifacts, and the terms you are suggesting. Do you agree to this?

James kept arguing:

> Donna, go back and read. We get an agreement, then I help liquidate. Tell John to go ahead and sue. I am tired and broke. You don't seem to be able to understand that when you froze my assets you took responsibility. I am only doing this for you and my lawyer insists that if I am successful in bringing any deal you will both have to indemnify me. So to involve you in any pre-discussions would be as stupid as what I am trying to do for you. It's take it or leave it time!

Actually, it wasn't take it or leave it time—the circular debate via e-mail continued. James said he was a superb officer of the Titanic company and whatever he did that broke up our marriage had nothing to do with business. I said he had to help me pay the credit card bills. He said he couldn't help because I took his assets—like the television and the car.

I was tired of the argument.

While all this drama was going on with James, I was trying to get my life on track. Once again, I was producing the Showboat employee newsletter, the Crew's News. But I was still considering taking a full-time job, and went on two interviews. One was for a publishing company in Malvern, Pennsylvania. The company wrote newsletters targeted to a variety of fields, which were sold by subscription. It needed editors to research and write the newsletters—a job I could do in my sleep.

Should I take the job? I analyzed the pros and cons. Although the steady income would be nice, it wasn't high enough to get me out of my financial jam.

I'd be working in an office with people around me, but I'd have to punch a clock—something I never did, not even at Atlantic City Magazine. My working hours would be 8:30 a.m. to 5 p.m. But at 5 p.m., I would be done—that would be a new experience. I'd have to sell my home and relocate, but at least Malvern was an upscale suburb of Philadelphia, where I might meet a professional man, with a real career, who'd be a suitable husband.

I acknowledged to myself that, even though my marriage to James was a disaster, I wanted to try again. First, however, I made myself go to a clinic for an AIDS test. My husband had not been faithful, and I did not know the extent of his extramarital adventures.

I was back on the market.

My sister, Tracy, came down to visit, and we went out to a local bar. I hadn't forgotten how to strike up a conversation—I met a man who owned a small construction company. He bought me a couple of beers. He asked for my phone number. And a few days later, he called me.

The guy lived in a winter rental in Sea Isle City, New Jersey, which was 40 minutes south of Atlantic City. He invited me down and took me to dinner. Then he did what guys do—tried to get me in bed.

I did something I'd never done. I cried.

"I don't think I can do this," I said. "I just left my husband. He was cheating on me."

"I'm not your husband," the guy said.

"I can't do this," I repeated, and left.

I wasn't ready to be on the market.

A phone bill arrived in the mail for James' voice mail account—an account I didn't know he had. I opened it and found call after call from someone in Pennsylvania. The phone number matched the one printed on the receipt for my husband's new Gateway computer, under the name Sylvia Banning.

The evening of Thursday, April 29, 1999, I dialed it. A woman answered the phone. "Hello," she said. Her voice was deep and raspy.

"Is this Sylvia Banning?" I asked.

"Yes, it is," she replied.

"I'm Donna Andersen," I said. "I'm James Montgomery's wife, and I'd like to suggest that you don't give him any more money."

"It's too late," the woman replied. "I already gave him $92,000."

I almost dropped the phone.

I knew about the computer. I knew about one, and possibly two, wire transfers for $6,000. But $92,000? How had this happened? And what did James do with the money?

I needed information from this woman. But where did I start? It was, to say the least, an awkward situation. But Sylvia Banning was anxious to talk to me.

"How did he talk you into giving him so much money?" I asked her.

"He told me I was investing in a Titanic show. He showed me all the artifacts he was buying."

"How long have you known him?"

"Almost two years."

"Was this a romantic relationship?"

"Sure was. Although there wasn't a lot of romance. Mostly we met in motel rooms."

Sylvia had questions for me as well. How long had I been married to James? Was I involved with the Titanic? Was I taking James to court? Sylvia was trying to get her money back from my husband. James told her he couldn't pay because he and John Glassey were suing each other. Of course, that hadn't happened. At least not yet.

We talked for an hour. It became clear that we were both trying to recover our money from James Montgomery. The best thing to do, we decided, was cooperate. I gave the woman my phone number.

After I hung up, I sat at my desk in shock, trying to absorb all that I learned. My husband had cheated with her for almost two years. That was practically our entire marriage. And all the times he told me how much he loved me—well, he was saying the same thing to her.

I was not angry with Sylvia. Not at all. She was a victim. James lied to her, as he lied to me.

The next morning, before 7 a.m., the phone rang. It was Sylvia, with more questions. Did I go with James to Florida? What exactly did I do for the Titanic?

Sylvia said James talked about me, although he neglected to mention that we were married. Sylvia was suspicious early on, but James swore that he was single. How could he be married when his wife had died so recently? In fact, to prove he had no wives hiding in the closet, James sent Sylvia a copy of Gale Lewis' death certificate.

According to James, I was nothing but an incompetent employee who couldn't get anything done, so he asked Sylvia to do work for him. Then he asked her for money. When he failed to repay Sylvia as he promised, she reported James Montgomery to the FBI.

I then understood the true nature of my husband's relationship with me. James wanted my money. Everything else was a lie.

Chapter 15

Sylvia Banning, who lived in northeastern Pennsylvania, had filed for divorce. She'd been married for many years and had two children whom she loved dearly, but her relationship with her husband was never going to work.

Unfortunately, Sylvia was not in a position to leave the marital home. Although she once had a solid career, she had been seriously injured and was no longer able to pursue it. She couldn't afford to move out, and her stubborn husband wouldn't leave either. So in May 1997, more than six months after filing for divorce, Sylvia was still living—uncomfortably—in the same house with her husband and children. She slept on the couch.

Sylvia had emotionally checked out of the marriage and taken legal action. According to her friends, she was a free woman, available to find a new companion. They talked her into placing a personal ad on America Online. Sylvia wrote in her AOL ad that she was 41 years old, had short blond hair and blue eyes, and was the mother of two children. She'd filed for divorce but it wasn't final.

One of the men who responded to the ad was James Montgomery. James said he was a 49-year-old widower, originally from Australia, and the owner of numerous companies. He made himself sound financially well off. He did not mention the fact that he was married.

Sylvia and James started corresponding every day. Within a few weeks, they talked on the phone. Sylvia told James how she wished she could afford to take her kids and leave the house. But her son, Kevin,* was 15 and would soon be going to college. Her daughter, Allison,* was eight and needed surgery. Sylvia's only income, independent of her husband, was the paltry sum she earned at a menial job a few hours a week.

James had a solution. "I'm starting another company," he said. "I need someone to do research and make phone calls for me. Are you interested? I'll pay you."

"Can I work from home?" Sylvia asked.

"Yes," James said. "Everything can be done over the phone or online."

James' new business was called the Southern Florida International Institute for Continuing Education—he used the acronym "SFIICE." He said his business was affiliated with the United Nations and the Australian National University. The company would bring college-age students from Asia—primarily China—to the United States to learn English so they could become qualified to attend college in America.

James needed someone to contact colleges and universities all over the United States and gather information on their admissions programs for foreign students. To Sylvia, it sounded like a good opportunity to earn money and still be available for her children. She agreed to do it.

James told Sylvia that she was getting in on the ground floor of what was sure to be a big, successful enterprise. He couldn't pay much to start, but eventually, James promised, she would do very well financially. He sent her Lotus Notes software to use for his work. Sylvia installed the software in her home computer and started.

As the summer progressed, Sylvia and James had plenty to talk about—on topics both business and personal. Sylvia enjoyed the male attention—she certainly wasn't getting any from her soon-to-be ex-husband. In fact, when Sylvia visited her favorite psychic, Maggie Kay*—a woman whom she'd consulted for four years—James showed up in the tarot cards. "The relationship will be fine," Maggie predicted, "as long as it stays as it is and no money changes hands." Sylvia did not tell the psychic that she was working for James, even though she had yet to meet him.

In August 1997, during one of their daily phone calls, James steered the conversation in an unexpected direction. "You're the type of person that someone would want to marry," he said. "Will you marry me?"

"What?" Sylvia asked, stunned.

"You heard me," James said. "Will you marry me?"

"Yeah, funny, funny," she replied. "That's a real joke."

"I'm not joking."

"Well I don't think the commonwealth of Pennsylvania is going to look kindly on bigamy."

"I'm not married."

"Well, I am. Remember?"

After the call, Sylvia was still shaking her head about the marriage proposal when she heard that cheery AOL computer voice announce, "You've got mail!" It was an e-mail from James. He wanted to prove to Sylvia that he had "no wives hiding in the closet." Attached was Gale Lewis' death certificate.

Sylvia called James. "Okay, I see the death certificate," she said, "but I still can't marry you. I'm not divorced."

"Someday you'll get your divorce."

"We haven't even met!"

"We will," James said.

Then James started a little game. He'd call Sylvia, trying to disguise his voice and introducing himself as James Montgomery's attorney. "I'm calling about a prenuptial agreement," James-as-attorney said. "You'll have to sign one. My job is to protect Mr. Montgomery's assets."

"I don't want his money," Sylvia said, playing along. "I don't care about any money he had before marriage. But any money that comes in during a marriage will be community property."

"That's fair," James replied.

The business—and mild flirting—continued. Finally, Sylvia and James set a date to have lunch on September 15, 1997. James said he had a meeting that afternoon, so he couldn't drive all the way to Pennsylvania—could Sylvia drive to New Jersey? They agreed to meet at the Red Lobster restaurant at the Hamilton Mall in Mays Landing. It would take Sylvia two hours and 45 minutes to get there.

That morning, Sylvia's daughter, Allison, woke up feeling sick. Sylvia called her next-door neighbor and best friend, Madeline Lombardelli,* who had listened to her talking about James all summer. Sylvia thought she should cancel the lunch date. "Don't be silly," Maddy said. "Allison's not that bad. She can go to school."

Sylvia made the drive to Mays Landing, arriving at 11:30 a.m. She had a pleasant lunch with James—he paid—and left by 1 p.m. She was back by the time her kids came home from school.

Sylvia called colleges and universities all over the country for James' new company. Just about every week, James wanted to meet with her to go over the information she gathered, although to Sylvia it seemed that he was also pushing a personal agenda.

Sylvia, however, was distracted. Her daughter needed dangerous surgery. While attending to her child's medical issues, Sylvia was sometimes unable to complete work for James when he wanted it. He was impatient, but Sylvia explained that she needed to care for her daughter. If James had a problem with that, he could find someone else to do the job.

James backed down. He continued to give Sylvia work, and agreed to meetings according to when she could make the trip to Mays Landing—he didn't have time to drive to Pennsylvania. During one of Sylvia's visits in the fall of 1997, James showed her his home. It was an attractive brick townhouse nestled in the woods. "I'd invite you in, but Gale's parents are visiting," James apologized. "I don't want to set off my mother-in-law."

"What would set her off?"

"Anything. She's still trying to hold on to her daughter. I have enough problems with them; I don't need any more."

"That's too bad."

"Yeah. Sometimes when they visit, I just get a motel room. It's easier than being around them."

A month or so later, in November 1997, Sylvia drove to another meeting with James in Mays Landing. She hadn't slept well on the couch the night before, and was worried about falling asleep on the drive home.

"I know where we can go," James said. "We'll order food, and you can rest."

James took her to a motel, and that afternoon, even though Sylvia didn't intend for it to happen, their relationship became physical.

Afterwards, on the way home, Sylvia had mixed emotions about the encounter. She no longer had feelings for her husband. But although she'd filed for divorce, it certainly wasn't final, so she was still technically married, which created some Catholic guilt. Plus there was the issue of mixing business with pleasure—she thought it was generally a bad idea.

Still, she hadn't been sexual in a long time. She was human. She missed it.

A few weeks later, James wanted to stop by Sylvia's home. He was going to be nearby, he said, so he asked if he could come and install a new version of Lotus Notes into her computer.

"Why don't you send it to me in the mail?" Sylvia asked.

"The disks might break," James explained. "It would be better if I updated the software and took them back with me."

"Oh, okay. If that's what you want to do."

Sylvia and her husband owned a 100-year-old home that was originally built with only two bedrooms, so they carved an additional bedroom out of the basement for their son. That's where Sylvia's computer was, which she had told James during one of their conversations.

When James arrived, Sylvia was alone—her husband was at work and her kids were in school. They went downstairs to the bedroom in the basement. Installing the software update didn't take long. Even though James said he came all that way to her home just so the disks wouldn't break, it obviously wasn't true. He sat a little too close, touched her a little too often, and then made his move.

"Ever since that afternoon in the motel," he said, "I haven't been able to get you out of my mind." He led her to the bed.

Afterwards, Sylvia made lunch. They were sitting in the kitchen when Sylvia's neighbor, Maddy, stopped by. Sylvia introduced James, the three of them chatted awhile, and James left.

As soon as he was out the door, Maddy voiced her disapproval. "I don't like him and I don't trust him," she said. "He's a weasel."

Allison's surgery took place in February 1998, and after three days in the Children's Hospital of Philadelphia, the eight-year-old returned home, where she was supposed to recuperate for 15 weeks. James called to find out how she was doing. Although he'd never met the child, he asked to speak to her on the phone.

"Allison, this is the man that mommy does work for," Sylvia said to her daughter as she handed her the cordless phone. "He wants to say hello."

"Hello," Allison said into the phone.

"Hello, Allison, my name is James," James said to her. "I understand that you've spent some time in the hospital."

"Yes," Allison said.

"Are you feeling better?" James asked.

"Well, it kinda hurts."

"Yes, I'm sure it does. But you're a very brave girl. Your mom tells me that you have a birthday coming up. Is that right?"

"Yes."

"And you'll be nine years old."

"Yes."

"What would you like for your birthday?"

"A dog."

"A dog! Well, I happen to be an expert on tiny black and white dachshunds. I will get you one."

"Really?"

"Yes. I will. Let me speak to your mother."

Allison gave the phone back to Sylvia. "Mom, he's going to get me a dog!" she said excitedly.

Sylvia took the phone and walked into another room. "What did you say to her?" she demanded.

"I said I'd get her a dog," James said.

"Well, that's a problem. My husband doesn't want anything to do with a dog."

"This wouldn't be just a dog. It would be a tiny black and white dachshund. They aren't really dogs, you know. They're little people."

"It's a dog, James. We can't have a dog."

But from that moment on, every time James spoke to Allison, he promised her a dog. He also made promises to Sylvia. He sent her a post card from Paris. "Miss you, lover," he wrote. "Someday we'll be here together."

Sylvia resumed working for James, in between playing games of Monopoly, Life and checkers with her daughter. Eventually, Allison was well enough that Sylvia could get out of the house.

James asked Sylvia to meet him in Berlin, New Jersey. He gave her directions to the Berlin Motor Lodge, which was an old, two-story motel on an insignificant highway. It looked like most guests did not spend the entire night.

When Sylvia arrived, James had been cleaning his briefcase; papers and photos were spread out on the bed. Sylvia picked up one of the photos—it was a close-up of a woman on what was obviously her wedding day. The woman's dark blond hair was styled in an up-do, and a tulle bridal veil perched toward the back of her head. She had sparkling blue eyes and a broad smile. She was the picture of happiness.

"That's Gale," James said.

Sylvia knew that Gale was James' wife who died. "What a shame," Sylvia thought. "She was pretty." She handed the photo back to James, who put it into his briefcase, along with the other papers he scooped up off the bed.

"I brought the letters that you wanted," Sylvia said.

"Good," he said, pulling her down to sit on the bed beside him. "We'll look at them in a little while. But first, we have something more important to do."

"James, I don't have time for this," Sylvia said. "I've got to get back home."

Sylvia was having second thoughts about their previous physical encounters, and wanted to limit her relationship with James to business. Her real interest was making money. Not that James was paying her a lot—only sporadic checks for $100 or $200. But although James said money was tight at the moment—everything he had was invested in the new venture—he promised all Sylvia's efforts would eventually be well-compensated.

"I've been thinking about offering you stock in SFIICE," James said. "That means once our revenue starts coming in, you'll be entitled to dividends. Would that interest you?"

"How much money are you talking about?" Sylvia asked.

"Let's just say you wouldn't have to worry about paying for Kevin's college."

At home, Sylvia's husband was becoming downright nasty, and now, in addition to everything else, he complained about the phone bills she incurred making calls for SFIICE. What Sylvia really wanted was to take her kids and get away from him. If stock ownership would allow her to do that—well, yes, she was interested.

James, however, kept wanting to mix business with pleasure. He repeatedly asked Sylvia to bring letters and reports to him at motels located between Atlantic City and her home in Pennsylvania. Sometimes she met him, sometimes they had sex, but usually she blew him off. When she did, James became angry. But he never stopped trying to arrange encounters. It seemed like the more she refused him, the more he pursued her.

Sylvia did offer to meet James in his Atlantic City office, but he wouldn't allow it. "I do not want to parade you in front of my employees," he said. "What I do with my time is none of their business."

This seemed odd because Sylvia thought of herself as an employee, although she wasn't making much money. James promised to reimburse her phone expenses, but, as usual, he was slow coming up with cash. On several occasions, Sylvia emphatically demanded payment, and James wrote her a small check. But he owed her far more than he paid.

Then, in early April 1998, James started talking up a new project—a Titanic exhibition. "It's truly a phenomenon," James said. "The whole world is going nuts over the movie."

"I saw the movie," Sylvia said. "I didn't like it."

"Well, you're not normal, because everybody else loves it. I'm working with a local man called John Glassey. He was an executive at the Resorts casino in Atlantic City, and worked on television productions with Merv Griffin. John and I both saw the Titanic exhibit in Florida, and we both thought it was boring. We believe that if we can add some Hollywood sizzle to an exhibition, we'll be beating the crowds away."

"If you say so," Sylvia shrugged.

James then asked Sylvia to be part of the project—he was certain it would be a winner. If she invested just $1,200 to help start the Titanic company, James said, she'd be a shareholder and quickly earn 10 times that amount—or more.

Sylvia could also help him with the show. James was working with a memorabilia dealer based in Allentown, Pennsylvania, named Charlie Schalebaum.

Allentown was located between where Sylvia lived and Atlantic City—she could pick up and deliver boxes and envelopes to Schalebaum. James would pay her, of course.

It was another opportunity to earn money, and high returns on a small investment would go a long way toward helping her get out of her marriage, Sylvia thought. She gave James the $1,200, although she did not tell him that it came from a cash advance on her credit card. She also started making trips to Charlie Schalebaum's warehouse.

A couple of weeks later, James wanted Sylvia to print out SFIICE documents, pick up boxes from Schalebaum and meet him at a motel in King of Prussia. When she arrived, James had just gotten on the phone. He was ordering a new computer from Gateway.

"Hold on, I'll have my assistant talk to you," James said into the receiver.

He gave Sylvia the phone and a piece of paper. "Here's what I'm ordering. Talk to them," he said. Then he ducked into the bathroom.

Sylvia gave the sales representative all the item numbers and the shipping address—James' office in Atlantic City. James came out of the bathroom and looked through his wallet. Then he wrote on a piece of paper: "I forgot my credit card. Can you use yours?"

Sylvia looked up at him sharply in surprise.

"Can't you do this when you get home?" she asked.

"I just found out about this deal," James explained in a low voice. "If I don't order today, I'll miss it. Just put it on your card, and as soon as the bill comes in, I'll pay it."

Sylvia hesitated.

"You have nothing to worry about," James pushed. "I'll write you a check as soon as you get the bill."

Sylvia gave the sales rep her credit card number.

"James, I need this money back right away," she said when she hung up the phone.

"Of course," James said. "You'll get it."

Sylvia handed James the SFIICE printouts and got ready to leave.

"Don't you want to stay awhile?" James asked.

"I can't. The kids are coming home from school and I told Maddy I'd be there," she said. Ignoring James' scowl, she got in her car and drove away.

When Sylvia arrived home, James called to ask questions about the SFIICE work. "Oh, by the way," he said, changing the subject, "I'm having the computer sent to your house."

"Why?" Sylvia asked.

"It's safer. Nobody is at the Atlantic City office."

"Where's your secretary?"

"She's hardly ever here anymore. I think she's out looking for another job. So it would be best to have the computer delivered to your house. I don't want anything to happen to it."

A few days later, three big boxes arrived at Sylvia's house. James wanted her to bring them to the motel in King of Prussia. Sylvia asked her neighbor, Maddy, to help her load them in the car. When Maddy found out that the computer was for James, she was furious.

"Are you out of your mind?" Maddy yelled at Sylvia. "I hope you didn't pay for it."

"No," Sylvia said, in a tone that implied, "Do you think I would be that stupid?"

"I'm telling you, I don't trust that guy," Maddy said. "He's got shifty eyes. He's a weasel."

Sylvia, too, had misgivings, but she wasn't about to admit them to her friend.

James was waiting for her at the motel in King of Prussia with lunch, and offered some to Sylvia. She ate a little and then said, "The computer's out in the car. You have to hurry up and get it, because I've got to get back home."

"Can't you stay awhile?" he asked.

"No. I can't."

James silently unloaded the boxes from her car. He was angry again.

By the end of April 1998, things suddenly started looking good for James and his business ventures. The Titanic project was a go. Although she was still working on SFIICE, James gave Sylvia more and more tasks related to the exhibition.

James sent Sylvia information via e-mail to print out and bring to Schalebaum, an old guy who did not own a computer. James also sent envelopes and boxes to be delivered to him. Sylvia thought this was stupid—why didn't he just ship them directly to Schalebaum? But on this issue, she was the employee and James was the boss, so she did as she was asked.

Sometimes James drove to see Schalebaum himself. One day, before James got on the road, he sent an e-mail to Sylvia with the text of a letter for Schalebaum. He wanted Sylvia to format the letter, print out several copies and bring them to him at a motel in Allentown.

Sylvia arrived at the motel with the letters. James looked them over and told her more about the Titanic exhibition. By the time the show's run in Atlantic City was finished, he said, Sylvia would be able to walk away from her marriage with the kids whether her husband gave her a divorce or not.

"I can't wait," Sylvia said. "And I can't wait to see the look on his face when I leave."

"It's coming, Bubba," James said. "You'll see. Now, if you'll wait for me, I have to go over and see Charlie, and then we can go out to lunch."

"Oh, okay," Sylvia said.

"But first I want to get cleaned up. I left really early this morning, and I'd like to take a shower." James handed her a stack of papers. "Why don't you look through this stuff? I'll be right out."

Sylvia sat at the small table in the motel room and leafed through the papers. Stuffed between the pages were two photographs—pictures of a giant bouquet of red roses.

James came out of the bathroom wearing nothing but a towel. Sylvia showed him the photos. "What's this?" she asked.

James took the photos and looked at them. "They're roses," he said, sadly. "I sent them to the wife of my mate from Special Forces. He was sent out on a mission and got killed. She was pregnant, which I didn't know. She just had the baby—a daughter—a couple of months ago. I'm the godfather."

"I didn't think you were Catholic."

"I'm not, but she is, and she named me as the godfather," James replied. "I don't know anything about kids. I didn't know what I was supposed to do, so I sent her flowers. I was trying to be nice."

Sylvia had a feeling that something was amiss with James' story, but she wasn't sure what.

"Maybe you can help me," James said, approaching her. "You're so good with kids. You must know what to do."

James started to kiss Sylvia. His towel slipped to the floor.

"I thought you had to see Charlie," Sylvia said.

"He can wait," James said.

This time, Sylvia did not resist. An hour later, as they were both cleaning up in the bathroom, James suggested that Sylvia come with him to see the memorabilia dealer. "I'll talk to him, and then we'll go to lunch. You can leave your car here."

"Okay," Sylvia said.

James called Schalebaum. "My secretary came up from Atlantic City with the papers," James said into the phone. "I'll be by to drop everything off."

"What the hell did you tell him that for?" Sylvia asked when James hung up. "What?"

"That your secretary came up from Atlantic City."

"Well I don't want him to know you're my girlfriend."

"I work for you from Pennsylvania. I don't work from Atlantic City."

"What difference does it make?"

Sylvia didn't know why James was lying about something so stupid. "If that's the way you feel about it, I don't care," she shrugged.

They got in the car and drove over to Schalebaum's warehouse. "Wait here," James said.

"Why?" she asked.

"Just wait here," he said, getting out of the car.

Sylvia sat in the car and fumed. She'd met Schalebaum before. She spoke to him every time she delivered envelopes and boxes for James. Why was James making her sit in the car?

Before long, James came out and they went to lunch. Afterwards Sylvia drove home, wondering what had happened.

In June, James came up with some of the money that he owed Sylvia. But he did not pay for the Gateway computer as he promised, and he again stopped paying her for the work she did. His excuse was that all his assets were invested in the Titanic show.

In August 1998, James called and asked Sylvia for money again.

"You have to do this for me," James said, his tone somewhere between imploring and ordering. "I need you to send $1,860 to a man in Kentucky."

"Who is he?" Sylvia asked. "What's it for?"

"You don't need to worry about that," James replied. "All you need to know is that it is important for everything that I'm working on."

This pissed Sylvia off. In fact, recently James was pissing her off more and more frequently. "Look, asshole," Sylvia snarled at him. "Whatever is going on, it's your problem, not mine." She slammed down the phone.

Two minutes later, Sylvia's phone rang again. She knew who it was.

"What?" she spat into the receiver.

"Please don't hang up," James asked.

"What do you want?"

"Look, Sylvia, I really need your help," James said, his tone conciliatory. "I'm doing everything I can to pull this business together, and right now it's critical to get this guy his money. It's long and complicated, and I don't want to burden you with an explanation. This is for us, for our future, for you and Kevin and Allison."

"What are you talking about? We don't have a future."

"When you get your divorce, we'll be together."

"We will?"

"You'll move down here with me."

"Well that's not happening. I am not uprooting two kids who have lived here in Pennsylvania all their lives to move to New Jersey."

"But you want to provide for your kids, don't you?" James asked.

"You know that I do."

"Well, this is your chance. If you help me get the show going, you'll have enough money to do whatever you want."

Sylvia still had a gnawing feeling that something wasn't right, but James kept talking, kept telling her how once everything came through she'd have no problem taking care of her kids. Sylvia sent the money. In fact, as James continued to tout the profits she'd earn, she took additional cash advances on her credit cards for $3,500 ... $4,000 ... $9,000 ... to invest with him.

Then Sylvia received really bad news. Her attorney was disbarred for legal malpractice—embezzling funds from his clients' estates. Her divorce proceedings stopped.

Throughout the spring, summer and fall, James kept telling Sylvia's daughter that he was going to buy her a miniature dachshund.

In November 1998, Allison had a follow-up appointment with her doctor in Philadelphia. James suggested that Sylvia bring Allison to Mays Landing for lunch after the doctor visit. "Maybe she'll get a dog," he said. He'd found a miniature dachshund puppy in a local pet store.

Sylvia had her doubts. She didn't know anything about dogs, and she didn't know how her husband—who was no longer being divorced—would react. But

James pressed.

"Just come to Mays Landing," he said. "I'll buy you and Allison lunch at the Great American Grill. Then we'll walk next door to the pet store and Allison can meet the dog. I've already paid for her, but if the dog doesn't like Allison, the store is not going to allow us to take her."

Sylvia couldn't imagine that happening—any puppy would like her daughter. She gave in, knowing the dog was a done deal. She drove Allison to Mays Landing after the doctor visit, and James met them for lunch. Then they walked into the pet store and saw a cage with a big sign on it: "Allison's my new mommy." Inside the cage was a tiny, five-pound dachshund.

The storeowner brought the dog and Allison to a playroom. As Sylvia expected, the dog loved Allison and jumped excitedly all over the little girl. The little dog also liked Sylvia, but would not go near James.

Allison was ecstatic. She continued to play with the puppy while Sylvia walked around the store picking up supplies—a bed, pet carrier, bowls and food. James had told her she'd have to pay for the supplies, and estimated the cost at about $100.

James stepped outside the store to make a phone call. Sylvia went up to the cash register with the supplies, and the storeowner rang everything up.

"That will be $706.22," she said.

"Seven hundred dollars!" Sylvia repeated, astonished. "For this?"

"This plus the dog," the owner replied.

"But he paid for the dog!"

"I don't think so," the owner said. "But let me check. What's the name?"

"James Montgomery."

The storeowner searched her records. "We don't have any record of the dog being paid for. And there's no credit card on file for James Montgomery."

"Just a minute," Sylvia said. She walked outside, where James was still on the phone.

"I have to talk to you," she said to him.

"Hold on," James said into his cell phone. Turning to Sylvia, he asked, "What is it?"

"I thought you said that you paid for the dog."

"I did."

"Well they don't have a record of it."

"The woman was supposed to put the charge on my credit card."

"They don't have your credit card information."

"Look, Sylvia, I don't have my credit card with me. And I've got to get back to this call. You'll have to deal with it. We'll clear it up later."

Sylvia was furious, but she was also stuck. After Allison's painful surgery and weeks of recovery, Sylvia did not want to disappoint the child by not buying the dog. She went inside and paid the bill with her credit card.

Sylvia was still angry when they packed the dog and pet supplies into the car, although she tried to hide it from her daughter. Then James said he was driving north to a hotel in Bordentown, New Jersey, because he had to be in New York

City early the next morning. He needed Sylvia to do some work for him before the meeting. "Could you follow me to Bordentown?" he asked. "Would Allison be upset?"

At first Sylvia was shocked—after the stunt James just pulled with the dog, he was asking her to go to a hotel with him? But she quickly realized that it might be an opportunity to find out what the hell was going on. "No, Allison won't be upset if I explain it to her," Sylvia said. "And she'll have the dog to keep her company."

So Sylvia piled Allison and the dog into her car, and drove an hour and 15 minutes north to Bordentown. At least it was on her way home.

They got two adjoining rooms in the hotel. In one room, Allison played with her new puppy and watched television. In the next room, Sylvia and James worked on his computer. Every time James went to the bathroom, or to the vending machine to buy a Diet Coke, Sylvia searched his computer. She wasn't sure what she was looking for. She'd know it when she found it.

Allison was asleep when James and Sylvia finished working.

"Thank you for doing this, Bubba," James said.

"You're welcome," Sylvia said, standing up.

"Where are you going?"

"To bed," Sylvia said. She walked into the adjoining room and locked the door behind her.

James started asking Sylvia for more money, more frequently. When Sylvia declined, James explained that she was already a shareholder in his company—Jersey Shore Productions—and showed her stock certificates with her name on them. He also explained that because her investment was lower than that of the other partners, she was in the minority recovery position. That meant the other investors would get paid before she did. If she increased her investment, however, she would be paid at the same time. James advised her to do this—she'd get all her money back more quickly when the deals worked out, and she'd easily be able to put her kids through college.

Sylvia was torn. Instinctively, she didn't trust James. But he had an amazing ability to make her believe what he wanted her to believe—which was that he was helping her out of an unhappy marriage and funding her kids' college educations. She took more cash advances on her credit card and sent him the money.

In November 1998, James asked for money again. Sylvia held off. But by the end of the month, his requests became increasingly insistent. He'd worked out a deal to open the Titanic show in Florida. He was moving down there to supervise the launch—and as soon as Sylvia was divorced, he wanted her to move to Florida with him. As a Florida resident, he said, she'd easily be able to send her kids to state colleges. But in order for all this to happen, he needed her to come up with $20,000 right away.

Sylvia didn't have that kind of money. The only way she could get it was by taking even more advances on her credit cards, which she didn't want to do. Plus, she was no longer in the process of divorce, so her involvement with James was now officially an affair—which could pose problems later. She did not respond to his request.

James started an e-mail campaign to convince her to act:

From: Futron0 I
Subj: Think!

I don't screw around with people's lives, manipulate or make promises I can't keep.

So, your silence yesterday stopped me cold - I never got to explaining things that would have answered some of your questions.

Firstly, about us. I don't know! The only time we have ever spent together is so unusual - I don't know what it would be like to be able to call you on a normal telephone, see you without sneaking around, spend more than 24 hours with you. But, I would like to find out - so I started making the offer. It puts me at risk, so I must care enough to make it.

I, too, think it would be crazy for you to try & do anything until you have been through the divorce courts. This was the plan I was going to outline to you yesterday - read carefully and think.

1] You commit to moving to Florida once the divorce is final and the house is sold — that changes the way you approach divorce!

2] You beg, borrow or steal up to $20,000 before lunch time on Monday and place it into my JSP stock [this is illegal insider trading] - which automatically becomes $30,000 along with the $30,000 you already have in January. This does two things:

i] gives you the financial independence to live in Florida should we decide that we can't live together

ii] guarantees you a job - I was going to suggest coordinating the schools program — given your organizing abilities.

You come to Orlando as soon as you are divorced - we try living together for 3 months or so to see if it works - and we see where it goes from there. BUT, you haven't come to Florida and been stuck if it doesn't [your stock guarantees your place even if we fight!] ... You have your freedom and your future secured - Allison has a chance of growing up normally.

Write me back with your reactions - I am in and out of meetings all day but have my Toshiba with me.

Sylvia wrote back. What if she couldn't come up with the money?

"It doesn't affect us," James replied. "It does affect your ability to guarantee a job and Allison's college and so on. If you can do it—do it!"

Still, Sylvia hesitated.

Then James wrote to Sylvia that he'd renegotiated his financial obligations. He didn't need $20,000 after all—he only needed $15,000! He didn't need the entire sum all at once—he could take it in increments! And, according to his attorney, James could legally give her a loan of $15,000 in the first week of January, which she could repay when she cashed in her stock! James was only asking Sylvia for money temporarily. "You only have to find it for five weeks," he wrote. "Go, go, go, go!"

In the meantime, life with her husband was unbearable. Sylvia desperately wanted to get out, and investing with James seemed to be the only opportunity she had to get enough money to leave. On Monday, November 30, 1998 she took cash advances of $6,000 on two credit cards and sent the money via wire transfer to James' First Union bank account, which he could access in Florida. The money was supposed to be deposited into his account on Wednesday, December 2, 1998.

With that, James packed his car for his move to Florida. He planned to stop at a hotel near the Philadelphia airport Monday afternoon. He wanted Sylvia to drive there from her home, bring work she'd completed, sign legal documents and spend the night.

When Sylvia arrived, she pulled out the documents that she'd brought for James and asked about the legal papers. Reading them, she saw that the agreement seemed to give James all kinds of ways to get out of paying. Sylvia refused to sign it. James tried to persuade her, but she held her ground. Shortly after that, Sylvia left. She never had any intention of spending the night.

In the morning, James started his drive to Florida. He arrived in Orlando on December 2 and went to a First Union bank ATM machine to check his account balance. The money Sylvia sent wasn't there. James called Sylvia from his cell phone and demanded to know where it was.

"I don't know," Sylvia said.

"You're sure you sent it?"

"Of course I'm sure. The woman gave me a receipt."

That evening, the money still hadn't arrived. James sent an e-mail to Sylvia:

> As of 1900 tonight it still had NOT been transferred I don't care what she wrote you or told you etc., etc.— I am in a meeting now to try & prevent more damage—not a happy camper—know its not your fault but I am furious.

The next morning, James went four times to a First Union bank branch located near his new apartment complex—Brittany at Waterford Lakes. Each time he inserted his bankcard into the ATM machine, the balance was unchanged. Then the money appeared in his bank account. In fact, he received two wire transfers from Sylvia, for $6,000 each.

James could now pay the rent, and he signed the lease for his new apartment. But he still wanted Sylvia to come through with the rest of the money, which he told her by e-mail on December 7, 1998.

> Just finished breakfast with Orlando attorneys. Good chance we could even wangle Kevin's undergrad year into UCF in Orlando [if he

wanted!]— it's now v. important that somehow or other you pull off the last 3K by Tuesday night—that should take me off any insider trading appearance.

Ignoring the alarm bells ringing in her head, Sylvia took another $3,000 credit card advance and sent James the money.

Sylvia had a talent for crocheting, which at some point James discovered. So for Christmas, James asked her to crochet a blanket for the poor baby daughter of his military buddy who was killed in action. Sylvia loved children. It was impossible for her to say no.

James bought the wool, and Sylvia made a white blanket decorated with hearts in three shades of pink. She crocheted the baby's name—Janna—into the blanket in maroon. Sylvia also hand-knit a white baby jacket with pink ribbons, along with a matching hat and booties. She sent the handmade items to James, along with his Christmas gift—a tiny portable TV with a two-inch color LCD screen.

James didn't get Sylvia a Christmas present. But he did promise that they'd be together soon. He wanted to take her to Australia. He also wanted Sylvia to plan on living with him in Florida starting in March 1999.

In fact, James said, moving to Florida would help her divorce. If she became a property owner, he explained, she would qualify for benefits under the state's homesteading laws and could legally take her daughter to Orlando. And James had a plan for her to become a property owner. He said that he and his Australian partner, Archie Turner, and Johnny Stuart, from On Stage Entertainment, were personally purchasing the parking lot behind Wild Bill's Wild West Extravaganza—that's where the Titanic show was being launched and his Titanic lifeboats would be displayed. When the show opened, Jersey Shore Productions would pay them rent for the parking lot. James could get Sylvia in on the deal. All she had to do was come up with $10,000 by the end of the year.

Sylvia couldn't do it. She had just pulled together $15,000 for James and was tapped out.

Three weeks later, James excitedly told Sylvia that she'd soon start seeing returns on her investment: The Titanic Experience was scheduled to open at Wild Bill's on February 17, 1999. That's when the income would start. But until then, James was strapped for cash. Sylvia, in the meantime, had applied for and received another credit card. In an e-mail, James asked her, with a touch of embarrassment, for a personal loan of $4,250 so he could buy their tickets to Australia. "I haven't borrowed money in the last 14 years!" he wrote.

Sylvia couldn't believe it. James called and said he'd flown back to Atlantic City. He didn't have a car because he'd loaned his to a friend, and the driver who was supposed to pick him up never showed. Could she come and take him to his motel?

"Can't you just call a cab?" she asked him.

"It's impossible to get a cab around here; they just go to the casinos," James said. "I need to get to the motel. John Glassey is picking me up in the morning, and we're going to a meeting. Besides, I thought we could spend some time together."

"I can't stay there. My husband's working the late shift, but I have to be home before he gets here. And the weather's supposed to turn bad. Can't you figure something else out?"

"Well I also need the SFIICE updates that you have. I certainly can't get them from a cab driver."

So late in the afternoon of February 9, 1999, Sylvia printed out reports with the latest SFIICE information. Then she started the three-hour drive to Atlantic City. At least it was late enough that she'd miss the Philadelphia rush hour traffic.

Sylvia got off the Atlantic City Expressway at Exit 2, which put her onto Albany Avenue, one of three highways that led into the casino resort. James was not at the airport; he was waiting for her, in the dark, on the Albany Avenue bridge. This was a small drawbridge over a narrow part of the Intracoastal Waterway. Sylvia pulled over, stopping traffic behind her because there was no shoulder on the road, and James quickly climbed into her car. She then continued over the bridge into Atlantic City. James directed her to make a series of turns until they were back on Albany Avenue heading out of town to an Econolodge.

Once in the motel room, James started pulling things out of his bags, including two china dinner plates—octagonal in shape, with large, whimsical flowers in peach, pink and pale blue. "Would you take these with you?" James asked.

"Why are you carrying plates around?"

"I'm tired of buying Styrofoam plates when I need to eat in a motel room, so I thought I'd bring some from home. But they're too heavy, and I don't want them to break."

"What am I going to do with them?"

"Just hold on to them for me."

Sylvia changed the subject. "You said I'd start getting money back in January. Where is it?"

"The sellers of the car park are giving us a hard time. But we're working on it. As soon as the deal is finalized, the show will open and you'll start seeing returns on your investment."

"You better be telling me the truth, James."

"Of course I'm telling you the truth. I don't like this delay any more than you do. It's hurting me too."

Sylvia looked at her watch. She had to leave. "Do you want this SFIICE stuff or what?" she asked James.

"Yes, but I thought we'd relax for a few minutes."

"I don't have time. I've got to get back to Pennsylvania."

"I thought you were going to spend the night."

"I told you over the phone that I couldn't do that."

"Then what was the sense of coming down here?"

Sylvia could not contain her vexation. "I drove to Atlantic City because you said you needed me to pick you up," she said, incredulous. "And you wanted the SFIICE stuff."

"Well if you're just going to drive down and turn around you shouldn't have bothered," he retorted.

Now Sylvia was angry. "I don't have time for this bullshit," she yelled at James. "I shouldn't be traveling. We're supposed to get snow, and I need to get home. I'm not going to get stuck in a storm."

She picked up her carryall, got in her car, and drove back home. James was left at the Econolodge.

When she arrived home, Sylvia noticed that her carryall felt heavy. She opened it up. Inside were the two dinner plates; James had stuck them in her bag.

James had a new crisis. Things had gone sour with his partners on the Titanic show, John Glassey and Donna Andersen, and they were suing him. Donna, apparently, was more than just a ditzy secretary, and John had turned against him.

So he had a new proposition for Sylvia: Did she want to buy out John's share of the Titanic show? "With what you've invested so far, all you need to put in is another $13,000, and you can have all of his stock," James said. "You'll be listed as an owner of the Titanic show and artifacts. Once this show gets going, you'll get an even bigger share of the profits."

"Where am I supposed to come up with that kind of money?" Sylvia asked.

"It's only for six weeks," James said. "It will allow me to tie up loose ends with John and the courts. Then the money will start flowing from the show. You have to do this, Bubba. It's the best way to get the money you want."

James kept up the pressure in an e-mail he sent on Sunday, February 14, 1999—Valentine's Day:

> Going like crazy. Your $13,000 has now become critical, Bubba—you just have to do it, to make things worse I think Monday is a bank holiday—let's stay in touch with e-mail, lover. We are so close to making it all work—please make it work for us!
> Later lover—at least all this pressure is keeping my mind off of us.

Sylvia was close to panic. She had already given James so much money—$50,000? $60,000? $70,000? With all the cash advance fees, wire transfer fees and interest charges, she wasn't even sure what the total was.

She couldn't put any more money on a credit card. But maybe she could get a home equity loan. For that, she'd have to talk to her husband. James had sent her financial projections for the Titanic show. Sylvia showed them to her husband, explaining that they had an opportunity to invest with the company she'd been working for. Their investment would be returned within six months. Plus, their money would double, or perhaps grow even more. Her husband looked at James' financial projections and agreed to the investment. He co-signed an application for a $13,000 loan from Household Finance.

The money came through on February 18, 1999. Sylvia deposited $8,500 into James' First Union bank account, and sent him $4,500 in cash via Federal Express.

Then James asked Sylvia to come to Florida. He said he needed her help with SFIICE.

Sylvia hadn't visited Maggie Kay, the psychic, since November. In her last reading, Maggie warned Sylvia not to give anyone money. James appeared in the tarot cards, and although the psychic didn't see anything overtly wrong, money issues kept coming up, and she didn't like what he seemed to portray. Maggie told Sylvia to watch her back.

By February, the cards showed that James was evil, and Sylvia confessed that she had given him money. A lot of money.

The psychic threw a fit. "What is wrong with you?" Maggie yelled. "I told you not to give anyone money."

She turned another tarot card. The message was more bad news. "You'll never see your money," she predicted.

"James told me his partners—John and Donna—were suing him in court," Sylvia said.

"He's lying. They are not the problem. He's the problem. He's the one telling the lies."

Maggie turned another tarot card. "You're going down to Florida," she said.

"Yes. I'm going down to see him," Sylvia said.

"You shouldn't go."

"I have stuff I have to find out."

"You might get hurt," the psychic said. Then she turned another card. "Well, you'll probably get away with going down there. But you're not going to have a good time. And you'll find out things that you knew all along but didn't want to admit."

When Sylvia arrived in Orlando, Florida on February 23, 1999, it was cold. In fact, the low temperature for the day was only 41 degrees—setting a chilly new record.

James picked Sylvia up at the airport in a black Pontiac Grand Prix. She'd seen the car before—James had told her it belonged to his Special Forces friend who died. As they left the airport, James said he needed to stop by Valencia Community College. They pulled off the highway, into a driveway and then into a parking lot. James told Sylvia to wait in the car while he went into a building.

As soon as James left, Sylvia opened the car's glove compartment. She found insurance and registration documents. The car was owned by a Kimberly Goodson.

James came back out. He wanted something from the trunk. Sylvia pulled her suitcase out, so James could get what he needed. When James was back inside the building, Sylvia opened the trunk again—she'd left the lid partially ajar. Inside she found medical records and a mammogram, all belonging to Kimberly Goodson. It was quite clear that the owner of the car was a woman, not James' army buddy.

James finished his business at the college, and they drove a half-hour to his apartment in a brand-new complex on the outskirts of town. At the entrance was a pond with a fountain in the center that shot water about 12 feet into the air. They passed a clubhouse and swimming pool, then pulled up in front of James' building.

His apartment on the second floor was nice, but empty. There was a bean-bag chair on the floor in the living room. A nondescript table in the eating area. An inflatable mattress on the bedroom floor. In the room that James used as an office, his computer was on a table and papers covered the floor. A third bedroom was completely empty—except for more papers on the floor.

"The furniture hasn't arrived yet," James explained. "I'm making do."

The next day, James left for a business meeting. As soon as he was out the door, Sylvia started looking through papers. She found printouts of e-mail correspondence with women who responded to a personal ad James apparently placed on the Internet. So despite proclaiming that he and Sylvia were a couple, James was aggressively searching for companionship.

Sylvia walked to the shopping center across from the apartment complex—she'd seen a pay phone there. She had to tell her neighbor, Maddy, what she'd found. Neither of them was surprised.

For the next three days, every time James left the apartment, or for that matter, went into the bathroom, Sylvia searched his papers and computers. She found e-mail exchanges between him and several more women. She found correspondence indicating James was trying to get money from all kinds of people. She found Christmas cards from James' family addressed to "James and Donna." As she suspected, James was married.

After every find, Sylvia took another walk to the shopping center to call Maddy. The women realized that it was unlikely James had any intention of paying Sylvia back. If she were going to get any money, she'd have to come up with a plan. They decided that the only thing that might keep James around was if Sylvia convinced him that she loved him—and told him she was pregnant.

In reality, this couldn't happen—Sylvia had taken care of that possibility years earlier. But she never told James. So there on the inflatable mattress on the floor, she had sex with James—something she'd frequently avoided.

On her last day in Florida, James was sorting through a pile of photos. "Isn't this a strange picture of Gale?" James asked, showing Sylvia a picture.

Sylvia looked at the photo. The woman had dark brown hair and hazel eyes. The last time James showed her a photo of his deceased wife, the woman had blond hair and blue eyes. This was a different woman. James was lying again, but Sylvia didn't point this out to him.

When she returned from Florida, Sylvia revisited Maggie, the psychic.

"You had a terrible time," Maggie read from the tarot cards. "You found out some things, but there is more to be found. There is much more going on than you know. You're going to get a phone call and you'll be very surprised by it. Then again, maybe you won't be surprised."

Sylvia was in trouble and she knew it. Her phone calls with James became verbal battles. "I want my money back," she yelled at him. "If you don't give me my money back, I'm going to report you."

"Go right ahead," James retorted. "I have legitimate businesses. You invested in my businesses. There is nothing you can do."

"Well, then, you'd better account for every penny I've given you. Because I have proof of every transaction. You still owe me for the computer I bought you. I've got to pay my credit card bills."

"Well, I don't have the money now. It's all invested in the show."

"Then uninvest it."

"It's not that simple."

"You could pull the money out if you wanted to."

"I told you, it's not that simple."

Sylvia switched tactics. "You know, I haven't had my period in awhile. I might be pregnant."

"Are you serious?" James asked.

"Of course I'm serious. Do you think I would joke about being pregnant?"

"When will you know?"

"I have an appointment with the doctor in a couple of weeks." This was true, but Sylvia was certain the appointment would not reveal a pregnancy.

"Well, tell me what you find out," James said.

"You'll be the first to know."

James promised Sylvia that she'd have her money by April 17, 1999.

Shortly after telling James she might be pregnant, Sylvia made another call—to the FBI. On March 23, 1999, Sylvia spoke with a young agent in the Scranton, Pennsylvania office. "I feel like a total and utter fool," she began. "But I'm being badgered by my friends to tell you that I have given money to a man who I think is a con artist."

Sylvia then told the agent, in general terms, what happened. She met the man, James Montgomery, on the Internet. She was working for him, helping him start a business to bring Chinese students to the United States to learn English. They became romantically involved. Then he started a Titanic show—she saw artifacts in his possession. He asked her to invest in the show, and promised her stock in return. She demanded her money back. James said he'd pay her by April 17, but she didn't think he was going to do it.

The agent listened and took notes. She told Sylvia that if she didn't get her money by April 17 to call them back and they would see if they had a case.

Sylvia knew she had to maintain contact with James. So when he went to Australia at the end of March—without her—she called him. James had given her the phone number where he was staying—with his daughter, Margaret Riley. No one was home, so Sylvia left a message on the answering machine.

"Hi James, I hope you had a nice flight," Sylvia said. "I have something very important to tell you. I've just come back from the doctor. How would you like to be a father? Anyway, I miss you and I love you. Call me as soon as you can."

A few days later, James returned her call. "Are you sure that you're pregnant?" he asked excitedly.

"Well, I have another doctor's appointment," Sylvia lied. "This time they're going to take a blood test instead of just the pregnancy test. But I'm sure it will come back positive."

Then James put his partner, Archie Turner, on the phone. "I hear congratulations are in order," Archie said.

"If that's what you call it," Sylvia replied.

"How are you feeling?" Archie asked.

"Tired."

James came back on the phone, and demanded that Sylvia call him as soon as she finished her next doctor visit. He didn't care what time it was; he wanted to know right away. Sylvia promised to call him.

Then she paid another visit to the psychic. Maggie knew that Sylvia had called the FBI, and predicted she'd be calling them back. The psychic emphatically warned Sylvia never to see James again—it was too dangerous—even though he had bought the story that she was pregnant. Maggie also repeated that Sylvia would soon receive a surprising phone call.

On April 28, 1999, Sylvia contacted the FBI again. She told them that James Montgomery hadn't paid her.

On April 29, 1999, Sylvia received a phone call from James Montgomery's wife. That was me.

Chapter 16

Every day, several times a day, Sylvia Banning and I spoke on the phone. Asking each other questions, telling each other what we experienced, we started to unravel the tangled web of James Montgomery's lies.

James told me that he stayed out-of-town so he could be on time for early-morning business meetings. That's why I put his motel charges on my credit cards. In reality, he was booking motel rooms hoping to have sex with Sylvia.

James told Sylvia that his wife died tragically at a young age, leaving him a widower—free to fall in love with her. He didn't tell her that he remarried within a few months. According to him, I was merely an employee, and a lousy one at that.

James told me he was traveling from Orlando to Atlantic City so he could go on to New York in a last-ditch effort to sell our Titanic artifacts. I used my last remaining credit to buy his plane ticket. He arrived in Atlantic City, called Sylvia and went to a motel.

Every conversation between Sylvia and me brought new revelations. I was astounded by how James twisted facts and half-truths to serve his agenda. And I was humiliated that he did much of it right under my nose.

Sylvia realized much more quickly than I did that James was a con artist. She also realized that her only prayer of getting her money back was by using James' own tactics against him. That's why she cooked up the pregnancy story—and kept embellishing it. She wanted to maintain contact with James, and hoped that some paternal instinct, or some threat of exposure, would move him to return her cash.

Sylvia forwarded to me many of her previous online exchanges with James, which, in light of her scheme, proved to be entertaining reading. In an e-mail to him on March 27, 1999, she really laid on the lies:

> I love you honey I really do and I'm not going to make myself upset over this because it's actually not worth the health of the baby. And I want this baby no matter what. I want it because it's yours and mine. Because we made him out of love.

Sylvia followed that up by telling James how much she wanted to be with him. She dreamed of them becoming a family, together forever. James, however, had reservations about the togetherness idea. On April 9, 1999, he wrote to her:

> Bubba! You can't listen to all those hormones rushing around—you have to be a little realistic.
>
> You are still married.
>
> We are committing adultery.
>
> And, you are pregnant.
>
> Now that still worries a lot of people. For openers, it is a court martial offense in the military. Some prudes like Rupert Murdoch would stop doing business with me if they ever knew.
>
> Bubba—we are getting there—but we aren't there yet! Your typical answer is, "you don't care what they think" BUT I have to—it's my business—our money—it could cost me the schools program—Florida is the heart of the Bible belt—they don't necessarily think like you and me!
>
> Just think a little! We are adulterers in the eyes of both the law and the community—and I am a guy who broke up a family!
>
> Bubba—from the start I said I HATE all this sneaking around but until we are free it's a fact of life for us—particularly NOW and in FLORIDA.

James points out that Sylvia was married! James worries about adultery! James hates sneaking around! What a joke! But he had taken the bait. He believed that Sylvia was pregnant and pining for him. The con artist was being conned—it was delicious.

Sylvia and I agreed not to tell James that we were in contact with each other. We provided each other with moral support in our separate battles to hold him accountable. We also set out to learn what else James was doing.

We were fairly certain that James was living in Florida with Kimberly Goodson, the mother of his child. James called Maddy, Sylvia's next-door neighbor, and "K Goodson" came up on the telephone's caller ID screen.

We quickly discovered even more women were involved. One of them called Sylvia and demanded that she leave James alone. The woman did not identify herself and quickly hung up the phone. But the call gave Sylvia an opportunity to pick a fight with James.

"Who the hell is this bitch calling me?" Sylvia yelled when she got him on his cell phone.

"What are you talking about?" James asked.

"Some woman just called me. She told me to leave you alone."

"That's ridiculous."

"It's not ridiculous. I just hung up from her."

"Well, I don't know what it's about."

"It's about another woman."

"Someone is playing games, maybe the mob in Atlantic City. There is no one in my life but you. And that's by my choice. Because if I wanted to be with another woman, I would do it."

"So you are seeing someone else!"

"No, I'm not. I told you that I choose to be with you."

"Then who called me?"

"I have no idea. But I do know that you sound like you're paranoid."

With that, Sylvia pretended to back down. She pretended to let James reassure her. All the while, Sylvia and I were digging for information and planning our next moves.

Sylvia went to the FBI, bringing Maddy with her for moral support. In a conference room of the William J. Nealon Federal Building in Scranton, Pennsylvania, Sylvia told her story of being swindled by James Montgomery to agent Deryck Bratton. She brought with her a carton of documents—printouts of the work that she did for SFIICE and the Titanic exhibit, and credit card statements showing more than $92,000 in cash advances and expenses that she paid on James' behalf.

"Isn't this illegal? Some kind of misrepresentation?" Sylvia asked.

"No one else has called to complain about him," Bratton said.

"Well I know he took money from his wife," Sylvia said. "She said he took over $200,000 from her."

"So why did you keep giving him money?" Bratton asked. "Didn't you ever think of stopping?"

"I thought that if I gave him more money, the businesses would get going and I'd get my money back," Sylvia explained. "I've stopped now, and I'm trying to get him to pay me."

The meeting didn't go well. Sylvia sensed that the FBI agent thought she was a stupid woman who cheated on her husband and got in trouble. He seemed to have no interest in pursuing the matter.

"Seeking a smart one," read the ad that James posted on Love@AOL, which Sylvia found on May 4, 1999 and forwarded to me. I'd gotten used to the idea that James was aggressively cheating on me. Still, seeing the lies in his ad, I felt sorry for any woman who responded.

Filling out the AOL questionnaire, James said he was six feet, two inches tall with an average body style, "about 10 lbs over." In reality, he was at least 35 pounds overweight, and it was all in his protruding gut—not a body style that I'd call average. He also claimed an income of $100,000 or more—yeah, of other women's money—and a marital status of widowed. He said he wasn't sure that he wanted children.

Then the questionnaire asked, "What celebrity do people say you resemble?" James' answer: "Sean Connery in all respects." I almost choked.

"I can't believe he's still pulling that Sean Connery bullshit," I griped to Sylvia.

"Why not?" she asked. "It's a great hook. He just keeps lying until he catches someone."

Sylvia, Maddy and I debated how to respond to James' ad. The consensus was that Maddy should send an e-mail to James to bust him:

> WELL, WELL, WELL. Look what you find when you look at the personals. So you want to get BACK into a relationship with a slim, intelligent woman. FUNNY I thought you were already VERY happy and content with the relationship you are in now!!!! I don't know what GAME you are playing but the GAME is OVER!!!! You can either tell Sylvia or I WILL.
>
> As for this baby, if it were me, I wouldn't want any part of a lying, manipulating weasel like you, but Sylvia wants this baby. You can BE SURE I WILL do everything to see it arrives happy and healthy. It will give me great pleasure to see you support it until it turns 18.
>
> You know, Sylvia may think you are something special, but I, for one, think you are pond scum. Wonder if you told K. Goodson about the NEW addition to the Montgomery clan. And the BS about you calling from the base is just that. You HAD to be at K. Goodson's house for the number to come up on my caller ID box. Sylvia may swallow that story, but I do not.
>
> I EXPECT a response to the things I have typed here. You had better be very polite when you do or I may not keep my side of the bargain and give you time to explain it yourself. I particularly want you to explain the fact that you are NOT sure you want children. HHHHMMMM, seems strange for a man who will be a father in a few short months.

James immediately deleted the Love@AOL ad. He gave Sylvia the lame excuse that someone else posted the ad in his name and without his knowledge. Sylvia hung up on him. Five times James called, and five times she slammed down the phone.

Sylvia then sent James a nasty e-mail accusing him of seeing other women. She told him to send her money so she could pay her bills and get a divorce. She wrote that she was tired of being screamed at, tired of the games and lies, and wanted the truth for a change. If James didn't want to see her but wanted to see their son—she now "knew" it was a boy—that could be arranged, but he'd be paying support until the child was 18.

In his reply, James tried to defend himself. He protested that he was lying awake, wondering what had happened to their relationship. Yes, Sylvia had problems, but she was getting a divorce and a baby, both of which she wanted, while his life was being ruined. He took offense to her accusations.

> Your last note virtually called me a liar and said that you want to get on with your life without me and all the variables of how I can interface with the child. I know you are in a lot of shit — some of it because of

your lunatic husband—some of it I caused.

    BUT, just for a minute walk in my shoes. Just for a minute imagine that I am telling the truth ... and that I am doing everything I can to raise funds ... watching what I had two years ago slowly going down the drain ... all because I fell in love with a married woman who lived too far away with a crazy husband and a wacko neighbor next door. Now imagine that I have been telling her the truth and I get this crap continually thrown at me—I yell at her because she is too dumb to see how her so-called friends are manipulating her and how the things she does make it that much more difficult to raise the money she so desperately needs.

    BUT, I remember holding her on a floor with no furniture and I love her—then I think of this week and I don't know her anymore.

When she forwarded James' message to me, Sylvia attached her own note: "You don't know how much I want to tell him that I know that he's married and that he's been FUCKING other women. I can even give him names. God how pathetic he is. I just don't understand why he keeps holding on."

Sitting in the waiting area of one of Atlantic City's biggest law firms—Cooper Perskie April Niedelman Wagenheim & Levenson—I looked around at the dark wood paneling and photographs on the walls. I'd asked my uncle, Dennis Daly, an attorney with the New Jersey Casino Control Commission, to help me find a divorce lawyer. After making inquiries among his colleagues, one of the recommendations he received was for Julie Davis Lisa, who practiced family law at the firm.

Julie Davis Lisa stepped off an elevator and walked toward me. She was a woman about my age with short blond hair. She wore a business suit that flattered her trim figure. I, too, dressed in a business suit for the meeting. We shook hands, and Julie led me to a small conference room.

I told the lawyer my story: My husband, James Montgomery, fathered a child with one woman during our marriage, and had an affair with yet another woman. He took more than $92,000 from that woman—Sylvia Banning—and his sole purpose in marrying me was to bleed my bank account and credit rating. I used Quicken software for my financial records, and coded all the expenditures I made on his behalf as I went along. Between the cash I laid out and the debt I incurred, James owed me $224,702.

My biggest concern at the moment, however, was the Titanic artifacts. They were my only hope of paying off the debts, and many of them were still in my husband's possession. I knew for a fact that he traveled abroad, and would be traveling again. I worried that the artifacts would disappear.

Julie had a standard set of questions that she used for initial divorce interviews. My case was like nothing she'd ever heard, and the standard questions were useless. So she asked new questions, and listened carefully to my answers.

I decided to hire her, which meant I had to come up with a $3,500 retainer.

I approached my brother, Doug. His company was revamping its marketing materials and needed copywriting. He agreed to pay me for the work in advance. I sent Julie a check, and she got started.

My long-time friends, Betty Davies and Ed Galm, were getting married on May 15, 1999. For their first date, nine years earlier, Ed took Betty to the Renaissance Faire in Manheim, Pennsylvania. They were both intrigued by all things reminiscent of Merry Olde England, so they planned a medieval wedding. Guests were encouraged to attend in period attire.

What to wear to a costume wedding? Hanging in my closet was the floor-length brown velvet jacket embroidered with heavy gold braid. James gave it to me shortly after I met him. The jacket had a royal flair, and was an excellent start for a costume. But I'd need a long gown—preferably in gold—to wear beneath it. I didn't expect to find a suitable gown at the mall.

My friend, Sheryl Ginsburg, was also invited to the wedding and shared my fashion dilemma. The only solution, we realized, was to make our dresses.

I hadn't made a dress since high school. Despite the drama in my life—cheating husband, financial meltdown, career crisis—I spent days at my sewing machine, carefully stitching the gown's long seams. I had to reach deep into my brain to remember how to install the zipper. But I did remember, and the gown came out beautifully. It felt good to work on a project that was blessedly normal.

The wedding was in Maryland at the Cloisters, a small castle outside of Baltimore. Although it was built in 1932, its owners had fallen in love with, and replicated, medieval architecture. The exterior walls were random-sized blocks of stone, and a turret with a four-story spiral staircase rose from the center of the building. Many of the castle's accents had been salvaged from medieval structures in Europe. The Cloisters was the perfect backdrop for Betty and Ed's fantasy wedding.

The ceremony took place in the garden courtyard under brilliant sunshine. Three little winged fairies—Betty's young nieces—led the bridal procession. They wore short gauzy dresses in pink, aqua and lavender, and dropped rose petals from small baskets. Following them were four young nephews dressed as mini-Robin Hoods and Betty's brother as Merlin. Then came the bridesmaids—Betty's two sisters and her oldest niece—all wearing simple gowns in shades of blue and purple, and headpieces of distinctly medieval design. Finally, Betty's father, the king, wearing a robe, crown and sword, escorted the bride.

Betty's gown was regal—nothing like a modern bridal dress. She wore a white silk chemise topped by a robe of champagne satin. The front of the robe featured a panel of textured cream satin, fastened by large pearl buttons. Betty's long blond hair was curled in ringlets and she wore a tiara of tiny pearls and rhinestones. She looked radiant.

Prince Edward was waiting for her before a covered walkway of stone and timber. A big man with shoulder-length, wavy black hair, he wore a long gold tunic, topped by a layer of deep purple fabric upon which a griffin had been appliquéd like a coat of arms. Draped across his wide shoulders was a mantle of luxurious mauve silk. At his waist was a gold-hilted sword in a scabbard, which he had ordered over the Internet from Spain.

Most of the guests, like Sheryl and me, were in costume. Some people looked like nobility, others looked like peasants. There were even a couple of jokers. After the ceremony, we all stepped inside the castle for the reception. With good food, good music and good company, Betty and Ed's wedding reminded me that love and marriage could, in fact, be magical.

I returned from the magical wedding to an e-mail from my husband. James wrote that he hoped to send me a check for $850 by the end of the month. He also rumbled about getting a court injunction against John Glassey and me to prevent the sale of any Titanic artifacts until we took responsibility for the show's debts.

Sylvia, in the meantime, actually got James to wire her $2,000.

James did not, however, pay his $97 cell phone bill after I had stupidly kept his account open, which was, of course, in my name. And, he ran up another $132 in calls.

"Once again, you have cost me money," I furiously wrote to him in an e-mail. His reply, written on May 19, 1999, was laden with crap.

> I never used the phone except to talk to you. I have never received anything from you—you have got to stop making me the enemy. However hard it is for you, multiply it by 10 for me! ... Donna you cost me in a hundred ways every day ... What I did to you in our private life is unforgivable in your eyes—that is your choice. What you and John did to me in business is not only unforgivable but illegal.
>
> Donna you know how I feel about you and always will. I have never deliberately hurt you, but you are pushing me into protecting myself. You have appropriated nearly all the tools I need to keep going and kept me from any chance of making us whole again.
>
> I am not the enemy in the business. I am a way out if you will stop vilifying me and work with me rather than against me. Donna the voices of others are getting stronger every day—they tell me I am wasting my time trying to talk with you as you are so blinded with anger. I can still hear your voice but it's getting softer by the day. Don't answer this with a string of the bad things happening to you—trust me I can give you as many back—instead recognize it for what it is ... my last real effort before I give in to those other voices.
>
> I love you—and I always will.

My reply, written on May 20, 1999, was short: If you have a bona fide offer for the artifacts, bring it on and we'll all walk away. In the meantime, stay away and do not call.

That same day, my attorney, Julie Davis Lisa, drafted a letter to James. His belongings had been moved to a secure storage facility, she wrote, so there was no reason for him to appear at my home. If he did show up, I'd call the police.

Who was James Montgomery? What was he doing? Sylvia went back to Maggie Kay, the psychic, for more information. Maggie immediately knew that she had visited the FBI and was talking with me. As the psychic turned the tarot cards, she saw more and more disturbing information about James Montgomery:

He probably had two more wives.

He took women's money as a game.

And he killed Gale Lewis.

When Sylvia told me what Maggie said, my hands trembled. Was it true? I remembered the first time I met James at that restaurant in Mays Landing. He showed me his wedding photos—his wedding to Gale. He looked at me with sadness in eyes. They hadn't even celebrated their first anniversary, and she was gone.

Had he killed her?

Had I been sleeping with a murderer?

I went to Florida with this man. Alone. I remembered the miles of scrubby forests. The swamps. The public warnings not to feed the alligators.

Had I gotten out just in time?

Maggie told Sylvia that we should raid James' bank accounts. She also had another message, a spiritual one. This entire debacle—involving me, Sylvia, Maddy, James and who knows how many other people—was meant to be. There was a larger purpose.

I wish I knew what it was.

Because Sylvia sent multiple wire transfers to James' bank account, she had his account details—including his PIN number. With this information, Sylvia could call First Union Bank's customer service telephone number, and using its automated account information, monitor how much money James had.

She called several times a day. She said she was "dialing for dollars."

On May 24, 1999, Sylvia had news for me. "I just checked his account," she said. "Pukeface has more than $10,000."

"That fucking bastard," I said. "I wonder where he got it."

"You mean what woman he took it from. And of course the fucker told me yesterday that he couldn't give me any more money because he's broke."

"Fucking bastard," I repeated.

"I think we should take it," Sylvia said.

"What do you mean?"

"Use it to pay our credit cards."

"How are we going to do that?"

"It's easy. Just call the credit card companies and make a phone payment. I do it all the time. Give them his account number."

"You can do that?"

"Sure. They don't care where the money comes from to pay the bill."

This was a great idea. Because of James I had $69,000 in debt, and Sylvia owed more than $92,000. The least he could do was pay some of it.

I called the USAir Visa card and made two phone payments—$2,000 and $1,000. I made two more phone payments to the AT&T Mastercard—$1,000 and $1,500. Sylvia applied $3,000 to her Citibank card and $2,000 to another card.

We wiped James out. Even if it represented only a fraction of the debt he piled on us, it was a small victory.

Memorial Day weekend, the official start of the summer season, always drew thousands of visitors to the Jersey Shore, especially when good weather was predicted. Not good, but absolutely perfect weather was forecast for the holiday weekend—sunny skies, temperatures in the 70s, comfortable humidity. So multitudes of people drove the Atlantic City Expressway to the shore. On Sunday, May 30, 1999, the crowd included Sylvia Banning, my husband's mistress, who came to visit me.

Our plan was to go through James' boxes and boxes of papers. He had at least 30 file cartons—some of them contained books, but others held a paper trail of his past. For two years, I'd ignored the boxes in my basement. Then, when I came back from Florida, I moved the boxes, along with his clothes, trinkets, computer parts and other jetsam, out to the storage unit. One of the boxes, I was shocked to discover, contained three bottles of vodka, and the bottles weren't full. Apparently, his claims of not drinking were also lies. But I got rid of everything. I wanted no reminders of him in my house.

Now, however, the boxes might contain information that we needed.

Sylvia pulled up in a blue, four-door sedan—a typical mom car. Before she arrived, I wondered what I would feel upon meeting her. She did, after all, have an affair with my husband. Would I be angry? Jealous? Sympathetic?

When I actually went outside to greet her, the only thing I felt was curiosity.

Sylvia and I were the same age, although she looked more like a mom than I did. She was of average height and average weight. Her blond hair was short and curly. Her blue eyes squinted when she smiled.

"It's good to finally meet you," I said, a bit self-consciously. "How was your drive?"

"Not bad," she replied. "This is Allison."

"Hello Allison," I said to the child, who was now 10 years old. I was surprised when Sylvia told me she was bringing her daughter, given the nature of our mission. But she said Allison would be fine.

Sylvia wanted to see James' office, so I took her down to the basement. James' desk was still in the corner where it had been since I assembled it. The television and tables were still there. But his paperwork, books, pictures and baseball caps were gone. All were in storage.

Sylvia stood in the center of the room and looked around slowly. "Yeah, this would have worked really well for him," she said.

Her observation hit me hard. For two years, James sat in his office, in my home, plotting and scheming. And I never knew it. What an oblivious, trusting idiot I was.

We went upstairs into the kitchen, and Sylvia opened a bag she brought. "Are these yours?" she asked.

She pulled out two dinner plates from my china service. I hadn't even noticed that they were missing. "Where did you get these?" I asked in shock.

"James brought them to me."

"Why?"

"I have no friggin' clue."

Then she pulled jewelry from her bag—bracelets and necklaces. "How about these? Are they yours?"

I recognized several of the bracelets—costume jewelry that once belonged to Gale, but James had given to me. Then I saw the gold-link bracelet I received from David Hansen, the guy with anger problems that I dated before James—I didn't know it was missing either. Sylvia also had a necklace of tiny pink beads and crystals, accented by larger pink and gold beads. I had an identical necklace—a gift from James. Apparently, James picked through my jewelry chest, looking for things he could steal and give to other women. And, when he did actually spend money on gifts, he bought for all his women at once.

The day's revelations were just beginning.

Sylvia, Allison and I got into her car for the 12-mile drive to Black Horse Self Storage. Our route took us over the Albany Avenue Bridge, which was located less than a mile from my house. Sylvia recognized the place where she picked James up after he flew to Atlantic City in February. We continued driving out Albany Avenue, which turned into the Black Horse Pike. Just before we reached the storage facility, we passed the Econolodge, where Sylvia met James several times. "I had no idea that this place was so close to your house," she said.

At the storage facility security gate, I punched my access code into the keypad and it slid open. We drove to the storage unit, which was locked with a padlock. I got out my key, opened the door and we stared at the mountain of file cartons. "Well, let's get started," I said.

It was slow going. Each box had to be opened. Each piece of paper—and there were thousands—had to be looked at. Many of the papers appeared to be benign. But throughout the afternoon, the pile of stuff that we wanted to save grew taller and taller.

We found photos of 20 to 30 different women. I recognized one—Gale Lewis. She was the only woman with dark hair. Among the rest of the women, there was one redhead and three with light brown hair. The rest were blondes. All were slender and attractive.

We found faxes and printouts of e-mail. One of them was a letter from Gale Lewis:

My Dearest Mr. James,
    Still wasn't entirely awake when you called the second time (around

I I :00 am??) this morning. Still not entirely with it! Despite that did get some things done this afternoon:

 • Wire transfer of $4,000 to your account will be done Monday morning … paperwork all done at my bank.

 • Used my cash advance on my gold Visa to cover the cash I need to pay bills … so ok til April there.

 • Opened the SuthunSun account at NationsBank and have signature card to mail to you … need to know which address you want me to send it to.

The letter was dated February 24, 1995. James and Gale got married in September 1995. That meant that James had done to Gale exactly what he did to me—wiped her out financially before they even got married!

Then there was a letter from a woman named Jody. It was dated April 29, but there was no year. Jody wrote:

Since the first of March I have found out that pain was only a four-letter word. Kathleen, Colleen, Robin, Felicia, Siegrid … people who you justified either for business reasons or my not being there for you at the times they were. I could believe that your having me with you was "proof" of my permanence. I don't know when that changed for you … what came first … the all-state search or my falling out of grace?

I can't think that making me miserable is part of your excitement … the latest Bubba, Darwies, Mouse who react so predictably to your dynamism and sexuality are enough. I'm wondering if the lady who's so clever, so funny, so close-by has become important enough to allow this exposure. I remember feeling competitive with Kathleen. The competition time is over … even if I were 35 and gorgeous.

Stapled to the letter was a handwritten sheet entitled "James 1991-1992 ONLY." It was a list of dates and dollar amounts. January 14—$2,000. January 25—$2,000. March 11—$2,000. During that year, Jody gave James a total of $36,750.

In a different box we found a fax that James sent to Jody, telling her he was going to be in Los Angeles, and he wanted to get together with her. He gave her a new fax number—it was for the machine in my home. That meant James was still in touch with this woman five or six years later, while married to me.

Then we found a printout from a different, unknown e-mail address. It was entitled *To Bubbles and Eternity*.

I am feeling incredibly hot and sexy tonight and I think I will be very good to myself. I have a bottle of Ballatore Gran Spumante on ice. And I think I will use the Irish Galway crystal flutes; I only use them on very special occasions. I'll wear my finest black satin gown. The one with the thin straps and the deep plunging lace V insert, mmmmmmmm see through across my breasts. I think this will really get a reaction from him.

The story went on to describe a sexual encounter in a bubble bath, in the style of a steamy romance novel, full of references to "my delicate rosebud" and "your shaft so hard with desire." The date on the e-mail was Sunday, March 16, 1997—two months after my New Jersey wedding to James. I didn't know who the author was, but apparently James was sleeping with her and had encouraged her to write an erotic fantasy—just as he had encouraged me.

Then I found another fax, dated August 3, 1996, that James received from a woman named Vanessa Martinelli.* It was free-verse poetry entitled *Donna's Idea.*

"Who the fuck is Donna?"
I asked this
in the most controlled manner I could.
I try
not to betray too much emotion.

The poem described a man, obviously James, sensuously kissing Vanessa to distract her from asking too many questions about Donna. But Vanessa would not be deterred:

And I said,
getting back to this Donna chick
It seems like she and Burton really got the swell end of the stick
in *The Bet*

Reading the poem, I knew exactly what had happened. About the time that James and I became engaged, he was also having sex with Vanessa Martinelli, who, I could tell by the fax number, lived near Atlantic City. James sent her *The Bet*—the first of the erotic stories that he sent me. But he forgot to change the names of the characters. So Vanessa received this sexy, tantalizing story that mentions James, Burton—and Donna. When she confronted James about it, he admitted to nothing except sexual prowess:

And then he turned to me
and kissed me
and said
"see if your lieutenant can make you
rub against the sheets that way."

Another e-mail printout was dated a few weeks later—August 26, 1996. It was from a 24-year-old man named Aaron. An "escort."

Aaron thanked James for responding to his ad and described his services. "Most clients and I enjoy fucking, sucking, licking, massaging, touching, stroking, kissing, cuddling, talking, taking a shower, showing off, jacking off and more," he wrote. He quoted his fees—$125 for the first hour, $50 per additional hour, plus travel expenses. Aaron also sent a photo. He looked like a kid.

Apparently James and Aaron were negotiating. In another e-mail, dated September 2, 1996, Aaron wrote, "Yes, I could travel to AC. And actually, two hours would be just $175, although you're welcome to tip me. When did you have in mind?"

So, not long after James had proposed to me, telling me, "I don't have a gay bone in my body," and just before we started planning our Australian wedding, he was searching for a male prostitute.

I was amazed, and eternally grateful, that my AIDS test was negative.

By the time Sylvia and I finished looking through the boxes it was getting dark. We went back to my house with several file cartons of papers to review further—evidence of James' duplicity. In the living room, Allison watched *Austin Powers: International Man of Mystery*—a parody of '60s secret agent movies that seemed somehow appropriate. In the dining room, Sylvia and I talked about what we found. We used a lot of swear words.

The documents indicated that, in addition to fleecing women, James had been lying about his income, credentials and connections for a very long time.

James claimed in all his resumes to be a founder of E! Entertainment Television—which started out as the Movietime channel—and the Sportsline interactive website. Well, we found a check stub from Movietime dated September 1, 1987. The $2,750 was in payment of "consultancy for August services of James Montgomery." Another check stub from Sportsline USA Inc., dated August 8, 1995, was for a $10,000 consulting fee. Obviously, James was a hired hand, not a founder.

In a fax written on July 21, 1997, to a potential business partner, James stated, "CelebAM is funded—it has been since I had my first contract on the site nearly a year ago." This was a lie. CelebAM, James' vision of an electronic theme park on the Atlantic City Boardwalk, which he used to entice me when we first met, was never funded, and he never had a contract.

But if James had earned money, or convinced people to give it to him, maybe he banked it. Sylvia found pieces of paper that seemed to indicate hidden assets. In a letter he referred to his private Swiss bank, Julius Baer. A small sheet of notepaper, stamped "Berner Kantonalbank"—another Swiss bank—included two names and a California phone number. Finally, on a tiny scrap of paper, two numbers, handwritten in a distinctly European style, looked like account numbers.

Along with financial documents, we found military papers, but none were originals. Sylvia considered this evidence of her theory that James was never in the military. One photocopy was a Royal Australian Navy Officer's Certificate of Service. It was awarded to a surgeon lieutenant I'd never heard of. Then we found another copy of the certificate, with white-out covering the surgeon lieutenant's name. James apparently used the document to create a forgery. Perhaps all the military documents he sent to me were forged as well.

Even if he wasn't in the military, James did have a collection of weapons. We found a photo of James with his partner, Archie Turner, kneeling on the floor of a house. Spread out on a blanket between them were 11 rifles, seven pistols, and what seemed to be two machine guns. I'd previously found two handguns hidden in his office.

Who was this man? Everything we found presented more questions than answers.

Sylvia and her daughter spent the night. The next day, after they left, I tried to come to terms with the magnitude of my husband's betrayal.

James Montgomery proclaimed his love to me—just as he had proclaimed his love to 20 or 30 other women who had discretionary income and access to credit. I was just another pawn in a long line of women who heard the words "I love you" and believed them.

Why had this happened to me? All I ever wanted was what everyone wants—companionship, happiness, love. I was a good, considerate person. I worked hard. I treated people fairly. I did not deserve to be so exploited.

I paced up and down the hallway, my thoughts tumbling over each other, building into a mountain of pain and confusion. I leaned my back against the wall and slid to the floor, talking to myself. I felt like I should cry, but I could not. My dog, Beau, worriedly licked my face.

I was angry. I was outraged. Yet all I felt was numbness. I decided to call my therapist, Elaine Anderson. Luckily, she was available to do a session with me right then, over the phone.

I lay on the bed in my spare room, the meditation room, and told Elaine what Sylvia and I found in James' papers: Correspondence to his business associates that was full of lies. Letters from women asking for their money back. Stock certificates made out to many of these women. Proof that the corporation issuing the stock certificates was defunct.

The dam within me began to crack, and then it burst. I cried. I groaned. I choked. Emotional pain rose from deep within me to the surface of my awareness, like pus rising from a deep infection. Painful energy traveled to various parts of my body—my hands, my eyes, my heart. My hands clenched. I struggled to breathe.

I don't know how long it went on. But slowly, the pain dissipated.

As she helped me clear the negative energy, Elaine heard spiritual messages. My experience, she heard, was part of a huge karmic exercise. James had been defrauding women for a long time, probably many lifetimes. My assignment was to bring it to an end, and spiritual assistance was gathering to help me.

Guidance said there was an important reason for my pain. A larger perfection would, in time, be revealed.

While Sylvia and I were at the storage unit, searching for information about the activities of James Montgomery, an e-mail arrived from him, questioning my activities. He'd discovered that money was missing from his bank account.

I did not reply.

Two days later he sent another e-mail, informing me that he'd sent me a check for $850, but the bank was withholding payment, pending investigation of his missing money.

This time, I did reply:

> What the fuck kind of bullshit are you pulling now? I have spent the last two-and-a-half years paying your way, supporting your grandiose dreams of being some big-shot entrepreneur. You owe me about $225,000. You graciously deign to send me a measly $850. And now you tell me that the bank is going to hold payment on the check? You asshole.

James called a couple of times. I hung up on him. So James sent me another e-mail on June 2, 1999: "The money taken was considerable and not mine. If I don't get a reply from you that you will stop hanging up on me by noon which is 1700 here I will be forced to stop the check. I WANT to help, you are making it impossible for me."

That same day, the two payments that I'd made to the AT&T Mastercard from James' bank account were rescinded. He simply had the payments reversed and got his money back.

Then a green envelope arrived in the mail, postmarked from West London, England. It was a card. On the front was an illustration that James apparently thought was funny: a crocodile and an alligator, mostly submerged in a river, eyeing each other suspiciously. Inside, James wrote, "I DO keep my promises." A check for $850 was enclosed. I took it immediately to the bank.

Too late. Payment on the check was already stopped. James won again.

James' boxes contained not only papers, but floppy disks—dozens of them. Because James used a PC and I used a Macintosh, I couldn't open them. But Sylvia could—James had even given her the software that he used. She spent June 4, 1999, printing documents off the floppies, finding more evidence of more liaisons with more women. "This stuff is sickening," Sylvia said.

Several of the disks were labeled "Lois." James apparently was involved with Lois Brown,* a Florida woman, in 1993 and 1994. She must have invested in CelebAM—100 shares of stock were issued to her on December 1, 1993. At some point—either before or after the investment—her involvement with James became sexual.

Lois, like many of us, was encouraged to write an erotic story. She sent him the beginning of a story called *At Sea*, in which James and Lois, sailing on a tall ship, rescue two young women with long raven hair and skin the color of maple syrup, who had been cast adrift at sea. The story was "to be continued," with implications of carnal adventures to follow. Lois also wrote a document called *Post Climax Disposition*, which described fantasies of sexual encounters with James, in graphic detail. In a note dated January 12, 1994, she wrote, "James has been here every day ... except yesterday ... since Saturday. I think I must be in heaven."

Three weeks later, however, her tone changed. In an e-mail dated February 7, 1994, she wrote that she couldn't live with James' lifestyle—his disappearances, his constantly changing plans, his lack of stability. But a week later Lois changed her mind again. She wrote:

> Is it our fate to stay together? It seems so ... I know I was so miserable without you, I could barely function ... I thought I could give you up for a more "normal" life without you, but the harder I tried to let go, the more I wanted to be in your arms, listening to your whispered words of love ... I fully expected you to walk away, even thought it would make it easier if you did, I told myself it would be for the best if you did ... but I'm so glad you couldn't ... can we put all that behind us and start fresh?

I read more of Lois' correspondence and, based on what I knew of James' modus operandi, I filled in the blanks. They did get back together, but James was as unreliable, and as secretive, as ever. Lois learned that he had some kind of involvement with a woman named Cecelia Portnoy, but James would not explain it. Instead, when questioned about her or some other matter, James flew into a rage. He accused Lois of being a "lying, conniving bitch" who was trying to "rationalize her position." Then he told Lois how much he loved her, and how hurt he was.

At some point Lois had enough and decided to date another man. Unfortunately, she told James, and he used it against her. He wrote:

> Lover, our special world came about because we were totally open with each other—he introduced you to his family—I introduced you to my fears and my dreams—I made you part of mine ... not in some polite fashion but totally, we shared the heartache ... the real physical depths of struggling together ... it wasn't secure ... it wasn't nice BUT it was us ... it was us against the rest of the world ... if I wanted to settle for a truck salesman's life, I would have ceased trying to create things and stopped chasing the impossible dreams ... then like our friend I would have turned my energies to bottles and broads.

By April, James convinced Lois that the flaws in their relationship were her fault—she had hang-ups that needed to be addressed. His behavior, however, did not change.

Although Lois wanted to trust James, wanted to believe that there were no other women in his life, she still had doubts. In an e-mail dated June 12, 1994, she wrote:

> Surely you can understand why I feel insecure ... your erratic pattern of traveling, the amount of time I see you, the way the dates for everything keep changing and getting pushed forward is so far from the

'norm' that it breeds doubt … it could so easily mean what I fear the most … and I am so scared of giving you my heart and getting it broken.

James continued to insist that Lois' suspicions were wrong. He wrote:

> There are no 'current women' in the sense that you continue to torture yourself with … you tried other men—you found out that what we had was so special - you were as locked in as I am! At least, you believe that I love you … that's a starting point—hold onto it and the fact that I am going to come for you my lover … then all the rest doesn't matter.
> Because it IS so special and it IS worth fighting for—and that will be so much easier when we are together ALL the time.

Then the truth came out. Despite all the self-righteous denials, James lived with Cecelia Portnoy during the entire time he was seeing Lois. She fired off an e-mail stating what she discovered:

From: Lois
To: FUTRON01

> For starters, I have asked you over and over again to tell me exactly who Cecelia Portnoy is, and how she fits in your life, since she is the most obvious and since I have suspected since over a year ago that she meant more to you than a friend's wife … I haven't been playing games … I have been trying to give you every chance in the world to tell me yourself what is going on so I wouldn't have to go into detail, but you won't do it. You insist on me telling you what I know before you will address any of it. This, in itself, gives the impression that if I don't know about something in particular, you can get away with telling me anything you want to. So here goes…
> You told me she was the wife of Donald Portnoy, a friend of yours that was subletting your apartment, right?
> a) According to your apartment manager, no one lives there except you and Cecelia, and the two of you have lived there together for quite some time.
> b) According to Tom Portnoy, there is no such person as Donald Portnoy … and Cecelia is actually Tom's ex-wife.
> c) According to Tom Portnoy, Cecelia is James Montgomery's fiancée, lives with him at his apartment in Tampa, and has for some time.
> d) Cecelia is registered in Tallahassee as a Director of CelebAM (which seems rather strange for someone who isn't involved … and funny her name hasn't been listed as a Director on any of the paperwork I have seen! Why where you hiding this fact from me, if she doesn't mean anything to you?)
> e) Cecelia was seen walking your dog, Harold James, outside your

apartment building (no biggie ... just that you told me he was at Homestead).

Lois was crushed. She poured out her feelings in an e-mail on July 21, 1994:

From: Lois
Subj: no more ...

I give up ... it's over for us ... if there ever was an 'us' ... I feel so betrayed, I just can't even put it into words. You have lied to me about everything ... you never loved me, you were just a good actor ... a very good one ... and I was so in love with you, I wanted to believe in you so badly ... I really wanted us to have a future ... I just keep asking myself why, why, why ... is your ego so fragile that you have to have a multitude of women to constantly bolster it? As much as I adored you, as incredible as our sex was, it just wasn't enough, was it? I just keep asking myself if you said the same things to all of them ... if you called them all your "Princess" ... if they all thought they were the only one ... how can you live with yourself?

I fell in love with the man I thought you were ... the man you made me believe you were ... but it was all just a dream, and that dream has been shattered for the last time. Always before, I would let you explain it all away, and I believed you because I wanted to believe you ... but no more. I can't take it any more ... you can delete me from your list ... go on with your other women, and I will go on with my life. I am going away for awhile ... away from the bedroom that holds so many memories, and I will try to forget you ever came into my life. The only thing that was ever real was CelebAM ... at least I think it was real ... so you don't have to worry bout me causing you any problems with that ... I wish you luck ... I know it is your dream, and you see, I would never want to shatter your dream the way you have shattered mine, because I truly loved you more than anything else in the world.

I'm sure you will label all this as drivel, but I had to write you one last note ... I had to let you hear—whether or not you want to believe or whether or not you give a damn—how much you have hurt me. Please don't try to contact me ever again with anything other than updates on CelebAM. I have lost ... but you have lost more ... no other woman could ever love you the way I have, and I believe that with all my heart. Goodbye.

James did go on with other women. While managing relationships with Cecelia and Lois, he was also in contact with a woman named Siegrid—an e-mail to her, dated March 16, 1994, was signed "Later Lover." In November 1994—after the fallout with Lois Brown—James was sending his erotic stories to a woman named June.

He was also having a liaison with Debra Patrick,* who lived in Florida. This, however, was something like having a harem, because Debra suffered from multiple personality disorder—she identified her other personalities as Barbie, Tammy, Marian, Kate the Cowgirl, Thomas and the Observer. The Observer wrote a long e-mail to James on November 20, 1994. Here's how it began:

> Thank you very much for calling, we love it when you are there and talk to us. We get so lonely sometimes that it's a big ache in the heart. But we are used to it really, so don't worry about us doing anything rash. Debra has just about everyone under control, especially in public most of the time. Barbie got out as she was waiting to get Chinese take out and bought $85 worth of sex toys, what a bad girl she really is … The problem is when she is out, then nothing else gets done, no work, and she buys things, stupid things. Not like Marian. Marian will buy beautiful and elegant things we can't afford either, like that serpent's egg. She, and we, are very glad that you have it. Do you wear it every day? It makes us all feel good that you have it. Marian is the one that dresses us almost every morning; that's why we look good. I can tell when Marian doesn't feel good, because we all look terrible; it looks like we don't care what we have on. Unfortunately Barbie is really a bimbo, no sense at all, and dyslexic as you have found out. Debra is more the numbers person, pays attention to detail, and Marian could care less about anything but being taken care of and being a haughty bitch.

Debra spent the five years before meeting James living alone, avoiding emotional involvements, focusing on holding her fractured personality together so she could function in the world. But with James, she dreamed of having a child, being a mother, her life revolving around him and the baby. She said in an e-mail:

> I am so attracted to you, by the third phone call I was lost. Like a moth to a flame. What is it that makes me want to be with you? The sex by phone or in reality is incredible, touching my soul every time. But it is more than that, it is your mind, your intellect, and what else?

Since falling in love with James, Debra felt she could reveal her deepest fantasies—like she wondered about being sexual with a woman. James encouraged her. He was all for the idea of a ménage à trois—he wanted to watch Debra with a woman. He'd even help arrange it.

All the tangled e-mails indicated that James was involved with multiple women at all times. Then we found video evidence as well.

Among all the papers in the boxes were several hi-8 videotapes. I couldn't view the tapes because James' video camera—the one I bought—was broken. But Sylvia's neighbor, Maddy, had the right kind of camera. Sylvia borrowed it to watch the tapes. Most of them were programs James had recorded off of television. One, however, Sylvia marked, "Destroy."

It was a homemade sex tape. First, it showed James having sex with a woman who had short, wavy brown hair. We didn't know who she was. Then the tape showed James having sex with Sylvia. Viewing it long after the encounter, and knowing what she knew, Sylvia was humiliated and enraged.

Then the tape showed Kimberly Goodson holding her new baby. "Janna is seven weeks old, and will be eight weeks old on Friday," Kim said to the camera. "She's seeing Daddy for the second time."

Based on the age of the baby, the scene had to be recorded during the week of June 8, 1998. If the other scenes were recorded about the same time, that meant that while I was struggling to help my husband get the Titanic show off the ground, he was busy having sex with at least three other women.

Sylvia was waiting for James at Philadelphia International Airport. She bought a ticket for him to fly up from Florida back in April, but never sent it. Now that Sylvia had an exotic surprise for him, she mailed the ticket.

They drove directly to a hotel. On the way, Sylvia told James that she'd been thinking about one of his sexual fantasies, a wish he'd expressed many times. His fantasy, Sylvia said, was about to come true. He was in for a real treat. James could barely contain his excitement.

Once in the hotel room, Sylvia undressed James, and partially undressed herself. Then she told him to lie on the bed and close his eyes. "Actually, this would be better if you were blindfolded," Sylvia said.

"Okay, lover," he replied.

Sylvia blindfolded him. She also pulled out some soft bondage ropes and tied him to the bed. Then, as he lay naked, spread-eagle and blindfolded, she sat on the bed and massaged him so that he got an erection—she knew exactly how to do that.

"Your surprise is coming," Sylvia told him.

She got off the bed and opened the bathroom door, where Maddy and I were hiding. We slipped into the room without saying a word. I sat on the bed at James' right side, and Sylvia sat on his left. Maddy sat between James' legs. In her hands she held a razor strap and a paring knife, although James couldn't see them. All he knew was that several people had joined him on the bed—he thought he was in for an orgy.

"I'm going to take your blindfold off very slowly," Sylvia whispered into his ear. "But I don't want you to open your eyes."

James complied with her wishes.

"Okay, open your eyes," Sylvia commanded.

The look on his face was priceless—total shock, surprise and fear.

There I was—the wife whom he had, indeed, been hiding in the closet. And there was Maddy—the neighbor that James detested.

For the first time in his life, James was speechless. Sylvia loved every minute of it. Then he asked Sylvia if this was a joke.

No, but it was a dream. Sylvia had the dream a few days after printing out the correspondence from James' multitude of women. She woke up with a sense of vicarious satisfaction, and couldn't wait to tell me about it. I thought her dream was hysterical. We got Maddy on the phone, and kept coming up with increasingly devious ways to embellish it—such as an untimely end for his private parts. "I think they belong in a blender," I said.

At least, in the midst of our trauma, we were laughing.

The Atlantic City Civil Courthouse, built in 1975, was a multistory red brick building of modern design. I entered it for the first time in my life on June 7, 1999 and went up to the second floor, where family court cases were heard. As I stepped from the elevator, I was surprised to see a lounge with tables, chairs and vending machines—did that mean I should expect a long stay?

I met my attorney, Julie Davis Lisa, in the corridor. We entered one of the courtrooms and took seats in the gallery. Looking around, I decided the courtroom was more utilitarian than imposing. The judge's bench and adjacent witness stand were plain, light-colored wood—perhaps maple. Wood paneling in a similar maple color covered the walls surrounding the bench. The same paneling was used for wainscoting around the room; above it was faintly textured white wallpaper. Tables for the plaintiff and the defendant, each with two standard swivel office chairs, faced the judge. Behind the tables, a railing separated the actors in legal dramas from the spectators.

My case was called, and the judge ordered everyone else in the gallery to leave. Julie had requested an *ex parte* hearing for a court order to recover the Titanic artifacts that James Montgomery had in his possession. *Ex parte* meant secret—James, the defendant, was not notified of the proceedings.

This was unusual in a divorce case. The judge, William C. Todd III, said that in five or six years on the bench, he had never granted an *ex parte* hearing. But after reading my complaint for divorce and my certification—my account of what happened—the judge understood why we wanted it.

Julie and I had been working on the divorce complaint for two weeks. She was incredulous as I told her the details of my story. I knew it all sounded bizarre—fraud, multiple women, possible murder, a baby out of wedlock, the sinking Titanic—but everything had truly happened. I had enough experience as a journalist to recognize a story when it flattened me like a steamroller. Eventually I'd be writing a book—something I never before had any desire to do—and creating a website. My story might even be good enough to become a movie.

First, however, I had to get through the court battle.

In New Jersey, couples can get a no-fault divorce after living apart for 18 months. I wasn't interested in that. My husband was at fault.

Typical causes of action in a New Jersey fault divorce were extreme cruelty, adultery, desertion, addiction, institutionalization, imprisonment or deviant sexual conduct. My divorce complaint had a few of those issues, plus some that were much more rare. We claimed:

1. Extreme cruelty. James constructed a web of lies and misrepresentations, carried on numerous affairs, did not contribute financially to our marriage, forced me to incur $69,000 in credit card debt, and used my money to entertain other women.

2. Adultery. James cheated with Kimberly Goodson, which resulted in a child being born.

3. Breach of contract. James repeatedly told me that he would be responsible for his business and personal expenses. I relied on his promises, paid his bills, but he never reimbursed me.

4. Fraudulent inducement to marry. James lied when we met and throughout our courtship. He lied about when Gale Lewis had died, his age, his ownership of the townhouse where he was living, his assets and his earning capacity. James knew he was lying and intended for me to believe him. I did.

5. Fraudulent inducement to continue the marital relationship. James kept telling me that his business endeavors would benefit us both so that I kept giving him money.

6. Deceit and fraudulent representation. I believed James' lies and was damaged because of them.

The complaint demanded "judgment against defendant for compensatory damages, punitive damages, attorneys' fees and costs of suit."

The issue on that day in court, of course, was the Titanic artifacts. I estimated the value of what James had at about $30,000. In my certification, I stated that I was the majority shareholder of the corporation that owned them, and I was worried that James and the artifacts would disappear.

Judge Todd was willing to sign an order forcing James to return the artifacts. He and my attorney discussed the logistics of enforcing it, which were complicated by the fact that James was in Florida, where a New Jersey order would be considered "foreign." I needed to retain a Florida attorney and have the order validated by a Florida court.

Then there was the problem of how I would physically take possession of the artifacts. The judge doubted the local sheriff would want to be responsible for them, and he didn't think shipping them through the mail was a good idea. I'd already told Julie that I would fly down to Florida to get the items. James had the tiny shard of stained glass from the Titanic wreck, some post cards and books, a few of the miniature models from the Cameron movie, and small pieces of the White Star Line china. I could easily put everything in a carry-on bag. The judge suggested that James be required to turn them over to an officer of the court, or that I accompany sheriff's officers to James' location to collect everything.

My hearing only lasted 20 minutes, and round one was a win for Donna. As we left the courthouse, Julie worried about me going to Florida and confronting James. "I don't know if it's a good idea for you to go with the sheriff to his home," she said.

"But Julie," I replied, "what a great scene for the movie!"

During the day, while engaged with people—Sylvia, my lawyer, my clients or my new softball team in Philadelphia—I was able to hold my emotions together. But at night, when I was alone, my anger, fear, frustration and grief rose to the surface.

How could my husband be so evil?

How could I have been so stupid?

I was an honorable person—what had I done to deserve this?

I sat on the daybed in my meditation room, with Beau curled up beside me. I chanted "om," trying to reduce my stress. Some evenings I wrote in my journal—just about every entry started, "Dear God, please help me." I pleaded with God and Guidance to explain why all this was happening to me. When I started to cry, Beau frantically licked my tears away. Even the gliders tried to distract me—scurrying across my pages as I wrote in the journal, chewing the edge of the book.

My little guys—Chuckie the chinchilla, and the two sugar gliders, Donald and Jamie—were no longer relegated to the basement. I moved them into the spare bedroom, probably more for my comfort than theirs. Eventually, I started letting them out of their cages. The pets loved this. The chinchilla, being a rodent, liked to chew, which was detrimental to the furniture in the room. The sugar gliders, being arboreal animals, climbed the curtains and perched above the two windows, close to the ceiling. They're also social animals, so sometimes they jumped on me.

When the sugar gliders first arrived in my home, Jamie, the female, was the more aggressive of the pair. That changed over time—probably due to sexual maturing. By June 1999, Donald was always chasing and mounting her. She never looked like she enjoyed it, and I suspected that I knew why. Once I saw Donald's sex organ—it was about an inch long. Considering that his entire body, not counting the tail, was four inches long, he struck me as being extremely well-endowed. Maybe sex wasn't fun, at least for Jamie.

One day about a year earlier I'd noticed what seemed to be a black, shriveled piece of string hanging from Donald's back end. It looked biological, like a piece of skin. What was wrong with my pet? Did he have parasites? Were his intestines falling out? He was a little buddy. I hoped he wasn't dying.

I took him to the veterinarian. The diagnosis: Donald's long penis was necrotic at the end, which meant dead. This sometimes happened to sugar gliders who were sexually frustrated—they mutilated themselves. Apparently all the time Donald spent chasing Jamie still wasn't enough, or somehow she was getting away from him. The vet recommended that nothing be done. Eventually, the dead part fell off.

It didn't seem to stop Donald, though. He kept chasing Jamie, even if he was missing some of his masculinity.

"I have just seen one of the forged checks in your name to Citibank????" James said to Sylvia in an instant message on June 10, 1999.

"My name?" Sylvia asked, feigning ignorance. "Where did that come from?"

"It is being scanned—I will send you a copy."

An hour later James sent her a copy of the check. "Any comments?" he wrote. "It's out of my hands now and with First Union and the FBI's check fraud squad."

Sylvia did not flinch in her e-mail reply:

> All I have done is cry since you sent it. Is this some kind of a joke? First of all it's not even my address. Second of all is this your way of not having to pay the $13,000 back that my husband will not get off my back for? I don't know but I'm going away tonight and I won't be back until Monday late or Tuesday. I have no choice. And yes it's about the baby. Since you haven't asked or cared to find out what's going on I needed to recall the doctor because something is wrong. I'll try to find out next week what's going on so I can't deal with all of this right now.

"If you're not involved and it's some sort of trick by Atlantic City you have to help me!" James wrote back. "My account has been looted by this and other checks—it's in the hands of the fraud squad! What's wrong with the baby?"

A few days later, on June 14, 1999, Sylvia sent an e-mail to answer him.

"Well I have a big one for you," she wrote. "We are having twins. And boys to boot. They are identical. I just returned home. Everything has worked out well with the tests that they had to do. I am going to try and send the ultrasound to you."

At 10 p.m. that night, after Sylvia told him he was the "father" of twins, a process server banged on the door of Kimberly Goodson's home in Florida. James was served with my complaint for divorce, along with an order to appear in Pinellas County court the next afternoon regarding the Titanic artifacts.

As I flew through brilliant sunshine into Tampa, Florida, the morning of June 15, 1999, I was apprehensive about confronting my husband.

My new Florida attorney had arranged a hearing in Pinellas County court regarding Judge Todd's order on the Titanic artifacts. It would take place in the chambers of Judge Nelly N. Khouzam.

I met my lawyer at her firm's office, and she drove me to the courthouse in Clearwater. We entered the chambers. The judge, a slight, attractive woman with brown hair pulled back from her face, sat at a large desk of dark wood. Pushed up against the desk, forming the shape of a T, was a long wooden conference table. My attorney and I sat on the left side of the conference table. The other side was empty.

James did not show up. He did, however, appear via telephone, as did his attorney. The lawyer apologized, saying he had just been called that morning and had prior commitments. James also said he had another meeting—he was on his way to see the mayor.

"Then you must be right in the neighborhood," Judge Khouzam noted.

The hearing didn't take long—James agreed to deliver the Titanic artifacts to my attorney by the end of the day. At that time, he would sign a consent decree—already prepared by my Atlantic City attorney—in which James and I agreed that the artifacts would be safely stored until the next court hearing, which was scheduled for June 30, 1999.

I'd won again, although it felt like a hollow victory, compared to all the problems I faced. My attorney and I talked about my situation as we drove back to her office along Clearwater Harbor, where the sunshine created diamonds of light that danced on the water.

"You're alive and you're healthy," my lawyer said. "Everything else can be repaired."

Intellectually, I knew she was right. Emotionally, I vacillated between anger at my husband's treachery, hope that I'd find justice and consuming fear that my entire life would collapse.

In honor of Fathers Day—June 20, 1999—Sylvia faxed to James an ultrasound picture of their twin sons. Sylvia, of course, was not pregnant. But Maddy had once been pregnant with twin boys, although, tragically, she lost the babies. Maddy still had an ultrasound of them, and suggested that Sylvia send the picture to James to convince him that the babies were on the way.

"They can't be boys," James said when Sylvia spoke to him on the phone. "I only have girls."

"How can you say that? You have one daughter," Sylvia said. She was referring to his grown daughter in Australia, Margaret Riley. Sylvia knew that the baby Janna, his "buddy's daughter," was actually fathered by James, but she hadn't yet confronted him about that lie.

"I'm telling you, I only have girls," James insisted.

Sylvia called me, laughing—James was arguing about the gender of babies that didn't exist. We were still conning him. Next, we hoped to get him arrested.

My partner in the Titanic materials, John Glassey, asked his good friend, an FBI agent named Jody Petracci, to look at the evidence we had of James Montgomery's swindling. Sylvia and I made an appointment to meet her at my house on June 22, 1999.

I spent days going through all the documents that we found, putting together a synopsis of James' pattern of defrauding women. The rough outline of the story was this:

James Montgomery married his first wife, Patricia Heywood, in November 1971, in Sydney, Australia. They were already in business together—she was the "Pat" in Jaypat Productions. A newspaper blurb called their marriage "the computer match of the year." James and Pat divorced in October 1976.

In the late 1980s, James came to the United States. He had a romantic relationship with Colleen Jessick,* a Hollywood scriptwriter. James kept coming up with ideas for television shows and movie scripts, and convinced Colleen to write treatments. None of the ideas were produced.

While continuing the relationship with Colleen, James married Kathleen

Maloney in March 1990 and moved across the country to Kathleen's home outside of Boston, Massachusetts. During this time he won a contract to build a public information system for video terminals to be installed in Florida tourism centers. He spent a lot of time in Florida, and stayed there when he and Kathleen separated. The tourism system was never built, and by this time, James was living in the United States illegally.

While in Florida, James had a romantic relationship with Jody McClure, whom he'd originally met in California. She gave him $36,750 during 1991, plus incurred credit card debt on his behalf. James continued to see her into 1992, and promised her stock in CelebAM.

In 1992, James also started a relationship with Cecelia Portnoy. They lived together in Tampa, Florida, through July 1994. James and Cecelia had a joint checking account, and articles of incorporation for CelebAM listed her as a director and officer. She was issued 200 shares of CelebAM stock.

While living with Cecelia, James became involved with Lois Brown. Lois apparently invested in CelebAM as well; James gave her 100 shares of stock on December 1, 1993. By January 1994, Lois was writing about their hot and heavy romance, although it was impossible to tell what came first—the money or the sex. Later in 1994, James began a relationship with Debra Patrick, the woman suffering from multiple personality disorder. He was also seeing Kimberly Goodson, although it was unclear when that relationship started.

At the same time, James was talking to Gale Lewis, who he met online. He moved to Mays Landing, New Jersey, to live with her in early 1995. They got married on September 14, 1995. Two weeks later, on September 28, 1995, James finally filed for divorce from Kathleen Maloney, his wife living near Boston. He committed bigamy when he married Gale.

Gale, who was not working, incurred substantial debt on James' behalf while pursuing several failed business ventures. She and James were home alone when she died suddenly on May 17, 1996. The cause of death on the death certificate was listed as coronary artery thrombosis. James posted his online ad—"Finished grieving" it proclaimed—shortly thereafter.

When I met James on July 21, 1996—two months after Gale died—he was living in the Mays Landing townhouse. Although he claimed he owned the townhouse, he did not. James signed a six-month lease with John Lewis, Gale Lewis' father and the executor of her estate.

After James proposed to me, he was still searching for women and men on the Internet, and still seeing Vanessa Martinelli, who lived outside of Atlantic City. By the time James and I married on October 10, 1996, I had already given him thousands of dollars. Over the course of our marriage, I spent in excess of $200,000 on his business ventures and incurred $69,000 in debt.

During our marriage, James had affairs with Loraine Moyle,* of Ocean City, New Jersey; the woman from *Cats* who bought him a Velo computer; and Sylvia Banning, who gave him more than $92,000. He was still in touch with Jody McClure and Kathleen Maloney.

And, James also continued to see Kimberly Goodson in Florida—I unknowingly paid for many of the trips. He and Kim had a child on April 17, 1998. I discovered this and left James in February 1999.

He was currently living with Kimberly Goodson—although he also seemed to be involved with another Florida woman named Sharon Decamp.* Sylvia thought Sharon might have been the woman who called and said to leave James alone.

James' papers indicated that he contacted even more women, but those involvements appeared to be shorter and less costly. They were the lucky ones.

Promptly at 10 a.m. on June 22, 1999, the FBI agent, Jody Petracci, arrived at my house. She was a tall, mature woman, probably in her late 40s, with short dark hair. She wore a blazer and skirt. I, too, dressed for the meeting in a skirt and top. Sylvia was in slacks.

Our evidence was arranged in neat piles on my dining room table. I created 12 separate reports on James' activities—eight of them related to his involvement with specific women. Attached to each report were copies of documentation—marriage certificates, stock certificates, invoices and e-mails in which women pleaded for their money back.

We told the story, and answered, as best we could, Petracci's questions. At one point, she asked if we had any photos of the women. I opened up the folder containing all the pictures, the bevy of attractive blondes and light brunettes, plus one redhead.

"He definitely seeks out a particular profile," Petracci commented.

I gave the agent the photo of James surrounded by weapons, and told her that he left two guns in my house. She asked to see them.

Jody Petracci spent two hours listening to our story, going over the information we presented. When the agent got up to leave, she stated, "This man has to be stopped."

James offered me a divorce settlement. He retained an attorney, who contacted my attorney.

"Mr. Montgomery is willing to give you all the Titanic artifacts so you can do what you want with them," Julie Davis Lisa told me. "He would not be responsible for the debts, and he would not be responsible for any money you gave him. You would just go your separate ways."

"Are you kidding me?" I asked. "He takes a quarter million dollars from me, and thinks he can just walk away?"

"I'm obligated to communicate the offer to you," Julie said.

"I understand that. But I'm not accepting it. The debts are killing me, and I want him to pay them."

Then I told Julie how Sylvia and I tried to make James responsible by using his accounts to pay our credit card bills. My lawyer was not pleased to hear this. "You shouldn't do that," she said to me. "The court isn't going to like it."

"Well, it didn't work anyway," I said. "James had all the payments reversed." But I was angry. My husband swindled more than $200,000 from me, and I was reprimanded for trying to get some of it back? What kind of system was this?

On June 30, 1999, we were back in court, in front of Judge William Todd. This time, James was represented by an attorney, Stephen A. Browndorf, of Northfield, New Jersey.

The hearing was about the Titanic artifacts; all parties agreed they'd be kept in storage and in a bank vault—except, of course, the lifeboats, which were to remain where they were. The judge then wanted to find out the other issues of the case.

For me, the big issue was fraud. My lawyer explained that James Montgomery had a history of meeting women on the Internet, convincing them to give him substantial amounts of money, and then disappearing with the money.

Judge Todd questioned me about this. As I answered him, my voice had a thick, controlled quality. My husband's actions were an outrageous betrayal, which I had to describe in an unemotional, matter-of-fact way.

"How many women do you know of?" Judge Todd asked.

"Fifteen or 20," I replied.

"How do you know about this, did these women get in touch with you?"

"My husband's papers were left in our house, which I didn't look at during the course of our marriage. I finally looked at them, and was amazed at what I discovered.

"You still have all those papers?"

"Yes."

"You're saying your husband has bank accounts with some of these other people?"

"There's one bank account, yes, that has another woman's name on it, whom he lived with before. That account is still in use; I don't know what happened to the woman. There are other documents that indicate he owes other women money and has not done a good job of paying it back."

"You have the names of 15 or more women that you believe he may have been involved in soliciting money from on some fraudulent basis?"

"I'm aware of at least three different women he had affairs with during our marriage. I assume there was money involved there as well. I haven't gotten in contact with them yet."

"One of these women you have been in contact with?"

"Yes."

"What's her name?"

"Sylvia Banning."

"How much did she say she gave him?"

"Ninety-two thousand dollars."

"When did she say that happened?"

"Over the past year or so."

"When was the last time you and your husband were living together?"

"February."

"So she gave him money when you were living with him?"

"Absolutely."

"At the time you didn't know anything about that?"

"No."

"And you're concerned that some of these other women may be in the same situation?"

"Yes. And I'm also aware that he's been sending money to the woman he had the child with during our marriage. I have checks to that effect. In fact, she has access to the checking account and writes the checks herself."

"Assuming he did what you suggested, am I correct in assuming that you don't know what he did with the money?"

"That's true."

"Is one of the things you're concerned about that you gave him money?"

"Sure."

"How much did you give him?"

"Two hundred thousand dollars."

"What did he do with that money?"

"Mostly I paid his expenses as he was trying to get his business ventures going. Some money I just gave him as checks, and other money, I essentially paid all his expenses during the course of our marriage. Business expenses. That figure does not include food or the mortgage, which I also paid."

"What kind of business enterprises was he involved in?"

"His original intention in coming to Atlantic City was to establish an entertainment center called CelebAM on the Boardwalk, which never got anywhere. He had also been trying to establish the same business down in Florida, ever since 1990 or 1991, and never got anywhere. He tried to get different projects going in the casinos, he tried to develop a theme park at the Gateway property, any number of different projects were going on, none of which panned out."

"Do you work?"

"I have an advertising business called Donna Andersen Copywriting. I work out of my home. I've been doing that since 1982."

"How much do you earn in that business?"

"Well in 1997, my gross receipts were close to a half-million dollars. I essentially stopped working in my business to work with my husband, so I'm in the position now of having to rebuild. Last year's receipts were like $100,000."

"Putting aside the Titanic artifacts and that corporation, do you own anything yourself?"

"I own my home."

"Just in your name?"

"Yes."

"How about your husband, do you know what he owns?"

"I don't believe he owns anything. Well, there's a 1977 MG in the yard, worth about $3,000."

"You think that the Titanic artifact business has some value now? If things were liquidated, there would be some money generated by that?

"Yes, and we've been trying to liquidate them, but not everybody's in the market for a $100,000 antique."

"If you were able to liquidate that, what should happen to the money that should be generated?"

"I think I should get it all."

"Why?"

"Because essentially, I've been defrauded. My husband made virtually no money during the course of our marriage. He misled me from the very beginning."

"And you say that over the course of your marriage you probably provided him with more than a couple hundred thousand dollars?"

"Absolutely. I have it itemized."

"So if I could magically bring this to a conclusion today, and you were told that you could take the Titanic artifacts, pay for the debt, keep whatever was left, and go on your way, and not have to worry about any debts that he may have created with other women or investors, would you be satisfied?"

"I'm not sure. I'd have to think about that."

"What else would you conceivably want?"

"I think that there's more money out there. I think punitive damages are in order."

"You want more of the money that you gave him back?"

"Yes."

The judge turned to my husband's attorney. "Mr. Browndorf, is all of this new to you?" he asked. "Are you aware of this claim?"

"I read the complaint," Browndorf replied. "About the truthfulness of it I have no knowledge. My client denies it. If they want to litigate this thing, we can. I want all bank records from before they got married. I want to see where she gets this money she claims she has. And as far as the court's proposal to give her all the artifacts and walking away ..."

"I wasn't proposing that," Judge Todd interrupted. "I was just trying to find out what her position was."

"It is a proposal my client will be willing to accept," Browndorf continued. "And the fact that she wants compensatory and punitive, and so forth, and she indicates he doesn't have anything else—if he has nothing else, she's just going to be spinning her wheels. Unless she thinks she's going to find something that she doesn't know about now, and I obviously don't know about. But if she wants to go through it all, we can litigate this."

I was not about to let James Montgomery simply walk away. The litigation began.

Chapter 17

A gaping hole ruptured the place within me where love and partnership were supposed to be. Three years earlier I thought the hole was filled. But the man who promised to be my forever husband was a lying, cheating mirage. Now the mirage was gone, leaving only the hole.

Perhaps it was time to fill the emptiness. I felt emotionally stable enough to bait the hook and go fishing for companionship again. So I returned to what I knew—the personal ads. I was not afraid. I was certain that I would never again be deceived as James Montgomery had deceived me.

Since I last tried Internet dating, America Online had upgraded its personals technology with a user-friendly display and photo capability. On July 5, 1999, I posted my personal ad in the Philadelphia section. "Are you a professional who lifts more than a phone?" I asked. "Can you execute a play on the court as well as the corp? I'm looking for an athlete with brains, or brains with moves. Please, no used-to-be or thinking-about, if you get out there and sweat, we're off to a good start."

As with my past forays into online dating, my inbox quickly filled with responses. I replied to every man who seemed suitable. One was a guy named John, who described himself as 35 and single with no kids. He was five feet, 10 inches tall and in good shape because he was active in paintball and dek hockey.

My first question to him: "What is dek hockey?"

"I still haven't come up with a streamlined answer," John said in his e-mail reply. "So here goes another attempt: Dek hockey is street hockey played in a rink, on a plastic surface—called a dek. It is played on foot. A good analogy is dek hockey is to ice hockey what softball is to baseball."

John was half-owner of a dek hockey rink, and he was about to open a paintball field. Although he wasn't a fan of action movies or violent video games, he did have an aggressive side. "I still love to light up an opponent," he wrote. "That goes for both paintball and dek hockey, dress me in a certain uniform and another person comes out! EEEKK! Can you recommend a good shrink?"

John's e-mails were clever and entertaining. He did a riff on personal responsibility. Then he made fun of himself for getting on a soapbox. It was a nice mix.

John asked about me—what do I do in life?
My reply:

> At the moment I'm working on rebuilding my life after a mercifully short but disastrous marriage—that's a whole story in itself. In fact, I expect that one day it will be a movie.
> What a story! We have white-collar crime. We have murder. We have multiple mistresses. We have psychics and card readers. We have the Titanic. We have dream sequences in which several women take revenge by following the path of Lorena Bobbitt. What do you think? Tom Clancy's formula might work.

Although John cringed at the mention of Lorena Bobbitt, he was intrigued enough to keep writing to me, and I kept replying. His e-mails were waiting for me just about every morning. It was a pleasant distraction.

Progress was slow in rebuilding my life. With the return of the Showboat Crew's News account, I had two casino newsletters—not as good as four, but better than none. Embarking on a campaign to find more clients, I bought 100 personalized pens for a mailing—"Need a Writer? Donna Andersen Copywriting." Making money was my priority.

Turning the Titanic materials into cash would certainly help, so John Glassey and I kept trying to do something with the collection—either mount an exhibition, or unload it. We pitched everyone from shopping malls to Las Vegas casinos to Ebay.

At the same time, I lived the parallel existence of a vigilante pursuing a criminal, as Sylvia and I tried to figure out what James was doing and how to make him repay the money he took from us. Sylvia was good at the game. She had James convinced that she didn't know me and was in love with him, the father of her soon-to-be-born twin boys. James told her he was coming up from Florida for a meeting, and asked her to arrange a car and hotel room. Sylvia was not about to go anywhere near James, but instead of blowing him off, she wrote in an e-mail that she couldn't help him because her credit cards were maxed out. She closed her note with, "I wish you were here with me. I miss you so much."

Sylvia forwarded his reply, preceded by her note, "READ AND PUKE!!"

"Bubba, you were the real reason for the trip—so guess it's not to be," James wrote.

Somehow Sylvia convinced James to send her another check. Then she ramped up the pressure, telling James that her husband filed a lawsuit for the return of the $13,000 loan. After her "court appearance," Sylvia told James that the judge gave her two weeks to produce the money or stock certificates as proof of her ownership interest in James' company. In the meantime, she kept dialing for dollars—monitoring the balance of James' checking account.

Tiny Jamie perched inside the sugar glider cage, even though the door was open and she was free to roam the spare bedroom. She looked frightened.

Donald wasn't with her, so I checked all the usual sugar glider hiding places: Behind the books on the dresser. Inside the pillow shams on the daybed. Between the ruffles of the curtain valence. He was nowhere to be found. I looked in new places, like the closet—maybe I left the door ajar and he crept in. I moved furniture—maybe he got behind something. After a half-hour of fruitless searching, I started to panic.

Then I saw it—a hole in the window screen. I didn't know who chewed it — Donald or Chuckie—but Donald escaped to the giant locust tree that was right outside the window. My heart sank.

I went into the sunlit backyard and called Donald, knowing it was useless—the little pets never came when I called. They didn't even know their names. But maybe he was still in the neighborhood. Maybe somebody would find him. I made up flyers with a picture of a sugar glider and posted them on telephone poles. Two children whom I frequently met as I walked Beau tried to help—they got out their butterfly net and searched the trees near their home. They didn't find Donald, and neither did I.

I put the small wooden glider nest box, which was usually attached to the inside of their cage, outside. Maybe Donald would seek shelter in it, I thought, kidding myself. That night, the temperature dropped and it rained heavily. Donald had never experienced cold or rain. I knew he did not survive.

Three days after Donald left, on July 15, 1999, he reappeared—in a session with Elaine Anderson, my energy therapist. Donald came into my life, and then ran away. It was an allegory of my experience with James.

Lying on Elaine's therapy table, I cried over Donald. But as I focused on the pain, I tapped into another, far deeper loss. My tears also fell over my sadness at losing love. Or at losing in my efforts to find love. My heart's anguish was deep and old, buried under layers of internal sediment. Slowly the wretched energy found a path to the surface of my awareness and drained away. Releasing the sugar glider, in a way, helped me to release James.

I heard Donald's words. He was happy to be out of the cage. He was happy to be in the trees, even if he only lived for a little while. He was happy that I put a house outside for him, although he said he wouldn't be there. My little pet sent me his love, which Elaine described as a pure love. She asked me to receive as much of it as I could.

I told that Elaine I'd taken Donald to the vet a year earlier because of the black string hanging from his backside, which turned out to be his shriveled, necrotic penis. With that, Elaine saw another correlation between Donald and James. As the sugar glider had mutilated his penis, James had mutilated his soul.

We asked Guidance a question: What happened to James? Why did he live a life of deceit? We were told that James spent too many lifetimes as a warrior. The gore, death and deception—it pushed him over the edge to the dark side. It became his twisted way of life.

My role, Guidance told us, was to contribute to a tremendous healing. Guidance explained that the lack of integrity between men and women, and the squashing of the feminine principle, were huge wounds in the collective consciousness. The wound manifested in many ways: The overemphasis on sexuality—raw sex, not the sacred conjunction. Men conning women, and women conning men. The acceptability of lying and deception in so-called romantic relationships. It all pointed to a chasm of integrity, a rift that needed to heal. I was shown that my whole life was set up for this experience—crushing deception, followed by recovery and growth. It was my purpose.

July 19, 1999 was my 43rd birthday. The previous year had been horrible. My husband deceived me, scammed me and cheated on me. I needed comfort. I needed love. I hoped someone in my family would reach out to me. But on July 19, I received birthday wishes by phone. No invitations.

I called my childhood friend, Pam Breyer, and she and her husband took me out to dinner. Although I had a lovely night with them, as far as my family was concerned, I felt like I was down and being kicked.

Eight weeks earlier, my brother, Doug, hosted a birthday dinner for our sister, Tracy. I went to the dinner—an 85-mile trip each way—but I had to leave early. I had deadlines—several jobs to finish. I needed the money. Doug called the next day and reamed me out for leaving early, which turned into an opportunity to criticize me for marrying James.

"Well Doug," I said, "James told me that he loved me. No one, including no member of our family, ever said that to me before. I wanted to believe him, and I did." My brother seemed surprised at what I said.

The day after my birthday I talked to Tracy on the phone, carefully avoiding the topic of my disappointment. She asked me what was going on in my divorce. I told her a few things, and then mentioned that Sylvia had seen a psychic, and the psychic advised us to raid James' bank accounts.

With that, Tracy was all over my case, telling me that I'd better not do anything illegal, and if I had listened to everyone's advice and not married James, none of this would have happened. Now, she said, I was in all kinds of trouble, and the best thing for me to do was to just walk away.

This was not what I needed to hear. I hung up. Then, steaming, I sent her an e-mail:

> That's exactly what he's counting on—me rolling over like the rest of his victims without a fight. It's not happening.
>
> I told Doug about a month ago—after he reamed me out for leaving your birthday dinner early (I had to work)—that the main reason I fell for James was that for the first time in my life I felt like someone loved me. And believe me, I never felt that from my family.
>
> And so I've had a shitty year. And my birthday has come and gone, and not one member of my family even suggested that they might like to get together to celebrate. Point proven once again.

Tracy replied immediately with another lecture—if I was feeling alone, I was to blame. She wrote:

> You have to give to receive Donna!
>
> Doug told me of your conversation. You have this "poor me, nobody loves me attitude," complaining that people don't love or care about you, yet, you don't make the effort to find out what's going on in the lives of the people in this family. Instead, you say things like "nobody tells me anything."
>
> With the exception of the last two or three weeks, you would NEVER call me to just talk. See what's going on in my life, when I would continually call you for updates, to find out what's going on, to find out how work is going, etc.
>
> I know what's going on in the family because I MAKE THE EFFORT to find out. I send e-mails to our family. I make phone calls.
>
> You generally call when YOU need something from us. Last year on Father's Day you wanted Doug to give you $80,000 overnight. When he said no, you told him that the two families could never be together again and you hung up on him. You didn't talk to him for months. It caused major stress in the family all the way around — everybody. Yet, the next time you called him was because you needed money. No apology, nothing. I don't know if you've apologized to him since, but if you haven't, you ought to.
>
> We all tried to show our love and concern for you when you rushed into marrying James. You didn't want to hear it and told us all to go to hell. Look where you are now. Donna, I'm sorry, but when almost everyone you know, friends and family, have reservations about a man and what you're doing, you can't spit in their eye and tell them all to go to hell ... especially now when everyone's suspicions are turning out to be correct, and then some. The intuition of at least 15 or more people should not have been ignored!
>
> I personally feel like you owe the whole family an apology. We were trying to look out for your wellbeing, when it came to James. I'm looking for you to say, "You were right Tracy, and I'm sorry I was too pigheaded and stubborn to be open and objective enough to see if what you were saying could have had some merit."
>
> Donna, I understand that James showed you love and that's why you got suckered into that marriage. This family would be happy to show you more love if they felt they were going to get some in return.
>
> Keeping your current attitude and actions is NOT going to accomplish what you want. We want you more a part of our lives, but you need to make the effort too!
>
> Love,
> Tracy

I couldn't believe what I was reading. My life was shattered, and all my sister cared about was being right. And she wasn't.

Not one person expressed any doubts to me about James before we married. Maybe they talked to each other. But nothing was said to me until my brother's birthday party in March 1997. By then, I was already married—twice. James had cleaned out my savings and put me in debt. I was in over my head and believed my only hope of recovery was for him to make good on his promises. So yes, they said something and they were right—but their misgivings were expressed too late to do me any good.

What did she want me to do now, grovel?

I didn't. I sent Tracy another e-mail stating that I was embarrassed that I had to borrow money from Doug to start my divorce. It wouldn't happen again. And after everything collapsed, my friends were much more supportive to me than any member of my family.

"It's amazing that I express what I feel and everything turns out to be my fault," I wrote. "That's the shit I got from James. I don't need any more of it."

I sent the e-mail, but it didn't make me feel any better. I had a huge lump in my chest—like I was weighed down by a giant, invisible tumor. I couldn't breathe. Later, I pulled out my journal to write. I got as far as, "Dear God, please help me." Guidance jumped in:

> It was an oversight. Your family loves you—they're just
> busy—your e-mail will make them realize that they have ignored
> you. You were right to bring it up—it will cause self-examination.

I did not sleep at all that night.

The next morning, Tracy wrote back. Her opening line was, "Do you want to be a part of this family or not? It seems to me that you don't." Then she dissected every statement I'd made in my e-mail, and pointed out how I was wrong, contradicting myself, and I'd put my family through hell.

I did not reply.

James Montgomery, through his attorney, Stephen A. Browndorf, filed an answer to my divorce complaint on July 22, 1999. He denied everything.

James denied constructing a web of lies and misrepresentation. He denied carrying on numerous affairs throughout our relationship. He denied promising to repay me for the expenses I paid on his behalf. He denied using my credit cards and forcing me to incur debt. He denied asking me for money. He did, however, admit to committing adultery with Kimberly Goodson.

Then James filed a counterclaim. He said I was guilty of extreme cruelty toward him throughout our entire marriage. My specific acts included:

A. I failed to exhibit that kind of love, emotional warmth and affection associated with a marriage partner.

B. I destroyed his immediate family life and caused the disintegration of the family unit.

C. On occasions too numerous to list, I treated him with scorn and derision, and acted in a cold and contemptuous manner towards him.

D. I criticized and berated him and acted in a hostile and mean spirited manner towards him.

E. On more than a dozen occasions, I became hysterically violent, struck and assaulted him, threw objects, destroyed his objects and caused general mayhem to him and his property.

All I could do was laugh.

James then accused me of theft for fraudulently diverting funds from his personal bank account for my own benefit and personal use. His lawyer filed a complaint with the bank, First Union, to get the money refunded. Browndorf also filed a third-party complaint against John Glassey and the Polytechnique Group. My business partner and my corporation became part of my divorce.

I had my own reading with Maggie Kay, the psychic, on July 23, 1999. I went to her home, located not far from where Sylvia lived. Hers was a narrow, two-story structure, probably built in the 1920s or 1930s. Maggie only charged $10 for her readings. She lived modestly.

Maggie opened the side door when I knocked. She was about as tall as me, with a medium build and thinning red hair. Although she had to be well into her 60s, she had an air of vitality.

We sat in her cramped kitchen, at a table pushed up against a window that overlooked the street. I couldn't believe what I saw on top of the table—a crystal ball. Maggie brought out two decks of cards, regular playing cards and tarot cards. They were so worn that the pictures were almost invisible. Each time she turned over a card, it conveyed information for me. She started talking about James immediately.

"There are about four wives out there. He's a Bluebeard. And you're all nice people," Maggie said. "He looks like Satan. He is Satan. He's a psycho. He's a Ted Bundy, only in a different way. Sociopath is written all over him."

Then Maggie started talking about all the victims that she saw—two in Florida, one in Georgia, Kansas, Seattle, New Mexico, Texas, California, Germany and one in Australia. He duped a lot of women, but many were too embarrassed to come forward. "He's working on an older lady now," Maggie said. "She lives in a big house. It looks like Spanish décor. This one's from Florida."

Maggie again urged me to raid James' bank accounts as soon as possible. She said he had two Swiss accounts, with $6 million in one and $9 million in the other. And the numbers written on the scraps of paper we found in his boxes were indeed account numbers. I should call the banks, say that my boss, James Montgomery, asked me to check on the balances, and then once I found the accounts, a computer expert could crack them.

"Remember the movie *Ghost*, how the guy got into the accounts and transferred money?" Maggie asked. "Well, you be the ghost. You get in it and transfer the money." She told me to open a dummy account, transfer his money into it, and then siphon the money back to the United States. She assured me that I wouldn't go to jail—all I had to say was that I was following my husband's instructions.

"You're going to win out here," Maggie said. "But you can't always follow your lawyer's advice."

Maggie saw that the FBI was investigating James, and wondered why they were dragging their feet. She wanted us to raid the accounts before he was arrested and all his money was confiscated.

She repeated that James had murdered Gale Lewis. "There's three murders under his belt," Maggie said. "He don't shoot them, but you know poison does the job too. Who's the one who died in a mental home? New Jersey, that's where she's from. Wait until they start uncovering things on him. But I guarantee you he'll kill himself before he goes to jail. He could be dangerous. Does he ever carry a gun?"

"Yes," I replied, thinking of the two that were in my home.

"Don't go in a remote place with him. I think that's why Gale got it. Only he didn't use the gun. If they were ever to dig her up, look out. So far, I don't see you getting murdered or anything, but don't go no place remote with him. Because he might lock you in the car and put the gas on. See, he does it clever, that it doesn't look like murder."

Maggie turned another tarot card, and then asked me about my family. I told her that my mother had died, my father was still alive, and I had two brothers, Doug and Greg, and a sister, Tracy.

"Your mom—she's probably helping you get even with him," Maggie said. "She died from cancer? Your mother went to heaven. They gave her a little job; she works in the library part-time. What a nice spirit she is. She's telling me she joined the choir, her mother and her. She says, 'You know, we sit by that Elvis guy, and sometimes we sing better than him. And Frank came here, and he's not the big shot he used to be. I like Gene Autrey and Roy Rogers.' She's going to help you.

"Allan—he has a second wife. She's nice to you. At least you don't have to take care of this stubborn mule. He loved your mother. He still thinks about her.

"Doug worries about you, and Greg is a high achiever.

"Tracy ..."

"We're having a big fight right now," I interjected.

"Well it's not your fault," Maggie said. "She didn't want you to marry him. She sees him as evil. You didn't tell her about your plans, did you? About raiding his accounts? That's what she's against? You fight fire with fire. Lawyers don't always know everything."

James, Maggie repeated, thought Sylvia was having twins, and had no clue that she was on my side, although he was trying to trap her. He wouldn't succeed, because Sylvia was a better liar.

"He's met his match," Maggie said. "You're too naive for a guy like James.

But that's okay; God sent Sylvia into your life so that you two will get rewards. It was a blessing that you and her connected. When you're dealing with a demon, you have to think on his level. You're not capable of that. But Sylvia is so desperate, she is."

Maggie turned another card. "He's shrewd. He's good. So don't feel like you've been stupid," she said. "You've just been an honest girl. And he did show you an opportunity to make money, but it wasn't real."

So how did James get me to go along with his schemes? Maggie thought that he hypnotized his victims. In fact, he might even use drugs.

"You know that stuff they use to induce date rape?" she asked. "He might put something like that in your drinks, so that you obey certain subliminal suggestions. There's medicine like that, and when you hear his voice, you automatically think you have to do what he says. None of his victims were stupid. They're schoolteachers, stockbrokers, business owners, rich widows, rich divorcées. He put some drops in your beverage or food. So that when he's talking to you on the phone, there's key words he always says."

Words like Bubba? Or Nuffles? Or Darwies?

"He brought me orange juice every morning," I told the psychic.

"It was in there," she said. "And it weakens your senses. It won't kill you, but you obey a certain voice."

Maggie saw that I had a lot of heartbreak with this man, but things were going to get better. In fact, she saw a nice love interest coming into my life. "Such a young, beautiful girl, you could have had any man you wanted. Why were you so lonely? He's the dealer of lonely hearts."

"Why did he marry me?" I asked.

"Look at you. He never had it so good," Maggie replied. "Flattery, ego, for the moment he did love you. Then when he saw he couldn't get nothing more out of you, love dies.

"He was born in hell," Maggie said. "And that's where he's going to land."

My attorney, Julie Davis Lisa, filed a motion for *pendente lite* relief—temporary financial support from my husband while our divorce case was still in progress. Because James had always promised that he would repay the expenses I incurred on his behalf, I kept meticulous records, which we submitted to the court. We also submitted a copy of his signed agreement to pay me. As of July 29, 1999, James owed me $215,569. The minimum payments on the credit card debt and home equity loan added up to $1,700 per month, including $850 in finance charges. It was killing me.

At the hearing a month earlier over the Titanic artifacts, my husband's lawyer informed the judge that James would not be available to participate in any proceedings from July 5 through August 11, 1999, because he would be traveling in Australia and China. "If the defendant has the financial capability to travel the world," my attorney wrote, "he certainly has the capability to contribute to the debt he incurred."

A hearing on my motion for support was set for August 27, 1999.

Sylvia and I, however, weren't waiting for any court hearing. She calculated how much money James owed her. The credit card charges, cash advance fees, interest charges, penalties—by July 29, 1999, they added up to $118,478.

James was still trying to convince Sylvia that she'd get her money back. He sent his latest business proposal with a note that said, "Confidential stuff—and our future!" The new scam was the International Institute of Continuing Education (IICE). It was essentially the same as the Southern Florida International Institute for Continuing Education that Sylvia did work for, elevated to an international stage. The idea was still to teach Chinese students English well enough for them to attend universities in English-speaking countries. Now, however, the programs would operate in both Florida and New Zealand.

In the proposal, James sought two investors to put in A$200,000 in exchange for 15 percent of the IICE stock. James projected fabulous returns: The investors would get US$600,000 in December 2000, and the company would have a market value of US$6.75 million by September 2001. IICE would go public within three years.

Yeah, right.

James' IICE proposal said the company had been funded by the principals for 18 months, which apparently meant that James and his partner—Archie Turner—had some cash. So Sylvia continued dialing for dollars.

The balances in James' accounts did seem to be increasing. But how were we going to get the money? We'd learned the hard way that paying our credit cards out of his account wasn't going to work—James got all that money back. As we were talking on the phone about the problem, I suddenly remembered James' blank, signed checks! In his grand gesture a year earlier, he stood next to me at my desk, told me that he wanted to make sure I had money, and signed six of his checks. I still had them. We could fill out one of his legitimate checks—no forgery needed—then cash it. We had a plan.

I mailed Sylvia two of the checks. She kept an eye on James' account, and when the balance got up to $11,000, we decided to strike. She wrote a check for $11,000, payable to cash. Sylvia brought the check to the bank. Luckily, she got the same cashier she'd dealt with every time she was putting money into James' accounts. The woman wrote out two cashier's checks with no questions. Sylvia took them to other branches and cashed them.

Sylvia called me as soon as she got home. "I did it," she said. "I got the money."

"Whoo hoo!" I screeched into the phone.

"Yeah. The fucker. All we need is a couple hundred thousand more and we'll be fine."

Well, $11,000 was better than nothing, which is what James would have given us. We split our take, and I had money to pay my bills for a few months.

I did not tell my attorney, or my sister.

Sometimes I felt like I was leading multiple lives. With Sylvia, I stole my money back from James and tried to find out what other crimes he had committed. With my lawyer, I prepared my court case, accusing James of fraud. For my career, I rebuilt my business and looked for a job at the same time. I was still corresponding with John, the dek hockey guy—all the other men who answered my online ad had disappeared. I participated in two sports, rowing in the mornings with three other women in a quadruple scull, and pitching softball in the evenings.

My co-ed softball team, the WB17 Frogs, qualified for the league playoffs. Suddenly, instead of playing one game a week in Philadelphia, I had three. After playing on Monday, Tuesday and Wednesday for two consecutive weeks, the Frogs won our division. We'd be playing another three-game series for the championship. I was pleased because as the starting pitcher, my contribution helped the team.

At least I had something to feel good about, because everything else was horrible.

Before James and I married, he convinced me to give him $10,000 to buy an option on Central Pier. Atlantic City was legalizing slot machines on the piers, and James said a casino company would surely want to buy Central Pier. We'd make a lot of money.

Three years later, I suspected that the option never existed. I had a friend who once worked for the owners of the pier, Abraham and Robert Schiff. I called her, explained what my husband had told me, and asked if there was, in fact, an option to buy Central Pier.

She burst out laughing. "The Schiff brothers never sell anything," she said.

I felt like a total idiot. My husband deliberately conned me.

I wasn't the only one. In James' records I found a receipt from a Nissan dealer in Florida for service to a car owned by Claudia Micklin.* Who was this woman, and why did James have receipts for her car? I called her to find out.

Claudia was not romantically involved with James; she was actually a friend of Kimberly Goodson. She told me a truly convoluted story: James asked to borrow Claudia's leased Nissan in August 1994. He was going out of the country, and said he would drive the car to the airport and leave it in the parking lot while he was abroad. Instead, he gave the keys to Debra Patrick, the woman with multiple personality disorder. Debra looked in the glove compartment, discovered the car belonged to a woman and concluded that James was cheating on her. Infuriated, she hired someone to "steal" the car and drive it into the bay. It was wrecked beyond repair, and Claudia was responsible because the lease was in her name. Claudia tried to sue James, but she was never able to find him to serve papers.

Claudia described Kimberly Goodson as a "neat person." Then she told me that Kimberly Goodson and James Montgomery had gotten married in February.

I almost dropped the phone.

"February?" I asked, incredulous.

"Yes, they just decided to do it," Claudia said. "They've been seeing each other a long time, since before I came to Florida in 1992."

I was in shock. I left James in February. I didn't file for divorce until June. We were still married. James married Kimberly Goodson anyway. So along with being a compulsive cheater, my husband was a bigamist—again. And, he'd been seeing Kimberly Goodson all through his marriages to both Gale Lewis and to me.

I called Jody Petracci, the FBI agent, and told her what I learned. Then I asked what was going on with the investigation of my husband. She didn't know—it was being handled by the Scranton FBI office.

"Well, nobody has called me," I said. "My husband's attorney wants copies of all the evidence of fraud that we have. I'm concerned that once I turn it over, and James sees it, he's going to permanently disappear."

"I can understand your concern," the agent said.

"So what would motivate the guys in Scranton to do something?" I asked.

Jody promised that she would call them, but I was beginning to doubt any action would be taken, and James would get away with his crimes. He was a bigamist. He was a con artist. Couldn't the authorities see what he was doing? Why didn't they care?

Frustration. Anger. Fear. Helplessness. Rage. I was so worked up that I needed therapy. On August 12, 1999, I had a session with Elaine Anderson over the phone. I told her what I'd learned: James had lied to me about the option for Central Pier so he could steal $10,000 from me. He caused Claudia Micklin's car to be wrecked, which cost her $25,000. He committed bigamy with Kimberly Goodson.

"This is unbelievable," I said to Elaine. "What kind of person does this?"

"It sounds like he might be a sociopath," she said.

Sociopath—Maggie had used that word. What in the world was a sociopath?

With Elaine's help, I released tremendous emotional pain, anger and resentment. Feeling calmer and more peaceful, I patched up my relationship with my sister, Tracy. My brother, Doug, invited me to his seven-year-old son's birthday party. Then I went to another family event—my cousin's engagement party. I resolved to strengthen my ties with my relatives.

In the meantime, I continued corresponding with John, the dek hockey player. I learned that he was writing a book, a novel loosely based on his experiences. John had 180 pages completed—I was impressed. He, however, was self-deprecating about it—to him, writing was a hobby.

So what was the book about?

"Scratching my head: Hmm, a, him, haw ... mmmm. Let's see," John wrote. "It is a retrospective; the main character looks back upon his life to make sense of its recent unraveling. It is about loss; although, it is written, hopefully, in a humorish style."

Well, he sure kept making me laugh.

After Elaine described my husband as a sociopath, I had to find out what she meant, and researched the term on the Internet. Sociopaths, I learned, were people who did not have a conscience. They were glib and charming, but thought nothing of lying, cheating and stealing. They did not feel love or empathy for other people, although they were good at pretending they did.

I was reading a perfect description of my husband, James Montgomery.

Sociopaths were also called psychopaths—I thought psychopaths were serial killers. Another term, antisocial personality disorder, was the official diagnosis for the condition listed in the manual of the American Psychiatric Association. Researchers estimated that three to four percent of men, and one percent of women, had antisocial personality disorder. I was shocked. That meant there were millions of them in the United States and more millions around the world.

I read *Without Conscience—The Disturbing World of the Psychopaths Among Us,* by Robert D. Hare, Ph.D. Here's how it started:

> Psychopaths are social predators who charm, manipulate, and ruthlessly plow their way through life, leaving a broad trail of broken hearts, shattered expectations and empty wallets.

The book described exactly what I experienced. It was written in laymen's terms, and I could not put it down. I read it with an orange highlighter in my hand. Some of the passages I marked:

> Psychopaths have a narcissistic and grossly inflated view of their self-worth and importance, a truly astounding egocentricity and sense of entitlement, and see themselves as the center of the universe, as superior beings who are justified in living according to their own rules.

> Psychopaths show a stunning lack of concern for the devastating effects their actions have on others.

> Psychopaths are not disordered or out of touch with reality, nor do they experience the delusions, hallucinations, or intense subjective distress that characterize most other mental disorders. Unlike psychotic individuals, psychopaths are rational and aware of what they are doing and why. Their behavior is the result of choice, freely exercised.

© 1993 Robert D. Hare, Ph.D., *Without Conscience,* Guilford Publications, Inc., New York, NY

Many psychopaths were criminals and locked up in jail, but many more were not. Because they did not look or act crazy, psychopaths often lived freely in society, using and ruining people, then moving on without facing any consequences, just like my husband.

I could not believe that millions of these disordered individuals were on the loose, and no one knew about it. After my first-hand encounter with such a predator, I knew that I had to tell my story, and warn people to be on the lookout for them. The fastest way to do it, I thought, would be a website. I'd never written a website before, but I was sure I could figure it out. What should I call it? After experimenting with headlines and titles, I came up with Lovefraud. The domain www.lovefraud.com was available, and I bought it.

Sylvia and James engaged in another online battle of wits and will. On August 18, 1999, Sylvia had her neighbor, Maddy, send James an e-mail to inform him that Sylvia was in the hospital due to complications with her pregnancy. Maddy wrote:

> The complications are due to stress! WE ALL KNOW WHO IS CAUSING THIS STRESS. Quite frankly I don't understand why she is even still speaking to you.
> Your lack of concern for her wellbeing is reason enough for her to stop speaking to you. You promised her months ago that this money would be returned and you do what you always do. NOTHING!
> We have tried calling you since last night and all day today and your cell phone is not on. This only goes to show again your lack of concern. I as usual will help Sylvia as much as I can. You as usual will do what you do best, being INDIFFERENT.

James wrote back the next day—he was in Atlantic City and was trying to find out Sylvia's condition, but claimed no one answered his calls. Sylvia countered that James didn't answer their calls. Sylvia, of course, was lying, but was James?

Apparently not. I scheduled another reading with Maggie Kay, the psychic, and left for Pennsylvania the afternoon of August 20, 1999. When I got just 10 blocks from my house, my cell phone rang. My security alarm had gone off.

I quickly returned to my house, which already looked like a crime scene. Several police cars were parked at all angles in the street, and officers went behind the house to check the back door. All the commotion woke up Beau, and he bolted through his dog door to find a female police officer in the yard. He charged her; she stuck out her foot; my dog bit her on the shoe.

The cops told me what Beau did. They also told me the policewoman was the chief's sister.

"Well, she was in his yard," I said.

But why did the alarm go off? Afraid that James may have tried to get in—he did not know about my security system—I asked an officer to look through my house. Nothing was amiss. After the police left, my neighbor noticed that the screen on one of my front windows, easily accessible from the porch, was raised. Someone had tried to go through the window.

In my reading the next morning, Maggie said it was James. "He rented a car so you wouldn't know what the car looked like. He saw you leave, thought it was a good opportunity. He knew right away where to go, so he wouldn't be in there too long."

Maggie said James had cash, or information that would lead to cash, hidden in my house. "It wouldn't be in your safe," she said. "Where did he spend a lot of time, basement or attic?"

"His office was in the basement."

"Then that's where I'd look. Do you have cans or something?"

Yes—I had cans in the storage room.

"Maybe that's where that big bank account is. In cans. It won't be in a jar, because you could see it. Coffee cans. Check them, you might get a nice surprise. It looks like cash, or a paper worth a lot of cash."

Maggie repeated that James had money in Switzerland. I'd already called the bank, and learned that the numbers I had were not proper account numbers. The bank representative even looked under James Montgomery's name, but found nothing.

This time, Maggie said that James didn't have four wives—he had eight. I was the only legal one. "Out of all the women, believe it or not, lucky you, you're the one he really loved," Maggie said. "He feels bad about that. Why not? You're a beautiful woman. And you know if he wasn't such a lazy bastard, and he used his mind legitimately, he could be a successful businessman. But it takes too much time. He wants the fast buck.

"You got taken for $250,000? Where did you get that from? Your life's earnings. He has a big sin on him. God don't sleep. His hand is slow, but it's sure. I think he's going to go to prison through the IRS."

Maggie saw good things for me, however. I'd soon recover my money. Plus, several men wanted to come into my life. I hoped that she was right on both predictions.

When I got home, I went directly to the basement and opened every coffee can. I pulled at loose ceiling tiles and unscrewed wall vents. I looked every place I could think of, all over the house.

I found no cash, and no clues to his bank accounts.

A new judge, Charles M. Middlesworth Jr., heard my motion for *pendente lite* relief on August 27, 1999. My attorney, Julie Davis Lisa, requested $3,000 per month to be applied toward my $68,000 in credit card debt.

Judge Middlesworth asked if we complied with the case management order to turn over copies of all my credit card statements. Stephen A. Browndorf, my husband's attorney, immediately went on the offensive. "They only turned over the credit card statements through May of 1999 because the subsequent statements would prove that she stole money from Mr. Montgomery's bank account," he said.

"Your honor, we provided the credit card statements from January of 1996 through the date of the order," Julie replied.

"We have a claim against her for stealing another $11,000," Browndorf added.

Julie turned and looked at me sharply—she, of course, was in the dark about the most recent heist. I shrugged my shoulders, as Maggie instructed me to do.

"We're not going to conduct a damages trial here, and we're not going to conduct a criminal case," Judge Middlesworth said. "We're here on your motion. You're seeking an order compelling the defendant to pay half of credit card payments and counsel fees."

"Actually we're asking that Mr. Montgomery be responsible for all the credit card payments," Julie said. "Mr. Montgomery is a con man. He talks people into doing this kind of thing, into giving him money, to support him."

My attorney was just getting warmed up. "Ms. Andersen has been married to him for two-and-a-half years, she is now in the hole over $68,000, her credit is on the verge of being ruined because of this massive credit card debt that she incurred because of Mr. Montgomery," Julie said. "He convinced her to support him, to pay business expenses—his car payment, his car insurance—on the promise that he put in writing that he would pay her back. And now he's disappeared."

Julie told the judge that James married again, two weeks after I left him. And, he was now saying that he didn't live in America. "All through this marriage he was committing act of fraud after act of fraud upon Ms. Andersen, and now she's got nothing to show for it but debt."

My husband's attorney was not going to allow these statements to go unchallenged. "As to the allegations that he's a con man, a gigolo, whatever, all they are is allegations," Browndorf said. "As far as these claimed expenses go, she claims everything is his expense. The cable bill is his expense. The car is his expense. If you look at the case information statement, she owns the car. It's listed in her name and she uses the car, and she put it as an expense that she paid every month for herself. She also itemizes her storage bills."

"Let's stick to the credit cards," Judge Middlesworth said.

"She claims that she incurred all the expenses at his urging and she had no control," Browndorf continued. "If you look at this compilation, it's easy enough to tell that Ms. Andersen is not a naive or stupid woman. She managed to save all these records for a four-year period, compile them and set forth her case. If these expenses were incurred on Mr. Montgomery's behalf, they were also incurred on her behalf.

"If she didn't know when she married him, she had to know within a year— this man had no assets. This man had no income. So throughout the course of the marriage, for two-and-a-half years, she paid the bills, she financed everything, the cards are all in her name, she had to say yes, spend this money, go do this, go do that. And then she made all the payments. She knew he doesn't have it. But now she comes to court and says, 'I know he had no assets beyond the Titanic artifacts. And I know he has no income. But I want him to pay $3,000 a month, even though the payment is only $1,700. I want to reduce the debt some more.'

"He doesn't have it. She says we should go prove what his present income is. He told you what his income is. He doesn't have any. What he has is an opportunity to possibly make some money, sometime in the future, if the project he's involved in works. The people he's working for said, 'We'll pay your travel expenses; we'll pay your living expenses; you put this together. If it works, we'll give you 20 percent.'"

"So that's his response? He has no money?" the judge asked.

"He doesn't have any," Browndorf said. "The money that she took, the $11,000, two different times, wasn't his money. It was money that was given to him by investors to finance the trips to China and to Australia and to New Zealand, trying to put this together. So she's already got $22,000 of his money, which she's going to have to account for eventually."

"Did your client apply $11,000 or $22,000 to the credit card debts?" Judge Middlesworth asked my attorney.

"I know that $11,000 or $22,000 has not been deducted from these credit card debts," Julie answered. "These debts that are listed on Exhibit B are the debts that are the outstanding balances."

"What are the minimum payments on these debts?" the judge asked.

"The minimum payments amount to about $1,700 a month," Julie answered. "There's $850 per month of finance charges."

"Here's what I'm going to do," Middlesworth said. "I'm going to order the defendant to pay half of the minimum payment each month on these accounts."

"Your honor, she has all the money," Browndorf protested. "He has no income or assets to pay her."

"She doesn't have any money," Julie interjected.

"The whole marriage was that way," Browndorf said.

"I'm not going to hear any more arguments, counselor," Judge Middlesworth said. "I made the order."

So James was supposed to pay $850 per month. I was disappointed, but it was better than nothing.

Why was I nervous? I was calling women whom James victimized. I was trying to find out the truth about him. Sylvia and I had become best buddies, and were working together to bring James down. Maybe these women would also be happy to talk to me.

But the truth was, I never knew how my efforts to reach out to James' victims would be received. I spoke to Lorraine Moyle from Ocean City, with whom James had many early morning "meetings." She listened to what I said, but did not want to get involved. Some women whom I contacted via faxes and letters never replied.

Kathleen Maloney, I learned from the documents I found, had been married to James in the early '90s. She lived outside of Boston, Massachusetts. Would she be willing to tell me her story?

Then there was Jody McClure, of Marina del Rey, California. From papers I found, I learned that she was involved with James during 1991 and 1992. She gave him at least $36,750. Five years later, James contacted her again while he was married to me.

I reached both women by phone. After the initial surprise of hearing from a wife of James Montgomery, they told me their stories—tales of woe that were far worse than I expected.

Chapter 18

Kathleen Maloney sat by herself at a tall cocktail table in a waterfront Mexican restaurant in Marina del Rey, California. It was dinnertime and the place was busy—groups of friends were drinking margaritas at the bar; families at tables were eating quesadillas and burritos.

The restaurant was about a mile from her hotel; wanting to stretch her legs after a long flight, Kathleen walked there. It was a Sunday evening in June 1988, and she just arrived in the Los Angeles area on a business trip—a week of training on software that she used in her work as a project administrator for the Boston Gas Company. The training started the next morning. She took herself to the Mexican restaurant for dinner. She wasn't looking for a date.

Kathleen was an attractive woman of 45. Expertly applied eye shadow and mascara framed her brown eyes. Her short, thick blond hair was perfectly cut close to her head and around her ears, drawing attention to her dramatic earrings. Her figure was trim and toned—a result of healthy eating and exercise, like walking to the restaurant.

As she sipped a cocktail, the bar area filled up. Two men came in, dressed in casual clothes but carrying briefcases, looking for empty seats. The only ones left were at Kathleen's table.

"May we join you?" one of the men asked in an Australian accent.

Kathleen gestured toward the empty chairs. "Sure. Be my guest," she replied.

The man immediately noticed Kathleen's accent. "Where are you from?" he asked.

"Boston," Kathleen replied. It sounded like "Bah-ston."

"And what brings you to Los Angeles?" he inquired.

"Business—I'm here for a seminar. It starts tomorrow."

The man introduced himself—he was James Montgomery, and he'd come to Los Angeles from Australia to make movies.

The men ordered cocktails and struck up a conversation, although the Australian did most of the talking. With a bald pate, ruddy complexion, gray beard and apparent beer belly, he wasn't much to look at, but Kathleen never put a lot of store in looks. James Montgomery was interesting. He was charming, clever and entertaining. Eventually the other man left, and James invited Kathleen to dinner—he knew of a delightful place frequented by the Hollywood set.

James included himself in the Hollywood set. He said he launched Movietime, a cable network that aired movie trailers, entertainment news and interviews. He was the producer and on-camera host of a show called *Power Breakfast,* interviewing studio executives about their upcoming projects. But James left Movietime and was on to his next venture—an action adventure film starring the colorful Brian Bosworth, a former linebacker with the Seattle Seahawks pro football team. James was the executive producer, and the project was at a critical juncture, about to be green-lighted.

They drove to the restaurant in James' silver convertible sports car. The roof was down; the weather was pleasant. As they followed the hostess to their table, James slowed and tilted his head toward someone on the other side of the room. "There's Steven Spielberg," he said. Kathleen looked, but could not get a clear view of the man's face. Still, it was a thrill. She felt like she was experiencing Hollywood.

Dinner was pleasant, and James kept the conversation going. He talked about how difficult it was to get a movie made. Finding the right person to pitch was like peeling an onion—he had to get through one layer to move on to the next layer. But he was doing it. He was certain his movie would hit the big screen—and he had more scripts lined up to produce after his first one. Kathleen was fascinated—she'd never met anyone in the movie business.

When they finished their coffee, James drove Kathleen back to her hotel. "How long will you be here?" he asked.

"Until Friday morning," Kathleen answered.

James pulled out a business card. "Call me the next time you're in town," he said.

"I don't know when I'll be back here, but I'll do that."

"I enjoyed talking with you."

"It was fun," Kathleen said. "Thanks again."

The very next day, James Montgomery called Kathleen at her hotel. He had to drive to San Diego for business in a couple of days, and suggested getting together for breakfast before he left. Kathleen agreed. Then, as her week in Marina del Rey drew to a close, James took Kathleen out for dinner again. He continued to regale her with his stories and charm her with his cleverness. He also exuded sexual magnetism, and Kathleen's business trip turned romantic.

At the end of the week, she flew back to Boston. James called a few times, but the calls eventually dwindled, which wasn't surprising—after all, Kathleen lived clear across the continent. The encounter should have been a fling, nothing more.

Kathleen married young, at age 22. Seven years later she divorced, and had not remarried. Not that she was alone. Kathleen had many friends and dated frequently—in fact, she was never home. She'd had several long-term relationships. Her last, of five years, ended about a year before she met James Montgomery.

As Christmas approached, Kathleen was shopping in a Crate and Barrel store and saw a cute little wooden ornament—two small dolls, wearing Dutch hats, sitting on a bench and holding a heart. On impulse, she bought the ornament and sent it to James in California. He called to thank her, and wished her a Merry Christmas.

Three months later, in March 1989, Kathleen and three girlfriends were planning a skiing vacation in Lake Tahoe, Nevada. "Why don't you call your friend in California?" one of her friends suggested.

"We're not going to California," Kathleen said. "We're going to Nevada."

"Well, Los Angeles is only a few hours from Lake Tahoe," the woman said. "Who knows? Maybe he'll drive up to see you."

So Kathleen called. To her surprise, James did want to get together, and suggested meeting in Reno—the city she'd be flying into. When she arrived on Friday, March 10, 1989, James met her at the airport. Kathleen's friends caught the bus to Lake Tahoe, while she drove off with James. She spent the first weekend of her vacation in Reno with him—they did some sightseeing, gambled a bit and stayed at Harrah's Casino Hotel.

James seemed totally fascinated by Kathleen. He asked many questions about her life: How long had she worked at Boston Gas? (27 years.) Where did she live? (She owned her own home.) What did she drive? (She just bought a brand new Toyota Camry.)

The man also talked endlessly about his life and projects. He served in the Australian Special Forces and fought in Vietnam, where he earned several military decorations. In fact, he was still in the military, and occasionally participated in clandestine missions. James talked about his successful advertising career in Australia, where he owned a television production business called Jaypat Studio. But he'd come to Hollywood for bigger and better things.

Kathleen was intrigued. An Australian. A war hero. A movie producer. James Montgomery's life certainly seemed bigger than those of the men at the gas company.

The weekend whizzed by, James went back to LA and Kathleen joined her friends for several days of skiing. While she was at Lake Tahoe, James called constantly. In fact, he wanted to see Kathleen again before she flew back East. Would she like to meet him in Fresno, California? It was halfway between Lake Tahoe and Los Angeles. She could rent a car and drive there.

Flattered, Kathleen extended her vacation, sent her skis home with her friends and drove to Fresno. She and James toured the area—although Fresno had almost a half-million people, it was in the middle of the agricultural San Joaquin Valley. They saw almond, pistachio and citrus orchards, vegetable fields, sheep ranches and dairy farms. And scattered among the farms—small oil wells. The landscape was so different from what Kathleen was accustomed to, as was the man who accompanied her.

As soon as Kathleen got home from California, her phone started ringing. Acting like a smitten teenager, James called her four or five times a day, often talking to her in baby talk. Divorced and dating for almost 20 years, Kathleen had never experienced such attention from a man in his forties. It had to be love.

Only a few weeks after they were together in California, James called Kathleen with good news—he was traveling to New York City, and while on the East Coast, he wanted to swing by Boston to see her again.

Kathleen picked James up at the Boston airport during Patriot's Day Weekend, April 15-17, 1989. The holiday commemorated the Battles of Lexington and Concord, the first skirmishes of the American Revolutionary War, but became more famous for the Boston Marathon. Kathleen suggested they take part in marathon festivities—James wasn't interested. He was barely interested in seeing Harvard Square. All of his focus was on her, and in scouting Boston as a possible place to establish his business.

Kathleen lived in an inner suburb of Boston—the city center was less than 10 miles away. Her home, built in 1946, was traditional in style, like a large, two-story bungalow. James wanted to see all of it—the living room, dining room, kitchen, three bedrooms, two baths and garage. The house also had a basement apartment with a full kitchen and bath. The tenant, Kathleen mentioned, was getting married in a few months and would be moving out.

Somehow James worked into the conversation that he was thinking about relocating to Boston. If he did, Kathleen said, he could stay with her for awhile. "This is doable," James said.

Kathleen invited her mother over for dinner to meet her new beau. James was gracious, making a good impression. After the whirlwind weekend, James went back to the West coast. But even with him gone, Kathleen felt swept up by his energy, his charisma, his focus on achievement. The man had big plans. And it sounded like his plans might include her.

In a way, it was overwhelming. This man was different, funny, charming, exciting. He was larger than life. Kathleen had heard about men like this, and had seen such colossal characters in movies. But she never thought one would actually come into her life. Kathleen felt herself falling in love.

James called as soon as his plane touched down in California. And he continued to call, multiple times a day. He kept her apprised of his business negotiations and happenings in Hollywood. James called to tell her that comedienne Lucille Ball was rushed to the emergency room of the Cedars-Sinai Medical Center. She had an aneurysm and underwent heart surgery. A week later, James reported that Ball's aorta ruptured. She lost consciousness, and by the end of the day, was gone.

Suddenly, James decided. Life was short. He was making the move to Boston right away.

Kathleen was shocked. She thought they might get together sometime in the future, but now? They barely knew each other. This didn't bother James. Boston was a good, untapped market for him—the sooner he established himself, the better. He and Kathleen were simpatico. They were adults, capable of making their own decisions. Why should they wait?

James quickly proposed a plan. He'd ship some clothes to her home. Then he'd rent a truck to drive across the country with the rest of his belongings. Kathleen could fly to Los Angeles and make the trip with him. Driving cross-country with her new beau—to Kathleen, it sounded like a romantic adventure. Spontaneous. Exciting.

As they discussed the idea further, James mentioned that he was short on cash—could she help him put their plan into action? Could Kathleen lend him $2,500?

Shocked by the request, Kathleen refused.

But James persisted. He called back, explaining that all his money was tied up in the movie. He offered collateral—cameras, a car—that were worth more than the amount of the loan he was asking for. Not that she needed the collateral, James said, because she could trust him to pay her back.

Kathleen insisted to James that she was not giving him money. But the calls kept coming, and his pleas increased in intensity. Finally Kathleen relented and sent him money, although not as much as he requested.

Then a massive carton arrived at her house, about the size of a refrigerator box. It was packed so tightly that it fell apart upon delivery, spilling clothes in the breezeway between Kathleen's house and the garage. James was moving in.

Kathleen arrived at Los Angeles International Airport late in the afternoon of May 12, 1989. James picked her up at the airport in a yellow Penske rental truck. They got on the road immediately, although that evening they only drove 60 miles, to San Bernardino.

As they approached the city, the radio was full of news about a terrible tragedy that struck earlier in the day at the Cajon Pass in the San Bernardino Mountains. A runaway train with six locomotives and 69 cars derailed and plowed into a residential area. Four people were dead. Seven homes and the entire train were destroyed. James somehow found it significant that their time together began with a train wreck.

The next day, James and Kathleen drove toward the border between California and Arizona, near Lake Havasu City—the home of the original London Bridge, which had been moved there from England. It was the second most-visited tourist attraction in Arizona, after the Grand Canyon.

Kathleen knew the bridge wasn't far from their route. "Let's stop and see it," she suggested.

"We don't have time," James replied.

"What do you mean, we don't have time?" Kathleen asked. "What's the big rush?"

"No," James refused.

He was adamant. He didn't want to see the majestic Grand Canyon, either. James did, however, want to stop at the Martin and Osa Johnson Safari Museum in Chanute, Kansas. He said the museum was critical to a movie he was making called *I Married Adventure.*

The movie was based on Osa Johnson's book of the same title. Osa was only 16 when she married Martin Johnson in 1910. From 1917 to 1936, the couple traveled to the most remote and exotic locations in the world—the wildernesses of Kenya, the Congo, Borneo and the South Pacific Islands. Their trips were the original camera safaris—they made documentaries such as *Headhunters of the South Seas* and *Captured by Cannibals,* and shot thousands of still photographs. Between safaris, they toured the United States giving lectures.

So James and Kathleen drove across miles and miles of flat land to Chanute, Kansas. The town's population was under 10,000, and the Safari Museum, located in a dilapidated old house, was its only attraction. They looked at the artifacts and James talked to the curator. A couple of hours later, James and Kathleen were back on the road, driving straight through to Boston, stopping only to eat and sleep. They made the entire cross-country trip in less than five days.

Jody McClure pulled her red hatchback into the parking lot of her apartment building in Marina del Rey, California, on May 12, 1989. It was a long day, but a good one—she just watched with pride as her son gradated from college. Jody opened the door of her apartment and immediately knew something was wrong. Her live-in lover, James Montgomery, was gone.

His clothes—gone. His electronics equipment—gone. His mounds of papers—gone.

Jody was shocked. She was crushed. She had no warning at all.

She found a tape, two hours long, in which James repeatedly told Jody how much he loved her. But apparently he didn't love her enough to talk about their relationship in person. He vanished.

James moved into her apartment a year earlier, in May 1988. She'd met him almost a year before that, in August 1987, at a Beverly Hills cocktail party sponsored by Who's Who International. It was a singles networking event for professionals over 40.

Jody, at the time, was 56. Previously married to a doctor, she'd been divorced for 10 years. Jody's divorce settlement was substantial—her assets added up to about three-quarters of a million dollars. That included a home, which she rented out, worth a half-million dollars. The mortgage was only $30,000, and other than that, she had no debt.

For her career, Jody traveled the world. She was an international tour manager for travel wholesalers, and often took extended trips to exotic locations like India, Australia and New Zealand. Jody's lifestyle was comfortable and exciting. She loved skiing, which kept her in good shape. She'd enjoyed several *petite amours* since her divorce, but in August 1987 she wasn't attached, which was why she was at the singles event.

As they stood among the Who's Who International crowd, James told Jody that he worked at the new Movietime channel as a producer and on-air talent. He also brought up his military background, which included two tours of Vietnam and secret missions during the 1983 Grenada invasion.

Jody was intrigued, and agreed to meet him again. When they did, James told her about his advertising work, for which he earned a Clio award. He showed her articles he had written on sales promotion that were published in Australian trade magazines. He talked about his production studio in Melbourne. The man presented himself as extremely successful, and, even though he was 10 years younger than Jody, attracted to her.

James lived in his own small, but well-located, apartment in Los Angeles, and told Jody how much he paid in rent. Jody later discovered that the figure was exaggerated, and at that point she should have walked away from him. But, already hooked, she overlooked her new beau's misrepresentation.

A couple of months after James and Jody met, he stopped working at Movie-time—never saying exactly why. No matter. James was on to bigger and better things—producing an action adventure movie that would be the acting debut of the former pro football star, Brian Bosworth.

James worked his movie deal day and night, and kept Jody apprised of his progress. He'd produced documentaries before—Jody saw one about the indigenous people of Australian islands, and *Strike Swiftly,* his television series about the Australian army reserve.

Military connections were still important to James—he frequently wore his Special Forces beret and shirts. During a big Veterans Day ceremony at the Los Angeles National Veterans Cemetery in Westwood, California, he stood right in the front row. James' photo appeared in the newspaper.

James and Jody became an item. He seemed to be smitten, and he frequently asked her to marry him. Jody didn't want to remarry, but in May 1988, she agreed to live together, and James moved into her apartment.

Jody often accompanied James to meetings on the movie project—she met Brian Bosworth and his agent many times. But putting the deal together required money, and James was running out of it. He stopped contributing toward household expenses, and soon Jody was paying all the bills. He also needed money to keep the movie project going—the deal was always just around the corner. In the summer of 1988, Jody cashed in stocks to support them and fund the movie.

Then Jody had a big financial decision to make. The home she acquired in her divorce had not been upgraded in many years. If she wanted to continue renting it, she should make substantial renovations. It would be a lot of work, and because she spent so much time traveling, Jody would not be around to oversee it. She didn't know what to do.

James had a solution. He recommended that she sell the house and put the money into other investments, including his movie. Jody hesitated—the house was her nest egg. But slowly, James convinced her that it would be best to get rid of it. She did, and gave him more than $100,000 to finance his movie.

Some of the money went to paying screenwriters—one whom James mentioned was a woman named Colleen Jessick. But despite all of James' efforts, the

Bosworth movie stalled. Then the award-winning director James was courting decided he wasn't going to get involved. The whole project fell apart.

James blew through all of Jody's money and had nothing to show for it.

James didn't tell his new love interest, Kathleen Maloney, anything about Jody McClure, or her money, or the collapse of the Bosworth film. Instead, he raved that Boston would be a great place for him to set up his movie business. He talked constantly about his big plans, and promised that Kathleen would be part of them. In fact, Kathleen would be a big part of his life—he was already hinting at marriage.

First, however, he needed a place to work. "Your tenant has to go," James said. So although the tenant in her basement apartment planned to stay for another four months, and pay four more months of rent, Kathleen asked him to move out. James quickly turned the apartment into his office.

The next thing James needed was funding. Although Kathleen didn't have excess cash lying around waiting to be invested, she did have equity in her home. Her mortgage was down to $14,000, and the house was worth at least $160,000. A week after James moved in, he started suggesting that Kathleen refinance her home.

She resisted. But James carefully explained the issues with his Bosworth movie—which weren't his fault. He was personally on the hook for fees to the screenwriters, and if he didn't pay, the writers union would sue him. That would make it impossible for him to move forward with the Bosworth movie, with *I Married Adventure,* or for that matter, any movie.

James reminded her that their relationship had started with a bang—the train wreck. It meant, in his view, that they were destined to make an impact. He had the talent, and if she could just help him get started, they would soon be reaping the entrepreneurial rewards. James kept up the pressure, and in June 1989, Kathleen capitulated. She refinanced her $14,000 mortgage into a $60,000 mortgage. Still, being financially responsible, she took money to pay off her car and her small home improvement loan. The rest she gave to James.

Kathleen wanted to invite about 15 people over for a cookout on her back-yard deck to meet James. She had plenty of experience with entertaining, and planned a menu of summer favorites—steak, burgers, potato salad, baked beans, corn on the cob. James nixed it. He was going to serve bangers and mash—a traditional English pub dish of sausage and mashed potatoes.

"This is a barbecue," Kathleen protested. "No one will eat it."

"Yes they will," James insisted. "This is how we do barbies in Australia."

Kathleen could not talk him out of the sausage and mashed potatoes. James made up invitations on his computer, telling guests to bring nothing but a bag of chips. On the day of the barbecue, James made his bangers and mash, using a huge box of instant mashed potatoes and jars of prepared gravy. Kathleen was mortified.

What she didn't know about was even worse. As the guests arrived—each carrying a bag of potato chips—James handed everyone a copy of his biography. A friend of Kathleen's from England asked James how he liked living in America. His caustic reply: "If you had read my bio, you'd know."

There was more. One of Kathleen's co-workers from the gas company was an Israeli. All Israeli citizens must serve in the military—they are conscripted at age 18 or at the conclusion of 12th grade. James, wanting to make an impression, brought the man into his basement office to show off an Uzi submachine gun.

A few days later at work, the Israeli asked Kathleen, "Do you know that James has an Uzi?"

"What?" she asked, astonished. "You're kidding!"

"No," he replied. "I saw it."

When she got home that evening, she confronted James about the Uzi.

"It's gone," James said.

"What do you mean, it's gone?" Kathleen asked. "What did you do with it?"

James said something, but it wasn't an answer to her question. Kathleen never saw the Uzi.

James took over the downstairs apartment. He set up his computer, phone, fax machine, television, cameras and other electronic gadgets. Books, diskettes, videos, magazines, catalogs and photos lay in piles on his desk, on shelves and on the floor. Then there were the papers—faxes sent, faxes received, computer documents printed out in triplicate or quadruplicate. He even dragged a shopping cart into the apartment, which he filled with what Kathleen considered to be crap.

Kathleen kept a tidy house, and James' mayhem drove her nuts. She stopped going downstairs. Because James didn't necessarily want to walk upstairs every time he had something to say to Kathleen, he bought a set of walkie talkies. James called for Kathleen constantly, and if she didn't respond right away, he demanded to know why.

Usually, James called Kathleen with an assignment—like making an airline reservation for a flight to California. A month after arriving in Boston, James flew back to Los Angeles, saying he had business meetings. It was the beginning of a pattern—every month, he took a trip to California.

James talked frequently about getting married, but he hadn't formally proposed. That changed in the fall of 1989, when he took Kathleen to a Legal Sea Food restaurant—several were in the Boston area. He arranged for the waiter to deliver a rose to their table, and with that, James asked Kathleen to marry him. He did not, however, give her an engagement ring—it was a detail that he'd take care of later.

Kathleen wasn't ready to get married, but the relationship was hurling forward, out of her control. James was so sure of his direction, so confident in his ability to create what he wanted—it seemed like she just was along for the ride. James proposed. It was unthinkable for her to say anything but yes.

Still, Kathleen didn't tell anyone that she was engaged. She was not over the moon with excitement, as she was for her first marriage. And there was no ring on her finger.

About a month later, James and Kathleen had dinner with a couple from the Power Squadron, a volunteer organization that offered boating courses and safety inspections for vessels. James joined and became an active member, teaching a class every weekend. During conversation over dinner, it came out that Kathleen and James were getting married.

"Congratulations!" the woman said. "I didn't know you were engaged!"

"Well, we hadn't said anything," Kathleen replied. "We're waiting for James' immigration papers to come through."

James didn't react, but gave his fiancée the blackest of looks. When they left the restaurant, he flew into a rage. "What a stupid thing to say!" he ranted at Kathleen.

"What are you talking about?"

"They don't know that I'm not an American citizen."

"I didn't know that."

"You shouldn't have told them!"

"What difference does it make? You're getting your papers."

James insisted that Kathleen had made an unforgivable error, one that could jeopardize everything he was working towards. "Don't ever mention my citizenship status again," he commanded.

Shortly before Christmas, James called—he was out of town again—and asked Kathleen to invite people over for Christmas Eve. Kathleen didn't really want to—she was busy enough planning a turkey dinner for Christmas Day. But James insisted. It was their first Christmas together, and he wanted to share it with friends. She finally agreed, even though he was away and she'd have to do all the work.

James also informed her that he ordered a goose.

"A goose?" Kathleen had asked, incredulous. "We're not having a goose."

"I ordered a goose," he insisted.

"James, nobody eats goose. It's too greasy."

Once again, James would not be swayed. He was going to cook his goose.

James returned from his trip on December 23, and the next morning, presented Kathleen—finally—with a heart-shaped diamond engagement ring.

"Oh, it's beautiful," Kathleen said, slipping it on her finger. Then she got to work with last-minute cooking, vacuuming and gift-wrapping. While putting a bow on a Christmas present, she looked at the brand new ring on her left hand. The stone was missing.

Kathleen retraced her steps through the entire house to look for the diamond. She checked the kitchen. She opened up the vacuum cleaner bag and sifted through the dirt. No luck—the stone was gone, and James was angry.

"It couldn't have been set right," Kathleen protested. "A stone doesn't fall out just because you're wrapping gifts. You'll have to go back to the jeweler."

"I didn't get it at a jeweler," James said.

"Where did you get it?" Kathleen asked, surprised. James didn't answer. When Kathleen's friends arrived later, wanting to see the non-existent ring, he was visibly annoyed. A sour expression stayed on his face all evening.

By Christmas morning, James was in better spirits; he added a Santa hat to his usual attire—nylon gym shorts and a t-shirt. He enjoyed opening the gifts Kathleen bought for him—clothes, a winter scarf and gloves, a Pictionary game. James gave Kathleen a book on photography, earrings to match the engagement ring that had already lost its stone, and another pair of earrings that he had custom-made from two of his Special Forces pins. At that point he casually mentioned where he had been on his most recent trip—in Panama, as part of the American invasion force.

The United States invaded Panama on December 20, 1989. Almost a year earlier, General Manuel Noriega, the country's *de facto* ruler, was indicted by the U.S. Drug Enforcement Administration; he ignored the charges. Then Noriega attempted to rig the national election in May. After a tense standoff in which a U.S. marine was killed, the Panamanian legislature declared on December 15, 1989, that "a state of war" existed with the United States, and President George H. W. Bush authorized the invasion. In its opening hours, U.S. Navy SEALs were charged with preventing Noriega's escape by destroying his private jet at Punta Paitilla Airport. The SEALs were ambushed, with four killed and eight injured. "It was a fuck-all disaster," James said. The dead soldiers, he told Kathleen, were his men.

James, however, was home, and guests were coming for Christmas dinner. So after opening their gifts, Kathleen went to work on the turkey, stuffing, gravy, side dishes and multiple desserts. Preparations were difficult because she had limited counter space and no kitchen table—James had dragged her old table downstairs, put it next to his desk and covered it with papers. He replaced it with a portable kitchen cart on wheels, which didn't have nearly the surface area of a table.

Kathleen was pulling the turkey out of the oven when she heard James behind her. "Where can I put this?" he asked. He was holding a roasting pan containing his goose, which he just took out of the oven in the downstairs kitchen.

Kathleen looked around—there wasn't a square inch of counter space available. "Do you really want me to tell you where to put it?" she asked sarcastically.

James turned on his heel, angry, and took the greasy bird back downstairs to carve. At dinner, he was the only one who ate any goose.

A week later, James informed Kathleen that they were having company on New Year's Eve. He had tracked down a local Special Forces veteran who served in Vietnam. The man's wife was in Greece, so James had invited him, and his seven-year-old son, for dinner.

Kathleen was annoyed—after all, she never met the man or his son—but as the hospitable hostess she cooked another holiday dinner. All night long, James pumped the man with questions about his time in Vietnam. Like most Vietnam vets that Kathleen knew, he didn't really want to talk about what he saw and did—it was a bad experience. But James persisted, and the man reluctantly answered his questions.

James, in the meantime, told the vet about his service during the war working with the Montagnards, the hill people of Vietnam. James showed photos of the indigenous tribesmen. He was not in any of the photos. He couldn't be, James explained, because he was taking the pictures.

James kept telling Kathleen about his business ventures, although she had trouble keeping his plans straight. He was still flying to California every month for meetings about his movies. He met people on Cape Cod who were writing papers about non-lethal defense technologies, such as weapons that could stop mechanical systems or interrupt electronics without injuring people. James was trying to get an association going with them—perhaps to use their work as the basis of a movie. So far, however, nothing was working.

When Kathleen questioned him, James always had an excuse for why his plans hadn't materialized, but his reasons didn't make any sense to her. James attributed this to her lack of business knowledge, so he took Kathleen out to dinner and patiently explained about venture capital. He showed her tables of projected revenues and expenses, and anticipated profit margins. The best way for her to reap the benefits of what she'd already invested, James said, was to make sure he had enough money to see his projects through. He encouraged her to unlock the equity in her home and put it to work. Her money would grow exponentially! The interest was tax deductible! She couldn't lose!

In other words, he was running out of cash.

But mortgage rates at the time were high—over 10 percent. "No way," Kathleen said. With this, James became sullen. He pouted around the house. "If you loved me and trusted me, you would help me out," he complained. Eventually James succeeded in making Kathleen feel guilty, and she refinanced again. Now her mortgage was $80,000.

Then James wanted Kathleen to get a new car—he was enamored with the Nissan 300Z, and drove Kathleen to a dealership to look at it. She wasn't into sports cars, and had no interest in buying the Nissan. So James had another idea. He convinced a leasing company to buy her car. The company would provide cash right away, which Kathleen would repay through the lease. Again she resisted—why should she lease a car that she already owned? James responded by proclaiming his love, talking about how they were a team, asking her to help him. It was only a temporary situation—he'd repay everything when his plans were funded. James kept up the pressure for weeks, until Kathleen finally relented.

James was thrilled, thanked Kathleen for believing in him, and began planning a wedding and a honeymoon trip to Australia. Because Kathleen had such good credit, she could, James said, put the entire trip on her credit cards. The charges wouldn't be there for long, he said—just until his movies got going.

The end of February 1990 was snowy in Boston—James shot video of Prudence, the basset hound Kathleen had bought him, joyfully playing in white stuff. The video would introduce his family in sunny Australia to his wintry new home in America.

James and Kathleen planned a three-week visit to Australia in March, which was the beginning of autumn Down Under. But first, on their way to Australia, they'd stop in Las Vegas to get married. Kathleen suggested that they invite some of his California friends to their wedding.

"No," James said. "I can't see putting people out of their way just for a wedding."

"James, people are generally happy to go out of their way when friends get married," Kathleen replied.

He wouldn't have it. In fact, James didn't want to tell anyone in California that they were getting married. But he did want to take care of business while he was on the West Coast, so they flew into Los Angeles on March 1, 1990 and checked into a hotel in Marina del Rey—the same one Kathleen stayed in almost two years earlier when they met.

The day before their wedding, James left for meetings in San Diego. With time to kill, Kathleen went for a manicure. At least she had a new engagement ring— James returned from one of his trips to California with a ring that he said came from a movie set. Later in the afternoon, she was in their hotel room, waiting for James to return so they could have dinner, when she heard news reports that a minor earthquake had hit the area. If the ground had trembled, Kathleen completely missed it—she didn't even see any glasses rattling or pictures shifting. But James called to tell her that the earthquake had struck hard where he was, knocking out power, and he was marooned. She should go ahead and have dinner without him.

Kathleen was not happy—they were getting married the next day, and she wanted to have dinner with her fiancé. But James insisted that he was stuck and he'd get back to the hotel as soon as he could. Later that night he called again— he still couldn't travel. He'd find a place to spend the night and would be there in the morning, so they could drive to Las Vegas.

The next morning, James picked Kathleen up in a red hatchback. After a four-hour trip to Las Vegas, and checking into another hotel to freshen up, they went to the Little White Wedding Chapel to get married. It was the most famous wedding chapel in town, where many stars, like Frank Sinatra and Mia Farrow, had tied the knot.

James and Kathleen stood in the back of the chapel while the minister, a middle-aged, red-haired woman in a white robe, adjusted the video camera. James wore a black suit jacket with a red handkerchief in the breast pocket, an open-collared white shirt and gray trousers. Kathleen wore a white suit, belted at the waist. She carried a single red rose, still in its plastic wrapper.

A scratchy recording of the *Wedding March* began, and James started walking up the aisle. Kathleen took a couple of quick steps and caught up with him, slipping her arm through his.

"No, you're supposed to stay," James said. "I'm the first one." Then he turned to the minister and said, "She blew it, didn't she?"

"What?" the woman asked.

"She blew it. I'm supposed to come first, and then her. She blew it."

"No, most people walk up together."

"Really? I had a different script." He was not about to admit an error.

"It depends on what you want to do," the minister replied, and quickly began the ceremony. "Dearly beloved, we are gathered here in the Little White Chapel in Las Vegas, Nevada, on the third day of March, 1990."

James took Kathleen's hand, placed it on his arm, and patted it.

"We're here in the presence of God to join James Alwyn Montgomery and Kathleen M. Maloney in matrimony, which is an honorable estate instituted by God."

James pulled Kathleen's hand up to his heart, squeezing her fingers.

"If there is any just cause why you can't be joined together, will you speak it now?" the minister asked. She paused for a moment, and then continued. "James, do you take Kathleen to be your lawfully wedded wife?"

"I certainly do," James answered, with sincerity.

"Do you promise to love her, to honor her and comfort her, in sickness and in health?"

"As I have in the past, I will in the future."

To the same questions, Kathleen softly, or perhaps apprehensively, replied, "Yes, I do."

Then the minister told the couple to face each other, and asked James to hold Kathleen's hands. He took them gently and brought them to his lips, kissing her fingers. "Repeat after me," the minister said. "I, James, take you, Kathleen, to be my wedded wife, to have and to hold from this day forward, for better or worse, for richer or poorer ..."

But James made a correction to the script: "for better or worse, for richer ... and richer," he said, emphasizing the word "richer." James placed the ring on Kathleen's finger, and repeating after the minister, said, "With this ring, I thee wed. I pledge my love and devotion, as long as we both shall live."

Then James switched scripts all together. Sliding the ring up and down on Kathleen's finger, he said, "At this point I want to stop and say, that this ring belongs to a bunch of guys who never made it out of Vietnam." He gulped, then continued. "On behalf of them, as well as me, will you take this ring?" He brought her fingers to his lips and kissed them again.

Kathleen said her wedding vows. "With this ring, I thee wed, and hereto I pledge my faith and loyalty, so long as we both shall live."

James, wearing his new wedding ring, gently clasped Kathleen's hands and looked deep into her eyes. "This ring is for a bunch of guys who never made it back. You married a whole team of people."

The minister brought the ceremony to its conclusion. "Inasmuch as James and Kathleen have come together in holy wedlock and witnessed the same before God, according to the power vested in me by the state of Nevada, I now pronounce that you are husband and wife." Then after a short benediction, she said,

"You can seal this covenant with a kiss."

James kissed Kathleen passionately as the minister said, "Now those who God has joined together, let no man cast asunder."

With that, James turned directly to the camera and pointed, like the recreation of an "Uncle Sam wants you!" poster. "Proody, this one's for you," he exclaimed.

"What rotten woman would cheat on her husband in 36 hours?" James narrated, facetiously, as he slowly panned the newly married couple's honeymoon apartment in Australia with his video camera. "I see a dozen pink roses up there, and there's no way in the world her husband would buy a dozen pink roses."

Kathleen and James were staying in a tiny rented apartment in South Yarra, a suburb of Melbourne, Australia's second-largest city. Although the trip was mostly an opportunity for Kathleen to see Australia and meet her new family, James did want to spend time on business. So along with clothes, he's carted briefcases, computers and paperwork halfway around the world, accounting for most of the couple's 10 pieces of luggage.

James' partner, Archie Turner, lived in Melbourne, and James scheduled a meeting only a couple of days after their arrival. Luckily, while James was busy, Archie's wife, Paulette,* was available to show Kathleen the scenic areas outside of the city. Melbourne was located on the southeastern coast of Australia, where the Yarra River flowed into Port Phillip Bay. Paulette and Kathleen drove along the western edge of Port Phillip, then they picked up the Great Ocean Road, which hugged the contours of the rugged coast.

The day was sunny and mild, and the landscape was breathtaking. Sandy beaches were flanked by rocky cliffs that tumbled into the sea. The women stopped to see Bells Beach, known as a surfer hangout. The waves that day were devoid of surfers, but bathers sunned themselves at the water's edge. Unlike the cold gray of Boston's North Atlantic Ocean, the Bass Strait off of Victoria, Australia, was a brilliant shade of turquoise. To Kathleen, it was absolutely beautiful.

The next morning, James and Kathleen walked a few blocks from their apartment to South Yarra's famous Prahran Market. The market, which opened in 1891, featured stall after stall of fresh fruit, vegetables and flowers, along with baked goods, prepared foods, meats and seafood. James, wearing a new football jersey with "MONTGOMERY" and a huge number "45" emblazoned on the back, circled all the stands in the market three times, searching for the best price on scallops.

Leaving the market, James and Kathleen strolled down the street along the storefronts until something caught James' eye. In the window of Grant's Bookshop was a volume with a bright teal cover entitled *Australia's Armed Forces*. He asked the clerk to show him the book. Leafing through the pages, he came across photos of Australian soldiers in the jungles of Vietnam. "There's your old man," he said to Kathleen, pointing to the picture.

"Where?" she asked.

He answered with gibberish that made a reference to the Australian army and ended with a statement to the clerk, "I'll take it."

A few days later, the Turners invited the Montgomerys to their home for dinner. Large quantities of wine were consumed by all, and James turned on the video camera to record after-dinner banter.

"There is nobody at this table, over the age of 21, who isn't smashed," James narrated. "It is the dreaded, unbelievable, alcoholic crowd that is going to control the future of this country."

Then Paulette, Archie's wife, set a bowl on the table containing something she found down the hall—a large dead insect with eight spindly legs.

"Show it to James," Kathleen said.

"If that is a spider, I'm going to scream," James threatened. "I'm also going to get my bloody Beretta."

James wore a yellow polo shirt with a green and gold patch of the Australian Army Training Team Vietnam over the left breast. It did not give him courage.

"He's afraid of nothing in this living world, except spiders," Kathleen said.

"It can only live as long as I get my hand on a bayonet or a Beretta," James countered. The spider lay motionless in the white bowl. James stood up and started a slow tai chi dance, chanting over the spider.

"This is our hero," Kathleen said. "Two world wars, and he's afraid of spiders."

"You who we're about to send to another life," James intoned to the spider, "You must understand, I cannot live with you in my life." He dumped the spider onto the tablecloth and, still chanting, picked up a carving knife.

"Don't mess up my tablecloth," Archie warned, laughing.

James chanted some more, and poked at the spider with the knife. Satisfied that it was quite dead, he dropped the knife and sat down. Everyone laughed, amused by the performance, which was recorded for posterity by the video camera. And that seemed to be James' objective. As Kathleen taped more of the conversation, James always wanted to be the star of the show. In fact, when Kathleen asked Archie's teenage son to explain his school blazer and its emblems for her family back in the U.S.—she'd never seen anything like it in Boston—James pirouetted like an overweight ballerina in the background.

"He always has to be in the picture," Kathleen commented.

Then James told Kathleen that there was something else he wanted her to photograph.

Archie disappeared for a few minutes. When he returned, he carried a large, heavy bundle wrapped in an old white and blue coverlet. He opened the bundle onto the floor. It was a collection of weapons.

Kathleen had never seen so many guns, but no one seemed to think there was anything unusual about a pile of weapons on the dining room floor. Archie didn't ask his kids to leave. His wife didn't object. James arranged the guns in rows on the coverlet.

Kathleen counted 20 rifles, pistols and submachine guns, plus several bayonets. They were mostly military issue weapons that saw action in conflicts ranging from World War II to Vietnam: A Russian SKS semiautomatic carbine. A Japanese Arisaka bolt-action rifle. German and Italian Mauser rifles. An M-14 rifle, which the United States used briefly in Vietnam. An Uzi carbine. And a CAR-15, or Colt Automatic Rifle-15, which was used by the U.S. military in the 1960s and 1970s.

The collection included pistols and handguns: A Colt .45 semiautomatic—the primary sidearm of U.S. soldiers. An old German broom handle 7.65 semiautomatic pistol. A Smith and Wesson .357, an Ingram 9 mm SMG, and an Uzi 9 mm automatic pistol. There was also a Glock handgun—primarily used by police officers.

James and Archie weren't specific about why they had the guns, or even who owned them. Kathleen didn't ask questions. She just took the requested photographs.

A steady rain fell in the marina where the Ace, a cabin cruiser owned by Bob Montgomery, James' brother, was docked. Bob and his wife, Laurel—both of them psychologists—lived in the Melbourne area. They invited the newlyweds to join them for a day on the boat.

Everyone huddled in the cabin, watching the videos James recorded of snowy Boston, waiting for the skies to clear. Melbourne was known for its changeable weather—the locals talked about "four seasons in one day." Sure enough, the sun came out. Captain Bob ordered the rain shields rolled up, the lines cast off, and he piloted the boat out onto the bay for a cruise.

Bob invited a few other friends for the voyage. One man stepped aboard wearing a cap from a Royal Australian Navy ship—he'd served on the ship as a naval surgeon. James soon started regaling the doctor about his experiences in Vietnam.

Bob's head jerked around. "When were you in Vietnam?" he asked incredulously.

"While you were off at Berkley protesting the war, I was in the jungle fighting it," James replied. "I never told you."

Bob stared at James in disbelief, but let the comment pass.

James continued schmoozing the doctor, buttering him up for his big request. James liked the doctor's hat—dark blue with heavy gold braid on the brim—and he wanted it. At first, the doctor refused. But James persisted. "What can I do to get that hat?" he asked. Eventually the man relented. James became the owner of the hat.

Back at the dock after their pleasure cruise, Laurel put out a buffet, including large steamed yabbies. They looked like lobsters, but were freshwater crayfish native to New South Wales, Australia. With the yabbies she served champagne in silver-plated goblets. Then it was time for the highlight of the celebration—a three-tiered wedding cake, topped not by a bride and groom, but by toy male and female superheroes.

Fueled by champagne, the guests serenaded the newlyweds with the first two lines of *Here Comes the Bride*—no one knew any more of the lyrics.

"The groom will now cut the cake with this knife," Laurel said.

James took the knife and held it between his hands, clasped in prayer position. He started chanting, "Ummm, gah, om."

Remembering the spider incident, Kathleen rolled her eyes. "Oh no," she said.

"Ummm, gah, hah!" James karate-chopped the wedding cake, sending the superheroes and the top two layers of cake tumbling to the deck. Kathleen was shocked; the rest of the people on the boat burst out laughing.

Later, Kathleen and James were at his brother's house when Archie and Paulette Turner stopped by. "Oh, by the way, James, Colleen Jessick called for you," Paulette said. "I told her that you just got married. She says congratulations, and she wants the two of you to stop by for drinks when you get to Los Angeles."

James' mother, father and sister lived in Sydney, so that was the next travel destination. James said he had a bit more business to take care of in Melbourne, so Kathleen drove ahead with Paulette Turner—a 10-hour trip. Alone for a day in Sydney, Kathleen wandered around the city and took herself to see the famous Sydney Opera House.

Kathleen and James rented another serviced apartment in the King's Cross neighborhood of Sydney, which had always been the city's entertainment mecca and red light district. In World War II, it became a playground for soldiers and sailors on leave. During the Vietnam War it was a wild scene, fueled by drugs and crime. Among the carousers was James—and hundreds of American servicemen who flocked to the area every week.

"This is R&R city," James said, taking on the role of the video tour guide for King's Cross. "We used to bring the guys back out of Pleiku, plop them down here. This was the only place that made any bloody sense in Australia."

The camera was also rolling when Heather Azzopardi, James' sister, hosted a small, informal wedding party for James and Kathleen in the backyard of her home. At the party were Heather's husband and two young sons; James' mother, Vera Montgomery, who also lived in the home; James' sister, Robin Swann—James asked Kathleen to pay for her flight from Queensland; and a few friends.

James entertained the guests with stories of his exploits and business ventures. When the newlyweds flew back to the U.S., they'd stop for a few days in Los Angeles to check on his movie that was about to start production. "I've got a problem with a writer," he said.

James continued to cast himself as the star of his honeymoon movie. Like Laurel, Heather brought out wedding cake for the newlyweds—a heart-shaped cake frosted with yellow icing and decorated by chocolate morsels and tiny silver dragées. "Kathleen and James" was written in icing on the top. James placed his bride's arm through his and escorted her to the table in the dining room where the cake was displayed.

"I'd just like to welcome you to the family," Heather said to Kathleen. "And congratulate you. And hope you're very, very happy together, and sorry that you're so far away. Wish we could see more of you, because we miss you."

"Thank you," Kathleen replied.

"Well geeze," James said, clasping his hands behind his back, staring at his feet and pretending to be embarrassed. "I run out of words at a time like this."

"Camera shy," Kathleen said facetiously.

"Do you want to cut the cake love?" James asked.

"Sounds like a good idea."

James picked up a knife. "I've got five bucks that says from the top of the piano, I can hit the cake ..."

"Don't do it!" Heather reprimanded.

James persisted. "Five bucks? Ten bucks?"

Kathleen took the knife out of James' hand and cut the cake.

"I want a kiss on the lips," said Robin from behind the video camera. "A kiss! A kiss! Let's see some real passion!"

James traced the outline of Kathleen's bare shoulder and neck—she was wearing a scoop-necked white shift—with his tongue. He kissed her ear, put his hand on her shoulder, looked directly at the camera and proclaimed in a boy-like voice, "We is married."

Toward the end of the nearly 14-hour Qantas flight from Sydney to Los Angeles, James stood in the back of the plane talking with a stewardess. Kathleen walked up, and the stewardess became testy. Kathleen quickly realized that her new husband was a little too familiar with the woman. In fact, he seemed to be hitting on her. Kathleen was angry, and let James know it.

By the time they reached baggage claim, James was in a foul mood. He yanked his luggage off the carousel—because he'd bought so much stuff in Australia, including a new $400 briefcase, they now had 12 pieces to claim, which he piled onto a cart.

"I'm going to go get a car," James proclaimed. "They don't have taxis at the international terminal."

"What are you talking about?" Kathleen demanded.

"There are no taxis here," James insisted. "I have to go get a car."

James stormed away, leaving Kathleen to watch over their 12 pieces of luggage—except one of James' bags was missing. "Serves him right," she steamed to herself.

About a half-hour later, James returned.

"Well you took off without counting your bags," Kathleen said. "You're missing one."

Now James was really in a rage. "Did you report it?" he demanded.

"No, I didn't report it. You left me with all these bags. I couldn't move."

Eventually the lost bag was recovered, and they piled everything into the car James brought back—the same red hatchback that they'd driven to Las Vegas.

James had explained previously that the car belonged to his good friend, an older woman named Jody. The woman traveled out of the country frequently for her work, and when she was away, she let James use her car and apartment. In fact, that's where they would spend the night—in Jody's apartment. James drove Kathleen to a high-rise building in Marina del Rey—not far from the hotel they stayed in before their trip to Australia. He took out a key, opened the door and let Kathleen in.

Although the apartment wasn't big—only one bedroom—it was immaculate and nicely decorated in shades of white. The woman who lived there had a large wine collection, which she displayed in distinctive wine racks.

James showed Kathleen the bedroom. First she noticed the comforter on the bed—when James moved to Boston, he'd wrapped a computer in one just like it, staining it with grease. Then, on the night table, she noticed a Christmas ornament—two little Dutch dolls on a bench holding a heart.

"Isn't this the ornament that I sent you?" Kathleen asked, shocked.

"Oh, I don't know," James replied. "You certainly can't expect me to remember something like that. Now I've got a meeting, but I'll be back later. You relax. Just be careful not to touch anything." Then he was gone.

Kathleen strolled around the apartment. What did he mean, don't touch anything? He certainly didn't care what got touched, or for that matter, spilled on and ruined, at her house. Tired, she decided to lie down—small, upright airline seats were not conducive to sleeping. Three or four hours later, James returned, and they spent the night in the bed of his friend, that older woman, Jody McClure.

But as they were leaving the next day, Kathleen picked up the little wooden Christmas ornament and stashed it in her purse.

Back in Boston, James' movies fell by the wayside as he pursued a new business opportunity—a contract to develop, install and maintain a computerized tourism information system at visitor welcome centers in Florida. James and his business partner, Archie Turner, had somehow received an inquiry for the project and jumped on it. They started working on a proposal to develop the technical aspects of the service—hardware and software—as well as plans for marketing it to both tourists and corporate sponsors.

This necessitated another infusion of cash—not something that Kathleen was happy about. But James had a solid opportunity for a real, four-year contract with the state of Florida. He said no one could put together a business plan comparable to his. It was time to play for all the marbles—the more money Kathleen could put into the venture, the less he'd have to get from investors and the more profits they would retain. James recommended that she take all the remaining equity in her home and invest it in his "Futron America" corporation. That would mean a new mortgage of $160,000.

By this point, Kathleen knew that something was amiss with her husband, but she couldn't figure out what it was. He talked a good game, but had nothing to show for it. The details of his stories didn't add up. For example, she once found a photo of a woman among James' papers, and asked him who it was. James said the woman debriefed him after his mission to Panama, but she didn't look at all military. Kathleen found another photo of a woman—this one pornographic. She furiously asked James to explain it. He indignantly retorted that it was a girlfriend from his past, and he kept the photo for old time's sake. She had absolutely no reason to be angry about it.

Then there was the engagement ring, supposedly from a movie set, which James said was so valuable. Kathleen took it to a jeweler for appraisal, and found out the stone was a fake and the ring was worthless. Embarrassed, she bought her own ring.

Kathleen was not happy in her marriage, but she was trapped. She didn't have proof that James was doing anything wrong. And if she ended the relationship, she was sure that she'd lose all the money she had already given him.

And now James wanted more.

But this wasn't some pie-in-the-sky movie; it was a real contract with a state government. In fact, the Florida contract seemed to offer her only possible chance of recovering her money. If she didn't prime the pump, nothing would happen. Kathleen reluctantly agreed to the refinancing.

To firm up plans for the venture, James needed to return to Australia for meetings with Archie and other potential partners. He asked Kathleen to accompany him. He also asked her to finance the trip by maxing out a new credit card that he encouraged her to apply for. Feeling like she had no choice, Kathleen took a $10,000 cash advance.

So in September 1990, they flew back to Australia. The trip was much shorter than their first one—only 10 days. They had dinner with Archie Turner and a few other people. For one meeting at their hotel in King's Cross, James asked Kathleen to leave. Her presence, he said, would be inappropriate. She spent the day at a museum.

After they returned to the U.S., James submitted the first draft of his proposal to the Florida Department of Commerce, Division of Tourism. Officially, he responded to a request for proposals for a Public Access Videotex System (PAVS) in all official State of Florida Welcome Centers.

Department of Commerce officials had questions about the proposal, like, "who is Futron America?" James responded that the company didn't really exist, but it would soon. The key executives would be Archie Turner, the president, and himself, vice president.

James described himself as a naturalized U.S. resident with experience in film, television, data processing—including electronic funds transfer—and marketing. His last public venture, he said, was launching the Movietime Channel, a basic cable network. Archie Turner would become a U.S. resident before the year was out, and the rest of the corporation's shareholders would be Florida residents and companies. They planned to employ minorities in both the work force and in management. The new service would be promoted so that, when fully operational, PAVS would generate profits for the state of Florida.

James flew to the capital of Florida, Tallahassee, in pursuit of the contract. After he left, Kathleen found a fax on the dining room table. It was sent to James by Colleen Jessick, the writer in California. Reading it, Kathleen realized she found a critical piece that explained the puzzle of James.

Her husband was having an affair with Colleen Jessick. Maybe that's why James called her "Colleen" on their wedding day.

Kathleen was furious. She picked up the phone to call the writer in California, which was three time zones behind Massachusetts. It was Saturday, October 13, 1990—Columbus Day weekend. She woke Colleen up.

"Is this Colleen Jessick?" Kathleen demanded.

"Yes," the woman replied sleepily. "Who's calling?"

"It's Kathleen Maloney. I'm James Montgomery's wife."

No response.

"I have here a fax that you sent to my husband," Kathleen continued. "From the content, it seems that you're having an affair with him."

"What are you talking about? James isn't married."

"He is married, and you know it. You called him at Archie Turner's home in Australia last March when we were on our honeymoon. Archie's wife told you that he was married. She told us that you asked us to stop by for cocktails when we got to Los Angeles."

Suddenly Kathleen remembered James storming off as soon as they touched down in Los Angeles, saying he had to find a car. And then taking her to the apartment in Marina del Rey, dropping her off, and leaving for four hours. Had he gone for a tryst with Colleen Jessick—as soon as they returned from their honeymoon? For that matter, what about the day he went missing before their wedding? Had he spent it with this woman?

Colleen didn't admit to anything. She just insisted that she didn't realize James was married. She'd been having a hard time financially, and James gave her money.

"Well, that was my money that he gave you," Kathleen said.

After a moment, Colleen answered. "I guess I owe you, then."

"Yeah, you do."

Kathleen hung up the phone. Then she started thinking about the apartment in Marina del Rey. James always said the woman who lived there, Jody McClure, used to be his neighbor, and they were nothing but good friends. James had lied about Colleen Jessick—was he lying about Jody McClure?

She found a phone number and called. Jody answered.

Kathleen introduced herself as James Montgomery's wife. Then she asked Jody about the nature of her relationship with James.

"James is living in Boston," Jody said.

"He's living in my basement," Kathleen replied.

"Oh, no," Jody said. "He lives with a family at the army base."

"Jody," Kathleen said impatiently, "He lives downstairs. He's been living here since he left Marina del Rey."

The line was quiet for a moment. Then Jody spoke. "We were living togeth-er. I went to my son's college graduation, and when I got home, James was gone."

"Yeah, well I flew into Los Angeles and he met me at the airport in a moving truck. We drove across the country to Boston."

Jody was silent. Then she asked, "What kind of truck?"

"A yellow Penske rental truck."

"I saw that truck in the parking lot. I didn't know he rented it."

Kathleen kept talking. She told Jody that they'd driven from Marina del Rey to Las Vegas in a red hatchback to get married.

"That's my car," Jody said. She was deeply hurt—Kathleen could hear the pain in her voice. But there was more. Kathleen told Jody that she and James spent the night in her apartment when they returned from Australia. They slept in her bed.

"You know that little Christmas ornament of the Dutch kids sitting on a bench?"

"Yes," Jody said.

"Well I gave that to James. I sent it to him for Christmas two years ago. And then I walk in and see it in your bedroom. I took it."

"So that's where it went."

Instantly, Kathleen knew what had happened. She sent the ornament as a gift to James. James turned around and gave it as a gift to Jody. She wondered if it was the only thing James ever gave the woman.

After the phone calls, Kathleen was so angry that she was yelling at James, even though he wasn't there. But James was returning from Florida that evening, and he wanted Kathleen to pick him up at the airport. She had two words for him, and they weren't, "yes, dear."

James took a taxi home from the airport Saturday night, and as soon as he walked in the door, Kathleen confronted him: She found the fax from Colleen Jessick. She called the woman on the phone. Then she called Jody McClure. She accused him of cheating on her. She used a lot of choice words.

James denied everything. Colleen Jessick was a business contact, and Jody McClure was a friend. Kathleen didn't know what she was talking about, and she sounded like she was paranoid.

James had plans to fly to California on Monday. On Sunday, he holed up in his basement office, quiet as a mouse. Then he tried to talk some sense into his wife. He loved her. He told her that he loved her 10 times a day. Why couldn't she just believe him?

By Monday, Kathleen was calm enough to take him to the airport. She was glad to see him go. When she got home, she went downstairs and started search-ing through James' papers and records—something she should have done long ago. But who knew? James was the one acting like a lovesick puppy. He was the one pushing to get married. Yes, Kathleen had noticed incidents that seemed a bit strange, but when she questioned him, his explanations were always plausi-ble. Now he left Colleen Jessick's fax on the dining room table, yet totally denied its suggestive contents.

With a start, Kathleen suspected that James purposely left the fax for her to find. But why? What else would she find in his office?

Personal ads. Kathleen discovered that James had been placing singles ads in local newspapers, describing himself as a 6-foot-2 retired Australian military officer who was also a Hollywood screenwriter. Apparently cheating with women he knew wasn't enough—he had to find new conquests.

Credit reports. James seemed to be looking for a new sugar mama. He had Equifax reports on several women whom Kathleen did not know.

Video8 tapes. Kathleen knew that James often recorded television programs, and of course, they'd used his camcorder in Australia. What else was on his tapes? She couldn't play them, because both the camera and tape player were gone—James must have taken them with him.

So Kathleen bought another player. When James called, acting as if everything was fine between them and they just had a little spat, she let him know.

"I'm watching the movies," she said.

"What movies?"

"From our honeymoon. It seems that you took the tape player, so I bought another one."

"Take it back!" James ordered.

"Why? You don't want me to know that you were recording us in bed?"

"I took that of us so I'd have it to remember our special time."

"Don't be ridiculous. Because right after us on the tape, there's another broad that you're fucking in Australia on our honeymoon. Is that what you were doing when you stayed in Melbourne while you sent me to Sydney? In fact, there are two other women besides me. Who are you kidding?"

"Take that thing back!" he screamed into the phone.

"Shut the fuck up," Kathleen said, disgusted. She hung up.

Jody McClure sat in her attorney's office on Wilshire Boulevard in Los Angeles, California. James agreed to meet her there to discuss the money that he owed her.

She was still shaken by the phone call she received from Kathleen Maloney—James' *wife!* He'd lived with Kathleen in Boston ever since the day he disappeared—May 12, 1989. They married six months ago. James had been in touch with Jody almost the entire time—she saw him during his visits to California. He never bothered to inform Jody that he was involved with another woman, let alone married. Now he was saying that he and his wife were separated.

Was it true? Jody had learned that James did not always tell the whole and complete truth. Take, for example, the job he had at Movietime when she first met him. James never said why he left the company. Long after the fact, Jody talked to one of his former co-workers—James had been unceremoniously fired. Apparently he drank all day long—his big glasses of Diet Coke were generously spiked with vodka, and after he left Movietime, empty bottles were found everywhere.

Jody's thoughts were interrupted by James' appearance in the office. He actually showed up! Jody was half expecting him to disappear, as he had before.

The two of them, and her attorney, got down to work. James produced a letter of agreement that he was prepared to sign. He agreed that he owed Jody $180,000. He committed to pay half of the amount by Christmas 1991, and the second half by Christmas 1992. He offered Jody the right to attach a lien on his stock for the yet-to-be-formed company that would operate the Florida Public Access Videotext System. In return, he wanted Jody to refrain from disclosing the debt to the Florida Department of Commerce or other potential clients. She would also give up any interest in James' other ventures.

The attorney advised against accepting James' letter, and recommended that Jody insist on a promissory note. She did. So for two hours, Jody, James and the attorney haggled over the terms of an agreement.

The lawyer drew up the promissory note. It stated that James promised to pay Jody $180,000. He was required to make payments of $30,000 three times a year in 1991 and 1992. The agreement spelled out how interest would accrue if any payments were late or missed, and what would happen if James defaulted.

James surprised Jody again. On October 26, 1990, he signed the agreement.

From a hotel lobby in Tallahassee, Florida, Kathleen picked up the phone to return a call. Trying to decide what to do about her marriage and her money, she'd flown down to Florida over Veterans Day to salvage—what? She didn't even know.

James had been calling Kathleen consistently ever since he left Boston. He said he still loved her. He kept reassuring her that the videotext contract with the state of Florida was coming through, and he'd be able to repay all the money that she'd given him. They could work everything out.

James arranged a lunch for Kathleen to meet his future clients at the Florida Division of Tourism. He liked to do business over lunch, especially since he didn't have an office or a place to live—he was staying at the local Ramada Inn. He invited eight state workers, including his main contact and several young women who worked as office support staff. One of them, a single mother about 26 years old, seemed to be overly impressed with her husband.

James was doing his best to placate Kathleen. Then Kathleen picked up her husband's messages from the hotel answering service. One was from Jody McClure. Kathleen spoke to the woman for about an hour.

"By the way, James, you had a message," Kathleen said back in the room. "I returned the call for you. It was Jody McClure."

James didn't react. Instead, he continued with the day's plan—attending the city's annual Veterans Day parade. Kathleen and James stood together, watching high school bands and war veterans march through downtown Tallahassee. Afterwards, James met some Vietnam veterans who invited them to a barbecue at their "hooch." During the war, soldiers called any Vietnamese hut or simple dwelling a hooch. The Tallahassee Chapter of the Vietnam Veterans Association appropriated the term for its small headquarters near Lake Ella.

The barbecue drew quite a crowd—many of the vets arrived on Harleys. Kathleen didn't usually hang out with bikers, but everyone was friendly and she enjoyed herself. She chatted with a middle-aged woman named Felicia Cottman,* a fellow Northerner who had recently moved to Florida.

When it got dark, the party moved inside the hooch and a deejay started spinning dance music. James walked up to the table where Kathleen and Felicia were talking. "I'm getting tired," he said.

"It's not that late," Kathleen replied. She was not anxious to go back to the hotel with her so-called husband.

"Well I've been up since before dawn and I have a lot of work to do," James said.

"You mean you have phone calls to make?" Kathleen asked, sarcastically.

"The party's just getting started!" Felicia chimed in.

"That's right. You should stay," James said to Kathleen.

"Yeah, Kathy, stay. We'll have a good time," Felicia said. "I'll drive you back."

Kathleen stayed. She and Felicia had a few more beers and talked. Felicia sensed tension between Kathleen and James; Kathleen admitted that they were having problems, but didn't go into detail. After a couple of hours of socializing, they left and Felicia dropped her off at the hotel.

"Where were you?" James demanded as soon as she walked in the door.

"Where do you think I was?" Kathleen replied, dumbfounded. "At the hooch."

James was pissed. He launched into a tirade about how she should have come home earlier. Kathleen wasn't buying it. To her, it seemed like James was just trying to pick another fight. Fine. She flew back to Boston.

A few days later, on November 15, 1990, James received a letter from the tourism research administrator for the Florida Department of Commerce. The letter announced that James' company, Futron America, had won the contract for the videotext system. After the purchasing department completed its procedures, a contract would be prepared.

The deal was not yet ready to move forward—James still had to find investors to fund the project. He kept issuing reports to Archie Turner, the official president of Futron America, about his efforts. James sent copies to a standing distribution list, which included Kathleen. Reading between the lines, Kathleen realized that James spent Thanksgiving with Felicia, the woman she chatted with at the hooch, and was also hitting on the young single mother she met at the lunch in Tallahassee. In fact, he seemed to be taking the girl's money.

In February 1991, Kathleen flew back to Florida, still trying to find the truth about her husband's activities. Although James now rented an office in a brand new professional building in downtown Tallahassee, he had not found investors, so he did not have the state contract. At one point, James was at a meeting and asked Kathleen to go to his office. While she was there, Kathleen searched the place, and amid the rubble of James' paperwork, discovered that her husband had run a credit report on Felicia Cottman.

Was James trying to get money out of her?

What else was he doing?

Back in Boston, Kathleen tried to investigate. She asked a friend who worked for the Immigration and Naturalization Service whether James was in the country legally. According to INS records, he wasn't in the country at all.

"What do you mean?" Kathleen asked. "He's in Florida. I was standing right next to him when he came through customs."

"When was that?" the friend asked. Kathleen gave him the date.

"We have no record of him coming into the United States on that date."

Another friend arranged for Kathleen to meet with a prosecutor. Kathleen told him about the money James had taken from her, and showed him documents related to the Florida contract. The prosecutor said the business documents appeared to be legitimate. Because they were married, and she had given James the money, it was unlikely that any criminal charges could be filed.

James, in the meantime, continued to update Kathleen on his "progress." Now, both she and Jody were copied on his incessant reports. They arrived by fax, when fax paper came in rolls—Kathleen would come home and find yards of paper spilling from the machine. She ripped the faxes off and threw them away without reading them.

Kathleen flew to Florida one last time in July 1991. She stayed with a friend in Bonita Beach, which was several hours away from Tallahassee, and didn't tell James she was coming. Still, she wanted to let her husband know that she was tracking him and his associates.

July 14, 1991 was James' fiftieth birthday. Kathleen called everyone she'd met from the state tourism office—James included their contact information in his reports—and invited them to a surprise birthday party at a Chinese restaurant. They all thought the party was a nice idea.

James, however, was furious. "You're crazy!" he screamed into the phone when Kathleen called to tell him.

"What's crazy, James? It's your fiftieth birthday. I just thought it would be nice to have a party."

"You'll ruin my birthday," he bellowed.

Of course, there was no party, and Kathleen had called the state workers just to piss James off. She didn't know if any of them showed up for it. But obviously the Florida contract wasn't going well, and James blamed Kathleen—she had jeopardized his delicate negotiations by calling the state officials about the birthday party.

Kathleen didn't believe him.

Losing hope that she would ever get her money back, Kathleen had to take stock of her life. Before she met James, she had a $14,000 mortgage, a small home improvement loan, a car payment and no credit card debt. Now she had a $160,000 mortgage, was leasing a car that she had previously owned outright, and carried a staggering $25,000 in credit card debt.

Kathleen considered declaring bankruptcy, but she didn't want to lose her home. She could keep up with the payments, but it took all of the money she earned.

Thanks to James, Kathleen was going to be in debt for a long time.

James kept Jody McClure apprised of his progress with the Florida contract—that was how he was going to pay back her promissory note. He hit some snags—investors weren't coming through as they promised—but he was still optimistic.

James was not, however, optimistic about his marriage.

In his conversations with Jody, he said that his wife, Kathleen, turned out to be a world-class bitch. She gave him nothing but problems and disparaged his military service. She even contacted several of the Florida state employees directly, and it took him weeks to repair the damage she had done to his negotiations.

Finally, James confessed to Jody that he made a huge mistake. He never should have left her. He apologized, and wondered if they could rebuild their relationship. Via fax and long-distance telephone calls, James pleaded his case. He missed Jody and knew that she was loyal to him. Could they try again? Would she come to be with him?

James wanted to relocate to Tampa, Florida. He could still pursue the state contract from there, but he believed the city offered other business opportunities as well. In October 1991, Jody succumbed to James' pleas. She packed up everything she owned and drove across the country, from California to Florida. James found a lovely apartment with a gorgeous view in a high-rise building on Adalia Avenue in Tampa, and they moved in.

Jody believed that James would soon be building Florida's Public Access Videotex System—after all, he already won the bid. Archie Turner, James' business partner and the actual president of Futron America, had arrived from Australia—he was living in a motel not far from their apartment. All they had to do was come up with the funding and the project would start. James assured Jody that he had investors lined up.

Helping James, Jody believed, would ultimately help herself—when he started making money, she could collect on her promissory note. So Jody was willing to pay their living expenses while he finalized the contract. In fact, since she still traveled frequently for her job, she even let Archie drive her car while she was away.

Nine months and $50,000 later, Jody realized that her lover, James, was involved with a mob of other women. James had discovered the latest computer innovation—online dating—and despite the fact that he and Jody were living together, he actively sought women for long-term relationships. Jody found the evidence—copious printouts of his correspondence with the women—in June 1992. At the time, James was preparing to travel to Australia. The reason, he said, had something to do with his visa. She quickly surmised that, first, James wanted her to find the correspondence, and second, he was going to Australia with one of the other women. But who?

She made a list of the women whose names she found on the correspondence. Colleen Jessick—apparently she was much more than what James described as a "writing partner." Felicia Cottman, who he originally met in Tallahassee. Cecelia Portnoy—she lived in Palm Beach. Kim Goodson—she was a schoolteacher who lived and worked nearby, and her faxes were genuinely funny. The more Jody searched James' papers, the longer the list of women grew. Eventually, there were 30 names on it.

To discover who was going to Australia with James, Jody put her travel industry experience to work. She knew which flight James was on. So she called the airline, pretending to be the first woman on the list, confirming her reservation on James' flight. The airline had no reservation. Twenty minutes later, Jody called the airline again and pretended to be the second woman on the list. Again, she wasn't on the flight. Jody repeated the phone call every 20 minutes, crossing names off until she had her answer. James was going to Australia with Cecelia Portnoy. Jody did not confront James with what she learned. But she did decide that the relationship was over.

On the day James left for Australia, Jody took him to the airport. "Have a good trip," she said when they arrived at the Qantas door, putting her arms around him. James disengaged from her embrace quickly. He was anxious to get going, and Jody knew why—he didn't want Cecelia Portnoy to see him with her. So Jody left him at curbside check-in, went back to their apartment, and started packing.

Virtually everything in the apartment was hers—all the furniture, all the housewares, all the linens, all the pictures on the walls. She packed everything. She went through James' office and filled an entire suitcase with letters from other women. While cleaning out the bathroom Jody got another shock—she found his hidden collection of gay porn magazines.

Jody was just about ready to leave when Archie Turner unexpectedly dropped by. James' partner, at that point, was angry about the lack of progress with the tourism contract. In fact, he was downright surly, and wrote letters to his wife ranting about what a bastard James was. Jody begged Archie not to tell James that she was leaving, and she was pleasantly surprised when he didn't.

When Jody finally drove away, on June 20, 1992, only two things were left in the apartment—a mattress and a typewriter. Jody took James' American Express card and used it to charge her expenses for the trip back to California. When she got home, she mailed the card back.

Shortly thereafter, Jody received a phone call from Archie. James did not have the money to pay the apartment's electric bill, and the power was going to be turned off. Could she please pay the bill? Astounded at his audacity, Jody, in no uncertain terms, refused.

Kathleen Maloney was shocked to hear from Paulette Turner, Archie's wife, that Jody McClure had moved to Florida to be with James. She told Jody that James cheated on both of them. She told Jody that she slept in her bed with James. In fact, he still kept trying to talk Kathleen into moving to Florida so they could work on their marriage. Why in the world would Jody go back to him? Kathleen didn't know what spell James had cast, but she felt badly that Jody allowed the man back into her life, moved from California to Florida, and invested more money in him.

Then Kathleen received a five-page letter from Jody, explaining that she'd left James, telling what James had done, and asking Kathleen to call her.

Although Kathleen was appalled that Jody went back to James, she could tell that the woman was heartbroken and needed someone to talk to. A few days after receiving the letter, Kathleen called. Jody was terribly upset, crying on the phone. She told Kathleen what James had put her through—taking her money while building a harem of 30 women, purposely leaving the correspondence for her to find, and then taking Cecelia Portnoy to Australia. He lied to her again and again and again, and never owned up to anything.

"Jody, I hate to say I told you so, but I told you so," Kathleen said.

"I know," Jody wailed. "I just didn't want to hear it."

After that first call, the women kept in touch from time to time, as they both tried to rebuild their lives.

More than three years later, in the fall of 1995, Kathleen was quite surprised when James served her with divorce papers. Even though she had plenty of reasons to divorce him, she had taken no action. She paid for everything during their marriage; she refused to pay for the divorce.

The one-page petition claimed that the parties had no liabilities subject to equitable distribution, and even though Kathleen was carrying nearly $200,000 in debt due to James, she did not respond. There was no point in arguing with him; she'd never get her money back. The divorce was granted by default.

Then, in August 1997, James contacted Kathleen out of the blue. He was going to be in the Boston area and he wanted to have dinner with her. They met at the Pillar House restaurant. James told Kathleen that the woman he married after her, Gale Lewis, had died in his arms. He did not disclose that he had already married again.

As they were leaving, James tried to kiss her. Kathleen wasn't interested.

After leaving Florida, Jody heard nothing from James for six months. Then he started sending her copies of his plans for his latest moneymaking scheme—he was going to build an electronic theme park for adults called CelebAM, which was short for "Celebrate America." His ideas were cutting edge, far ahead of anything in the entertainment field! He was certain to succeed! He would repay her all that he owed and more! He wanted to get together and tell her all about it!

As the voluminous faxes arrived, Jody laughed. James' grandiose plan called for a massive investment in a huge venue. If James couldn't put together a deal when he had a state contract in hand, how in the world was he going to pull this one off? If by some miracle James' plans came to fruition, Jody could collect on her promissory note. But she wasn't counting on it.

Three or four times in the years after she left him in Tampa, Jody did agree to meet James in public places for coffee. She never brought up why she left him, or the money he owed her. When he suggested that they go to bed, Jody politely declined. It was a game she played, treating James like an old acquaintance who didn't matter very much. Her game seemed to infuriate James, which was her objective.

Still, her entanglement with James had shaken Jody to her core. She left him in June 1992, but could not even think about another relationship with a man for five years. She, the divorced wife of a California doctor, was sharing an apartment with a girlfriend and driving an ancient red hatchback. How could she face the humiliation of explaining this to another man? How could she admit the terrible, ego-smashing things that she allowed to be done to her? How could a caring, decent, super-intelligent man feel anything but disgust and pity for a jerk like her?

Then in the spring of 1998, Jody met a new man, a doctor. For the first time in almost 10 years, Jody felt like she was alive. After dating him for a few weeks, she wrote him an eight-page typewritten letter explaining her history with James Montgomery.

The doctor spent an afternoon patiently asking Jody questions, trying to fathom how this international, sophisticated woman could have allowed it all to happen. After that, the topic hardly ever came up.

By the time I contacted Jody McClure in September 1999, she and the doctor were engaged to be married.

Chapter 19

Violence erupted in East Timor, a tiny country I never heard of, in September 1999. East Timor was located, not surprisingly, on the eastern half of the island of Timor, 400 miles from Australia. The other half of the island was part of Indonesia. On August 30, 1999, the people of East Timor voted for independence from Indonesia, and anti-independence militias went on a rampage. More than 1,000 people were killed; women and girls were raped; and almost all of the country's infrastructure, from schools to the electric grid, was destroyed.

James told Sylvia that because he was already in Australia, the U.S. Special Operations Command asked him to file a report on the troubles in East Timor. He sent it to her:

> Pro-Indonesian militias control the Ermera district, 19 miles south of Dili, and the towns of Maliana and Liquica. In reference to Maliana, UN Mission in East Timor (UNAMET) spokesman David Wimhurst said September 3, "It is very clear that the militia are in control."
>
> There are two basic questions. First, will the UN Security Council approve a peacekeeping mission in Indonesia? Most agree that at some point a peacekeeping mission will be necessary, but there is no agreement as to when. Even if the UN does launch a peacekeeping force, logistics would require a month or more to deploy the force – while the roof could blow at any moment. Only Australia has volunteered 2,100 troops as an interim force while New Zealand has said it will join a UN operation.

Was James in East Timor? Despite the official-sounding nature of his report, it was unlikely. So we tried to learn what he was really up to. Sylvia looked for other women, and the screen names he used to lure them. I looked for money. Through Internet searches I located every major bank in Eastern Australia—Sydney, Melbourne and Queensland—and sent them a message:

I am writing to inquire about the status of my husband's account with you. He is very ill and we need to get his affairs in order. Unfortunately, I do not have his account information. My husband's name is James Alwyn Montgomery, and his date of birth is 7/14/41. Our marriage certificate is recorded at the Registry of Births, Deaths and Marriages, Sydney, NSW. The date is October 10, 1996. I would be happy to send you a copy if you require it. Thank you for your help.

Several banks told me the procedures I needed to follow to make an inquiry. I got started, hoping to find a pile of cash.

While Sylvia and I were investigating James, it appeared that the FBI was not. Almost three months had passed since we met with the FBI agent, Jody Petraccci, in my home, but no investigator called me. No one called Sylvia. The court ordered me to turn over my evidence of James' fraud to his attorney. I was stalling—I didn't want to tip James off—but I was running out of time.

Perhaps I had something that would get the FBI's attention. I called Jody Petracci.

"Not long after I met James, he faxed me some papers entitled 'Ruff Workin September,'" I said to her. "It's a list of terrorists, drug runners and money launderers, with addresses and phone numbers. I don't know if it's real, but do you want it?"

"I think we would be interested in that," the agent replied, in a tone that sounded like a major understatement.

I sent over a copy of the list. Maybe it would inspire the FBI to do something.

My court case wasn't making any progress either. At a case management conference before Judge Charles Middlesworth Jr. on September 21, 1999, the attorneys were still debating James' contribution to my credit card debt. Stephen Browndorf, my husband's attorney, argued that I could keep running up the cards, costing his client money. By this time I was in credit counseling, so all of the cards except two were closed. The judge modified the order—James still had to pay $850 per month, and I had to pay all new charges within 30 days.

Then my attorney, Julie Davis Lisa, complained about James' case information statement. He was supposed to list all his income, expenses and assets on a standard form. The form he turned in was virtually blank.

"He has no assets and no income," Browndorf explained.

"His bank records indicate he's eating sushi and buying clothes, so for him to come back and say he doesn't have any budget is ridiculous," Julie countered.

"He doesn't have any income," Browndorf repeated. "He can't earn income in the U.S. He filed no income tax return in the U.S. and never has. Under Australian law, you only have to file income tax if you earn $10,000 in country—in Australia. If he earns money in China—he doesn't have to report that any place."

The judge interrupted. "For this divorce proceeding, he has to report all his income—no matter what the source."

"I'm looking at his bank account," Julie interjected. "If he's going to receive $29,000 in one month, he's going to have to report that somewhere, in some fashion."

"It ain't his money," Browndorf said.

"Another month he got $6,000, another month $3,000, and I only got the last three months," Julie said. "I think there's an explanation, whether he's an Australian citizen, an American citizen or a Chinese citizen."

"I gave you an explanation; you just don't like it," Browndorf countered.

"It doesn't make any sense," Julie replied.

Judge Middlesworth intervened. "That's the same problem I have with him saying, 'I didn't file a tax return; I have no income,'" he said to Browndorf. "He obviously has living expenses. But he didn't detail any of his living expenses whatsoever. Maybe someone else is paying them for him, but that does not mean he doesn't have any living expenses. If he's learned how to live for nothing, then he has an asset that is very valuable, and would be subject to equitable distribution."

Julie and I laughed. Browndorf did not.

"He has no home; he has no rent; he has nothing there," Browndorf insisted. "He has no telephone. There are motels he's staying at that somebody else is paying for."

"If he's living in a hotel, that's the expense, and if somebody else is paying for it, that's the income," the judge stated. "You can't say they net out to zero and therefore he has no income and no expenses."

Browndorf finally conceded that James would be back in the country on September 29, and he'd try to get my husband to provide his financial information. Then the attorneys argued about turning over credit card statements, bank statements and business records. The court finally set a deadline of October 12, 1999, for all information to be provided.

After training three mornings a week all summer long with my rowing buddies in the quadruple scull, we entered the masters' quad event in the King's Head Regatta, slated for September 26, 1999, in King of Prussia, Pennsylvania.

I'd been corresponding all summer with John Zunski, the dek hockey player. When I told him about the regatta, he finally suggested getting together. King of Prussia wasn't far from where he lived.

Although I liked the idea of meeting—and wondered what took him so long to ask—I knew finding each other at the regatta would be extremely difficult, which I pointed out in an e-mail. There were hundreds of people milling around, no easy meeting places, and all the rowers were dressed alike.

"You're right, muddling my way through a sea of tall, muscular blondes would be tortuous," John wrote back. "But it is an adventure I'd be willing to undertake!" Still, he agreed that a prior meeting would be helpful, and suggested getting together on Sunday afternoon a week earlier, in Sea Isle City, New Jersey.

While growing up, my family frequently vacationed in Sea Isle; it was a typical Jersey Shore resort—bursting with people during the summer, dead the rest of the year. John said he'd be waiting for me in the pavilion overlooking the beach at the end of John F. Kennedy Boulevard, the main route into town. "I'll be the guy reading the John Irving book," he wrote.

After a 40-minute drive, I parked right on Kennedy Boulevard—with the tourists gone, it was easy. I walked up to Sea Isle's version of a Boardwalk—an elevated asphalt promenade along the beachfront. Sitting on a bench facing the ocean, with his feet up on the rails in front of him, was a guy reading a book. I walked over to him.

John heard me coming and jumped up. "Donna?" he asked.

"Yes," I said. "I take it you're John?"

"That's me."

In his initial e-mail, John told me he was five feet, 10 inches tall and 175 pounds. Seeing him in person, it was obvious that he had told me the truth; this was already an improvement over my husband. He had straight, fine brown hair that hung to his ears, brown eyes and glasses. John told me that he looked younger than his 35 years, and it was true. I would have pegged him at 27. He even dressed like a kid—he was wearing baggy nylon shorts and a t-shirt.

"How about we go for a walk?" John suggested.

"Okay," I replied. We started down the promenade, which was practically deserted, even though it was a pleasant, sunny day. I asked John about the book he was reading—*The Cider House Rules*. He told me about the story and his fascination with John Irving, and from that point on, conversation never lagged. Before long we were back where we started. Just down the ramp was an outdoor bar in an oversized gazebo, where we sat and ordered beers.

"So tell me about this New Age stuff," John said. "I'm really fascinated by it."

I was surprised by the request, and unsure of how to respond. "'New Age' is a pretty broad term, and there's a lot to it," I said. "I don't think of myself as an expert, but I guess I've had some experiences."

"Like what?"

"Well, I see someone, Elaine, who I refer to as an energy worker. In my sessions with her, I sometimes get glimpses of what happened in my past lives. So I guess you could say I believe in reincarnation, and I believe that we're all connected energetically to each other."

"Cool! Are you familiar with Joseph Campbell?"

"I've heard of him, but I don't know anything about his ideas."

"He did a TV series, and I have the tapes. They really resonate with me. Campbell says, 'Follow your bliss.'"

"Well, that's certainly a New Age concept."

John invited me to dinner. We walked to the Dead Dog Saloon, just a few blocks away. Our animated conversation continued, and John asked if he could come to my regatta the following Sunday—at least now he knew what I looked like. I agreed to meet him. During the week, our plans for after the regatta evolved to include a paintball game at his new facility. It would be an interesting date.

On Sunday, my teammates and I arrived in King of Prussia two hours before our 1 p.m. race to check in and rig our boat. I kept looking for John, but didn't see him anywhere. By the time we were called to launch, he still hadn't shown up.

My heart sank. Not again, I worried. I didn't want to be blown off. Again.

We were carrying our boat to the dock when I heard my name called. "Donna! Good luck!" John finally made it—he had a hard time finding the place. I was excited—and relieved.

My crew placed our boat in the water and paddled the three miles upriver to the start. This was my first head race rowing in the bow and I was nervous; it was my responsibility to steer our course. But there was no time to dwell on my anxiety. The race officials called our boat into the chute. "Twenty meters to start," we heard through a bullhorn. "Ten meters to start. You're on the course."

We took a power 10—10 hard strokes—then settled into our racing cadence. Roll up to the top of the slide, drop the oars in the water, push with the legs, pull with the arms. Repeat. Repeat. Every five or 10 strokes, I looked over my shoulders to make sure we were going in the right direction. Stay on course; don't hit a bridge.

We rowed at a good clip, and cranked up the speed to sprint at the end. After 17 minutes of full power rowing, we crossed the finish line, exhausted. We came in second, which was good for a medal.

My teammates and I were thrilled. John was impressed.

After the regatta and a stop at Starbucks—my date, I learned, was addicted to Starbucks coffee—I followed John's white pickup truck to his rink, Echo Valley Dek Hockey. The facility was located in rural Phoenixville, Pennsylvania, behind a small water park.

The rink was outdoors, in an open field surrounded by trees. It was 160 feet long, 80 feet wide and enclosed by a wall—the lower half was wood, the upper half was chain link fence. A small building attached to the rink housed an office and pro shop. Two sets of bleachers were filled with spectators—a tournament was underway.

Teenagers in helmets and pads wielded hockey sticks as they chased a small plastic ball up and down the rink. I didn't know anything about hockey, so I couldn't follow the game. But I could certainly see that John ran quite an operation—between players, officials and spectators, there had to be 200 people at Echo Valley Dek Hockey.

John just stopped by to check on the tournament—everything was running smoothly. So we left and drove down the street to his paintball field, a property occupied by an old, two-story house in a state of semi-disrepair. On a few acres of wooded ground behind the house, trenches and dirt hills created terrain suitably rough for paintball skirmishes. Precast concrete barriers and drainage pipes provided cover.

Ten of John's friends were there, ready for a game. We all suited up in one-piece coveralls—military-style camouflage—and masks. Then we were each issued a paintball gun and a supply of ammunition—gelatin balls filled with fluorescent paint that splattered on contact.

The players were divided into two teams—John and I were on the same team—and we played Capture the Flag. One team was supposed to sneak across the playing field, get the opponent's flag and return to base, all without getting hit by paintballs. After a few rounds of that, we started a new game—Speedball. The idea was for one team to wipe out the other by hitting everyone with paintballs. John and I were on opposite teams, and as soon as the game started, he was in hot pursuit of me. Before long I was splattered with paint.

By this time it was getting dark, and I had a long ride back to Atlantic City. I shed my paint-splotched coverall and John walked me to my car. I got in and lowered the window.

"Thank you," I said to John. "I had fun."

"Me too," he said. Then, after a slight hesitation, he asked, "Can I see you again?"

"I'd like that," I replied.

"All right," he enthused. Then he stuck his head through my car window and gave me a quick kiss.

I smiled. This man was so unpretentious and so sweet. So different from my husband. He was also a lot of fun. I liked him.

James was still trying to manipulate Sylvia. He sent her e-mail from Christchurch, New Zealand—"This is a great city to raise kids," he wrote. James also told Sylvia that, in honor of an "old Aussie custom," he bought two loose opals, one for each baby. He wanted to meet Sylvia in Philadelphia when he returned to the U.S. In fact, he wanted to spend the night with her.

"Over my dead body will I spend the night!" she wrote to me. But she led James to believe they'd get together.

"OK," James e-mailed to her. "Find a motel/hotel for me close to the airport—that last one was hopeless."

The hotel was hopeless? What hotel? When did he stay in a hotel, and who was he with? Sylvia took the opportunity to pounce:

> What do you mean by hopeless? I haven't stayed with you in Philly since October of last year. The last two times after that we stayed in The Holiday One I think it's called in Hammonton or a town close to there. I came to New Jersey! Something you'd like to tell me about?
>
> Miss you and love you — ME

"Think he'll even say who he was with?" Sylvia asked rhetorically. "No way! The fucker! Now I got him even more. Oh, yes, I love it. This is very good therapy."

Then Sylvia's pregnancy ended. All along, the twin boys were scheduled to "die" on September 28, 1999. That was in memory of their true short lives—it was the date that they were originally lost by Maddy, Sylvia's neighbor. Sylvia told James that she fell and lost the babies. James decided that he was conned and sent Sylvia a furious e-mail:

You can make the smartest person believe the dumbest scam if he really wants to believe ...

When I thought you were in danger some months ago—I asked some friends from the Philly NIS to keep an eye on you—they tell me I am being scammed—they have now been to your town four times! You are incredibly active for someone whose doctor won't let her drive and the smallest pregnancy in the world for month and twins. Just give me the Drs. name & tele #—we will take care of the rest.

The checks will keep coming. You didn't have to do this. The main reason I was coming back was you—I am canceling my plans to return to the U.S. No more bullshit please—you don't need to do it to get your money back.

Sylvia, however, didn't give an inch. She stuck with her story, accused James of stalking her and calling her a liar, and said that his informants couldn't be any good if they didn't know her doctor's name. Then she told James her intuition about him had always been right—all he cared about was money.

On the night that Sylvia "lost" her twins, I was working late in my office when I heard Jamie, the sugar glider, making strange noises. I went into the next room to investigate. Jamie was sitting in her cage, and I noticed a huge bulge in her abdomen.

It looked like a lump, and my thoughts immediately turned to the worst. When Herbie, the hedgehog, had a lump, it was cancer and he died. Did Jamie have cancer? Was I going to lose another pet? I was afraid that I contributed to Jamie's illness. I knew that sugar gliders were social animals, and if they didn't have a glider buddy, they sometimes died of loneliness. Donald was gone, but I hadn't gotten Jamie another companion. I couldn't afford it.

I worried myself to sleep.

The next morning I brought Jamie in her cage to the veterinarian. I woke my nocturnal pet and made her get out of her sleeping pouch. As she scrambled around the cage, the vet saw a tiny foot protruding from the bulge in Jamie's abdomen.

"It looks like she has a baby," he said.

"A baby! You're kidding!" I exclaimed. "Donald escaped almost three months ago. And the end of his penis fell off."

"Well, apparently, it still worked."

I was relieved—and thrilled.

Sugar gliders were marsupials. After just 16 days of gestation, an immature sugar glider, called a joey, was born and crawled from the vaginal opening to the mother's pouch. There the baby stayed, growing, for about nine weeks.

So before Donald left, he impregnated Jamie. (Just like a guy, I thought.) Then, 11 to 12 weeks later, there was a tiny new fur ball in my family. I saw the baby for the first time on October 3, 1999. Jamie was sitting on a perch in the cage, and the little creature, about two inches long, was lying in the bottom of the sleeping pouch, crying. I just caught a glimpse of it; then mom went to take care of her baby.

I was amazed at the miracle of life, and hoped my new pet would be a good luck charm.

"Congrats, Mama Marsupial," John wrote to me upon hearing about the newest member of my household. "Have any ideas for names?"

I decided to call the baby "Hope."

John and I continued with our e-mail friendship. I learned that he had been in a relationship for eight years; it ended a few months before he answered my personal ad. I also learned that besides the dek hockey rink, John worked nights at a small manufacturing facility as a computer operator. Mostly he babysat the computer while the backup software ran, passing the time by working on his novel. John sent me e-mail when he got home from work, which was 5 or 6 a.m. So when I sat down at my computer every morning, a message from him awaited me.

In one of them, John invited me to join him and his friends for the annual bonfire at the dek hockey rink, which was slated for October 23, 1999. "I'd love to see you in the flame's shadows," John wrote. "It would be-witching."

Before the bonfire, however, John went on vacation to Disneyworld in Orlando, Florida, with his sister and her family. Toward the end of his trip, he asked, via e-mail, if he could visit me when he returned. I was available, so we made plans to get together on October 13, 1999—a Wednesday.

John arrived that afternoon with a gift for me—a gray Mickey Mouse t-shirt, with his ears drawn as yin and yang symbols. I introduced John to my family—Beau the dog, Chuckie the chinchilla, and the sugar gliders, Jamie and Hope. John was fascinated by the gliders—especially the tiny baby, who clung to her mother's back.

We talked, laughed, went out to dinner, came back to my house—and then John became romantic. He kissed me; he caressed me; he spent the night. He was a wonderful lover, the best I'd had in years. Better yet, I felt like I could trust him.

Yes, the baby glider was a good omen—I felt a bit of hope. Perhaps my life was starting to turn around.

The turn of the century was approaching, and eBay, the Internet auction site, planned a special millennium promotion to sell "Great Collections." Each week, for the 10 weeks approaching the millennium, collections of items from one decade of the 20th century would be prominently featured. I contacted eBay about including our Titanic collection in the promotion. EBay wanted to do it.

I'd already sold a few things on eBay—like James' $600 Porsche Design briefcase, another expensive, frivolous purchase made with my money but without my knowledge. I took the briefcase with me when I left Florida and sold it for half-price to some guy in Japan.

EBay would feature items from the Titanic decade—1910 to 1919—during the week of October 29 through November 5, 1999. The auction company was going to provide plenty of free promotion for our sale. James, through his attorney, agreed to let me take the Titanic artifacts out of storage so I could photograph them. Then James refused to give his consent for the eBay sale.

My husband's attorney, Stephen Browndorf, said James was negotiating to sell the collection for $500,000 to a buyer who was somehow connected with Rupert Murdoch, the Australian publisher. My lawyer asked for proof that the deal was under discussion. James refused to provide any.

Then James' attorney said my husband would not engage in any negotiations unless I accepted the proceeds of his phantom sale as full and complete settlement of all my claims against him. And if I didn't accept the settlement offer, Browndorf would stop being my husband's attorney and James would default in the divorce litigation. That meant there would be no one to deal with, making my case more difficult.

The October 12, 1999 deadline for James to turn over information about his financial circumstances arrived. He provided nothing.

James was still under court order to pay $850 per month toward my credit card debt, plus another $1,500 toward my attorney fees. By mid-October, I should have received $4,050, but he paid me nothing—even though the bank records we subpoenaed showed that from June 2 to September 3, 1999, James received deposits of $55,955.

So on October 15, 1999, my attorney filed a motion on short notice for court approval to sell the Titanic artifacts on eBay and served Browndorf with the papers. Browndorf immediately resigned as my husband's attorney. A week later we were in court, at 1 p.m. on Friday, October 22, 1999. James, now officially acting as his own attorney, did not show up.

I was not surprised. My husband's antics indicated that he did not take the divorce proceedings seriously, so I thought our request for the eBay sale would be a slam dunk. I was wrong.

"Have you been able to serve your motion papers on the defendant?" Judge Middlesworth asked.

"No. I served them on Browndorf," my lawyer replied. "He was still Mr. Montgomery's attorney at that time. I then spoke to Mr. Browndorf to get information on how I could reach Mr. Montgomery. And I left him messages on Wednesday and Thursday at the telephone number listed in another letter. Then yesterday I got some e-mail addresses, so I e-mailed the information to Mr. Montogomery.

"Just now, at about 11:45, I got a phone number for Mr. Montgomery in China, and my office called Mr. Montgomery and said that we were in court in front of Judge Middlesworth on the motion, and said, 'Do you want to take the phone number?' Mr. Montgomery said, 'I don't need the phone number,' and hung up.

"In my e-mails to Mr. Montgomery, I wrote the court may allow you to appear via telephone, here's the phone number for Judge Middlesworth's chambers, so while I didn't serve the papers on Mr. Montgomery directly, I feel that I served them on his attorney of record, while his attorney was his attorney, and furthermore, I don't think this would be a surprise to Mr. Montgomery, because we filed a consent order allowing Ms. Andersen to take the artifacts out of the storage facility and photograph them and describe them for the purpose of putting them on this eBay auction. And I think that Mr. Montgomery is trying to play games, by having his attorney file a substitution of attorney when he gets our motion, and by not responding to our messages and e-mails, and definitely now, he's aware that we're in court. And if we aren't able to get this project going, we're going to miss our chance to exhibit the items on eBay.

"Mr. Montgomery's only response was, 'Well I have a deal I might be able to work out for $500,000. I'm not going to tell you anything about it, but I'm not going to make the deal unless you agree to take this and go away, without providing any discovery.' So it wasn't even a real settlement offer that we could sit and consider, and then when I didn't take the deal, now Browndorf is no longer Mr. Montgomery's attorney, and now you can't get notice, and too bad for you. 'I'm in China; I'm out of reach.'"

Julie took a breath, and Judge Middlesworth spoke. "I think my question was, did you serve the defendant with the papers?" he said. "I didn't mean to unleash the floodgates."

Julie laughed, a tad embarrassed. "Sorry," she said. "No. I did not serve the papers on Mr. Montgomery."

The judge asked why it was so important to sell the Titanic artifacts on eBay, and why it was critical to sell them between October 29 and November 5. My attorney replied that eBay was the most well-known Internet auction, and the Great Collections promotion was a one-time opportunity. I said that if everything sold, the proceeds would cover our $190,000 in debt.

"What do you propose would happen if you sell everything for $190,000 and then the defendant turns out to have had a bona fide offer for a half-million dollars?" the judge asked.

"I don't believe the defendant has a bona fide offer for anything," I replied.

"I ask you to assume that's what happens," Judge Middlesworth pressed. "How do you propose the defendant to be compensated, if that turns out to be the case?"

For two and a half years, I'd seen James lie about his deals. I knew he was lying again. But I couldn't think of a reply.

Julie jumped in. "He can't wait until it's too late, and then get back with his proof and say, 'I could have had a bona fide offer.' Now is the time for him say, 'I've got a bona fide offer.'"

"That's why the notice issue is so critical," the judge stated.

"I agree. But I don't know what else I can do. I've got a guy who says, 'I'm in China; I'm out of reach.'"

"That gets back to my question of why is it so critical to sell these items during this particular two-week period."

The judge and my attorney went around and around—what was the rush?

Why did the artifacts have to be sold on eBay? Weren't there other auction sites? And Judge Middlesworth didn't agree that my husband had been properly notified about our motion to participate in the auction.

"I think I'm getting stuck in a game here," Julie said, frustration apparent in her voice. "Browndorf is his lawyer until he files a substitution of attorney."

"I'm not saying you did anything wrong," Judge Middlesworth said. "I'm just saying that I don't think the record here supports a conclusion or a finding that Mr. Montgomery has had service of this application."

Sitting at the plaintiff's table, I couldn't believe what I was hearing. My husband did not show up. James did not submit his financial information to the court, and he refused to pay me as Judge Middlesworth had ordered. He hung up on my lawyer's secretary when she called to tell him about today's hearing. James was using legal shenanigans to jerk me around. And all the judge was worried about was making sure James properly received the legal papers.

"He knows we're here," Julie said.

"How do you know that he knows we're here?"

"Because my secretary talked to him. And I sent him e-mails and messages. If he doesn't want to pick up his message, he's the one walking out on this litigation. And Ms. Andersen shouldn't be left hanging for that."

"If he does default in the litigation then you can proceed without him."

"Meanwhile, we lose our chance of selling the items on the Great Collection."

"Have you had anybody appraise these items?" the judge asked.

"No, we haven't. We don't have any money to do that. All of Ms. Andersen's money is wrapped up in this project. She's in debt. We were in front of your honor before about that issue. Mr. Montgomery was ordered to pay *pendente lite* support. He hasn't paid anything. He's not going to pay anything. His lawyer told me on the phone when I talked to him that he's not going to comply with the order. He's not going to comply with any discovery."

With that, Judge Middlesworth said he would permit us to continue making plans on the assumption that the sale would proceed on October 29. In the meantime, my attorney was required to serve James with the papers, and prepare evidence detailing why I would suffer irreparable harm if we did not sell the items on eBay. Another court appearance was set for 9 a.m. on October 29, 1999.

I left the courtroom completely frustrated. It was obvious that James was lying. It was obvious that he was not negotiating in good faith. It was obvious that he had no respect for the legal system. Yet there I was, unable to move forward, because the legal system protected the con man's rights—rights that the con man didn't even care about.

A clear, crisp evening was forecast for John's bonfire. We'd been exchanging e-mails all week—mine were now addressed "Dearest Donna" and sprinkled with romantic innuendo. The bonfire flames weren't the only ones burning.

John sent me directions to his home in Royersford, Pennsylvania. He lived in a nice development, and gave me a tour of his two-bedroom, two-bath condo.

It was furnished in early bachelor—a sofa from one relative, table and chairs from another. The only furniture he actually bought was a king-sized waterbed and the wall unit that surrounded it. Obviously, the guy had his priorities.

First on our agenda was another paintball game. I got splattered. Then, after a casual dinner in a local bar and grill, we drove to John's dek hockey rink, site of the bonfire. A massive pile of wooden pallets was ignited, and we, along with a group of John's friends, drank beer and stared into the flames. The real fireworks, however, took place later that night on the waterbed.

I stayed with John well into the next afternoon. When I finally got home, Beau let me know that my absence was noticed by jumping all over me. I told this to John in an e-mail that I sent thanking him for the lovely weekend.

"You can mention to Beau that absence makes the heart grow fonder," John replied. "He may wag to that one. I'd like to hear his opinion. I, too, am wagging my tail about the last two days. It was a hooter. Oops, Freudian slip. I mean it was a hoot."

John continued to make me smile.

I wrote my certification—my personal statement—for yet another set of court filings in support of the eBay auction. It was laced with frustration.

"If I am not permitted to proceed with the sale of the Titanic Artifacts on eBay, I will be forced to file bankruptcy," I wrote. "As I have stated previously to this court, James Montgomery is a con man. He is a sociopath. He makes money, and gets his jollies, by professing his love to women, convincing them to support his business schemes, bleeding them dry and then leaving them. I was a victim of this fraud. But I was not the only victim."

I included information about other women my husband scammed. I reiterated that James had no legitimate buyer for the Titanic artifacts, and our best hope of recovering our money was through the eBay sale. I pointed out that James had not complied with previous court orders.

"The court has ordered James to pay me, and he has essentially thumbed his nose at the American legal system," I wrote. "This court can imagine my frustration that my criminal, con man husband's rights of notification are being placed before my rights of survival."

My lawyer did not use much of the certification that I wrote—venting was not a good legal strategy. She drafted a brief that laid out an argument according to New Jersey legal precedent, and sent the documents to my husband at the hotel in China and his rented Florida mailbox. I suggested that we also ask Sylvia to notify James via e-mail. She was still in touch with him—that's how we got James' phone number in China.

Sylvia was happy to forward the e-mail—to her, it was another opportunity to needle James. He had already surmised that Sylvia had passed on his phone number. He wrote to her, "You majored in bullshit and betrayal but I will eventually get money back to you—just don't count on me for chit chat."

So Sylvia wrote back:

> Yeah okay whatever. If my number wasn't left all over the place I wouldn't be having the hang ups and the nonsense that is going on. And if you are calling me a LIAR! I'm not.
>
> I blew Donna off and if no one can contact me all the better. I didn't do anything and I didn't marry her, you did. And all that you ever did was scream at me about being married!
>
> You did this not me and it's not my fight it's yours. I want everyone to leave me alone. I didn't ask for this mess nor did I create it. I have enough problems with PA courts I don't need them from NJ. You think whatever you want to, you always do!

My lawyer wrote a short e-mail to James, advising him of the hearing scheduled for October 29, 1999, at 9 a.m. She sent it to Sylvia with a note at the top: "Please forward this to Mr. Montgomery via e-mail. This is a court order."

James replied to Sylvia:

> This is NOT a court order, this is Donna's lawyer—you are being bluffed—you live in PA—the judge sits on CIVIL matters in one county in NJ. Just do what everyone else does and do nothing! I am about to leave the last phone link that is reliable for five days anyway.

Not surprisingly, James did not show up for the hearing on October 29, 1999. We, however, brought reinforcements—John Glassey. After my lawyer made her arguments for why we should be allowed to sell the items on eBay before the divorce was final, Judge Charles A. Middlesworth asked John for his views.

"EBay has just chosen to do this decade by decade thing; it's a big promotion," John said. "We were selected to be in the 1910 to 1920 group. This is a great opportunity for us to find out if there is a market to sell it in that way. And that opportunity is just here now, and if we're not available, they're just going to pass us by and fill in someone else. The longer we go away from when the movie was out, *Titanic*, a lot of the items in this exhibit will decrease in value. So the longer the timeline goes, the less the value."

"What exactly is the extent of your personal financial interest in the exhibit?" Judge Middlesworth asked John.

"I have about $100,000 out. That was all cash."

"Do you know what Mr. Montgomery's investment in these artifacts is?"

"I never saw Mr. Montgomery put money into this project," John replied. "All the money that was brought to the project was from three sources: myself, the English fellow, and the original investors, who ended up forfeiting the project.

"I know that Mr. Montgomery and Ms. Andersen put money on their credit cards, and whenever we got money into the company, we tried to pay off their credit cards. But of personal knowledge, he never had gainful employment during the time I was working on this project with him. So I don't know where he was getting any money to put in this project. I don't think he put any personal money into it."

After a few more questions, the judge said he'd permit the sale.

Halloween was John Zunski's favorite holiday of the year. For Halloween 1999, he turned his living room into a crypt. It was pitch black, except for candles and strobe lights. Synthetic cobwebs hung from the ceiling to the floor. Somewhere he got a full-size, fake wooden coffin, and in it lay one of his young employees, who was dressed up and proclaimed to be "Miss Dead America."

All week, in our e-mail exchanges, he asked what I was going to wear. I finally suggested that we go as the Addams Family. I'd be Morticia, and he could be Gomez. "I'd love to be Gomez, that is, of course, if there are perks for me," John wrote. "I always wanted to see what Morticia hid under that dress of yours, I mean hers."

"Of course there are perks for you," I replied. "But you have to kiss my arm, my neck, etc. etc."

As if John needed a reason to kiss me. He had already confessed that, during our first walk on the Sea Isle City promenade, he felt like he knew me well, and had an almost uncontrollable urge to hold my hand. But he did control it, not wanting to scare me off. Now, anytime we went out, he took my hand.

So I put together a Morticia outfit. I pulled an old black gown out of my closet—it had a plunging neckline and a slit on the side. I went to a party store and bought a long black wig, a black feather boa and the longest fake eyelashes I could find. I also went to Macy's, where my credit card still worked, and bought new black lingerie—including a garter belt and stockings.

I drove to John's house and put on my costume—banning him from the bedroom while I dressed. John wore a suit, white shirt and a fake moustache. Then we waited—John had told friends to stop by, and put flyers in his neighbors' doors. But only a few people came over, so John decided to take the show on the road.

He and a friend loaded the coffin into the back of his pickup truck. Four of us squeezed into the front seat, and another car followed. John drove to a friend's house, put the coffin on the front lawn, rang the doorbell and then ran back to the truck, waiting to see the reaction of the homeowners. The gag was repeated at a few stops, and then the coffin fell apart.

That was it, game over. Plus, since I'd been sitting so close to him in the truck, John put his hand on my thigh, and discovering what was under my black gown, decided he'd have more fun at home. We got back to his condo and he pulled the black wig off of my head—it did look ridiculous. He kissed my arm, my neck, my lips, pushing me into the bedroom. Pulling back the covers on the waterbed, John revealed what he had hidden between the sheets—a dozen roses.

After all the court battles, the Titanic sale on eBay did not go well. We made only $11,000 in the auction—nowhere near the $190,000 we hoped for. Our big-ticket artifacts received no bids at all. They apparently weren't nearly as valuable as James claimed.

I was disheartened. Frustrated. Frequently I had trouble sleeping. Either I couldn't fall asleep, or I woke up in the middle of the night and remained awake, my mind churning.

I asked God, spiritual guidance, anybody, for assistance. One evening, while meditating, I received a clear message from Guidance: "Go through the records again—you have missed something. Look in the blue folder." I did have two blue folders in my file drawer, but they just held bills to pay. I tore my office apart and searched through every box, looking for another blue folder, but found nothing.

According to Maggie Kay, the psychic, I was supposed to be sitting on a pile of cash by the holidays. Well, it was almost Thanksgiving, and there was no end and no money in sight. I was still sending letters to the Australian banks, with no luck. The court would not allow me to do an asset search on my husband until the divorce was final, which wouldn't happen until January or February, giving him plenty of time to hide money. I was working, but not to capacity, and I didn't feel the desire or initiative to start growing my business again.

I was tired.

At least there was one bright spot—my new weekend lover, John Zunski. Sometimes he came to Atlantic City; sometimes I went to Royersford. I wasn't sure if John had long-term potential—I thought I'd have more in common with an executive-type guy. Still, John was loving, entertaining and physically comforting. He was my oasis of normalcy amid the ridiculous daily drama of my life. And he still sent me clever e-mails:

From: Dekhd
Subj: Gutter Speak

Dearest Donna,

I'm sure after this weekend you will not have to be reminded of my affinity for Gutter Speak. You may see me in a new light, albeit a blue one. Although, I promise to be on my best behavior until Saturday night, or whenever else you choose for me not to be. ;)~

Please refrain from typing in French, granted I have no way of judging your spelling or grammar, I still would be inclined to kiss and lick my monitor screen; a truly disgusting thought considering how dirty it is.

My salty one, you think Beau licks you for salt. HA!

As always you have all my moral support as you grease the frying pan for James' frying. As the saying goes: too much is almost not enough!

Until I read your words,

I bid you, my salty one, adieu,

John
Not only am I in your heart, I'm on your delete key; I know where I stand ;)~

I asked John if I could join his family for Thanksgiving. Although things were fairly patched up with my family, I'd learned that it was best not to talk to them about the odyssey of my divorce. So I went with John to his parents' home, where I enjoyed a delicious turkey dinner and easy, non-judgmental conversation.

Afterwards, John and I returned to his condo. He wanted me to hear one of his CDs—*Christmas Eve and Other Stories* by the Trans-Siberian Orchestra. The band was part progressive rock, part classical and part heavy metal. The album was a Christmas story, sprinkled with strains of traditional carols, in a rock opera style. The band's first-ever live performance was scheduled for the Tower Theater in Philadelphia, and John got us tickets.

He put the CD on his stereo, cranked up the volume, and sat on the sofa beside me. The music started with piano chords, soon joined by a deep, operatic male vocalist, singing of an angel on a mission from God. Then came a heavy electric guitar riff, followed by more piano, more vocals, and more electric guitar, incorporating strains of *Silent Night*. I was transfixed.

John pulled me close, then closer. Halfway through the album, he pulled me to the floor, and we made wonderful love to the magical music.

As anticipated, James did not show up for his deposition. On November 30, 1999, my attorney filed a motion to enter a default against him.

According to our favorite psychic, Maggie Kay, who Sylvia consulted the next day, we would clean out James' bank accounts. Before long, we would have all the money we wanted.

I actually found a bank account in Sydney, Australia. A customer service representative conveniently gave me the address of the branch where my husband's account was located. Pretending to be the diligent, concerned wife, I corresponded with the bank branch to find out how to submit a power of attorney. My husband, I told her, was dying, and I needed to tend to his affairs, which would include transferring the assets to me and closing the account.

"James is heartsick," Maggie told Sylvia in her reading. "He has a feeling that you're up to something, but he can't figure out what it is, because he believes you love him. But he was planning to kill you after the babies were born."

She had more predictions: When I went into divorce court against James, the judge was going to "fry his ass." By the end of January, or mid-February, all our troubles would be imaginary. And after the divorce was over, John would propose to me.

For three Christmas seasons I pretended to be a happily married woman in love with my husband, while trying to figure out how to pay the enormous bills incurred by said husband. By Christmas 1999, I was still struggling financially, but at least I was truly in love.

John and I settled into a nice, comfortable romance. Every morning during the week, we exchanged cleverly written e-mails sprinkled with lusty innuendo.

On weekends we were together, enjoying animated conversations and indulging our lust.

Especially on Sunday mornings, when we'd sleep late, make love and shower together. It was like being on vacation—all we needed was a cabana boy to bring us towels. We started calling these leisurely mornings "Cabana Sundays." John named himself "Raul" and volunteered for the job of cabana boy. I'd never experienced someone who seemed so thrilled to be with me. My love life was delightful, and for the first time ever, I looked forward to the Christmas holidays.

John's family exchanged gifts on Christmas Eve—attendance, he said, was "mandatory." I dropped Beau off at Dad's house on the evening of December 23, 1999, then drove up to John's. All week, he'd been telling me about his Christmas decorations, although they did not include a Christmas tree. I had a spare tree—the small artificial one that I'd brought to Florida the year before. I arrived at his condo about 10 p.m. with the tree, decorations and gifts.

"Hello, love!" John greeted me at the door. "Merry Christmas!"

Holiday music was playing on the stereo. I looked around for his decorations, and saw garlands and a few candles—it was a good thing that I brought the tree. I set it on a low table in the living room and decorated it, which took all of 15 minutes. Finally, I was ready to relax. John was always good at helping me unwind. He led me into the bedroom. The lights went out and the passion started.

"I have a surprise for you," John said.

Suddenly the room was bathed in a soft, multicolored glow. John had lined the wall unit surrounding his waterbed in tiny Christmas lights. Music drifted in from the stereo. The effect was enchanting.

"Do you like it?" he asked.

"It's beautiful!"

Our passion continued, with new tenderness and new energy. It felt so good that I didn't want to stop, even though we hadn't implemented birth control.

We used natural birth control, meaning we took precautions when I was ovulating, which included December 23, 1999. But that night, surrounded by holiday music, bathed in multicolored light and making love to a man I loved, I didn't want an interruption. In my heart, I hadn't given up my desire for children. All I ever wanted was a chance for a normal family. I was 43 years old and running out of chances. John and I hadn't discussed a future. In fact, he'd said that he didn't really want children. But he didn't ask about my pregnancy risk either. Maybe he'd changed his mind.

Ecstasy overcame us. Then we fell asleep, our bodies caressed by the glow of Christmas lights.

I woke up on Christmas morning as excited as a kid. Employing my best shopping skills, I managed to put a stack of presents for John under the little artificial tree, courtesy of a Macy's one-day sale. John had three presents for me— two books and a big mystery gift. I unwrapped it, and found a compact stereo to replace my old one that didn't work.

I was deeply touched. "This is fabulous," I said. "Thank you so much, John."

For the first time in my adult life, I felt full, happy and complete on Christmas morning. I snuggled with John on the sofa. "You know," I said, kissing him, "this is the best Christmas I've ever had." We kissed some more, and before long, the Christmas spirit moved us to the waterbed. The romp, unfortunately, made us late for dinner with my Dad.

The next day, Sunday, we drove to the home of my younger brother, Greg, in North Jersey. Two weeks earlier, his wife, Trish, had given birth to their first child. Holding the infant made me think about the chance John and I had taken a few nights earlier. Was I a little bit pregnant? If so, what would happen?

Then we had to go back to work. I thought I'd soon see John again—December 29 was his birthday. "Do you want me to come up?" I offered.

"Nah, don't worry about it. I'm not taking off of work."

"But it's your birthday!"

"Well, when you have a birthday at Christmas time, you get used to not celebrating it."

"That's terrible! Birthdays should always be celebrated!"

"Really, it's no big deal. I'll see you on Friday."

Friday was New Year's Eve, 1999—the end of the millennium. All the casinos, bars and restaurants in Atlantic City were trying to outdo each other by throwing the most lavish—and the most expensive—parties. It was nuts—$700 per person to go to dinner? Forget about it.

Ads for one casino party, however, caught my eye. A really fun dance band, Johnny O and the Classic Dogs of Love, was playing at Trump Marina, and the tickets were reasonably priced. So John and I had a nice dinner at Chez Donna, then danced the night away at the casino.

The entire world was supposed to celebrate the new millennium, and before I met John, I worried that I would spend the holiday alone. Again. But I did have a date for the biggest party night of the century. I had a good time. I even won money in the slot machines.

I dared to hope that the new millennium would be better for me than the old one.

Chapter 20

My divorce trial was scheduled for January 20, 2000 before yet another judge—Max A. Baker. At that time, my attorney would ask the court to award me $908,000—the money James had taken from me, which was $227,000, plus triple that amount in punitive damages. We would also ask for his shares in the Polytechnique Group corporation, which owned the Titanic artifacts, along with attorney's fees and authorization to sell James' MG, which was still parked in the driveway next to my house.

As we prepared for the trial, I vacillated between confidence that the money would come through to save me, and terror that it wouldn't. Charging fraud and demanding punitive damages in a divorce was unusual, but my case seemed strong. I had thorough documentation of the money taken from me, and plenty of evidence that James did it intentionally—to me and other women. Sylvia Banning, Jody McClure, Kathleen Maloney and the parents of Gale Lewis, James' deceased wife, all agreed to testify for me. They all wanted to see James held accountable for his actions.

Still, after watching the court fastidiously protect the rights of my con man husband when we wanted to sell the Titanic artifacts on eBay, I wasn't sure that justice would prevail. So I was taking matters into my own hands and going after the money in the Australian bank. I asked Sylvia to help, offering to split whatever money we found.

The bank required a power of attorney letter, drawn up by my solicitor—the Australian term for lawyer. I was not about to ask my divorce attorney to do it; I didn't even drop her a hint about my plans. Nope, my lawyer in this matter was named Sylvia Banning.

I designed conservative-looking stationery on my computer for "Sylvia Banning, Attorney at Law," and got it printed. I found a standard power of attorney letter on the Internet and copied it onto the stationery. Sylvia and I signed the letter. It was notarized and sent to Australia, along with copies of my passport and marriage certificate. I did everything asked of me, and awaited the bank's final response.

Would it work? Would I gain access to the account? I didn't know.

In the meantime, the FBI was finally investigating James. Jody McClure, Kathleen Maloney and John Lewis were all interviewed. Would law enforcement take any action? I didn't know that either.

The uncertainty surrounding every issue of my life made me nuts. Hoping for answers, I visited Maggie Kay, the psychic, on January 12, 2000. As she turned the cards, she confidently predicted that my troubles would soon be over. I would definitely gain access to the Australian bank account, which she said was fat with a million dollars.

"Clean it out," she advised. "You might have a little apprehension that you might get involved with something illegal, but you're not. You're his wife. How many wives raid bank accounts? Are you supposed to face him in court?"

"The divorce trial is next week," I replied.

"Get that money out before then."

Maggie studied the cards further. "I'm trying to figure out how you're getting away with this," she said. "Unless it's easier in Australia. Because you're getting away with it. After you clean that out, you're going to have to watch for your life. He'll be stalking your place. Just get the police on him and put him in a nuthouse where he belongs. Because you're the one that's getting power of attorney. There's not a damn thing he could do to you.

"Don't worry, I don't see you getting rubbed out," Maggie assured me. "By the time he gets around to it, he'll be in prison, in shackles. If he shows up for this hearing, there's a possibility that they might haul him off to jail."

Every time she turned a card, Maggie made another prediction:

• I would find two bank accounts in Australia, one large and one small.
• James was going to try to get the divorce trial postponed.
• James was being watched by either the FBI or CIA.
• James changed his mind; he's not coming to the divorce hearing after all.
• I wouldn't go to prison, even after taking his money.
• My husband's big thrill was taking women over.

"By the end of the week, with a little magic, you're feeling wonderful," Maggie predicted. She turned another card. "There's the ocean. Across the waters—there's the first quarter moon—money being transferred. By the time he finds out, he'll be scared to come near you, because that bench warrant will be on him. He'd have to change his appearance drastically before he could show up."

"Maybe it would be an improvement," I joked.

"I doubt it. His black heart shows on his face," Maggie said. "Your guardian angel protects you from harm. Thank God I don't see no danger."

Several times Maggie said my boyfriend, John Zunski, wanted to marry me. "John is very serious about his feelings for you," the psychic said. "Are you serious about him? You may end up marrying him. It's coming into play here. I think you and him are not only soul mates, you're twin flames."

Although Maggie's prediction gave me hope that maybe, just maybe, my quest for romantic partnership was over, I didn't want to scare John off, or put any pressure on him. I never told him what the psychic said about us getting married.

We'd already had one scare—after our unprotected sex at Christmas, I thought I was pregnant. But the scare only lasted a few days, and afterward, we agreed that we wouldn't take any more chances.

Everything was ready for my day in court, but I was nervous. Could I explain what happened and have it make sense? Would the judge think I was a complete fool for falling for James' lies, or would he recognize that I'd been conned by a professional? Would my husband actually show up? The possibility of James making an appearance scared me—I knew how convincing he could be.

I was also scared about my plans for James' Australian bank account. The bank sent me the final "Authority and Indemnity" instructions—all I had to do was sign it, have it witnessed (by Sylvia again), fax it in, and I could take the money. I decided to hold off until the divorce was almost final—I didn't want to give James an opportunity to show up in court and accuse me of theft, even though he had been quite happy to steal from me for two-and-a-half years. I decided to do it the day before my court date, January 19, 2000.

When that morning arrived, Julie and I finalized the strategy for my testimony. First, I'd discuss my pre-marital assets, including my home, business, savings and good credit. Then meeting James and the representations he made to me, such having as a net worth of $2 million to $3 million. Then the financial arrangements during our marriage—he ran up the bills; I paid them. Then the Titanic. Then the break-up, and discovering a string of women who were also conned. Finally, Julie wanted me to prepare a summary statement about how the marriage affected me.

I wrote out my statement. "Marrying James was the most devastating experience of my life," it started. "This man proclaimed he was head over heels in love with me on a daily basis. It was all nothing but a lie, a calculated lie so that I would marry him and pay for his pursuit of his ridiculously grandiose dreams."

Then the trial was postponed.

Julie called me with the news early that afternoon. There was a conflict in the court schedule—the postponement had nothing to do with James or me. As I hung up from the call, I felt like all my emotional energy—anticipation, fear, anxiety—had no place to go. My feelings turned into numbness. I had to live another month in limbo, waiting for my fate to be decided.

On the day that I should have had my divorce in hand—January 20, 2000— I faxed the final authorization document to the bank in Australia. I would soon have access to my husband's account. With the money I planned to pay my debts, cover my living expenses and write my book. A week later, I gathered the courage to inquire about the balance in James' bank account. The customer service representative in Australia cheerfully told me the amount. Contrary to what Maggie predicted, it was not a million dollars. The account held A$6,300.

I was stunned. Crushed.

That little bit of money was not going to allow me to focus on my book. Once I split it with Sylvia, it wouldn't even cover my expenses for a month.

Apparently, Maggie was wrong.

My troubles would continue.

What was I going to do?

I was able to make one decision—still not wanting to jeopardize my divorce, I let the money stay, temporarily, in my husband's account. I'd raid it closer to my court date.

Beyond that, my brain was filled with conflict.

Perhaps James really didn't have any money—I saw, up close and personal, how quickly he spent it. But how could that be? He had taken a total of more than a million dollars from me, Sylvia, Jody McClure, Kathleen Maloney and the Lewises. I assumed he took money from other people too. Did he really blow it all? Was there nothing left?

Perhaps when I got my official divorce, I'd find his stash through an asset search. Yeah, right. Who was I kidding? The court might not grant me a judgment. And even if it did, James knew how to cover his tracks. There would be no paper trail.

Three days before my divorce trial, on February 13, 2000, I raided the bank account in Australia. I instructed the customer service officer to wire transfer the entire balance to an account that I'd opened just to take James' money.

The next day, February 14, 2000, Sylvia had another reading with Maggie. She still predicted that at the last minute, we'd find plenty of money. The psychic saw Sylvia and I as two little pirates, cleaning James out. She suggested that we try banks in Seattle, where she said James had married a rich widow, who apparently put her assets in his name. He also married another woman in Georgia. "He has two more pigeons on the wire, but it's going to blow up in his face," she said.

Sylvia told the psychic that she was coming to Atlantic City to testify. "No you're not," Maggie said. "You will not be in that courtroom."

The next day, James' money arrived from Australia. With the currency exchange, an Australian dollar was only worth 63 cents. So the total that showed up in my new bank account—$3,838—was even less than I anticipated.

John Zunski arrived at my house around 7:30 a.m. on February 17, 2000. He was accompanying me to my divorce trial for moral support. John Glassey would also be there as a third-party defendant, dragged into the fray by my husband.

Sitting in the courtroom at the plaintiff's table, I felt strangely detached. I'd been working toward this day, this moment in time, for months. Now it was here.

My attorney, Julie Davis Lisa, addressed Judge Max A. Baker. "It is our intention this morning to show that Mr. James Montgomery married Donna Andersen to use her financially, and once she had no financial resources left, he set her up to find out that he had a child during his marriage to Ms. Andersen, and at that time their marriage broke up," she said. "This is a pattern that Mr. Montgomery engages in."

Julie named the witnesses who would testify to the same experience—Kathleen Maloney, who gave James over $200,000. Jody McClure, who gave him between $200,000 and $300,000. The parents of Gale Lewis, who died while she was married to James. And Sylvia Banning, who gave James more than $100,000. "Sylvia Banning was supposed to be here this morning," Julie said. "Unfortunately she had to be in bankruptcy court."

It was true. A day before the trial, Sylvia called me and said she just found out that her final bankruptcy hearing was scheduled for the same day as my divorce. Maggie was right. Sylvia would not be in the courthouse to testify.

"It's our intention this morning to prove that Ms. Andersen was defrauded by Mr. Montgomery to the tune of $227,000, and that she has now become financially depleted: massive credit card debt, her house mortgaged to the hilt, and she's lost her savings. We're going to ask your honor to award her damages based upon breach of contract. Mr. Montgomery said that he would pay all her expenses, as well as all her credit card debt. As part of the fraud damages, we're going to ask your honor to triple her damages, as this is a course of conduct that he has engaged in with the intention of defrauding women."

My attorney was then ready to present my testimony and our exhibits. After I was sworn in, she began asking me questions.

"How and when did you meet Mr. Montgomery?"

"I met him via the Internet in June of 1996."

"I'm showing you exhibit one, page one. Can you identify this document?"

I looked at it. "Yes, that's a personal ad that Mr. Montgomery placed on America Online."

"And did you answer this ad?"

"Yes, I did."

"What about this ad attracted you, so that you decided to answer it?"

"Well, Mr. Montgomery told me in the ad that he was in his late forties. He said that he was involved in the development of Atlantic City. He said he was a film and television writer and producer, who had experience in Hollywood. He said that he was emotionally and financially secure. He implied that he had considerable social standing. And the one line at the end of the letter that appealed to me said, 'Life together must be a two-way street; make mine a happier journey, and I guarantee you will not feel any potholes along that highway.' So he sounded like a substantial individual."

"And did you respond to his ad with a written response?"

"Yes, I did. I answered the e-mail, and I realize now that with that very first e-mail, I essentially set myself up as a target."

"What was it about this e-mail that you think set yourself up?"

"The very first paragraph. It says, 'I've been doing business with a few of the casinos and quietly taking my earnings to the bank.' I told him I was 40 years old and had never been married, and I told him I was attractive."

"Looking through the other pages of exhibit one, pages five through eight, do these represent the initial e-mails exchanged between you and Mr. Montgomery?"

"Yes, it does."

"What specifically were representations that you relied on in deciding to meet him?"

"Well, I specifically questioned him about his age, because he sent me his resume and it seemed to have an amazing amount of accomplishments on it and so I said to him, 'Are you a child prodigy or are you really in your forties?' And he wrote back saying that he was a genuine baby boomer, and that his driver's license says he was born in 1948.

"In those e-mails, he also claimed that he had a net worth of $2 million to $3 million," I continued. "He claimed that he was in the process of establishing CelebAM on the Boardwalk, which was supposed to be an attraction that would have been built in the old Convention Hall. He claimed that he owned movie costumes that would be on exhibit in this entertainment place. He claimed that he was politically well-connected. He claimed that he was part of the Australian Special Forces attached to the United States government, and still going on missions. He claimed that he had won the Australian equivalent of the Medal of Honor while serving in Vietnam. He claimed that he owned a townhouse in Mays Landing. He claimed that he was an American citizen. And he claimed that he was in the process of establishing a themed construction business in Atlantic City. A lot of those, I later found out, turned out to be highly exaggerated."

"Were some of them, in fact, false?"

"Oh yes. He was not in his forties; I later found out that he was like 55 or 56 years old at that time. He had no money. He did not own the townhouse; it had been owned by his previous wife. And he was not an American citizen."

Julie then questioned me about the money I gave James—$10,000 to invest in the construction business, called the Polytechnique Group. Another $10,000 to buy the Central Pier option, which didn't exist. Putting our trip to Australia to get married on my credit cards. Building an office for him in my basement. Continuing to pay his bills.

"Did you and James ever discuss the fact that you were putting out all this money and using your credit cards to pay his expenses?" Julie asked me.

"Oh, absolutely. It was the source of several arguments."

"Tell me about exhibit three." This was the handwritten agreement that James signed promising to repay all the money I had given him.

"Exhibit three took place when we were having an argument about the money, because we fought about it consistently," I explained. "James kept saying, 'Don't worry about it; it's all going to come through; you're going to get your money.' And so I said, 'Okay fine. If that's it, then let me put it in writing.' So I wrote this down, and he signed it. I wrote, 'James Montgomery agrees to pay all the expenses that I paid on his behalf and he agrees that he's responsible for all the credit card debt.' And he signed it."

We went over my Quicken printouts, itemizing all the money I spent on James. The summary did not include personal expenses, such as the mortgage or food, only business expenses.

"What kind of expenses are on here, for example?" Julie asked me.

"The biggest ones are probably his phone bills," I answered. "I mean, in 1998, my phone bill was $9,000, because James had two cellular phones and two land-based lines in the house. The phone bills were just, like, ridiculous. I bought him a lot of airline tickets for his traveling to different places. And business expenses, supplies, computers—he's always buying computers."

"What kind of business was he running?"

"He told me he was attempting to get CelebAM established. He was always getting dressed up and running off to meetings. I have no clue if he actually went to these meetings. He was also trying to establish a television network dealing with Suburban Cable in Philadelphia. Anything that came along, he would come up with an idea for a get-rich-quick scheme, so to speak."

I testified about those schemes—the Polytechnique Group and the Titanic exhibition. For more than two years, my husband was coming up with brilliant ideas that never worked.

"How were you financially situated toward the end of 1998?" my lawyer asked.

"Desperate."

"Why?"

"All my credit and my savings were gone. I wasn't making any money. The credit cards were just about maxed out. James wasn't bringing in any money, and the Titanic show was not working out."

"Tell me what happened that you wound up in Florida."

"James made the acquaintance of a man by the name of Johnny Stuart, who owned On Stage Entertainment in Las Vegas. On Stage Entertainment also owned properties in Orlando, Florida. James told me that he had worked out a deal with Johnny Stuart to open the Titanic show in Orlando, in one of his facilities there. And so we were packing up and going to Orlando to try and open the show."

"And was there a show?"

"No, there was not. He never, in fact, had a contract with Johnny Stuart."

"So by February 1999, when you separated, what was your lifestyle like?"

"We were broke. I was absolutely desperate. The show was not going forward. There was no funding."

"What was going on with your business?"

"I had no business, except for one little newsletter that I did via phone as a subcontractor."

"What was yours and James' relationship like by February 1999?"

"Well, the same," I sighed. "We fought about money, but every day he'd say, 'I love you, I love you,' and all this other stuff, so I was just hanging in. But I was disturbed, extremely disturbed by the fact that I was broke, we were broke, and that my lifestyle was terrible."

"What happened in early February that led to your leaving Florida?"

"There was another show, another Titanic exhibition, being opened in Florida by a company called SFX. James seemed to feel that we could compete against a $7 million show." This was, my tone indicated, ludicrous.

I continued my story. "I thought our last chance was try to sell some of the things that we had to SFX. So I took the last $300 available on my credit cards and bought him a plane ticket so he could fly up to Atlantic City, and then go on to New York, to have a meeting with SFX. He was supposed to leave on February 9. On the way to the airport, we had an argument. I also asked him where were some rings that he had given me, because my intention was to take them to a pawn shop, and see if I could get some money for them. He told me that they were in a locked box in the apartment.

"So when I got back to the apartment, I went looking for the locked box. And it was there. I found a key; it was lying in the drawer. I open up the box and inside I find a birth certificate for a child that he had with another woman during our marriage. I find pictures of him with this child. I find a receipt from a computer that he was using, that he told me had been acquired from a business associate, which in fact had been bought for him by Sylvia Banning. And I found another receipt of another computer that had been purchased for him by another woman."

Julie then asked me to identify the birth certificate, photos and receipts, which she put into evidence.

"Once I found this stuff, I started going through every piece of paper I could find in his office, and I found a bank statement which indicated that Sylvia Banning had wire transferred money to him."

"What happened when you found these records?"

"I didn't tell James what I had discovered, because he was back in my house in Atlantic City, and I didn't want him to trash the place. So I packed up everything in the apartment, and sent back all the rental furniture, which had been rented in my name. I sold my car and took his car, which had been leased in my name. I packed the truck up, packed up all the pets, and as soon as I knew he was on the plane coming back to Orlando, I got on the road."

"What happened when you got home? Did you do any investigation?"

"The next thing that happened was I inadvertently got a phone bill in the mail. It turned out that James had a secret voice mail account during our entire marriage that I knew nothing about. The phone bill came in. Inside I found all these phone numbers for Pennsylvania, which is where Sylvia Banning lived. And I called her up. I said, 'This is Donna Andersen; I'm James Montgomery's wife; I'd like to suggest that you don't give him any more money.' She said, 'It's too late; I already gave him $92,000.'"

Someone in the courtroom gasped.

I described what I knew about Sylvia and James—they got romantically involved, then he pressured her to invest in the Titanic show. After I contacted Sylvia, we compared notes and started working together to find out what my husband was really doing. We became friends.

"She was a victim like me," I said. "I have no hard feelings toward her whatsoever."

I described more of what I learned from the piles of papers that James left in my house, and from talking to the other women: James married Gale Lewis before he divorced Kathleen Maloney, committing bigamy. He committed bigamy again when he married Kim Goodson 10 days after I left him, because he was still married to me.

My lawyer asked me to identify documents related to Kim Goodson—checks James wrote to her, which probably came from money I put into his bank account. Copies of his auto insurance that listed Kim Goodson as a driver of his MG, while he was married to Gale Lewis. A quote from an auto transportation company to ship the MG back to Kim Goodson, while he was married to me.

I described the relevance of more documents—United States immigration forms that indicated James was in the country illegally. Correspondence from lawyers demanding that he pay his bills. Printouts of more personal ads that James posted online while married to me, claiming he was widowed, and the five different screen names that he used.

"Describe some of the things that you found out about James," Julie said.

"What I found out was that James is an extremely skilled con man," I replied. "What he does is he gives you 'proof' to establish his credibility, 'proof' in quotation marks—letters from other people that will vouch for him. He makes you think that other people believe in him. When he wants you to give him money, he has to have an answer right away, before you have time to think about it. He lies fluently and proficiently, without blinking an eye. Any opportunity that comes along, he tries to twist to his advantage. And he preys on sympathy. Every time he had a problem it was somebody else's fault. He never did anything wrong."

I testified that when James did have money coming in, he gave none of it to me. Julie presented subpoenaed bank records, which proved that between December 1998 and September 1999, while I was broke, James had plenty of money. "When Mr. Montgomery received this money, over $117,000, did you receive any of that?"

"Two hundred dollars," I said. "He was ordered to pay half of the rental fee for the storage unit for the Titanic artifacts and for the bank vault storage, so he sent me $200."

Julie wanted me to reiterate my requests to the court. "You're asking for breach of contract, focusing on a fraud claim," she said. "Why do you think you have a fraud claim?"

"I think James set me up," I replied. "His entire purpose in getting married to me was simply to take my money. In fact, Sylvia and I met with the FBI in June, and turned over all the evidence that we had to them."

With this, Judge Baker asked a question. "Has he been reported to any law enforcement agencies?"

"Yes," I answered.

"What's going on with that?" the judge asked.

"I understand he's under investigation," I replied. "Sylvia did have an interview with the FBI at the end of August. I recently found out that the FBI had contacted Jody McClure and they've also been in touch with the Lewises, and they've been in touch with Kathleen Maloney."

My lawyer continued with her questions. "You feel that Mr. Montgomery misrepresented who he was and his businesses?"

"Absolutely," I answered.

"What he owned?"

"He was an expert at creating a web of lies."

"And the fact that you gave him money?"

"I thought we were building our future together. Since I was able to help in the beginning, I would do that, and it would all come back to me."

"So now, you're out money."

"Yes."

"And what about emotionally?"

"Well, James pretty much destroyed my life," I said. "I used to be self-sufficient. I had a business; I was making good money. I could do anything that I wanted to do. Now, my business is gone. I'm facing probably close to $100,000 in debt between the credit cards and the attorneys fees. I have to ask my family for help. I have to rely on friends to help me out. I've had to sell personal belongings just to try and make ends meet. A couple of weeks ago I had to overdraw my checking account to buy food. This is ridiculous. And to know that the entire thing was just a calculated scam on his part, just absolutely makes me sick.

"When I first met James, he said that he was head over heels in love with me, he talked about having children, he's promising me the world—and everything was a lie. He continued the charade throughout our marriage. He'd bring me flowers, he'd buy me t-shirts, he'd buy cards all the time, and if we had a fight he'd stand there with tears in his eyes telling me how much he loved me. Essentially what he loved was my money. I was just a cash cow to him.

"I found out that, at the same time we were engaged, he was soliciting a male prostitute; he continued to post ads on the Internet throughout our entire marriage. He met a woman in Ocean City at the same time he met me, and continued to have a sexual relationship with her. He met Sylvia Banning and continued to have a sexual relationship with her, two or three times a week. I don't know how many people he's been with. When I came back from Florida I had to go get an AIDS test.

"One of the things that upsets me is that James may have taken away my last chance to have children. I met him when I was 40 years old, I'm 43 years old now, and I may not be able to do this."

"Let me interrupt you," Judge Baker said. "Ms. Lewis is on the phone. Is now a good time?"

The judge swore in Loretta Lewis, who was calling from South Carolina— asking her over the phone to raise her right hand and promise to tell the truth.

Loretta began her daughter's story. When she met James Montgomery over the Internet in the fall of 1994, Gale Lewis was unemployed, taking temporary jobs as a management consultant. James started living with Gale the following spring, and before long, Gale had accumulated $20,000 in credit card debt, racking up $400 a month in interest charges. Upon learning that, the Lewises paid off their daughter's credit cards. It was the beginning of the cash drain.

"During the course of Gale's relationship with James, did she or James ever ask you for money?" my attorney asked Loretta.

"It was an ongoing thing. He had her call us for money all the time."

"How much do you think you gave them over the course of time that James was involved with Gale?"

"I tried to keep track of the money sent to New Jersey, but it distressed me so much that I asked my husband to be sure to keep an itemized record. Which he did. It's over $100,000."

"What reason did Gale give when she called you to say that they needed money?"

"He needed money for this radio station, or he needed money to do this or money to do that. And we sent it."

John Lewis, Gale's father and the executor of her estate, then testified that he and his wife sent their daughter, while she was with James, about $130,000. When Gale died, she had another $44,000 in credit card debt and $89,000 due on her mortgage.

After Gale's death, James expected to live in her townhouse free of charge. Instead, John Lewis drew up a six-month lease. "He signed it under protest, but he signed it," he said.

"He signed it under protest?" my attorney asked.

"Yeah, well, he didn't like it," John Lewis said.

"Mr. Lewis, did you give Mr. Montgomery a credit card that he could continue using?"

"He had one in a joint name, with Gale, I think that was for CompUSA. He asked me to leave that open, so I did not close that one, until after I got a notice from them that it was overdue, so that's when I closed it."

"And how much was owed on that?"

John Lewis consulted his records. "Let me see. The amount due on that was $8,223."

Then John Lewis said he sent $4,000 directly to James not long after Gale died. "He had to have that deposited in his account in Florida, because I think he was in Australia someplace, running out of money."

After establishing the amount of money they had given to James, my attorney had no more questions for the Lewises. Kathleen Maloney was on the phone, calling from Boston, Massachusetts.

Kathleen stated that she met James in 1988 while on a business trip to Marina del Rey, California. At the time she was 45 years old, made a good living, and had been divorced for 15 years. James told Kathleen that he was an executive producer, making an action movie. Kathleen went back to Boston, and from time to time James called her. She once met up with him while on vacation in Lake Tahoe, Nevada. Then James asked her for money.

"I was kind of taken aback, and I said, 'Gee, well, no,'" Kathleen testified. "And he called back; he really needed the money. He's got collateral, he had a car, and he has some cameras, all this type of thing, that would be mine; I could trust him. My girlfriend said, 'Absolutely no, you're crazy.' So I said that. I insisted that I wasn't going to give him any money, but the calls kept coming, the frequency of them, and finally, I ended up sending him like $2,500, less than he originally asked for."

In April 1989, James traveled to visit Kathleen, telling her that he wanted to check out the film opportunities and see if he could work from Boston. Two weeks later, all his plans changed—he wanted to move from California to the East Coast. She flew to California in the beginning of May 1989, and drove with him back to Boston. James moved into Kathleen's home.

"He wasn't there a week when he started talking to me about remortgaging my home," Kathleen said. She only owed $14,000 on her home, but by June she refinanced to $60,000. "I didn't have any credit cards. I didn't have any debt at all. And at that point, James needed this money to help him get established, and settle his problems with the Writers Guild in California. He was being sued for breach of contract because the movie fell through, and all these people had to get paid."

"After that, did you continue to give him other money?" my lawyer asked.

"That same year, he wanted to remortgage again," Kathleen replied. "This was when the rates were over 10 percent. I said no way. And he was like pouting; he'd act like a little kid. Stupid me went along with it and remortgaged again. Now we're up to $80,000. And we didn't go through my credit, we went through a loan company, probably the worst thing I could have done."

"Did you have to use your credit cards?"

"He didn't have any credit cards. All he had was American Express. He kept applying for credit. And he wanted me to get these cards. He said, 'You can get a card with Sears; you can get a card with anybody.' I think he did get a credit card with Sears. But I ended up with all these credit cards."

"What do you think the ballpark was?"

"We got married in March 1990; he wanted to refinance again. Now this time we went to the max; my mortgage was $160,000. And he had applications for two credit cards that he wanted me to sign. Which I did. I filled out the applications, got credit. And took a $10,000 cash transaction from the credit card company. And that was September, because we broke up in October. When he was gone, in January and February, and I'm looking at my life, saying, 'Oh my God.' Instead of going bankrupt, which I should have, I took out a home improvement loan for $25,000 to pay off all the credit cards. So now I have a $160,000 mortgage and a home improvement loan. He also sold my car back to a leasing company. So now I have the car on lease. The mortgage payment alone was $1,700 or $1,800, plus $300 for the home improvement loan, plus the car payment.

"Did you have to dip into your savings also?"

"There was no savings. Everything was gone. To this day I have nothing. I should have gone bankrupt, and I didn't. Don't ask me why. I have no idea. Maybe because I lived in my house for so long, I didn't want to lose it. I didn't know where I was going to live. I was too proud to do it; I don't know. All I know is the quality of my life went right down the sewer."

"Did you ever ask James for the money?"

"He never had any money."

"When your relationship broke up, why did it break up?"

"Well, the fact that I found him involved with so many women, that I found videos of him and women; he's like cheating on our honeymoon. I mean he was cheating the day we got married. The day after we got married. The man has the morals of a snake."

Jody McClure was the next of my witnesses to call in. She told of meeting James at a cocktail party for professional singles in Beverly Hills, California in August 1987. James was working for the fledgling Movietime network, after running what he described as a successful sales promotion agency in Australia.

At that time, Jody said, she was 56 years old, divorced and financially comfortable. "I probably had easily three quarters of a million dollars in assets, and a very interesting and unusual job. I was an international tour manager and traveled all over the world."

"Did you have any debt?" my attorney asked.

"None. Zero. I think I owed less than $30,000 on a half-million dollar home."

Jody and James started living together in May 1988. She soon began giving him money. "It started slowly," Jody explained. "In the summer of 1988, I started cashing in some of my stocks to help support, not only our living expenses, but his endless need for money involving this movie project he's now involved in. He's going to have written and produced an action adventure film, and it became one of those 'almost' things, it almost happened. In Hollywood, this is not surprising. The star was the big football hero from Seattle called Brian Bosworth, and I met Brian many times, and his agent, so these things happen. The director, who was almost signed, was a famous director whose name probably I shouldn't say. It was close. It took a lot of money to get to that point."

"Besides cashing in your stocks, how else did you find money to give James?"

Jody explained how, at James' urging, she sold her home and gave him the proceeds.

"You gave him $100,000?" Julie asked.

"Well over $100,000; I can't remember now. But it was over $100,000 in cash."

"How long were you and James romantically involved?"

"It ended in May of 1989, when he just disappeared. He left me. I know you and I discussed where he went at that time, but you haven't asked that question. The point is he left."

"We talked to Kathleen Maloney a little while ago," Julie said. "She said that she came and picked James up in Marina del Rey in 1989."

"Right, the same identical day—May 12. She apparently flew out and had met him. I had no idea of this connection at all. She believed he was single and in love with her, and she drove back with him to her home in Boston. All of which I found out months later."

After James left, Jody said, she was still in touch with him, on and off. In October 1990, he signed a promissory note, confirming that he owed Jody $180,000. By this time, James was married to Kathleen Maloney. A year later, James and Kathleen were split up, and Jody was living with James in Florida. Once again, she was giving him money—$2,000 here, $3,000 there, until it added up to $50,000, in addition to the promissory note, which James Montgomery never repaid.

"What was the net effect of this relationship with James on you financially?" my attorney asked.

"Oh, it was horrible. What can I say? He took enormous amounts of my money. I owe some company $700 or $800 for a word processing machine that he bought under my name. I just cracked and refused to pay for that one, and I've never, ever been able to get it off my credit record. I lost an enormous amount of money."

"What about your house?"

"Well, the house is gone; it was sold. Obviously I made some money on that house, the money he took from me. At any rate, financially, my relationship with James was beyond anything I ever dreamed a human being could do to another. I was one of the early people involved in a relationship with him, and I had no concept that anyone could be that evil."

"Did you think you were eventually going to get your money back?"

"Of course I did."

"Did he tell you he would work to help you get your money back?"

"James never said, 'I'll go out and scrub floors or drive cabs.' He was always going to make it in one of his endless projects."

Finally, Sylvia Banning was on the phone to testify. She said she met James online in May 1997, when she was 41 years old, and met him in person in September 1997.

"Did you and James begin a romantic relationship at that time?" Julie asked.

"Yep," Sylvia answered. "Well, not right away. It took a little bit, but yes, afterwards we did."

"Did you know that he was married?"

"No, I did not."

"What representations did James make about his age, his employment, background and his social status?"

"He sent me a death certificate of Gale Lewis and told me he had nobody hiding in a closet. He told me he was 49 years old. He said he owned numerous companies and named a lot of them that I can't remember, and I didn't understand. Actually he made himself sound very, very well off."

"When and how did you start giving James money?"

"He talked about Donna Andersen as basically a glorified secretary, kind of, that's the way I took it. I figured she didn't do a whole heck of a lot, because I had done quite a bit of work for him. He talked about John Glassey as a partner. He said that he wanted me to buy John Glassey out, and that if I gave him the money, I wouldn't have to worry about college for my son. The companies were lucrative, that it was something I should do if I wanted to put my son through college, which I do."

"How much money did you start giving him, and did it increase?"

"It would vary at different times. Like in the beginning, it wasn't a lot. It was like something here or there. Then it got more frequent and more intense. The money amounts would vary. The times would vary. Sometimes I blew him off and didn't give him what he wanted. I was starting to get a little leery about the things I was doing."

"I have in front of me an exhibit that is a bank record showing a $6,000 transfer from you to James. Is this something that you would do?"

"Yes. What I would do is I would take the money off my credit card. I would deposit it into my account, then drop it into his. Sometimes I would just make direct deposits to his. Or mail him money through the mail."

"There's a series of e-mails that we have as exhibit 15, and Donna previously testified that they were e-mails that you forwarded to her. Do you know the e-mails that I'm talking about where James is asking you to put money into an account?"

"Yes. That was the way it went. It was like, he had to do this because we're on a deadline, and he needed this because he was going to court, and if I didn't get this much, then the deal or something else they needed for the exhibit would fall through. That was typical."

"Did you feel pressured to give him money?"

"Yes."

"Did he say he was going to pay you back?"

"Oh yeah, most definitely. There would be returns on anything that I invested. I asked at numerous points for stock, which he never has to this date produced. Often I asked him for my money back, now he's got a song and a dance, well, this happened, and Donna and John are being rotten about things, I still need more money to buy them out as partners, and it just went on and on and on."

"How much money do you think you gave James over the course of your year-and-a-half relationship?"

"I think the bottom line is like $115,000, with interest, penalties, charges for taking the cash advances, all total."

"What is the net effect of your having taken out all these credit cards and loans?"

"I had to declare bankruptcy, and I've been to court twice about it. Today and in December."

"Did you think you were investing in his businesses?"

"Yes, I did. I thought I was buying John Glassey out. I didn't know too much about what he was doing with Donna, I mean, that didn't seem to faze him in the least. So I thought her interest in this was minimal. But I came to find out it was not."

Through two-and-a-half hours of testimony, John Glassey had been patiently sitting at the defendant's table, even though he wasn't the defendant. Judge Baker finally turned to him. "Is there anything you want to add to this?" the judge asked. "Anything you want to tell me about?"

"No, the pattern was the same with me," John said. "James purported to have all these projects going on, misrepresented the facts consistently, took money from me for the Titanic show. Always had excuses and delays, etc. Took money from a fellow in England, who's listed in the documents. And always had a reason why it was not coming to fruition."

"Ms. Lisa, I sort of jumped in," the judge said. "Do you have any questions for Mr. Glassey?"

"Did James ever tell you where he was going to put any of the money that he made off the Titanic shows?" my lawyer asked.

"The first thing was to reduce all the debt that had been accumulated, that I had put forward and the other investors had put forward, and then the profits would be divided 50-50 once it was in the profit mode."

"Did he ever say anything about offshore accounts?"

"Yes. He told me he wanted to have all of his funds sent to a Bermuda bank account, that he was not going to have any accounts in the United States, and he wasn't going to pay U.S taxes."

With that, the testimony was finished. Judge Baker called a 15-minute recess. When the trial resumed, he would give his verdict.

During the recess, I sat in the corridor next to my boyfriend, John. We didn't sit there for long. The bailiff soon called us to return. I hoped it was a good sign.

"I have had an opportunity obviously to listen to Ms. Andersen as well as the various other witnesses, all of whom have had direct contact with Mr. Montgomery," Judge Baker began. "At the outset I am satisfied that this was an application appropriately brought for divorce on behalf of the plaintiff, alleging various grounds for divorce, extreme cruelty as well as adultery.

"The plaintiff has testified in detail as to the actions of the defendant. I am also satisfied that the defendant has committed adultery with a Kim Goodson, and that therefore, it is appropriate for me to grant the final judgment of divorce in favor of the plaintiff on both the grounds of extreme cruelty as well as the grounds of adultery.

"There were no children born of this marriage, and unfortunately, as I heard in the story related by the plaintiff, and confirmed by Mr. Glassey as well as the other witnesses, there were substantial debts created by this relationship and a substantial dissipation of assets that the plaintiff had acquired prior to the time that she met Mr. Montgomery. I am clearly and completely satisfied that Mr. Montgomery met and got involved with Ms. Andersen for the sole and complete purpose of using her assets for his own personal and selfish gain. I believe, having listened to all the witnesses today, that it was Ms. McClure who said it best when she described Mr. Montgomery as simply being evil. It is clear to me. Unfortunately there are people in this world who for whatever reason, simply prey upon other people. It is clear to me from the testimony that Mr. Montgomery had a pattern, had figured out a way to find people who were, notwithstanding their success in life and their intelligence, vulnerable. He preyed upon that vulnerability. And unfortunately was extremely successful at it.

"Therefore, I am satisfied that the relief requested by Ms. Andersen is appropriate. It is clear to me that the testimony, the voluminous documents, the work that has been done, was necessary in order to piece together what apparently was a series of events perpetrated by Mr. Montgomery on a series of innocent, vulnerable women, to take advantage of their emotions, to cheat them out of whatever they owned. He has, in my opinion, based upon the evidence, committed fraud, breached the contract that he had with Ms. Andersen, for the sole purpose of defrauding her of whatever it is that he could take from her, and use for his own personal benefit."

Judge Baker then awarded me everything that I asked for: He gave me all of James' stock in the Polytechnique Group, so we could sell the Titanic artifacts. He made James responsible for all the credit card debt. He gave me permission to sell the MG. He ordered James to pay my attorney fees. He said James had to repay the $227,000 he took from me.

All that was left was my request for punitive damages.

"I am satisfied from the testimony that the $227,000 does not include normal living expenses that you would expect that married people pay for, food and those kinds of things," Judge Baker said. "These were in the nature of extraordinary expenses that Mr. Montgomery convinced Ms. Andersen to pay, as part of his intentional fraudulent scheme. I am also satisfied that this was not a business venture gone bad, where two parties enter into it knowingly, with their eyes open, and therefore lose their money. It is clear to me, based upon the testimony of Ms. Andersen as well as the other people that have testified, that this is the way Mr. Montgomery lives his life, and this is apparently the way he funds his lifestyle. That he met Ms. Andersen for the sole and complete purpose of defrauding her out of her assets. And unfortunately he was successful.

"Therefore, I do believe it's appropriate for me to assess and award punitive damages against Mr. Montgomery. I will award a punitive damage award against Mr. Montgomery in favor of Ms. Andersen in the amount of $1 million."

A million dollars!

I looked over at John Glassey. He had a big smile on his face, and gave me a thumbs up.

"Thank you, sir," I said to the judge.

Afterwards, my boyfriend, John, wanted to take me out for a celebratory lunch. We decided to go to a small restaurant near my home that served great food. But as we drove over, I was subdued.

"You won!" John said. "You crucified him! That's terrific!"

"Yeah," I replied.

"Aren't you happy?"

"Sure," I said. "But I'll really be happy if I can find his money."

Chapter 21

As I poured dry pasta into a big pot of boiling water, I heard laughter coming from the living room. In celebration of my divorce, I hosted a small dinner party on February 27, 2000. Sheryl Ginsburg, my graphic designer, and Bill Horin, my photographer, were there. I also invited a woman who played on my original Erasers softball team and her husband. The special guest was my new love, John Zunski, who was meeting my friends for the first time.

Everybody was enjoying themselves, which warmed my heart. The last time I hosted a dinner party, I was with James. On that occasion, my husband delivered a monologue and our guests nodded. I did not hear the friendly repartee that was currently drifting into the kitchen.

We sat down to eat, and the lighthearted conversation continued. John joined right in. Reticence was never one of his traits; John was proud of his ability to go on a colorful rant when necessary. Most of the rants were related to dek hockey. John played as a goalie; sometimes he didn't like a call and was vocal about it. The referees, who were his employees, ejected him from his own rink.

Usually John was funny. But as the six of us sat around the dining room table finishing dinner, John made a joke, sexual in nature, which was a bit too explicit for polite conversation. I was embarrassed, but didn't say anything.

A few minutes later, he did it again.

I didn't know if any of my guests were uncomfortable with John's comments; no one reacted. The rest of the evening was pleasant, and after everyone left, John helped me clean up. His inappropriate words were on my mind, but I couldn't think of any way to bring up a conversation about them that wouldn't sound judgmental, so I said nothing. The next morning, when we woke up, I was still stewing over the incident.

"What's wrong?" John asked me.

John was psychic like that—he knew something was bothering me, even though I hadn't said a word. If I denied there was a problem, he would know I was lying. So I took the opening and told him—his comments at dinner were too explicit, and I was embarrassed.

John was upset—not at me, but at himself. He agreed that he shouldn't have said what he said. He was angry with himself for embarrassing me. I wasn't happy about upsetting him, but I did feel he needed to be aware that he'd crossed a social line. Both of us felt terrible.

We discussed the matter in our next few daily e-mails. John wrote that the problem "touched on my biggest fear/phobia regarding us, which is that I'm out of my element, not intellectually, but socially." He also felt that he'd just reclaimed who he was, after giving up parts of himself to fit into his previous relationship, and he didn't want to do it again. I tried to reassure him—he didn't need to change who he was. But it didn't hurt to know how to handle social situations.

We survived the first rough spot in our relationship. We both expressed our opinions, fears and expectations of the future. Although it was uncomfortable, I felt like the episode brought us closer together.

With my divorce, John Glassey and I could finally liquidate the Titanic artifacts without asking anyone's permission. John worked out a deal to rent one of our lifeboats to SFX, the company exhibiting the authentic artifacts from the wreck. I worked out a deal with a British auction house, Henry Aldridge and Son, in Devizes, Wiltshire, to include our artifacts in their annual Titanic auction. The sale would take place in April, on the anniversary of the ship's sinking, and we heard it was the best way to move Titanic memorabilia. So on March 1, 2000, I FedExed three cartons of our stuff to England.

I was desperate to sell everything and get out of debt. I was also desperate to find James' money and collect the $1,253,287 awarded to me by the court. But one morning, I woke up with my stomach in a knot—again. I was terrified that it was never going to happen. This was not good. With all the self-help books I'd read, the psychics I'd seen and the spiritual messages I received, I knew that if I didn't believe the money would come, it wouldn't. My fear was working against my wellbeing. I needed to align my subconscious with my desire to find the money, and get all the energy flowing in the right direction.

All the gurus said to visualize what I wanted, and it would materialize. I desperately hoped they knew what they were talking about.

Clint Eastwood stood in the driving rain, his thinning gray hair plastered over his high forehead, the most forlorn man on the planet. Playing Robert Kincaid, a photographer for National Geographic, he gazed at the woman he loved, who was sitting in her husband's pickup truck, with so much longing that it was painful. Slowly he nodded, accepting her decision that she would not be running away with him. Meryl Streep, portraying Francesca Johnson, a fiery Italian girl who became an Iowa farm wife, almost did get out of that truck, almost did escape to join her true love, but she could not abandon her family.

My lover, John, lay on the sofa, his head in my lap, as we watched *The Bridges of Madison County* on a Sunday afternoon. It was a bumpy ride for him, because I sobbed through the second half of the emotional movie, and as my stomach heaved, his head bobbed up and down.

The passion between the man and woman in that movie was deep and palpable. When the film was over, John wrapped his arms around me. I was overwhelmed. I could not talk without crying.

I always cried at sad movies. In fact, I cried at sappy McDonald's commercials. But for many years, I did not cry over my own emotions or my own pain. Instead, an internal wall separated me from my life. I'd knocked out a few blocks, but it was still there.

John and I held each other while I calmed down. After an hour or so, we went out to dinner and visited Borders Books and Music to browse and sip coffee. Back at home that night, the movie was still with me as we went up to the bedroom.

John pulled me into his arms and held me close. "I love you," he whispered softly into my ear. "I love you. I love you."

I wanted to be in the moment like he was. I wanted to be totally focused on him, on my love for him, while I was with him. "I feel the wall coming down," I whispered back.

"Let it come down," he breathed.

I relaxed into him, into our love. I felt it envelope me, soothing my desperate hunger for connection. So this is what it's supposed to feel like, I thought.

Shortly after that Sunday, John asked if I'd like to go to Montana. A good friend of his, Travis Hawes,* had moved there. Travis invited John to visit. John invited me to go along, offering to pay my way. Imagine that! A man wanted to go on vacation with me, and he was footing the bill!

Of course I wanted to visit Montana. After all the trauma of the past year, I needed a break. We decided to go at the end of May, and John started making the arrangements.

My only current paying project—a job for Showboat—was cancelled, which caused me mixed feelings. On the one hand, given my financial state, any loss of income was bad. On the other hand, I really wanted to get back to writing my book. Suddenly, I had the time.

Sitting at my desk, I read the few pages I had composed after I got my divorce. What should come next? For ideas, I navigated to the Lovefraud.com folder on my Macintosh, which I created when I bought the domain name. In it were eight documents and one additional folder labeled "To investigate." I'd changed the color of the folder to blue. With a start, I remembered the message from Guidance that I'd received back in November, "Look in the blue folder." I'd looked all over my house and through all my file drawers and found nothing. But there it was on my computer—a blue folder.

Inside was one document called "Unidentified deposits." It was an e-mail that I'd sent to my lawyer requesting further details of two wire transfer deposits that I'd found in my husband's bank records. Who was wiring money to James? Or was he wiring money to himself? Had I found anything useful?

What I'd learned about his finances so far was not promising. According to the asset tracing company I hired, James Montgomery stopped paying his bills in 1993—three years before I met him. Eighteen different creditors—including American Express, Sears, Discover, Chase, Citibank and GTE Florida—had put his accounts into collections or charged them off. He was, the agent told me, a "career debtor."

I wished I had known that before I married the man.

While trying to decide how to proceed in the U.S., I launched another effort in Australia. I retained a solicitor named Leon Davis, from Sydney. He did a quick search of property records—nothing. To search for bank accounts, I'd have to send the solicitor my court order. I'd already called all the major Australian banks with my husband-is-dying ruse, but maybe, with a legal judgment, he'd get better results.

I was also in touch with an asset search company based in England that used more unorthodox methods of finding accounts. The company was highly recommended, but my contact wouldn't tell me exactly what they did—I got the impression serious computer hacking was involved. John Glassey and I agreed that when we sold the Titanic artifacts, we'd use some of the money to pay the company to hunt down my ex. I felt like I had to try.

During the 13 months since I left my husband, I focused on forcing him to pay the debts he piled on me. I doggedly pursued him and his money. But it was becoming apparent that my pursuit would not prove fruitful anytime soon, if at all. I was stressed, exhausted from the stress, and uncertain that anything would be accomplished. I began to think that if I stopped resisting my reality and started solving my financial problems, I'd be better off.

I owed American Express $10,473. I called the company and explained to the customer service representative that the debt had been incurred because of my ex-husband, and the judge in my divorce had found him guilty of fraud. I should not be held responsible for the debt—they should go after him. The representative said they'd launch a fraud investigation. A few weeks later, American Express sent me a form letter:

> Dear Donna Andersen:
>   According to documented company records, you released your account number to your husband. Our cards are non-transferable, and by releasing your account number, you accepted liability for any charges the person might make. Based on this information, we will not be able to handle this as a fraud dispute; therefore, this case is closed.

My hands shook as I read the letter. The judge found James Montgomery guilty of fraud. My husband was ordered to repay the credit cards and everything that he took from me—plus $1 million in punitive damages. I had a judgment, a court order. And it meant nothing to American Express?

Maybe it would mean something to the FBI. On March 24, 2000, I sent a letter to Deryck Bratton, the agent Sylvia met with almost a year earlier.

Dear Mr. Bratton,

Judge Max Baker has found James Montgomery guilty of every complaint I made against him. It has been one year since the activities of James Montgomery have been reported to your FBI office. Yet he is still at large, and still defrauding women. Quite frankly, I find this appalling.

You may want to know that I am in the process of developing a website to warn the public about James Montgomery and others like him. The callous lack of response by law enforcement agencies is certainly one of its major themes. And I assure you, with my experience as a journalist and marketer, this will not be an obscure website.

This was the sixth letter I'd written to Bratton, and for the first time, I got a response. He called me, and during our brief conversation, his words were a mixture of apology and defense. Bratton said they were still working on the case. It wasn't exactly a definitive statement, but I interpreted it as good news. If the case were over, I was sure he would have blown me off.

The issue, not surprisingly, was a chain. As my energy therapist, Elaine Anderson, dealt the Star+Gate cards during our session on March 29, 2000, they identified the biggest problem I faced with an illustration of a heavy, black chain. I thought the interpretation was obvious—debt weighing me down. Elaine agreed, but also saw another meaning—the chain was a series of connected links, the information and insights I was putting together.

In the weeks prior to seeing Elaine, I spent a lot of time crying, meditating and asking for guidance. One evening I sat cross-legged on the floor, trying to access the message buried in the painful block that I could feel in my heart. After an hour, words finally rose to the surface of my awareness: "I can't do what I want to do." I knew what the message meant. I'd always felt so responsible, pushing aside my own desires in order to do what was expected of me. In fact, for most of my life, I didn't even know what I wanted. That hidden belief—"I can't do what I want to do"—limited how I lived my life.

"I need to live now," I said to Elaine. "I can't postpone living until my financial situation is solved."

"Sometimes we keep waiting to live until this or that happens because we don't want to accept what is," Elaine replied. "It's our need to control. But how much control do we really have?"

"Well I have none," I said resentfully. "I took James to court and won. The judge awarded me over $1 million. But what good has it done me? I've been putting all my time and energy into looking for his money. Maybe someday I'll find it, but I don't know when. So right now, I've got to go back to work."

"That's probably a good idea."

"I've been getting the message that I should keep doing the advertising work. There's more information I need that will help me with what I really want to do, which is build my website about sociopaths."

I told Elaine the Internet domain name I'd reserved—Lovefraud.com.

"The problem with sociopathy is that no one knows what it is," I said. "Everyone thinks a sociopath, or a psychopath, is a serial killer. Sometimes they are, but usually they aren't. They're just lying, cheating, heartless bastards. The disorder needs to be named and exposed. These people are truly evil."

"There is a dark side, a shadow side. You're shining a light on it."

"I just want it all to go faster. If I could find his money, I'd work full-time on writing my website and writing my book."

Elaine laughed. "We always want things to move faster than they do. But there is a higher perfection," she said. "You have to stay in a place of trusting that."

Even though Elaine encouraged me to be patient, as I lay down on her massage table, we decided to focus on asking for relief from the debt. She lit incense and turned on her healing music. She walked around the table, requesting spiritual guidance to join us. Stopping at the foot of the table, she pulled my toes and squeezed my legs—not hard, but her touch caused me intense pain. She worked my shoulders and massaged my face, which was where I stored a lot of tension. Elaine then put her hand on my lower abdomen. "What do you have to say to release the helpless rage?" she asked.

I didn't know I had helpless rage, but there it was. As I paid attention to it, I felt alternating anger, despair and hatred of James and what he had done. I saw his face—crocodile tears running down his cheeks. I saw him making his speech at our wedding, telling the world about "this lovely creature that I've married."

"You son of a bitch!" I screamed, over and over. I cried. I raged. I pounded the table with my fists.

Then I started feeling another sensation in my abdomen—a pregnancy, a child. And it came to me—in one lifetime, I had been James' mother. He was a monster. He was rotten. He turned on me, criticized me, degraded me and physically hurt me. I did all I could for him. Nothing helped.

"He was unreachable," Elaine said.

In that lifetime, I felt like I failed as a parent. James grew up to be a criminal. I knew nothing but anguish.

"Let the struggle of these two souls be turned over to the light," Elaine entreated.

I felt the tension ease out of my womb, but it seemed to slide around to my back, between my shoulder blades. And there it stayed, like a massive muscle knot. "It's stuck in my back," I said.

Guidance told me that I was still carrying the burden. In fact, I had been carrying the burden for so long that it was part of my identity. They told me to let it go, but the knot wouldn't budge. "If I let go of the burden, I don't know what to replace it with," I said.

"Ask Guidance," Elaine said.

I did, and the answer came back: "Joy." Still, I couldn't get the energy block to move.

"They don't want you to hold onto this as a burden," Elaine said. To encourage me to shift my energy, she put on different music—a woman singing, "Turn it over to God."

I cried as I lay on the table. Then my back arched, and the negative energy started to drain.

"The burden is nothing; it's paper; it's nebulous," Elaine said. "Let it dissipate."

Slowly, my sense of over-responsibility, carried for many lifetimes, melted away. I felt lighter, and the spirit of John, my boyfriend, joined Elaine and me. He was one of the few sources of joy in my life.

"He really likes you," Elaine said.

"Yes," I agreed, feeling my lover's energy. "He thinks I'm funny."

In the physical world, I still had to ease the burden of my credit card debt, and I'd learned that calling the customer service reps was useless. I decided to take my case directly to the top officials of the credit card companies—with the Internet, it was easy to find out who they were.

I drafted a letter to Kenneth I. Chenault, president and chief operating officer of American Express. "I have been a victim of fraud," I wrote. "Unfortunately, this particular crime doesn't quite fit in with your company's definition of fraud."

My ex-husband, I explained, was a career con man who swindled all my assets. I proved in my divorce that he defrauded me, the judge found him responsible for all my debts, and awarded me $1 million in punitive damages. I intended to find Montgomery's money, but until I did, making the credit card payments was difficult. I asked for a one-year moratorium on my debt and interest payments.

I sent similar letters to the presidents of credit card operations at Citibank, Bank of America, Wachovia and Associates National Bank. Two weeks later, every one of my letters had been answered, although not by the presidents. None of the companies gave me a one-year moratorium, but some of them did adjust my terms:

• American Express issued a $500 goodwill credit to my Optima account, and reduced the interest rate to 6.9 percent for the life of the balance.

• Associates National Bank reduced my interest rate to zero percent for one year, and set my minimum monthly payment at $50.

• Bank of America also reduced the interest to zero percent, setting the minimum payment at $94.

• Citibank reduced my interest rate to 5.0 percent, after pointing out that my divorce decree was not binding on them and suggesting that I "contact Mr. Montgomery directly to make arrangements for repayment of these charges." As if I hadn't thought of that.

• Wachovia's letter said a customer advocate would call me, but the company did nothing.

I was wanted back on the pitcher's mound. At the Philadelphia Advertising Club, I ran into some of my old softball teammates, and they urged me to play again. Just as important, with my new focus on making money to solve my problems, I hoped for contacts that would lead to business opportunities.

But what kind of business did I want? My real mission, my destiny, was to develop Lovefraud.com, so I didn't want to lock myself into being responsible for newsletters again. I didn't want to manage the clients, designers, printers and problems anymore. The solution: I would focus on freelance copywriting. I'd be a hired gun.

I started to feel hopeful. I had a direction for my career. I'd be playing ball again in Philadelphia every week; I could use the trips for business as well. And our Titanic auction was coming up. If we made good money, it would really take the pressure off of me.

The auctioneers, Henry Aldridge and Son, considered our artifacts to be important to their sale—our Titanic card case was displayed in a full-color, half-page photo on the back of the auction catalog, and four of our items were featured on the inside front cover. They held the auction during the British Titanic Society convention in Southampton, England on Friday, April 14, 2000, the 88th anniversary of wreck.

On that day, the U.S. stock market crashed.

For two years, stocks had been skyrocketing on the strength of the "new economy"—the Internet. People were making paper fortunes on wild valuations of web media companies, e-tailers and "Internet pure plays." But despite the "irrational exuberance" in the stock market, 80 percent of 350 companies that had gone public with Internet business models were not showing any profits.

The morning of April 14, 2000, the U.S. government announced a 0.7 percent increase in the Consumer Price Index, sparking fears that the economy was overheating. Investors immediately bailed out of the market. The Dow Jones Industrial Average dropped 618 points—at the time, its largest decline ever. The NASDAQ fell 355 points, a one-day loss of almost 10 percent. The technology bubble had burst.

In Southampton, the Titanic auction went on as scheduled, but the regular collectors of expensive artifacts were not calling in bids—they were trying to salvage their portfolios. The auction was a bust. Only half of our items sold, and none of them brought the prices we'd hoped for. We made $7,740.

Once again, the Titanic sank. I couldn't believe my bad luck.

While my divorce was underway, my lawyer, Julie Davis Lisa, subpoenaed my husband's bank statements from First Union. Now that I had a judgment, I studied them carefully for clues about where James' money might be. I also studied statements from the bank in Australia. I requested copies of checks from Australia as well, but before they arrived James found out that I raided his account and angrily told the bank that he wasn't dead. The bank wouldn't help me any further.

From the information I collected, however, I determined that one of the mystery accounts I found on my computer—in the blue folder—belonged to James. On April 24, 2000, I sent my lawyer an e-mail requesting that she subpoena all the records for that account.

She wouldn't do it. Now that the discovery phase of my divorce was over and I had a judgment against my ex-husband, Julie explained, I was a "judgment creditor." I had to abide by the Fair Debt Collection Practices Act, and I no longer had the right to subpoena information about James' bank accounts. So the legal system gave me a judgment, and then, when I tried to collect it, tied my hands behind my back.

Even getting money from the accounts we knew about was burdensome. First my lawyer sent a writ of execution to the sheriff's department. The sheriff would levy James' bank account. Then I'd have to get a court order for the money to be turned over to me. I was also trying to get my judgment recorded with the Florida courts so I could go after any money James might have there. Plus, I needed an official copy of my divorce judgment to send to Australia.

But taking all these steps could, in the end, prove fruitless. According to a professional debt collector that I spoke to, with my judgment I could indeed get court orders to freeze my ex-husband's bank accounts. Then my husband could declare bankruptcy, and not be liable for the judgment. The banks would give him all his money back.

This was confirmed by another attorney in Florida. Generally, he explained to me, individuals who file for bankruptcy can have court-ordered judgments discharged—meaning they don't have to pay. Debts due to fraud, however, were an exception. The United States Bankruptcy Code prohibited a debtor from discharging liabilities incurred through "false pretense, false representation or actual fraud." At least I wouldn't have to worry about James getting away with not paying my judgment by declaring bankruptcy, because the judge said James defrauded me.

I retained the Florida attorney, and sent him my divorce decree. After reviewing it, he realized that I had a problem—there was no mention of James' fraud in the paperwork. My divorce lawyer had accurately written up everything that the judge decided—James was liable for the debt, he had to repay me the $227,000, and he had to pay $1 million in punitive damages. But she included nothing about the fact that James had committed fraud. It wasn't usually necessary in a divorce case.

"If your husband files bankruptcy, you might have to re-litigate the whole thing and prove again that he defrauded you," the Florida attorney told me. The best solution, he said, was to amend my divorce decree to include the court's findings of fraud.

That meant going back into court. This was a problem, because I'd just received a letter from the collections manager at Cooper Perskie April Niedleman Wagenheim & Levenson, where my lawyer worked. They would not represent me any further until I paid their bills, which added up to more than $20,000.

In the meantime, I found out through my U.S. asset search company that the mystery bank account in the blue folder was for James' International Institute for Continuing Education, and had a balance of $7,780. The business was incorporated on August 17, 1999, with James as the registered agent and director, and a woman named Sharon Decamp as the other director. Sylvia and I had previously found evidence of James' involvement with Sharon Decamp. In fact, Sylvia called the woman to warn her that James was a con artist. Sharon blew her off.

In my collection of subpoenaed bank records, I had proof positive that Sharon Decamp was giving James money. On May 15, 2000, I sent another letter to Deryck Bratton of the FBI:

> Dear Mr. Bratton,
> From bank records obtained through my divorce proceedings, I have discovered that James Montgomery has been taking money from Sharon Decamp of Florida for the past year. The dates and amounts I have found are as follows:
>
> | | |
> |---|---|
> | 4/27/99 | $2,000 |
> | 4/19/99 | $7,500 |
> | 5/7/99 | $7,500 |
> | 5/20/99 | $7,500 |
> | 6/3/99 | $2,000 |
> | 6/21/99 | $8,000 |
> | 7/1/99 | $9,750 |
> | 8/6/99 | $3,000 |
> | 8/16/99 | $3,000 |
> | 8/13/99 | $2,000 |
> | 11/9/99 | $7,500 |
> | Total | $59,750 |
>
> I'm sure this is only the tip of the iceberg. Montgomery appears to be living with Ms. Decamp in Florida. All of this has transpired after Montgomery was reported to your office. How much more evidence do you need?

Deryck Bratton did not reply to my letter.

The lack of response from law enforcement agencies no longer surprised me. Every day brought me another disappointment, a new problem, a further setback. With mounting frustration, I began to believe that unorthodox methods were the only ones that worked. The asset search guys in England, who apparently had some dirty tricks in their bag, would probably be my best bet.

I e-mailed all the identifying information I had about James Montgomery to the lead agent. Searching for Montgomery's money would be expensive, he told me, and possibly fruitless. We could try going after one hot target. "But you are going to have to resign yourself to the possibility of writing off a good several thousand dollars in return for nothing at all," the agent wrote. "Nevertheless, I am keen to help—assholes like Montgomery really get under my skin!"

I wanted to move forward, and my agent started drafting a proposal. All of the agent's cases had code names—he called the James Montgomery investigation "Project Gila."

"Gila monsters were unpleasant lizards with a poisonous bite," he explained, "much like Mr. Montgomery."

Chapter 22

As John and I were flying to Montana on May 25, 2000 for our vacation, I spent much of our five-and-a-half hours in the air analyzing my ex-husband's travel patterns. I brought along James' bank records from our divorce, and by studying his ATM withdrawals and debit card purchases, I hoped to determine where he had been, and when. My objective was to supply as much information as possible to my overseas agent for Project Gila. I wanted the agent to find James' accounts and raid them.

According to the bank records, from August 1999 through March 2000, James never stayed anywhere for more than a month.

In August, James went from Australia to Florida to Atlantic City to Georgia to Florida and then to Christchurch, New Zealand.

He spent most of September in Australia, then went to New Zealand, back to Sydney, and returned to the U.S., arriving in Florida on October 1, 1999. A week later, he was in Atlantic City—that's when he signed the papers to dismiss his attorney in our divorce case. The next day he was back in Florida; then he went to California and on to China.

In November he was in Australia and New Zealand, returning to Florida on December 1, 1999. By December 18, he was back in New Zealand. James was in Florida again at the end of January; afterwards he spent February and March back and forth between New Zealand and Australia. On March 11, 2000, he was in China, then he returned to Sydney and New Zealand.

Or maybe not. To my surprise, on several occasions, the bank records showed transactions in two different countries during the same period of time. Even James, with his supreme confidence in his superhuman abilities, couldn't be in two places at once, so that meant someone else had access to his accounts. But who? I didn't know.

I brought my laptop computer (which James had purchased for me, with my credit cards) on the plane. I composed an e-mail to send to my agent, summarizing what I discovered. All I had to do was send the e-mail, and I'd be ready to forget about James and enjoy my vacation with John.

Rugged peaks filled the view from my tiny jet window as we descended into the Bozeman, Montana airport. Bozeman, in the Gallatin Valley, was surrounded by mountain ranges. We certainly weren't in flat, sandy New Jersey anymore.

The Bozeman terminal looked like a giant frontier cabin. The interior walls and columns were covered in brown and tan fieldstone, and massive exposed wood rafters supported the high angular ceiling. The look was thoroughly Western—and that was before I saw the eight-foot grizzly bear statue by the luggage carousel. We picked up our rental SUV—John's friend, Travis Hawes, recommended that we reserve a four-wheel drive vehicle. The rental company gave us a dark green, four-door Dodge Durango, and we drove the 10 miles into town.

The city of Bozeman was founded by John Bozeman in 1864—his objective was to make money off of starry-eyed travelers streaming west in search of gold. The town still had a frontier air about it. Main Street was lined with plain one- and two-story buildings, many of them brick. One was a former railroad warehouse that had recently reopened as a hip new bar and grill called the Montana Ale Works. "You can't miss it," Travis had told us. "I'll meet you there."

We expected to spend the weekend in Bozeman with Travis, who, when he arrived at the Ale Works, looked like he was a few years older than John. But Travis told us that we'd all be visiting his friends who lived at Flathead Lake.

"You'll love Flathead Lake. It's really beautiful," Travis said.

"How long will it take to drive there?" I asked.

"Only about five hours," he replied, in the same tone that someone in New Jersey would say, "only about 15 minutes." In the American West, everything was far apart, and four- to five-hour trips were as normal as a daily commute.

After dinner, we followed Travis to his small rented house in the foothills outside of Bozeman. It was still light enough to enjoy the view from his back porch—low mountains, tall evergreen trees and native vegetation, just beginning to bloom. The view did not include neighbors, roads or buildings of any kind. That was why people escaped to the West—to bask in the unspoiled landscape.

I still had one bit of official business to complete—I logged onto AOL and sent my e-mail for Project Gila. With that, I was finished. It was time for the party to begin.

Travis cracked three beers. Slowly the sky darkened, and our host built a little campfire in his yard. We sat around it, chatting and enjoying the cool evening. John and Travis kept drinking, although I soon had my fill. When I finally went to bed, exhausted, they were still at it.

The next morning John looked like the cloudy skies—his face was a dismal shade of gray. But there was no time for him to recover from an overabundance of alcohol. We had a long trip ahead of us, so we loaded up our rental SUV and got on the road. Travis drove, because John couldn't.

Our first stop was a shopping center on the edge of Bozeman to pick up food and other necessities. Travis and I left John in the car and went into the store. After making our purchases we walked back across the parking lot to the SUV. John was sitting on the running board by the open passenger side back door, trying to get fresh air. Then, as I watched, John leaned over and puked.

When he recovered, John started laughing. "You should have seen the look on your face," he chortled. "Shock. Horror. It was priceless."

At least John felt better after purging his stomach, because our first stop, one of the places he really wanted to see, was only 30 miles west of Bozeman.

The Madison Buffalo Jump was a high limestone cliff on the edge of a valley carved eons ago by the Madison River. For 2,000 years, buffalo jumps throughout the West were critical to the survival of Native American tribes. Before Europeans brought horses and guns, the tribes stampeded herds of bison off the cliffs, so that the animals plunged to their deaths. The bison were butchered, providing everything the native people needed to stay alive: food, clothing, tools and housing.

The gray clouds thickened as we drove into Madison Buffalo Jump State Park. Empty land, wrinkled during some prehistoric shudder, stretched in all directions. Much of the land was covered by low grass that was just starting to turn green, with occasional accents of scrubby evergreen trees. Then a massive, dull-gray trapezoid of stone rose up from the ground in front of us. It was the buffalo jump.

We were the park's only visitors. It started raining as we walked up the gently sloping land leading to the cliff. What struck me most about my first tourist stop in Montana was the vastness of the land. The scenery was so rugged, so majestic, and so unlike New Jersey—the most densely populated state in the nation, where towns and strip malls piled on top of each other. As we got on the road again, the overwhelming sense of space only grew. Interstate 90 picked its way westward, finding level valleys between the mountain ranges. We saw flat, fenced pastures with small herds of cattle munching on new spring grass, undulating hills rising behind them. Two hours into the trip, the land grew more rugged, and the flat pastures were ringed by sharp mountain peaks, still dusted with snow.

Every bend in the highway brought another stunning landscape. The rain stopped, and the sun broke through the clouds, creating dappled patterns of light on the slopes. I frequently asked to stop the car so I could take photos.

"It's really beautiful out here," I said to Travis.

"Yeah," he agreed, "people who visit here get kind of punch-drunk on it."

The shadows were beginning to lengthen when we reached the lowest tip of Flathead Lake, which was 28 miles long and 15 miles wide—the largest natural freshwater lake west of the Mississippi River. I thought I'd seen my share of spectacular landscapes for the day, but Flathead Lake was staggeringly beautiful. A glacier that melted after the last ice age created the lake, and mountains rose directly from its water. The road hugged the curving, forested shoreline.

Travis' friend didn't live directly on the lake; her home was up another winding road, at the top of a hill. Pitched in her front yard was a large hunting tent—accommodations for John and me. This was nothing like the compact model I brought to the Philadelphia Folk Festival. It was made of heavy white canvas and was the size of a small room—both John and I could easily stand inside it. Two low cots were already set up, along with a wood-burning camp stove that had an exhaust pipe through the roof of the tent. Northern Montana in the spring was still chilly, but with the stove and our down sleeping bags, we were toasty warm that night.

The next day John and I went to the lake. At an elevation of nearly 3,000 feet, both the air and the water were too cool for swimming, so we walked hand-in-hand along the water's edge. The beach was covered with glistening rounded stones of all sizes, which had been worn smooth by the action of the water. John and I filled our pockets with the prettiest ones we could find—shining reminders of our trip.

"I really like Montana," John said.

"It sure is beautiful," I agreed. "Every time we drive around a bend there's another magnificent view. I'm just amazed."

"You know, I really feel like I belong here. I might want to buy property out here someday."

This surprised me. "Are you serious?" I asked.

"Well, there's really no reason for me to stay in Pennsylvania," John answered. "The only reason I'm there is for my parents, and they're getting older. One of these days they'll be gone."

"What about the dek hockey rink?"

"I never considered that to be permanent. At least not for me. I made an agreement with my partner to run it for 10 years. When the time is up, who knows?"

That night John and I had the hilltop property to ourselves—Travis and his friends had already moved on to other destinations. By now, our tent felt downright romantic, and we let our passions run wild, which was challenging on a cot. Unlike sheets on a bed, my sleeping bag was not tucked in, so as John pushed close to me, the bag and I kept sliding, until I was doing a backbend off the end of the cot and my head poked out from under the wall of the tent.

We burst out laughing.

"Come back in the tent," John said, pulling me up.

"What a ride," I joked. "This gives a whole new meaning to Cabana Sunday."

"Visit the House of Mystery!" the billboard proclaimed. "Just ahead on Highway 2!"

John and I left Flathead Lake early on May 28, 2000, heading for Glacier National Park. After the fourth billboard touting the House of Mystery, I finally asked John, "What do you think it is?"

"I have no idea," John said. "It might be stupid."

"Well, we're on vacation. We're allowed to do stupid things. Why don't we stop and see it?"

"All right. I have no problem being stupid."

I anticipated an old haunted house, perhaps a two- or three-story Victorian, with an overgrown cemetery in the yard. So when we arrived at the House of Mystery, I was surprised to see an isolated, one-story commercial building with a rust-colored gable roof, surrounded by a large parking lot. It looked like a road-side convenience store. We walked in and discovered a tourist-trap gift shop. We were the only customers.

"Where is the House of Mystery?" I asked the clerk.

"It's out back," she replied.

"What is it?"

"It's a small house built on the Montana Vortex."

"Vortex?"

"Yeah—the Earth's gravity and magnetic fields are different here, so when you're inside the house, you can lean way forward or sideways and not fall down."

It sounded bogus, but the admission was cheap enough—$6 each—so we decided to check it out. The clerk pointed us toward a path that led into the woods behind the gift shop. It was a self-guided tour with a series of stations where signs explained strange phenomena of physics. To our surprise, the signs were telling the truth.

At one station—just a marker along the path—we could lean approximately 30 degrees sideways, without holding on to anything, and because of an invisible energy field, not fall over. At another station, two poles, exactly the same size, were erected upright and plumb on level grade, eight feet apart—yet one pole appeared to be four inches taller than the other. The space between the poles was called the "line of demarcation," and the laws of physics seemed to be different on the two sides of the line.

Then there was the House of Mystery itself. It was actually a large, one-room shed, with gaps between the horizontal plank siding and windows without glass. The entire building appeared to be crooked. A rope hanging from a rafter with a weight on the end did not dangle straight down—it drifted sideways, as if pushed by a strong wind. A broom in the middle of the floor stood upright, with no apparent supports. On a narrow wooden track, marbles rolled uphill. The energy, or gravity, or something about the place definitely felt skewed.

In less than a half-hour, we walked the path and experienced the distorted energy fields. Since John and I were the only ones taking the tour, I suggested that we go back to the beginning and walk it again. This was a mistake—I soon started feeling lightheaded, even nauseous. The spinning energy of the vortex made me dizzy. We cut the repeat tour short, bought drinks in the gift shop, and left. I pushed my seat in the SUV into the recline position, and gradually recovered as we drove the remaining 13 miles to our next destination—Glacier National Park.

The park's mostly unspoiled wilderness covered 1,584 square miles and extended to America's border with Canada. It had two mountain ranges, 27 glaciers, 130 named lakes and hundreds of species of animals—including grizzly bears, black bears, wolverines, moose, elk, bighorn sheep and mountain goats.

Glacier National Park was also the home of a civil engineering marvel—the Going-to-the-Sun Road. This 50-mile mountain road, completed in 1932, traversed the park from one side to the other, climbing the Rocky Mountains and crossing the Continental Divide. John heard that it was one of the most scenic roads in America, and we were there to drive it.

We inquired about the road at the Apgar Visitor Center, which was just inside the west entrance to the park. "You're in luck," the ranger told us. "The road opened this weekend. We just finished removing the snow."

Snow? It was Memorial Day weekend, and back in Atlantic City, people were on the beach.

"How much snow was there?" John asked.

"At Logan Pass it can be 80 feet deep," the ranger replied. "It takes about 10 weeks to remove the snow. Some of it we blast out with dynamite."

"How long does it take to drive the road?" I asked.

"Two or three hours, depending on how often you stop," the ranger said.

It was still morning, so before traveling the Going-to-the-Sun Road, we had time for a hike. The ranger suggested a trail that began right behind the visitor center. "It's a nice hike," he said. "But watch out for bears."

We started walking the narrow trail, with me nervously looking for bears. It took us across meadows and up a gentle slope. As the terrain became rockier and more forested, we crossed narrow streams filled with rushing water from the spring melt. Eventually we reached a hilltop clearing ringed by tall, gray tree trunks—once magnificent, now dead. It seemed like a good place to turn around. When we arrived back at the visitor center, I relaxed—we hadn't seen any bears. We hadn't even seen any chipmunks.

I thought driving the Going-to-the-Sun Road would be far less stressful. I was wrong.

The narrow, two-lane road followed the southern shore of Lake McDonald, which was the largest lake in the park. Then the road started climbing into the mountains. That's when it got scary.

The Lewis and Livingston mountain ranges featured a vertical rock cliff known as the Garden Wall, and much of the Going-to-the-Sun Road was literally carved out of it. The road clung to the mountainside, and its outer edge dropped off thousands of feet to the valley below. We were traveling from west to east, so the mountain was on our left. I was in the passenger seat, looking through my window over a ridiculously short stone border—not even a guardrail—at a plunge to certain death below. John, in the meantime, did not have his eyes on the road; he was craning his neck to look at the mountaintops as he drove. I was tense.

Still, the views were magnificent. About halfway along the road we drove through a tunnel that brought us to "The Loop," the road's only switchback; from there we had a dramatic view of Heavens Peak. Further along we stopped at a scenic overlook so I could photograph Bird Woman Falls, which cascaded 492 feet down the mountain. Finally we reached the highest point along the way, Logan's Pass, which straddled the Continental Divide at an altitude of 6,646 feet. Then we descended from the mountains back to the prairie, until the Going-to-the-Sun Road ended near the east entrance to—and our exit from—Glacier National Park.

The next day John wanted to drive another of the most scenic roads in America—the Beartooth Highway. To do it, we had to travel from where we were, almost at the northern border of Montana, to the town of Red Lodge, which was almost at the southern border—a distance of more than 400 miles.

The Beartooth Highway was a 69-mile section of Highway 212 along the Montana-Wyoming border. The road's elevation was over 10,000 feet—significantly higher than the Going-to-the-Sun Road. It would bring us right to the northeast gateway of Yellowstone National Park, where we planned to spend a few days.

The trip was long. But as usual, plenty of stunning scenery entertained us—every time we rounded a bend I caught my breath. Montana's sheer beauty put me in a good mood—especially since I was sharing it with someone I truly cared about. I felt peaceful, which was something I hadn't experienced in a long time, if ever. I hoped peace would soon become a permanent part of my life.

I was watching the grassy plains roll by as we approached Red Lodge, when a small sign by the side of the road caught my eye. "Look honey," I said, a bit flirtatiously, "a wedding chapel!"

John immediately took both hands off the steering wheel and held them up towards me, making the sign of the cross with his index fingers. He hissed, as if he was warding off a vampire.

I was shocked. What was that about?

Saying nothing, I turned back to looking out the window, but my peaceful state of mind was shattered. John kept telling me that he loved me. Why was he warding me off like a vampire? I didn't know, but I decided I was not going to raise the question. We were on vacation. We had three days left. I didn't want to spoil it.

I put the incident out of my mind.

Beartooth Highway lived up to its reputation for extraordinary beauty. Each turn brought dramatic mountain views—when they weren't obscured by fog. Driving was also dramatic, because in several locations, the road wound its way up the steep slopes with a series of hairpin turns and switchbacks—road conditions that I thought only existed in TV commercials for sports cars. Once again, John was looking at the mountaintops while driving, and I was looking out my window at the valley floor far below us. It was another white-knuckle ride.

Suddenly, at the highest point of the highway, we broke through the fog into brilliant sunshine. The road leveled off onto a wide alpine plateau. In one direction we saw acres of brown and tan rocks, seemingly devoid of vegetation. Looking in another direction we saw snow-covered mountain peaks that appeared to be at the same altitude as us. Mist shrouded the view below, but fluffy white cumulus clouds decorated the blue sky above us. I was in awe.

As John and I descended the mountains and got closer to Yellowstone, we drove through a part of the forest where the natural surroundings were seriously damaged by a past fire. Charred, naked tree trunks, which had once been mighty conifers, were silhouetted against the hilltop sky. I knew that fire was often part of a forest ecosystem—in New Jersey, pitch pine cones only opened to release their seeds with fire. Still, I hated to see the blackened landscape.

The charred trees came to an end and we arrived at the northeast entrance to Yellowstone National Park. We had reservations to stay at the Lake Yellowstone Hotel, but to get there we still had to drive 50 miles into the park.

Yellowstone was more than twice the size of Glacier National Park. It covered 3,470 square miles, mostly in Wyoming. Early explorers had recognized the area' s unique geological formations and extensive wildlife, and proposed that the region be kept for the public as a wilderness. So in 1872, Yellowstone became America's first national park.

The Northeast Entrance Road followed small streams that flowed through picturesque pastures, with mountain peaks constantly providing a scenic backdrop. Consulting our park map, we saw that we were close to the Grand Canyon of the Yellowstone, and decided to hike the North Rim Trail alongside it.

The color palette of Montana's stunning landscape had been mountain gray, forest green, spring grass green and Big Sky blue. Spread before us in the Wyoming canyon was an equally stunning landscape painted in gold, yellow, beige and rust. The canyon was 20 miles long, 1,200 feet deep and 2,000 to 4,000 feet wide. Although its origins were not precisely understood, it formed about 10,000 years ago as a result of lava flows and erosion. Observation platforms scattered along the edge of the canyon offered us panoramic views of its full majesty. From Inspiration Point, we saw the starkness of the deep rock trench, bisected by the frothy blue and white of the rushing Yellowstone River. Lookout Point offered us a dramatic view of the Lower Falls, where the river cascaded 309 feet.

I was content admiring the views from the platforms, which were sturdily built and surrounded by nice, safe railings. John, however, wanted to get up close and personal with the rock walls.

"I'm going down to that ledge," he said, pointing to an outcropping about 100 feet below us on the cliff wall.

"Don't you think that's a bit dangerous?" I asked.

After my remark, of course, he had to go. I watched, with some trepidation, as John worked his way down the rock wall. He posed there, I took his picture, and he climbed back up.

"You're really a daredevil, aren't you," I said.

"Yeah, I guess I am," he admitted.

The sun was setting as we drove to the Lake Yellowstone Hotel. I expected a rustic-looking cabin of logs and stone, similar to the ranger station we passed as we entered the park. To my surprise, the hotel was a long, Colonial-style building with bright yellow clapboard siding. The front was enhanced with twin Greek Revival porticos supported by three-story Ionic columns. The hotel had been serving guests since 1891, and was completely restored in 1991. In its full-service restaurant, we had our first nice dinner of the trip. Then we walked down the long corridor to our room on the first floor, where we put the big brass bed to good use.

Buffalos were really big animals, especially when they were grazing 50 yards away, and the only thing separating them from me was a puddle.

What we called a buffalo was technically the American bison. These creatures could grow to more than six feet tall, 11 feet long, and weigh more than 2,000 pounds. At Yellowstone, about 3,000 bison roamed freely, munching on grass anywhere they wanted. John and I saw several of them as we hiked away from our hotel the next morning. I kept my eye on the animals—more people were killed in Yellowstone by bison than by bears—but they never looked up from their breakfast.

Our hike took us partially into the hills—we didn't go far, because we also wanted to see the Old Faithful geyser that day. This required driving—the geyser, while still in the park, was about 40 miles from our hotel.

All of Yellowstone National Park was served by essentially one road that was shaped like a figure eight. On our way to Old Faithful, we periodically found ourselves in a long line of vehicles, completely stopped, while small herds of buffalo took a leisurely stroll across the road. Even the recently born calves—easy to spot with their orange fur—had no fear of cars or people.

Other animals absolutely loved people. At a scenic overlook by the side of the road, adjacent to a small waterfall, chipmunks had learned to beg for food. They obviously hadn't learned to read, because signs clearly stated, "Please don't feed the wildlife." The cute, furry critters begged anyway, and obliging humans tossed them peanuts and crackers.

A crowd of people was already gathered around the Old Faithful geyser when John and I arrived. The average interval between Old Faithful's eruptions was 91 minutes, and the next show, according to a sign by the tourist information booth, would be in a half-hour.

Geysers were caused when underground water was heated to the boiling point by volcanic rock, then forced to the surface in a tremendous burst of steam. They were generally located in areas of active volcanoes, and that was the case at Yellowstone. The park sat on top of the Yellowstone Caldera, a massive chamber of partially molten magma and the site of a devastating volcanic eruption 640,000 years ago. The caldera might someday explode again, which would cause an incredible loss of life. But on May 30, 2000, the only sign of volcanic activity was Old Faithful, which erupted right on schedule. It started with a couple of preliminary squirts, then a tower of steaming water burst 145 feet into the air. Slowly, the volcanic energy dwindled, and after a couple of minutes, the column of water petered out.

Scientists have discovered about 10,000 geothermal features in Yellowstone National Park, and the next day, John and I visited the most amazing of them—Mammoth Hot Springs. That's where Yellowstone's volcanic activity turned into performance art, with hot pools of water that danced in vibrant colors and limestone sculptures that grew of their own accord.

At Mammoth Hot Springs, located in the northwest corner of the park, hot water didn't burst into the air like a geyser, it seeped to the surface through ancient limestone deposits. And it wasn't exactly water—it was a weak carbonic acid solution that dissolved limestone on the way up, creating a calcium carbonate solution that leaked out of fissures in the earth and solidified as it dripped. The resulting structures, called travertine terraces, looked like petrified waterfalls in shades of white, yellow, tan and orange.

All of Yellowstone National Park was a tribute to the power of nature, but at Mammoth Hot Springs, John and I, along with other human visitors, could actually see nature working. Throughout our entire trip, we'd been spellbound by the sweeping landscapes, and at our last stop in the park, we glimpsed the primal energy that created them.

After touring the hot springs, John and I were on the road again—our flight back to New Jersey left the next day, and we had to return to Bozeman. For our last night in Montana, we went to the Chico Hot Springs Resort, only 34 miles from Yellowstone's north entrance—or in our case, exit. We stayed in a quaint room in the main lodge, which originally opened as the Chico Warm Springs Hotel in 1900 and was listed on the National Register of Historic Places.

The resort had two open-air pools that were fed by heated water from deep within the Earth—user-friendly versions of the geysers and hot springs we'd seen in Yellowstone. The temperature was around 100 degrees—perfect for relaxing.

After our soothing soak, we had the last dinner of our vacation in the hotel's gourmet restaurant. The food, the wine—everything was delicious. Then we retired to our room furnished with antiques, and enjoyed another wonderful sensory experience in a week that was full of them.

"John is in love with you. I hope you know that."

A week after returning from Montana, on June 9, 2000, I had a reading with Maggie Kay, the psychic. A dozen times, as she turned the cards, she predicted that John and I would get married.

"John is crazy about you. He fell for you from the minute he laid eyes on you," she said. "You and John have a future, and you will marry him. You'll have a beautiful home. You're still young enough; you may have a child. Nice little boy. Oh, he can't wait for you to come home. He's a nice guy. How did you meet him?"

"On the Internet."

This surprised Maggie. "He had a broken heart. But now, she broke it, and you put it back together again. John came into your life at the right time. You know what I like about him? He gives you credit for using your head. He don't meddle. He comes from a nice family. Did you meet them?"

"Yes."

"They're hoping that you two get married. Once you straighten this out, you're going to consider it. You make a nice couple, make a nice baby. I think it's one boy, unless it's twins, then you'll get one of each. And I'll bet your John says, 'Ah, forget about the money; we'll get by with what we have.' He's not a mercenary. Comparing John to James is like comparing a racehorse to a jackass."

As she turned the tarot cards, Maggie saw that I was still searching for James' money. "Who's the computer specialist that's helping you?" she asked. "He has a British accent."

"That's my search agent."

"He's going to come through for you. He knows his stuff. You were a little leery of him at first, weren't you?"

"He came highly recommended."

"How did you meet him?"

"Through a business associate."

"That was a find. That's a gift from God. He's not a fraud. When he tells you something, he's going to do it. And he has pretty terrific international connections."

Maggie predicted that my agent would find six good bank accounts, adding up to about $1.7 million. "Clean them all out," she said. "What could James do to you? He owes you the money. And you got a court injunction.

"I think four accounts are going to put you on easy street," she continued. "You'll kind of break even. And then if you want to go after the other ones you'll get really rich. I can't see how they're going to get a hold of you. Actually, the way it's going to be done, they couldn't trace you. This agent knows his Ps and Qs."

James, the psychic said, was still playing his games. Maggie saw that he was in China. She saw that he was using multiple identities. And the women—the psychic still saw James involved with a bevy of women located throughout the United States, from New Hampshire to New Mexico. "He's got three more pigeons on the line," Maggie said. "He's a diseased man to do that. Thank God you didn't get any disease from him."

"What kind of disease?"

"Social. He's loaded with venereal warts right now. Some gal got a payback on him. If he don't take care of them his dick will fall off with cancer."

The psychic paused and thought about it. "You know," she said, "that's poetic justice."

After the reading, I felt hopeful. Maggie saw my financial problems coming to an end. She saw me happily married—although I again decided not to tell John her predictions. I didn't want to spook him. But all her good news gave me the strength to keep going, keep climbing the mountain of problems that my life had become. Soon, Maggie told me, I'd be sitting on top of the world, wondering if everything I'd experienced was a bad dream.

I felt like I was making progress, albeit slowly. My lawyer in New Jersey went back to work for me and filed a motion for an amended judgment of divorce that stated my ex-husband committed fraud. Now James could not get out of paying it by declaring bankruptcy.

Project Gila moved forward. I authorized my agent to search banks in the United States and Australia for any accounts James might have. The fee was £3,000 for expenses, which was paid from the proceeds of our Titanic sale. He would also get 10 percent of any money he found.

In the meantime, I moved forward with another fundraising option—selling James' 1977 MGB roadster. I found a website for MG enthusiasts and placed an ad for the car, asking $2,900. I also placed an ad in the local weekly newspaper.

I had to be ready to close the deal if someone wanted the car. From the New Jersey Division of Motor Vehicles, I learned that to get legal title, I had to supply a copy of the divorce decree and a letter from my attorney specifying the VIN number.

I gathered all my documentation and went to the Motor Vehicle office, which was always so crowded that they gave out numbers for service, like in a supermarket deli. I settled into a hard plastic chair to wait. When my number was called, I went to the window and explained my situation to the clerk. James had bought the car in Florida and drove it to New Jersey. He conned me out of $227,000. The judge had awarded me the car in the divorce. I needed a clear title so I could sell it.

The clerk looked over my paperwork. "All right," she said. "We can do this. You'll have to pay a registration fee of $38.50 and the sales tax."

"Why should I have to pay sales tax? I didn't buy the car."

"You have to pay sales tax in order to title the car."

"But the car was bought in Florida."

"New Jersey has reciprocal sales tax arrangements with Florida."

"My husband bought the car. He should be responsible for the sales tax."

"Someone has to pay the sales tax in order to get a title," the clerk repeated.

I could feel frustration and fear mounting within me. "How much is it?" I asked.

The clerk turned to her calculator. "It's $210," she said.

I didn't have $210 for sales tax. I could hardly buy groceries.

"I can't do this," I said, gathering up my documents. I barely held on to my composure as I walked back through the crowded waiting room. When I got outside the door, the tears began.

I was angry. I was frustrated. I was broke. How was I ever going to get out of this hole?

A couple of weeks later I sold the car for $1,600 in cash. It was less money than I wanted, but the buyer was willing to deal with the title problems, so at least I didn't have that aggravation. But I still couldn't pay my bills.

With embarrassment, I had to bring up the topic in my daily e-mail to John. "I'm afraid I may have to ask you for some financial assistance," I wrote. "This last round of bill paying wiped me out. I feel very badly about this. I was always able to handle things myself, and now I can't. Really sucks."

John generously came through and loaned me $2,000.

My rowing partners from the previous summer—all women of a certain age—saw a long-held dream come true. They bought their own quad, or quadruple scull, and named it the "Hot Flash."

Because I had been a substitute member of the crew—rowing in place of a woman who had knee surgery—I was not included in the purchase. I didn't have the money to participate anyway. When the ladies moved over to the club where the boat was stored—Brigantine Rowing Club—I went with them, but I was now the fifth person in a four-person boat. To continue my total-body workouts and get more time on the water, I found a new rowing partner—Mary Steinacker, a schoolteacher.

We were an unlikely rowing pair—I was 5 feet 8 inches tall, she was only 5 feet tall. Height was important in rowing because it affected the length of a stroke, which affected a crew's ability to row in unison. We had to learn to compensate for our differences.

I didn't know Mary very well, but rowing together three or four mornings a week provided us with ample opportunity to get acquainted. Mary could only be described as bubbly. She was always laughing. Even at 6 a.m., her laugh rang out across the bay.

I scheduled my rowing for the days that I didn't have a softball game in Philadelphia. I'd learned the previous year that despite my efforts to preserve my youth, if I rowed at six in the morning, I didn't have the stamina to pitch a full softball game at six in the evening.

Often I didn't have to pitch the full game anyway. The team had recruited another female pitcher, and we split the mound duties. When we were both there, I was the starter and she was the closer. This frustrated the batters who faced us, because by the time they got used to my pitching, we switched, and her style was totally different. While we pitchers kept a lid on our opponents' offense, the guys on our team were hitting machines. Halfway through the season, our WB17 team sat comfortably in first place.

For the first time in my life, I was in a relationship with a man that I cared about as my birthday approached. In 2000, my birthday, July 19, fell on a Wednesday. John worked nights, so if we were going to spend my birthday together—which I really wanted to do—he'd have to request the night off. He forgot to do it.

John was accustomed to his birthday being lost in the blur of the Christmas holidays, and to him, it was no big deal. He didn't understand why I wanted my occasion to be marked, but said he'd ask his boss about taking Wednesday off. I tried not to think about it, tried to give him the benefit of the doubt, hoping he would work it out. But I had a sinking feeling that even though I had a boyfriend and lover, I would be alone on my birthday. I was not happy.

When John came to Atlantic City on Saturday, July 14, he was tired, and had just had a major argument with his partner, so I didn't bring anything up. We went out to dinner, came home and went to bed—to sleep —at 9 p.m.

I went rowing early the next morning with my new partner, Mary. When I got back, John was still sleeping. Around 11 a.m., we went to a little café around the corner from my house for breakfast. As we drove over in his truck, I took John's hand, as I always did. He pulled away. I noticed, but didn't say anything.

My sister was coming down that afternoon to help celebrate my birthday. The plan was for the three of us to go to the Resorts Casino, which was hosting an exhibition of Fabergé eggs. Then we would get something to eat—preferably at an outdoor bar with music.

John and I had a couple of hours to kill before Tracy arrived. We lounged on the porch. Screwing up my courage, I asked the question:

"Did you get off Wednesday?"

I was hoping against hope he would say yes.

"No, I can't," he said. Then he started to say, "I thought next weekend we could ..."

I wasn't listening.

"This is not good, John," I fretted. "All I ever wanted was someone to take me out for my birthday. I guess you can't understand this because you don't care about your birthday."

"No, I don't understand it," he said. I glanced at him, and could see pain all over his face. Then he dropped the bomb. "Do you feel like we're trying to put a square peg into a round hole?"

I started to go numb.

"No, I never thought that," I replied slowly. "What do you mean?"

"Earlier, I started rolling my eyes. You were talking about James again. It's like you can't put him behind you."

"I don't even remember what I said," I replied.

"It was about him being a compulsive spender."

"You never said it bothered you for me to talk about him. It doesn't mean anything. I'm just so grateful you're not like him."

"What do you mean?"

"James was a pain in the ass. Even before I knew what he was doing to me."

"Well, I'm going to go out on a limb here. I think you want to get married. I don't want to get married. As far as I'm concerned, marriage is just a piece of paper you get if you plan to procreate. I don't want to procreate, so I see no reason to get married."

The numbness spread all over me. I looked down at the porch floor, not really seeing anything.

"I do want to get married," I said. "I liked being married. I would do it again."

"That's what I thought. I knew this was coming. I knew it when we were in Montana. When we were driving down Beartooth highway you made that comment about wanting to go to the wedding chapel."

The memory flashed in my mind—John taking both hands off the wheel of the Durango and making a cross at me, protecting himself from the vampire.

"Yes, I did notice your rather violent reaction to that, but I decided to ignore it."

"Maybe it's the distance. Or maybe I don't know if I'm in love with you. I don't know. But when I feel like this, I just withdraw."

By this time I was in emotional overload. "So is that all this was, vacation romance?"

"No," John said. He looked pained.

"Well, I did notice that you talk about the future without including me. You were talking earlier about wanting to buy property in Montana, and you didn't ask my opinion."

I paused, but I couldn't look at John. "Well then, why don't we just break it off right now?"

"Okay," he said.

John got up and sat next to me on the couch. I did not want to touch him, and really didn't want to be near him.

"Well, you might as well go home."

"Okay," John said. He bolted into the house and went upstairs to get his bag. I followed him into the house, but stayed in the living room.

"I don't think I have anything of yours," I said. "I'll give you your $2,000 back as soon as I can."

He came down the steps and put his arm around me. I turned away. "This is just too hard," I said.

So John left. The entire episode took 15 minutes.

For awhile I was in shock. I cried a little. Tracy arrived, and I told her what happened. She was surprised. "What do you want to do?" she asked.

"I guess we'll stick to the plan."

Tracy drove to the casino and paid my entrance into the Fabergé show. We walked slowly through the display of intricately jeweled and enameled eggs. Their beauty didn't register with me.

Then we went to a local bar for pizza. We spent a little bit of time talking business. Tracy now worked at my brother's company, Pierce Technology Corporation. They had submitted a proposal for a massive website development project for a big financial services firm. If Pierce got the job, they would need my help on practically a full-time basis.

By the time we finished the pizza, my emotions were crumbling. "I'd better go home now," I said.

Tracy drove me back. "Do you want me to stay?" she asked.

"I think it would be best if I were alone."

Tracy hugged me, and then left. As soon as she was gone, I started to cry violently. "Not again," I wailed. "Please, God, not again."

I spent a miserable night. The next morning, I talked to my friends, Sylvia Banning and Sheryl Ginsburg, on the phone. For months, I'd been telling them about John, about how different he was from my ex-husband. How comfortable I was. They both met John, and liked him. I was so upset that I could barely get through the conversations. They were shocked.

But I didn't have time to dwell in my pain. I'd spent $70 of my limited funds on a ticket for the Philadelphia Ad Club summer outing, an all-day event at a Pennsylvania country club, which I'd heard was one of the best networking opportunities in the advertising industry. I couldn't afford not to go.

A few times during the 90-minute drive to the country club I started crying— luckily I had the foresight to apply waterproof mascara. Somehow I held myself together and chatted amiably with other attendees, trying to meet as many people as possible.

The drive home was much more difficult. I could no longer contain my pain. My love was gone. Why did this happen to me again?

A few days later, I regretted my swift and abrupt reaction to John's words.

Maybe we just needed to talk. Maybe our relationship didn't need to be over. I sent John an e-mail, hoping to open a dialog.

It took John a few days to reply, and his answer did not make me feel better. "I'm not going to fight for something if you're not comfortable with the arrangement or if the arrangement is going to keep you from what you really want in life," he wrote. "Obviously, you want marriage; I don't want to keep you from that."

John did not believe that we had a future together.

Months earlier, I made an appointment for a session with Elaine Anderson, my energy worker, on my birthday. We both thought it would be a powerful thing to do. When July 19, 2000, my 44th birthday, arrived, I truly needed therapy.

I told Elaine that John and I broke up. I told her how we'd just spent a wonderful vacation in Montana, and then in 15 minutes the entire relationship was over. Elaine had sensed John's loving energy in prior sessions. She was totally surprised. Still, she felt that the universe had a plan. "It was perfect," my therapist said. "John was meant to be with you for that period of time."

Then I brought up my real fear. "I think I've lost my last opportunity to have children," I said. "All I ever wanted was a normal life. A family. And now it looks like I'm never going to be able to do it." As I talked, I could feel pain and bitter disappointment welling up within me.

The other issue, of course, was my continuing financial trauma. I wasn't making enough money. I was searching for James' assets, but that also cost money. I was so desperate that I had to ask John for help, and he gave me $2,000. Now I owed him money, along with my other debts.

"But he helped you," Elaine said. "If you can stay in a place of gratitude for that, the universe will send you more help."

"Well, there is a chance that my brother's company, where Tracy works, will get a big job. If they do, I'll have a lot of work."

"You need to focus on yourself now, almost to the point of being selfish," Elaine advised. "Stay peaceful; find the place of inner calm and knowing that there is a higher perfection. Do what you have to do, and maintain calm and serenity."

"How can I maintain inner calm when I don't know if I'm going to survive?"

"Everything is not available for you to know yet. It is all in process and in motion, but it has not gelled. Your eyes are wide open, and you are seeing better. You're coming into your own."

When I lay on the table for the energy work, Elaine wanted me to get in touch with my anger about the end of my relationship with John, but my anger was under so much pain and sadness that I could barely find it. Anger wasn't the issue. Profound disappointment was. Disappointment that I would never have the life that I always wanted. Disappointment that my dreams of a family were doomed to die.

"Maybe you're not going to do that in this lifetime," Elaine said. "Maybe you're going to give birth to something else." She worked on healing my womb, clearing out the chakras. I wept; I moaned; I felt the pain of my hopes and dreams collapsing: I would never have a normal life.

John's spirit joined the session. Elaine picked up his fear—fear that he could not fix my problems. She also heard messages from Guidance. They told her that the path my soul chose might not include what I thought I always wanted—a family. There was a larger perfection, and it was still unfolding. "Stay focused on gratitude," Elaine said again. "Gratitude keeps you open for the universe to give you gifts."

It was hard for me to hear her advice, let alone do what she said. I was overwhelmed by the loss of my most cherished dream. The session came to a close, but for the first time ever, when I left Elaine, I was still upset. That night, I wrote in my journal:

> I feel like a failure. I feel like I can't be the woman I want to be. I'm just a bitch that nobody wants, unable to make a connection except with a con artist, who only wanted my money. A total failure. That is what this is about. Who cares a flying fuck about the book and the spiritual journey?

My heart was broken, more shattered than when I discovered my husband was cheating on me. With James, I knew that I didn't want to spend the rest of my life married to him, and was relieved that I finally had an excuse to leave—although when I discovered his infidelity, I didn't realize that it extended to every aspect of our marriage. With John I was happy. I wanted the relationship to continue. I hoped we'd stay together—and my hopes were thrown into a meat grinder.

Luckily, I didn't have time to dwell on my pain because I was busy with work. I was commuting several times a week to the office of Pierce Technology Corporation, my brother's company, in Iselin, New Jersey. Pierce had won the bid to develop the financial services firm website. It was a huge project, and I was brought on to assist.

I had other jobs as well. Sheryl Ginsburg and I were working on newsletters and promotions for Dover Downs Slots. Showboat needed a few more issues of the Crew's News. I even got a call out of the blue from a local advertising agency for copywriting assistance. I said yes to everything—I desperately needed the money—and worked day and night to meet my deadlines.

Weekends, however, were miserable.

For almost a year, my weekends were delightful respites with my lover. Companionship. Laughs. Romance. Now weekends were filled with painful rumination as I kept asking myself, what happened? And why?

Maybe I hadn't told John often enough how much I truly liked him. I admired his poetic spirit it was so unlike my thoroughly rational and responsible approach to life. I wistfully wished I had his ability to live fully in the moment. Often, during the days between our weekends together, I'd think of him with a loving smile. Maybe I should have told him so. Maybe I should have more often spoken those three special words, "I love you."

But gradually, I came to realize that the issues keeping us apart weren't mine. They were John's. He had his own fears. He had his own demons from the past, and he was the only one who could come to terms with them.

With this realization, I was filled with compassion. I'd been dealing with my inner troubles for years—even before my marriage to James. If John chose to start down the road to healing, I knew it would be a journey of painful soul-searching. I also realized that I was further along that journey than he was, and maybe he wouldn't catch up. In those moments, I thought it might be best if we went our separate ways.

Then I felt the fear. Fear that I was alone again. Fear that I'd continue to be alone for a long, long time. In my panic, I imagined talking with John, explaining why I reacted as I did, telling him that I missed him, asking if we could try to work things out.

Three weeks after our breakup, I composed an e-mail to convey my thoughts. John had maintained his distance during our relationship, which I'd noticed. I assumed it was because of my financial problems. "But since you were paying for our entertainment, which I greatly appreciated," I wrote, "I didn't feel it was appropriate to make any demands. In fact, because of my financial problems, I didn't feel like I could ask for anything—including more attention."

Still, I cared deeply for John, and I told him so. I missed making love with him, and my relationship with him was the nicest I'd ever had. But I'd spent a lot of years waiting around for men who couldn't decide whether or not they wanted me. I didn't want to do that again.

"If you were just there to support me through the most difficult year of my life, I will be forever grateful," I wrote. "Do I know for sure what we should do? No. But we've been too happy for our love and relationship to end so harshly. Let's not let that happen."

I sent the e-mail on August 5, 2000. I received no reply.

The voices in my head were at war. I replayed dialog with John—actual conversations that we had, and conversations that I imagined. I sank into despair about my sorry history of unfulfilling relationships. I demanded an answer from the universe, with fear in my heart: Would I always be alone?

The endless mental chatter left me exhausted. I needed help. So on August 20, 2000, I sat in my rose-colored meditation room, preparing for a telephone session with Elaine Anderson.

I already realized that I had created part of my problem with John myself. Rereading the letter I wrote, one sentence jumped out at me: "Because of my financial problems, I didn't feel like I could ask for anything—including more attention."

That was the energy I'd created. Because of my debts and lack of steady income, I felt I was deficient, inadequate, damaged goods. Therefore, in my mind, I was not deserving of love. This was nothing new with me—it was part of a larger story that I told myself all my life: Nobody wanted me. I looked back through my old journal writings, with my litany of woe regarding romantic relationships.

"It's everywhere," I said to Elaine as we started talking. "I wrote it in my journal time and time again. Nobody wants me. I even believed it when I was a kid. That's why I read books all the time. It was an escape. I could get away from the pain and loneliness if I could read a good story."

"It's something you came into this life with," Elaine said. "An issue that needs to be healed."

I'd felt the negative belief all week as tension around my chest. As I lay down on the daybed, the tension became oppressive, a mountain of fear pressing down on me. I couldn't breathe.

"What are you afraid of?" Elaine asked.

"I'm afraid no one likes me," I replied. "I'm afraid no one wants me."

"Guidance says that you believe there's something wrong with you."

The pain of recognition shot through me. Instinctively, I curled up on the daybed. My hands were over my womb, my knees were up—like lying in a fetal position on my back. The energy pressed down on my chest, my womb and my legs, wave after wave of tension and emotion.

"I'm having trouble breathing," I said.

"It's collapsing," Elaine replied.

"The pain is from a past life. I'm feeling raped and beaten."

"Say, 'don't hurt me.'"

"Don't hurt me," I whimpered.

Then I saw that I was being raped. By my father.

"Why is John here?" I asked. "Was it him?"

"Yes, the father was John," Elaine replied softly.

In that life, my mother died when I was 10 years old, leaving my father and me. Although we had been a happy family, with my mother gone, my father fell apart. At age 13 I started to develop, turning into a pretty woman with long golden hair—just like my mother. My father went over the edge and started raping me. He told me that it was my fault he was raping me.

"What do you believe is wrong with you?" Elaine asked.

"I'm a bad girl," I replied. "But I'm trying so hard to be good."

When I was 15 or 16, I got pregnant by my father. Again, he told me that it was my fault, and I had to have an abortion. The abortion was butchered, and I bled to death. John couldn't stand what he did to me. He hated himself for raping me. After I died, he killed himself.

My confusion from that life was trapped within me. My mother died, abandoning me, and then my father raped me. I died with the belief that something was wrong with me. Because the experience was so traumatic, I attached a massive amount of energy to the belief. Elaine and I talked about how it translated into my present life.

"What did you believe was wrong with you?" she asked.

"I wasn't pretty. I was too smart. No one wanted me."

"Guidance is telling you to let go of the belief that there is something wrong with you," Elaine said.

"That's why I fell for James," I said. "He was telling me that he loved me and wanted me."

"You were desperate for it," she said. "That's why people like him succeed. We're all the walking wounded on this planet. We need it so badly that we believe what we hear—even when it's a lie."

This time around, my pain involved breaking up with John. I heard Guidance telling me that the relationship was perfect for what it was, very healing. For the past year, I needed someone to play with, and I played with John. But if he were not able to travel further with me, then I shouldn't wait for him.

"So why did Maggie predict that we would get married?" I asked.

"Psychics read off of the energy at the moment, but that doesn't necessarily take into account the decisions people make," Elaine explained. "When she read it, that's how it looked."

My relationship with John was fun and safe, but when I was honest with myself, I admitted that we might not be right for each other over the long term.

"It was perfect for the time; it was what you needed at the time," Elaine said. "You weren't ready to relate to someone of equal magnitude. You felt too many risks to be fully committed. Guidance says the important thing is to realize that you did not have a true perception of yourself."

"I believed in my own defects," I said. "This colored my entire life."

"Guidance has a message for you. Can you hear it?"

I could not.

"You came into this life believing that there was something wrong with you," Elaine said. "The belief was reinforced through many experiences in your life. You have to see who you really are, and not believe the lies and misperceptions you've been believing for so long. Guidance says to relax into yourself. Let your true nature come out. Let people see who you really are. You are perfect."

"That's all very nice," I said. "But changing this will take time. What am I supposed to do now? I'm tired. I think they've asked a lot of me."

"Complain," Elaine said.

I did. "What do I do about it now?" I demanded of Guidance. "I have a real problem. It's called $80,000 in debt. Who's going to want me now?"

"You're not going to like this," Elaine said. "Guidance says it's no big deal."

I was floored. How could $80,000 in debt not be a big deal?

Elaine told me what she heard. "They repeated, 'It's no big deal.' Do not wear it like a defect. There is nothing wrong with you. If you do not hold this like a big deal, there are lots of solutions. You can make lots of money. You can find the money. It can be written off. Someone can give you the money."

I couldn't believe what I was hearing.

"Are you willing for it to be no big deal?" Elaine asked me.

This made no sense to me.

She asked again, "Are you willing for the debt to be no big deal?"

"So if $80,000 in debt is not a big deal, what is a big deal?" I retorted.

Elaine was quiet for a moment, and then she answered. "The idea that you believed there was something wrong with you. Changing that is a big deal. Changing your consciousness. The important thing is to learn to distinguish between you and an experience in your life. The debt is something you are dealing with. It is not who you are. There is no reason for you to wear it like a defect."

"I'm having a hard time with this."

"Here's what is important," Elaine explained, "learning to distinguish between you, yourself, your soul, and the experiences of your life. Things that happen to you are not who you are. Trust the magic. There's a lot of magic around all of this."

Slowly, I came to grips with the idea that I'd have to release my ideas.

"You'll probably have to grieve for awhile," Elaine said. "Grieve for all the sadness you've had in your life."

After the session, I gave in to my addiction and read a book, trying to distract myself. When I was finally too tired to finish another page, I went to bed.

I started to cry. The grief that jammed my heart came pouring out. My dog, Beau, jumped on the bed, upset. Frantically, he licked away my tears, trying to comfort me. Then someone outside lit off fireworks, which were always guaranteed to frighten the dog, and I had to comfort him.

The day after my session with Elaine, I felt lighter, although I was still trying to get used to the idea that $80,000 in debt was no big deal. Guidance wanted me to treat my financial problems as an annoyance. According to them, getting rid of my debt was the energetic equivalence of getting rid of the bugs in my pantry.

Little moths lived in my pantry—arriving, I surmised, with my groceries. When I first saw the moths, I didn't take steps to eradicate them. They were fruitful and multiplied, and before long, a few moths became an infestation. I finally put all my food in plastic bags, and when I saw the bugs, sprayed them.

If my debt was no big deal, then I had to change my thinking about how I was living. I had assumed that my life was on hold until that problem was solved. With the debt relegated to no big deal, I could work on building a life for myself, on making myself happy, on surrounding myself with people I liked, regardless of my financial problems.

Maybe a miracle would happen. Maybe I would meet someone who would pay the bill. There were plenty of dotcom millionaires out there, for whom $80,000 was no big deal. Maybe a shift in attitude would make all the difference.

To my amazement, as the pain of disappointment, rejection and smashed expectations caused by my breakup with John receded, what I felt was more love for him. Not the "miss you, wish you were here" kind of love—a euphemism for the hunger of loneliness. I felt love for John that translated into concern for his happiness, his growth.

Somehow, I wanted to express to John what it all meant to me—our happy times together, my role in our sudden separation, how our love affected me, even if our relationship was over. The best medium for expression, it seemed, was poetry. Poetry was not my usual style—I was a journalist and advertising writer. Normally my objective was to be clear and concise, not metaphorical. But I worked on the poem for days, and it captured my feelings.

I e-mailed the poem, called *John's Garden,* on September 5, 2000.

John's Garden

I always dreamed of a garden
A paradise all my own
An earthly slice of heaven
Where my favorite flowers would grow
In springtime there would be crocuses
Peeking from under the snow
And then perennial daffodils
Nodding brightly, row upon row

In my mind I could see the color
From the warmth of the summer sun
Impatiens in pink, red and orange
With white and blue ageratum
Then as the days turned cooler
I'd plant hardy chrysanthemums
And even the stillness of winter
Would be the promise of spring to come

For years, I fought with my garden
I tilled and planted seeds
But no matter how hard I tried
All I could grow was weeds
I wondered, why am I failing?
What does my garden need?
There was emptiness in my heart
And my dream began to recede

Then, when I wasn't looking
My flowers started to sprout
The colors of my inspiration
In the physical world came about
The blooms grew strong and pretty
Each fragrant new day eased my doubt
This is beautiful! This is wonderful!
My joyful heart wanted to shout

My garden was a place of magic
Where I lost the cares of the day
My soul felt the peace and beauty
My heart was happy and gay
At times it was my sanctuary
Fountain of strength to make my way
And always it tickled my senses

As among the flowers I lay

Perhaps if I had been watching
I might have seen the approaching gale
But I was fully enraptured
By the Eden of my fairy tale
The wind blasted through my garden
Blinding rain soon turned to hail
The storm pelted my delicate blossoms
Ground them into the mud of the vale

I gazed at the wreck of my garden
No more playfulness in the sun
Plants broken, flowers shredded
Within I felt totally numb
In anguish I yanked up the stalks
Pulled the roots out, every one
And to the stack of dead foliage,
Asked, my God, what have I done?

Pictures of my lovely garden
Come unbidden to my mind
Pink impatiens, blue ageratum
Bursts of passion, vibrant and fine
I remember the sweet satisfaction
The easy being, so sublime
For it was a bountiful garden
And it lives still, somewhere in time

One day I'll have another garden
I feel deep in the seat of my soul
The emptiness that poisoned my heart
Is transformed to a light of gold
For now I have learned to plant flowers
And until my existence grows old
I'll remember the gift of that garden
Tender blossoms arranged in a bowl

The next day, I received a reply. John wrote:

> What a beautiful poem. It's sad that its inspiration is so painful. I don't know what else to say. I'm sorry that I can't give you what you'd like, but I guess it's all about timing; maybe we simply met at the wrong time. I think that us both being on the rebound worked against us, or probably more accurately against me. I'm still not anywhere close to

being mentally prepared for any kind of serious commitment; I doubt if I will be for a long time.

Despite all that, I hope that things are going as well as possible. I hope that everything works out. I often wonder how you're making out with your book. You deserve the best.

After receiving John's reply to my poem, I decided to take a big emotional risk. I sent him an e-mail saying that I would be at a party not far from his home on Saturday, September 9, 2000. Maybe we could get together for a proper goodbye.

The party was being thrown by a young couple who played on my Philadelphia softball team, WB17. We'd won the league championship, and it was a celebration.

At the end of the regular season, our team had the best record in our division, which got us into the playoffs. We had to win two out of three games to advance to the championship. With the other pitcher and I sharing the mound duties, and solid hitting by the guys, we did.

For the championship games, we again had to win two out of three. I anticipated that I'd pitch half of each game. But our other pitcher also played on another team, and she didn't show up for the first two games of the finals, leaving me the only pitcher. I did well, but WB17 and our opponent split the series. The trophy would be decided by the last game.

As I was throwing my warm-up pitches before the final, important outing, I was relieved to see the other pitcher pull up in her car. At least I wouldn't have to carry the pitching burden by myself.

"If you don't mind, I think I'd like to show them something different and start her as pitcher tonight," our coach said to me.

"That's fine," I said. "In fact, if you want her to pitch the whole game, it's okay with me."

"Are you sure?"

"Yeah, sure. They've seen all my stuff."

"Okay. I really appreciate you doing this for the team."

So she pitched. The guys hit. I kept the scorebook. We won. And that's why we were having a party.

It was slated to begin in the afternoon. I wanted to attend the party for a few hours, and then drive over to see John. But he hadn't replied to my e-mail. So Saturday morning, I nervously picked up the phone and called him. John had a new Saturday routine, I learned. After getting off from his nighttime job and taking care of morning dek hockey business, he went home and slept for a few hours. Then he went hiking. He didn't know when he'd be back from his hike, but if I wanted to call him after the party, maybe he'd be home and I could stop by.

I was thrilled. Maybe he'd take me to bed. What to wear?

I settled on a casual summer dress—a sleeveless shift in a bright floral pattern—and little black heels. At the party, the male members of my softball team were amazed—they'd never seen me in anything but black workout shorts and a red t-shirt. But I hadn't dressed for them.

As the team enjoyed burgers, potato salad, baked beans and beer, the afternoon slid into the evening. About 8 p.m., I found a private spot and called John on my cell phone.

No answer.

So I went back to the party. Twenty minutes later, I tried again. Still no answer.

That familiar fear came back. Was John standing me up? Was he really not interested in seeing me after all?

Finally, the fourth time I called, John picked up the phone. "Hello?"

"Hi, John. It's Donna." I tried to sound nonchalant.

"Oh, yeah. Sorry, I came back from hiking and fell asleep."

"Is it okay if I come by?"

"Yeah, sure. I'll be here."

I quickly left the party. As I drove to Royersford, I imagined what would happen. John would put his arms around me. He'd apologize profusely, saying he'd made a terrible mistake. He wouldn't be able to resist me, and would discover the sexy lingerie that I was wearing under my summer dress. We'd go to bed. I might even get pregnant—the timing was right.

None of my fantasies came true. Instead of a wild embrace, John gave me a peck on the cheek. Then we sat at his kitchen table and talked. I told him about the website that I was working on. He told me that he wanted to move to Montana and be a fire monitor, watching for wildfires in the wilderness.

Eventually I related to John what I'd learned in my sessions with Elaine about our past life together, when he was my father and abused me. He seemed to believe me. It explained a lot—why he felt an instant attraction to me when we met. Why he didn't want children. Why he couldn't stay with me.

"Elaine really helped me overcome this," I said. "I feel so much better. Maybe you should see her. She could really make a difference."

"Oh, I don't know," John replied, unenthusiastically.

"What are you going to do about it?"

"What I do with everything bad that happens in my life. I'll cope."

The phone rang. It was close to midnight. The phone never rang at that hour when I was with John. But John was now chatting with a woman from Montana, whom he'd met online. John told her that he'd call back.

"I want to show you something," John said after hanging up. He brought out two photos. One was his old girlfriend. The other was the woman from Montana.

"Don't they look alike?" he asked me.

They did.

"I'm sorry. Is this freaking you out?"

It was.

We chatted a bit more, although we were running out of things to say. To me, it was time for our goodbye sex. I stood up. "I'm getting tired," I said. "Are you taking me to bed?"

John looked uncomfortable. "I don't think that's a good idea," he said. "How about if I give you some money for a motel?"

So much for the last of my fantasies.

"That's all right. I'll make it home."

John walked me to my car. Finally, he put his arms around me and kissed me.

"It's better to be able to say goodbye," I said to him.

"Yes, it is," he replied. Then he added, "I'll always love you."

"I'll always love you," I repeated.

I got into my car and drove off. On the way back to Atlantic City, I berated myself for my stupid imagination. Sex, right. Pregnant, right. But I did not cry. I accepted the reality that John and I had once shared a love, but it was time to move on.

Chapter 23

While I walked toward the lunchroom at Pierce Technology on September 21, 2000, my cell phone rang. I'd forwarded my calls, as I always did when I worked at my brother's office. "Hello, Donna Andersen," I answered, identifying myself to the caller.

"Can I speak to James Montgomery, please?" a woman asked.

I stopped in the middle of the corridor. What might this be about?

"I'm sorry, he's not available. Can I help you?"

"I'm calling about his storage unit. We haven't received this month's rent."

Storage unit—I knew James had one in Florida. If I handled this right, I could find out where it was. I turned and walked back to my temporary desk. "I'm James Montgomery's wife. Let me have your information and I'll find out what's going on. Can you give me the address again?"

The storage unit was in Clearwater, Florida.

"And what is the balance due?" I asked.

"The total is $111.23," the woman replied. "That's the normal rental of $101.23, plus a $10 late fee."

"All right. Give me your name and phone number and I'll get back to you tomorrow."

I looked at the yellow legal pad where I just wrote down the location of James' storage unit. Knowing him, it was filled with boxes of papers—papers that might tell me where his money was.

How the woman got my phone number was a mystery. Maybe James provided it when he rented the unit, although that would be pretty stupid if he were trying to keep it secret from me. Maybe it was a miracle and my luck was finally changing.

A few weeks earlier, my agent in England sent me an e-mail—he found two bank accounts for James. One was another account at the First Union Bank in Florida, and it had a balance of $1,007.84. The other was at the Commonwealth Bank in Sydney, Australia. That account was protected by a high-security pass code, and he was unable to determine the amount of money in it. "It could be that this account contains quantities of money Montgomery wants to protect," my agent wrote. He said he'd try to get more information.

Maybe I could help. Maybe bank statements for the accounts were in James' storage unit.

During the 90-minute drive home from Pierce that evening, I decided that I would go to Florida and clean out the storage unit. Then I couldn't believe I made that decision. But I was desperate, and desperation was making me take actions that were contrary to my nature.

The next day I started putting my plan into action, contacting the storage facility about James' unit. "I spoke to my husband, and we've decided to close it," I lied to the woman who answered the phone. "I'll be there next week to pay the balance and take care of it."

"When will you be here?" she asked.

"On Thursday."

"All right."

Next I made flight reservations on Spirit Air—a one-way ticket from Atlantic City to Tampa. Then I went online to find a U-Haul dealer close to Tampa International Airport and reserved a 10-foot moving truck. My plan was to pay the balance on the storage unit, break into it, load everything into the truck and drive back to New Jersey.

I never stole anything in my life. I was terrified, but determined.

All summer long, I trained with my rowing partner, Mary Steinacker, in the double scull. We learned to compensate for the difference in our heights, and our boat was cutting nicely through the water. We decided to put our training to the test by racing in the King's Head Regatta at King of Prussia, Pennsylvania on September 24, 2000. Early on that bright, sunny Sunday morning, I picked Mary up. While we were driving up the Atlantic City Expressway, with my cruise control set at 71 mph, I told her about my plans to go to Florida and raid James' storage unit.

With all the drives I made to Philadelphia, including three times a week during the softball championship, I never noticed that the speed limit dropped to 55 mph as I approached the Ben Franklin Bridge. I was speeding, and with no one else on the normally busy highway, it was easy for a cop to see it. He pulled me over and gave me a ticket.

One more aggravation—but I did not want to get upset and ruin my race. "Maybe it means we'll row fast," I said to Mary.

Maybe it did. Just like when we trained, Mary and I started the race at a good pace and gradually increased the stroke rate—rowing faster as we progressed down the course. The result: We won the gold medal for our event.

But that night at home, I got angry—the ticket came with a fine I couldn't afford. Then I realized its significance. Any police officer would consider emptying James' storage unit to be theft, regardless of the fact that he owed me more than $1 million. Unlike my ex-husband, I was a law-abiding citizen, and I was afraid of the plan I made. My fear of breaking the law, and of getting caught, was swirling within me. My fearful energy attracted the speeding ticket.

I needed to get the negative energy out of my system. I focused on releasing my fear, so I could implement my plan with impunity.

My plane touched down in Tampa on September 28, 2000 at 9:40 a.m.—right on time. I took a taxi to the U-Haul dealer—it turned out to be a small gas station on a four-lane highway in an industrial part of town. The gas station had my U-Haul reservation, but did not have my truck. "Can you come back in a couple of hours?" the manager asked me.

"No, I can't," I replied, angry—and anxious about a wrinkle in my plan. "I have a reservation. I told you when I was coming. Where is the truck?"

The manager went into the office, made a phone call, and came out again. "It will be here in 15 minutes," he said.

I waited with my overnight bag under the gas station's canopy, between a rack of tires and a soda machine, getting more nervous with each passing minute. Finally the truck arrived. The manager filled it with gas and completed the paperwork. I signed the forms, jumped into the cab and pulled out onto the street. I immediately realized that I hadn't adjusted the side view mirrors and couldn't see cars coming up behind me.

What an idiot. I had to slow down, calm down and be careful.

I pulled off of the highway into a parking lot. After adjusting the mirrors on both sides of the truck, I organized my information on the front seat. From MapQuest, I'd printed out directions to a Home Depot store and to the storage facility. I studied them, got back on the highway and headed for Home Depot, where I bought a 24-inch bolt cutter.

Next stop: the storage facility.

After years of preparing brochures, ads and post cards for my customer, Black Horse Self Storage, I was familiar with all the features and benefits that storage facilities could offer. When I walked into the office of the one my ex-husband used, I immediately checked the walls behind the counter. Unlike my customer, this facility did not have closed-circuit television monitoring the storage buildings. This was good, at least for me.

"Can I help you?" the woman behind the counter asked.

"Yes. I'm James Montgomery's wife. I'm here to take care of his outstanding balance and close the unit."

"What's the unit number?"

"C-184."

The woman didn't question me or ask for identification. I didn't have to whip out the wedding photo that I tucked into my wallet to prove I was James Montgomery's wife. She just looked through her records and said, "That will be $111.23."

I paid her cash and scrawled some illegible signature on the bottom of a form. "I haven't been here in a long time," I said casually. "Where is the unit again?"

"You can drive right up to it. Just go through the gate on the left side of the office. It will be about halfway up the row on your right."

My heart was thumping as I slowly drove along a row of identical orange roll-up doors and found the unit, a standard 10-foot by 10-foot space. I continued driving to the end of the building, turned the truck around and came back. I parked just past James' unit, as close as I could to the building, blocking any view of my activities from the office.

A regular padlock secured the door to the storage unit. I looked in all directions—no one was around. Retrieving my big red bolt cutter from the cab, I quickly cut the lock and put the tool back, hiding it under my overnight bag. Then I rolled open the door.

It was filled, as I expected, with boxes. There were also plastic storage bins and a few small pieces of furniture—bookcases, rocking chairs—but nothing that I couldn't handle by myself. Much of James' stuff I'd seen before. But at least half of the contents I didn't recognize—women's clothing, children's toys. It didn't take long to determine that they belonged to James' most recent wife, Kim Goodson, and their daughter, Janna.

Well, I couldn't stand there and sort it out. I had to take everything.

Speedily, I carried box after box out of the storage unit and into the truck. Even though I was hot and thirsty, I did not stop moving. In an hour and a half, the job was done and I was on the road, heading back to New Jersey.

When I got home three days later, the contents of James' storage unit took over my basement. I did a cursory initial sort, looking for financial records. It was easy to tell which boxes belonged to James and which belonged to his wife. James apparently scooped stacks of papers off the floor and tossed them into the boxes. Kim Goodson's records were organized, dated and placed neatly into folders.

Much of James' paperwork related to the Titanic exhibit—I knew that was useless. I also found documents about a community event that James put together for Flag Day, June 14, 1999. It was the same ploy that he used in Mays Landing, New Jersey, three years earlier—creating a special event with a veneer of patriotism so he could make political and business contacts. Who would turn down a request to meet with him about honoring the flag of the United States? He claimed to be a member of the Special Forces to gain entrée to sponsors, and roped in his new father-in-law, who apparently was a veteran and a member of the local American Legion post. Of course, James Montgomery wasn't even an American citizen, but I doubted he disclosed that detail to his sponsors.

I found documents related to James' Southern Florida International Institute for Continuing Education, the schools for Chinese students to learn English, including the names and addresses of investors. I set those papers aside for further investigation. But I did not find what I really wanted—bank statements or financial information of any kind.

Kim Goodson, I could tell from her boxes, was a shutterbug. She commemorated every important event by taking photos, and the photos were all sorted and stored in albums. Each album was marked with a start date and end date. They included many pictures of James.

After all that I'd learned about James, I didn't think anything could shock me. I was wrong. James first showed up in the albums dated 1992. The visual evidence confirmed that he maintained his relationship with Kim Goodson through two marriages—to Gale Lewis in 1995-1996 and to me in 1996-1999—and through relationships with all the other women whose letters I'd found.

Obviously, not one of the relationships with women meant anything to James. Each of us served some kind of purpose for him, that was all. I could not fathom the emotional emptiness that allowed James to say, over and over, "I love you," when what he should have said was, "I'm using you."

Work kept me busy and distracted me from my emotions. But as soon as work subsided, emotions swept over me, and I was never sure what they would be. Some days I was happy. Some days I was bitterly resentful. Some days, within hours, I flopped back and forth between the two.

Resentment started winning out. My approach to life had always been honest, upstanding and moral. I tried to do the right thing—and look at what happened to me. In my mind, I did nothing to deserve the sorry state of my existence.

Then I thought, maybe I did.

In all the sessions I had with Elaine, I was always the victim. Bad things happened to me. I never did anything wrong. But maybe I had past lives in which my behavior was less than honorable—maybe even despicable. With that thought, my stomach tightened and I had trouble breathing. The tightness stayed with me for days, until, on October 14, 2000, I could stand it no longer. I had a telephone session scheduled with Elaine in a couple of weeks, but I couldn't wait that long. I went into my meditation room to try to move the energy myself.

I lay down on the floor. Before long, an image formed in my mind of a square-rigged sailing ship on the high seas. I was on the ship—a slave trader. I was one of the white men taking captured Africans away to the New World to be sold to the highest bidder.

The Atlantic slave trade flourished for more than 400 years. It was at its height during the 18th century, when the traders were mostly English, Brazilian, French and Dutch. Europeans rarely went into the interior of Africa to capture the slaves themselves. Rather, slaves were delivered to the coast by other Africans. Sometimes the slaves were members of tribes that had been defeated in wars among kingdoms and chiefdoms. Sometimes they were people who were simply in the wrong place at the wrong time, captured by thugs who went into the lucrative slave business. At least 12 million Africans were packed into ships like barrels of rum for transport to North America, South America and the Caribbean. Ten to 20 percent of them died along the way.

I was a willing participant. In that lifetime, I flogged the slaves and raped black women when I felt like it.

I started to cry.

Then, another image came to mind—the captain of the ship, or the guy making the deals for the slaves, was James. He went to the Africans and lied, making all kinds of promises to trick them. He double-crossed anyone to make a profit. And I was an accomplice. At times, my conscience bothered me, but not enough to stop him, or stop myself. I went along with James' plans.

As I did in this life. While we were together, I was under his spell again. He tried to convince people that he could pull off a new theme park, or a Titanic exhibition, or a hot air balloon ride, and I went along with his plans.

With that realization, I became angry. I'd covered for my lying, cheating husband. I never told anyone that despite all his bravado and grandiosity, he was broke. Even after our divorce, I didn't want to tell James' family and business associates what had really happened, reasoning that it might force him even further underground and jeopardize my chances of finding his money.

It was time to shake things up.

A week later, I sent fat manila envelopes to James' brother, two sisters and adult daughter—documentation of what James Montgomery was really all about. The documents included my original complaint for divorce, which accused him of marriage fraud and adultery. I sent the plaintiff's trial brief, which summarized the facts of the case, including how he walked away from a court of law. And I sent the final judgment of divorce, in which the judge found him guilty of fraud and awarded me a settlement, including $1 million in punitive damages.

"James is a criminal sociopath," I wrote in my cover letter. "That means he is a prolific liar, has no conscience and will never change."

My emotional stability was disintegrating. One thought permeated my mind: My life was ruined. On October 24, 2000, my anger boiled up into rage— rage against God. I wrote in my journal:

> Dear God,
>   I really hate what you've done to my life. My life is ruined. It's over. I have no chance of having the only thing I ever wanted—a family. I liked being married. I wanted to try to raise a child. Why have you done this to me?
>   I hate you. I hate what you've done to my life. I really don't give a shit about the higher perfection—my life sucks. It's ruined. I am unhappy and miserable. Why have you done this to me? What did I do to deserve this? I am so angry. I am so angry. I have so much resentment. What am I supposed to do—be philosophical? Say, "Well, my life is ruined, but that's okay. The human race will benefit."
>   This is not fair. Why won't it get better? Why won't you take the pressure away? Why can't I have a nice, normal, regular life? Why can't I have a nice, loving man? A family?

My tirade was interrupted by a message in my head from Guidance.

Will you let us talk? Just listen. You are getting yourself upset needlessly. It is not that bad. You are beautiful. You are intelligent. You will find love. You may find love tomorrow—get yourself in the right frame of mind.

Donna, please be patient. It will go away. That is one of your lessons—patience. You have gotten yourself in trouble many times because of impatience. Try to learn patience—it will help you tremendously.

You are not a failure. You have made a choice. You never really wanted children and all you want now is a lover. Relax. Lovers are easy to come by. Just switch your energy.

The pressure will go away—you will find the money. We want you to work on Lovefraud.com. It is your destiny. It is coming to closure. Please be patient.

I stared at the message from Guidance that I'd just channeled, telling me that everything would be fine. I did not believe it.

Trying to find the reasons for my suffering, I journaled frantically. I lamented my loneliness, rued the disappointment in my life, and prayed for deliverance. Guidance kept telling me to have patience, everything would work out, not to let my problems consume me.

Before my telephone session with Elaine Anderson on October 26, 2000, I e-mailed her what I had written in my journal—my questions, demands and pleas to Guidance, and their responses. When we got on the phone, she said that I was hearing Guidance correctly.

"The messages are very clear," Elaine said.

This did not make me feel better. "It's all very nice that Guidance has this cosmic mission for me, but in the meantime, here on Earth, in this lifetime, I'm miserable," I complained. "All I ever wanted was a family. My life is ruined."

"I don't think you were meant to have children in this lifetime," she said.

"So then why did I want kids? Why did I get all these messages that it would happen? The guides have admitted on several occasions that they've lied to me. Why should I believe them now?"

"Your trust with the universe has been broken," Elaine said. "Let's work on that. Lie down and get comfortable, and let's get you breathing."

I lay on the daybed in my meditation room. When I started deep breathing—in through my nose and out through my mouth—I focused on allowing the pain and disappointment locked deep within me to rise to the surface. "I'm so tired," I said, my voice breaking. "I'm so disappointed and I'm so tired."

Elaine thought I should go back to the lifetime when I was on a slave-trading vessel and release the energy from that experience. But I knew that wasn't the past life I needed to work on. "There's another one," I said.

Gradually I started getting images of the Roman Coliseum and gladiators. Then I realized I was a Roman guard when the Christians were being thrown to the lions. "This is so horrible," I recoiled, appalled. "It is so awful. It is unbearable."

During the first 300 years of its existence, the Christian church was sporadically subject to persecution in the Roman Empire. Often, it was the result of mob mentality—if natural disaster struck, Christians were blamed. But at times, persecuting Christians was official government policy—such as in 250 A.D., under Emperor Decius, and between 303 and 311 A.D., during the reign of Emperor Diocletian.

Romans had already been killing slaves, prisoners and criminals in their magnificent arenas for hundreds of years. Over time, the spectacles, as they were called, evolved from punishments to public entertainment. People sentenced to the most vicious forms of death were burned alive or thrown to the wild beasts—*damnatio ad bestias.*

As Rome conquered the world, ferocious beasts from distant lands were brought to the spectacles—including lions, tigers, panthers, leopards, wild boars, bulls and bears. Sometimes the damned were tied to a post or cart, defenseless against the hungry animals. Sometimes they were dropped into a cage full of beasts. The animals attacked, mauled and mutilated the victims, ripping their flesh.

Christians were considered to be guilty of "hatred of mankind," in part because they refused to attend the spectacles and make sacrifices to the Roman gods. This was an act of treason against the state. Yet often, Roman officials were reluctant to execute them. Some officials offered Christians a chance to live—all they had to do was make a sacrifice, such as burning incense, to a Roman god or emperor, and they would be released.

Hundreds of Christians refused. They wanted to be martyrs. They wanted to die for their faith, following in the footsteps of Jesus Christ. They would rather be mauled by lions, in the name of their god, than burn a little incense in front of a statue of the emperor.

As a Roman guard, I witnessed this in horror. I watched the Christians ask for death, rather than recant. I watched them passively wait for the animals, even try to attract their attention, until the beasts lunged at the Christians' throats. I was traumatized.

"You had to shut down," Elaine said. "It was so awful that you couldn't allow yourself to feel it."

"These people are dying for their god," I said, appalled. "What kind of god is that? What kind of god would allow his people to die like this?" I was shocked, appalled, numb.

"You didn't want to have anything to do with a god who allowed this," Elaine said softly. "It broke your trust with the universe."

Then I realized that James was in that lifetime as well. He was one of the captains of the guard, in charge of throwing the people to the lions. And he liked it. He got a charge out of it. He thought it was great fun. "He rapes the women before sending them out," I blurted out. "He says they're going to die anyway, so what the hell."

I felt the massive energy attached to this terrible memory. It was a huge disturbance in my energetic field—Elaine saw it as green and black—that I'd carried with me for so many lifetimes. The energy was centered in my back. "It's the burden," I said. "It's the burden moving."

As the energy shifted, I relived the memory of what I witnessed. Words came out of my mouth before I knew what they were. "This is horrible. The worst part is the kids. The lions get the kids first, because they can't run fast. And the mothers are screaming. James makes sure the lions are nice and hungry when he lets them into the ring."

"You wanted to stop James, but you couldn't," Elaine said. "You couldn't do anything. This was much bigger than one person could handle, but you've been carrying the pain of it all these years."

"James always found these situations where he could get away with his evil schemes. He really doesn't care."

"He's so distorted. He has his own agony that he runs from."

The horror of the callous, vicious killings overwhelmed me. That's why my trust with the universe was broken. How could I trust a god who allowed that to happen? An answer formed in my mind that was addressed to all of humanity. "I love you," I heard. "I trust that you're going to grow up."

"Free will," Elaine said. "He won't take any of it away, no matter what we do."

"But what about me?" I railed, with anger and resentment. "What about my circumstances in this lifetime? I feel like I shouldn't be in this position. I feel like my life is being frittered away, while the universe slowly lays out its plan. Guidance has no sense of time, so what do they care? I'm by myself. I have nothing. There are no bright spots in my life, nothing to look forward to."

"Just be patient."

"What do they care? It's all very well and good for them to tell me to be patient, but I'm the one who's alone. Spirits make lousy lovers."

"They're trying to make you laugh," Elaine said. "Let's listen for guidance."

I paused. "They're telling me to get a life," I said. Guidance wanted me to find pleasure in day-to-day occurrences. They wanted me to enjoy myself, make time for fun and joy in my life.

Elaine said rowing was important, not because of the competition, but because it got me outside with nature. "Nature is very healing for you," she said. "That's what nature is for."

"I take my dog for a walk by the bay in the mornings," I said. "It's nice." Thinking about Beau, I choked up again. "I worry about my dog," I said. "I worry that he'll leave me."

"Guidance sometimes lives in our pets, so it can be close to us," Elaine said. "Your dog will stay with you as long as you need him, and then he will pass. After that, there will be another dog. Everything is unfolding beautifully. You might as well make peace with it, because it is on its own timetable."

"It's hard not knowing what is going to happen."

"Yes, it is. That's where you have to trust in the universe."

"Well, there are times when it's very difficult to be philosophical about what's going on in your life. At least before, I had John. I had something to look forward to."

I felt another emotional blow. "You know, that was the first time I felt like someone loved me," I said quietly, almost a whimper. "Having that taken away was worse than when James left. I always knew James was full of shit. But John loved me.

"I saw him in the beginning of September," I continued. "He's already moved on. He's talking to some woman who lives in Montana. He didn't even want me any more."

Sadness welled up within me and I really started to cry.

"John was good for the moment, a playmate," Elaine said.

"I'm just so tired and angry."

"It's understandable. But Guidance is showing me everything unfolding beautifully. I would be angry too if that wasn't happening. But it is all unfolding, in its own time. They want you to make room in your life for joy. Look for it in the small, day-to-day things. It is all unfolding. Changes are coming."

I forced myself to be optimistic. "You know, I was thinking about feminine energy the other day," I said. "I was thinking that I've been trying to get out of my problems by my usual method—doing things. Taking action. Taking control. Being in the masculine. But the energy of the feminine—opening to receive, waiting for fruition—is also powerful."

"That's one of your lessons, becoming more aligned with feminine power."

"It's weird. With the masculine, you make plans, and with the feminine, you wait for things to happen. If you're supposed to create your future by your thoughts and plans, but you're supposed to wait for things to happen, how can you get anywhere?"

"That's the balancing of the masculine and feminine. You take a step, and then you back off and wait. It seems like the masculine and feminine are contradictory, but actually, they're complementary."

I was quiet, thinking about what I'd heard from Elaine, and from Guidance. Trust the universe. Employ feminine energy. According to Guidance, my job was to heal my life. Stop worrying about the debt and James. Start finding joy in my daily existence. Come to terms with the idea that events were proceeding on God's timetable, not mine.

I didn't want to change. I didn't want to give up my views and attitude. But my current approach to solving my problems sure wasn't working, so I thought I might as well try something different. Guidance agreed:

> *Let the universe support you. That is the lesson. All will be fine. Make each day pleasant. Meditate. Trust your intuition.*
>
> *Yes, your life is upside down—but that is good. You needed it for your higher good. You will enjoy life. You can enjoy it today—just decide to enjoy it. All will be fine. Just relax and trust. Open to receive. It is coming; there are many gifts. God has many gifts for you, and he will give you the tools to complete your assignment. It will be very valuable. It will take time. Do not worry. Relax, enjoy life and trust your intuition.*

The banquet room of a local country club was filled with women in business suits. The event was a "legislative breakfast" sponsored by the Atlantic County Advisory Commission on Women. A former customer suggested I attend, so I sat at one of the large round tables, drinking decaf and listening to speeches about community efforts on behalf of women. The only men in the room were politicians.

One of them was Frank A. LoBiondo, the local Republican congressman. As he talked about helping women, I wondered if he could help me.

James, of course, had been involved in Republican politics while living in New Jersey, trying to ingratiate himself into becoming a person with connections. He proudly played his voice mail for me so I could hear that Frank LoBiondo returned his call.

When the speeches were done, I approached LoBiondo, one of many people trying to get his attention. I quickly told the congressman my story, and asked him to find out what was going on with the criminal prosecution of James Montgomery. He asked me to send a letter to his office with the pertinent information.

I drafted a letter that day:

November 13, 2000

Dear Rep. LoBiondo,

Perhaps you remember my ex-husband, Australian-born James Montgomery. He was active in Atlantic County politics, working on the 1996 election campaigns for Freeholder Joe Nickles and other Republicans. I know he was in touch with you on some issues. In fact, he wanted to invite you to our wedding. I vetoed the idea because I did not want to be upstaged.

Montgomery is a con artist who funds his lifestyle by meeting women on the Internet and defrauding them. He has taken more than $227,000 from me. I can identify seven more victims from whom he has taken another $810,000. The judge in my divorce issued a court ruling that Montgomery committed fraud.

I am writing to you because it seems that law enforcement officials are reluctant to apprehend him.

Sylvia Banning of Pennsylvania initially contacted the FBI about Montgomery in March 1999. Then, working together, Sylvia and I turned over substantial evidence to an FBI agent from the Linwood office. Because the case was originated in Pennsylvania, the FBI office in Scranton continued the investigation, with Deryck Bratton as the lead agent. Mr. Bratton told me that Montgomery is defrauding women all over the United States.

I understand from Mr. Bratton that the case has been turned over to U.S. Attorney David Barasch in Harrisburg. Ms. Banning has called Mr. Barasch on many occasions to find out if he will prosecute. So far he has refused to return her call, let alone give an answer.

Enclosed are documents detailing Montgomery's crimes. I respectfully ask you to look into this matter. When will the U. S. Attorney prosecute?

Donna Andersen
cc: David Barasch, Deryk Bratton

My British search agent sent me an e-mail on November 14, 2000. Although his team had located James' account in the Australian bank, they could not get the critical information I needed—the account number. My only option was to try going through the Australian courts.

In the meantime, going through the American courts was proving to be an exercise in frustration. I had a judgment against James for $1,295,453. It was dated March 17, 2000. My divorce lawyer drafted a writ of execution for the Atlantic County sheriff to seize James' bank accounts back in May. It disappeared. No one knew what happened to the document. We had to start all over again, and then found that his First Union account had only $517.38 in it.

By this time, I'd gone through the boxes of paperwork that I recovered from James' storage unit more thoroughly. I still found no financial records. But I did find numerous floppy disks—perhaps they contained electronic clues. One by one, I opened and examined them.

To my surprise, I found that in March 1999—immediately after I left James—he was looking for a full-time job in Australia. In response to an ad for a corporate project director, James wrote:

> I will match my organizational technology and people handling skills with the best. I was a pioneer in computerized critical path planning for special events, acting as a consultant for both the Florida Division of Tourism and for the Atlantic City Convention and Visitors Bureau for their major international events—many included TV coverage [Miss America Quest, Daytona].

People handling skills? Yeah, he was an expert at lying and manipulating people into doing what he wanted. Consultant in Florida and Atlantic City? Never happened.

James sent the same letter to apply for a job as CEO of Hamilton Island Airport. Hamilton Island was located off the coast of Australia in the middle of the Great Barrier Reef. In that letter, James added that he was a consultant to the FAA—Federal Aviation Administration—in Atlantic City. I couldn't believe it. His total involvement with the FAA amounted to one visit to its facility with me, when I was asked to submit a marketing proposal. And what James wrote for that proposal was unusable.

Two months later, James apparently gave up the job search and found a new source of revenue named Sharon Decamp. James created two loan agreements on computer-generated stationery for SFIICE, his Southern Florida International Institute for Continuing Education. One stated that Sharon Decamp loaned

James $15,000 on May 10, 1999, and as collateral held a demitasse cup and asparagus plate from James' Titanic Experience collection. The second document said that Sharon Decamp loaned James $15,000 on May 20, 1999. This time, the collateral was three post cards and the shard of glass from the wreck. I couldn't tell if Sharon gave him $15,000 and the collateral changed, or she gave him two loans adding up to $30,000.

In any event, according to the loan agreements, James was supposed to repay the money by the end of June 1999. By then, of course, I had a court order for the return of the Titanic artifacts. I could picture what happened when James had to retrieve them from Sharon Decamp. He probably blamed "the mob in Atlantic City"—that would be me—for ruining his plans, and used it as a convenient excuse for not being able to pay her back.

I assumed that James' relationship with Sharon was not strictly business, even though at the time, he was married to both Kim Goodson and to me. And the disks held further evidence that James and Kim Goodson had indeed been intimate throughout his two prior marriages.

In June 1996, about the time I first started corresponding with James, Kim spent a week with him in the Mays Landing townhouse owned by Gale Lewis. Gale, of course, had just died. Kim visited him there again at the end of July, and was supposed to stay until August 13. At this point, James and I were engaged to be married. He told me he was going on a military mission to the Middle East, when he was actually staying in the townhouse with Kim. A few days into the second stay, Kim figured out that James and Gale were actually married. Furious, she left and went back to Florida. On August 10, 1996, Kim sent James the following message:

> Let me see if I understand: Gale was fatally ill, you lived in her spare room, she worked for CelebAM, you'd been there since about May 95 when you left Tampa? You "married" her with napkins? announcements? reception? rings? etc? to give her legitimacy and respectability ... the only people who think you are "married" are her family in Sumter ... and a few people in Mays Landing ... At the time you got a place to live, the dog stayed on where he had been, and she got ?? in May when you told me a member of the team had died and you had to go to Fort Bragg, you were really going to Sumter to bury Gale ... After she died and you had the townhouse and her vehicle and problems since her father is now dying and you weren't "married" to begin with ... My question: If I show up a year from now with a 5-month-old baby ... calling it your child ... won't impinge on the business? If you tell me something or I ask a question ... you will tell me the truth but it may not be the whole story rather only the part that I need to know?

In his reply, James expressed no guilt and no remorse. Instead, he went on the offensive:

You don't want to talk with me. You "probably will never see me again." Telling you I loved you didn't change things. It makes it a little difficult to deal with your hypotheticals. You have made the decision for us … so live with it!

But as he did with so many women, James reeled Kim in again. He flew to Florida to visit her right before Thanksgiving. By that time, James and I had gotten married in Australia; he told me he was going to Florida on a business trip. James saw Kim again from January 1 to January 5, 1997; they met in Orlando. This was two weeks before our New Jersey wedding, when he told me he went to Sumter, South Carolina, to spend time with the parents of Gale Lewis.

According to the evidence, James made many, many trips to see Kim Goodson while he was married to me. But even more upsetting than the infidelity was the undeniable proof of James' taste for promiscuity and porn. He had a massive collection of pornographic photos: men with women, women with women, men as women. The pictures made me want to vomit.

And then there was his continuing Internet search for short-term and long-term relationships. In October 1998, he was looking for women in California—that was when he was supposedly there on Titanic business. He was also looking for men. James wrote the following ad:

> This is all about fantasy sex, so unless we share the same fantasies—it's not going to be the special moment I have been scripting in my head for so long. Your role must be exactly what you are looking for, so that it works for you too…
>
> I want a man who wants to experience sex as a woman, to be kissed on the mouth, to play with, taste and suck my cock. So my fantasy was the opposite of me—slim, smooth and aching to be able to feel totally feminine without any hang-ups or fears. Frankly, I am jaded with fucking women. The thrill of that first time just isn't there anymore. I WANT a man to fuck like a woman. The thrill of the totally forbidden!
>
> I am in my mid-40s—a Sean Connery look alike in all respects … think of The Rock … so you will be kissing a man with a beard—totally masculine to look at—hairy chest—and touch! An imagination responsible for a couple of Emmy's that will create a total fantasy sex scene for us both.
>
> Please don't reply if each and every part of this isn't for you—but if it is—we are part way to making your fantasy into reality!

James in Atlantic City

The ad received responses from several interested men.

I was revolted.

I finished looking at the disks on November 17, 2000. The porn, James' solicitations—I felt so betrayed. So unclean. Agitated, I paced around the house.

I had to do something. Get out. It was Friday evening—I called a friend and asked her to meet me for a beer. We went to a local bar. I told her what I found. She was shocked.

I wished I could drown my sorrows. Unfortunately, it wasn't as easy as guzzling a few beers.

My internal stability was crumbling. I needed another session with Elaine, and scheduled one for November 20, 2000. As soon as we got on the phone, I started bitching. I was angry and disappointed. Even though she was not physically with me, Elaine could see my disappointment, layers and layers of it, stuck in my stomach.

"Guidance lied to me," I accused. "They don't care about me. They don't care how much I suffer."

"Guidance does care," Elaine said. "You're receiving their messages accurately, although sometimes you may be misinterpreting them."

Apparently, Guidance was indeed aware of all the disappointment I carried around within me, the result of dashed expectations, of my life not looking like I wanted it to look. Guidance said I struggled with this over many lifetimes. I kept trying harder, kept trying to do the right thing, and kept getting disappointed. Now I had pools and pools of disappointment, lifetimes worth, stuck in my stomach. Guidance wanted me to release the disappointment. So to help me, they piled on even more disappointment, so much disappointment that I could no longer contain it. The dam would burst; I would collapse and give up my expectations.

With that I would be free.

My expectations, Guidance said, were causing many of my problems. I was supposed to take on a new way of being, one without expectations. "By giving up your expectations, you are free to be who you are, regardless of the events in your life," Elaine explained. "You can stay calm and connected. You are you, your soul. You are not the things that happen to you."

I'd already accomplished a lot, according to Guidance. I'd made shifts in consciousness, and set new events in motion. "They're saying this is one of your most abundant lifetimes," Elaine told me.

"Define abundant," I commented sardonically.

She laughed. "It's not like we would define abundant."

Earlier in the day, before the phone session, I got the feeling that my soul wanted to move fast, so it was willing to take on many hard lessons at once. Toward the end of our call, I started feeling excitement. But as soon as I hung up the phone, my mood returned to disappointment, resentment and despair. I couldn't remember much of what was said. I was shaky, spilling things and yelling at my dog.

I felt shell-shocked.

Later, as I tried to remember what Elaine and I talked about, I realized that I had to let go of my resistance. I had to give up my expectations and let the universe do what it will—because it was going to do that anyway. And if I was honest with myself, I knew that everything was going to work out, and it would all be easier if I changed my attitude and trusted that God/universe/Guidance cared about me and would help me. I had to keep clearing the negative energy until I felt the excitement in my soul. Because my soul was excited; my soul knew the importance of my work, my mission, and how much I'd already accomplished.

I faced a struggle between my soul and my ego, and I'd be better off if I lost the ego, lost my attachment to results, and lost my expectations. Then I could open my life to miracles.

James was still on America Online, and still, I assumed, trolling for victims. On December 4, 2000, I sent an e-mail to AOL's Community Action Team, advising them that James had defrauded me and multiple other women that he'd met online. I was told to speak to an AOL member services representative.

The representative explained that it was not a violation of AOL's terms of service to lie and con people. "We don't monitor your e-mail," she said. "The way we know if a person is committing a violation is if it is reported."

So what constituted a violation? Pedophilia, extremely objectionable images, or committing a crime on AOL.

And what happened if a member committed a violation? First, someone had to report it. Then the member would be notified that he or she had committed a violation. If the member accumulated four violations, the account was suspended for 30 days. The gist of what the AOL representative told me was that James might be a criminal, but it didn't mean they'd terminate his account. It was up to other members to look out for themselves—buyer beware.

Two days later I received two responses to the letter that I wrote to Congressman Frank A. LoBiondo complaining about the lack of prosecution of my criminal ex-husband.

One letter was from LoBiondo. He said he contacted the Justice Department on my behalf, and would get back to me as soon as he heard from them.

The second letter was from the U.S. Attorney's office, which was part of the Justice Department. It was written by Assistant U.S. Attorney Martin C. Carlson, chief of the criminal division:

November 28, 2000

Dear Ms. Andersen:
    Your November 13, 2000 correspondence to the United States Attorney David M. Barasch has been referred to me for response. In this correspondence, you state that you were formerly married to a man named James Montgomery, an Australian national. According to your correspondence, your ex-husband, Mr. Montgomery, defrauded you and other women, taking both their moneys and manipulating their affections. While many of the activities which are the subject of your complaints have occurred elsewhere, one of the women who was allegedly

involved in this activity resided in the Middle District of Pennsylvania.

Your November 13 letter states that you "understood that the FBI office in Scranton ... has presented its case to [this office]," and then asks whether this office intends to pursue federal criminal fraud charges in this matter.

Thank you for your correspondence. I appreciate the opportunity to provide you with information concerning our office's position in this case, and to clarify some misunderstandings on your part.

As I am sure you can appreciate investigative and prosecutive decisions involve a careful, sensitive assessment of all facts and circumstances presented by a particular case. In each instance, we must assess the credibility and motivation of witnesses, and determine whether the admissible evidence proves a violation of criminal law which can be established beyond a reasonable doubt, the highest, most exacting burden of proof defined by law.

Moreover, in making these decisions we must be mindful of the fact that this office may only pursue criminal conduct occurring within the Middle District of Pennsylvania. Thus, we simply lack the authority to prosecute crimes which allegedly occurred in New Jersey or other jurisdictions. Rather, we may only prosecute crimes which allegedly occurred in this jurisdiction.

In this case, as you may know, federal authorities in Scranton have conducted a thorough investigation of these allegations over the past 18 months. At the conclusion of this lengthy investigation, on October 25, 2000, representatives of the FBI and the professional staff of this office met to review the evidence. At the conclusion of the review, it was the consensus of the investigators and prosecutor assigned to this matter that a criminal prosecution of this alleged misconduct in this district would be inappropriate. Therefore, prosecution of this case was declined by our office.

In reaching this declination decision our office considered the quality of the evidence as it related to alleged misconduct in the Middle District of Pennsylvania. We recognize, therefore, our declination decision does not in any way preclude you from contacting state or federal officials in New Jersey, and asking these officials to consider evidence related to alleged misconduct in that state.

While this office is not prepared to pursue a criminal prosecution of your ex-husband at this time for his alleged misconduct in Pennsylvania, I trust that this information will be of some assistance to you. Please feel free to contact me if you have any further questions concerning this matter.

Martin C. Carlson
Assistant United States Attorney
Chief, Criminal Division

I was shocked.

These people had the nerve to talk about "misunderstandings," and the audacity to question the "credibility and motivation of the witnesses." No one had contacted me since Sylvia and I met with the female FBI agent in my dining room. The FBI did, however, interview Kathleen Maloney, Jody McClure and John Lewis, all of whom testified during my divorce. Judge Max Baker believed us, declared that James Montgomery was guilty of fraud, and awarded me everything I asked for, plus $1 million in punitive damages, which I was struggling to collect. I'd forwarded the judge's decision to Bratton of the FBI. James Montgomery was a criminal.

I sent a copy of the U.S. Attorney's letter to Congressman LoBiondo. "My ex-husband has an obvious pattern of defrauding women," I wrote in my cover letter. "Does this mean that because he operates all over the country, not in one location, he is immune to prosecution? What office has the authority to deal with a pattern of crime on a national level?"

If I could find James' new wife, Kim Goodson, maybe I could find James. From the papers I retrieved from the storage unit, I learned that Kim Goodson's family still lived in the Clearwater, Florida area, and Kim was active in the Aviation Institute and the Civil Air Patrol. With that information, I formulated a plan.

On December 14, 2000, I called the home of Kim Goodson's parents. An older gentleman answered the phone. "Is this Mr. Goodson?" I asked.

"Yes," he replied.

"Hi. I'm calling from the Aviation Institute. I wonder if you can help me. We sent Kim a Christmas card, but it was returned. Do you have an address for her?"

"She's in New Zealand."

"New Zealand!" The surprise in my voice was genuine.

"Yes. Wait a minute; I'll get her address."

He set down the phone. I waited nervously, hoping this was the break I'd been waiting for. Mr. Goodson came back and gave me her address—Kim Goodson was living in Christchurch, New Zealand.

"Thank you so much," I said. "We'll be sure to get a new card out to her."

"I'm sure she'll be happy to hear from you."

"Well, we certainly want to keep in touch. Thank you again."

"You're welcome. Merry Christmas."

"Merry Christmas to you."

Yes. Merry Christmas indeed.

Mental health professionals know that many people suffer from the blues, even depression, during the holidays. As a prime candidate to be one of them, I decided that the best way for me to cope was to be around people, so I took advantage of every opportunity I had to socialize, even if I had to buy a ticket to do it.

I went to every Christmas party sponsored by the professional organizations that I belonged to. My younger brother, Greg, invited me to his home for dinner on a Sunday afternoon and I accepted, even though he lived 80 miles away. Greg seemed surprised. The following week I made the trip again for his son's first birthday party.

My brother Doug invited me to attend the Pierce Technology company Christmas party. I accepted that invitation also, even though it was at a restaurant in New York City and I had to ride almost three hours on a bus to get there.

For Christmas Day itself, I asked Doug if I could join him and his family. They always spent the holidays at a condo in a Vermont ski resort. I'd never been there, but for Christmas 2000, I wanted to get out of town. Doug and I did a bit of cross-country skiing on Christmas Eve, while the kids were downhilling on the mountain. On Christmas morning, the kids plowed through a mountain of gifts. I helped them put toys together and played with them—something I'd never done before.

A week later, of course, was New Year's Eve. I had no expectations of a date, and no plans to mark the occasion at all. I spent the evening at home, waiting for the terrible year to end. I went to bed long before midnight, praying that 2001 would be better.

Chapter 24

On the first business day of the New Year, Tuesday, January 2, 2001, I woke up tense. The holidays were over; it was time to get back to reality. My reality wasn't good. I had one paying job—another newsletter for Dover Downs Slots. Beyond that I had no work—and a mountain of bills.

I could ignore my worries as long as I was busy. But as soon as I finished whatever I was doing, my thoughts sprang to my troubles, and I was bulldozed by fear, pressure and loneliness. By this time, I was having almost daily conversations—telepathically, I realized—with the spirit guides. Their advice: Distract myself. Any effort I made to stay calm and peaceful would hasten my progress in my most important project—healing my life.

I tried to follow the advice, but faltered. Internal turmoil was always at the edge of my awareness—or with the slightest instigation, rolling over me. Desperate for relief, I scheduled another telephone session with Elaine Anderson for January 5, 2001. But that morning she called to cancel my appointment.

"Sure, I understand," I said. But when I hung up the phone, I freaked out. How could she say that something had come up? Didn't she know that I was on the edge of collapse? Despite my efforts, I could not stay calm; hopelessness overwhelmed me. I went into my meditation room and prayed for deliverance. Guidance did not offer me consolation. Instead, I was told that I was stubbornly hanging on to my drama. "Live lightly, adjust and be flexible," they said. "Watch for opportunities, for messages and for God's grace."

Great. The spirits, comfortably reclining on some heavenly cloud, were offering pithy advice. Here on Earth, in my life, I was shaking with trepidation. I didn't want tough love. I wanted to escape the fear. Guidance told me to allow myself to feel the fear, then let God's grace take its place.

With nothing to lose, I tried following their suggestion. I lay on the floor in the meditation room. Immediately, my mind's eye filled with images of being whipped. Torture. Crucifixions. I had once trusted in God, proclaimed his goodness and the rewards of heaven. People believed me, followed me—and I lead them to their deaths.

It was an image from a past life during the time of the early Christians, when I was involved with the new religious movement. The terrible memory started to surface. Because of me, many people died. And because of that, I lost my faith.

The life I just saw, I realized, preceded my lifetime as a guard at the Roman Coliseum. In that life, I'd returned to the planet, to Rome, in hopes of rectifying my error. I wanted to save other Christians condemned to die in the spectacle, *damnatio ad bestias*. But I wasn't able to save Christians the second time around either, and I lost my faith again.

My session with Elaine was rescheduled for January 12, 2001. I knew it would be important.

The Grand Design, by Paddy McMahon, was billed as a "simply stated, user-friendly guide to living in the universe." The work was in two volumes, and I was voraciously reading the second book.

McMahon channeled the information from an enlightened entity called She-baka, who incarnated as a king of Egypt from 712 to 698 B.C. The books discussed the nature of the soul, the stages of spiritual evolution, and the purpose of life on Earth. This planet, the book said, was "a platform for growth in consciousness."

I read and re-read the pages, highlighter in hand. The section on unconditional love spoke directly to the issues I faced.

Unconditional love, the book explained, meant accepting people and situations as they were, without judgment. This included accepting myself. But even while accepting a situation, unconditional love did not require me to like it or stay in it. Unconditional love for myself meant respecting myself, so I did not have to continue to live with a situation that I did not want.

But I'd been fighting my situation for two years, without success. How did I get it to change? How could I do what I wanted to do? McMahon, channeling Shebaka, provided an answer:

> If you are truly loving unconditionally, or, more accurately, being unconditional love, that question will never arise. A solution to enable you to do what you want will present itself. That's the way the loving energy of the universe, of God, works. There's no element of chance in it; it's as inevitable as night following day. It's the unfailing way of the universe.
>
> An unavoidable conclusion from what I'm saying is that, if you're in a situation that irks you, that you find intolerable in some way, or even simply that you don't like, it's a sure indication that you're not loving unconditionally. In that case, unless, of course, you want to stay in the situation as it is, I suggest that you look at it, determine what it is about it that you find intolerable, or that you don't like, and then hand it over unconditionally to your guides, divine consciousness, the god within, whichever is most comfortable for you. If you allow yourself to trust in the process with no reservations, no conditions, I promise you that the outcome will be a source of wonder and joy to you.

So how should I hand over a situation unconditionally? The book suggested asking myself the following questions:

> (a) Are you looking for a specified outcome?
> (b) Are you looking for an outcome within a particular time limit?
> (c) Are you saying to yourself that because you've been doing everything "right," life owes you what you would consider a favorable outcome?
> (d) Are you stipulating that you won't be able to get on with your work of, say, service to humanity, unless your situation changes in a particular way?
> (e) Are you leaving the outcome completely open, knowing that, whatever it is, it will bring the best possible solution to your situation in a way that you will find not only enjoyable but better than anything you could have envisaged?
> If the answers to any or all of the questions (a) to (d) are "yes," then you know that the process is still conditional as far as you are concerned. If you can give a positive answer to (e), then your handing over is unconditional.

My answers to the quiz were yes, yes, yes, yes and no. I completely flunked it.

James' First Union bank account, with a paltry $517.38 in it, was levied back in November. Almost two months later, on January 8, 2001, the judge signed an order for the bank to turn over the money. The cash was a step closer, but I still didn't have it.

In the meantime, I made up a spreadsheet of my debts. Not counting my mortgage and attorneys' fees, I owed $54,205 due to James' fraud. Every month, I had to come up with $1,029 just to make the minimum payments.

Perhaps, I thought, I should try a different approach to easing my financial problems. Perhaps I should simply ask for assistance.

I sent letters to American Express, Wachovia, the Associates, AT&T Universal card, Bank of America and Citibank. When I wrote to the companies previously, I hoped to find James' money and pay my debts, but my hopes were rapidly diminishing. So I asked the companies to treat my debts as fraud—as the judge in my divorce said they were. I asked for the debts to be forgiven.

My only alternative, I said, was bankruptcy.

I lit two candles and a stick of incense. After a few minutes of meditation, I called Elaine Anderson on January 12, 2001, for my rescheduled phone session.

I'd sent Elaine recent transcripts from my journal, which included the imagery of a past life as one of the early Christians. She said I was receiving the messages clearly. But even with all the advice from Guidance to stop worrying, I railed again against the instability of my life: I had no work, no relationship, and

I was always 30 days away from insolvency. Emotional turmoil welled up within me. "I've had enough," I lamented. "I'm afraid that the other shoe will fall. Another catastrophe to push me over the edge."

"You've been through all of this and kept your head held high," Elaine replied. "Whatever happens, you'll deal with it, and understand that you are not the circumstances."

"I just wish I had some joy. There's no joy in my life."

"Joy is always in the present moment."

I thought about that. "Yesterday I went out to dinner with the women I row with. I enjoyed that," I admitted.

"Look for those moments of joy in your life," Elaine said. "You're unraveling and unraveling disappointment. You're learning to trust."

Elaine wanted to start the energetic work. I arranged my telephone headset and lay down on the daybed. "Let's talk about the early Christians," she said.

I started to breathe deeply—in through my nose, out through my mouth—but it was difficult. I felt like concrete blocks weighed down my chest.

"There's a disturbance in your solar plexus," Elaine said.

Terrible details of that life, which I'd glimpsed a week earlier, formed in my mind. I saw an image of myself. I was a young man. I was being whipped. Other people were being killed, and it was my fault.

I was a leader in the early Christian movement. I was so sure that I knew everything. I was so sure that I was talking to God. I was so sure in leading these people. Now we were all being killed, and I couldn't do anything about it. They looked at me, pleading for their lives, and I was helpless.

"It's awful," I said. "It's just so awful." I felt so guilty, so responsible.

Although one to two billion people practice some form of Christianity today, the religion started out small, spreading slowly by word-of-mouth through the ancient Roman Empire. During that period of antiquity, people followed many different religions and cults. Nearly everyone at the time was a pagan, meaning they believed in a multitude of gods and spirits, including those of Greek and Roman mythology. Christians, however, said there was only one God, and all others were false. Some pagans, hearing the story of Jesus Christ rising from the dead, thought the Christian God must be extremely powerful and converted to the new religion. But other pagans rejected this message—at times violently. And although Christianity started out as a sect within Judaism, many Jews also opposed Christianity.

In 202 A.D., the Christian church was making converts and gaining strength, which led to anti-Christian feelings among some populations. Emperor Septimius Severus enacted a law prohibiting the spread of Christianity and Judaism. This was the first universal decree against Christianity, and violent persecutions broke out in Egypt and North Africa.

I didn't know if my life as a young church leader took place during one of those purges, or during some other persecution. And I didn't know exactly where I lived—all I saw was an image of dry, hilly terrain, and my feet wearing leather sandals on a dusty dirt road. I remembered not what I saw, but what I felt. And I felt the presence of James.

At first I ignored it, thinking that it was probably my imagination; I was always looking for James in my past lives. Finally, the memory was too strong. "I'm not seeing James again, am I?" I asked.

"Yes," Elaine replied, softly. "You are."

Suddenly, I remembered—James was in the form of a woman, and she betrayed me. Because of that, all these people, including myself, were dying.

I never meant for it to happen.

Christianity, during that lifetime, was the latest rage. A fad. I was a charismatic young man, full of promise. A handsome specimen. If I was honest with myself, I wasn't even sure that I believed in the one God. But the new religion seemed like a good racket, a good way to make a name for myself.

"I knew there was danger, but I didn't take it seriously," I said to Elaine. "At first the Romans didn't care. Then there was a new general, and he decided to persecute the Christians. All of a sudden, it got serious."

Deadly serious. The general decreed that the new religion had to go, and they cut me down—along with everyone who followed me. I was angry, but I was angry with myself, blamed myself. All these people were trapped, and there was nothing I could do. All for a woman who seduced me. "These people are dying because I wanted to get laid," I said.

"You fell in love with her," Elaine said.

And she betrayed me. Walked away; never looked back. For money.

One by one, the soldiers took away the Christians. They were tortured and killed. Hanged. Crucified. Being a leader, I was one of the last. They wanted me to hear everyone suffer. The screams. The wailing. Then the silence.

I didn't see any of those Christians rising from the dead. I lost my faith in God.

I was filled with hatred for that woman. Filled with remorse. Filled with anger. Filled with doubt. This God business was for the birds. I vowed that I would never, ever, let this happen to me again.

"This is just so awful," I whimpered.

The energy trapped within me became a full-body tremor. Tension was everywhere—my stomach, my face, my throat, my mouth. I pushed my feet into the daybed and lifted my hips. All my muscles contracted. Little cries escaped from my throat. Tears streamed from my closed eyes. I held on to the headset with my left hand, and my right arm was crossed across my chest, between my breasts, my hand clenched in a fist.

"What was so awful?" Elaine asked.

"It made me feel stupid," I blurted out. "I was stupid. I fell for her. I was young, self-confident, cocky. I thought nothing could happen to me. I was on top of the world. I felt stupid."

"You were in love with her," Elaine said. "And you shut down. You decided you couldn't trust people. You couldn't trust God. You couldn't trust love. You couldn't trust yourself. And that was ground into you."

"I hate that bitch. I have so much hatred."

"Feel the hatred. What does it feel like?"

Waves of emotion rolled through me. Hatred—my heart was tight. The area around my heart was constricted. "That bitch," I cursed. "She just walked away. Never looked back. For money. All for money."

The negative energy roiled within me, gradually escaping. Through much of the process I was silent, feeling the charge drain off. Slowly, slowly. My lower back, around my kidneys, hurt.

"We store our fear in our kidneys," Elaine said. "This was truly awful for you. They knew you were a leader. So they made you watch everyone else get tortured and killed. And then they tortured and killed you."

Gradually, the energy dissipated.

I became conscious of Beau. He was outside in the yard, barking. He must have been barking for a half-hour. Then he barreled into the house through his dog door. He was at the bottom of the stairway, still barking. I heard the dog door bang again, and he was outside barking. I did nothing about it.

Slowly, as my fear, anger and hatred subsided, I felt calmer.

"What does it feel like?" Elaine asked.

I thought for a moment, trying to name the sensation. "It feels empty," I said.

"Be in the emptiness. Guidance is helping you transmute the fear. Just be in the emptiness."

I thought about James, the woman. "She didn't care. She just walked away, never looked back," I said.

"She really went cold."

"What does this mean in regards to sociopaths? I still haven't figured out their purpose."

"There's an opposite for everything in reality."

I realized that the woman who was James didn't know what was going to happen either. Another person lied to her—the general, or an agent of the general. She never thought all those people would get killed. It was much more than she bargained for. In fact, it was the reason she, James' soul, went cold.

She knew the story of Judas. Like him, she betrayed me, and everyone, for her pieces of silver. But unlike Judas, she didn't commit suicide. Instead, she closed off her emotions and went on with her life. And that became the pattern of her soul. Disconnected. Shut down. Living by manipulation.

The horror of it, the guilt of it—well, she decided she would never feel guilt again. She had to push it aside. It was the start of James' career as a sociopath.

"Do you think this was the beginning of the struggle between James and me?" I asked Elaine.

"I think so. Don't you?"

"Yes," I answered. "That was why we kept having involvements over so many lifetimes. To try to get at this."

"This trauma has been locked away in your soul, in your energy, for hundreds of years," Elaine said. "You actually had to relive some of it in order to unlock it."

"This lifetime doesn't look so bad by comparison," I commented wryly.

"No," she agreed, with a slight laugh.

"So what was the original purpose of this experience?" I asked.

"I asked that," Elaine said. "But whatever it was, it got lost in the drama, the awfulness of everything."

Guidance told me that it was a situation where events got out of hand. No one was spiritually present; no one could stop what was going on. Everything ran amok. Free will turned into disaster.

"So what now? I asked. "What do I do now?"

"Let's ask that."

I listened for awhile. "I'm getting that I should do nothing," I said.

"That's what I'm getting," she said. "You need to do nothing. This has shaken up your soul. You're still vibrating. Just let it settle."

I thought of all the horrible things that happened in the world, the horrible things that people have done to each other. It was still going on—the day before, the former president of Bosnia surrendered to a United Nations tribunal, facing charges of genocide and crimes against humanity.

"That's why the universal consciousness has been so wounded," Elaine said. "And this is how it is healed—one soul at a time."

When the session was over, I stood up, unsteadily. Beau was still outside barking. I held onto the handrail going down the stairs to let him in. He was obviously worried. I petted him with two hands, rubbing him tightly. Then I gave him a treat—a nice rawhide bone.

I thought about going out to a convenience store for my own treat—ice cream—and Beau and I got into the car. But it was cold, and the windshield was covered with frost that needed to be scraped. I decided to find something to eat in the house. It was best that I do nothing.

In the days after my session with Elaine, I felt shaky. I cried without knowing why. At night I had bad dreams. Guidance said I was recovering from the seismic shock of unearthing the root of the drama between James and me. To recover, I should simply allow myself to be in the flow of life.

So I joined a new local gym. I attended an early-morning seminar sponsored by the Philadelphia Advertising Club, where I met a potential new client. I went to a seminar in New York City, where I met another potential client.

Business was still slow. My lack of work made me nervous, but provided me with time to sort through the avalanche of papers I'd recovered from James' storage unit.

For the first time, I read the documents related to SFIICE—the Southern Florida International Institute for Continuing Education. This was the work-at-home opportunity that James used to snag Sylvia Banning—I thought it was nothing but a scam. Well, if it was a scam, it sure was an elaborate one, involving people and companies across four continents.

One company was called Global Eco-Learning Publishing and Communications Pty. Ltd.—GELPAC for short. According to the corporate overview that I found, GELPAC, based in Australia, developed education programs on environmental issues that were recognized by the United Nations. The company also taught an English as a second language course that was formally accredited by the Australian National Training Authority. A man named Robert Palmer was the co-founder and chairman of GELPAC. The company's chief executive, to my surprise, was James' old friend and business partner, Archie Turner—the best man at our wedding. In October 1998, GELPAC, through Archie, was considering a joint venture with the Minsheng Group Ltd. of China, and the Shanghai Chinese Nation Relief Foundation, to develop environmental education programs in Shanghai. I found photos of Archie apparently meeting with a variety of Chinese officials.

James was not involved with GELPAC, but he was involved with a different company that also offered English as a second language programs to the Chinese. According to the correspondence I found, the relationship between GELPAC and James' company was intertwined in ways that seemed to indicate conflicts of interest. "Communication in e-mail is between thee, Archie & me; on letterhead is to share with your folks," James wrote to an executive of the company. "This is primarily your company—despite titles and other shareholders— what you say goes!"

I found two documents that outlined the company's business plan. One was a spiral-bound original. The other was identical—except that James had added his name and bio to the executive team:

> James Montgomery is the CEO, JAG Inc., of Florida in the USA. He has an extensive background in commerce as well as a strong academic background. He has been involved with the application of modern technology, notably cable TV and the Internet, to education. Better known as the founder of 'E!' basic cable TV network and CBS: Sportsline.com, his group is developing a similar institution in Florida. JAG has a memorandum of understanding enabling JAG to place Chinese students in their Florida facility and the company to place South American students of JAG's in Australia and New Zealand. Documents detailing JAG's activities are available.

So now, besides his standard E! television and Sportsline.com crap, James claimed a "strong academic background." What did that mean—he went to school? And applying technology to education? Probably the closest he ever came to that was buying books over the Internet.

I didn't believe him, but maybe other people did. Which meant that maybe they gave him money, money that I could claim.

Kim Goodson was living in New Zealand—I assumed it meant that James was living there as well. Unfortunately, this did not help my case in Australia.

I received a fax from my Australian lawyers on January 21, 2001: The court was probably not going to freeze James' bank accounts based on the information my search agent found—I needed more evidence of James' money, such as a bank statement. And if James was living in New Zealand, the Australian court might refuse to hear my case based on a lack of jurisdiction.

"I can appreciate the client's frustration; this is someone who is clearly experienced at rapidly moving himself and his assets from jurisdiction to jurisdiction," my lawyer wrote. "No country's bankruptcy laws are much good at dealing with this type of person."

In other words, my lawyers were not optimistic about recovering my money.

After reading the fax, I retreated to the meditation room, in turmoil again. What was I supposed to do? Give up? Throw in the towel? Let my con artist ex-husband win?

Yes, Donna, you do.

That was the answer from Guidance. My spiritual growth was important, they said, not the money. They advised me to let go of my expectations. I should forget about finding James' money, and rebuild my financial situation the old-fashioned way—by getting to work.

I spent the next two days alternately holding back tears and crumpled on the floor, wailing. My nose ran, dripping down my throat and onto my shirt. Beau worriedly licked my face.

It was time to give up. But give up what? Did I sell my home? Did I look for a job? I was out of energy, out of hope, and overcome by disappointment and failure. "Dear God," I asked. "What do you want me to give up?" I recorded the answer in my journal:

> *There is a difference between giving up expectations and giving up your hopes and dreams. Yes, give up the expectations. Expectations actually limit your options, because you do not see opportunities when they arise. But keep your long-term plan. The plan for your book and website. Whatever happens in the meantime is immaterial. If you get a job—so what? If you move—so what?*
>
> *This is a time of transition. There will be changes. The journey will lead you forward. Just follow the road. Listen to us. Know that God supports you and honors your efforts.*
>
> *What to give up? Give up your ideas of how things should be. Work with how they are.*

I was tired of the struggle, tired of whatever it was I'd been fighting. I forced myself to feel unconditional acceptance of my circumstances. Did I like them? No. Did I want them to change? Yes. But I accepted where I was.

I accepted that I didn't know what was going to happen. I accepted that I was alone. I accepted that I didn't have any money. I wanted all of these situations to change. But I accepted that I didn't know when they would change, and right then, this was my life. I was tired of arguing.

On Tuesday, January 23, 2001, I said, "I surrender."

Chapter 25

Within days of saying, "I surrender," three potential opportunities for work appeared. A friend I met at a women's networking organization, the contact I made at the Philadelphia Advertising Club, and a former client all mentioned possible assignments. "See, it's starting," Guidance told me.

You have let go of the worry—that enables us to help you. Your worry is like a big psychic wall, an energetic block. When you let go of the worry and expectations, it's like clearing away the haze, static and interference. It allows the energy to work. Keep at it. Exercise and meditate every day. It keeps the channels clear. It enables your soul to send out the energy, and it allows the universe to respond. The clearer you are, the faster you can get results.

Guidance was reiterating universal cause and effect—the energy inside me attracted circumstances to my life. Still, it was up to me, using my free will, to decide how to respond to the people and events that crossed my path. It made me wonder how many times the universe presented me with opportunities and I missed them.

I focused on watching for opportunities on January 28, 2001—Super Bowl Sunday. My sister, Tracy, and I went to watch the football game at Champps, a big, popular sports bar in Marlton, New Jersey. By opportunities, I specifically meant men suitable for dating.

Champps was packed. The Baltimore Ravens and New York Giants battled on multiple TVs suspended from the ceiling. Hundreds of men and women drank beer and ate bar snacks, with one eye on the game and the other on the room full of opportunities.

As Tracy and I stood at the bar with our Coronas, I noticed a man looking at me. He was wearing a white baseball cap on his short, brown hair and a t-shirt that showed off his broad shoulders and trim waist. He was about my height, and probably a few years younger than me. Younger, I knew, could be fun.

The guy sidled up to me. Literally. He took sideways steps through the crowd, almost like he was doing the tango, and stopped in front of me.

"Hi. I'm Mark."

I had to laugh. "Well, Mark, you're certainly direct."

"Yeah. I learned it in the Navy."

"You did?"

"Yeah. I used to go on shore leave with buddies from the ship. I noticed that the black guys always had women around them, and I didn't. So I asked them. I said, 'How do you do that?' And they said, 'Honkie, all you got to do is approach a woman. Just go up and say hello.' So that's what I do."

I laughed again. "Your buddies were right. A lot of guys are afraid to take that first step."

"So what's your name?"

Mark Granata* and I spent the rest of the evening chatting. I learned that he actually lived in Baltimore, and was in New Jersey with a group of co-workers. From time to time, we got distracted from our conversation by the football game—especially when three touchdowns were scored on three consecutive plays in only 36 seconds. In the end, Mark's team, Baltimore, beat New York, 34 to 7.

As I put on my coat to leave, Mark asked for my phone number, saying we'd get together the following weekend. I gave it to him, and he gave me a quick goodnight kiss. Driving home, I wondered whether Mark would actually call—after all, he lived nearly three hours away from me. Maybe he would. Maybe he wouldn't. Regardless, I enjoyed the attention.

When I wrote about the encounter in my journal, Guidance assured me that I would continue to attract attention. Because my energy had shifted so dramatically, I would have many, many opportunities.

> *It's like the energy of a teenage beauty queen.* American Beauty. *Everyone tells them how beautiful they are, and they believe it, so they attract plenty of attention. Belief is everything. You never believed that you were beautiful and attractive. That energy is changed, and your beauty radiates from the inside. Men of good fortune will be drawn to you. Men of substance.*

The next day I was back at work, with plenty to do. My contact from the Philadelphia Ad Club came through with a project. Dover Downs Slots wanted a series of promotions. My brother's company had assignments for me. I was busy all week, and grateful to the universe for the work.

Mark did show up, albeit a week late. He drove from Baltimore to Atlantic City, arriving the afternoon of Saturday, February 10, 2001. We chatted. I showed him around my home. He was impressed with my work—the AT&T and Showboat posters hanging in my office—and by my rowing medals. We went out to dinner, and afterwards were faced with a decision: Now what?

The date became romantic. I was pleasantly surprised—Mark turned out to be quite the lover. We were entangled well into the night, and again the next morning. As he put his coat on to leave Sunday afternoon, Mark talked about visiting me again the following weekend.

In the days after our rendezvous, I felt blissfully alive. My heart was joyful. The physical contact was wonderful—I'd needed it badly. Still, the magnitude of my happiness surprised me. When I wondered why I was in such good spirits, I realized that I was learning to enjoy the moment.

The following weekend, Mark stood me up. I was disappointed, but not terribly surprised. It didn't matter. I enjoyed the time I spent with him, and that was enough.

No, no, no, no and no. The credit card companies responded to my request that my balances be treated as fraud and forgiven. Every company respectfully declined.

Citibank wrote: "Although your divorce decree reflected Mr. Montgomery would be responsible for the credit card debt, a divorce decree is between the parties of the divorce and is not binding on Citibank (South Dakota), N.A."

The Associates wrote: "While we understand the circumstances as outlined in your letter and the accompanying court documents, we are unable to treat your account balance as fraud. Because you engaged in the transactions, received associated goods and services, and accepted the balance by making monthly payments, we must treat this as a valid debt."

Wachovia wrote: "Our Fraud Department has completed their investigation of your fraud claim. They have concluded this is not a fraud matter since the parties involved were married at the time the account was opened and the balance was incurred."

American Express wrote: "I certainly empathize with your situation concerning your ex-husband. It is particularly disheartening to learn that although the court decided in your favor, the situation has not been resolved to your satisfaction. Unfortunately, American Express is not in a position to enforce the judgment of the courts."

So the banks had more authority than the courts, and if the banks said fraud wasn't fraud, then it wasn't. I was incredulous. I was also staggering under the weight of the debt.

Maybe the banks would help me if I appealed to their own self-interest. Sociopaths, who had no conscience and no sense of responsibility, in all likelihood cost banks plenty. Credit card issuers probably wrote off millions of dollars in losses every year because of sociopaths who got credit cards with no intention of paying them. And I was sure that other victims like me carried huge debts due to sociopathic con artists. We carried them until we collapsed and declared bankruptcy. If the banks wanted to protect their assets, they should support my efforts to educate the world about sociopaths.

I sent a third round of letters to Kenneth I. Chenault, chairman of American Express, and the other credit card companies, explaining the sociopathic personality disorder and how prevalent it was—perhaps 12 million cases in the United

States. I was building the website. I was writing the book. I could work much faster if the banks would treat my debt like any other case of fraud and write it off. In fact, the banks should do more.

February 19, 2001

Dear Mr. Chenault,

I recently received a letter stating that American Express will not treat my case as fraud.

The charges in my divorce complaint include Fraudulent Inducement to Marry and Fraudulent Inducement to Continue the Marriage. The New Jersey Court has found that my ex-husband, James Montgomery, committed fraud against me, ordered that he reimburse me, and awarded me $1 million in punitive damages because of the fraud—which I have been unable to find. It would seem to me that this is fraud.

The letter stated that, "although we have obligations to our Cardmembers, we also have an overwhelming obligation to our employees and shareholders to preserve the veracity and profitability of our business." Well, the interests of your employees and shareholders would be better served by assisting me.

James Montgomery is a sociopath. Sociopaths (also called psychopaths or antisocial personalities) literally have no conscience. They appear to be charming, but they are only manipulating other people to get what they want. They are con artists. In the extreme, they can be serial killers.

Why should you care about this? Because sociopaths are probably responsible for many of the financial losses American Express and other credit card companies incur every year.

Sociopaths: Human nightmare

I, like most people, once knew nothing about sociopaths. But because of my devastating experience with Montgomery, I have done significant research on this character disorder. Here are some shocking facts:

• According to experts, up to 3 percent of men and 1 percent of women are sociopaths. They cannot be rehabilitated.

• Sociopaths can be found among all demographic groups—rich, poor, urban, rural, all races, all professions.

• Many sociopaths, especially those from middle- and upper-class demographics, blend easily into society. They are impossible to recognize, until they begin their hurtful pattern of behavior.

• There appear to be both genetic and environmental causes of the disorder. Some experts believe that because of breakdowns in social institutions and family structures, the number of sociopaths in America will rise.

• Obligations and commitments mean nothing to the sociopath—including obligations to pay credit card debt.

Looking for victims

I learned, far too late, that my husband had a pattern of defrauding women. I know of eight confirmed victims, from whom he took more than $1 million, and seven more suspected victims. Recent developments, I believe, make it easier than ever for sociopaths like my ex-husband to operate:

• Career women. Many women work hard, make a lot of money, and are so busy that their personal lives are empty. They are ripe targets for talented sociopaths willing to prey on their emotions. All of Montgomery's victims that I've spoken to are professionals.

• The Internet. Montgomery is on the Internet constantly, trolling for victims. The Internet allows him, and other con artists, to work anonymously, and to string along many potential victims at a time.

• Easy availability of credit reports. Before meeting Montgomery in 1996, I had absolutely sterling credit and my only debt was my mortgage. He pulled a credit report on me. Furthermore, one of his previous wives—another victim—said he was always receiving TRW reports.

Institutional ineptitude

Throughout my ordeal, I have been absolutely astounded by the inability of the justice system, banks and other institutions to take action against fraud.

In many preliminary divorce court hearings, I was forced to take extra steps, and incur additional cost, to protect Montgomery's rights—even though he stopped participating in the proceedings early on. When the judge awarded me punitive damages of $1 million, my ex-husband could have avoided paying it simply by declaring bankruptcy. The only exception to this is in a case of fraud. So I went to considerable trouble and expense to have my divorce judgment amended to include the court's findings of fraud.

Law enforcement officials have been practically useless. They'd much rather go after guys who rob convenience stores. And for well over a year, I've been trying to get America Online to close Montgomery's account. They tell me that they can't.

My conclusion: Rules are made for people who follow the rules. Since sociopaths see no need to follow the rules, if they're smart enough to stay out of jail, they can act with impunity.

Extensive problem

In talking to people about my run-in with a con artist, I have come across many others who have had similar experiences. And this is just among my circle of acquaintances. I suspect that this problem is far more extensive than people realize.

But many people who have been victimized by con artists are not willing to talk about it. Being conned carries the same stigma that being raped once had, when the prevailing attitude was "she asked for it." Victims often just try to put the crimes behind them and move on—especially because there is so little support available from the nation's social structure.

My response: Lovefraud.com

I have identified a desperate need for information about sociopaths. Most people do not know what a sociopath is. And nobody realizes the extent of the problem. The population of the United States is more than 270 million. That means there may be 12 million sociopaths living among us, 12 million people who really don't care what they do to someone else. This is a huge problem.

Even when the media do stories about con artists and serial killers, the critical link—identifying sociopathy as a character disorder that people should watch out for—is missing. My background is in both journalism and marketing. I intend to do something about it.

I have already started writing the book. I have already reserved the Internet domain name, lovefraud.com, and am in the process of constructing a web site. Its purpose is to alert people to the danger of sociopaths—the 1 to 4 percent of the population who literally have no conscience, and for whom "love" is simply another tool for getting what they want.

One of the sections I hope to have in the web site is a registry of known con artists. Why? Because the justice system moves too slowly, if it moves at all. Sociopaths are able to keep plying their trade because they continuously move on to new, unsuspecting victims.

By raising awareness of the problem of sociopaths, and helping people find out if someone is a con artist, I hope to provide a tool whereby people can protect themselves. Because once you've been victimized, it's too late.

You can help

How long will it take me to complete these projects? Quite frankly, it depends on how much time and energy I need to put into getting back on my feet financially. If I have to declare bankruptcy to get through this, well, it's just more fodder for the book.

Therefore, I again ask for you to treat this like any other case of fraud and write off this debt. American Express has already written off debt incurred by Montgomery. Your company issued him a Platinum Card in 1987. When he failed to pay, you attempted to sue him. Since then, Montgomery discovered it was much better to convince his love interests to charge items on his behalf than to get his own credit card.

In fact, if your company were really progressive—and self-interested—American Express would underwrite my work. Because the story is so sensational (you've heard very little of it), and because of how I intend to link the story to the character disorder, the widespread problem of sociopathy might finally see the light of day.

Lovefraud.com could only be good for American Express and other credit card companies. The more people are aware of the dangers that could lurk behind a charming smile and sweet nothings, the less likely they are to get in trouble. And the longer it takes for me to complete my work, the more people will be victimized.

Donna Andersen

I mailed my letters to the credit card companies on February 20, 2001. Would they work? I wanted the banks to act in my favor, but was terrified that they wouldn't. A battle raged within me. Was I feeling hope—or despair? I didn't know. I just knew that I was exhausted.

After struggling through the workday, I desperately needed to get out of the house, so I decided to go to the gym. During the eight-minute drive to get there, I almost turned around three times. I was losing my composure.

Somehow, I made it through my workout. But when I got home, pain and despair overwhelmed me. Climbing the stairs to the second floor of my home, I started whimpering, then wailing: "I'm so tired. Why do I have so much pain? Why is it so hard? It's not getting any better."

Deep cries started in my chest and took over my awareness. I leaned against the wall in the hallway, unable to stand on my own. Then, still in anguish, I gathered myself and made my way down the hall into the meditation room. Beau followed me in, upset, licking my face. I went to pet him, and he backed away.

My pain turned to anger. Rage. I pushed Beau out of the room and closed the door. Kneeling on the floor, I placed a pillow on the daybed, envisioned James' face on it, and beat it as hard as I could. I imagined it bloodied. I screamed in rage, in fury. I pounded until I lost control.

Over and over. Pounding and screaming. Losing control.

Beau barked frantically on the other side of the door.

I didn't know how long it went on. Finally, I sat back onto my heels, and slid to the floor. Curled up, fetal position, I prayed to God. "I'm so tired," I said. "What am I supposed to give up? What am I supposed to give up?"

The resentment. You still hate and resent everything that's happened. You want it over. You must remember that you selected these lessons for your own growth. When you resent, you are only resenting your own path back to God.

You still have not accepted your role in the fraud. That is what the credit card companies are telling you, although they do not interpret the message correctly. You have responsibility for the circumstances of your life. You have attracted the experiences for the growth of your soul. You want someone to take it away. If you accept, without judgment, they will go away. The lesson will have been learned, and you will no longer have any need for the circumstances.

Stop resisting. Go with the flow. The energy is moving; let it carry you forward.

Maybe Guidance was right. I had nothing to lose by putting their words into action. I gathered myself, opened the door, and Beau rushed in, licking me wildly. I hugged him while we both calmed down.

That evening, I went to sleep saying a new affirmation, "I accept my responsibility for my circumstances." Then I added, "and now I want love and prosperity."

I felt an internal burden lift.

The psychic took a deep breath and began my reading. "Wow, you have more than one angel around you," she said. "I see you really going through it. A lot of upheaval in your life."

Upheaval? That was an understatement.

The psychic, Gena Wilson, described the angels around me. One wore yellow, the color of thinking. "You're in your head a lot," she said. "Mental, mental, mental." Another angel wore pink, the color of emotions and love. "I feel like you've come into more balance between thinking and feeling."

I begrudgingly agreed.

"That was really wonderful for you," the psychic continued. "You had to go through that to get more in touch with your heart. You've always had a lot of love in your heart, but it's been kept down, so to speak, by overanalyzing, and thinking, thinking, thinking. Living in your head, mental, mental. It's easier for you now to make yourself vulnerable to someone, but it still isn't a piece of cake. You don't want to be hurt. I mean, none of us do. But it's like you have a guard around you, around your heart."

The psychic saw a third angel wearing deep green, the color of healing. "Her gown sways," Gena said. "It's like chiffon over silk, with a lot of drapes. It's very pretty. And her wings are just white and fluffy and huge. Angels are big. But she's bringing you a little bouquet of pink flowers. Bringing you love to heal your heart."

This angel, Gena said, had been helping me throughout my ordeal.

"Actually, she's your guardian angel. Your life lesson in this lifetime was to bring you back to love. Understanding love in a different level. Understanding love of self, love of another human, love of God, love of animals. And the differences in the loves. It's like a big, beautiful spider web that creates the whole of existence."

I traveled to Baltimore on February 24, 2001 for the reading. My friend, Betty Davies, told me about Gena, and said she was a pet psychic. I was worried that my pets were upset by my trauma, and I wanted to know how they were doing. I asked Betty to arrange an appointment. She planned a small psychic party in her home.

I didn't know that Gena read people as well as pets, so I was surprised when she asked me if I had any questions about my life. But it didn't take me long to think of one. "This whole trauma thing is still ongoing," I said. "I have a settlement of $1.25 million that my ex owes me. Am I going to find the money?"

"He's squirming like a worm, isn't he," the psychic stated.

"I don't know. I don't know where he is."

"Oh, he's squirming. He's hiding and squirming like a worm. He is a worm. I see him vanishing. He's good at doing a disappearing act. And he's going to be hard to nail. But I do see handcuffs going on him, eventually. He's definitely going to be caught. But it's going to be awhile. He's a fast talker. God, he's sneaky, and he's unbelievable. He's got like, magic almost, the way he can vanish. Or disappear. Whew, he's frightening. Not that he's harmful."

"No, he is harmful."

"I'm talking about, he wouldn't kill somebody."

"He may have killed somebody."

I told the psychic about Gale Lewis, the wife before me who died suddenly, but Gena insisted that James didn't kill her. Still, he was a ruthless user.

"That wickedness about him; he can slide around and be so slimy," Gena continued. "I don't think that you're going to recover nearly as much as you would hope to. It's going to be such an uphill climb, a battle all the way to get anything. It's like you can't get blood out of a turnip."

"Does he have money?"

"I don't see him having money. I see him using other people's money."

"Does he have the money he took from everybody else? Or is it all spent?"

"Some of it's spent, and some of it's—you know how you can launder money through other means? That's what he did with it. But he'll keep his mouth shut. He has connections where he can do that kind of stuff. When I look at his mouth, it's sewn up. He'd sit in prison for 10 years and then get out and go get his money. He's rotten. A rotten apple. But he's so charming, isn't he? And seductive in his way, his demeanor, he looks so innocent. People just give him anything."

Gena saw that James crashed into my life, demolished everything and left. She saw that I felt like a fool for trusting him, but said I needed to stop blaming myself. James was very good at what he did. Conning people was his profession, and he was an expert at it. Cunning. Charismatic. I wasn't the first woman he tricked, and I wouldn't be the last.

I asked if I should declare bankruptcy. The answer was a definite yes.

We moved on to talking about my pets. Beau, she saw, was joyful and loving. My dog felt my emotions and was protective of me, like a big brother. He never liked nor trusted James, and his attitude was, "Bring him back here. I'll kick his ass."

Next I asked about Herbie, the hedgehog who died. Gena said he had a wonderful life with me, and was thankful that I took care of him so well. He was now in St. Francis' garden—young, healthy and having fun.

Chuckie, my chinchilla, loved to run, Gena said. He wanted a bigger cage, or more opportunities to run around the room. He also wanted a mate. That scared me. Chinchillas bred, well, like their cousins the rabbits, and the last thing I needed was a house full of fur balls.

"He says, 'I need space. I want to move.' Other than that, he's happy," Gena said. "And he knows that you'll do something about it. He's like, 'I know she likes me. One way or another, she'll figure it out.'"

Finally, I asked about the sugar gliders—Donald, who chewed through the screen and escaped, never to be seen again. Jamie, whom Donald impregnated before he left. And Hope, the baby.

Donald, Gena said, thought long and hard before deciding to go through the window. The tall trees beckoned him, and he wanted an adventure. He may have lived in the trees for quite awhile, but eventually he froze to death. "He had to learn the lesson," Gena said. "But he's fine. He's okay. He's looking down from pet heaven, saying, 'Oh, I wish I would have stayed. I made the wrong decision.' But he had his adventure."

Jamie and Hope were homebodies. They were loved, safe, secure and warm, and they weren't going anywhere. Gena saw that Jamie's hand was injured—a loose thread from her glider pouch had twisted around it like a tourniquet. Although I quickly cut the thread, the tissue in Jamie's hand was dead. Hope, she said, was not very bright. "When I feel her," Gena said, "she just feels like, if she were a person, she'd be a little slow, or mentally retarded. Does that make sense?"

"It's kind of hard to tell with sugar gliders," I replied. "But they're happy I guess?"

"Oh yeah. Definitely."

"James brought all these pets home."

"They're better off with you."

"Were they for me? To help me?"

"Oh, definitely. And they have. They really are your family now. It's been good for you to have them."

With that, emotion welled within me and my eyes teared. "How much longer is it going to be hard?" I asked, plaintively. "I've run out of energy."

"I know," Gena replied sympathetically. "Bless your heart. You've been through it. God, you've been through it."

The psychic was silent for a moment, and then she continued. "It's like the trauma of a sudden death. The initial shock is a wave. And then, even though you move further away from it, it still comes back and grabs you and hurts. And then you move a little bit beyond it. I feel like you're coming out of the second wave of intense pain. But you're not going to really end it all until you let go of it. Until you say, 'I'm really over it. That part of my life is over and done with, and one way or another, I've resolved it.' It may end up that you have to let it go and move on. Not give it any more energy. I see by September things getting better, and then another full year before you say, 'I'm really ready to put this down and let it go.'"

"Am I wasting my time even looking for the money? Should I just stop? They found an account in Australia."

"I feel like when they catch him, he is going to have some money in his name that they can get a hold of. So hang in there, because you're going to get some money. It's just not going to be as much as you wanted."

"So what do I do between now and then?"

"Just allow yourself to grieve, to be angry and to hurt. Honor it. Accept it."

Gena was quiet again, feeling what I'd been through. "Talk about an experience that has gotten you totally in touch with your emotional body—this has been it," she said. "And that needed to happen for you. We don't always choose easy lessons. That one was definitely a devastating, hard lesson. I don't think you ever felt this much emotion in your life."

"No. I was frozen over."

"So look at what it's given you, not at what it's taken from you. Make a list. Look at how you grew, and at all the things you learned about yourself, and are free of, because of it. Instead of focusing on how horrible it was, start to look at it in the other light. That will help you.

"You're really going to be okay. Even two years from now, you're going to look back at this like it's a bad dream. If you wanted to stop it all now, you couldn't if you tried. The wave of emotion is still there. It's deep and raw. You are progressing, but it takes time. Earth time is a great healer. It really is."

Back in November, my asset search agent located an account for James Montgomery in the Commonwealth Bank of Australia. At the end of February 2001, my Australian legal representatives prepared to go after the money.

Under the Australian legal system, I had two representatives—a solicitor and a barrister. My solicitor, Leon Davis of Sydney, was my prime contact. He retained a barrister who appeared on my behalf before the court.

I'd been working with Leon for months to get my judgment registered in Australia, and before going to court, he wanted to be paid for the work he'd already done. His invoice was A\$3,500. It wasn't quite as much money in U.S. dollars, but I still didn't have it.

I decided to stop paying the credit cards—the companies had turned down my last request to treat my debts as fraud. I also decided that if this final attempt to find James' money failed, I'd declare bankruptcy.

My barrister prepared an affidavit for the Supreme Court of New South Wales that outlined the basics of my case: The New Jersey court found my ex-husband guilty of fraud and awarded me a money judgment. My search agent had located an account in an Australian bank with James' name and U.S. address. I asked the court for an order to help me collect the money.

Even though we were going to an Australian court for money in an Australian bank, I thought James was living in Christchurch, New Zealand—that's what I learned from his new wife's family. My solicitor wanted to retain a private investigator in New Zealand to track him down. I agreed, and e-mailed Leon photos of James.

In the meantime, I was still trying to get James held accountable in the United States. The letter I received from the Department of Justice, in which they told me that they wouldn't prosecute in Pennsylvania, said I could seek investigation in New Jersey. So on March 12, 2001, I wrote another letter to my congressman, Frank A. LoBiondo, and asked him to get the case transferred to New Jersey. After all, a New Jersey family court judge found that Montgomery had defrauded me. Surely with the resources of the FBI, a U.S. Attorney should be able to prove the case. "Because he commits crimes in many jurisdictions," I asked, "does that mean he can commit crime with impunity?"

Back in Australia, my barrister went to court on April 4, 2001. He won an "asset preservation order"—James Montgomery was restrained from dealing with any assets in New South Wales up to and including A\$2,150,000—the amount of my judgment in Australian dollars. We had to serve Australian banks with the preservation order. We also had 30 days to serve the order on James.

I was afraid it was not enough time to locate him. Guidance tried to reassure me, telling me everything would be fine, but I was also afraid that they were setting me up for another disappointment. Guidance didn't want me to worry about it:

> *What you want is an ending. No matter which way it goes—*
> *you will have your ending. If you have to give up finding the*
> *money, it doesn't matter. The burden will be released, either via*
> *finding the money or bankruptcy. Then you can start over.*

When I walked into my session with Elaine Anderson on April 12, 2001, she immediately felt the change in my energetic field. My business was doing well. In fact, my work was more interesting than ever—I had a variety of clients, not just casinos, providing me with diverse creative challenges. The Australian court had seen the merit of my case and issued an order in my favor, and a private investigator was looking for James. If my ex-husband weren't found, I would declare bankruptcy. Elaine agreed it was the best thing for me to do.

Yet there was a hole in my life. Although I'd enjoyed my fling with the guy I met on Superbowl Sunday, I was alone. Again. Still. This was my everlasting issue, rooted in some deep pain. My goal for the session was to excavate it.

I shuffled the Star+Gate cards as I spoke, then handed the deck to Elaine. When she positioned them on the felt layout, a green circle turned up as my "The Issue" card. The green circle meant pain in the heart chakra. It also meant unity and participation. These were exactly the issues I wanted to work on.

"Why do you feel alone in this lifetime?" Elaine asked as I lay down on her massage table. "What is your belief?"

"Nobody wants me," I replied. "I felt like no one wanted to be my friend in grade school. In high school, I did have opportunities to bring boys into my life, but I didn't see them. I was oblivious. I was clueless. I didn't know how to act."

Memories of another lifetime arose in my awareness. Suddenly, I felt like I was being slapped in the face. There on Elaine's table, I actually recoiled from the slap.

The blow was delivered by my husband. I was so confused—all I wanted was to love and be loved. The love we once had disintegrated. He would slap me, then make up, and when I thought everything was okay, abuse me again. I withdrew and started to fear love.

Reliving the emotion, I felt deep sadness. Slow, quiet tears rolled down my cheeks. Every once in awhile a wave of heartache hit and I emitted a tired "oh" of pain.

I felt the pain in my heart as if it were pushing up behind a wall. Slowly, it released—a thin, tight stream of energy squeezing through a hole in my heart about the size of a nickel. A backlog of pain, like too much water behind a dam, slowly squirted out. The hole didn't get any bigger; I could only process the energy as it escaped through a pipe that was too narrow.

The pain took a long time to drain. Then I felt the energy shift around to my back, my upper right shoulder. It was localized in a spot about four inches down from my neck, and two inches to the right of my spine. It was a small hole, like one made by a bullet.

Elaine put her arm under my shoulder blade, holding the spot where I could feel the energy.

In my mind's eye, I caught a glimpse of another past life, this one involving Native Americans during Colonial times. I could see an Indian in the forest. Elaine thought I was a soldier; she saw me in uniform. I was shot because some pompous British general wanted to fight a traditional war, and the Indians weren't cooperating.

On the broad plains of Europe, armies faced each other in formation, with soldiers standing shoulder to shoulder. The first line fired rifles at the opposing forces, then knelt and reloaded while the line behind them fired over their heads. In contrast, the traditional warfare tactics of Native Americans were raids and ambushes. By Colonial times, they had acquired guns through trade with the settlers, so their stealth tactics became even more deadly. The tribes took advantage of terrain and cover, used intelligence from scouts, and planned surprise attacks to consistently outfight the British and Colonists.

In 1755, during the French and Indian War, British General Edward Braddock—described as intemperate, arrogant, lazy and obstinate—planned a European-style assault on Fort Duquesne, a French outpost located in what was now Pittsburgh, Pennsylvania. But the French and their Indian allies, hiding in a forest, ambushed Braddock and his troops first. The British dissolved into confusion and disorder.

Even though he was on a narrow frontier road deep in a forest, General Braddock tried to get his soldiers to reform into lines. All this did was create easy targets for the unseen enemy. His heavy artillery was ineffective among the trees. When American militiamen took to the woods to fight, they were mistakenly fired upon by the British regulars. After short, intense combat, the remains of British column fled the battlefield. Braddock led 1,300 men into battle, and nearly 900 were killed or wounded. Braddock himself was shot in the lung, and died three days later.

I didn't know if that particular battle was the past life I remembered—Colonial American history held more accounts of similar incidents. Wherever I was, I tried to tell the general that we had to change tactics. He refused.

"That is not how you fight a war," the general bellowed. "We are not going to fight this way. I will not have my soldiers crawling around on their bellies like the savages." He wanted us to march in regular columns at the appointed time, with drums, flags and bugles. Not creep through the woods. In the meantime, we were all getting killed or wounded.

I lost my arm, or the use of my arm. When I became disabled, I was furious. I was angry at the pigheaded general who insisted on fighting by the old rules, even though they didn't work. He wouldn't listen, and my life was ruined. Unable to work, I started drinking, and my life spiraled downward. I looked unkempt. I became the town drunk, begging for food.

Crippled, I tried to approach women, and they laughed at me. "You've got to be kidding," they said. "How are you going to take care of me?"

In my mind, I pleaded my case: You don't understand! I was young! I was handsome! I went off to war to become a big hero!

Some hero I was. As I drank myself into a stupor, I became more and more lonely. The lonelier I got, the more I drank. I was always in a fog. And that's how I died, in a fog.

Sadness overcame me. Sadness, loneliness and grief over a life ruined because some idiot general insisted on fighting the old way. Suddenly, I felt a flash of intuition. Was that general James?

It was.

Elaine saw how he was overwhelmed—this style of fighting went against all his military training. This was not what he learned. This was not how a proper war was fought. James was actually devastated by what happened. All his soldiers were being killed. He was shamed.

In that battle, James learned about not playing by the rules, which eventually sent him over the criminal edge. Even though I was injured, lost my arm, and my life was ruined, I maintained my integrity. James went further into the blackness, and had several subsequent lifetimes in which not playing by the rules paid off for him.

Elaine and I talked about sociopaths—the world did not know the extent of the problem. I'd just seen a television documentary about Atascadero State Hospital in California—a prison where sexually violent predators and serial rapists were sent after they completed their prison sentences because they were too dangerous to release into society. Many of these criminals were probably sociopaths. But the entire 90-minute program never once mentioned the words "sociopath" or "psychopath." There was only an oblique reference to the fact that some of the men felt no emotional connection to other people.

Then, Elaine and I both started to feel the consciousness of the sociopath.

It was bleak, empty, horrible. No belief in anything, no trust in anyone, no connection to anyone, no love for anyone. Just seeking momentary pleasure wherever and whenever it could be taken.

How to describe the desolation? Closed, emotionally cold, completely severed from human connection, even amidst family and crowds of people. It was like being separated from everyone by a gray screen, punching through the screen to take, but not feeling anything. Not truly seeing the eyes of other people, the eyes of people they hurt, maimed, killed.

They had no eyes.

"This is hell on earth," Elaine said.

It was a horrible existence. A dead, cold, unconnected, unloving existence. Seizing what they wanted, no matter how much it hurt someone else. And not caring. If someone was dumb enough to be a victim, sociopaths rationalized, it was not their problem.

"What does this mean?" I asked. "What conclusion should I draw? Yes, I have benefitted spiritually because of the awful things James did to me. But that does not mean what he did was right, and he should remain free to keep doing it."

"Let's ask Guidance about that," Elaine said.

The answer, we both heard, was about consequences.

Shining a light on sociopathic behavior was important for two reasons. First, making people aware of sociopaths would help them avoid the predators. By exposing the masquerade, sociopaths would have fewer opportunities to perpetrate their frauds. Second, it was important to make sure sociopaths faced consequences for their actions. In feeling consequences, they had a chance to heal. It was their only way out of the hell. Would they heal in one lifetime? Probably not. After all, they were sociopaths. They did not want to change.

My quest was over. On April 19, 2001, all my efforts to find James and his money collapsed into ruin. I heard from my lawyers in Australia. The Commonwealth Bank had no account in the name of James Montgomery.

My hopes were pulverized. I was in shock.

If I had settled with James back in 1999, my divorce would have cost me $3,500. Instead, I spent $40,000 in lawyer and investigation fees, and got nowhere. Had I put the money toward my credit card debts, they would have been almost paid off.

The struggle was over, and I lost.

I shut the door of my mediation room and sank to the floor, crying.

I was angry at Guidance—they lied to me again. "We're waiting for more money to be in the account," they said. Yeah, right.

It was over. I lost. He won.

An argument raged within me. This was supposed to be some kind of spiritual victory. I lost, but I'm not supposed to care. Well guess what—I did care. James made a total fool of me. I could have settled two years earlier and saved myself a lot of aggravation.

"You lied to me again!" I screamed at Guidance. "You continue to lie to me!"

I got on my knees and pounded the bed in rage. "I have no hope. It's gone. Why did you lie to me?"

I knew what they'd say—"the victory is spiritual." You've got to be fucking kidding me. I lost. He won. Evil triumphed. James was just too good. I was a mouse pursued by a hawk. I was an ant under a bulldozer. I never had a chance. A hopeless cause. Why did I bother? What did I accomplish? Nothing. I wasted my time. No victory. No hope.

He won.

I raged at Guidance again. "You think it's so funny. The struggle between good and evil—and evil wins. What is the fucking point? So what's in this for me?" Guidance replied:

> *Understanding.*

"Understanding of what?"

> *Understanding of what really matters.*

"Like what?"

> *Truth. Love. Peace. Now you can have peace. The turmoil is over. We're in the denouement. Now you can move on. Now you can put all of this behind you.*

"I could have done that two years ago!"

> *No, you couldn't. This was a spiritual journey. Your spiritual victories are many—his are none. That's all that matters.*

"You lied to me through it all. You said I'd do well with the credit cards. You said I'd get money from the bank. You lied all the time."

> *For your own good.*

"WHAT GOOD? How can there possibly be any good for me?"

> *You have to let go of expectations. You have to focus on God, on what really matters.*

"This is stupid. None of it has any point. I might as well quit. My life sucks. I have nothing. I just drift—no goals—no family—no lover—no reason. Suffering with no reason and no benefits."

I cried harder.

"You know, I'm really beginning to hate you," I railed at Guidance. "I hate this life. I hate God. I have nothing. You've taken it all. Why don't I just give up? Why don't I just die? What is the point? Evil wins. That's the lesson. Evil wins."

Beau was outside in the yard barking loudly, and I went downstairs to let him into the house. My dog bolted through the door, obviously distressed. I was in no condition to comfort him.

I stumbled back upstairs to return to the meditation room, but on the staircase to the second floor, I started to cry uncontrollably, collapsing against the wall. I crawled up the remaining steps on my knees. At the top of the staircase, I lay on the floor, wailing.

Evil wins.

In June 2001, Timothy McVeigh, who blew up the federal office building in Oklahoma City, was going to be executed. So what? He'd already killed 168 people.

Slobodan Milosevic, who was president of Serbia and Yugoslavia, was arrested and going on trial. So what? Genocide had already killed thousands of people in Croatia, Bosnia and Serbia.

Justice? What justice? Evil wins.

Guidance said there was no evil. So what was this? Why did James succeed? Why were all those people dead? Why was Gale Lewis dead?

The feds wouldn't prosecute James Montgomery. Evil wins. So what is the point?

> *You're too upset now. You don't want to hear the truth. That's okay. You need to grieve. You have much to grieve. You have been wronged in Earthly terms—this is true. But your spiritual gains are priceless. You don't want to hear this now, and we don't blame you. But you have your ending. It is time to move on. It is time for you ...*

"But you lied to me!" I raged again. "Constantly! Consistently! Why should I believe anything you say to me?"

> *You know what to believe.*

"I could have just skipped all of this aggravation by accepting defeat two years ago. That would have been easier."

> *But it was not your journey. This was a journey of discovery. You have learned much. It will serve you well.*

Slowly, my crying subsided. I was tired. In fact, I was exhausted. I sat on the daybed in the meditation room, totally wrung out. Dazed. Shell-shocked.

I didn't know how long I sat there. But slowly, from deep within me, I felt a tiny twinge of happiness. I was astonished.

"What is this?" I asked Guidance.

> *God's love. God's peace. The struggle is over. It doesn't matter if you win or lose—it matters that you give up the struggle. Time heals all ills. That's why you stay alive. The secret of joy is riding the wave of life as it shows up.*
>
> *You have your answers. The money is gone. It doesn't matter. Your career is doing well. You will continue to find work, work that you like. You will continue to find peace and happiness. You will find love.*

Chapter 26

Tracy and I walked into Warmdaddy's, a blues club in the Old City section of Philadelphia. The place was packed, with the crowd clapping and cheering as a band belted out the heavy electric sound of Chicago-style blues.

"This is it," my sister announced.

We'd been walking around the bars and clubs of Old City for an hour, looking for the next stop for our Saturday night on the town. First we went out to dinner. Then we saw a movie presented by the Philadelphia Film Festival at the Ritz East theater. The movie, *A Question of Faith,* was about a monk in a California monastery who was visited by the angel Gabrielle. The monk's superior didn't believe his story, so the monk prayed for a miracle. He slowly morphed into a woman and, without the help of normal human processes, became pregnant. The film was filled with heavy themes of truth, loyalty and faith.

On Saturday night, April 28, 2001, I didn't need any more abstruse debates about meaning and faith. A week earlier, I was forced to accept the bitter truth that I'd lost my battle with my ex-husband. I was exhausted from the struggle. I wanted to forget about it all and have fun.

From the movie theater, Tracy and I walked up Second Street, stopping into several bars and clubs: The Plough and the Stars. The Khyber. The Tin Angel. The Continental. Tracy was looking for the right vibe. None of them had it, until we walked to Front Street and into Warmdaddy's.

The club was long and narrow, with a bar on the left and dining tables on the right, separated by a railing. We made our way into the dark, crowded room and stood along the railing, looking for seats at the bar. There weren't any.

A tall, nice-looking man wearing a rust-colored cotton shirt and black jeans waved us over. He was also standing, but his jacket occupied a chair. We were welcome to put our coats there as well.

We gratefully accepted, ordered beers, and chatted with the man. He said he was a jazz and blues musician, a drummer, but that night all he played was air guitar. Occasionally, inspired by the thumping music, or perhaps by Baker's 7 Year 107 Proof Bourbon Whiskey, he'd grab one of us for a dance, right there by the bar.

The man's name was Terry Kelly, and he looked like he was about my age. Terry was a lean, 6 feet, 4 inches tall, and had blond hair, deep-set blue eyes and chiseled cheekbones. He struck me as a fun-loving guy—perhaps a hearty party-er, judging by the bourbon and occasional cigarettes. But hey, it was Saturday night, and the man was certainly energetic and entertaining. He was also buying us drinks.

Eventually the topic of marital status came up. I was divorced. He had recently separated from his wife. He gestured with his left hand, where the indentation of a wedding ring was still visible. In the subtle movement I saw sor-rowful resignation.

The band ended its second set, and Tracy picked up her coat to leave. I decid-ed to stay, even though it was late and I had been up rowing that morning at 6 a.m. Terry and I chatted—we were in similar lines of work. I created advertising materials, and he owned a company that manufactured specialty papers to print them on. We were both into physical fitness—Terry worked out religiously in the gym, which I could tell as I touched his shoulders when we danced together. The band came back for the third set; we danced and clapped some more. In fact, we closed the bar, something I hadn't done in years. Then we went for a cup of cof-fee, which was not easy because almost everyplace nearby was closed. After-wards, Terry took me to my car and asked for my phone number.

I drove home to Atlantic City. I didn't know if the man would call, but it had been a long time since I was out so late, and I had fun.

Three days later, Terry Kelly did call. Not only did he want to take me out on a date, but he had work for me. His business was launching a new product that needed marketing. Was I interested?

My answer was yes—yes to the date, yes to the work. We made plans to get together the following weekend.

My congressman, Frank A. LoBiondo, contacted the U.S. Department of Justice on my behalf, inquiring about initiating an investigation of my ex-hus-band in New Jersey. Arthur Radford Baker, unit chief for the Office of Public and Congressional Affairs, replied to LoBiondo. The congressman forwarded his let-ter to me, which I received on May 3, 2001.

Baker wrote, "Ms. Andersen had ... been interviewed in the past by the FBI's Newark Office about her allegations. At that time, it was determined that the matter was not a substantiated violation of Title 18 of the U.S. Code and an inves-tigation was not initiated."

Baker was wrong—an investigation was initiated. Yet nothing my husband did amounted to a violation? Title 18 was the federal criminal and penal code of the United States of America. The code listed 123 "chapters" that described almost every type of crime—none of them applied?

Chapter 33 stated it was illegal to falsely wear military uniforms of the U.S. or friendly nations, military medals and decorations, and badges of veterans' organizations. James Montgomery did all of that.

Chapter 43 stated it was illegal for someone to "falsely and willfully represent himself as a citizen of the United States." James Montgomery did that.

Chapter 44 was about firearms. James Montgomery left two guns in my house and no licenses.

Chapter 47 stated that it was illegal to claim to be a citizen of the United States in order to vote in any federal, state or local election. James Montgomery did that.

Chapter 63 was about fraud. It was illegal to communicate via wire, radio or television to defraud or obtain money on false pretenses, or defraud people in connection with securities. James Montgomery certainly did that, taking at least $1 million from me and other victims, and issuing worthless stock.

And about the meeting with the FBI—I distinctly remembered Sylvia Banning and I going through all of our evidence with the FBI agent, the "Newark Office," in my dining room. As the agent walked out the door with the information we provided, her last words about James Montgomery were, "This man has to be stopped!"

The message from the United States Department of Justice was clear. They couldn't be bothered pursuing some guy who went around defrauding women.

I read the letter and yelled at Arthur Radford Baker as if he were in the room, which he wasn't. All afternoon and evening, frustration at the apathy of law enforcement agencies mounted within me. Finally, at 9 p.m., I went into the meditation room and sat on the daybed to try to release the tension.

Chuckie, my chinchilla, who was gleefully out of his cage, hopped over to me, settled onto my knee and went to sleep. It was difficult to release emotional tension without disturbing a sleeping chinchilla. By the time I put Chuckie back in his cage, my tension turned into anger—anger that was eating me up. I had to do something. I dropped to my knees and pounded pillows on the daybed.

"What do you mean he didn't violate the law!" I raged to unhearing and uncaring authorities, while Beau barked on the other side of the closed door. "He pretended to be a war hero and an American citizen. He took at least $1 million, probably more. He left a trail of bankrupt women. And nothing he did was illegal?"

James was out-and-out evil, and no one cared. I understood why people felt helpless in the face of evil, especially when those who were supposed to "serve and protect" did nothing of the sort. That's why, I realized, people give up, slink away and lick their wounds.

Well, maybe I'd have to go away, but I wouldn't go quietly. If I couldn't get any money from my ex-husband, at least I could make trouble for him.

I'd recently received the report from my private investigator in New Zealand. Although he never physically found James—my court papers were never served—he came up with interesting information:

1. James Montgomery's address in New Zealand, which I'd gotten from Kim Goodson's parents, was actually a commercial building.

2. New Zealand corporate records indicated that James was a director and shareholder of two companies—the International Institute for Continuing Education Ltd., and IICE Homestay Ltd.

3. Shareholders in the companies included a local property developer who

owned the commercial building. The developer was, coincidentally, working on a multi-million dollar project for the city government, and probably would not want to be associated with someone who was guilty of fraud.

4. Yet another shareholder was a solicitor with a longstanding Christchurch legal firm. Doing business with James could be damaging to him as well.

5. The home address that James listed on his International Institute for Continuing Education Ltd. disclosure form was actually the address of his partner in Australia, Archie Turner.

James seemed to be involved with legitimate businessmen. Could I use this information as leverage? In other words, could I subject my ex-husband to blackmail?

Terry Kelly pulled up in front of my house in a beige Lincoln Town Car. It was Sunday afternoon, May 6, 2001. Our plan was to first discuss his new product launch, then go out to dinner.

Terry owned Decorated Paper, a small manufacturer located in Camden, New Jersey. The company made heavyweight, glossy paper for annual report covers, menus, specialty packaging and other uses. His new sheet, called Stellar Cover, had a tough, ultraviolet coating that made it water- and scratch-resistant. Stellar was a different and exciting product in the industry, and Terry wanted a clever campaign to introduce it.

As we sat in my living room, Terry described Stellar Cover. "It's so shiny you can see yourself in it," he said. "You can splash it with water or alcohol and the ink won't smear. You can get greasy fingerprints on it and wipe them off. You can print on it, foil stamp it, emboss it."

Terry's description was energetic and fun—an approach that I thought we could take in marketing the product. In my mind, I began to picture a series of clever cartoons featuring the Stellar surface resisting scratches, repelling liquids, behaving indestructibly. As an example of my idea, I showed Terry the Mambo book on my coffee table.

Mambo was the crazy Australian surfwear brand with the theme, "Art Irritates Life." I'd visited a Mambo store while in Australia with my ex-husband, and was captivated by the colorful, wild designs—like Picasso on acid—and brash slogans. "Beauty is trouser-thin." "Be master of your own nudity!" Terry loved Mambo, and loved the idea of using it as a model for his own marketing.

Still excited by the productive brainstorming, we went out to dinner. Earlier in the week, Terry had asked me to make a reservation. He lived in Cherry Hill, New Jersey—about an hour away—and was not familiar with Atlantic City.

"Where do you want to go?" I asked.

"Someplace nice," he replied.

"Do you want to go to a casino?"

"I've never been to a casino."

"Well, they all have first-rate restaurants."

"All right. That would be good."

I made a reservation at Casa di Napoli, a gourmet restaurant at Showboat. Because I did work for the casino, I knew the restaurant was excellent. I also knew that for paying customers—those without casino comps—it was expensive. But Terry seemed like a man who had sophisticated taste. When he said he wanted "someplace nice," I assumed Casa di Napoli, known for its Northern Italian cuisine, was what he meant.

It was early and the restaurant wasn't crowded, so the maitre d' seated us in a cozy, upholstered banquette. Terry ordered a martini and I ordered a glass of wine as we looked over the menu. I wasn't sure what I wanted for an entrée, but I knew that I wanted the Caesar salad, which was made fresh tableside.

Terry and I continued to chat about his marketing program as we ate the salad, which was, as I expected, exquisite. The conversation then progressed to our personal situations. Terry had been married for 26 years, although he was unhappy for a number of them. He had two children, one in college, one graduated from college. Six weeks before I met him, his wife asked for a divorce.

It was my turn, and I figured there was no point in keeping secrets. I told my date that my former husband was a con man who had swindled me out of more than $227,000. The court had found him guilty of fraud and awarded me everything that was taken from me, plus $1 million in punitive damages. Although I tried for more than a year to collect the money, I failed, and I was on the verge of bankruptcy.

Terry almost fell out of the banquette.

"I've never heard a story like that," he said.

"Yeah, it's pretty unbelievable," I agreed. "I plan on writing a book. It might even be movie material."

"You seem to be holding up all right."

"I've had some rough times, but I guess I'm coming to terms with it all."

Over coffee, we made plans for me to accompany him to discuss the Stellar Cover marketing ideas with his graphic designer a few days later. Then Terry picked up the check, dropped me off at home and left. I didn't know what kind of impression I'd made, or what he thought of my revelations.

My blackmail letter to James needed to be crafted carefully—I didn't want to spill too much information, and an overt threat could backfire and create problems for me. So after writing a few drafts, I sent the following e-mail on May 10, 2001—my first communication with my ex-husband in two years.

Hello James,
    I've been following your progress with great interest, and I understand that your latest business ventures are actually becoming successful.
    I'm sure you deserve much of the credit. I'm also sure your business partners and clients — especially those in high places — will be very interested in knowing all about your true talents.
    Therefore, I have prepared your complete biography for them. It

includes a history of your many dealings and involvements here in the United States. I'm sure they will find the status of your dealings with me to be particularly enlightening.

I will also be including a nice photo of you and Archie Turner, which is attached. After all, you and Archie have been working closely for years.

If you want me to make any changes to the information I provide them, please advise me within **48** hours.

The "nice photo" was of James and Archie surrounded by the cache of weapons. I sent the letter to several e-mail addresses that I had for James, and copied Archie as well. I requested receipts to notify me when the e-mails were opened. Two days later, on May 12, 2001, I received them. The game was on.

I went into the meditation room and tapped into Guidance. I was able to pick up his reaction:

> *He is pissed. He's in a rage. He cannot stand the challenge. But he's ill. He doesn't have the energy to fight, and he is concerned about protecting the assets for his daughter. His mind is going 100 mph—revenge—tactics—strategy—what will buy you off? What have you been doing? He knows how much money you can make. He knows John Glassey has connections. What have you been doing? He's in turmoil.*
>
> *He's trying to figure out how much you'll take to shut up. He's trying to figure out how to go after you. He knows you found his accounts before—what are you doing? What do you know? He's in a panic.*

Throughout May, I was in communication with Terry Kelly, but we spoke only about his marketing project. He didn't call to chat. He didn't ask me out. Maybe my revelations scared him off. Maybe he wanted to keep our interaction strictly business.

Finally, right before Memorial Day, Terry invited me to the Brandywine River Blues Festival at the Chaddsford Winery in Pennsylvania. Chadd's Ford was nearly a two-hour drive from Atlantic City, so he said he'd pick me up between 11 a.m. and noon.

Memorial Day dawned sunny and mild—perfect weather for a festival. I was ready at 11 a.m. Forty-five minutes later, Terry had not arrived. Disappointment started creeping into the edges of my emotions. I'd been stood up so many times in the past, and I worried that it was happening again. I lay down on my bed, trying to keep from sinking into depression.

Shortly after noon, Terry's big Lincoln pulled up in front of my house. Relieved, I went downstairs to meet him. He was walking up the porch steps with papers in his hand.

"Hi!" I greeted him. "How was your trip?"

"There was a lot of traffic," Terry said. "More than I expected."

"Yeah, that happens on Memorial Day weekend."

We chatted a bit more, then Terry said, "I have something I want to show you. Can we sit down?"

"Sure."

We sat on the wicker porch sofa and Terry handed me the papers—his personal income tax return.

"I think what you went through with your ex-husband was terrible," he said. "I just want you to know that I really do have a business and I do make money."

I was stunned. I looked at the top page of the form—Terry reported a solid upper middle-class income to the government. Even more important, he thought enough of me to put my mind at ease.

"Thank you, Terry, this is really thoughtful of you," I said, handing the tax return back to him.

"Don't you want to look it over?"

"No. I've seen enough."

We embarked on our journey to the festival. Animated conversation filled our long ride to Chadd's Ford, a tiny township located halfway between Philadelphia, Pennsylvania and Wilmington, Delaware. The somewhat rural area was dotted with Colonial-era buildings, and was the site of the Brandywine Battlefield, where the Continental Army lost a major battle during America's Revolutionary War. The Chaddsford Winery was in a massive, red Colonial barn set far back from the road amid landscaped grounds. The barn now housed a winemaking and barrel aging cellar, tasting rooms and a retail shop.

By the time Terry and I arrived, the festival was in full swing. A white and yellow striped tent was pitched on the gravel driveway in front of the barn. Under it was a low stage, a small dance area, and white plastic tables and chairs. More tables and chairs surrounded the tent, occupied by people enjoying the vineyard's products.

Terry and I sampled a few wines in the tasting room and bought a bottle. We stopped by the food concession for platters, then found an empty table in the sun for our instant party. We hadn't eaten any lunch, so the food and drink disappeared quickly. Terry bought us another bottle of wine.

The blues band—with lead guitar, base, drums and harmonica—was cooking, and before long, inspired by the visceral music, we were dancing. This was quite a challenge on the loose gravel. I slipped and Terry caught me, which led to moments of bump-and-grind.

We laughed. We clutched. We enjoyed ourselves immensely.

A few hours later, after consuming our fill of wine and blues, we headed back to Atlantic City. It had been a wonderful day, with the attraction between Terry and me growing as the hours passed. He was handsome, fun, sophisticated and, I soon learned, passionate. Back at my house, there was kissing on the couch, and soon, we were ravenous for each other.

"Shall we go upstairs?" I asked.

Terry was a wonderful lover—gentle and strong, uninhibited and considerate. When he touched me, caressed me, the sensation was more than physical. I felt a deep, emotional and spiritual sharing. It was what I sought for so long—the sacred conjunction.

I met with a lawyer to start my bankruptcy proceedings on June 1, 2001. My financial situation was not good—work was slow again. I was stressed. In fact, I was so stressed that I broke out in acne all over my body, like a teenager.

Well, if I was incurring stress, I might as well go all the way. I took the next step in my campaign to blackmail James, e-mailing him copies of letters that I drafted for one of his New Zealand business associates—and his wife. I was sure my communication would piss James off. But my real objective was to forcefully encourage my ex-husband to buy me off. To add to the pressure, I e-mailed copies of everything to James' partner, Archie Turner.

Eight months earlier, when I sent my divorce papers to James' family, I also sent a letter to Archie asking him to reimburse me for the expenses I paid on his behalf, which amounted to $3,735. At that time I received no response.

Archie did reply to my e-mails, however, on June 6, 2001. "You have a gripe with James—I suggest you limit your communications to him," he wrote. "When I met you it was as a friend of James—I do not expect to be billed by the families of friends for staying with them, especially after being invited when they were a couple."

But James did not reply to any of the blackmail e-mails. So, on June 14, 2001, I went ahead and did what I told my ex-husband I was going to do. I sent his complete biography, including a copy of my final judgment of divorce with the findings of fraud, to seven of his business associates. I also sent a letter to Kim Goodson, stating that her marriage to James was not legal. When they married, James was still married to me.

A few days later, I asked for a message from Guidance: What about James?

> *Turmoil—there is turmoil on the other side of the world. Big problems. Yelling and screaming. Doubt and anger. You have lit a firestorm.*

How about the money?

> *We don't know. He has the money—yes—but this is about winning.*
> *Oh, what a mess he's in. Everyone is angry. He's being cut off. He's trapped. He's cornered. He is without options. He has no incentive to give you the money. He doesn't care about the pressure from the other people. He doesn't care about Archie.*

The letters were sent. Maybe they created trouble for James, but I had no more options for extracting money from him. The battle was over.

At least my love life was moving forward. After our wonderful date at the blues festival—and the romance that followed—Terry Kelly started calling almost every day. Every weekend, he drove to Atlantic City to wine and dine me—and take me to bed. I enjoyed him immensely.

Terry was what I called a "live wire." He was energetic, extraverted and funny. In fact, we made a great team—he cracked jokes and I laughed at them. Still, he read social situations accurately; he knew when to make wisecracks and when to use discretion. On June 16, 2001, Terry accompanied me to a family party. He was personable. He smoked cigars with my male relatives and made a good impression. I didn't have to worry about him fitting in.

The next afternoon, we were sitting on my back deck. I had a bottle of deep burgundy nail polish, and I flirtatiously asked him to apply it to my nails. Terry was game, and did a reasonably good job.

"What else can you do?" I asked him.

"What do you mean?"

"Can you fix anything? Take care of a lawn?"

Terry hesitated. Then he said, "Well, yeah."

"So what can you do?"

"Oh—plumbing. Electrical work."

"That's good to know."

"I was afraid you'd say that. There's a little guy sitting on my shoulder, saying, 'Don't tell her! Don't tell her what you can do!'"

I laughed. "Too late. Now I know."

Even though mechanical skills were a big plus, what I truly treasured about Terry was how sweet and caring he was with me. He grew orchids, and brought me a few blooming plants. Although I tried not to talk too much about my dismal financial situation, when I did, he listened compassionately, then did his best to distract me from my worries. In fact, within two weeks of us becoming lovers, Terry asked me to go away on vacation with him—his treat. We started planning a weeklong visit to Quebec, Canada in July.

I was happy. I was thrilled. I was ecstatic.

Terry enjoyed the finer things of life, and wanted to share them with me. We went to nice restaurants and drank good wine. He was fun and easy to talk to— we spent a lot of time laughing. Our physical loving was fabulous—the more time we spent with each other, the more fulfilling it felt. Sometimes we indulged in sex toys. With my ex-husband, such accessories were repugnant. With Terry, they were fun.

I was falling for him—emotionally. This was new for me. For the first time in my life, my heart lead the way. But it was easy, because my new beau was genuinely romantic. On June 24, 2001, after another weekend of enjoying each other's company and passion, we lay in the afterglow of our lovemaking.

"See what happens when you meet a crazy guy in a bar?" Terry asked.

"You looked like fun," I replied.

"This is more than having fun, isn't it?" he asked, hesitantly.

"Yes, it is."

"There are so many unhappy people out there. I'm so happy."

"So am I."

We were quiet for a few moments. Then Terry said, "I'm melting."

I caught my breath, touched by his honesty. "That's not a bad thing, is it?" I asked.

"No, but it's scary. You're not going to take advantage of me, are you?"

"Do you want me to take advantage of you?" I teased.

"Yes," he replied, getting the joke. "But sometimes I'm too generous. People tell me I'm too generous. But you appreciate it. You give back."

"I do appreciate it. You treat me very well."

"It's my pleasure."

"You brought me all those pretty orchids. I do appreciate it. They're beautiful."

"Well, I don't know what's going to happen. But I'm not going to put a stop to it."

"I guess we'll see," I said tenderly.

I slipped my hands under Terry's life vest and dug my fingers into his chest.

I was about to go for my first ride on the back of a wave runner—a personal watercraft—on June 29, 2001. Terry bought two of them, hoping his grown kids would join him, and rented slips at the Sunset Marina on the bay in Margate, which was 10 minutes from my house.

Terry gunned the throttle, and I held on tightly as we skimmed over the Intracoastal Waterway behind Margate, on our way to Atlantic City. We slowed to a putter in the "no wake zones" among the bayfront homes and docks, until we reached my neighbor's house. After a short visit, we retraced our voyage back to the marina, bouncing off the waves, getting drenched by saltwater spray.

Afterwards, we were both in need of a shower, which, as had become our custom, we took together. Terry washed my hair, then used the body puff and liquid soap to wash my skin. I did the same for him. It was always sensual, but that evening we had no time for carnal distractions—we had a dinner reservation.

I wore a low-cut lime green shift with spaghetti straps. My hair, which usually took hours to dry, was up in a damp twist on the back of my head. Handcrafted earrings, bought when I had money, dangled to my bare shoulders. Terry wore slacks and a silk Tommy Bahama shirt with a yellow tropical plant motif. We were a bit overdressed for the casual restaurant—but we didn't care. We dressed for each other.

Our dinner conversation ranged over many topics, including some that were very personal. Terry's mother had been stricken with Alzheimer's disease at an early age, and spent the last six years of her life in a nursing home, not recognizing her husband and family, which was hard on Terry's father. Terry talked about his own disintegrating marriage. Then he posed a question to me.

"How come you never got married?"

"I did get married."

"I mean, before you were 40. Before the con man."

How could I explain? "Well, I never really felt any emotions until I was 30," I said. "It was like I was internally numb, disconnected. I didn't really know what emotions were, what it was like to feel real affection for someone."

"That doesn't make any sense. You're so sweet and affectionate."

"That's because of what I've been through with my ex-husband. My therapist said I was cracked open. I hate to admit it, but as terrible as that experience was, it did have benefits. It broke down my emotional walls."

When we got home after dinner, Terry put music on the stereo—Art Blakey and the Jazz Messengers. Blakey was a drummer who created a bluesy, funky style of jazz called "hard bop." "This is how I play the drums," Terry said. "Maybe if you listen to it, you'll get to know me better."

Blakey's style was push, push, push—pushing the musicians, keeping the beat going. Terry and I sat together on the porch in the warm night air, listening to the pulsing music streaming through the open windows. After awhile, Terry took my hand and led me upstairs to the bedroom. He unzipped my lime-colored dress and pulled it to the floor. We tumbled onto the bed, kissing, stroking, touching gently, pressing hard.

Later, as we lay together, Terry had a question for me. "Do you know why you weren't able to feel anything?" he asked.

"Well, it goes back a long, long way." In my mind, I wondered where to begin an explanation. This lifetime? Past lifetimes? It was such a long story, so involved, and so integral to my life.

"Before I got married, my sister was involved with this personal development organization called Global Relationship Centers," I started. "Tracy kept trying to get me to attend their weekend program. I didn't want to go, but I finally did. At first I thought it was stupid. But I eventually saw the value of it. Over the course of the weekend I was able to get in touch with some deep, personal issues. One of the things I realized was that I never heard the words, 'I love you,' spoken at home."

"Neither did I," Terry said.

And the moment arrived, the moment we were hinting about, afraid of, hoping for. I wanted the moment; we both wanted the moment.

"I do love you, Terry," I said.

"I love you," he responded.

Love was offered and accepted. We lay close, arms around each other, overwhelmed by the magnitude and the magnificence of it. We started to kiss again, with more passion, more tenderness. Then we lay, our lips touching, not quite kissing, but trembling together, with energy and emotion passing between us.

"We've both been so starved for love," Terry said. "And afraid of being hurt. That's why we were reluctant to say 'I love you.'"

There were sounds—small whimpers of longing and relief. So many years of going without, of indefinable pain and emptiness, knowing something was missing, but what?

We kissed deeply, caressed each other tenderly, taking in the emotion. Love, happiness, gratitude, joy. "Thank you, God," I said in my mind. "Thank you, God;

thank you, God."

One a.m., 2 a.m., 3:30 a.m. I didn't want to go to sleep—I felt like I was going to miss something, like I wanted to soak up every second of being with Terry. It was 4:10 a.m.—and Terry had to get up at 4:30. He was taking scuba lessons, and he was going on his first quarry dive.

"Goodbye sweetie," he said tenderly. "I'll see you later."

"Be careful," I said. "If you start feeling bad in the water, get out. If you feel tired when you get home, take a nap." I didn't want anything to happen to my love. I turned over for a bit more sleep—I had to get up at 6 a.m. to go rowing. I was amazed at the energy I had, even with so little rest. It must have been the energy of love.

Terry returned late in the afternoon. I was standing in the driveway next to my house when he arrived. I'd asked Terry for help with a maintenance project—not for me, but for Chuckie the chinchilla. I found a bigger cage for him—my neighbors discarded it when they moved. But it needed to be adapted. Could he help me?

Terry agreed, and came walking up the driveway carrying a small, open toolbox. He wore shorts and a tank top, and the setting sun backlit his tall, lean, muscular frame as he moved confidently toward me. "Yes!" I thought to myself, admiring the view.

The cage, however, was a project for the next day. For the moment, we relaxed on the porch with Havarti cheese, crackers and Mer Soleil wine—a rich, creamy and fairly expensive chardonnay.

I planned an at-home dinner—grilled scallops, couscous and a salad of avocado, mango and arugula. Terry helped—he made the scallops, mincing the garlic for the marinade much finer than I ever did. He set the dining room table—using the good china from the breakfront and placing one of my blooming African violets on the table as a centerpiece. Following his lead, I pulled out my formal silverware—a remnant of my marriage.

Our meal was delicious, but for me, that was secondary. I was having a fine dinner at home with the man I loved. Jazz on the stereo, smooth wine and pleasant conversation—this was truly the good life. I was filled with emotion, love and gratitude.

After dinner, we sat on the porch sofa to finish the last of the Mer Soliel. It started to rain, but we were reasonably sheltered, enjoying the mist and emotion.

We went to bed—our favorite place.

"Where were we?" Terry asked. "Oh yes, we were in love."

Passion again—sweet and pleasant, even though we were both operating on very little sleep. Our lovemaking was becoming more and more satisfying. Years earlier, I'd read in *The Art of Sexual Ecstasy* that a woman needed to open her inner channel. It was the channel of emotion, the channel of being. I tried many times to do it, but I always seemed to clamp down, unable to stay open to receive. On that night, my inner channel was open. It was wonderful.

Sweet nothings—no—sweet somethings. When we talked at night, it was communication with emotional substance.

"I hope I'm being tender enough for you," Terry said.

"You are, honey, you are."

And all of a sudden, all the pain of the past didn't matter anymore.

That night, we slept. Toward morning, I felt Terry stroking me gently. Our chatting gradually became coherent, and we reluctantly left the bed. Terry made Sunday breakfast—omelets filled with sautéed mushrooms, along with red and green peppers. We ate on the porch, watching shoobies—Jersey Shore-speak for tourists—riding bikes down the street. Again, the good life.

The rest of the day was equally pleasant, and Terry left early Monday morning. Thinking about the progress of events, I realized that I was healing. My financial situation was still terrible—work was unsteady, and I was unable to get any money from James. But I had attracted a man who wanted to give to me. And I was able to receive.

For 4th of July weekend, Terry arrived bearing gifts. He stopped at a gourmet supermarket and bought bruschetta, cheese, French bread, crab cakes, sushi and two desserts—Grand Marnier cake and key lime pie. We cracked a bottle of pinot noir and enjoyed the feast. Then we sat on the living room sofa, making out like a couple of teenagers.

"I met you and I saw this beautiful, wide-open woman who needed to be loved," Terry said. "I find it hard to believe that you were once so emotionally unavailable."

"I was. But that's over now."

In bed that evening, after more wonderful closeness, words blurted out of my mouth before they entered my brain. "Don't leave me," I said, with tears in my eyes.

"What?" Terry asked.

"Please don't leave me," I repeated, plaintively. The emotional plea came from somewhere in the pain of my past.

"I'm right here," Terry reassured me. "Don't worry, I'm right here."

We clung to each other, holding each other as tightly as we could.

"I don't know how you were before, but now you're wide open," he said. "I trust you."

"I trust you," I replied. "We trust each other."

"I've never felt like this before. I think I'm in trouble. I know I'm in trouble. And I don't care."

The next day, Terry suggested attaching hooks to the inside of my closet door so he could hang his clothes. We went to the Lowe's Home Improvement store and stood in the hardware aisle, debating the racks of hooks.

"I don't want six hooks; it's too many," I said. "How about three hooks?"

"Six hooks would be better," Terry replied.

"If you need more than three hooks, I'll give you a closet."

"If you give me a closet, I'm never leaving."

Chapter 27

"Happy Birthday!" my lover called as he opened the front door. Terry was taking me out to dinner on July 19, 2001. Finally, at age 45, I had a date with a man I loved on my birthday. My lifetime dream was coming true.

I was only partially assembled—makeup but no dress. It was 4 p.m. and I'd been working like crazy all day. I'd recently picked up a new client that required a lot of attention. Plus other projects, stalled for weeks, finally became active. I was beyond busy—and we were leaving for our vacation to Quebec in four days.

Throwing on a powder blue cotton bathrobe, I ran downstairs to greet my lover. Terry looked handsome in a light tan sport coat, cream-colored crew-neck shirt and brown slacks.

"Happy Birthday, sugar," he said, presenting me with a dozen red roses.

I opened the little card attached to them. "They're from Terry!" I said, in mock surprise.

"How about that!" he exclaimed, playing along.

We kissed—a delightful kiss.

While Terry arranged the flowers in a vase, I ran upstairs to finish dressing. My form-fitting scoop-necked red dress, with tiny black polka dots, hung to mid-calf, but was slit on the left side up to my thigh. Very sexy—and under it I wore a red bra and matching panties from Victoria's Secret. Finally ready, I flew back downstairs, where Terry was practically dancing with excitement. He wanted me to open my presents. Three small boxes, tied with beautiful fabric ribbons, graced the coffee table.

"You can open them in any order," he said.

The first box revealed an artisan necklace. It was a flat, narrow collar of hammered silver, with a double thread of brass entwined around it.

"Oh, Terry, it's beautiful!"

"I knew you liked handcrafted jewelry."

Terry put the necklace on me. With the low neckline of my dress, the jewelry shone against my skin. "It's perfect," he said.

I opened the remaining gifts. Terry selected earrings to complement the necklace, and a silk scarf hand-painted in royal blue, purple and magenta. His taste was exquisite. Then he gave me two artistic birthday cards, both decorated with hearts. "Because you're close to my heart," he said.

It was all so wonderful—the flowers, the gifts, the cards.

"Thank you so much," I gushed, with genuine appreciation.

Our dinner reservation was in Cape May, which was at the southernmost tip of New Jersey, an hour's drive from Atlantic City. Cape May was America's oldest seaside resort—the entire city was a National Historic Landmark. Many of its Victorian homes, decorated by gingerbread, were converted to bed-and-breakfasts or gourmet restaurants. We had reservations in the critically acclaimed Ebbitt Room in the Virginia Hotel.

We arrived early, so we ordered cocktails in the hotel's tiny lounge. Terry pulled out a small camera. "Try to look sultry," he said.

"I can't," I replied, "I'm too excited." All I could do was grin.

The hostess led us to our table, right in the center of the small, sophisticated dining room, and handed us menus and a wine list. I surprised myself by ordering a filet mignon, while Terry selected lamb chops. Looking over the wine list, Terry asked, "Have you ever had a French Bordeaux?"

"I don't know," I answered.

"Do you feel like having something deep, with character?"

"Sure." I'd ordered steak, so I knew red wine would be appropriate.

My date selected a bottle, and asked the waitress to have it decanted. Terry explained the purpose of decanting—exposing the wine to oxygen allowed its full flavor to come out. When our wine arrived, Terry swirled it around in his glass, allowing it to oxygenate further, and then demonstrated the correct way to drink it—blowing bubbles in his mouth.

"I don't think I'll try that," I said, remembering how I'd recently spit wine across my dining room table when he cracked a joke in the middle of my sip.

Terry liked good wine, and the crop for the year 2000 was highly rated. "People start spending $100 and $200 for a bottle of wine," he said. "The problem with getting to that level is that you then don't want to drink less expensive wines. It's hard to go back."

"I know about that one," I said. "You get to a certain level, and it's hard to go back."

Terry understood that I was referring to my own situation. "Yes, it is," he agreed, sympathetically. Then he searched his pockets. "I have something else for you."

He pulled out another gift—art glass in the shape of a heart. The iridescent color shifted among magenta, green and gold, like carnival glass, and the top was embossed in a crosshatch pattern. The heart fit snugly into the palm of my hand.

"Because you have a piece of my heart," Terry said. "Not the whole thing, but a piece, a chunk. Maybe more will come."

I was touched, thrilled, relieved, in love. When my ex-husband made similar gestures, he was conning me. This time, the gesture was real. I knew Terry's love was genuine, because I could feel it.

After dinner, for the hour-long ride back to Atlantic City, I held Terry's hand, sometimes nibbling on his fingers, which I knew he liked. I stroked the back of his head. By the time we reached my house, we were both so consumed by desire that we barely made it to the bedroom.

The physical expression of our love was sensuous. Boisterous. Playful. Finally, exhausted and satisfied, I wrapped my arms and legs around my lover and squeezed him as tightly as I could. This man had just given me the most wonderful birthday of my life, and I wasn't letting him go.

Our Air Canada flight departed from Newark Airport at 10:10 a.m. on July 24, 2001. The flight went first to Ottawa, Canada, and then on to Quebec. Since Ottawa was our point of entry into Canada, we had to pick up our luggage from baggage claim and push it through customs.

"Where are you going?" the customs official, a young blond woman, asked.

"Quebec," Terry replied.

"Are you staying with friends or relatives?"

"No."

"Where are you staying?"

"At the Frontenac Hotel."

The young woman then directed us around a corner and asked us to sit down. We saw offices with closed doors and a loaded luggage cart, but no travelers and no officials. We waited. Then a young, dark-haired man in a uniform asked for our passports. He disappeared into an office and we continued to wait. After 10 minutes, he reappeared.

"You can go now," the customs official said. "Your name matches that of a wanted criminal, and we had to check you out."

"Whose name?" I asked. "Mine?"

"No, his," the official said, indicating Terry.

We pushed our luggage cart to the concourse. "This is amazing," I said, laughing, to Terry. "All the times I was traveling with a criminal, nothing happened. Then, when I'm traveling with you, I get stopped."

After a two-hour layover, which we passed in the airport's food court, it was time to continue our journey to Quebec. We joined the security line with our passports, boarding passes and hand luggage. I put my purse and camera bag on the conveyer belt for the x-ray machine, walked through the metal detector, and picked them up on the other end.

Terry put his carryon on the conveyer belt. It stayed in the x-ray machine longer than usual, with the security officials examining its contents on the monitor. Finally the supervisor, a matronly Canadian woman with her dark hair pulled up in a bun, asked Terry to bring his bag to the inspection table. From about 10 feet away, I witnessed the exchange.

"What do you have?" the woman asked.

"A lot of electronics," Terry answered. "Camera, battery charger, phone charger."

The inspector rooted around Terry's carryon. "Is this your shaving kit?" she asked, pulling his red leather kit out of the bag.

"Yes," Terry answered.

"What is the cylinder?" she asked, pulling a vibrator out of the kit and holding it up for all to see.

"Oh, my God," I said, under my breath, but loud enough for Terry to hear me. He glanced at me, but maintained his composure. The inspector apparently did not know what the device was. Taking it from the woman, Terry turned it on so she could hear it buzz.

Laughing, I turned away, and walked toward our departure gate. The further I walked, the funnier the scene became to me. By the time Terry joined me, I was sitting in the waiting area, hysterical, with tears running down my face. I continued to laugh helplessly until we boarded our small commuter flight to Quebec.

As the taxi carrying us to our hotel passed through the stone arch of Porte St.-Louis—one of the gates in Quebec's original fortification walls—I felt like I was transported to the Latin Quarter in Paris. Quaint three-story buildings with masonry or stone façades flanked both sides of the narrow streets. Bay windows and hanging baskets filled with flowers protruded from the buildings. Shops and restaurants were identified by tasteful wooden signs—all of them in French.

My visit to Quebec with Terry, I was certain, would be much more romantic than my visits to Paris with James.

Quebec, founded in 1608, was the only walled city in North America. Le Chateau Frontenac, the city's most distinctive hotel, towered above the fortification on the St. Lawrence River. It looked like a massive castle, with multiple rounded turrets crowned by conical roofs. Terry had booked us into the landmark hotel—on the exclusive concierge level, no less.

Walking into the hotel, I felt like I was entering a royal residence. The formal lobby stretched to the right and left, with polished wood-paneled walls punctuated by arched windows, a wood-coffered ceiling, chandeliers and thick Oriental carpets. Because of our status as concierge guests, we were whisked to a private check-in desk on the 14th floor. "You're staying with us all week!" the representative noted, surprised. Obviously, most VIP guests only stayed for a few days.

After stopping in our room, which, like many old European hotels, was small and traditionally furnished, Terry and I went out to explore the neighborhood and find a place for dinner. We settled on Café de la Paix, just a block from the hotel, which served French and French-Canadian comfort food in a distinctly European atmosphere. We placed our order and started sipping our wine.

"I didn't tell you the rest of the story," Terry said.

"What story?"

"From the airport."

"What happened?"

Terry just shook his head. "I can't tell you."

"Why not?"

"Well, not now."

After dinner, we returned to our room, and I changed into the fluffy white Frontenac bathrobe and sat on the bed.

"So here's the rest of the story," Terry said.

Back at the security station in the Ottawa airport, after I turned away from the scene, the matronly inspector continued her search of Terry's shaving kit. Under the vibrator, she found a silver-studded black leather cock ring.

"What's this?" the inspector asked, pulling it out and holding it up.

Again, Terry kept a straight face. "It's a collar for our pet," he answered.

"Why do you have it?"

"We miss the pet."

I lost it. I lay on the bed in our hotel room, laughing so hard that I couldn't move. In fact, I could barely breathe. I chortled; I guffawed; I convulsed; I almost rolled off the bed.

Fifteen minutes later, when I could speak, we riffed on the topic. "We'll get a leash," I said. "I'll take you for a walk, and you'll take Beau for a walk."

Terry joined me on the bed, sliding his hands under my Frontenac bathrobe, kissing me between my continued chuckles. Slowly my hysteria subsided. We talked about priorities, and how they change.

"What are your priorities now?" I asked.

"My emotional life—you," he answered.

Terry always told me the contents of his heart, and his words, which I knew were sincere, warmed my heart. Both of us were bursting with love and joy, which fueled our physical passion. We kissed; we caressed; we pressed into each other as hard as we could, until fulfillment washed over us.

Then we slept, in peace, appreciation and possibly a few giggles.

Quebec was in full bloom. Purple, white, pink, magenta, red, yellow—layered bursts of color filled the flowerbeds of the Joan of Arc garden. The lush garden, with more than 150 types of plants, adjoined the Plains of Abraham, a hundred-acre plateau carpeted in grass just outside the walls of Vieux Quebec—Old Quebec.

Terry and I finally stirred ourselves to walk to the garden after our first leisurely morning in our hotel. The private lounge down the hall served an expansive Continental breakfast. After eating, we went back to our room for quality time in bed. Since we'd done the same thing the night before, and the housekeepers had yet to visit, we needed to request more bath towels. It was a request we made several times during our stay.

The in-room fireworks weren't the only ones scheduled for the day. We had tickets to see literal explosions in the sky that evening at the Loto-Québec International Fireworks Competition. Every year, Quebec invited teams of pyrotechnics artists from around the world to create dazzling displays of fireworks synchronized to music. To add to the spectacle, the show took place at the dramatic Montmorency Falls, which, at 275 feet high, was taller than Niagara Falls. The waterfall was breathtaking when we arrived while the sky was still light—how would it look under the burst of fireworks?

The show began at 9:30 p.m., not with a bang, but with multitudinous explosions of color, light and sound. From our seats in the Montmorency Park grandstand, we had a clear view of the display, and the music, punctuated by the boom of the fireworks, enveloped us. I always loved fireworks, and these were, by far, the best I'd ever seen. Teams from South Africa, China, Spain, Italy and the Czech Republic all tried to outdo each other in pursuit of the grand prize.

Each team selected dramatic, emotional music. One performance was set to the theme from *Star Wars*. With the opening bars of the music, rockets with flaming tails launched from either side of the waterfall. Then, as the music shifted to a quieter tempo, glowing orbs drifted silently in the sky, like UFOs. When the music took on the ominous character of Darth Vader, trouble, in the form of violent explosions, burst in all directions, until the triumphant finale turned the night sky red.

The next performance was set to the classical *Carmina Burana,* a composition for choir and instruments. As the choir started singing in Latin, the tension in the music was almost palpable, and understated fireworks scattered across the sky captured the mood. Then, as the intensity of the music increased, towers of sparks burst from the base of the waterfall, and a spinning pinwheel of light suddenly materialized from an island in the river.

I gasped. I cheered. And as the crescendo of each performance filled the night sky with a barrage of red, blue, purple, green and white fluorescent explosions, simultaneously and in rapid succession, I felt the exhilaration of the moment.

The fireworks were emotional, sensual, fulfilling—just like my bursting romance with Terry.

Over thousands of years, the Sainte-Anne-du-Nord River carved mountains of Canadian rock into a spectacular tourist attraction. At Canyon Sainte-Anne in Beaupré, Quebec, which Terry and I visited on July 27, 2001, the river flowed through an ancient forest and then cascaded down a narrow gorge and over a 250-foot waterfall. A trail led to three slender footbridges that were suspended over the canyon. Walking across them, I felt like I was in a Tarzan movie—massive trees grew along both edges of the gorge, and turbulent water rushed below. I was even protected by a muscular, good-looking man.

One stop along the trail was called "Rocky Flats." This described the formation precisely—a large outcropping of rock protruding from the canyon wall. Visitors could walk across the flat top, but because of good-sized crevices, we had to watch where we stepped. Carrying my camera, I was a bit off balance. My foot slipped into one of the crevices and I fell.

"Terry!" I called, panicked.

Terry turned, rushed back and grabbed my hand, pulling me to my feet.

"You almost gave me a heart attack!" he exclaimed when I was safe.

"I'm sorry," I said. "Thank you for rescuing me."

Our next sojourn was even more of an adventure.

Further up the Sainte-Anne-du-Nord River was another natural attraction called Les Sept-Chutes, or the Seven Waterfalls. As the name implied, this park offered dramatic views of the river spilling down seven waterfalls, along with a hydroelectric plant that dated to 1916. Our tourist brochure extolled the beautiful flora and fauna along the park's five kilometers of easily accessible walking trails.

We must have picked the wrong trail. Following a sign with a simple arrow and the word "*chutes*," or waterfalls, which pointed down a wooded hill, our hike started out easily enough, but soon became steep and difficult. We had to watch our footing carefully so we didn't slip on loose stones, and sometimes we held on to trees to stay upright on the incline. The trail went on and on. We had no idea how long it was, if we should keep going or if we should turn back. Terry and I were alone in the woods, struggling down the hill, and it was getting late.

Finally, we came to a rough gravel road, a hint of civilization. Then a truck appeared. We flagged it down—it was affiliated with the park—but the driver told us we couldn't board. We had to go to the official truck stop, somewhat like a bus stop. Not knowing how much further it was to the truck stop, and frantic about missing a ride back, we quickened our pace, slipping and sliding down the rutted road. Around a bend we found, to our surprise and relief, the truck stop, with other people waiting.

We bounced back up the hill in the truck, without ever seeing the seven waterfalls.

In the middle of the St. Lawrence River was a picturesque island, Ile d'Orleans, where Terry and I spent the next day of our vacation. The island was only 10 miles from Quebec, but in appearance and sensibility, it was a world away. Ile d'Orleans was a farming community famous for its produce, and as we drove the historic Chemin Royal, the road that followed its circumference, we passed manicured fields of strawberries, cabbages, apples, potatoes and grapes.

Tourism was also important to Ile d'Orleans—bed and breakfast inns and art galleries were scattered all along Chemin Royal. One of the galleries, located in a historic cottage, featured handcrafted textiles. Terry picked a jacket for me to try on. The fabric was a cream-colored nubby fleece, sprinkled with flecks of black. He then selected a scarf to go with it, hand-colored in gold, tan, olive green, steel blue and wine red.

"Those colors look great on you," Terry said.

"You think so?"

"Yes."

I hesitated—although I liked them, I wasn't prepared to spend money on a new jacket and scarf.

Terry knew what I was thinking. "I'll buy them for you," he said.

I couldn't believe how Terry was spoiling me—he'd already bought me a beautiful necklace of freshwater pearls, pale pink and elongated in shape. I was happy just being in his company, being in love with him—the gifts were surprise treasures. "Thank you," I said, "I really appreciate it."

That evening, we had dinner at La Goeliche, one of the best restaurants on the island, located in Sainte-Pétronille. The glass-enclosed dining room offered a spectacular view, and as we savored an exquisite meal, the sun set behind Quebec on the other side of the St. Lawrence River.

Simply by passing through Porte St.-Louis in the old fortress wall, the road changed names from Rue Saint-Louis to the Grand-Allée, and Quebec City changed from quaint to chic.

Grand-Allée was known as the Champs-Élysées of Quebec, and there was, to my eye, a striking resemblance to the famous Parisian boulevard. Grand-Allée was famous for its restaurants, which, on July 29, 2001, the height of summer, offered al fresco dining on the wide sidewalks. We visited the nearby art museum—Musée National des Beaux-Arts du Québec—and then selected a sidewalk café for lunch.

I felt so cosmopolitan. The gourmet lunch was light and delicious. Conversations in French buzzed around us. My dining companion was handsome and sophisticated. It was a taste of the life that I truly wanted.

I experienced that life again in the evening. Terry made reservations for us at Le Champlain, the most elegant restaurant in Le Chateau Frontenac.

"Can you wear something dressy?" he asked.

"How dressy do you want?"

"As dressy as you can get."

Before our vacation, I splurged on a dress for just such an occasion. It was leopard-print silk, sleeveless and with an open back, yet full and flowing from the waist down. Terry wore a light-colored jacket and tie. As we exited the elevator holding hands, we made a striking couple, and heads turned.

We stopped in the clubby St.-Laurent Bar and Lounge for cocktails. Then, from a window table in Le Champlain, we enjoyed an exquisite dinner, accompanied by champagne and another spectacular view of the St. Lawrence River.

Finally, our last full day in Quebec arrived. As had become our custom, we spent a leisurely morning in the hotel, then ventured out. On this day, we didn't go very far—we strolled around the Place d'Armes, just outside the Frontenac, and then went down the funicular to the tourist area near the river, Basse-Ville, or Lower Town, for some shopping. Wanting our last night in Quebec to be romantic, Terry arranged a horse-drawn carriage ride. We picked up our carriage right in front of Le Chateau Frontenac, and the horse and driver took us on a 45-minute guided tour of Vieux Québec. I didn't enjoy the ride as much as I thought I would—I was worried about the horse. It seemed to me that he should be running in a field, not dodging cars on city streets.

The driver veered a block off the regular tour route to take us to Aux Anciens Canadiens restaurant, where we had a dinner reservation. The building was the historic Maison Jacquet, the oldest house in Quebec, dating to 1675. Its five small dining rooms were all decorated in different themes. Only a couple of tables were occupied in our dining room, so the staff had plenty of time to be attentive. Whenever we requested anything from our waiter, a handsome young Canadian, his answer was, "perfect." That was exactly how I felt about my visit to Quebec with Terry.

On our last morning at Le Chateau Frontenac, I woke at 6:10. "It's not time to get up yet," I said, rolled over, and went back to sleep.

An hour and a half later, I stirred, and felt Terry's hand on my shoulder. It had been a very physical week, not counting the treks to see waterfalls. We always lay together after our passion, and on that morning, I could feel the energy still vibrating back and forth between us long after the culmination of our expression. Our loving was truly wonderful, more wonderful than I'd ever known.

Our flight home was without incident. We picked up Terry's car at the Newark airport and headed for Atlantic City, chatting about our trip. After all the fine dining, I was sure that I'd gained a couple of pounds. Terry was blessed with a naturally fast metabolism—one reason why he stayed so lean.

"Do women care about a man's appearance?" he asked.

"I can't generalize," I said. "Some women will put up with anything if a man has money."

"What good is that?"

"Well, we're not talking about people interested in emotional fulfillment here."

Terry thought about that for a moment, and he didn't agree. "I'm shooting for the heart," he said.

"Me, too," I said, putting my hand behind his head and stroking his hair.

"It's hard to find a heart of gold like you have," he said.

I paused to reflect on his words. "That's sweet of you," I replied. "But I think a lot of people have hearts of gold. They just have too many walls in front of them."

Mine, at long last, was crumbling.

Chapter 28

The pattern needed to be broken. Five times since I graduated from college and began living on my own I was in dire financial straits, and on August 16, 2001, I was there again. Even though I was working and had $14,000 in receivables, my clients were slow to send checks. It was almost as scary as having no work.

I requested a session with Elaine Anderson specifically to deal with the issue of money.

At least one part of my life was going well—Terry and I were still in love and having fun. We went on double dates with friends. On a Sunday afternoon canoe trip, Terry put all his energy into the scavenger hunt, even digging through trash cans to find items on the list. He continued to make me laugh.

I told Elaine all of this. Still, as we talked, I could feel the fear and tension building within me. I lay down on her table, and soon began seeing images of a past life.

"What are you afraid of?" Elaine asked.

"I'm afraid that I'm going to starve," I answered immediately.

I saw a rural countryside, perhaps in England. Then I saw a big, dark city. Dark stone walls, dark alleyways between buildings, and dirty, skinny children begging. The sight of them ripped me up.

"Can you tell who you are?" Elaine asked.

At first I wasn't sure, but then realized that I was a young woman. I had come to the city from the country, where things were bad, hoping for a better life. My younger brother was with me; I was responsible for him. I was afraid of starving and afraid of getting sick. Then my young brother did get sick, and there was only one way for me to earn money for a doctor—prostitution.

"That's the first thing that flashed into my mind when you saw this lifetime," Elaine said.

It was awful. I was sleeping with drunken, smelly men. I never knew when one of them would hurt me. I never knew where the next meal was coming from. I felt deep, dark fear and isolation. I had no hope, only despair.

"It was so degrading," Elaine said. "You really hated it."

Tension took over my body. My arms were tense; my legs were tense; my back was tense. Pressure slithered up my back and into my head, concentrating in the roof of my mouth. My face muscles were wound so tight that my mouth contorted and I started to get a headache.

"You were always on edge," Elaine said. "Such fear and tension. What else are you afraid of?"

"I'm afraid I'm going to die," I said.

My younger brother did die, so I prostituted myself for nothing. By then it was too late for me. I was damaged goods and I could never hope to have a husband. My life was ruined. So I stopped living. Rather than continue the degrading existence of a prostitute, I stopped eating and died, filled with fear, tension, disillusionment and despair. That's what froze in my body.

It wasn't supposed to happen. I had come to the city because I was promised a job as a maid. But the master of the house took advantage of me. His wife discovered his infidelity and threw me out.

"You were too pretty," Elaine said.

I started to cry. "I worked hard. All I wanted was a job."

Thoughts of James invaded the periphery of my mind. I tried to ignore them—it seemed that every time I saw a past life, I thought James was involved. Finally I could ignore them no longer.

"That wasn't James again, was it?" I asked.

"Well, you two have a lot of history," Elaine said. "It feels like it was James."

"He didn't care," I said.

"No, he didn't. He was just like he was in this lifetime, concerned only about his desires of the moment."

"If I were ugly he would have left me alone. He left his wife alone. I never intended for it to happen. I just wanted to be a maid and work hard."

James, I realized, was an uncle or cousin who lived on an estate. That's how I got the job. "He was a relative, so you felt safe going there," Elaine confirmed.

But the last time he had seen me I was a child; I grew into a lovely young woman. He had his way with me. I hated what he did. I hated what he made me do. And he had kinky taste.

When I lost the job, I felt no one would believe my story—that he raped me. So I just left, my little brother in tow. I put on his coat and hat, saying, "We're going to the city. It's big and impressive, and it's going to be fun."

The city was a disaster. I became a prostitute—using what I had learned from James. It was awful, humiliating and ultimately fruitless.

"I want to go home," I cried. "I just want to go home."

"You were too shamed," Elaine said. "It feels like you blocked that option."

Hopelessness, fear, tension, despair. The waves hit me again—full-body tension, pressure moving to the roof of my mouth, my face contorting. The corners of my mouth pulled down hard, making my headache worse. I couldn't talk. All I could do was process the emotion, the charge, the fear.

"James never knew what happened to you," Elaine said. "He didn't care. Tell him what happened to you. Feel the anger."

"I don't have any anger," I said. "Only black fear."

"Try to express what you need to say to his soul," Elaine said.

I never got to that. Another wave of emotion hit—energy in my back, my mouth, my throbbing head. I started to tremble. Slightly at first, but then a full-body tremor that escalated into convulsions, with my body jerking. Contractions in my abdominal muscles, making me jerk up. Again, again, again.

"My heart is broken," I said. "My heart is broken." I kept repeating those words, feeling the pain.

It took a long time to move all the energy. My hamstrings and my arms were tensed and poised in the air, probably six inches above my midsection. I wept. Pain in my mouth, in the right temple. And the headache. I never had a headache in a session with Elaine before.

"Your trust was broken," Elaine said. "You felt like there was no way out. And that's how your life ended."

The charge started to drain.

"Somebody has been trying to comfort you," Elaine observed. "Let's focus on it."

At first I couldn't. I was still crying from the pain and fear. But slowly the tears dried.

"Terry wants to make it better," I said. "He wants to take care of me, but he's afraid." I paused for a moment, becoming aware of more.

"He is amazed at what you've been through, and proud that you've come out in one piece," Elaine said. "He likes your sense of humor. In fact, he's amazed that you have a sense of humor at all, after what you've been through. He sees it as a sign of your strength."

"Well, we laugh a lot," I said. "Sometimes it's a three-ring circus when we're together. And we love each other."

"He's grateful that you're part of his life."

"So am I. He's wonderful. We get along fabulously. He took me to Quebec, and we stayed in the best hotel, and ate in the best restaurants. He paid for it. It was wonderful. Still, sometimes I wonder if he's going to take the pressure off of me. I'm so tired of the pressure."

I started to cry again. Fatigue overwhelmed me.

"Guidance is saying that he's already taken the pressure off of you."

"That's because we love each other. It's easier to deal with all of this when you have love."

"Look at how much you've healed. You can love. You can feel love. The circumstances of this lifetime were bad, but you've healed, and it's going to be different. You're creating a whole new life."

"I feel like he was part of that other life. Like he was an old boyfriend from the country, and tried to help me, but it was too late."

"Yes," Elaine said. "He was someone who cared about you. He went to find you, but didn't get there in time. He wasn't able to help you."

"He's not going to let me go this time. And I think we knew each other before—is that possible? Like we had a nice life together before."

"Let's try to feel one of those happy lives. We have them, but we don't always remember them, because they don't have the charge of the bad lives."

In my mind I saw a small, white house with a huge flower garden—a country cottage. "We had this calm, nondescript life together," I said. "Maybe in France. I've felt like we need to go to France together. Back then he was always telling jokes, and we were always laughing. We had a bunch of kids."

"Three kids," Elaine said.

"It was fun; he was always joking. He loved the flowers. And now we're happy to be together again. I've been through a lot, and he's been through a lot."

"What I feel from your two souls is relief. Relief at finding each other. You appreciate each other. Appreciation is the key. It opens many doors."

"What do you mean?" I asked.

"That's what Guidance is telling me. Appreciate. Appreciate. It opens doors. It keeps the channels of communication open. It keeps the heart open. If there is a problem, appreciation will enable you to solve it. Everything is in motion. This life is going to be different. You've healed so much that you're able to create a different life. You weren't ready for this before. Your other boyfriend ..."

"John," I said.

"Yes, John," Elaine continued. "That was one level. But you weren't ready for more, and neither was he. You've healed more, and grown. So now you can feel more love."

"It's getting better," I said. "The money will be better."

"Guidance says it already is better," Elaine said. "Just keep feeling the gratitude. Especially now. Any time something good happens about the money, keep feeling the gratitude. It will open doors. It will attract more."

"I feel like now is a time to get my financial situation stabilized, and get to know Terry."

"That's right," Elaine agreed. "It's time to laugh and to play. That is how you both will heal. The rest will come later."

Bankruptcy was easier than I thought it would be.

I retained yet another attorney, and he drew up the paperwork. My financial position looked bleak. My cute little house at the shore was valued on the tax rolls at $74,000, but my first and second mortgages amounted to $75,300. The Thunderbird that I originally leased for James, with 78,000 miles on it, was valued at $9,000, but the car loan was $8,688. I had $56,000 in credit card debt and attorney fees from my divorce. And my business wasn't stable—sometimes I had money, sometime I didn't.

Bankruptcy law allowed me to claim certain exemptions, so I claimed my home, car, household goods, clothing and professional tools like my computer. My goal was to get rid of the unsecured credit card debt and attorney fees, but keep my home and business.

The bankruptcy hearing took place not before a judge, but before a trustee in a small, low-ceilinged room in a suburban office building. At the front of the room, the trustee sat at a utilitarian table with a brown laminate top and chrome legs. Two chairs faced the table, for the bankrupt and his or her counsel. Two rows of chairs in the back of the room were filled with people waiting for their cases to be heard.

When my turn came, the trustee asked me how I had accumulated the debt. I explained that my ex-husband had defrauded me, as he'd done with multiple other women. I'd won a judgment in my divorce, but I wasn't able to collect it.

"How much is the judgment?" the trustee asked.

"One and a quarter million dollars," I replied.

The trustee looked up in surprise.

"How many women did he defraud?" he asked.

"Four testified at my divorce, but there are more."

"Where is your ex-husband?"

"He left the country. I retained collection agents and lawyers, but they couldn't find him and I was never able to serve my judgment. I finally had to give up."

My hearing lasted 15 minutes. The trustee signed off on my petition, and the credit card companies, which had been calling me early every morning, could no longer try to collect their debts.

Terry continued to visit every weekend, getting more acquainted with me and my family of pets. Beau, of course, joined us for every meal—now, instead of one person to beg from, he had two.

I resumed the treat trick—throwing a dog bone down the stairs to distract him while I shut the bedroom door for private time with my lover. Beau lay outside the door chewing his treat, and if the bedroom activity became overly rambunctious, he added to the noise by howling. Sometimes Terry and I just had to stop and laugh.

Beau knew that when Terry was with me, he wasn't allowed on the bed. The dog complied, except in two situations—fireworks and thunderstorms. The local professional baseball team played in a stadium located three-quarters of a mile from my house as the crow flies, and frequently capped home games with fireworks. My dog, terrified at the noise, jumped on the bed. Luckily, the fireworks only lasted 15 minutes; afterwards, we could coax Beau back to his cushion on the floor.

Thunder was different. When summer storms rolled through, it was impossible to know how long they would last. I tried everything I could think of to comfort or distract the dog. I gave him treats. I sat with him in the basement. Nothing worked. With every rumble in the heavens, he jumped on the bed and positioned himself between us, with his head on my pillow and his butt on Terry's. I realized Terry must really love us—he tolerated Beau's panic attacks.

In fact, he must have loved all of us. Terry made home improvements for the little pets. Now that Chuckie had a big new cage, we moved him, and the sugar gliders, from the spare bedroom to the basement. This gave everyone more opportunities to get out from behind bars and run around. Chuckie raced the length of the basement gym and ricocheted off the walls. The gliders preferred scampering along the steam pipes from the heating system, which were suspended from the ceiling. Once the heater went on, of course, the pipes would be extremely hot—the temperature of steam was 212 degrees. So Terry built a glider highway—a surface of boards along the pipes—so the little animals wouldn't burn their feet.

Although Terry was great with the pets, mostly he made special plans for the two of us. Even though it was still summer, he bought tickets to see Cirque du Soleil, my favorite troupe of acrobats, on October 6, 2001, in Philadelphia. I was thrilled—no man had ever asked me for a date so far in advance. Then he made reservations for us to spend October 18 through 21 at a bed and breakfast in artsy, tony New Hope, Pennsylvania. I was beginning to feel that maybe, just maybe, Terry was going to stick around.

When we saw each other on weekends, sometimes we cooked in, and other times we went out to eat. On August 24, 2001, we had dinner at one of my favorite local restaurants. Over an exquisite meal, I told Terry about my bankruptcy hearing and my session with Elaine. I described the past life that we shared, with our cottage and flowers and children. He liked that a lot. Then I told him about the life in which I had starved to death.

"I wouldn't let you starve," Terry said.

My attempt to blackmail James generated a response. Robert Palmer, chairman of Global Eco-Learning Publishing and Communications (GELPAC), contacted me from Australia. He was very interested in the document I sent—my final judgment of divorce, with its findings of fraud against James Montgomery. On August 28, 2001, we had a long chat on the phone.

Robert Palmer was legitimately in the education business, with more than 30 years of experience as a classroom teacher and principal. He was a successful education author—he wrote more than 200 teacher support and student activity books. He also had expertise in curriculum design, and was a consultant to higher education institutions.

James recruited Robert Palmer to be Director of Studies for his International Institute for Continuing Education (IICE) in New Zealand. The two men met multiple times at a pub in Richmond, Australia, a suburb of Melbourne. James didn't have an office—he told Robert that he was staying at a secret army location. Robert eventually agreed to take the job, although he didn't go along with James' much-repeated suggestion that he and his wife sell their home and move permanently to New Zealand.

"We were probably among the few people who didn't put any money into his projects, although we did put in considerable time and effort," Robert said.

When Robert arrived in New Zealand in 2000, he learned that IICE was operating out of a small back room in an office building—totally unsuitable for teaching. James had hired a man to make improvements to the facility, but the man was a drunkard, so Robert fired him.

Wanting to make sure that the school was complying with regulations,

Robert met with key officials from New Zealand's education and immigration bodies. He quickly learned that the compliance policies James had said were in place were, in fact, nonexistent. Because of this, Robert believed that his own situation could become precarious.

In New Zealand and Australia, whenever a foreign student paid money for an education course, the money had to be kept in trust. Students had a week to change their minds about the course, and if they did, all their money had to be refunded. When students stayed in the courses, the educational institution withdrew installments of the money at regular intervals to cover the cost of services as students received them. That way, if a student didn't complete a course, he or she could use any money remaining in the trust fund to continue studies elsewhere.

James told Robert that IICE had a student trust fund, and even gave him a bank account number. But when Robert called the bank to verify it, he learned that the number was for a personal account in the name of Kim Goodson.

Robert told me what a senior immigration official said to him: If students came in from China, and IICE failed because of a lack of funds, the person responsible would be Robert Palmer. Robert immediately began working closely with the authorities—not only to protect himself, but to protect the students.

"I was the insider," he said. "But I was standing up for what I believed in."

Without a trust fund, IICE was not allowed to operate. That didn't stop James. "He was signing up 200, 300, 400 Chinese students at a time, getting paid in U.S. dollars, and making promises he couldn't keep," Robert said.

Robert actually saw some of the cash. James once came into a meeting with two briefcases. He planned to give Robert a stack of completed student application forms for processing. But James didn't open the briefcase containing the applications. He opened—and quickly closed—the one that was stuffed with hundred dollar bills.

Six Chinese students arrived in New Zealand for the school's pilot program. They started asking about the benefits they were promised, like visas and transportation vouchers. Robert never saw documents that explained the student benefits; he asked Kim Goodson for a copy. She contacted James, who was, as usual, out of town, or out of the country. If there were problems, James indignantly replied, it was the fault of the Chinese.

Robert asked the students to show him the documents they received. They were written in both English and Chinese, so translation wasn't an issue. James promised the students that their visas and travel expenses were covered. He also promised that they'd receive their qualification in six months, when the course required a year.

With this, the New Zealand authorities came down hard on IICE. Apparently, so did others who had been duped. One of the students was the daughter of a provincial police chief in China. The girl told Robert that her father locked James up until all the money for his daughter's course was refunded. James apparently spent a week in a Chinese jail.

In the end, IICE collapsed. James wasn't allowed to bring in any more students, and had to reimburse money to the students who had arrived. Robert got the students enrolled in other schools. Then Robert provided information about what he believed was James Montgomery's fraud to government officials.

All summer long, I'd been rowing with my doubles partner, Mary Steinacker, preparing for the fall racing season. We continued to train in September, getting on the water before dawn so Mary could be at work on time.

The sky was still dark, just starting to show a few streaks of light, as we pushed off from the dock on September 11, 2001. Mary was in the bow; it was her job to steer us. She kept the boat in the middle of the bay so we didn't accidentally hit a channel marker in the blackness. Gradually, almost imperceptibly, the sun rose, promising a gorgeous day of blue skies, pleasant temperatures and low humidity. Gliding along on the water, we saw herons and egrets standing silently by the marshes, while seagulls and terns swooped not so silently overhead. Early mornings on the bay were so tranquil, so beautiful.

I was on my way to a 10 a.m. sales meeting when I heard a report on the car radio—a plane had crashed into the World Trade Center in New York City. The information was sketchy and disjointed—what were they talking about?

I reached Bayport One, a five-story office building overlooking the bay in West Atlantic City. I went up to the second floor, and the woman I was there to meet escorted me back to a conference room. We passed a group of her co-workers, who were all standing around a radio, staring at it, listening to the news from New York City. Both towers of the World Trade Center were hit by planes, and one of them just collapsed.

"What do we do?" I asked my potential customer. "Do you want to have our meeting?"

"I guess so," she said. Neither of us knew the protocol for a time of national emergency. But as we talked in the conference room, through wall-to-wall windows I could see jet after jet landing at Atlantic City International Airport, which was eight miles away and in the middle of the busy Northeast travel corridor. No jets were taking off.

I finished the meeting, went home and turned on the television. NBC newscasters Tom Brokaw, Katie Couric and Matt Lauer were sitting at the news desk, recapping what was known so far: Four domestic airliners had been hijacked. American Airlines Flight 11 crashed into the World Trade Center North Tower at 8:46 a.m. United Airlines Flight 175 hit the South Tower at 9:03 a.m. American Airlines Flight 77 crashed into the Pentagon at 9:37 a.m. Another plane, United Airlines Flight 93, smashed into a field near Shanksville, Pennsylvania at 10:03 a.m. The North Tower of the World Trade Center collapsed at 9:59 a.m. The South Tower collapsed at 10:28 a.m.

Nobody knew how many people were dead.

In a state of shock, I continued to watch the news. NBC had already produced a graphic: "Attack on America." Over and over, television stations aired video footage of the second jet crashing into the World Trade Center, the billowing black smoke from the tops of the buildings, and then the 110-story skyscrapers sliding to the ground.

My brother, Doug, had an office in lower Manhattan. Was he safe?

My other brother, Greg, was working a construction project at Newark Airport, from which one of the hijacked planes departed. Was he okay?

My sister was in Hawaii. When was she supposed to fly back?

I had no answers. Cell phones didn't work.

I spent the afternoon glued to the television, switching back and forth between NBC and CNN, which were broadcasting coverage of the horrifying event nonstop. Every time the phone rang I jumped to answer it. Both of my brothers were safe. Unfortunately, that couldn't be said for thousands of other people.

All day long, I struggled to breathe and cried for people I didn't know. Still, the tragedy felt strangely familiar. Evil boarded the airliners, betraying the trust of fellow passengers and crew, who thought everyone was on the jet for the same reason. Evil set plans in motion, with no consideration at all for the consequences. Evil ripped through innocent lives, leaving thousands of people dead, and many thousands more mourning family members, friends and colleagues.

It was my experience of evil, magnified by 100, or perhaps by 1,000.

I talked to Terry several times during the day. I was trying to be strong, but by early evening, I needed comfort.

"I don't want to be alone tonight," I said to him. "Will you please come over?"

In an hour, Terry was at my house. We watched more television, but it was the same footage of planes crashing into the Twin Towers that had been on all day. So we went to bed, clutching each other, trying to feel some sense of normalcy in the midst of such horror. I wondered about all those who had nobody to clutch, because their loved ones were incinerated by burning jet fuel, or crushed in the mountain of collapsing steel. Even though I didn't personally know them, I was heartbroken.

The goddess of the Earth, an African woman adorned in multicolored plumage, sprang from a hole in the stage floor, gyrating to rhythmic percussion. The goddess of air floated down from the ceiling on fabric streamers of sapphire blue. Then the goddess of water, looking like a Cambodian princess in jade green, sequins and an intricate silver headdress, danced through mist to the center of the stage. Finally, the god of fire in brilliant red and gold somersaulted from beneath the floor and joined the other deities.

So began *Dralion*, the latest show—part acrobatics, part mysticism—by Cirque du Soleil. The date planned so long in advance arrived, and, as usual, we went in style. Terry bought VIP tickets, which included a wine and hors d'oeuvres reception and the best seats under the massive blue and yellow tent.

Terry treated me like a goddess, and I felt spoiled. The week before, Terry had taken me to Longwood Gardens in Kennett Square, Pennsylvania—right down the road from Chadd's Ford, where we began our romance at the blues festival. Longwood Gardens was a 1,000-acre botanical preserve with formal outdoor gardens and fountains reminiscent of old Europe, and a massive conservatory so plants—even lawns—could grow indoors all year round. To me, the displays of roses, chrysanthemums, bonsai, water lilies, orchids and other flowers and plants were simply amazing. To Terry, they were examples of what could be grown with knowledge, time and the right conditions.

Terry developed a sense for trees, lawns and flowers with his property in Cherry Hill, New Jersey. He originally purchased six acres. Over the years, he sold some of them off, but still had a lot of land for a densely populated suburb, with a long driveway, big house, in-ground pool and a formal rose garden. Now that his divorce was underway, "Camp Kelly," as he called it, was for sale.

Like many, if not most, divorces, Terry's wasn't going smoothly. His children, even though they were both young adults, were not happy about the family's breakup. His wife, who had not worked during their 26 years of marriage, was squeezing him for everything she felt entitled to. To make matters worse, Terry's business wasn't generating the profits that it once did. Like many small American manufacturers, Decorated Paper was under the assault of cheap imports from China.

All of this bothered Terry tremendously. He was sad about the end of his marriage, but no longer felt there was anything to save. He knew the rule of thumb for men in the process of divorce—"it's cheaper to keep her"—but he wanted emotional fulfillment more than asset preservation. Still, sometimes his problems depressed him.

I thought Terry was being overly harsh on himself, and told him so. I made suggestions when I could. But mostly I just listened sympathetically as he talked. Terry appreciated my compassion. He left a note for me on October 10, 2001, after a weekend visit:

> Sweetheart,
> Thank you for holding me and talking to me and your patience with me. Your understanding and kind words make me feel good and give me the support I really need. I love you.
>
> Terry

Touched, I tacked his note on the wall near my desk. Thinking about our relationship, I realized that I'd come a long way. I didn't try to "win" Terry by proving my appeal, as I'd done in the past. The appeal that I thought I once had—success—was gone anyway. My business was shaky, and my accomplishments were overshadowed by my failures. All I had to offer Terry was love and emotional support—and that was enough.

Ten days later, Terry and I left for our long weekend in New Hope, Pennsylvania. He rented the carriage house of the Wedgwood Inn bed and breakfast—a tiny, two-story bungalow built in 1890. Downstairs was a light-filled living room with a comfy sofa, wood-burning stove, kitchenette and bathroom. Upstairs was a bedroom with an antique four-poster bed. The posts seemed to lean toward each other, and I worried that if the bed saw any activity—a likely possibility—it would collapse.

We drove to nearby Doylestown to visit the Moravian Pottery and Tile Works. The factory was founded by Henry Chapman Mercer, a proponent of America's Arts and Crafts movement. Mercer had lived on the property, and his house, called Fonthill, was one of the wildest buildings I'd ever seen. Constructed between 1908 and 1910, the entire structure was hand-mixed, poured-in-place concrete, which was new technology at the time. Mercer made up the home's design as he went along. In the end, it had 44 rooms, 10 bathrooms, 18 fireplaces, 21 chimneys, 32 stairwells and more than 200 windows of various sizes and shapes. The place was bizarre, but fascinating.

Back at our cozy little carriage house that evening, we snuggled on the sofa. "Tell me again about when we were married," Terry entreated.

Surprised at my lover's request, I described the past life I remembered from France. We lived in a small white cottage with a huge flower garden. We were very happy and had a lot of fun. Terry goofed with our three kids, and watching him, I affectionately laughed to myself.

When I finished, Terry was quiet for a moment. Then he said, "I love you so much. Sometimes when we make love I feel like I can touch your soul, and it feels so big. It feels like I'm touching the universe."

We went to the bedroom upstairs, and perhaps that night we both touched the universe.

I told my spiritual counselor, Elaine Anderson, how happy Terry and I were during my session on October 23, 2001. But as I spoke, I could feel tension building in my chest. Something wanted to be released. With ethereal music emanating from the CD player, Elaine walked around me as I lay on the table. "We ask that the personality we call Donna be surrounded with white light," she began.

I focused on breathing, and almost immediately, the tension grew. Tears fell from the corner of my right eye. Before long, I started to vocalize, "I'm so tired. I'm so tired. I'm so tired."

"Say what you're tired of," Elaine directed. "I'm tired of..."

"I'm tired of the instability. I'm tired of the financial pressure. I'm tired of having no money. I'm tired of being afraid. I'm tired of hating him."

I knew I hit pay dirt. This was the issue—my hatred for James. Elaine knew it too.

"Talk directly to James," Elaine instructed. "Say why you hate him. I hate you for..."

Words tumbled out of my mouth. "I hate you for ruining my life," I said. "I hate you for how you hurt me. I hate you for how you lied to me. I hate you for what you took from me. I want you to give back what you took from me. I hate you for what you did to Sylvia, and Kathleen, and Jody and Gale. I hate you for everyone that you hurt."

The hatred within me was intense, consuming—and I hadn't even known it was there. Deep, burning hatred, lifetimes of hatred, hatred for what he did to me and hatred for all he represented.

Elaine changed the music to a thumping drumbeat.

The hatred welled up from my chest, causing me to cough, even choke. Elaine started working on my throat chakra, helping to move the energy. "Feel the hatred. Growl at him," she directed.

I growled. Utter hatred at what he had done to me. Then I felt a flash of understanding about tribal hatred. I seemed to see, or perhaps be, a Native American looking at the ruins of his village destroyed by white men, feeling the bitter hatred at the evil of others. I felt a flash of understanding of the hatred that fuels long-standing ethnic rivalries. Hatred twisted upon itself, deep under the awareness.

My eyes were shut. I was aware of nothing but the pressure cooker of hatred in my heart. Slowly the steam released. Slowly it dissipated. Feeling it, being aware of it, allowed the negative energy to drain. White light absorbed all that hatred, and it was gone.

Then I felt deep, sorrowful sadness. Sympathy for all wronged people. Sorrow about the evil in the world. The sadness, buried under the hatred, flowed from my heart.

"Keep sinking through it until you get to what's under the sadness," Elaine told me.

What could it be? It seemed so deep, like hatred and sadness filled a hole to the center of the Earth. But I did get to the bottom, and there, to my surprise, I found love and hope.

"Love, hope—the bigger perfection that can hold it all, the Mother Theresas and the Bin Ladens," Elaine said. "The bigger perfection can hold the dichotomy. The bigger perfection can transmute what happened to you into good, can transmute evil into good."

We talked about September 11th. In the days following that shocking event, I felt like the souls of the 2,974 victims all knew in advance what would happen, and had volunteered to participate. The slaughter was meant to create an opportunity for the human race to make a change.

Elaine said she had received the same message. "It came to me in a dream," she said. "I dreamed that I saw all those souls floating above the Earth, circling the Earth, encouraging the human race to take advantage of their sacrifice to make things better." Elaine felt a parallel between what happened to me and the tragedy of September 11. "The planes already crashed into your towers," she said. "You've experienced this. You've been through it. You have been able to transmute evil into good.

"Guidance told me that you are going to use the energy that was tied up in hatred and put it into creativity," she continued. "It's not in your nature to hate. And your hatred wasn't just toward James. It was toward everything he represented, all the evil and deceit and darkness of the world."

At the time I was reading *The Other Side and Back*, by Sylvia Browne, the famous psychic. In the book, she described the "Dark Side." She wrote that God gave all spirits free will, but some spirits used it to reject him, and reject the light. Although God didn't turn away from anyone, people were free to turn away from God.

Browne referred to those who made this choice and joined the Dark Side as "dark entities." They existed in both human and spirit form, and all had the same basic qualities: They had no conscience, no sense of responsibility for their actions and no remorse. They didn't care about the people around them. And they lived by their own arbitrary, self-serving rules.

Then, on page 198, I saw, for the first time ever, the word "sociopath" in a psychic-spiritual-New Age book. Dark entities, Browne said, were sociopaths. She described their behavior, and it was as if she were repeating the profiles found in all the psychological literature: They were charming. They appeared to be loving and compassionate, but they were merely mimicking human emotions. They claimed common interests with others, but it was just a charade to earn their victims' confidence. They hurt others, then pretended to be sorry, to keep victims off-balance. And as soon as they felt like they controlled their victims, the mask came off and the pretense of sensitivity was gone.

Browne explained what happened to all souls, light and dark entities, on "the Other Side," which traditional religions referred to as "heaven." Periodically, light entities, from the comfort of the Other Side, decided to incarnate on Earth to gain knowledge and experience ourselves as the extensions of God that we are, Browne wrote. But before we were born, we created a blueprint for the life we were about to begin, based on what we wanted to learn. When we died, we returned to the Other Side and reflected upon the life that we just completed.

Dark entities, however, did not choose to go into the light of heaven. They chose a black abyss of nothingness on the Other Side, with no light, no love and no hope. They did not reflect upon their lives and plan what they wanted to do differently. Instead, they immediately incarnated again into another empty, hollow existence.

I felt such relief in finding a spiritual explanation for sociopaths. Everything Sylvia Browne wrote rang true for me, and matched the information I personally received from Guidance.

The holiday season arrived. Thanksgiving was wonderful—Terry and I spent it with my family—and Christmas was approaching. A year earlier, I forced myself to partake in holiday cheer—buying tickets to Christmas parties just so I wouldn't be alone. In December 2001, cheer flowed easily from my happiness.

We were excited about more than spending our first Christmas together. Terry sold his big home and bought a townhouse in Cherry Hill. He expected to make settlement and move in right after Christmas, and I'd be moving in with him for the winter. So along with holiday shopping, we bought things for his new home. The first purchase was a bed for Beau. The second purchase was a bed for us.

Christmas dawned cold and clear in Atlantic City, and Terry and I both woke up as excited as a little kids impatient to see what Santa brought. We put on bathrobes, made coffee and plugged in the Christmas tree lights. It was time to open our gifts.

I wanted to spend my limited shopping budget on gifts Terry would really like. When we were in a craft store in New Hope, he admired handmade martini glasses. They were somewhat Art Deco in style, with the stems assembled from pieces of clear, textured glass and black, etched glass. I called the store and had two of the glasses shipped. Terry was thrilled.

Shopping for me, Terry went overboard. He bought me lovely gold and ruby earrings, a leather skirt and leather pants, although I didn't quite see myself as a leather pants kind of woman. He bought me a naughty Christmas negligee—sheer red nylon with fluffy, white faux fur trimming the neckline and cuffs. He bought me a book called *Ten Poems to Change Your Life*.

My life had already changed dramatically. And soon, I hoped, it would change even more.

Chapter 29

Terry's furniture was packed in a moving truck, ready to be delivered to his new townhouse on December 28, 2001, as soon as his settlement was complete. I, too, had suitcases packed. I was also moving in, or at least bringing enough clothes to be ready for any business or social opportunity that might suddenly arise while I was there. Although I said nothing, I hoped that my visits would evolve into a more permanent arrangement. I hoped that my search for love and commitment was finally over.

I was excited about the new possibilities in my life, but as I waited for Terry to call, my excitement was tempered by heartbreak. Jamie, one of my sugar gliders, was missing. The night before, I discovered Hope, Jamie's daughter, sitting alone on the wooden glider highway that Terry built. She looked forlorn.

"Jamie!" I called, even though she had never before responded to her name. "Jamie! Where are you?"

My pet was not in her sleeping pouch in the cage. She was not on top of the bookshelves. With mounting anxiety, I looked in all the glider hiding places. They were empty.

"Not again," I groaned to myself. "Not another one."

Then I saw an opening around a steam pipe that went into the ceiling. It was tiny, but if Jamie was really determined, perhaps she could squeeze through it. If she did, she was lost somewhere in the walls of the house. My heart ached. I left the lights on all night, hoping she'd find her way back. But the next morning, Hope was still alone. I cried for Jamie and sent her my love, wherever she was. There was nothing else I could do.

At 3:30 p.m., Terry called. Settlement was finished; he was moving into a townhouse in the large, nicely landscaped Chanticleer development in Cherry Hill. Two hours later, I walked through the front door of my lover's new home for the first time.

The living room was dominated by a tall, Oriental-style breakfront of dark wood, which was actually part of Terry's dining room set. In its lighted cabinets behind glass doors, Terry displayed his impressive collection of art glass. For seating, Terry had an L-shaped sectional sofa of a beige textured fabric flanked by granite-topped coffee and end tables.

The living room flowed past an open central staircase into the dining room, which created a sense of space. A half-wall in the dining room separated it from the large kitchen, and a sliding glass door opened onto a good-sized elevated deck. The deck overlooked a dense stand of trees, giving the illusion of living in the country instead of suburbia.

"This is nice," I said to Terry.

"Let me show you the rest," he excitedly replied.

First we went downstairs. From the front, his townhouse looked like it was two stories, but it was really three. The basement was a finished family room, with sliding glass doors opening to a small yard under the deck. Terry furnished the room with a green leather sofa and love seat, along with a large oak entertainment unit that held a 35-inch television. The room even had a bar, installed by the previous owner.

We climbed the central staircase to the top floor. Immediately to the left was an open den area, which would be my office. Next to it was a small bedroom for Terry's daughter, in case she visited. To the right, double folding doors led to the master suite. Built-in drawers and cabinets, left by the previous owner, stretched across the entire back wall of the master bedroom, and above them an expanse of windows offered a view of the same trees that I saw from the deck. The suite included a large walk-in closet, and the master bath had both a tub and a separate stall shower, big enough for two.

It was a really nice townhouse.

Boxes were everywhere, so I started emptying the ones marked "kitchen." Terry's kitchen had three times as many cabinets as mine, and it was a good thing, because he had an abundance of dishes, glasses, silverware, serving pieces, storage containers and appliances.

"You sure have a lot of stuff," I said, trying to find a home for everything.

"Are you kidding? I had a big house. This is only half of what we had."

Judging by the art glass, original oil paintings, quality furniture, crystal wine glasses and the expensive suits in the walk-in closet, it was clear that Terry was accustomed to an upper-middle-class lifestyle. Unlike my ex-husband, whose plans were built on sand, my lover was a man of substance, a man who prospered in the world. As I put away the pots and pans, I allowed myself the luxury of hoping that maybe he'd help me climb out of the hole I'd gotten myself into, and move into the stable, balanced life that I wanted. He had already lent me money a few times when I was in a jam. I intended to work hard to pay him back, but it would be wonderful to have a safety net.

The kitchen was stocked with everything but food, so after a few hours of unpacking, we went out to eat. Later, we went up to our new bed, fitted with our new sheets, and celebrated the beginning of our new life.

Terry and I talked about how much we loved each other—something we did often.

"You just want me for my body," he said.

I thought about that. "Which answer would you prefer?" I deadpanned. "Yes or no?"

My lover laughed, and gave me a big hug.

But in three weeks, our plans for a new life together changed. Terry's daughter, who had been going to college in Boston, dropped out and came to live with him. Being that Terry's divorce was still underway, I felt it was inappropriate for me to be there as much as we planned. So I packed up my clothes and brought them home again.

I'd been working day and night since the beginning of 2002, and although I hadn't been paid yet, I knew money was coming in.

Terry's business, however, was struggling. The economy was already in recession the previous year, and the attacks of September 11, 2001, made it worse. By February 2002, orders for the specialized coated papers his company made practically dried up.

Terry was in turmoil. He didn't sleep. During the day he went to his factory, then left the building and called me from his cell phone, ruminating about his problems and trying to come up with solutions—one of which was closing Decorated Paper. If he did, 11 employees would be out of work. He felt like he was letting many people down—his employees, his family and me.

Terry was personally liable for the company's debt, so if he shuttered Decorated Paper, he might end up with no money and no income, facing bankruptcy. All of this, of course, was going on in the midst of his divorce, which added to his stress.

One of Terry's options was trying to sell the business. On Saturday, March 2, 2002, the owner of a competing company, Hazen Paper, based in Holyoke, Massachusetts, looked at the plant. Afterwards, Terry came to see me in Atlantic City, and told me about the meeting. Even if his competitor wanted to buy Decorated Paper, Terry didn't know how well he'd do financially. His outlook was grim, and we discussed the possibility of him selling the townhouse that he just bought and moving in with me. The conversation alone disturbed Terry—all of his adult life he was financially independent, able to buy what he wanted, when he wanted. He didn't want to impose on me. Unlike my ex-husband, he wasn't a freeloader.

As for me, I simply felt accepting about the situation. In fact, after my daydreams of Terry helping me out of my mess, I was surprised at my own sense of calm. It seemed that subconsciously, Terry wanted to change his life around, so the opportunity arrived for him to do it. I didn't know how things would work out. I felt like it almost didn't matter, as long as we were together.

"I love you so much," he said. "This isn't fair to you."

"Well, Terry, the good news is that I'm accustomed to financial problems. So it's not like I'm giving up anything."

"I am. I'm used to being able to spend money whenever I want. I'm used to fine wine and nice vacations. Trading down is hard."

"I know, honey. But as long as we love each other, we'll figure something out."

We were quiet for a moment. Then Terry asked, "Why do you love me?"

"Why do I love you?" I repeated his question slowly. "Let me think about that." There was no one dominant reason, but there were many reasons: He was handsome. He was tender. He was fun. He made me laugh. I loved how I felt when we were together, and I loved how I felt thinking about him when we were apart. With no easy answer to the question, I simply said, "I don't know; I just do."

"That would be my response," Terry said. "I don't know why I love you; I just do."

As we lay in bed that night, Terry's feet were cold—which was unusual, they were always warm. I draped my arm across his chest, and suddenly I saw myself in bed with him—as his wife, I suppose—before he was going off to battle. It was an image from a past life, and that time, too, he had cold feet. Terry got killed in the battle, and died thinking that he let me down.

We fell asleep; then Terry woke up, which woke me up. Again I put my arm across him, but this time I felt intense pain emanating from his heart. The pain traveled up my arm and into my eyes. Several times, I touched Terry's heart chakra, and my eyes immediately squeezed tight, like they did when I released energy during my sessions with Elaine.

Terry left early the next morning, and at lunchtime, he called me from work. "If you've ever prayed, pray now," he said. "Hazen is interested in buying the business." At 5:30 p.m., Terry called again. They were trying to work out the terms of an agreement.

Weights in hand, I pushed through *The Firm* video workout in my basement/gym/pet room on March 5, 2002. While I did lunges and flies, Beau sniffed excitedly at the bookcases, his tail wagging wildly. I'd seen him do it several times over the past couple of months. What was attracting his attention?

I put the video on hold and went to look. The three bookcases stood next to each other, but were not straight and plumb. Maybe it was because they were cheap—they belonged to James—or maybe it was because everything in my old house was crooked. So although the bookcases were jammed together at the bottom, at the top they were separated by a gap about an inch and a half wide.

When the sugar gliders were loose, they loved scampering across the tops of the bookcases—perhaps it made them feel like they were in the branches of a tree. They could easily jump across the gap between them. Or so I thought.

I looked on the low shelves where Beau was sniffing. The books all appeared to be in order. And then I saw why Beau was so excited—stuck in the narrow space between the cases was Jamie's body. She must have misjudged one of her leaps, slid down the pressboard and laminate crevice, and was trapped.

Frantically, I pulled books off the shelves so I could move the cases. Jamie looked like she had died of starvation or dehydration—her body was little more than a pelt. I was heartbroken, and furious with myself. Perhaps, if I had looked harder when I discovered she was missing, I could have found her. Perhaps I could have saved her.

Carefully, I retrieved her rigid body and wrapped it in a piece of silky gold cloth. Then I buried her under a tree in the garden, near where I buried Herbie the hedgehog, begging her forgiveness.

"I love you" in six languages was printed on the tiny scented pillow that I bought Terry for his birthday, March 10, 2002. That, and a book from Borders, was all I could afford. It wasn't much, but it was better than what Terry received for his birthday the previous year—a request for divorce.

The divorce wasn't going well. Even though Decorated Paper was practically defunct and Terry was no longer drawing a salary, the judge ordered him to increase the support he was paying his wife.

The divorce was also holding up the sale of his company. Hazen Paper originally planned to keep the business running, which would allow all the employees to hold on to their jobs. Because Decorated Paper was a marital asset, Terry's wife had to approve the deal. She wouldn't make a decision, her attorney wouldn't make a decision, and the judge wouldn't make a decision. Terry was hanging on, hoping that his buyer wouldn't lose interest while his wife's lawyer procrastinated. In the meantime, he started talking to a bankruptcy attorney.

When Terry visited me the weekend of March 22, 2002, his mood bordered on depression. Even a jazz festival in nearby Somers Point didn't boost his spirits. The first performance we saw was straight-ahead jazz—the music that pleased purists like Terry, but I couldn't understand. The second performance was smooth jazz, which I enjoyed, but he didn't. It was too predictable, he said, too simplistic. We heard one-and-a-half songs. Terry obviously didn't like it, so I suggested that we leave.

On Sunday morning, Terry was tense and agitated. As he sat in a rocking chair waiting for me—we were going to the gym—I thought perhaps he needed to process the frustration in his life. Acting on impulse, I put my arms around him.

"You have to allow yourself to feel it," I said. "Let it rip. Don't try to hold the feelings down." I stood next to the rocking chair in the living room, bent over him, holding him. I exhaled forcefully.

"What's the matter?" he asked.

"Nothing," I said. "I'm just picking up what you're feeling. I feel the pain, the emotion."

I held on to him. "What does it sound like?" I asked.

His voice choked with crying sounds. I was surprised—I'd taken a chance when I asked the question, and Terry responded. He was processing his emotions.

"Come on," I said. "Take your coat off. Sit with me."

We sat on the couch and I put my arms around Terry, rubbing the chakras in his chest. I hoped I was doing it right. "Allow yourself to feel it," I said to him. His pain traveled from him to me, as if we were energetically linked. "It hurts," I said. "It hurts so bad."

Terry made the crying, choking sounds, like someone trying to hold back tears. "I wasn't honest," he said.

"Honest about what?"

"Honest about myself. What I wanted. I didn't do what I wanted. I never got what I wanted."

"What did you want?"

"Music, I guess. But I wasn't allowed. My parents wouldn't let me. I ran away once. But I came back."

I felt Terry's pain in my heart, my stomach. It rushed up to my eyes. I tried to think of what Elaine would do. "Breathe in through your nose and out through your mouth," I said.

I did it—breathing in through my nose and out through my mouth. And Terry did it. Sometimes he emitted little cries. I kept rubbing his chest, turning the chakras.

Terry talked about passion—how he felt passion for jazz. He talked about the burden—it was so heavy, so many people wanting things from him. "I'm always supposed to have the answers. I'm always supposed to know what to do."

After awhile, as I held Terry, he fell asleep. Since he hadn't been sleeping well, I didn't want to wake him. Fifteen minutes later, Beau did it for me—he started barking.

We went upstairs to lie in bed. "That was some therapy," Terry said.

"Did it help?" I asked.

"Yes. I feel better. I feel lighter."

He lay close to me, pulled me tight. After awhile, he started to kiss me hungrily, almost forcefully. I too, wanted him desperately. Before long, we were entangled.

Sometime in the afternoon, we finally went to the gym.

"How are all your animals?" Elaine Anderson asked as soon as I walked in for my session on April 11, 2002.

I was surprised, yet not surprised. I wondered if Jamie would turn up at the session. "Well, the dog and the chinchilla are fine," I answered. "But I lost one of the sugar gliders."

"Aw," she commiserated.

"It was awful." I told her the story—Terry built a track on the heater pipes in the basement and I let them run lose. I came downstairs one evening and found Hope alone, and I thought Jamie had escaped. Two months later I found her body stuck between the bookcases. As I spoke, I could feel tension rising within me. It was anger—not at the pets, but at my situation. I was angry at Guidance.

"The guidance I get is wrong," I complained. "I ask them what to do, I make decisions based on what they say, and I end up spending time and money in vain. I'm not doing what I want to do, which is writing the book. I don't have the money I need to do the research. I don't have the money to build Lovefraud.com. Four different psychics told me I'd get money from James. But I got nothing."

"I have other clients who have had similar experiences with psychics," Elaine said. "I spoke to a psychic about it once. She said that it's very difficult to really predict the future accurately. We live on a free-will planet, so people change what they do. And then there are world events, like September 11th. That really changes things. The way this psychic explains it is, 'At this moment, with these circumstances, this is how it looks.' But things can change."

"Especially when you're trying to predict what a sociopath will do."

"Yes, really," Elaine agreed.

I could feel my anger rising as I lay on the massage table. Elaine put drum music on the CD player. "Your job is to release the energy from your emotional body," she said. Elaine touched my toes, and I almost jumped off the table. She touched my throat, and I jumped again.

"What do you need to say to the guides?" she asked.

"I'm angry," I accused. "You lied to me. You didn't tell me the truth." I paused, and as the frustration built within me, I realized my anger was bigger than I thought.

"How can you be angry at God?" I asked.

"You can be angry at God," Elaine said. "Tell him you're angry."

"I'm angry," I said, my voice filled with reproach—and pain. "This is so hard. Why is everything so hard? Why does it hurt so much? Can't you do better than this?"

I could hear God talking to me. "It only hurts because of your expectations."

"He said you made the plans for this life together," Elaine relayed to me. "You both worked on the plans."

"It's so hard. It hurts so much."

"It's much harder here than it looks from the Other Side," she continued. "It's much more painful. What else do you want to say to God?"

"I'm so tired," I whispered. "I need a break."

I lay quietly for a moment, feeling my anger and desperation. But Elaine felt something else.

"What do you need to say to the sugar glider that died?" she asked.

The question hit me with the force of a body blow.

"I'm so sorry," I whispered. I kept repeating it, crying, "I'm so sorry. I feel so bad. If I had looked harder, I might have found her."

"What does the sugar glider say?"

"She says it's okay. She wanted to go home. You know, she was my favorite. She had such a hard life. I felt so sorry for her."

"The sugar glider has a message for you."

"I can't hear it. I'm still in the pain and sadness."

"What did all this pain cause you to believe?"

I waited for a response to form in my mind. "I'm not good enough. There's something wrong with me."

"Yes," Elaine said softly. "The idea that you're not good enough turned into a belief. Every time something bad happens, you think it's because you're not good enough. It's a belief that's been reinforced many times in this lifetime. We get these ideas, and then they harden and attract more experiences. Let's work on releasing the belief."

An oppressive yet invisible weight pressed on my heart and chest. I made noises, like heavy breathing, guttural animal sounds.

"Let the guides pull it out of you," Elaine directed.

That surprised me. I didn't expect physical participation from the spirit world. But eventually the weight moved.

"The sugar glider says that things just happen," Elaine said. "She showed me the idea, but it's difficult to put into words. She just fell. It wasn't because she wasn't good enough, or you weren't good enough. She just fell. She fell and she passed. It's just the cycle of life."

"I know her arm was hurting her."

"That's why she fell. It doesn't mean you did anything wrong. It was time for her to go. Animals are sometimes more aware of that than humans are. She wasn't meant to be found."

"She's telling me how happy she was living with me."

"She was very happy. She loved the freedom you gave her. She loved running on the track. She had a nice, full life."

I felt another weight. This one was in my back, creeping up my spine into my right shoulder blade. My shoulder trembled.

"What is it?" Elaine asked.

"It's the weight of having to know what is going to happen."

God was talking to me again, telling me that I'd feel better if I followed his plan instead of my plan. I didn't need to know it all in advance; the information would come at the appropriate time. Like a boulder slowly sliding off my back, the heavy burden fell away. As the pain and tension dissipated, the vacuum, surprisingly, was filled with joy.

The subject of Terry's e-mail was, "Our Love." It was waiting for me the morning of April 24, 2002.

> Donna,
>
> Last night as I lay in bed I was deep breathing and meditating, our love energy came into full power. I don't know how long it held me but it was so beautiful, that feeling so strong, so intense. It was all I could "see." I could feel your love there. It was present. And my love was returning and running throughout yours. They were one. Oh, how sweet, how tender, how I love you.
>
> You are so good to me. Your love shines on me wherever I am—I feel it. And it has different facets. Sometimes it's calm and soothing, like summer ocean waves. Sometimes it's wonderfully strong, like a rapturous symphony. And the best part is that I can return your love with my love for you. You make me very happy.
>
> Your love,
> Terry

I was awestruck by his words, and amazed at the depth of his feelings. I, too, felt a warm energy in my heart, and joy at being alive, which was surely the result of Terry's love. I told him how I appreciated the sweetness and tenderness of his caring. I was truly happy.

The following week I received another e-mail:

> Donna,
>   I feel your love when you are so close to me. All I have is my love to offer you, since my fortunes are fading. I do feel badly that all this has happened and that I can't give you the things I would like to. You are so sweet to me. I'll always remember your beautiful soul and how you melt my heart when you smile at me. My dream is that I can have a lighter heart from these burdens and spend more time with you someday soon.

The burdens were becoming more difficult for Terry to bear. Because his wife and her attorney would not make a decision to approve the sale of Decorated Paper, he ran out of money to pay his employees and was forced to shut the plant down. Thankfully, Hazen Paper still offered to buy the business and hire Terry, but now planned to move production to the Hazen facility in Massachusetts. Terry accepted the offer and sold the business, but all his factory workers lost their jobs.

I repaid Terry the few thousand dollars that he lent to me. Still, he could no longer afford the mortgage on his townhouse, so, after living there for four months, he put it up for sale.

I drove to Cherry Hill for a mid-week visit with Terry on May 8, 2002. He was glum, and talked about seeing a psychiatrist—he was afraid that he was slipping into depression. I didn't like seeing him so unhappy, but I certainly didn't blame him. The man was losing his entire life and had every right to be depressed.

Two weeks later, I called him at his office. He sounded terrible.

"What's the matter?" I asked. "Are you sick?"

"I feel a little woozy," he replied.

"Maybe you should go home."

"I'm thinking about it."

Terry didn't call me that evening, but I didn't think anything of it—some nights I didn't hear from him. I did, however, talk to my sister, who wanted to go to the River Jam concert in Philadelphia for her upcoming birthday. I didn't know if Terry was up for such an excursion, so the next morning, I called his office at 10 a.m. to ask him. His secretary said he hadn't come in yet.

"Is he home sick?" I asked.

"I don't know," she replied.

I went back to work—I had plenty to do. Shortly after noon, the secretary called me. "Terry's in the hospital," she said. "He'd like you to call him."

"What's wrong?" I asked.

"I'll let him tell you," she said, sounding upset and flustered. She gave me the phone number and I called Virtua Hospital in Cherry Hill.

"Hello?" It was Terry, but he didn't sound good.

"It's Donna," I said. "What happened?"

"Well," he paused, "I tried to do myself in last night."

My breath escaped as if I were punched in the stomach. I expected him to say he had a virus, the flu, food poisoning. Not that he tried to commit suicide.

"I took a bunch of pills and alcohol," Terry continued. "Then somehow I drove over to my Realtor's house. She brought me here."

My mouth opened, but nothing came out. I didn't know what to say or think. So I didn't think, I took action. "What's the status now?" I asked, amazed at how efficient and heartless I sounded.

"The psychiatrist is supposed to come in this afternoon."

"Can I come up?"

"I'd like to see you."

"Okay, I'll be there in an hour. Maybe more than an hour."

Terry asked me to bring a razor and shaving cream. I put on makeup, packed clothes and fed the pets. I didn't know how long I'd be gone.

During the hour-long drive to Cherry Hill, I was frantic with worry. Would he have to stay in the hospital? What should I do? Should I have seen this coming? I was angry—not at Terry, but at his wife, the attorneys, everyone who was pressuring him. If these people had been reasonable, Terry might not have been contemplating suicide.

I found the hospital—Terry hadn't been admitted; he was still in the emergency room, lying in bed in a hospital gown. Monitors were attached to his chest, an IV was in his arm, and another monitor was on his finger. "Hi," I said. "How are you?"

He just smiled weakly.

The psychiatrist came in. "Mr. Kelly has treatable depression," she told me. Then, the doctor turned to Terry and said, "You will get over this."

She left, and the phone rang. It was Terry's divorce attorney. I got on the phone and spoke forcefully. "He tried to commit suicide last night," I said. "You have to get them to settle."

Someone—I wasn't sure who—decided that Terry could be discharged. A social worker came in to discuss further treatment. Because Terry had good insurance coverage with his new employer, he could choose an intensive week in a hospital, or outpatient visits with a psychiatrist.

"What do they do in the hospital?" I asked.

"They have therapy and activities all day," the social worker replied.

"Basket weaving?" Terry asked.

"Not much better than that," she said.

Terry nixed the hospital idea. We left with a prescription for Wellbutrin, an antidepressant.

Back at the townhouse, Terry took a shower. Then we decided that I'd go shopping for food and he'd pick up his prescription. To do that, he needed his car, which was still parked near his Realtor's townhouse elsewhere in the large Chanticleer development. He told me her house number and we drove there, but it was a totally wrong section of the development. He couldn't remember where she lived. Driving around the many curving parking lots, we finally saw his car.

I didn't know how Terry found the woman's home the night before while under the influence of drugs and alcohol. The fact that he did, I realized, was a gift from God.

The next day was Friday, May 24, 2002—the start of Memorial Day weekend. A year earlier, Terry and I had danced the afternoon away at the Chadd's Ford Blues Festival—the beginning of our love. Now our love was being sorely tested.

After a difficult night, we had breakfast together in Terry's dining room. "Why are you with me?" Terry asked. "You may have to find someone else. There are a lot of guys out there."

For the first time since the ordeal began, I started to cry. "Don't leave me," I said. "Please don't leave me."

"But I have nothing to offer you."

"I love you, and we'll get over this. Just don't leave me."

I kept talking to Terry—I understood why he felt bad, he had every reason to be depressed. Since it was a holiday, he certainly wouldn't get an appointment to see a psychiatrist. I convinced him to come to Atlantic City with me for the weekend.

When we arrived at my house, Terry moped in the living room. This wasn't good. I thought fresh air would help, so we went for a walk on the Boardwalk. Several times, right in front of all the Memorial Day tourists, Terry leaned over the rail in emotional agony.

For dinner that evening I suggested that we make hamburgers—one of Terry's specialties. Moving around the kitchen like a zombie, Terry slowly added his signature ingredients to the ground meat, shaped the burgers, and cooked them on the grill. Then he didn't eat—he sat at the dining room table so hunched over that his forehead was about one inch above his plate.

Terry didn't sleep that night. He lay in bed muttering, "No, no, no, no!"

"Who are you saying that to?" I asked.

"Myself," he replied. "I'm saying it to myself. I had it all, and now I'm ruined. I'm going to get slammed hard. It's all coming down on me."

I'd arranged for Elaine to do a phone session with Terry on Saturday morning, and counted the minutes until it was time to call her. I was in over my head. I had no medical training. I'd never been around someone who was suffering from depression like he was. My only source of assistance was *The Doctors Book of Home Remedies,* which recommended exercise and doing something—anything.

After the session with Elaine, Terry looked better and felt calmer. So I dragged him to a garden store to buy flowers for my yard—impatiens and ageratum—and to a grocery store to buy food for dinner. Then the depression kicked in again. Another meal, another episode of Terry with his head in his plate, another bad night.

Trying to make Sunday morning normal, I sent Terry to the store for bagels and newspapers while I made scrambled eggs. Afterwards, I made him go to the gym. When he got back, I made him help me plant the flowers we bought. He put a few plants in the ground, then walked aimlessly around the yard. Planted a few more, then walked around. He sat on the garden bench with his head in his hands. Finally he went into the house.

I didn't know what to do. Finish planting? Wait for him? I waited awhile, then started to dig holes. Finally he came out, picked up a shovel, and we got the job done.

"That was rough," I said. It was an understatement.

Afterwards, we sat on the porch and I made Terry pick all the little buds that fell from the trees out of my hair. After that I wanted us to shower together, as was our habit. He hesitated.

"Terry, we should continue to do what we always do," I said. He nodded. I got into the shower, not sure if he would follow me. When I opened the curtain to peek out, he was coming down the hall. The shower wasn't as playful as usual, but we got through it. At times I saw pain wash over Terry's face.

That night, I was awakened by Terry's tossing and turning. I tried to soothe him by rubbing his temples, his face, his chest. But he was truly agitated, worse than the previous two nights. He leaned out of the bed and groaned, "No. No. No." He lay back down and sat up again, "It's too hard," he said. "Too hard."

"Come on," I said to him. "I think you need to beat some pillows."

He followed me down the hall to the meditation room.

"Here's what you do," I said. I lay one of the pillows on the daybed, knelt on the floor, and started to pound it. Pound, pound, pound. "Do this until you lose control," I said.

I left the room. I could hear him wailing and groaning. Not wanting to eavesdrop, I shut the bedroom door. A little while later, I heard Terry go down the stairs. In the morning, he was dozing on the couch.

On Memorial Day, Terry wanted to go back to Cherry Hill. I drove us to his townhouse, and Terry went to his deserted factory while I slept. About 5:30 p.m., worried, I called Terry's cell phone. No answer. I called the factory phone, and he picked up. Yes, he was coming back. His voice sounded forlorn.

At dinner—sandwiches—he started again. "I had everything, and I lost it. I lost the business. I wasn't paying attention, and was spending money out the other end. It's my fault. I had my head up my ass."

"Okay, maybe you did," I said. "But now you have to deal with it. You have to pull yourself together for tomorrow." The next day, Terry had two meetings with his new boss.

Still, he kept denigrating himself. "I'm going down the tubes," he lamented.

That evening, when we went to bed, I rubbed Terry's chest, and he pushed my hand lower, which surprised me—he showed no interest in sex all weekend. I caressed him, but his efforts toward me were half-hearted. There was no emotion in his kissing. No desire to please me. Eventually, he stopped.

I started to cry.

"Why are you crying?" he asked.

For a year, I felt love and emotional tenderness from Terry. It was evaporating. For a year I felt warmth, joy and love pouring out of him. Now I felt nothing. Terry was an empty shell. I was terrified of losing him. I was also terrified of being alone again—so terrified that I could barely get any words out. Finally I said, "I can feel you slipping away."

He tried to comfort me, sort of.

"Please don't leave me," I pleaded. I cried for a while, lying on my side, with my arm draped over his chest.

Terry had to be on the road at 7 a.m. on Tuesday, May 28, 2002, for his business meetings. He woke up early, agitated again. He showered and put on khaki pants, a blue shirt and a blue striped tie. The shoulders of the shirt hung low—he'd lost so much weight that it no longer fit him properly. "You look good," I lied. "Come eat breakfast."

The litany again. "I had my head up my ass. I had everything and lost it."

"Look, it doesn't matter how this happened," I said. "The solution is the same. You have to make more money. That's the only way out, so you have to keep your job. Just focus on getting through today."

"Actually, I don't feel as depressed as I did. I guess I'm coming to grips with it all."

"That's good," I said, feeling a tiny bit of relief. "That's progress."

Terry left and I drove home, arriving in Atlantic City in time to do some work then rush off to a business luncheon. But at the restaurant, while I was supposed to be networking, my own fears caught up with me. Why was I losing love again?

I'd arranged a session with Elaine for Terry, but realized that I needed one for myself. Luckily, she was available to speak to me over the phone.

I was crying as soon as the call started. I'd spent all weekend trying to help Terry, but I was also upset for myself. Things were just starting to get better for me. Why couldn't I find comfort? Why did I have to deal with money problems again? Terry and I discussed him living with me so he could save money, but I wasn't sure it was a good idea.

Elaine firmly stated that he shouldn't live with me—it was the first time she ever gave me definitive advice on a decision that I needed to make. She said I should be Terry's friend and help him, but go on with my life. It was best to let him find himself. "There are many decisions yet to be made," she said. "It is not finished. It is not decided. You'll just have to see how he handles it, and what choices he makes."

She picked up on my anger and wanted me to release it.

"I'm not angry at Terry," I said. "I'm angry at God. I'm angry at Guidance. Why are they doing this to me again? I was just starting to get a little bit of stability and they knock me down again."

"Tell them how you feel," Elaine said.

I expressed my anger at the universe—I was thrown yet another catastrophe, and the love I found was being taken from me. I didn't want to be alone again.

"Terry is in a very powerful place now," Elaine said.

"What do you mean by powerful?"

"Life changing. He has the opportunity to change his life, to become closer to who he really is. It all depends on the choices he makes now. And those choices have yet to be made."

She said I should just wait and see what happens, see how he handles the situation. "What does Guidance say about it?" Elaine asked.

"The usual," I replied. "That it doesn't matter. If he goes away, I'll just move on."

On the one hand, I told Elaine, I was upset that this was happening to me again, but on the other hand, my soul was happy that I could help Terry.

"It's a reflection of the contradictions of being human," Elaine commented. "We can feel the pain, and feel the joy and excitement. How it comes out depends on which we choose to feed."

She said I had much to offer Terry, and that all the happiness we shared up to this point prepared him for this episode. I was a gateway for him. Because of what I had walked through, I could walk in this painful place with him. "When you asked, 'Why me?'" Elaine said, "Guidance answered, 'Who else? Who else has the strength to show him the way?'"

Elaine said Terry had a very good chance of coming through the depression. He had good insights and a high survival instinct.

The phone rang during my session with Elaine. Then my cell phone rang. Afterwards, I picked up the messages—it was Terry. I called him back, and he sounded much better.

"I'm sorry I scared you," he said. "I love you, and I'm not leaving our relationship."

Terry went to a psychiatrist and explained his situation. The doctor agreed that he had reason to be depressed.

Early in the morning on June 15, 2002, Terry called me in a panic. He already had a buyer for his townhouse, so he had to find a new place to live. Feeling pressure to make a decision, Terry reserved an apartment in a nearby complex. I went with him to look at it, and agreed that it was awful. Emotionally, though, Terry was spent—he couldn't look at any more places. So I went to look at a development called Tenby Chase in Delran, New Jersey. Although it was out of the way, the units were spacious and the property was well kept; it actually looked a bit like Chanticleer. In July 2002, Terry left his three-story townhouse and moved into a one-bedroom apartment there.

In the meantime, the psychiatrist turned out to be useless. For a couple of visits, Terry sat there, the doctor sat there, and nobody said anything. It was a waste of time and money, so Terry stopped going. He also flushed his antidepressants down the toilet. He'd beat the depression on his own.

As the summer progressed, life for Terry and me gradually stabilized. Most weekends, he visited me in Atlantic City. We cooked dinners, went to the beach, rode his wave runners on the bay.

In September, we went on our first getaway in almost a year—a weekend in

New York City. One of Terry's jazz idols, Elvin Jones, was performing at the Blue Note club in Greenwich Village. Jones was a drummer who began playing professionally in 1949, and was a sideman for some of the biggest names in jazz, like John Coltrane and Miles Davis. Although Terry wanted to pay for the entire trip, like he did when we went to Quebec and New Hope, he could no longer afford to. So we shared the costs—he bought the show tickets; I paid for our accommodations.

I searched the Internet for a hotel deal. A room at the Club Quarters in downtown Manhattan was only $124 plus tax—really good for New York City. It was located in the heart of the financial district, near Wall Street and the World Trade Center site. Although the memory of the terrorist attacks still upset me, we visited Ground Zero soon after our arrival on September 21, 2002.

Ten days earlier, New Yorkers observed the first anniversary of the attacks. The debris from that horrific day was gone—all that was left of the 110-story buildings was a 16-acre hole surrounded by a chain link fence. A viewing platform was erected at Fulton Street, and we joined the people who came to pay their respects on a sunny Saturday afternoon. Instinctively, everyone was quiet and reverent as they looked through the fence and remembered the tragedy.

We stopped at St. Paul's Chapel, located on Broadway at Fulton Street, directly across from Ground Zero. The chapel was the only building in New York City that dated from the Revolutionary War—George Washington actually worshipped there. Amazingly, the only damage the chapel suffered in the attack was a few broken windows. For eight months afterwards, St. Paul's was the home of a volunteer effort to serve the workers who sifted through the remains of the Twin Towers. More than 2,600 people died there, and most bodies were never found. Homemade flyers for missing people were still attached to poles and fences along the streets that surrounded the giant hole in the ground.

As we walked back toward our hotel, I was overwhelmed by a palpable sense of loss. Enjoying our weekend felt disrespectful. But we were in New York, so we did as New Yorkers did—went on with our lives, unbowed by terrorists' efforts to destroy them.

I had a plan. I wanted to make a lot of money with a new line of business so I could afford to write my book. My plan wasn't working. "I am so frustrated about not doing what I want to do," I complained to Terry when he arrived for the weekend on October 18, 2002.

"We'll get it back on track," my lover assured me.

That night I woke up and couldn't go back to sleep. Terry slept peacefully beside me. I touched his hand, and instantly, to my surprise, felt waves of love traveling up my arm to comfort me. I was astounded, and filled with gratitude. I told Terry about the experience in the morning.

"That's the way I feel love from you," he said.

A few days later in my session with Elaine Anderson, I talked about my frustration, and about feeling Terry's love.

"How is Terry doing?" Elaine asked.

"Much better," I said. "He sold his townhouse and moved into an apartment. The surprising thing is that he likes the apartment."

"You really helped him through that experience."

"Terry says he wouldn't have made it without me."

"No, he wouldn't have. You saved his life."

I was surprised. I didn't think myself capable of such an achievement.

When we started the breathing session, Elaine stood by my side as I lay on the table. "We offer up the frustration, the disappointment," she intoned. She motioned around my heart chakra, then my throat chakra. She put her hands around my face, massaging my temples, jaw and forehead. She pressed down my right arm, and put her left arm under the small of my back.

"Release the throat chakra," she said.

The energy was bottled up. "I feel like I'm afraid to speak," I replied. "Like my throat was cut, or I was strangled."

"Yes," she said softly. "Can you go back to that lifetime?"

It seemed to be several hundred years ago. "It was my husband," I said. "I was opinionated, and I couldn't keep my mouth shut." I paused. "I had what was known at the time as a sharp tongue."

"And he beat you because of it."

"Yes."

"Do you know who it was?"

I thought it was James, although I didn't want to say it again. But I had seen this lifetime before—that dark little cottage, probably somewhere in England or Europe. Yes, it was James.

Elaine agreed. "The emotion would just boil up and burst out of you," she said. "You couldn't help yourself."

"Oh, I was good, too. The words poured out of my mouth. Not like this lifetime."

"Yes," she said. "He would be enraged, and you could match him."

I felt it—how we battled, how I whipped the words out, and how he beat me.

"Did he strangle you?" Elaine asked.

"I don't know if he killed me, but he grabbed me by the throat."

The energy flowed out of my throat and heart charkas.

"I didn't want to say that it was James," I admitted. "I get tired of seeing him in my past lives."

"You did have a lot of lifetimes with him," Elaine said. "You kept trying with him. Why did you keep trying?"

I thought about it. Or, I waited for an answer, because I didn't know. Then it came: "I wanted to get back what he took from me."

"You have such a sense of fairness and justice, and it's all wrapped up in your experiences with him," Elaine said. "What he did wasn't fair. It wasn't right. You wanted justice. That's why he has such deep hooks in you, and why you kept trying. It was an affront to your sense of justice."

A pause.

"What did he take from you?" she asked.

"Well, this time he took $227,000. He took my self-respect. He took my ability to buy nice things and clothes and fix my house. He derailed my career."

"And you thought it wasn't fair. It wasn't just. But what did you feel? What was under your sense of injustice?"

"It hurt," I replied. Lying on the table, my heart and throat ached. Then a full-body pain overcame me, not physical, but emotional. The pain didn't move; it felt like I was trying to melt a rock.

"Allow yourself to sink into the hurt," Elaine said. She sat behind me at the head of the table, and put her arms around me, resting on my chest, close to my heart chakra. Her head was lying on the pillow, touching mine. She seemed to be trying to hold me like a child. She helped drain the pain away.

"Why did you keep listening to him?" she asked.

I couldn't answer for awhile. Then I replied, "I thought he knew more than I did."

"There's something bigger than that."

As the energy moved, I waited for the answer to come. Suddenly, I knew. "He was the one who talked me into leaving God," I blurted out.

"Yes," Elaine breathed.

"Oh, he was good. He had it all figured out. He thought he had a better plan than God."

"So because of him, you lost your connection to God."

"Yes."

"And then he hurt you, and nothing happened to him. So you wondered, 'Where is the justice? How can God let this happen? What kind of God would allow this?' So you lost your connection to God, and you lost James. And you've been trying to get back what you lost ever since."

I absorbed her words.

"Guidance wants you to release the hooks he has in you," Elaine said.

"How do I do that?"

"They can't do it. You have to do it. You have to use your free will."

I listened for assistance. "They told me that I can never recover what was lost," I said. "I can only let it go."

"What you're saying is very important," Elaine replied. "The guides are saying that you wouldn't want James' journey. You want this to end. You want to be finished with him. So let it go. They'll help you."

I lay there, and an image came to mind of a big, heavy hook, the size of a harpoon, jammed into my heart. It had to be worked, turned and twisted, in order to be released. I could see my heart—red and pulsing—with the hook being uncoiled, although I didn't see any blood. The energy moved, and my right hand and arm shook. Then my entire body shook. I imagined someone operating on me. Slowly, the energy dissipated, and the hook was gone.

Elaine sat by my left side. The real work of the session was finished. We talked a bit—I was always looking for the answers my rational mind needed.

"The guides want you to feel supported, to know there is support for your efforts," Elaine said. "You will have the support to give birth to your creation."

"So how do I get the book done?"

"Let's both ask Guidance about that."

The answer came to me—I just had to start and trust that the support would be there.

"Just go along with the flow of the universe," Elaine said. "If you can do that, the results are often far bigger than you can create in your own head."

Guidance said I needed to listen to my heart, not my head. And I needed to let go of expectations about the outcomes.

"You released the hook," Elaine continued. "But you're going to have to be with this for awhile so you absorb the new idea."

"What is the new idea?"

"Let's ask Guidance to clarify that."

Again, I waited for an answer. "The idea is that I am connected to God," I said. "I don't need to recover what James took from me—I can have my connection to God at any time."

As research for my book, I needed to find out about other women James was involved with, like Gale Lewis, the woman he married before me, who he claimed "died in his arms," and Colleen Jessick, who he said was his "writing partner."

I'd maintained contact with the Gale's parents, Loretta and John Lewis, who lived in Sumter, South Carolina. They were both in their 80s, and John was ill, undergoing treatment for cancer. I needed to speak to them before it was too late.

Terry and I decided to combine business and pleasure with a trip to South Carolina. We'd fly into Myrtle Beach and drive to Sumter, which was about two-and-a-half hours away. Then we'd travel to Charleston for a few days, where Terry's brother and sister-in-law, who lived near Atlanta, would meet us. Finally, we'd head back to Myrtle Beach for the end of our trip, where we would stay in a condo owned by one of my friends.

The Lewises agreed to talk to me, and Terry and I made all our reservations. But a week before the trip, John Lewis died. Loretta called to tell me the news, and I was truly sorry for her. Loretta graciously invited us to keep our plans to visit.

Terry arrived at my house the evening of October 25, 2002—we were flying out of Atlantic City International Airport early the next morning. He asked me about my session with Elaine. "What did she say about us?"

"She was glad that you were able to talk to her during your depression," I replied. "That was a difficult time."

"You saved my life," Terry said.

I was still stunned by the idea. "That's what Elaine said," I replied.

Terry was quiet, putting words together. "That's when I knew you really loved me," he said. "After I got busted down a few pegs, and you were still there."

"I do love you. I wasn't going to abandon you. I'm just glad we were able to work through everything and we're still together."

Our flight the next morning was uneventful. Upon arrival in Myrtle Beach, we picked up our rental car and drove over country roads, past small churches, farms and cotton fields, to Sumter, arriving shortly before noon. Loretta Lewis lived in a one-story, L-shaped home of tan brick in a quiet residential neighborhood shaded by tall deciduous trees. We rang the doorbell, and an older woman who I didn't know answered the door. It was Loretta's sister.

Loretta came out to greet us, and I was shocked at how much she had aged in the three years since I last saw her. She invited us into the house, and then invited us to see her flowers on the back patio. It was a ruse, she admitted, because she wanted to talk to me privately. Loretta told me that she had never spoken to her sister about the money James took from Gale, money that was supplied by her and her husband.

Great. The whole point of my visit was to interview Loretta, and she did not want to discuss what had happened in front of her sister.

Loretta did tell me a little bit there on the patio, as we sat by a pool that she didn't have the energy to clean. She and John "had words" about James—Loretta never trusted him. She described John, however, as a Good Samaritan who didn't want to think badly of her daughter's husband. John just wanted his little girl to be happy.

Loretta, prim and proper, refused to visit her daughter in New Jersey while Gale and James were unmarried and living together. She also wouldn't permit James to stay with Gale in her home before their wedding. Her dim view of unmarried couples was another surprise—what did it mean for Terry and me? I thought we were invited to spend the night. Did I get that wrong?

We chatted for almost an hour while Terry wandered around the yard. Then the two women served us a casserole for lunch—I recognized the silverware as Gale's formal pattern. In the afternoon, Loretta took us to the small Sumter County Museum. It was marginally interesting, and we talked to a man who told us about a nearby plantation that had been meticulously renovated. But I didn't get a chance to ask Loretta any questions.

Back at Loretta's home, we sat in the living room. It was packed with her furniture, plus furniture that I recognized from Gale's townhouse in Mays Landing—the traditional blue sofa, the plaid wingback chairs, the huge prints of shore birds that once hung above Gale's staircase. That evening, Terry and I took Loretta out to dinner. The restaurant she suggested turned out to be exceptionally loud, so again I couldn't interview her. We brought Loretta home, and as I wondered whether we had to find a motel, she said, "There are two rooms available to you."

They were furnished with the bedroom suites that were once in Gale's townhouse. My bed that night was the same one I slept in with James—the heavily carved four-poster with a canopy. It was flanked by the same nightstands that were in the master bedroom of the townhouse, upon which stood the same white and blue porcelain lamps. Gale's triple dresser and drapes were also in the room. It was unsettling to see all that furniture again, knowing how James lied to me about it.

The other spare bedroom contained the furniture from Gale's guest room. Terry honored Loretta's request to sleep there without complaint. He'd been an angel throughout the visit with the two old ladies, friendly and gracious, attentive as they spoke.

"You've been absolutely wonderful today," I gushed. "I really appreciate how kind you've been to Loretta and her sister."

"Of course," Terry said. "I love you."

The next day I again attempted to get Loretta alone so I could interview her. I suggested that we visit the renovated plantation that the man at the Sumter museum had told us about. As we were getting ready to leave, her sister appeared, all dressed up. Loretta had invited her to join us.

I looked at Terry, who was shaking his head in disbelief. "I'll be quick," I whispered. And I was, because the plantation was closed. We got back to Loretta's house, and somehow Terry shuffled Loretta and me into the garage so we could talk privately, while he kept her sister occupied.

Loretta Lewis told me more of her daughter's tragic story. It was a story that intersected that of Colleen Jessick, which I learned when speaking to the screenwriter.

If only Gale had listened to Colleen.

Chapter 30

Gale Lewis logged on to her computer, hoping like a giddy schoolgirl that a message from her exciting new romantic interest would be waiting for her.

Well over 100 men had replied to her personal ad on the Internet, and she met a few of them. One was a computer nerd from Philadelphia; another was a pharmacist at a local drugstore in Mays Landing, New Jersey, where she now lived. They were nice guys, and seemed to be interested in her. But she didn't feel any chemistry. Not like she felt with James Montgomery.

James was exotic—an Australian transplant who came to the United States to produce feature films. He was heroic, a Vietnam veteran who earned medals for his valor. He was romantic—always sending her poetry, some by famous authors, some that he wrote himself. And he was accomplished—he'd owned an advertising business and television production studio in Australia, and planned to build an innovative new electronic theme park in the United States.

But what was truly refreshing about James Montgomery was that he was not afraid of her.

Gale was an accomplished professional, and this often made men nervous. In her successful career as a manufacturing executive, she improved plant efficiency, reduced operating costs, implemented continuous process improvements and developed new technologies. She was responsible for adding millions of dollars to her employers' bottom lines.

At least, she used to be.

After eight years at Becton Dickinson in Sumter, South Carolina, where Gale had full responsibility for a line of surgical and medical instruments worth $300 million in sales, she was fired. It certainly wasn't for incompetence—Gale was named Sumter's manufacturing woman of the year, and an executive at corporate headquarters began introducing her as the next vice president. No, her skills and dedication were not questioned. Instead, she was told that she didn't relate well to others. Yeah, right—it was more likely that the guy who fired her was afraid she'd take his job.

Gale knew she didn't deserve to be let go, which made the blow even more crushing. When she came home and told her parents—she lived with them in Sumter—they'd never seen her look so broken.

That happened more than two years earlier, in 1992. A few months after she left—"pursuing other opportunities," according to the company line—she accepted a position as vice president for quality assurance and materials control at Wheaton Tubing Products in Mays Landing, New Jersey. With the cash from her substantial severance package, she made the down payment on a brand new townhouse in Mays Landing Village, not far from the Wheaton factory, and bought new furniture to fill it.

Her taste was traditional. For her living room, she selected a dark blue sofa and wingback chairs in a complementary plaid fabric. Her bedroom was also traditional, but with a touch of romanticism. She had a four-poster queen bed of dark, intricately carved wood, topped by a canopy of white lace. Blue and white drapes accented the windows, through which Gale could see the forest of oak and pine trees that surrounded her development.

Just as Gale got her new townhouse the way she wanted it, she lost her job at Wheaton Tubing. This time the whole factory shut down, but that didn't make the second hit to her career any easier. Since then, she'd had a few consulting assignments—the most recent was nine months as a plant manager in Champaign, Illinois. But that job was over in August 1994, and now, a few months later, Gale was once again unemployed.

Gale was 42 years old, with an oval face, smartly styled dark brown hair and hazel eyes. Although she had always struggled a bit with her weight, she'd lost 35 pounds off of her 5 foot, 7 inch frame, and was down to a size 6. Gale liked to dress well, with every outfit perfectly accessorized, and now, tall and slender, she looked better than ever. In fact, she recently went to a GlamourShots store for a makeover and photographs. In the best one, she was bare-shouldered, holding a fan of dark blue feathers in front of her, with glittering faux-diamond earrings drawing attention to her sparkling eyes. She had to admit that she looked like a model.

Gale sent a photo to James, and the exciting Australian gushed about her charms. He admitted that he usually preferred blondes, but for her—well, he said, it was time to make an exception. He wanted to meet her.

But where? Although many of the men who replied to Gale's Internet ad lived near her home in New Jersey, James was a thousand miles away, in Florida. James had a suggestion—he was planning a trip to California for meetings about one of his films, and, while he was there, he'd be at a dinner with the actor Charlton Heston as guest of honor. Would Gale like to join him?

Yes, she would.

Gale bought her own plane ticket—after all, she'd never met this man, and didn't want to feel obligated to him. But this was all so amazing—she was accustomed to factories, not film stars. She just had to tell her best friend, Patty Kornegay.

Gale and Patty met at the Camden Hunter Barn in Camden, South Carolina, where they both kept horses, in 1986. Gale was learning English-style show jumping, and rode her horse, Foolproof, in the Camden Hunt Schooling Show that October. The two women became friends, and many times Gale accompanied Patty to the Rolex Kentucky Three Day. The equestrian event, at the Kentucky Horse Park in Lexington, was an international Olympic trial, attended by thousands of spectators from around the country and the world. Patty and Gale enjoyed it from the comfort of the Kornegays' well-equipped motor home.

Although Gale had moved to New Jersey, she still spoke to Patty at least twice a week. She'd already told Patty about James, prefacing her announcement with, "I'm almost embarrassed to tell you this, but I met this guy on the Internet." After that, James Montgomery became Gale's main topic of conversation—he founded E! Entertainment television! He'd won a Clio for advertising! He rowed in the Olympics! He served as a Navy SEAL and was still in the military! He looked like Sean Connery!

Gale was smitten.

This was unusual—in all the years Patty had known Gale, she never saw her date anyone. Oh, there was that older Irish guy that she bought a horse with. But that relationship certainly didn't seem to be a romance.

So on their next call, after a few pleasantries, Gale made her big announcement, "I'm going to California to meet James."

"California?" Patty repeated, shocked. "I thought you said he lived in Florida."

"He does."

"So why the hell are you going to California to meet him?"

"He's going there for business. He'll be attending a dinner with Charlton Heston, and he's invited me to go with him."

"What kind of dinner?"

"I don't really know."

The whole idea didn't sit well with Patty. "Gale, why are you going to California? Why are you spending that kind of money for a flight out there? You're both on the East Coast. Meet on your own turf."

But Gale had made up her mind. She was going to California to meet the extraordinary James Montgomery. And she did.

After her trip, Gale told her mother, Loretta Lewis, about meeting James, but left out the small detail of flying to California. Instead, Gale told Loretta that they got together in New York City. But, surprisingly, she also volunteered the information that she slept with James on the very first night they met.

Loretta was extremely disappointed—that wasn't how she raised her daughter. But Gale was a 42-year-old woman who had been a rebellious youth. What could a mother do?

She could answer a question.

"Mom, how long did you know Dad before you knew that you were going to marry him?" Gale asked.

"Two weeks," Loretta replied.

Patty and her husband, George Kornegay, a funeral director, planned a wedding for his daughter in December 1994. Of course, Patty's best friend, Gale, was invited.

"Can James come?" Gale asked.

"Oh, please bring James," Patty replied. "We would just love to see him."

"James said he could wear his dress uniform."

"Well, most of the men are going to be in tuxes, so that would be fine."

After listening to Gale talk about this man for months, Patty expected him to drive up to the wedding in a big, shiny Mercedes. That didn't happen. Despite his claims of a James Bond persona, he was overweight and ruddy, and wore not a dress uniform, but a tux that Gale had rented for him.

Patty was not impressed.

Gale, however, was still wild about James. Her relationship with him was the one bright spot in her life. Gale still couldn't find a job, and it really bothered her. Companies told her that she was overqualified, or they couldn't pay her what she was worth. So she was all alone in New Jersey, away from family and friends, with nothing to do.

Patty didn't voice her negative opinion of James Montgomery. She didn't have the heart to crush her friend's excitement.

A month later, Gale and James both traveled to Sumter, South Carolina, so she could introduce him to her parents. The four of them went out to dinner, and James told Loretta and John Lewis all about his advertising work, movie work, the people he knew and his top-of-the-line computers.

At one point, Gale and her father left the table. "How come you're with Gale when all the rest of the men are not?" Loretta asked.

"Gale is just too high-powered for most men," James replied. "She's a competent professional. Other men are threatened. I'm not."

After dinner, they parted company—James was staying at a motel. As Loretta watched her daughter's beau walk across the parking lot, she thought he was the biggest liar she'd ever met. He put on too big of a sales job, and he was obviously older than he said he was.

The next day, Gale told her mother that she was broke and James was broke—all his cash was tied up in $10 million worth of property in Los Angeles. So they were moving in together to save money.

Aghast, Loretta asked, "Whose money are you going to save?"

In January 1995, James latched on to a new moneymaking scheme. He secured the rights to distribute HotSkins, a brand of form-fitting Lycra athletic wear, in Florida, Georgia and South Carolina. The product was geared toward young male and female hardbodies, skin-tight to accentuate every muscular cut. But James' deal was bigger than mere retail distribution. He negotiated a second contract to supervise a TV shoot and postproduction for a series of "Miss Hot-Skins Fitness" promotional pageants in Lake Tahoe, Nevada; Daytona, Florida and Oahu, Hawaii.

James was certain that he'd scored a real coup. The HotSkins product line included skin-tight bike shorts, short shorts, bodysuits, leotards, singlets and even thong bathing suits. When thousands of bikers descended on Daytona for

Bike Week, followed by more thousands of college students on spring break, HotSkins would be available only from him—and Gale. With Gale's inventory management skills, James felt that she could really contribute to the success of the venture.

James' plan was to set up as a vendor outside of one of the big Daytona hotels during Bike Week at the end of February 1995, and stay through spring break, selling HotSkins to the masses. In financial projections, he assumed they would sell 750 pieces per week at an average price of $28 per piece. This would add up to gross sales of $21,000 per week. Of that, 60 percent would go to the manufacturer, and 40 percent, or $8,400 per week, would be theirs. James believed the opportunity was limitless.

There was only one problem. He needed to pay for the merchandise in order to have it on hand to sell, and all his cash, as he explained, was tied up.

Gale approached her father for the money. John Lewis had done well in life. He worked his way up through the Army Corps of Engineers, building U.S. military bases. Much of his work was abroad—Gale and her younger brother, John Brett, spent five years of their childhood in Germany. Her father's last assignment before retirement was chief construction engineer for Saudi Arabia, Italy, Egypt and Jordan.

James wanted the Lewises to invest $25,000 in his new company called "SuthunSun." Loretta was totally against the idea—she didn't like James, didn't trust him, and believed the entire venture was a losing proposition. But John only thought about one thing—seeing his little girl happy. He agreed to a lower investment—$15,000.

While James was in Florida, Gale started making business arrangements from New Jersey. On February 24, 1995—just before Bike Week was set to begin—she sent James a note:

> • Wire transfer of $4,000 to your account will be done Monday morning … paperwork all done and at my bank.
> • Used my cash advance on my gold Visa to cover the cash I need to pay bills … so ok til April there.
> • Opened the SuthunSun account at NationsBank and have signature card to mail to you … need to know which address you want me to send it to. As I used SuthunSun, Inc., need to have tax ID number to the bank in 30 days.
> • Have contact for MC/Visa to get SuthunSun set up to accept charges.

Loretta thought the whole exercise was useless—all those college kids would bring three or four bathing suits with them, so there would be no reason to buy HotSkins. But Loretta did not want Gale to be attempting to manage an outdoor retail operation alone, so she and her husband traveled to Daytona as well.

It was awful.

Bike Week, Loretta thought, was appalling. To her, the bikers looked like big, hairy apes, with women riding on the back wearing nothing but a string. Then the college students started arriving, and the blatant sexuality was even worse. All the students were drunk. One day, as women were getting doused with ice water during a wet t-shirt contest near their merchandise booth, a young college guy went behind them, masturbated, and then got up on the stage and exposed himself to the crowd.

As for the HotSkins—the bulk of the shipment arrived late, so for the first few days they had virtually nothing to sell. Then, when the merchandise finally arrived, nobody wanted it. On the beach and around the pools, the college men were wearing baggy shorts and jeans with loose t-shirts, not skin-tight short shorts. The women wore bikinis with conservatively cut bottoms. Thongs were illegal.

Gale, Loretta and John manned the sales booth—James stopped by briefly a few times, but mostly he was off at other meetings. After two weeks of trying to sell, in weather that was either hot and windy or disintegrated into rain, Gale wrote a report:

> Our sales were worse than dismal. Potential (male) customers were primarily asking for five-pocket shorts, the HotSkins equivalent of "baggies." We could not accommodate any of those individuals, as we only had XS or S sizes 5-pocket shorts in stock and could not fit them, nor interest them in the short shorts, knee shorts, bike shorts or singlets. No men's tops were available to fill requests.
>
> Potential female customers looked at tops and short shorts and were leery of the sizing ... with even the large size being cut for the slim, tight athlete rather than the average figure (or bigger than average in some cases). Crew neck and t-backs seemed to be the design of choice, with a rare few considering the lace-backed tops, then discarding the consideration because they didn't care for the black of the lace. In this group, few asked about the bodysuits, unitards or leotards ... nor could they be lured.

In two weeks, Gale sold one bathing suit, and total sales figures were 90 percent less than James' projections. James blamed HotSkins for sending the wrong merchandise. He returned the unsold clothing and demanded a refund. The Lewises, however, never saw a dime of it.

The Miss HotSkins Fitness pageants never took place.

After the Daytona fiasco, Gale and James returned to her townhouse in New Jersey. James ditched HotSkins and decided that his CelebAM theme park project, no longer viable in Tampa, Florida, was perfect for the Atlantic City Boardwalk. Plus, he saw an opportunity to start a new television channel. James set up meetings with politicians and business leaders who could help him implement his grand vision.

To Gale, James offered a vision of an exciting working partnership—and marriage. Believing that she and James were working together toward their joint future of happiness and success, Gale did her part by paying their living expenses, mostly by putting them on her credit cards.

But in early May 1995, Gale received a disturbing e-mail. It was from a woman named Colleen Jessick, who lived in California. Colleen wanted Gale to know that she'd been in an intimate relationship with James Montgomery since 1989.

In the spring of 1989, Colleen Jessick took another meeting with a television producer, a long-time contact, in Los Angeles, California. The producer had a big office at the top of a high-rise on Wilshire Boulevard—Colleen wouldn't want to be there during an earthquake.

Colleen was a scriptwriter with many television credits—she'd written episodes of *Charlie's Angels, Fantasy Island, Falcon Crest, Kung Fu, Star Trek* and more. She recently finished the script for a three-hour television movie called *I Married Adventure*. It was the fascinating story of Osa and Martin Johnson, a young couple from Kansas who, from 1917 to 1936, traveled to the most remote jungles in the world, photographed the indigenous people and animals, and then brought the images back to audiences in America. Right after Colleen turned in the script, the development executive she was working for left the network, a new guy took his job, and all existing projects—including *I Married Adventure*—were canned.

She was meeting that day in the high-rise in the hopes of reviving her project. Colleen wore a nice tailored shirt, jacket and slacks, with a gold rope necklace and earrings. Although she was tall—5 feet 8 inches—she wore heels to make herself even taller. She curled her shoulder-length blond hair to frame her face and set off her green eyes. In Hollywood, she knew, visual impressions counted.

Her long-time contact had found an Australian producer who was interested in the Osa and Martin Johnson script—a man by the name of James Montgomery. The three of them had already met twice, discussing possible sources of funding and actors who might want to be attached to the project. On this day, while chatting before getting down to business again, Colleen mentioned that she wasn't married—she was living with a former lover who was now simply a good friend.

James, sitting on a couch across from Colleen, suddenly straightened.

"You mean you're running around free and single?" he asked.

Startled, Colleen answered honestly. "Well, yes," she said.

"Can I call you sometime?"

James really wasn't Colleen's type. She liked the Viking look—tall, broad shoulders, blond hair, blue eyes. Or perhaps really dark hair with piercing blue eyes. This guy was tall, but that was about it. Still, Colleen was free and single, so she gave James her phone number. He promised to call.

In mid-May 1989, before she ever got together with James Montgomery, Colleen received a call from someone named Jody McClure. The woman was hysterical on the phone. Jody said, through her sobs, that James lived with her, until she came home from her son's graduation and discovered that he had packed up and left. Did Colleen know where he was?

No, she didn't know where James was. In fact, Colleen was taken aback—she was only doing business with James, and felt Jody's call, and personal questions, were totally inappropriate. But the woman was obviously distraught, so Colleen gave her the phone number for the UCLA crisis center and urged her to get counseling.

About a month later, Colleen heard from James Montgomery—he was back in town, staying with a friend and offered to cook her dinner. Colleen preferred to go someplace public for a first date; James agreed to that. But the day before their date, Colleen jammed her foot and broke her little toe. All she could wear were her moccasins, and she certainly wasn't going to wear them to a restaurant. James again offered to cook, so Colleen accepted.

James was staying in Marina del Rey. It was a small apartment in a high-rise, but the view of the marina was fabulous. James said he once had a romantic relationship with the woman who lived in the apartment, but now they were just friends, and she let him stay there when he was in town. This did not strike Colleen as odd—after all, she herself was living with a former lover. And she never connected the woman's name with that distraught phone call that she previously received.

After a lovely evening of conversation—her date was interesting and charming—James leaned forward and kissed Colleen. She almost passed out. She felt energy in that kiss that she'd never felt before, and she'd been married three times. The kisses continued, and they ended up in bed.

Later, Colleen realized that this man, James Montgomery, understood ch'i, the concept of the "energy flow" or the "vital life force" in many Asian belief systems. Martial arts masters learned to focus ch'i for more powerful strikes, and to fight longer without fatigue. James pushed ch'i directly into Colleen, and it made her knees buckle.

Colleen decided to ask around—who was this James Montgomery? She called a friend who worked in casting.

"I've met this guy, a producer from Australia," Colleen said. "You know everybody who knows everybody. Can you find out about him?"

"What's his name?" her friend asked.

"James Montgomery."

"That's really funny," he said. "That name has come up several times in the last two or three months. Let me think about it."

The casting agent made some inquiries and then called Colleen back. "Well, I didn't find out a whole lot about him."

"So what did you find out?"

"He likes women who have money."

"Well, that leaves me out."

Colleen's third husband had left her financially devastated. The last Christmas they spent together, her husband bought her a mink stroller jacket monogrammed with her initials, diamond earrings and a case of her favorite champagne—Cristal. He wanted it to be the best Christmas they ever had—because afterwards, he planned to leave her. The guy charged all the expensive gifts to Colleen's accounts and took out a line of credit based on her assets. Then he was gone, and Colleen was broke. She hadn't had many paying script assignments since then, so money was still tight.

James Montgomery was living on the other side of the country—in Boston, Massachusetts—but flew to Los Angeles periodically. When he was in town, they got together. James told Colleen about his military service and his continuing involvement in covert operations. Either he was playing James Bond to get laid, she thought, or he was a really scary guy. Either way, it didn't matter. To Colleen, James was a fantasy relationship.

They usually met in his friend's apartment in Marina del Rey, and the minute the front door shut, they were peeling their clothes off. The sex was really, really good. Plus, Colleen had a chance to do something she'd always wanted to do—write erotica for a love interest. Her first piece was a short story called *The Bet,* starring James, Colleen and a fictional character named Burton.

"Do you think he wants to fuck me?" the story began. The character "Colleen" suggested a threesome, but James explained to Burton that he was Colleen's lover, and she would only have an orgasm with him. Burton then did his best to prove James wrong—but Colleen obeyed her lover and waited for his command before letting her passion soar.

James loved the story, and encouraged Colleen to write more—which she did. She sent them to him during the times that they were apart, which kept the embers smoldering until they were together.

One time while they were in the Marina del Rey apartment, their conversation led Colleen to a sudden insight:

"You're married, aren't you," she said to James.

"No, I'm not married. Why would you think that?"

"Well, you're so secretive."

"You know all about my business, including my special ops assignments."

"Yeah, but you're too secretive about your personal life."

James continued to deny it, but Colleen was almost certain that James was either married or sleeping with other women. Did it bother her? Most of their relationship was long distance—love affair by fax. She was enamored, it was exciting, but James really wasn't much more than a steamy pen pal.

One day, Colleen was sitting at her desk in the home she shared with her former lover, thinking about her current lover, when her mind's eye transported her to another place. Colleen had always been psychic—she started having visions when she was two years old, and she consciously developed her ability to communicate with beings in other dimensions. In fact, when screenwriting assignments were scarce, she supported herself by doing tarot card readings at a psychic bookstore. This particular image was so vivid that it seemed real.

Colleen and James were staying in an exquisite tropical paradise—perhaps

Hawaii or Florida. They were in an upstairs bedroom, romantically furnished with a four-poster bed that had a lace canopy and curtains. Beautiful French doors opened into the room, allowing a warm summer breeze to drift in. Through the doors, Colleen could see the silhouettes of palm trees as the evening slipped into night.

James brought in a bucket filled with cracked ice and a bottle of champagne. He poured the bubbly into two saucer-style champagne glasses of thin, delicate crystal. They toasted their marriage—and the beginning of their honeymoon. They were going to drink the champagne, then make love.

Colleen sat on the bed, propped up by multiple frilly pillows, sipping her champagne and talking about how happy she was. She looked up at James, and realized he wasn't drinking, and he wasn't listening. He was just watching her.

Suddenly, Colleen felt like she'd been hit by a Mack truck. Her heart started speeding up, beating harder and harder, like it was trying to explode from her rib cage. "Oh my God, James, I'm having a heart attack!" she screamed. "Call an ambulance!"

James sat down on the edge of the bed and watched her.

"Call an ambulance!" she pleaded.

He did nothing.

Colleen struggled to reach the phone on the table next to the bed. But she was too weak; she couldn't make her muscles move. "Call an ambulance," she whispered. Then she looked at James' icy eyes and realized that he had poisoned her.

It was the most terrifying vision that Colleen ever had. She believed it was sent to her as a warning.

The First Casualty, Colleen realized, was a really good script. It was the story of a journalist covering the Vietnam War who had to make heart-wrenching choices between his obligations and his love. James told Colleen that he wrote the script, and asked her what she thought of it. Colleen thought James had talent.

That was when she started taking him seriously as a producer, and agreed to work with him on spec—which meant for free, or for very cheap. He had a lot of great ideas for television shows and feature films. Many of them were based on his military and Special Forces background. They were action stories—exactly the type of scripts that Colleen liked to write.

One was a TV show about a military force that used non-lethal tactics—stopping enemy combatants without killing them. James learned about non-lethal techniques from a woman he met in Boston who was part of a military think tank—they were really being considered for development. Colleen was fascinated, and began researching that other world James lived in—terrorism, counterinsurgency, low-intensity conflict.

Perhaps James was living in conflict in more ways than one. On October 13, 1990, Colleen was awakened by a phone call from a woman who identified herself as James Montgomery's wife—Kathleen Maloney.

So he was married, and living in this woman's home near Boston.

Everything that Colleen faxed to James—including the erotic stories—apparently went to James' office in his wife's basement. On that day, however, James managed to leave one of her faxes on the dining room table before he left for a trip to Florida.

Colleen told the wife that she specifically asked James if he was married, and he denied it. That meant James was lying to both of them, because he told his wife that his relationship with Colleen was strictly business.

"He's using you for your Hollywood connections," Kathleen said. "You don't need him; he needs you." Kathleen also said that James was not in the military—he bought all of his Special Forces paraphernalia from magazines.

Now Colleen had proof that James was married; he could no longer deny it. But he did say that the relationship with his wife was over.

So Colleen had to evaluate—did she have a problem with this situation? She herself had no interest in marrying James. He brought her interesting writing projects. The sex was good. He was married—but probably not for long, because his wife was furious, and Colleen didn't blame her.

Colleen didn't break off the relationship. In fact, four months later, she was head over heels in love with James.

Colleen resisted falling in love with James—until she could resist no longer. In a fax that she sent on February 16, 1991, almost two years after first meeting him, Colleen confessed her feelings:

> I might as well tell you … I need you, James Montgomery … I need you and I've never wanted a man like I want you. No matter what I do to blot you out, I think of you day and night. Disgusting as all this truth is … I haven't slept with anyone else since we got back together … because I look at other men and only want you. The other women in your life don't matter. All that matters is that you keep coming back to me. And keep coming with me. You're like a powerful drug. My body hungers for your body … my creativity hungers for your mind. The truth is, I guess I'm not as independent as I wish or want to be … not since I met you … the truth is, I'd sell my soul to be with you, to work with you, to sleep next to you at night. (Why do I pretend? You probably knew that all along, too. Damn you for always being right.)

James was now living in Florida, trying to finalize his contract to build information kiosks for the state division of tourism. The contract seemed to be within his grasp, but there was always a detour, always a crisis, that prevented him from doing the deal—and making room in his life for Colleen. At least, that's what James told her.

They had brief discussions about Colleen moving to Florida, but never got past the wild idea stage. No matter what Colleen said to James, and no matter how powerful their physical and creative interactions, he refused to tell her that he loved her. Colleen only got crumbs of attention, and on May 12, 1991, James sent her a fax to explain why:

Hi darling –

> You have to understand the mentality ... there is no life you are
> excluded from ... in fact I have got this survival down to an art. I really just
> exist around getting the contracts thru and developing the finances. I don't
> lead a normal life, live normal hours and I never think about any future. I
> never seem to have enough time ... you are part of a world I don't think
> about ... I can't afford to ... it really is a little bit like AA ... just do it a
> day at a time ... sorry I am so down, maybe it will all end soon and I can
> get back to a semblance of normality. You do count ... I try not to think
> about us ... miss you very much when I dare to open that door!

James, Colleen believed, needed to direct his prodigious mind not toward thoughts of survival, but thoughts of success. If he visualized what he really wanted, she faxed back, his subconscious mind would bring it to fruition. Colleen wrote:

> The two of us, each in our own way, have very powerful minds and
> personalities. Can you imagine what we could do if we consciously linked
> all that up? I can. I have. I do. My loving you is not just about sex ... or
> even about just a normal relationship. I work best in partnership; that's
> part of my path. I know how to link with another, and in this process, I +
> I is not 2, it goes to the tenth power! Never before have I known a man
> with your potential for power ... and I want to link my power with that
> ... I think it would be fucking dynamite! One can do this without sexual
> connection, but when you add sex (kundalini) to it ... it simply goes off
> the charts!

Did the message get through? Maybe. Maybe not. For Colleen, the relationship swung between waiting and fulfillment, between exhilaration and crushing disappointment. She loved their lovemaking, and James continued to tell her how special their relationship was—he made a card for her with the sentiment, "two hearts beating in unison." But sometimes he asked Colleen, "Do you think I look like Sean Connery?" And she caught James in lies, which he explained away as acts of momentary expedience. By October 1991, Colleen was wondering what place she held in James' life, and whether his talk of sharing an apartment with her in Los Angeles was serious.

Then James offered to contribute $250 a month toward a two-bedroom apartment, so that he could have an office, a base of operations, in Hollywood. Colleen found one, moved in with her dog, a little pug, and installed a separate line for James' phone and fax. For a period of time, he visited more frequently.

Once James brought Colleen a beautiful yellow topaz ring, probably 10 carats. He said he found it at an estate sale. Colleen didn't care much for jewelry, especially ostentatious jewelry. Plus, she intuitively knew that the ring belonged to some other woman. She refused it.

James never did send her any contributions toward the rent, and eventually her lover's trips to Los Angeles fell off again.

Maybe what Colleen and James needed was a romantic getaway. She booked a hotel room in charming Santa Barbara, California. With its Mediterranean climate and backdrop of mountain peaks, Santa Barbara was known as the "American Riviera."

Their plan was for Colleen to pick James up at the Los Angeles airport and then drive the 90 miles up the coast to the resort together. James said he was flying into the LAX helicopter pad directly from a military mission, and told Colleen where to meet him.

Colleen arrived at the airport and asked for directions to the helicopter pad. When she reached it, she sat down and waited. And waited. And waited. More than two hours passed, and she was getting worried. Had something happened to James? Then she saw him walking toward her in full camouflage gear—except for his face, which was flushed bright red and distorted by an ugly rage. James ripped into her.

"Where in bloody hell have you been? I've been walking around here for two and a half hours! Do you have any idea how much danger you put me in? I'm one of the people who set up the antiterrorist system here! If anyone sees me in this uniform, my life could be in danger!"

Colleen was astounded. "You said you were coming in on the helo pad. I went to the helo pad."

"I told you where to meet me," James screamed. "Do you listen to anything I say? I should not have been walking all around this airport in this uniform. It could get me killed!"

Colleen had never seen such monsterous behavior from James, and his unreasonable accusations angered her. "If you're so worried about being seen in your uniform, why didn't you go to the men's room and change clothes? You've got luggage with you."

"That's not the point. I gave you explicit instructions ..."

"Well, maybe you gave me the wrong instructions. I went to the helo pad. I thought you were delayed. Did it ever occur to you to pick up a phone and page me?"

Finally, in silence, they walked to Colleen's car. She was stunned by what she had just seen, and seriously considered leaving James at the airport. But maybe there was a reason. Maybe he was under pressure from his mission, and he just needed to relax. She wanted to relax—she hadn't had sex in ages. Maybe they could put this incident behind them and enjoy their time together.

But as she drove along the highway to Santa Barbara, Colleen regretted her decision. She should have left the raging James at the airport. She should have picked up her daughter and brought her to Santa Barbara instead.

James tried to be nice during their time at the American Riviera, but for Colleen, the romantic getaway was already ruined beyond repair.

When he was in high school, James told Colleen, he went out with a lot of girls. One time, as he and a particular girl were leaving for their date, she said she forgot something at home. James accompanied the girl back to her home, and there, sitting in the living room, was every single girl that he was dating. He had told each of them that she was the only one. He was busted.

Colleen knew James was seeing other women. She had been willing to tolerate the lack of exclusivity, but not when he flaunted it. James once invited Colleen to stay with him in a hotel on the west side of Los Angeles, saying a guy he knew came into town for meetings and finished up early. He gave James his extra night in the hotel.

James implied that he hadn't seen the room until he and Colleen walked in together. But when she went into the bathroom, she noticed that a washcloth was on the vanity folded in the distinct way that James always folded his washcloth. Plus, there was a box of sushi in the mini-fridge, and an empty sushi box in the trash.

"So who really paid for this room, and who were you sleeping with here last night?" Colleen demanded.

"What are you talking about?" James exploded. "I told you how I got this room. I'm trying to have a nice time with you, and you have to go ruin it."

James kept ranting. Colleen left.

It had taken her a few years, but Colleen was realizing that James was a sociopath. He couldn't stay pleasant for more than three days. He didn't just have another woman, he had multitudes of them. Colleen once found a videotape of his sexual exploits—first there was a woman who was so fat she took up an entire queen bed, then another woman, then Colleen. She didn't know how or when he made the tape, and started looking for hidden cameras anytime they were together.

The man obviously had no qualms about going from one woman directly to another. Colleen once drove James to the international terminal at LAX—he was leaving for Australia. As she was about to pull up in front of the Qantas Airlines door, James suddenly said, "No, no, no, park down there!"

Colleen looked at him sideways—obviously he had spotted the woman who was waiting for him. "Oh, are you meeting someone here, James?" she asked cynically. "Taking the trip with somebody?"

Then there was that fight in Colleen's apartment. She didn't remember what the fight was about, but she sure remembered one statement James had made. With tears streaming down his face, he said, "I am the most miserable man on the face of the Earth. I live off of women. It's all I do."

James either said that to manipulate her, Colleen thought, or he had finally spoken the truth.

"James, it's a choice," she replied. "You can change it anytime."

He didn't. Colleen knew this for a fact, because faxes kept coming into his "Los Angeles office"—her spare bedroom—from a variety of women who were obviously enthralled with James.

"By the way, this came for you," she'd say, handing him a fax. "So who is she?"

"Oh, she's just a business associate."

"Come on, James, this is a woman you're having a relationship with."

"No, we're not having a relationship, although she wants one. She's madly in love with me. I can't control what women feel about me."

Yeah, right. One of the women sent James a fax to thank him for the erotica he had written just for her—a titillating story called *The Bet.*

"Do you think he wants to fuck me?" it began.

James was raging again. In the spring of 1995, he was standing in Colleen's bedroom during one of his intermittent trips to Los Angeles, and something set him off. Colleen didn't know what it was. All she knew was that James shoved her, she flew across the room and almost cracked her head open on the waterbed.

That was it. No man, Colleen believed, ever had a valid excuse for hitting, shoving or physically threatening a woman. She wanted nothing more to do with James Montgomery.

Her fantasy relationship was over. Maybe he was a James Bond, a globetrotting fighter of terrorists, but she'd seen his dark side, and it frightened her. As far as his potential to be a big-name Hollywood producer—well, in five-and-a-half years, Colleen did an awful lot of work for James and earned exactly zero, while he tried to use her skills and connections. James wanted Colleen to give him a co-author credit on the *I Married Adventure* script, even though he wrote none of it. Then Colleen and James took a meeting on a possible project, one that would have meant a great deal for her shaky finances. Afterwards, the woman they met with contacted Colleen. In a cagey, hesitant conversation, the woman asked, "Were you aware that James was meeting with us directly to cut you out of the deal?" And *The First Casualty* script, which had so impressed her in the beginning of her relationship with James—well, Colleen was convinced he stole it from some other screenwriter.

No, it was time to end it with James. But Colleen didn't want to become a statistic, another victim of domestic violence. She could not confront him. She had to stay calm, and keep him calm, for another day until he was out of her apartment.

Colleen pretended everything was fine until James left for New Jersey, where he now lived. On April 30, 1995, Colleen sent a break-up e-mail. She wrote that of course she still loved him, and they had many wonderful moments, but James had lost control of his temper and shoved her, and she couldn't take the chance of it happening again. His anger issues, she was sure, were due to his military service, so perhaps he could find a veterans' program to help him.

The e-mail spoke of Colleen's everlasting love and deep respect for James— but those statements were written solely for dramatic effect. Colleen no longer loved him and had lost respect, but she did not want violence from James, so she purposely flattered him. By writing as if she were still smitten, she hoped to keep him from retaliating.

James did not let go easily. He turned on the charm again, sending e-mails that finally proclaimed Colleen was the only woman he ever really loved.

Yeah, right—he probably said that to all the other women too. So Colleen's reply was more forceful. On May 5, 1995, she wrote, "I've packed everything except your clothes in boxes. After five-and-a-half years, you're still lying to me. Adults must be responsible and accountable for their actions. You seem to feel you're above all that."

In fact, to make sure James was held accountable, Colleen decided that the women who had sent faxes to James in his Los Angeles office needed to know the truth. She was sure they were being hurt—emotionally, financially and perhaps even physically—and she hoped to protect them from further hurt.

Colleen had been collecting contact information from the faxes that arrived in her spare bedroom, just in case. Now was the time to use it. She spent hours composing an e-mail advising the women of her relationship with James Montgomery: "I don't want to ruin anybody's life, but I'm providing you with this information so you can make an informed choice." The e-mail went to five different women.

One woman already suspected James was cheating on her and immediately ended the relationship.

One woman was absolutely clueless about James' duplicity. She had put so many charges on her credit cards for him—$75,000 to $80,000—that she didn't have the money to give her daughter a wedding. What was even more surprising was how James treated this woman—he took on the role of a gentle caretaker. He went shopping, cooked for her, did her laundry. Colleen never saw that kind of behavior from him.

One woman was Debra Patrick, who had the CIA connections James claimed. Debra told Colleen a truly wild story, saying that she needed a car and James had a Special Forces buddy with a car to sell. She made monthly payments to James to pass along to his friend. James' friend, however, was really another woman. James never gave her the money and the woman demanded the car, so he had to get it back from Debra. Debra figured out what was going on and hired someone to "steal" the car and dump it in the bay. The next morning, Debra called the police to report a "stolen" car.

"If I disappear," Debra said to Colleen in an e-mail, "call the cops because James killed me."

These three women kept in contact with Colleen for months, sharing their stories about James, helping each other get over the obsession. A fourth woman did not reply to Colleen's message at all.

The fifth woman was Gale Lewis. She responded only to Colleen's first e-mail. "Thank you for the information," she wrote. "I'm sure you mean well, but I'd rather not be involved."

September 14 was Gale Lewis' birthday—and, in 1995, it would be her wedding day as well.

Although the date had been set, Gale wasn't making any arrangements. Loretta couldn't understand why her daughter was so lackadaisical about what should be one of the most important events of her life, and chided her about getting the wedding plans underway.

Maybe Gale was depressed. She still had no job and no income. Although her fiancé, James, was meeting local movers and shakers, establishing a brand-new Lions Club, and making contacts through Vietnam veterans organizations, his business plans weren't working out either. Both of them were living off of her credit cards, which her daddy discovered in June 1995. John Lewis spent $20,000 to pay the cards off. The charges included a trip that Gale and James had taken to Australia.

Finally, Gale traveled to South Carolina to shop for a wedding gown. She and Loretta went to several stores, but found nothing that they liked. Flipping through a catalog, Loretta saw a champagne-colored gown with a fitted bodice, short sleeves, full skirt and long train. Gale agreed that it was beautiful, and they ordered it.

Gale's good friend, Patty Kornegay, was to be the matron of honor. Patty felt torn about the wedding. Convinced that James Montgomery wasn't who he said he was, all spring and summer she'd been tactfully trying to discourage the marriage. But the message wasn't getting through to Gale. As September approached, Patty realized that all she could do was try to make the day as wonderful as possible for her friend.

Two nights before the wedding, Patty held a cocktail party in honor of the bride and groom in her showplace of a home. An accomplished cook and hostess, Patty put out a lavish buffet of pork tenderloin, roasted asparagus and other delicacies for 25 guests. During the evening James held court, and Gale, smiling and laughing, stuck by his side.

The wedding was planned for 7 p.m. at the Patriot Hall in Sumter. The building, with six massive classical columns at the entrance, was once a high school, but had been converted into a performing arts center and gallery. The Lewises reserved a salon for the civil ceremony and reception.

About 40 guests were expected—all but one of them friends and family of the bride. For the groom there was only Lee Patterson, James' lawyer from Florida, who was the second choice for best man. James originally wanted the role to be filled by his dachshund, Harold James. Although James continually lobbied to have the dog at the ceremony, Loretta's response was, "Over my dead body."

The best man arrived the day before the wedding, and was invited to join other out-of-town guests at the Lewis home. Unbeknownst to Gale and her parents, James and Lee were working the crowd in the living room, trying to find investors for a new brewery. They were handing out business cards and copies of the prospectus. Patty saw what was going on and was furious, but not wanting to create a scene right before the wedding, she left the room and bit her tongue.

The evening of September 14—a Thursday—was warm and pleasant. Gale arrived at Patriot Hall early to dress, and Patty was there to assist her. Especially after witnessing the blatant soliciting by James and Lee, Patty had serious misgivings about her friend's marriage, but Gale was genuinely happy. As Patty helped the bride into her beautiful gown, and fixed flowers in her hair, Gale said,

"I thought I'd never get married." Her voice conveyed a mixture of joy and relief.

As much as she wanted to, Patty couldn't bring herself to stick a pin in Gale's happiness balloon. She resigned herself to putting on a good face for the evening.

Wedding guests were seated in the salon, a large room that exuded traditional Southern style—yellow walls decorated with raised molding, candelabra-style chandeliers, Oriental carpets and antique furnishings. At one end, a long, Federal-style table was ready to be laden with food. A judge waited in front of the fireplace, and the single musician, with her electric keyboard set to sound like an organ, played an interlude.

James strode purposefully forward and took his place next to the judge. As the music switched to Bach, the matron of honor entered. Patty, a slender woman, wore a peach-colored, two-piece dress with a scalloped neckline and a slim, tea-length skirt. She carried a small bouquet of flowers. Then, escorted by her father, Gale appeared in her magnificent gown with its long train.

"We have gathered together in the sight of God and the presence of this company," the judge began, "to witness the joining together of James and Gale in holy matrimony."

The ceremony was short. The judge recited the well-known verse of the Apostle Paul, which began, "Love is patient, love is kind and is not jealous; love does not brag and is not arrogant, does not act unbecomingly." James and Gale made their vows and exchanged rings, promising to have and to hold each other from that day forward, for better or worse, until death do them part.

"By the authority invested in me by the state of South Carolina," the judge said, "I pronounce you husband and wife, in the name of the Father, the Son and the Holy Spirit. What God has brought together, let no man put asunder."

Crash! At that moment, a tray of glasses for the reception fell to the floor and shattered. It was an ominous sign.

Ignoring the noise, the judge continued, "You may kiss the bride." The newlyweds kissed, then turned and were presented to their guests as Mr. and Mrs. James Alwyn Montgomery. A server brought them champagne in two crystal flutes. They toasted each other and sipped.

Servers poured more champagne for the guests and arranged platters and chafing dishes of food for the buffet. The musician switched her keyboard from organ to electric piano. After eating and drinking their fill, the guests drifted off, and James and Gale went to a hotel for their wedding night. The next day they returned to New Jersey. There was no honeymoon.

Two weeks later, James went to Florida. While he was there, he retained a lawyer to take care of the small matter of his two wives. James and Kathleen Maloney of Massachusetts had never divorced. When he married Gale, James committed bigamy.

Gale looked at her list of bills to pay for November 1995 with dismay. She needed $1,056 for her mortgage and condo fee, $430 for the car payment, $118 for the electric bill. Because of her husband, she now had three phone bills, which totaled $687. At least that was an improvement over October, when James' phone bills added up to $1,160. Besides that, she'd given James $5,300 in October, and now he wanted another $500.

Gale needed $2,968 to pay the monthly bills, and that was if they didn't eat, put gas in the SUV, or spend any other money. She sighed and picked up the phone.

"Hello?" Loretta answered.

"Hi, Mom, how are you?" Gale replied. They chatted for a few moments. Then Gale asked, "Is Daddy there?"

Gale's calls for financial help had become a regular occurrence. She'd ask for $2,000, $3,000, sometimes more. Loretta knew the requests were coming from James, and she objected to giving them money, but her husband, John, could never say no to his daughter.

It was one of the few things Loretta and John argued about in their 50-year marriage. Loretta was angry, convinced that her new son-in-law was a con man. John didn't want to believe it, and got tired of hearing her complaints. "Don't talk to me about it," he said.

For awhile, Loretta kept track of the money they sent to Gale and James. But soon, the total was so high that she just stopped writing it down.

Once when Gale called, Loretta knew immediately that she was upset.

"Mom, James wants me to give him a credit card," Gale said.

"Don't you do it," Loretta stated emphatically. She also advised Gale not to include James in her will until they'd been married for five years. Gale followed her mother's advice, but with the credit cards it really didn't matter, because James simply convinced Gale to put the charges on her cards for him. After all, they were in love and working together toward the fulfillment of their dreams and a big payday—the opening of his fabulous new electronic theme park, CelebAM on the Boardwalk, which would be promoted by his new television network.

James told Loretta and John all about CelebAM when the Lewises traveled to New Jersey for Thanksgiving 1995. It was the first time they'd visited their daughter since James had moved in; Loretta refused to visit Gale while they were unmarried and living together.

Gale prepared Thanksgiving dinner for the four of them, and they sat down at the round table in her dining room, under the tall cathedral ceiling. Instead of saying grace before the meal, the tradition in the Lewis family was for each person to name something for which he or she was grateful.

"I've been in the United States for eight years, but I was still an Australian," James said when his turn came. "I'm grateful to be sitting down to a Thanksgiving dinner, because I've never done it before."

James talked to his father-in-law about the incredible potential of his theme park project. He offered the Lewises one-half percent of CelebAM Inc. for an investment of $20,000. John agreed to invest, and on December 1, 1995, James issued John and Loretta Lewis a stock certificate, which included the notation that their stock was "undilutable." But he neglected to mention that the state of Florida had already dissolved CelebAM Inc. for failure to file its corporate annual report.

Ever since Gale moved to New Jersey, she and her friend, Patty Kornegay, spoke on the phone several times a week. That gradually stopped. If James answered the phone when Patty called, he said his wife was not available. If Patty did get Gale on the phone, her conversation was evasive. She talked about all the wonderful things James was working on—like launching CelebAM, starting the television channel and founding the first Lions Club in Hamilton Township. But Gale didn't sound like the confident, take-charge woman she once was. She sounded brainwashed.

Eventually, Patty only heard from Gale when her friend called from her car, using her cell phone. Sometimes Gale drove to the parking lot of the nearby Atlantic County Library, just so she could talk. She started to make comments indicating that her life wasn't as hunky dory as she thought it would be. Still, Gale never told Patty about her financial problems, or that James continually pressed her to ask her parents for money. But she did confide that, once she'd married James, she learned he had a terrible temper.

Patty didn't actually see Gale until Easter 1996, when the Montgomerys traveled to South Carolina and they had dinner together. Patty was shocked at how much weight Gale had put on. In fact, she was heavier than she'd ever been.

Loretta, too, was shocked to see how her daughter looked, but for another reason—Gale seemed to be exhausted. In the past, Gale dragged her mother along as she shopped until the stores closed. But during her visit in April 1996, as soon as they got to a store, Gale sat down.

"What's wrong with her?" Loretta worried to herself. "She's not acting right."

For the entire visit, Loretta fretted about her daughter—Gale sighed a lot, and had no energy. She was smoking more. After Gale and James returned to New Jersey, Loretta wandered around her home, crying.

Every time she thought of her daughter, she thought of death.

This was frightening. Three and a half years earlier, Loretta had a premonition about her son, John Brett, who was planning a dive trip. She and her husband were with John Brett, his wife and in-laws—nine people all together—at a Cracker Barrel restaurant. After dinner, Loretta and John Brett were alone in the restaurant's gift shop and she reached up to embrace him.

"Whose little orphan are you?" Loretta asked, as she often did when he was a child.

John Brett played along with the game, putting his arms around his mother and kissing her. "I's yours, Mama," he answered.

"I don't want you to go to Florida on that diving thing," Loretta said. "I want you to cancel it. I have a bad feeling about it."

"Oh, Mom," he laughed. "I've already paid for the trip."

As they were leaving the restaurant, Loretta rolled down the car window. "John Brett," she said. "Goodbye."

Those were the last words Loretta ever spoke to her son.

Two weeks later, on a Sunday morning, Loretta was reading the newspaper. Suddenly, in front of the newspaper, she saw a vision of John Brett. He was in the water, and he was dead. She also saw his wife above the water, looking down on him.

John Brett was diving with one of the best instructors in the business. But something had gone terribly wrong, and he'd suffered decompression sickness, also called the bends. Dissolved gasses turned into bubbles within his body, and at the age of 37, he was gone.

And now images of death came to mind whenever Loretta thought about Gale. "What's wrong with me?" Loretta berated herself. "Am I wishing her dead? I've already lost one child. Why am I thinking about losing another?" She had no answers—only more tears.

Loretta could tell as soon as she answered the phone that her daughter was feeling low. So after a few moments of chit chat, she asked, "Gale, what's the matter?"

"Oh," Gale sighed. "Everything is just going so slow."

She and James had returned from their Easter visit to South Carolina and got back to work on his projects, but nothing was moving forward. Now James was away on another business trip for the weekend.

"I'm trying to get some work done for him, but I need information off of his computer," Gale said.

"Well, just go to his computer and get it," Loretta replied.

"I don't have the password."

Loretta was silent for a moment. "Gale, a wife should have access to her husband's computer," she said. Loretta hesitated, then decided to press. "And I find it quite strange that your husband is gone only on weekends, when everybody else takes care of their business on weekdays."

They spoke a little while longer. After hanging up, Gale reflected on her mother's words, and then went to James' computer. She tried a few likely passwords, and surprisingly, one of them worked. Gale was in—and looking at messages between her husband and another woman, describing their recent sexual adventures in pornographic detail.

Shock. Bewilderment. Betrayal. All of these emotions collided within her as Gale read the messages, not believing what was in front of her eyes. But the evidence could not be denied; she'd only been married seven months, and her husband was already having an affair. As she waited for James to come home, Gale's internal state turned to anger. When he walked in the door, she confronted him.

If Gale expected James to be ashamed and repentant, she was wrong. Instead, he was enraged, furious that she had gotten into his computer and screaming at her. Terrified, Gale bolted from the townhouse, got into her car, drove to the library parking lot and called Patty.

"James is cheating on me," Gale blurted out, almost hysterical.

"How do you know?" Patty asked, concerned, but not surprised.

"I saw messages from some woman on his computer. And when I confronted him, he started screaming at me—as if I'm the one who did something wrong! He was out of control. I've never seen him like this."

Gale sounded frightened, and Patty was worried. "Listen. I want you to leave right now," she said.

"I'm not leaving. This is my house."

"Then throw him out. Change the locks. It's your condo, your home, you have every right to lock him out if you're afraid."

"I can't do that."

"Gale, this guy is no good. If you don't want to throw him out, then come home."

Gale hesitated.

"Please come home," Patty pleaded. "I'm begging you. George and I will come up and get you."

Gale started to calm down. "No. Really. I'll be all right."

"Well at least let me call your daddy."

"No. Please don't do that. I'll get this sorted out. I don't want them to worry."

Patty kept trying, but Gale kept refusing her help, insisting that she'd be fine. Finally, there was nothing left to say.

Gale returned to her townhouse, but James was not there. When he walked in later, he handed her $5,000.

"Don't you ever say that I never gave you any money," he said icily.

Luciano Pavarotti appeared at the Atlantic City Convention Center on May 4, 1996. The 64-piece New Jersey Symphony Orchestra played a Mozart overture, and then the world-renowned opera singer, wearing white tie and tails, took the stage to the ecstatic cheers of the sold-out crowd. Among the 15,000 opera fans were Gale and James Montgomery.

Pavarotti sang pieces composed by Bixio, Leoncavallo, Mascagni, Sibella and Verdi. He performed the love duet from Act 1 of Puccini's *Tosca* with soprano Mary Jane Johnson. On other pieces, Pavarotti was accompanied by the 130-member Festival Chorus of South Jersey.

It was the type of evening that Gale savored—an opportunity to wear fine clothes, like her royal blue beaded cocktail dress, enjoy a gourmet meal, and join the area's social elite for refined entertainment. Perhaps, if things started to turn around for her husband, there would be more of these evenings in their future.

Loretta Lewis was membership chair for a local community concert series, and one of her responsibilities was sending out brochures for the upcoming season. On the morning of May 17, 1996, she, her husband, John, and three other committee members were in the family room of her home, folding brochures and stuffing envelopes in preparation for the mailing. The phone rang; John answered it.

"It's James," he said. "He wants you on the line too."

Loretta went into the kitchen and picked up the extension.

"It's about Gale," James said. "She's had a heart attack. I called 911 and I'm following the ambulance to the hospital now. I'll call you as soon as I know more."

Loretta went numb. How bad was it? Was this why Gale had no energy during her last visit?

Only a few minutes later—minutes that seemed like an eternity—the phone rang again. Loretta and John both picked up immediately.

"Gale's gone," James said. "I pulled up behind the ambulance at the hospital and I knew from the looks on the guys' faces that they couldn't revive her."

John put the phone down and moaned. He came out to the kitchen, and as soon as he got there, Loretta fainted. John caught her. When she came to, her husband was holding her up and moaning, crying hard tears of grief for the loss of his little girl.

Loretta's committee members, and the brochures, were gone. But within minutes the doorbell rang, and two of Loretta's friends arrived to offer support and begin making funeral arrangements. Loretta was grateful for the assistance, because all she could do was cry, and all she could feel was pain.

Two days later James sat with John and Loretta in that same family room in Sumter, South Carolina. "I'm only going to say this once," James said, and proceeded to tell them what had happened.

His voice cracking with emotion, James said he was upstairs in the Mays Landing townhouse shaving that morning, around 10 a.m., and Gale was downstairs watching *Regis and Kathy Lee* on television. He could hear her laughing. Suddenly Gale screamed for him, and he knew that something was wrong. James ran downstairs, saw that his wife seemed to be suffering a heart attack, pulled her to the floor and called 911. The ambulance left the rescue squad building at 10:11 a.m. and James performed CPR until it arrived. Gale was dead on arrival at the hospital. The time of death was listed as 10:58 a.m.

Later, James accompanied Loretta and John to make arrangements for Gale's funeral. He told the entire story again, with the same cracking voice and emotion.

"He was only going to say it once," Loretta thought as she sat through it. "But he said it twice."

Kornegay Funeral Home was handling the arrangements for Gale's burial. Patty Kornegay would help prepare the body, doing her good friend's hair and makeup.

Gale's body was first picked up by a local New Jersey funeral home and embalmed, then shipped to South Carolina. When she saw her friend's body for the first time, Patty was horrified—Gale had bruises on the right side of her neck and shoulder.

"George!" Patty called to her husband, the funeral director, with urgency in her voice. "Look at these bruises!"

George Kornegay was in his family's funeral business for many years, but had also served as an army medic, worked in an emergency room, and had been a premed student. He saw a lot of bodies. Usually, in order for a bruise to appear, the injury had to be inflicted while a person was alive. "Those bruises had to be there before she died," George said.

Only a few weeks earlier, Gale had called Patty, hysterical. She'd confronted James about his affair, and saw a threatening side of him that she didn't know existed. During that phone call, Gale was terrified. So what exactly happened at the end of her life?

All Patty knew was that she was filled with regret. If only she'd been able to talk Gale into leaving her husband. If only she had driven to New Jersey to get her. If only she had called Gale's parents. If only something was different, maybe her friend would still be alive.

But at that moment, Patty had to be professional. She lovingly fixed her friend's hair and applied makeup to cover the bruises.

Gale's service was at 5 p.m. on May 21, 1996. Patty drove the Kornegay Funeral Home limousine to the Lewis residence, picked up Loretta, John and James, and brought them to the Trinity United Methodist Church in Sumter.

Standing before a massive stained glass window in the sanctuary, the minister offered traditional Christian prayers for Gale, such as Psalm 23, "The Lord is my shepherd, I shall not want." He recited a pastoral prayer, giving thanks for her 43 years of life. "As Gale has now left this Earth and marched off into the eternal, we ask that you receive her spirit into your care, and that you visit those who loved Gale in their sorrow."

The minister then offered a sermon, entitled *The Garden of Beautiful Memories,* in which he talked about Gale's life, based on the information provided to him by her parents and by James.

"She married James Alwyn Montgomery on September 14, 1995," the minister said. "These months of marriage brought the greatest happiness to both Gale and James. James found her to be an incredible businessperson whose personality and personal demeanor commanded the respect of persons from the gardener to the governor in New Jersey. She was deeply involved with her husband James in the shaping of their broadcasting company. She was a person of unharnessed energy, and thrilled to invest her mind and labor in the business they were building together."

Then the minister described Gale's last moments—the story had evolved since James first told it to Loretta and John. "At 9:55 a.m. Friday morning, Gale was talking and laughing with James," the minister said. "She mentioned she had some heartburn, and then she broke into a cold sweat. James immediately called 911, and before they could arrive, by 10 a.m., Gale died in the arms of her husband, James. She was unconscious before the emergency medical team arrived; she never suffered; the beginning of the alarm to her death was captured in some 90 seconds of her life. It was quick, it was painless and she died happy, with no idea that she had any illness."

Following the church service, the mourners went to the cemetery for the burial. Then, in a sad, final ride, Patty Kornegay drove the Lewises and James home. The limousine pulled into the driveway, and the Lewises got out of the car. James then launched into the story of Gale's death again for Patty's benefit. He could hear her laughing, he said. Then she cried out.

Patty looked at James directly in the face and interrupted. "I don't believe a damn thing you say."

James silently got out of the car.

Patty couldn't shake the feeling that something was amiss in the death of her friend. So 10 days after the service, she started making phone calls.

She called the New Jersey funeral home. The funeral director there knew James and his plans to start a Lions Club, and was highly skeptical of him. "Individuals don't start Lions Clubs," he said.

Next Patty called the Hamilton Township police department, which covered Mays Landing. She told a detective about the terrified phone call that she had received from Gale a few weeks before her death, and about the bruises on Gale's shoulder and neck.

The detective speculated that the bruises were caused by the paramedics when they attempted to revive Gale. But he said he'd look into the situation.

Unfortunately, Patty did not tell the detective that Gale and her parents had given James thousands of dollars. She didn't know about the money pit.

Less than a month after Gale died, on June 15, 1996, James posted a personal ad on America Online:

> Finished mourning! Ready to move on! Really!!
> Deeply involved in the development of AtlCity of 2000; late 40's Sean Connery lookalike, 6'2". From Hollywood Film & TV scene as writer/prod; now into Entert. Biz in greatest city in USA. Emot. & Fin. secure, Ex-Green Beret; no drugs, don't even drink! Daughter grown up. Hold several advanced degrees but I baby talk to my dog. No hobbies, just threw myself into work; time to change all that! The grieving is complete.

It wasn't James' first step toward moving on. On May 31, 1996, he contacted Kim Goodson, who lived in Florida, about a marriage license. They'd been in a relationship since 1992—a relationship that was not interrupted by James' marriage to Gale. Kim sent James an e-mail:

> Marriage License ... $88.50 ... 3 offices nearby ... open 9a to 5p ...
> mon-fri ... need drivers license and divorce decree if within 30 days ...
> license is good for 60 days ... performed by notary public or ordained
> minister ...

James' ad on AOL received plenty of responses from women such as Terry, Collette, Libby, Linda and more. On June 22, 1996, he printed out their responses, along with the ads posted by women that he considered replying to. James also printed out an ad placed by "NYC Hotties," who described themselves as an "uninhibited but sane New York City couple looking to meet 'a few good men' to assist him in quenching her sizzlin' and insatiable desires this summer!"

Continuing to investigate his options, James called Colleen Jessick again.

He'd already called once to tell Colleen that his wife, Gale Lewis, had died suddenly. Colleen didn't know James had remarried, and he didn't sound like he was consumed by grief. Instead, he proudly told Colleen that right before Gale died, he'd given her a truly special evening. They went out to dinner at a fancy restaurant; they drank champagne; they went to a fabulous concert by Pavarotti; they went backstage and met the opera star. "Gale was just so happy," James said. "She told me it was the happiest night of her life."

Most people would interpret that story to mean a loving husband did something wonderful for his wife. But it reminded Colleen of her sociopathic third husband. He bought her a mink, diamonds and champagne, giving her the best Christmas ever—then he left her, taking all her money. The man built Colleen up, then ended it.

James' story chilled Colleen. Then the terrible vision she'd had years earlier flooded her awareness—James pouring her champagne then dispassionately watching her die. With a shiver, she wondered, did James murder Gale? Colleen had a vague memory of hearing that Gale was part of the "horsey set" ... which made it sound like she had money. Had James secretly taken out a life insurance policy on Gale and murdered her to collect? How many crime stories had Colleen seen with that as a reason for murder? Should she call the police? She didn't even know where James and Gale had lived. And telling the police her fears and suspicions based on a "vision" would brand her as some kind of lunatic. All Colleen could do was hope that she was wrong.

So about a month after giving Colleen the sad news of Gale's passing, James called again. "Why don't you get on a plane and come to New Jersey?" James asked. "Put your little dog in his carrying case. You don't need clothes—I'll buy them for you. We'll get married."

This was bizarre. A year earlier, when Colleen contacted the five other women about her relationship with James, it set off days of frantic phone calls. James called Colleen. James called the other women. He begged the other women for forgiveness, told them Colleen was insane and nothing she said was true. It didn't work—he lost three places to stay and three sources of income. James turned his anger toward Colleen.

"You're the woman who ruined my life!" he shouted.

"Well, if your life gets ruined by the truth, there's something wrong with your life," Colleen retorted.

To Colleen, busting James back then, and the drama that followed, had been exhausting, sad and even frightening. But now, a wife she never knew about was dead, and James wanted her to drop everything, leave her daughters, business contacts and friends, move to New Jersey and marry him?

"James, your wife isn't even cold in her grave yet," Colleen said. "What are you talking about? Is there that little grief?"

"Well, you know there are things that nobody will ever understand. The relationship was already almost finished."

Colleen declined his offer. Later, she talked to a friend who was also psychic—they did readings together at the psychic bookstore.

"James called," Colleen said. "The woman he married is dead ..."

Her friend interrupted, not waiting for any details. "Colleen," she said, "he killed her."

Before Gale's death, James was planning an old-fashioned July 4th picnic for Hamilton Township. Spearheading a community celebration gave him an excuse to contact business leaders who could prove helpful to his entrepreneurial dreams. In the event's program, James dedicated the picnic to the memory of his wife. He invited Loretta and John Lewis to come to New Jersey as his guests of honor.

The Lewises had already been to Mays Landing during the first week of June 1996 to begin dealing with their daughter's estate. Gale's will, dated 1993, named John as the executor. James was not mentioned at all.

Apparently, though, James thought that he would be the beneficiary of his wife's passing anyway. While the Lewises were in Mays Landing after the picnic, the topic of Gale's townhouse came up. Loretta informed James that if he wanted to continue living in the townhouse, he would have to pay rent.

With obvious disappointment—his face looked like a droopy dog—James told the Lewises that he would not contest the will. Then he left for Australia.

Loretta and John stayed until July 14, 1996, sorting through Gale's belongings and straightening up the townhouse, which was a challenge because James left papers everywhere. As Loretta reached across a chair to dust a table, she looked down at a pile of papers on the chair and the first line caught her eye: "Finished mourning! Ready to move on! Really!!"

Appalled, she continued reading James' personal ad, along with the printouts of his correspondence with multiple women. She gave all the papers to her husband and told him to get copies made.

The personal ads weren't her only shocking discoveries. Loretta found electronic equipment used for bugging telephones. She found sexual devices that made her wonder what her daughter endured on the marriage bed. And, beneath the mattress in the guest bedroom, she found a handgun. A brand new clip of bullets was in James' drawer.

Several months after Gale died, Patty Kornegay could no longer stay silent about her misgivings. She went to visit her friend's parents. Sitting with Loretta and John in the living room, Patty related the story of Gale's frantic call after the confrontation with James, and how Patty begged her to leave, begged her to let them come get her. And Gale refused.

Loretta was upset. "I wish she had called us," she said. "I would have been up there the next day and he would have been out the door."

Then Loretta told Patty about the money they'd been giving James, by way of Gale. After she died, the Lewises used the proceeds from her life insurance policy to pay off $44,000 in credit card debt. Patty was shocked. She had no idea that Gale had run out of money and was living on credit cards, or that James pushed her to ask the Lewises for help. Her friend never discussed her financial situation. Still, Patty always had a sneaking suspicion that James was taking Gale for everything he could get.

That suspicion was just confirmed. What about her other suspicions?

"You know," Patty said, "I think James had something to do with Gale's death. I think there was foul play involved—he could have given her something. Potassium chloride causes a heart attack and can't be detected in an autopsy."

"Well," Loretta said, "People in our family do have heart disease."

Patty didn't force the issue. The Lewises had already suffered two tragedies—they lost their son, and then their daughter. She couldn't imagine the pain of contemplating that one of the deaths might have been murder.

For her part, Loretta remembered telling Gale that a wife should have access to her husband's computer, a comment that, she learned, apparently led to a terrible confrontation. What if she hadn't said it? What if Gale hadn't looked at the computer? Would the confrontation have been avoided? Then Loretta thought of the gun she'd found. Had James pulled it on Gale? Had her daughter suffered such a shock that it lead to heart failure?

Loretta also remembered the time Gale told her James was moving in to save money. She was so taken aback that her only response was, "Whose money are you going to save?" In hindsight, she wished she had been more direct, more forceful. She should have made her daughter think twice about the whole arrangement.

On many, many of the following days, Loretta cried for Gale. She never believed James Montgomery; she knew he was nothing but a con man. But James and Gale were married, and the Bible said not to put asunder a man and his wife.

Loretta couldn't escape the feeling that she failed her daughter, and now she could never make it up to her.

Autopsy reports are public record in New Jersey, and long after Gale Lewis Montgomery died, I requested a copy of hers. The cause of death, according to Lyla E. Perez, M.D., the Atlantic County medical examiner, was coronary artery thrombosis—a blood clot in Gale's coronary artery. Her death was determined to be natural.

The report contained no mention of bruises on Gale's neck and shoulder. The toxicology report found no traces of drugs that could have caused an overdose, such as amphetamines or barbiturates. There were no traces of poisons or other dangerous compounds. One surprising finding, however, was the blood alcohol level—.073 percent. In New Jersey, someone with a blood alcohol level of .08 percent was legally drunk.

I asked three doctors to review the autopsy report, including the new Atlantic County medical examiner, Hydow Park, M.D., and a nationally known forensic pathologist, Cyril H. Wecht, M.D., J.D. They all agreed that nothing in the report indicated that Gale Lewis was murdered.

Gale was declared dead at 10:58 a.m., and the autopsy was conducted the same day at 1:45 p.m. Bruises on a body are not always visible immediately after death. They sometimes take time to appear, which may be why Patty Kornegay saw them and the medical examiner didn't. But according to the experts, the bruises wouldn't have contributed to her death anyway.

According to the Centers for Disease Control and Prevention, heart disease was the second-leading cause of death for American women in their 40s, after cancer. Gale faced several risk factors of heart disease for women: Family history—her mother, Loretta, had heart problems. Gale smoked—and smoking was a greater risk factor for heart disease in women than in men. Gale had gained a significant amount of weight, which probably indicated overeating and physical inactivity. And then there was stress. Research has found that stress, particularly marital stress, increased the risk of coronary heart disease in women.

When the ambulance arrived shortly after 10 a.m. on May 17, 1996, Gale was almost intoxicated. According to the forensic pathologist, it was unlikely that the alcohol in her blood remained from the night before. That meant she was drinking in the morning—possibly self-medicating to cope with the downward spiral of her life.

When visiting her mother a month before her death, Gale showed symptoms of fatigue and listlessness, which were consistent with coronary heart disease. But she never told Loretta that she was ill. Perhaps she didn't know. From the time she married James until January 1996, Gale's lists of bills to pay included health insurance. The lists for March and April 1996 did not. On March 22, 1996, Gale received a letter indicating that she had not made her COBRA payment. Gale probably discontinued her health insurance because she could no longer afford it, and even though she felt bad, she may not have gone to a doctor.

Gale's heart disease could have been easily diagnosed and treated with angioplasty, a medical procedure that widens obstructed blood vessels. "There was no reason for this woman to die," said Dr. Wecht. "Her condition could have been handled with a stent."

James Montgomery may not have been directly responsible for Gale Lewis' death. But the circumstances that he created certainly contributed to it.

Chapter 31

Terry and I sat on the porch of a Victorian bed and breakfast in Charleston, South Carolina, drinking iced tea and nibbling cookies. Finally, on October 28, 2002, our vacation was truly beginning. Our last extended trip was to Quebec, early in our relationship. Since then we'd experienced rocky times—but we held on and were still together.

We toured the city's historic district, where magnificent three-story antebellum homes populated a waterfront neighborhood called The Battery. The homes were designed to capture ocean breezes, with large open porches, or piazzas, on every floor, one directly above the other. Terry and I agreed that the architecture was wonderful, and he photographed almost every house. "We might need these pictures for reference someday," he said. My heart did a little leap.

Our visit included several wonderful restaurants, such as Circa 1886 at Wentworth Mansion. The dining room was formal and intimate, the service attentive and the food exquisite. It was a perfect romantic evening. The next day we went to Middleton Place, a plantation established outside of town in 1741, and strolled paths that led to sunken gardens, ornamental ponds and the lovely Wood Nymph statue. From there we returned to Myrtle Beach, where we stayed at an oceanfront condo owned by a friend. The geographical distance from Charleston was only 80 miles, but the cultural distance was infinite. The main drag of Myrtle Beach, Route 17, was 16 miles of neon, flanked by every known American chain store, including four Hooters restaurants, and 50 miniature golf courses.

That evening was Halloween, and we joined our friends for a street party at Celebrity Square, where a dozen nightclubs opened onto a pedestrian mall filled with creatively costumed revelers. Terry dressed as a vampire, and with his high cheekbones, white face paint and a black cape, he looked the part. I was the sexy victim, wearing my silver leather miniskirt and black crocheted tank top, with bite marks applied to my neck—actually dots of lipstick. In one of the clubs, I waited while Terry went for drinks. A guy asked me to dance. I politely declined, saying that my boyfriend would be right back. The guy was persistent; he wanted to dance with me until Terry returned. I was amazed—in all my years as a single girl, nothing like it had ever happened. But I was in love. I was happy. I said no.

The next afternoon we traveled to Brookgreen Gardens in Murrells Inlet, 18 miles south of Myrtle Beach. We'd heard it was a nice sculpture garden. Actually, it was astonishing. *Fighting Stallions,* a dynamic aluminum sculpture of incredible realism by the park's founder, Anna Hyatt Huntington, marked the entrance. The Brookgreen Gardens collection included more than 1,200 works by 350 sculptors. Some of the statues were massive, such as *Pegasus,* which stood 15 feet tall. But even the largest monuments were displayed in appropriately dramatic settings—lawns that extended for acres.

Terry and I wandered along the walkways, and around each bend was another work of art set in another beautiful garden. We enjoyed the park so much that we returned the next day. Apparently many people shared our experience, because the entry ticket was good for a week. The artistic talent, combined with the natural setting, was a breathtaking tribute to all forms of beauty.

Brookgreen Gardens was a fitting end to our vacation. We felt renewed, connected and inspired. Perhaps, Terry and I dreamed, we'd one day build our own garden, and populate it with sculpture.

James Montgomery was opening a language school in China.

Robert Palmer, the former Director of Studies for James' venture in New Zealand, learned about the latest scam from one of his contacts. On November 30, 2002, he forwarded to me an e-mail that James sent out:

From: CEOIICE@aol.com

> Friday must have gone pretty well — will have pix later this week, we finished up with the Gen. Secy. of the Communist Party of Beijing as a guest for 25 minutes — he asked to be remembered to Dad!
> My debriefing with our JV Partner just turned into "now that we have this one going and you have spare time [I am Vice-Principal, Dir of Admissions and HR plus I am the teaching head of both the ESL and IT departments!!!] James we want you to move to your new school faster" -design [by Friday] your specs for 50 acres on Dao Xing Lake Shore [20/25 clicks NW of here at the foot of the Fragrant Hills] for 3,700 students from K to Uni prep.
> Well, I had nothing planned for Thursday night!
>
> James
> Beijing
> BUT tell us what we can do with your IICE company in your current premises -"can I please have till Saturday afternoon"

Robert Palmer also sent a photo purported to be James' school—a four-story structure of red brick in a boxy, contemporary design, complete with a running track and basketball court—but it was quite possible that the building had nothing to do with James. The e-mail sounded highly exaggerated—I doubted that James met with the general secretary of the Beijing Communist Party. And was James referring to his father? The man was long dead.

"What are you going to do?" I asked Robert.

"I am letting the Australian officials know, but quietly," he replied.

The second Christmas that Terry and I spent together was wonderful. Terry surprised me with a big Christmas present—an ergometer, or rowing machine, which would help me maintain my racing stamina during the off-season. The nicest present I got for Terry was a piece of clear, heavy glass, four inches square, that was etched with the outline of a heart in red. One word was engraved on the glass: Forever.

Terry didn't talk about forever. But he did talk about fixing up my house, even though he was living in his apartment. I hadn't made any home improvements since James started taking my money. Improvements were desperately needed, but I couldn't afford them—my business had dropped off again, and I was broke. Terry hated my bathroom and, now that he was earning decent money at the company that bought his business, offered to pay for a new one. I was thrilled. I never asked about his intentions, but to me a new bathroom was a strong indication of "forever."

We started shopping for tile, hardware and fixtures. Terry wanted a whirlpool tub. This was a challenge, because the bathroom was small—only five by eight feet. At the Philadelphia Home Show, which we attended on January 25, 2003, we found one that would work—it was practically the same size as a standard tub, with high sides and whirlpool jets.

After slogging through the show all day, we returned, exhausted, to Terry's apartment. That night, I dreamt that I was interviewing my ex-husband for my book. With my pad and paper in hand, I asked questions:

"Were you ever in the military?"

"Of course not," James answered, laughing.

"Did you only marry me for my money?"

"Of course. You were so naive." To James, swindling me was a big joke. He was quite proud of himself. I did not feel any anger or outrage. All I wanted was the truth.

A distant rumble broke through my consciousness and woke me up. James was gone. The noise came from Terry, my sweetheart and lover, snoring next to me.

At my house, on nights that Terry wasn't sleeping with me, I lifted my dog, Beau, onto the bed. He could no longer jump up. He sometimes whimpered and tried to bite his own back. One morning as I sat on the edge of the bed, my dog was in so much pain that he crawled into my lap, crying. I increased his dosage of steroids.

We'd already been to the vet—the doctor thought Beau had a blown disc in his spine. During that visit, he also did blood work, and found that Beau was anemic, possibly caused by infections around some bad teeth. The teeth were pulled, and it took Beau a long time to stop bleeding. Then he hurt his hind leg and had trouble walking.

My dog was 13 years old. I sensed he wouldn't be with me much longer.

I called the vet again on February 6, 2003. Beau was losing weight, which made tumors on his shoulder and chest more apparent. Based on his symptoms, the doctor said my dog probably had cancer or leukemia. Additional tests and chemotherapy were possible, but I didn't want to put Beau through that. The vet agreed. Beau had simply gotten old.

My dog still wanted to go for his walk three times a day, although the walks were much slower—he no longer dragged me down the street. His nose was still in the gutter, sniffing for treasures. But I saw confusion in my dog's eyes. Beau didn't hear very well and, wobbly on his legs, sometimes he tripped and fell. Beau looked at me, and seemed to be wondering what was happening. When I knelt to pet him, he buried his head into my chest, or between my knees. He never did that before.

Beau was at the end of his life, but I did not have him euthanized—I couldn't bear to make the decision to terminate it. I chose to love him and make him as comfortable as possible in the time he had left. "You're the best dog in the world," I told him, again and again.

So twice a day, I gave Beau his steroids. Hard, dry dog food was too difficult for him to chew, so I fed him soft canned food. The wag-o-meter—his tail—still spun wildly when he smelled people food, and he almost always caught pieces of cheese tossed his way. He still barked impatiently for his 5 p.m. walk. Beau was still the dog.

March 10, 2003 was Terry's birthday. He took the day off from work so he could help our carpenter demolish the bathroom.

Everything was ordered—our whirlpool bathtub. A slim-profile vanity and sink that fit the narrow scale of the room. Faucets and other hardware. We'd spent hours looking at wall tile and selected a basic white, accented by decorator tiles that had a central diamond pattern of blue, green and tan, and complementary pale green ceramic tiles for the floor. The overall look would be clean and white, with a dash of vibrant color.

Terry worked hard all day, then went to the gym to take a shower. I'd be doing the same thing—my house had only one full bathroom, and, by the end of the day, it was gone.

In the meantime, I cooked a birthday dinner—stuffed Cornish hens, braised carrots with walnuts, roasted asparagus. I even made a chocolate cake from scratch. I hadn't done that in years. Maybe decades.

The next day Terry went home to his apartment while I began life in a construction zone—circular saws buzzing, hammers banging, a radio playing and talking among the carpenter, plumber and electrician. My office was only 10 feet down the hall; the noise made it difficult to concentrate. Not that I had much to do. I was managing one project for my long-time client, Bob Rosenthal—stationery for his new real estate agency. My writing assignments had dried up, so I spent my time researching content for Lovefraud.com.

I also spent time sitting with Beau.

He was failing quickly. On Monday, March 24, 2003, as soon as we came through the front door from his morning walk, Beau collapsed to the floor, exhausted. Then, he didn't want his breakfast, although he did eat later, after a dose of steroids. That evening, when I went down to the basement to feed the small pets, Beau followed me. Everybody wanted peanuts. Beau sat in front of me, begging. Chuckie the chinchilla sat on my knee. The sugar gliders—Hope and her companion, Mojo—who I found through a rescue service—sat on my shoulders. I opened peanuts as fast as I could. When everyone was finished, I carried Beau up the stairs.

The dog spent most of the next day lying under the dining room table while the sun shone through the window onto the rack full of Terry's orchids. One of them, a phalaenopsis, had seven swollen buds; soon they would bloom. At 5 p.m., Beau asked for his walk. I wanted to cut it short, but he wanted to keep going along our usual route to a neighbor's house where he always begged for treats. When we got there, Beau somehow ran up the stairs. He got his reward—two biscuits and a dried pig ear. That evening, when I fed the small pets, Beau didn't beg for peanuts at all. He lay down immediately, and didn't move when Chuckie jumped on top of him. Crying, I carried Beau all the way up to my bedroom on the second floor.

Beau didn't ask for a walk the next day. He wouldn't eat his dog food.

By Thursday, Beau was noticeably worse. I carried him out to the yard, but he could only take a few steps. Again, he spent the day on his pillow under the dining room table, while the carpenter banged away in the bathroom. Between phone calls to Sheryl Ginsburg, my graphic designer, about the Rosenthal stationery, I went downstairs to talk to Beau and pet him. At the end of the day I told Sheryl that Beau was dying.

"Beau's been your friend," she said, sympathetically. "He opened your heart. He brought you in touch with the real world—he was something you couldn't control. He's been good for you, and you've been good for him. He's had a good life."

After the carpenter left, I lay with Beau under the table, stroking his head. "Beau, you're the good dog," I said. "You can go home. Thank you for being here with me."

Sometimes Beau seemed to be aware of me. Other times he jerked his head up and looked off in the distance as if he'd heard something. Then he put his head back down on the pillow, only to jerk up and look again.

I prayed. "Thank you, God, thank you God, thank you God," I said. "Thank you for bringing Beau to me. He helped me so much. He was my friend."

I called Terry and asked him to stay with me. I didn't think Beau would make it through the night.

He didn't.

A week earlier, I'd asked my father if Beau could be buried in the woods behind his vacation trailer near Sea Isle City. At 5 a.m. on March 28, 2003, I called again. Beau was gone.

Terry put Beau's body in the trunk of my car, and I drove to meet Dad at the trailer park at 6:30 a.m. I watched as Dad dug a grave, tenderly lowered my pet's body into it and filled it in. We found a decorative brick for a marker, and placed it on top of the grave, above Beau's head.

We turned and walked toward the trailer. "Do you want a Snapple?" Dad asked.

"Sure."

We sat on the porch, drinking our Snapples, and talking for a bit. "I really appreciate this, Dad," I said. "Thank you."

"He was a good dog," Dad replied.

When I got back home to Atlantic City, the phalaenopsis in the dining room had burst into beautiful lavender blooms.

Even with the noise of continuing bathroom construction, my house was strangely quiet. No dog running down the stairs, no dog barking. My mind played tricks on me. I saw Beau lying in his favorite spots, like under the coffee table, when he wasn't really there. I felt him coming into the kitchen to investigate when I fixed lunch or dinner. My dog's presence was still in the house.

I had to admit there were positive changes. Not taking him for walks three times a day, I had more time. When working, I was able to concentrate without Beau's frequent interruptions. And I slept better without him waking me up.

Still, I was lonely. My dog, I realized, had been my main source of company, except on weekends, when I saw Terry. My lover did his best to cheer me up, but he also knew how much Beau meant to me. On a Sunday morning two weeks after my pet died, as we ate breakfast in the dining room, Terry gave me another art glass heart, a small one with multicolored swirls, which he said was from Beau.

Terry also gave me a poem that he'd written as if he were Beau, talking about our life together—running on the beach, begging for food, sleeping on the bed. "Oh boy, it's great to be the Beau you love," he wrote. The poem was so touching that we both cried.

On April 15, 2003, I had a session with Elaine, and spent much of it mourning my dog. Sometimes the loss felt like it was on the surface of my heart, and sometimes it reached all the way through me. Elaine sat by my left side, with her hand on my arm. "Pets get deep into our hearts," she said.

"At the end, all Beau could do was lay under the table," I told her. "He would lay down his head, and then jerk it up, as if he heard something. I just kept petting him, saying how much I loved him and how glad I was that he was part of my life. He would look at me, but I wasn't sure if he saw me."

"He knew you were there," Elaine said. "He felt your presence. And he appreciated you being there. You helped him through the transition."

"Beau has been through a lot with me. He was such a good companion.

When I was really upset about James, he would jump on me and lick my face. He was always trying to comfort me."

As I lay on Elaine's table, I felt the energy of it. I could feel my dog licking my face, persistently, frantically, the way he always did when I was dealing with the trauma of James. I let him do it, let him kiss away my tears.

Finally, the session drew to a close and I got off the massage table. "I can't believe how long I spent on Beau," I said.

"It was necessary," Elaine said. "You and Beau were friends for a long time."

"You mean he was my dog before?"

"You were good friends. Beau offered to come back when you're ready."

"He did?" I asked, incredulous and delighted. "That's terrific. I'm so glad you told me that."

One day melted into the next, and spring rolled into summer. I did the little bit of writing work that I had. I rowed. I saw Terry on the weekends. I sat with the chinchilla and the sugar gliders.

Whether I wanted to or not, I was doing what Guidance advised me to do. I was living day to day.

My financial situation became frustrating again. Although I kept getting hints that the big jobs I wanted would come through, they didn't. I couldn't meet my expenses, and every month, Terry gave me money to help pay my bills. By early July, my frustration boiled over. It had been three years since my divorce. Why hadn't my situation improved? Why was I still paying for my mistake with James?

James, on the other hand, seemed to be enjoying himself. According to his profile on America Online, he was living it up in Beijing:

> The James saga
>   ... starts Down Under over half a century ago ... meanders thru SE Asia—free holidays with all expenses paid by US and OZ govts—into LALA land and Tampa—back to Asia and now reclining in luxury in downtown BJ ...
>   My Hobbies and Interests
>   ...have mainly been women! Marrying them and loving them ...
>   My Bank Account...
>   ...has been kept slimmer than me by the process above ... but wouldn't have it any other way! There ain't no god—just goddesses!! And, I do like to worship!!!

Robert Palmer, my contact in Australia, forwarded to me a flyer that my ex-husband was sending around about his education ventures in China. Now, James appended the title "Ph.D." to his name. James claimed that his company, the International Institutes of Continuing Education (IICE), was making strides in many directions:

• IICE operated one of the largest foreign study agencies for Chinese students, and had placed more than 2,500 students in overseas colleges.

• IICE offered an English as a second language (ESL) school in Beijing, in cooperation with the China International Publishing Group.

• IICE launched a postgraduate management training program with the State Economic and Trade Commission and the China Women's Development Fund.

• IICE added ESL to vocational education programs in Beijing, offering students a year of work experience abroad.

• IICE was involved with the only national television program on overseas study, and was planning an ESL radio program on China Radio International.

Knowing James, his claims probably held shreds of truth, but were highly exaggerated. Still, the fact that he was still out there brazenly scamming people, while I struggled, made me furious.

I felt anger in my stomach, tension in my jaw. I was angry at the universe. "I've paid enough," I raged. "I've paid enough." The negative emotion was chewing me up, so on July 31, 2003, I had a phone session with Elaine.

I lay on the daybed in the meditation room, allowing myself to experience my emotions. Underneath all the anger and disappointment, I discovered fear. Fear that if I had something, people would take it away. It was dangerous to have too much. I would be killed for having more than others.

I began to get an image of a place, a time. I could see a fire burning in the distance, lighting up the night sky. "I think I was an aristocrat in a past life," I said to Elaine. "I was an aristocrat, and people became angry and took everything. People in my family were killed. There was some kind of riot; they took everything." I had the feeling it was Russia, but didn't say it.

"Was it in Russia?" Elaine asked.

"That's what I thought."

"Who were you?"

"I was a young woman. It was some kind of riot."

"Who did you lose? Who was killed?"

"I'm not sure—several people."

"You lost your whole family."

I felt the emotion of the experience. "I was away," I said. "I was away when it happened. It feels like it was in the 1700s. Russia was very sophisticated then, and had connections with Europe."

Peter the Great, who ruled Russia from 1682 to 1725, implemented sweeping reforms to modernize and strengthen his country, with the goal of making it a European power. He mandated European-style dress in court. He built a navy. He changed how taxes were assessed. The Russian economy, however, was still organized as a system of masters and serfs—the masters owned the land, and all the people attached to it. A landowner could not kill a serf, but could transfer a serf to another landowner, while keeping the serf's personal property and family. Over the years, there were hundreds of rebellions against this bondage.

One of them was Pugachev's Rebellion in 1774-75, during the reign of Catherine the Great. Emelyan Pugachev, a disaffected Russian soldier, set up an

alternative government and abolished serfdom. The news of his revolt prompt-
ed bloody uprisings against landlords and government officials all along the
Volga River in western Russia. Although Catherine initially considered Pugachev
to be nothing but a nuisance, he eventually controlled so much territory that she
sent her army to crush the rebellion.

Elaine and I pieced together my memories, although I didn't know which
rebellion they were from. I was a young woman, brought up in a life of privilege.
I was on my way home from traveling when the mob, rioters, whoever it was,
came to my family's home. They took everything and killed everyone. A maid
traveling with me took me to her relatives in the country. I had to change my
identity. I couldn't speak the way I was accustomed to speaking; I couldn't
behave the way I was accustomed to behaving. But I didn't know how to act like
a peasant, or farmer, or serf—whatever I was. My jewelry became bribes to stay
alive. I had furs, but couldn't wear them, and I was cold.

"I don't think I lasted very long," I said.

The fear and terror of my life as a young Russian woman drained away, but
my body was processing something else. I felt incredible tension in my back, and
I reflexively pushed my body as hard as I could into the daybed. The pressure
shifted to my head.

"Make the sound," Elaine said.

A high-pitched "e-e-e-e" came from my throat, like a test signal from the
Emergency Broadcasting System. It seemed to go on forever. My body was
soaked in sweat. I had to stop sometimes to breathe.

"Keep going," Elaine said. "Keep releasing the energy."

"It's in my head," I said.

"What happened to your head?"

"I don't know." The sound continued—e-e-e-e. "It's from more than one lifetime. I have such a headache. It's a headache from trying to figure it out. Trying
to figure out the reasons why things are the way they are."

The tension came from my unanswered questions. Why did I suffer when I
did nothing wrong? Why did many people suffer when they did nothing wrong?
Why was there so much suffering? Why was life so unfair? For lifetimes, I made
myself nuts trying to figure it out, and my futile quest for answers caused the
build-up in my head.

Guidance said there was nothing to figure out. I interpreted their message:
"Just accept and you win."

Elaine laughed. "It's really difficult for us, as humans, to simply accept," she
said. "Things seem unfair, difficult, and it is our nature to want things to be different. We'd be better off accepting what is and staying in the moment."

"Like when I watch the birds in my backyard?" I asked.

"Yes," Elaine said. "It means you're living in the moment."

So what should I do about my personal situation, including my financial
problems?

Guidance said I was on the right track, but manifesting what I wanted was
difficult because of the current state of the world. They were talking about the

traumatic effects of September 11, 2001. A few weeks earlier, in my mind's eye, I saw an image of the catastrophe as a boulder thrown into a pond, sending shockwaves in all directions, even into the lives of people not directly affected. My plans had been on track to succeed before that terrible day, but everything was delayed because of the widespread negative energy in the world.

Guidance wanted me to separate myself from the effects of September 11. "Don't take the delays personally; don't feel like it's your fault," they said. "Everything got delayed." They recommended that I keep watching the birds.

The next day, August 1, 2003, Terry came for the weekend and brought me a present—a birdfeeder for the backyard. I had never mentioned a birdfeeder. He was psychic. I was amazed.

As we sat on the porch having dinner, I told Terry about the session with Elaine and releasing the fear from my past life in Russia.

"Does this mean you're going to start making money?" he asked, jokingly.

"I hope so," I said.

Then I told him about draining the energy in my head, which had been caused by the stress of trying to figure things out.

"There's nothing to figure out," he said. "All you have to do is focus on now. You have one now after another now, and then you have a life."

Terry, it seemed, had already learned the lesson.

While Terry was browsing through a Borders bookstore in September 2003, a book jumped off the shelf and into his hands. It must have happened that way, because the book was the missing piece of the puzzle I'd been looking for. *Excuse Me, Your Life Is Waiting,* by Lynn Grabhorn, explained the key to our experience of life: "We create by feeling, not by thought."

Many books had been written about the power of positive thinking, going all the way back to Napoleon Hill with *Think and Grow Rich.* According to Grabhorn, the idea that we can create what we want in our lives by thinking positive thoughts was close, but not quite on target. The real creative power was in our emotions.

How did it work? Through the laws of physics. Grabhorn explained that energy and matter were the same, just vibrating at different levels. This included people—our vibrations sent out electromagnetic wave patterns of energy. What was the source of our vibrations? Our highly charged emotions.

A basic law of physics, Grabhorn said, was that like attracts like. This applied not only to physical matter, it also applied to our life experiences. All of us were walking magnets, pulling toward us anything that matched our vibrations. She wrote:

> Our feelings go out from us in electromagnetic waves. Whatever frequency goes out will automatically attract its identical frequency, thus causing things to happen—good or bad—by finding their matching vibrations.

> Happy, high vibrations attract happy, high vibrational circumstances. Yucky, low vibrations attract yucky low vibrational circumstances. In both cases, what comes back causes us to feel just as high or low as what we had been transmitting (feeling), because it's an exact vibrational match to what we sent out.

Just a few weeks earlier, I'd seen the principle in action in my own life. I wanted to refinance my mortgage. A local bank was having a "loan sale," offering rates significantly lower than my existing mortgage. Through all my financial difficulties, I'd never missed a mortgage payment, and if I got a lower interest rate, my payment would be less. I could certainly afford to pay less than I was already paying. But I worried about the bankruptcy on my credit record. I worried that the bank wouldn't care that I'd been defrauded, and would see me as financially irresponsible.

My worries were victorious. The bank turned down my loan application.

According to the Law of Attraction, I created my disappointment—as I had so many times in my life. So I consumed *Excuse Me, Your Life Is Waiting*. And then I read it again. I wanted to get the message.

At the same time, another book related to energy was recommended to me. It was called *The Power of Full Engagement,* by Jim Loehr and Tony Schwartz. The book was directed more toward a business audience, and its premise was that "managing energy, not time, is the key to high performance and personal renewal." The authors wrote, "Full engagement requires drawing on four separate but related sources of energy: physical, emotional, mental and spiritual." All four needed to be managed, which meant using energy and then allowing it to be renewed. In other words, it was important to flex our energy muscles, and it was also important to rest.

To me, this was a novel idea. I built my life around being productive, and anything that wasn't productive was a waste of time. The concept that down time was important and actually enabled me to be productive—well, for me it was, in corporate parlance, a paradigm shift.

Strawbridge's, a department store in Philadelphia, was having a big sale on Oriental rugs. Terry's home improvement list—for my house—included new rugs for the living room and dining room. On October 18, 2003, I met Terry at the store to check out the rugs.

While driving to Philadelphia, I thought about the two books I'd been reading on energy and vibrations. The messages crystallized in my brain:

Everything that happens depends on my internal energy. I create it. The spirit guides tell me positive, hopeful messages, so that I become positive and hopeful. Then, filled with positive energy, I can attract good things. It's like priming the pump. To attract what I want to happen, I have to maintain the energy. However, if my energy isn't positive enough, or strong enough to overcome negative energy from other directions, the good things may not happen. What I experience depends on the quality and strength of my own vibrations.

Wow—that was much more insightful than the average highway daydream.

The Strawbridge's sale was for authentic, handmade Oriental rugs, selling for $5,000 to $20,000 each—far too extravagant for my house. So Terry and I went, instead, to the store's furniture department and found a perfect rug. It was the right size, the right color and on sale. Terry bought two of them.

We left the store and walked around Old City Philadelphia, then decided to have dinner at Amici, an Italian restaurant on Market Street. Almost as soon as we ordered, Terry wanted to talk about Lovefraud.

"I'll fund it," he said.

Just like that. I couldn't believe his words.

Our first course arrived—Caesar salad for me, shrimp and bean soup for him. "How do you want to do this financially?" I asked. "Do you want to make a new company?"

"Do you want to be partners?" he asked. "Fifty-fifty?"

"Sure."

It was done. Terry offered me the money to move forward with my dreams. All I had to do was get to work.

Chapter 32

Sociopaths live in all communities, among all segments of the population. They are male, female, rich, poor, all races, all religions, all ethnic groups. They are toxic, damaging, even deadly. But few people know they exist.

My mission was to tell the world about sociopaths, to shine a bright light of exposure on this darkest of personality disorders. Now that Terry had offered to fund the project, my work could begin.

The first step was building my website, Lovefraud.com. I'd been writing the content sporadically since my divorce was finalized in 2000. In November 2003, after Terry offered to help, I retained a web designer to start putting it all together. Within a few weeks, he showed me initial layouts. Lovefraud.com began to move from a concept into reality.

Many years had passed since I last hosted Thanksgiving dinner. With all the turmoil in my life, making an appetizer or a carrot and apple casserole for a family gathering was all I could manage. But the turmoil was in the past; Terry was part of my life; I had a new bathroom upstairs and a new recreation room in the basement—another of Terry's home improvements. I wanted to entertain.

Terry took off on Wednesday, November 26, 2003 to help me cook. When we woke up on Thanksgiving morning, he felt romantic, but I was visualizing my mental checklist of everything that still needed to be done. He could sense it.

"Your brain is buzzing," he laughed, waving his hand in the air like a bee flying. We got up and got moving. By 2 p.m., when our guests arrived—15 adults and six children—everything was ready, and we were sitting on the porch sipping wine.

The day was a blur. I organized the food, put out warming trays, poured milk for the kids, found serving spoons for all the platters. Terry kept mixing drinks. Dinner was delicious. At the end of the evening, I was happy, tired and looking forward to a week of leftover turkey.

Christmas was also lovely. I knew what most of my gifts would be because

Terry took me shopping—a winter coat and new clothes, which I desperately needed. My gifts for Terry included another hand-blown martini glass and a board game—Strip Chocolate. It was somewhat like Monopoly, although the goal was not to acquire items, but shed them. He couldn't wait to play.

But he had to, because the day after Christmas, we drove to Washington, D.C. for a long weekend. Even though we were planning a big trip—a vacation to France in April—we still wanted a quick holiday getaway. We visited the national Christmas tree, the National Archives and the National Art Gallery.

I also wanted to see the United States Holocaust Memorial Museum. I knew it would be disturbing, but I felt a deep obligation to be part of the remembering.

The Nazi party came to power in Germany in 1933, when 9 million Jews lived in Europe. By 1945, two out of three Jews were dead—nearly 6 million people, half of them Polish. One historian estimated that the Nazis killed 90 percent of the Jews in Poland, Estonia, Latvia, Lithuania, Germany and Austria. They also killed more than 50 percent of the Jews in Bohemia, Moravia, Slovakia, Greece, the Netherlands, Hungary, Belarus, the Ukraine, Belgium, Yugoslavia and Romania.

Other populations were targeted as well. The Nazis killed 2 million to 3 million Soviet prisoners of war, nearly 2 million ethnic Poles, more than 200,000 Roma (gypsies), more than 200,000 mentally or physically disabled people (most of them German), plus Serbs, homosexuals, Jehovah's Witnesses and political opponents. When these groups were included, the total number of Holocaust victims was between 11 million and 17 million people.

Exhibits at the Holocaust Museum unflinchingly conveyed the horror of the "Final Solution"—the Nazi plan to annihilate the Jewish race. After riding an ominous industrial-style elevator to the museum's fourth floor, where the permanent exhibit began, the first thing we saw was massive shocking photographs of the concentration camps taken by U.S. Army soldiers in 1945. The exhibit explained the Nazi rise to power that culminated in the totalitarian state, which made the slavery and slaughter possible. I was struck by the newspaper coverage of measures being taken against the Jews as it was happening, and how little the world did to stop the genocide.

Two simple displays poignantly captured the tragedy of the lives snuffed out. One was a mound of 4,000 shoes, covered with what appeared to be soot, that were piled outside a warehouse at the Nazi concentration camp in Majdanek, Poland. More than 78,000 people died there, including 18,000 Jews shot on a single day, November 3, 1943, during what the Nazis called "Operation Harvest Festival." The other heartbreaking display was the three-story Tower of Faces—6,000 photographs of people from Ejszyszki, a Jewish village in Lithuania that was totally destroyed by the Nazis and their collaborators. At one time, 4,000 Jews lived there. Only 29 survived.

The Holocaust museum was, as I anticipated, disturbing; I struggled to keep from crying in the middle of the tour. What kind of people could conceive of, and then implement, such methodical genocide? I had to assume that the perpetrators included plenty of sociopaths.

Afterwards, we walked around to the monuments on the National Mall—memorials to Thomas Jefferson, Franklin D. Roosevelt, the Korean War, Abraham Lincoln, and finally, the Vietnam War. To me, the Vietnam Veterans Memorial was just as emotional as the Holocaust Museum. I remembered the war and knew men who fought there—really fought, unlike my ex-husband, who I suspected lied about his service. This time, contemplating the senseless loss of life, I could not hold back my tears.

Walking back to our hotel gave me time to regroup for an evening at the Kennedy Center—dinner and the ballet. The rest of our Washington trip was more touristy and less emotional—the Smithsonian, Georgetown, the Spy Museum.

Back at home, Terry went to work on New Year's Eve, while I planned our private celebration. After searching my cookbooks, I shopped for the ingredients for Coquille St. Jacques, vegetable side dishes and our favorite dessert—Godiva Chocolate Raspberry ice cream. Terry was already at my house when I returned, using my computer to surf the Internet. I unloaded the groceries and changed into one of the pretty outfits he bought me for Christmas.

"You're all dressed up," he said.

"Well, it's New Year's Eve," I replied. "I thought we'd have a nice dinner and then play Strip Chocolate."

Suddenly, Terry was as excited as a teenager who had a date with the prom queen. While I cooked the scallops, he changed into slacks, a dress shirt and tie, and set up the Strip Chocolate game in the spare bedroom. We started drinking a bottle of champagne with dinner, and finished it around the game board.

We rolled the dice, advanced our game pieces, and then, directed by the cards we drew, removed clothing and painted chocolate on each other. The next morning, despite our best efforts to kiss the chocolate away, we found some on the bedsheets.

Development continued for Lovefraud.com. I created web pages about the *Key Symptoms of a Sociopath, How to Spot a Con, Fraud on the Web* and more. I developed a quiz, called *Are You a Target?*, that assigned a score based on the reader's answers to yes-or-no questions. I also developed a *Risk Calculator* to estimate how many sociopaths may live in a community. Depending upon which expert was quoting the statistics, the number of sociopaths in the population ranged from 1 percent to 4 percent. My *Risk Calculator* did the math, showing people how many sociopaths may be among their neighbors. The figure was always shocking.

Not only was I working on Lovefraud, but my writing business picked up. I had a new client, Midi Corp., based in Princeton, New Jersey, that created web-based compliance training programs for major corporations. On February 3, 2004, I went with them to a project kickoff meeting. After a drought of more than a year, I finally had big jobs for big clients that paid healthy fees.

On the way back from my North Jersey meeting, I stopped to spend the night with Terry in his apartment. When I returned to Atlantic City the next morning,

I discovered that my heat was off. I got the heater going, but not until that night, when I went to feed the pets, did I realize that the cold had affected my sugar glider, Hope. Her body temperature was way below normal; her fur was matted and her eyes glazed. Hope was close to death.

I cupped her tiny body in my hand and held her under my fleece sweatshirt, next to my chest. I focused my mind on sending her love and warmth. It was like a little sauna under my shirt, and after about an hour, Hope stirred. I offered her water on the tip of my finger and a slice of grape; she wasn't interested. Forty minutes later, she moved again and ate some sunflower seeds. The other glider, Mojo, jumped on me, and even though I was exhausted, I held the tiny pets in the pocket of my sweatshirt until 12:45 a.m.

The next morning, both sugar gliders were running around.

"I was so grateful that Hope recovered from being close to dead," I wrote in my journal. "I felt the love I have for my pets." Guidance responded:

> Hope is so grateful. She was scared and calling for you, calling for her mother. She felt so cold, couldn't get warm. Mojo actually tried, but then he despaired—he didn't think he could do it. He knew his playmate was sick and dying. He was afraid.
>
> But you came, and they are both grateful. She felt your love, and it gave her strength. She felt your warmth, and it enabled her to recover. But mostly it was the love, the healing energy that you sent to her.
>
> That is the power of the energy, your energy. Yes, it is that powerful. You can change your life. You can get what you want. You can be happy and one with all that is. Trust it. Trust the universe. Trust yourself.

The universe sent me another message about my pets. On March 28, 2004, our phalaenopsis bloomed. It was the one-year anniversary of Beau's death, and it was the same orchid that burst into flower on the day he passed.

Terry's daughter, Meghan Kelly, met us at the Charles de Gaulle airport in Paris on April 14, 2004. She was a French major, studying at the Sorbonne for the semester. We planned to spend a few days in Paris with her, then explore Provence in Southern France and end our trip on the French Riviera.

In her excellent French, Meghan directed the taxi driver to our hotel in the seventh *arrondissement*, near the Eiffel Tower and the Hôtel des Invalides. After flying all night, all I wanted to do was eat and sleep. We found a restaurant near the hotel, and although we were too late for breakfast, I was able to order an omelet, *bien cuit,* or well done—I'd been brushing up on my French ever since we decided to take the trip. Then I went back to the hotel for a nap, while Terry and his daughter strolled the neighborhood.

That evening, I felt refreshed, and we all took a walk to the River Seine. Near

Invalides, we found a restaurant for dinner. I ordered veal, but when I tasted it, the meat was dry. I sent the dish back, telling the waiter it was *trop bien cuit,* or too well done. He immediately launched into a torrent of words that I didn't understand, although I did hear him ask if I wanted something else. I gestured toward Terry's salmon, and the waiter turned in a huff and left.

"What did he say?" I asked Meghan.

"He said that's the way it was supposed to be prepared."

"That's crazy. It was overcooked."

Terry was laughing. "Our first dinner in a real French restaurant, and you send it back," he said. "I'm impressed."

The next day the three of us visited the Tuileries Garden, and Terry bought two small oil paintings of French street scenes from a young artist selling them on the sidewalk. We went to the Musée D'Orsay, which I'd visited before and thoroughly enjoyed again. Then we walked to the Latin Quarter, where I stayed during my first visit to Paris with James. It was much more lively in April than it was in January.

We ate dinner at Le Procope, which claimed to be the oldest operating restaurant in the world. It was founded in 1686, and over the centuries was patronized by luminaries such as philosophers Voltaire and Rousseau, novelists Balzac and Hugo, and the American statesman Benjamin Franklin. Afterwards, Terry wanted to see jazz, and we found Café Laurent, located in the Saint Germain des Prés section of Paris. The club was tiny—seats for about 30 people—and the band was good. It was the type of intimate jazz experience that Terry savored.

Terry and I took the metro back to our *arrondissement,* and when we emerged from the subway tunnel, the Eiffel Tower, with white lights tracing its form against the darkness, rose before us. It was beautiful and romantic.

"I'm so happy to be visiting Paris with you," Terry said, putting his arm around me. "It's something I've always wanted to do, ever since I heard the song *April in Paris* when I was 12 years old."

The lyrics told the story of finding love in Paris. For Terry and me, it was truly *April in Paris*—City of Lights, City of Love.

On the TGV, or *Train á Grande Vitesse* (high-speed train), we could travel from Paris to Avignon, a distance of 360 miles, in two hours and 40 minutes. First, however, we had to get to the train station. We had trouble with the hotel phone system when we tried to call Meghan, who was on spring break and was joining us for part of our trip to Provence. Then we almost went to the wrong train station—Paris had six of them.

The train certainly was fast—our ears popped from the pressure changes as we sped through mountain tunnels. When it stopped in Avignon, the doors opened, but we heard no announcement and saw no signs. We continued to sit in our seats, then realized that we'd reached our destination and got off, just before the train left for the next stop.

After picking up our rental car—I insisted that we buy accident insurance—we discovered that driving around France was going to be a challenge. There seemed to be a shortage of street signs. Leaving the airport, we couldn't tell what road we were on, couldn't find the road we were looking for, and went off in the wrong direction. At traffic circles, which were numerous, we saw posts full of arrows that pointed toward particular destinations, but it was difficult to determine which road each sign pointed at.

So began the adventure.

We didn't stay in Avignon but drove directly to Arles, an ancient city that was already well established in the day of Julius Caesar. Based on our bible for the trip—*Rick Steves' Provence and the French Riviera*—we booked rooms at the Hôtel de l'Amphiteâtre. The guidebook said it was located next to a Roman arena, and it was.

I didn't know that the Romans built arenas in France. When I glimpsed my past life as a guard at an arena, I assumed it was the Colosseum in Rome. But I could have been wrong. The Romans built more than 200 arenas, and ruins were found all over France, England, Germany, Switzerland, Spain, Algeria, Tunisia, Libya and other countries.

The arena in Arles, constructed around 90 A.D., was one of the largest and best-preserved Roman monuments in Provence. A double row of 60 arches formed the oval-shaped exterior, and stone bleachers inside could seat 20,000 spectators for gladiator and animal fights. After the Roman Empire collapsed, townspeople used the arena as a fortification, building houses inside and adding guard towers. When the citizens of Arles decided to restore the arena in 1826, they cleared out 212 houses and two churches.

We visited the arena on Saturday, April 17, 2004. There was no line and no guided tour—after buying our tickets, we were free to walk anywhere we wanted, including up narrow steps, with no handrails, to the guard towers. I couldn't help but think that such unfettered access would never be allowed in the United States, where too many lawyers waited to file slip-and-fall lawsuits.

From the amphitheater, we walked down the hill to Arles' famous Saturday morning open-air market. The town's main boulevard was lined with vendors selling fresh produce, cheeses, meats, preserves, clothes and souvenirs. Salesmen did their best to convince me to buy, even though I didn't understand everything they said. One enthusiastically demonstrated a hand-painted ceramic grater for garlic, cheese and whole spices, which I bought. Another, petting a lamb, offered honey throat lozenges to benefit a vaccination program for baby animals. I bought them as well. I enjoyed practicing my French, even if the practice was a sales pitch.

After lunch, we drove 45 minutes to Pont du Gard, a spectacular bridge that was part of a Roman aqueduct built in 40 to 70 A.D. The structure was a marvel of engineering—three levels of stone arches, one above the other, spanning 300 yards across a river canyon. It was constructed entirely without mortar—the stones were cut to fit together perfectly. Hundreds of people visited the aqueduct that day. In fact, it had been a tourist attraction for centuries—I saw graffiti dated 1839.

During Roman times, the aqueduct transported 4.4 million gallons of water daily to the city of Nîmes, which we visited next. In the center of the town's plaza was the Maison Carrée, considered to be the most complete and beautiful building that survived from Roman times. This temple, built around 16 B.C., was a wonderful example of classical architecture. A stone staircase led up to the front portico, where 10 Corinthian columns supported a triangular pediment. We ordered drinks at a café, and watched as two guys sat on the temple's towering portico eating sandwiches from the Golden Arches—McDonald's.

The next morning we visited Gordes, a tiny but extraordinary hilltop village that had morphed into a trendy tourist stop. We strolled its narrow, twisting medieval streets for about 15 minutes, which was enough time to see much of the town. After lunch at an outdoor café, we headed back to Avignon, where we put Meghan on the train so she could return to Paris.

The train station was outside of Avignon, and our hotel was within the old city, behind a massive fortress wall built between 1355 and 1368. The wall had eight portals, and we drove completely around Avignon three times before we found the gate that lead to our hotel. Then we struggled to find a parking space—few were included in the 14th century city planning.

After the stress of driving in circles, looking for parking, and realizing that we'd forgotten our umbrellas when it started to rain, we selected a restaurant based on the fact that a lighted sign in the window proclaimed "bar." Terry wanted a drink. A martini, to be exact.

"Rouge ou blanc?" the waiter asked.

Red or white? This was not a good sign. When the drink arrived, it was white vermouth—the Martini brand—and no gin. Terry sent it back and tried several times to explain what he wanted. The bartender didn't understand and couldn't make the drink. A group of Americans seated near us witnessed Terry's frustration. One woman in the group gave Terry the bad news: "You can't get a martini in France."

Avignon was located on the Rhône River, at the southern edge of the Côtes du Rhône wine region. Terry loved French wine, and wanted to go on a tasting tour. So the next morning, April 19, 2004, we headed off to the nearby Dentelles de Montmirail mountains, which were ringed by vineyards.

Our guidebook said the village of Vaison La Romaine was the hub of the region's wine road. The town had two distinct sections—a "modern" area on the banks of the Ouvéze River, settled in the 17th and 18th centuries, a medieval village on the adjacent mountaintop.

The medieval village was our destination, but we did not drive there—we parked in a dirt lot on the side of the mountain and walked up. When we reached the top, we passed through a fortified gate and stepped back in time. The streets, only about six feet wide, twisted between stone buildings packed closely together. Sometimes the streets turned into stairways. Sometimes they passed under stone arches. Sometimes they opened into tiny plazas with ancient flowing fountains.

I was starving, but most restaurants were closed—it wasn't quite tourist season. We found a boutique hotel called Fête en Provence, and its tiny dining room was open. Lunch was delicious, especially my dessert—three *petite crème brûlées* flavored with lavender. We enjoyed ourselves so much that we made a reservation to spend the night there.

With recommendations from our waitress, we got back on the mountainous wine road. We drove up to the private homes of winemakers, with their small tasting rooms, and stopped at large retail operations. All the tasting made me queasy, and the ride back to Vaison La Romaine made me even queasier. Somehow we got on the scenic route, which had narrow roads, hairpin turns and cliffs with no guardrails. It wasn't as bad as Beartooth Highway in Montana, but I was much happier to be walking when we arrived back in town.

Antibes was a small city on the Mediterranean coast, located between Cannes and Nice. According to the Rick Steves guidebook, it was a down-to-earth town on the tony French Riviera, so that's where we chose to stay.

The tourist area of Antibes—its Old Town and Port—was like a tourist area anywhere, with small stores selling everything from sodas to clothing to high-priced souvenirs. On the warm, sunny afternoon that we arrived, April 20, 2004, it was filled with crowds of visitors. A group of teenagers walked in front of us; one young woman had a single lock of hair on top of her otherwise shaved head, and a white rat perched on her shoulder. With the help of a friendly waitress, we made a reservation at the Hôtel Pension le Mas Djoliba, the top-rated place in our guidebook.

Le Mas Djoliba was once a manor house, and was set back from the road, surrounded by palm trees and other greenery, in a residential area of Antibes. The three-story main house had yellow stucco walls, a red tile roof, a covered outdoor portico and a kidney-shaped swimming pool. Our ground-floor room was large by European standards, and opened onto our own gravel patio. We planned to stay there for the last three nights of our vacation, and I happily settled in.

We walked a few blocks to the shoreline, and I was astonished at the beautiful turquoise color of the Mediterranean Sea—no wonder the French referred to the region as *La Côte d'Azur*. At a nearby bathing beach of yellow sand, some of the women were topless. In the distance, mountains tumbled into the sea. No, Terry, we weren't in Atlantic City any more.

Our hostess at the hotel recommended a nearby restaurant called *Albert 1er,* or Albert the First, for dinner. When we saw it, we were hesitant; unlike the small, intimate places we preferred, it was big and somewhat touristy. All around the restaurant, hanging just below the ceiling, were black and white publicity photos of famous customers—I recognized Marlon Brando and Leonardo DiCaprio. The stars came for a reason: The restaurant specialized in seafood, and it was excellent.

The next day, April 21, 2004, I just wanted to relax. Navigating around France was interesting but stressful; I needed a break from the driving. So we slept late. A real breakfast, not just continental, was available in the hotel dining room; I feasted on eggs. Then Terry and I took a walk, strolling toward the Old Town along the Promenade Amiral de Grasse, a waterfront rampart that protected Antibes from the sea. We reached the harbor, Port Vauban, which offered dockage for the biggest yachts I'd ever seen. The marina could accommodate a maximum boat length of 150 meters—nearly 500 feet. Several yachts, with ports of call such as Grand Cayman, looked like they were pushing the limit. One had an onboard helipad.

Terry wanted to take a boat out, and we inquired at a rental agency, Antibes Bateaux Services. We could only rent a skiff with a putt-putt outboard engine of six horsepower—anything bigger required a French boating license. We bought food for a picnic lunch, climbed aboard the skiff and headed out into the marina, poking along between the massive yachts towering above us. Suddenly the engine conked out. Terry got it going, but it conked out again. With no way to control the boat, we started drifting right into one of the big, luxury yachts.

A longhaired, sailor-looking guy leaned over the rail from above and shouted to us in French.

"Ne marche pas," I replied. It doesn't go.

The sailor called something else, but that was the end of my emergency French. He quickly figured it out. "Do you speak English?" he asked.

The guy was an Australian crewman on the yacht. With a line and boat hook, he pulled us around the yacht and up to the dock, then climbed in and got the motor started. He and Terry figured out that the fuel pump was defective. We motored slowly back to Antibes Bateaux Services.

The rental employee made some adjustments to the engine and it seemed to be okay, so we started out again. This time we got as far as the lighthouse at the mouth of the channel before the engine quit. We drifted helplessly again until, luckily, the guy from rental dock came by in a boat and towed us in. That was the end of our maritime adventure. From the safety of a park bench overlooking the Mediterranean, we laughed and ate our picnic lunch.

We had a reservation for dinner at our hotel that evening—the owner was also a chef. With no place to rush to, we indulged in afternoon delight. Even with our not-so-excellent adventure, the day was lovely and relaxing.

The village of Boit, located just outside of Antibes, was known for glassmaking, so of course, Terry wanted to go there. On April 22, 2004, we planned to visit the studios, then drive on to Nice. I was supposed to navigate while Terry drove, so I studied our map and planned a route—not realizing that the roads I picked were going one way in the wrong direction. We got on the road, and promptly got lost.

After several frustrating wrong turns, we found Boit and the studios, visiting three of them. In one Terry bought a beautiful art glass wall sconce—pale, frosted pink overlaid with ribbons of raised glass in black, white and tan. At the next studio Terry bought a piece that looked like a delicate rectangular vase of blue, gold and copper encased by a heavy envelope of clear glass. In the third studio, Terry wanted a truly exquisite piece that cost more than $700—so he thought it best to leave.

We missed the entrance to the highway to Nice and ended up near the airport. Terry turned in, intending to stop, study the map, and figure out where to go. As he started to make a left turn, a car sped up to pass us, and hit us on the driver side. It was only a fender bender, and luckily the people in the other car were Brits from Monte Carlo, so we could resolve everything in English, but once again, driving proved stressful. I was glad we purchased the accident insurance.

Finally going in the right direction, we entered Nice along the busy Promenade des Anglais, with the Mediterranean on the right and big hotels on the left. Nice was the largest resort in France, and that's exactly what it felt like—a big tourist city. I was amazed that it was so popular, because the beach was covered with rocks. Yes, they were round and smooth from the action of the waves, but the people who spread out beach towels and lay down on them had to be uncomfortable. Apparently most of the Côte d'Azur had rocks on the beach—we'd learned that the yellow sand in Antibes was imported.

After a few hours in Nice—hiking to the top of Le Chateau, a steep hill that offered a panoramic view—we got back on the road to explore further up the coast. Fifteen minutes away we discovered Villefranche, an unspoiled little town that was the antithesis of Nice. Squeezed between the mountains and a tiny, delightful harbor was a row of colorful buildings, a narrow road, and a pedestrian promenade that dropped directly into the water. Small boats tied up at bollards on the promenade.

We found a restaurant called Carpaccio for dinner. I ordered paella, which was excellent, but the dessert was exquisite—the best ice cream I'd ever tasted, and I'd eaten a lot of ice cream. An old woman came into the restaurant selling red roses, and Terry bought one for me. A delightful ambience, good food, a flower—it was all so romantic.

The next day, Terry wanted to return to Nice to visit the Marc Chagall museum. I was tired of the driving, or more precisely, tired of getting lost. I didn't want to go.

"I've been thinking about the driving and navigating," Terry said. "I think it's unfair to leave all the navigating to you. I think we should both look at the map before we leave."

"That would probably help a lot," I said.

I was amazed, and relieved, at Terry's approach to the problem. If I had attempted a trip like this with my ex-husband, driving around a strange country with hard-to-find street signs, it would have been ruined on the first day by him screaming at me, and continued downhill after that. Through all the wrong turns, Terry never criticized me, and his willingness to come up with a workable solution warmed my heart. He was a keeper.

I agreed to return to Nice, and we put our new plan into action, studying the map together before we left. It worked—we found Nice and the museum without a problem.

I was glad we went. Marc Chagall was a modernist painter, although to me he seemed to be part illustrator, part mystic. Between 1954 and 1967, he painted 17 large murals specifically for the museum in Nice. Each was a reflection on a message in the Bible, and each was extraordinary. The *Creation of Man* depicted, in Chagall's loose, vibrant style, an angel carrying to Earth a sleeping Adam, oblivious to the future of mankind. Chagall's art bypassed my brain and went straight to my emotions, eliciting a deep reaction within me.

A smaller room in the museum was dedicated to five paintings that were meditations on *The Song of Songs,* the book of the Old Testament that has been interpreted as portraying the relationship between God and Israel as the love between a husband and wife. Other traditions viewed *The Song of Songs* as sacred erotica. Chagall's five paintings, all with red as the dominant color, unabashedly celebrated the love between a man and a woman.

Terry and I returned to Antibes for our last afternoon in France, and spent most of it in bed.

Back in Atlantic City after the sensuous visit to France, the workaday world became reality again. Terry and I both returned to our responsibilities—and for me, a big one was Lovefraud.com. I continued to develop content, send it to my web designer and proof the pages. In May, I transferred the website files to my hosting company, although the site wasn't yet ready to go live.

My advertising business picked up, and on June 9, 2004, I had an appointment with an exciting potential new client—Comcast—at its office in a Center City, Philadelphia skyscraper. A mid-level communications executive who I knew from one of my previous accounts contacted me. The cable giant needed writing services.

Comcast had acquired Suburban Cable, the company that James said he was taking over—one of his more ridiculous claims—in 2000. Four years later, Comcast ranked number 89 on the Fortune 500 list of U.S. companies. It had 68,000 employees and was adding more—which was why I was called. The company expected to roll out many new services and needed to strengthen its internal communications program. It was exactly the type of work I did for Showboat.

This was big. An account like Comcast would finally put my finances on firm footing.

I met with the director and two of her assistants to discuss the parameters of the project. I did my homework and came prepared with a list of questions. As we discussed how to proceed, we were all getting excited at the project's potential. Then, as the meeting came to a close, without being asked, I told them my billing rate was $75 per hour.

As soon as the number was out of my mouth, I knew I'd made a mistake. That was the rate I used for Rosenthal Realty, a local business with a receptionist and five associate real estate agents. For one of the largest companies in the country, I should charge more.

I screwed up, big time. I lambasted myself during the entire ride back to Atlantic City. I continued to berate myself for days. My chest tightened and I had difficulty breathing. Why had I quoted such a low rate? Why was I afraid to ask for what I deserved?

I did not want to work for Comcast on the cheap, and struggled to decide what to do. Should I tell them that I made a mistake and that I wanted a higher fee? Should I not admit anything and just use the higher rate when I submitted a proposal? For days, the tension in my chest grew as I debated my options. "What a stupid mistake," I chastised myself. "You know better than that. It's Sales 101—know the cost."

Internal turmoil, I knew, would manifest bad results, so I tried to release the tension by meditating. I felt energy draining through my forehead and through my tightly pursed lips, but it seemed that as soon as some negativity was gone, more welled up to take its place.

In the end, I decided to be honest. I sent a proposal via e-mail. I quoted the project based on $85 per hour, and told the director that I used my national rate, which was only 13 percent higher than what I said in the meeting. The reply from Comcast was not good. A few days later the project was gone, and I beat myself up even more. My first stupid mistake was compounded by a second stupid mistake, and I ended up with nothing.

I felt like I was suffocating. After rowing one afternoon, I went to my meditation room to release the anxiety, with only partial success. But while lying on the daybed, an impression drifted into my mind of being in a store. I saw glass showcases; it was a jewelry store, and I was the owner. The memory felt like I was a Jew before the Holocaust, unfairly accused of cheating people.

A month after the Comcast disaster, on July 28, 2004, I had a telephone session with Elaine Anderson and told her what had happened.

"You were really hard on yourself about this Comcast," Elaine said.

"Yes, I was," I agreed.

"You were really beating yourself up. Far too hard. You weren't meant to have that work. It would have drained too much energy from your purpose."

"I was getting those messages."

"But you felt like you made an error, and you were really hard on yourself. You should not treat yourself that way."

"Yes, I made a mistake. I don't make them very often. I was always terrified of making mistakes."

"Where does that come from?"

"I don't know."

Pressure subtly grew in my head. My face frowned; my brow was totally furrowed. The energy was thick and heavy, moving slowly into my teeth.

"You have all this energy, this emotion, attached to making an error," Elaine said. "Why is that?"

The Holocaust image drifted into my mind again, but I didn't want to say it. I felt that I had been injured, that somebody had done something to my teeth. There was pounding, or pulling. Finally, I said, "I think there was some torture involved."

"Yes," Elaine replied. "What emotions do you feel with this?"

I couldn't respond; pressure overwhelmed my mouth, teeth and ears. At times I coughed. A sound escaped my lips; it was a cross between a moan and a gasp. "I don't feel anything," I said.

"You're numb."

"Yes, I'm numb. I can't feel anything." Finally, I had to acknowledge the image, "I think this might be related to the Holocaust." A tremendous heaviness, a weight, a black void was locked in my body's energy field.

"What are your impressions?" Elaine asked.

"This is so horrible," I said. "I don't see anything. I can't. Do you think it was the Holocaust?"

"It feels like that time period," Elaine said. "You don't want to remember. This was so traumatic; you went numb. But there is a lot of self-blame associated with this. You made an error; something happened to you and your family. It wasn't your fault, and whatever happened would have happened anyway, but you blamed yourself. Can you go into the feeling?"

I couldn't do it.

Elaine didn't push me. "Just surrender it to Guidance," she said. "Give it over to the angels."

I was surprised—Elaine had never called on angels before. The weight was in my chest, my heart, my stomach, hovering within my body and above it. I kept trying to release the weight energetically.

"Surrender it to the angels," Elaine said again.

I could feel it starting to move, starting to lighten.

"You're doing well," Elaine said. "Give it to the angels."

Slowly the weight, the big black disturbance, started to dissipate. It took a long time, but I could feel the tension draining away. We talked about that terrible experience of my past, and the energy block it created.

"You blamed yourself, and you had so much energy attached to this experience," Elaine said. "It wasn't your fault. I get the feeling that someone followed you home and found the hiding place. They took you and your family, and you blamed yourself for it."

"It felt like James was part of the experience."

"Yes. I got the feeling that he was one of the torturers."

"You know, I have such a reverence for life, maybe it came from this experience," I continued. "I hate to see anything injured or dead. Sometimes there are ants in my pets' food plates, but I won't kill them. I put the plates outside so the ants can go away, and then put the plates in the dishwasher. I even worry about plants. Last week I pulled up the pansies in the front garden. I hated to do it, hated to kill them. I thanked each plant for the pleasure it gave us."

I started to cry. "Why am I crying about plants?" I asked.

"It's related to your experience," Elaine said. "You saw such disrespect for life that you went numb. You can cry about the plants because it's safe."

As we talked, the energy continued to drain. "Guidance and the angels are depressurizing you," Elaine said. "When we first started the session, I was shown an image of how you were so hard on yourself about the Comcast error. It was like you had beaten yourself to a pulp."

"If I wasn't supposed to get the project, why did it show up?"

"It was supposed to help you trust your intuition, kind of a test," Elaine answered. "It was to help you learn to do only what is in line with your purpose, only what honors you. You would have taken the job—you would have felt irresponsible if you didn't. So Guidance helped you out."

The session had lasted two-and-a-half hours, and it was coming to a close.

"We thank guidance for the insight and assistance," Elaine said in her ceremonial voice. "We ask for continued help for Donna in pursuing her purpose. And so it is. Amen."

"Amen," I repeated.

As a cost-cutting measure, Hazen Paper Company, Terry's employer, was closing his office. Terry still had a job—he would just be working from home. So where should his home be? There was no longer any reason for him to live in his apartment in Delran, New Jersey. We were happy together. In August 2004, we agreed that Terry would move in with me.

I was thrilled! My sweetheart wanted to be with me all the time! After years of aloneness, followed by a scam marriage, I finally found companionship, togetherness and love. Terry was happy too, and we floated in euphoria for a short time—maybe an hour. Then we had to face the question: How were we going to do this?

My house was not very big, and it was full. Terry's apartment was also full, and its basement storage area still held boxes from the big home he once owned. How would we make room for Terry in my house? What would we do with all the stuff—his, mine and ours?

We rented a storage unit and decided to have an indoor yard sale. Terry's old pickup truck, a powder blue 1982 Ford 150, made the 65-mile trip between Delran and Atlantic City many times, packed with furniture, household goods, clothes and boxes. We initiated a complete purge of both of our homes, looking at everything we owned, in every closet and drawer, and deciding what to keep, store, sell or trash.

In the midst of the sorting and transporting, I planned two trips to gather information for the Lovefraud website. On October 5, 2004, I traveled to Atlanta, Georgia—staying with Terry's brother and sister-in-law—to interview a woman for *True Lovefraud Stories*. That's what I called my case studies.

A week later, on October 13, 2004, I traveled to Great Falls, Montana, to attend a workshop presented by Dr. Robert Hare, the world-renowned expert on psychopaths.

When Elaine Anderson first mentioned that James Montgomery might be a sociopath, I read Dr. Hare's book, *Without Conscience—The Disturbing World of Psychopaths Among Us*. According to the book, the symptoms of a psychopath—the term Dr. Hare preferred—included:

Emotional/Interpersonal:
- Glib and superficial
- Egocentric and grandiose
- Lack of remorse or guilt
- Lack of empathy
- Deceitful and manipulative
- Shallow emotions

Social Deviance
- Impulsive
- Poor behavior controls
- Need for excitement
- Lack of responsibility
- Early behavior problems
- Adult antisocial behavior

© 1993 Robert D. Hare, Ph.D., *Without Conscience*, Guilford Publications, Inc., New York, NY

The list was a perfect description of my ex-husband. And I realized that James Montgomery wasn't the first disordered person that I'd met. The description fit Don Clement Jr., who convinced me to "invest" in his used cars, then stole my money. I thought it also applied, in a different way, to David Hansen, the guy with the anger issues that I dated before James.

Dr. Hare developed an evaluation instrument, called the Psychopathy Checklist-Revised, with which professionals could rate an individual's degree of psychopathy. The workshop in Montana was to teach mental health professionals and prison officials how to use it. I didn't anticipate a career in evaluating criminals, but I did want to meet Dr. Hare, so I signed up for the workshop.

Great Falls, Montana was not one of the places I'd visited with my former boyfriend back in 2000. The city was located near the center of the state, on the northern Great Plains, and lacked the breathtaking vistas of mountains and lakes. The seminar was at a Hampton Inn near the airport. Approximately 100 people attended—many of them employed by Montana's prison system.

The basic philosophy of most corrections systems, Dr. Hare told the audience, was that offender problems were due to problems in socialization. Antisocial behavior was viewed by prison officials as resulting from inadequate parenting, disruptive social forces or simply bad luck. The strategy was to resocialize offenders to get them back on track.

Psychopaths, unfortunately, never were on track.

The core symptoms of psychopathy were strongly determined by genetics, Dr. Hare explained. Psychopaths experienced emotion as if it were a foreign language that needed to be translated. They had no loyalty to any person, group, code, organization or philosophy. Psychopaths were loyal only to themselves, and they weren't going to change.

According to Dr. Hare, when dealing with a psychopath, attempting to do any of the following was a waste of time:

- Correct deviant attitudes
- Instill a sense of empathy
- Get them to look at the victim's perspective
- Train them to be less self-centered
- Have them adopt a pro-social philosophy
- Focus on emotions

Psychopaths, Dr. Hare said, had a higher rate of recidivism than other criminals—after release from jail, they were more likely to reoffend. In fact, they often gamed the prison system by participating in treatment programs and modeling good behavior. To prison psychologists, they looked like they'd reformed, but they went out and reoffended at the highest rates.

"Are all psychopaths criminals?" Dr. Hare asked. "We have Enron and Worldcom." The audience laughed. Executives at both companies—once lauded as business visionaries—engaged in accounting fraud that cost stockholders billions of dollars.

"Are you married to a psychopath?" was his next question, and everybody laughed again.

Why were they laughing? I was married to a psychopath and lost almost everything—my money, my dreams, my self-respect. This crowd of therapists and prison officials thought it was funny! I was floored. I almost stood up to protest—but I didn't. If these people hadn't been married to a psychopath, they probably didn't understand just how devastating it was.

I did have a chance to speak with Dr. Hare; in fact, he graciously invited me to join him and the conference organizers for dinner. He agreed that more needed to be done to educate the general pubic about the problem of psychopaths. He also agreed to let me refer to his work on Lovefraud.com. It was an important step in preparing to launch the website.

Our moving sale would be in Terry's apartment, and for three weeks he lived amid our growing inventory. We had a lot of quality stuff—duplicate household appliances, too many decorator pieces, extra furniture. "When this is over," Terry promised me, "we'll go someplace nice to celebrate."

The sale was slated to start October 23, 2004, at 9 a.m. Our first customer arrived before 8 a.m. We expected this—the real buyers always showed up early, and the guy took all of Terry's Japanese vases and several other collectibles. People were in and out all day; we must have had more than 100 customers. We sold just about everything and made $1,700.

The next day, Terry rented a truck to bring the remaining big items to Atlantic City, including the pillow-top mattress that he bought before moving into his townhouse. The two of us manhandled the heavy, queen-sized mattress out of his apartment, into the truck, into my house and upstairs to the bedroom. With that, Terry was officially living with me.

Terry kept his promise for a celebration by getting tickets to see Acoustic Alchemy, a contemporary instrumental band fronted by two acoustic guitar players. The show was at Zanzibar Blue in Philadelphia on Saturday, October 30, 2004, and before it, we had a reservation for dinner at the swanky Grill Room in the Ritz-Carlton Hotel. To get there on time, we planned to leave at 4:30 p.m.

At 4:10 p.m., I was still at my desk. Terry was antsy, but I knew I would be ready on time. My outfit was laid out—I was wearing my black knit pants and tank top, covered by a beaded, sapphire-blue overshirt. All I had to do was put on my makeup.

"Are you ready?" Terry asked, impatiently pacing in his suit, tailored shirt and tie.

"Almost," I replied, as I sat at my dressing table. "I can't find my mascara."

A minute later, he walked into the bedroom carrying a narrow tube. "Is this what you're looking for?" he asked. "It was in the bathroom."

"Yes," I replied, although I didn't know how it got into the bathroom—I always put on makeup at the dressing table. I quickly finished, and was ready to leave at 4:34 p.m.

We pulled up in front of the Ritz-Carlton. The building was once a bank, and had the same classic architecture that we saw at the Roman Maison Carrée in Nîmes, France—six massive columns, topped by Ionic capitals, supporting a triangular pediment. A uniformed doorman smiled and held the door as we walked into the domed marble rotunda, now a lounge. We turned right to the restaurant, which also had a traditional, sophisticated look—high ceilings, crystal chandeliers, Oriental carpets, long white tablecloths and Chippendale-style chairs.

We were seated in a booth along the wall. The maitre d', a woman, unfolded the napkins onto our laps with a flourish. Our waiter was a middle-aged man who looked like he'd been working in sophisticated restaurants for decades. He asked if we'd like something to drink.

"We're having champagne tonight," Terry replied.

That was fine with me—I liked champagne. For dinner, I ordered a field green salad and wild sea bass. Terry ordered a salad with warm goat cheese and pork loin. In our dinner conversation, Terry complimented me, talking about how determined I was, and how I overcame all the crap that was thrown my way.

Suddenly, I had a flash of intuition: Terry was going to propose.

We finished our dinner and champagne, then decided to share dessert— warm chocolate cake with nut ice cream. I excused myself to use the ladies' room. When I returned to the table, the waiter had refolded my napkin. I sat down and opened it on my lap, in anticipation of our sweet dessert.

It was far sweeter than I expected.

"You know I love you," Terry said. "And I want to marry you." He put a small black velvet jewelry box on the table.

Despite my intuitive flash, I stared at the box in total disbelief. The only words that came out of my mouth were, "Thank you."

"Will you marry me?" Terry asked.

"Yes, of course," I said, still dazed. I looked up at him, then down at the box. "Open it."

"Thank you," I said again, reaching for the box. Inside was a beautiful diamond solitaire. We never discussed marriage. Terry never dropped a hint that he was thinking about marriage. I was in shock.

"It's a little more than one carat," he said. "A beautiful diamond for your beautiful heart. And your beautiful soul."

I just sat there looking at the ring in the box. "Thank you," I repeated.

"Put it on."

The ring fit perfectly. I modeled the diamond for Terry.

"It looks beautiful on you," he said.

"Thank you," I answered. It was all I could say.

"By the way, we're staying here tonight."

"We are?" I asked, totally surprised again.

"That's why your mascara was missing. I was running around grabbing a few things for you. I know you need your mascara."

"Oh, that's why I couldn't find it. Did you get a case for my contact lenses?"

Terry had forgotten about that. But the Ritz had toothbrushes and bathrobes, and they'd go to the store for a contact lens case and solution. He'd been planning the surprise, planning to propose, ever since he decided to move into my house. "I'm not going to be the live-in guy," he said. "I love you, and I'm not afraid to commit to you."

After dinner we walked, or perhaps floated, a few blocks down Broad Street to Zanzibar Blue. The performance by Acoustic Alchemy was wonderful, but my happiness was even more wonderful. My heart overflowed with joy. I kept looking at the diamond on my finger. It was still there. And unlike the gaudy engagement ring with the fake stone that I received from James Montgomery, the gem from Terry Kelly was real.

Chapter 33

Lovefraud.com was almost ready to launch. The basic design was complete; I was working with my webmaster to add content and fine-tune the website's functionality. On November 4, 2004, I sent him an e-mail: I wanted Lovefraud to go live by the end of the year.

Then I had an idea. The purpose of Lovefraud was to teach people how to recognize sociopaths. What better way to do that than to show one in action? I posted on Lovefraud a video clip from my wedding to James Montgomery—the toast of gratitude that he made to my family.

"I'm supposed to be thanking the parents of the bride," James had proclaimed. "I never got to meet, one of the sad things of my life, I never got to meet Donna's mother. Those of my friends who got to meet Donna over the last six months or so are absolutely spellbound by this incredible creature that I've married.

"To her parents, and more than her parents, to her complete family, to her two brothers and her sister, somewhere along the line, we all start with the same genes, and they did something so special with this lady, it is absolutely incredible. My heartfelt thanks go out to the people that created my Donna for me. I'd ask you to drink a toast now to the parents, and the family, the Andersens."

James spoke with such conviction, such seemingly sincere gratitude, that anyone would believe he was totally in love with me. But it was all a setup, carefully calculated to keep me funding his dreams of grandeur, as well as his trysts with other women. The video showed how convincingly sociopaths lie.

James used a continuous stream of lies to snare me: He had $2 million to $3 million in assets, when in reality he had no money at all. He was a Special Forces commando mentioned in the *Rogue Warrior* book. I read it—no Australian, no James Montgomery. He rowed in the 1964 Olympics in Mexico. James didn't even get the country right—the 1964 Olympics were in Japan. And all those messages of congratulations from VIPs that Archie Turner, James' longtime co-conspirator, read at the wedding were also lies. Either Archie or James made them up.

From time to time since I gave up my campaign to collect money from

James, I searched the Internet just to see if I could locate him. I did find ads that he posted—through much of 2003, James trolled for investors for his schools in China. I tried searching again on November 26, 2004, typing "James Montgomery" into Google.

I found a James Montgomery who was a blues harmonica player with bands like the Allman Brothers, a James Montgomery who was a 19th century British poet, and a James Montgomery Flagg, who was a 20th century American artist and illustrator. On about the 15th page of search results, I found a listing that said, "James Montgomery – New man at the helm." I clicked the link and read:

James Montgomery is the new man at the helm of the National Radio News service.

> While he has never had the distinction of working as a reporter, he has earned a living as a writer and media executive for the last three decades. He was a founder of the E! for Entertainment Cable TV Network in Hollywood and CBS:Sportsline.com in Fort Lauderdale – one of the first commercial websites.

Whoa! I'd heard those claims before. I kept reading.

> He spent fifteen years in advertising with Grey and Tinker in Sydney, Melbourne NY and Asia. He started his own agency in Melbourne and it reached top five billings status. He and Phillip Adams pioneered the Ad Degree Course at RMIT in the '80s.
>
> James is considered by many of his peers to have been the Australian pioneer of modern media planning, developing such concepts as Reach and Frequency evaluations using mathematical formulae. He launched one of the first media buying services – Sprint – for Unilever over 25 years ago.
>
> He was a partner in IICE Studios in Sth. Melbourne – a full TV production studio with 30 hours of prime time credits in Australian doco's and 100's more in Network soap. In LA, he worked as a writer for Paramount on several TV series including the Star Trek's. He has several feature film credits as well.
>
> James returns to his position at Charles Sturt University's Bathurst campus (and to Australia) after 25+ years overseas in the States with the last half dozen in China. His American wife and dual citizen 6yo daughter live with him in a 19th Century terrace in 'the Paris end of Bathurst'.

At the end of the announcement was a photo—it was definitely my ex-husband, although James had stopped using brown-in-a-bottle. His beard, and what was left of his hair, were completely gray.

James obviously wrote the news release himself—I recognized both the sloppy style and the flagrant exaggerations. He still claimed to be a founder of E!, even though, according to Jody McClure, he was fired from its predecessor,

Movietime, for drinking on the job. He still claimed to be a founder of Sportsline, when he was only a paid consultant. And calling his television facility IICE Studios—what happened to Jaypat Productions? Perhaps he didn't really want to be found; I assumed that when he left Australia, he owed people money. His television and movie credits? They belonged to Colleen Jessick.

I inferred from the announcement that my ex-husband's ventures in China had failed. That was no surprise, but I was amazed that James actually took a job. And I was ecstatic that the job was in Australia. Finally, he was within my reach. After waiting almost five years, I could serve James Montgomery with my $1.25 million judgment against him.

I immediately contacted my solicitor in Sydney, Australia, Leon Davis. We agreed that our first step was to hire a private investigator. I forwarded all the contact information I'd accumulated about James—his name, possible aliases, e-mail addresses, all past home addresses, wife's name, daughter's name, U.S. drivers license number, Australian passport number, bank accounts that I knew about, business addresses in New Zealand, known business partners, and information James posted himself on his America Online profile, in which he listed his interests as, "pubs, pubs, pubs." The document was 14 pages long—plenty of information for the investigators. I also sent a photo—the one of James and his long-time associate, Archie Turner, surrounded by weapons.

The investigation report came in on December 8, 2004. James Montgomery was, in fact, employed by Charles Sturt University. He lived in Bathurst, in a rented house. Bathurst was the oldest inland city in Australia, located about two and a half hours from Sydney. It was famous for the Mount Panorama motor racing circuit—a racetrack that used public roads—but with a population of 30,000, it was even smaller than Atlantic City. My ex-husband, it seemed, lived in the boonies.

The investigators searched Australian business records—James had been a director and shareholder of numerous Australian companies in the 1980s, but they were all delisted years earlier. A search for bank accounts revealed two. One had a balance of $99, the other a balance of $107. The bottom line: James had no assets.

Still, I was not letting him off the hook. I wanted to serve my judgment and perhaps force him into bankruptcy. I wanted him to face consequences for what he had done to me and the other women he swindled.

This required reactivating my case against James in the Supreme Court of New South Wales, Australia. Not to jeopardize the case, my attorneys advised me to delay launching Lovefraud.com.

Terry and I settled into a pleasant living-together routine. We usually had trouble getting out of bed in the morning because we'd rather stay there and cuddle. After pulling ourselves from beneath the covers, we each made our own breakfast and then went to work—me in my office, Terry at his desk in the basement rec room. We ate lunch together, went back to work and met again for dinner. Then sometimes we went to the gym, sometimes we watched TV.

But we also had an important event coming up. How would we get married?

We didn't want a big ceremony. In fact, we seriously considered standing before a judge with a couple of witnesses. But as soon as I told my father that Terry proposed, he was so happy for me, and so excited, that I knew we had to have a real wedding and reception. After all I'd been through, my family wanted to share my joy.

Terry thought it would be romantic to get married on Valentine's Day. A February wedding would also allow us to go someplace warm and relaxing—like the Caribbean—for our honeymoon, which was a priority. I knew from experience that planning a winter wedding was easy—the officiants, banquet halls and musicians were usually available. So we lined up our honeymoon first. We rented a cottage for a week on St. John in the U.S. Virgin Islands, from February 15 through 22, 2005. Then we turned our attention to the wedding, and by mid-December settled on a ceremony and luncheon at the Seaview Resort in Galloway Township, New Jersey, outside of Atlantic City. It would be a small affair—only 30 guests—on Saturday, February 12, 2005, the closest we could get to Valentine's Day. Invitations were in the mail before Christmas.

We found a non-denominational minister to perform our ceremony. We hired a jazz duo—piano and upright bass—for the music. We finalized the luncheon menu. Everything was coming together, and on January 13, 2005, a month before the big day, I figured I'd better find a wedding dress.

I didn't want a gown, just a fancy dress. I went to a store that specialized in eveningwear and prom gowns, then to a local bridal salon—no luck. A salesgirl suggested the King of Prussia mall, located on the other side of Philadelphia. That was a major excursion, so I sent an e-mail to my sister, Tracy: Did she want to go shopping with me the following Sunday?

The next morning, Tracy sent me links to wedding dresses available from Nordstrom.com. She picked one out. I liked it. The dress was only $170, I could have it in three days and Nordstrom offered free exchanges. I bought it.

On January 17, 2005—a day shy of what would have been my eighth wedding anniversary if I were still married to James—the dress arrived. It fit perfectly and looked beautiful.

That evening, I commented in my journal about how well everything was going—I located James; my business was doing well; Terry's business was doing well. I felt an energy shift, and good things kept happening. Guidance agreed:

> *Yes, your energy is running high, which is helping us to arrange all these good things for you. You have far more to do with it than you realize—by your energy, your love, your desire, your passion, you are making it all come to fruition. That is the real secret. We are guides—we are not creators. You are the creator. We can nudge, we can help, we can create opportunities, but you must actually do the creating.*

Once again, my statement of claim was filed with the Australian court. The lawyers converted the amount of my New Jersey judgment to Australian dollars—it totaled A$1,654,339. They added interest, at 9 percent per year, going back to the date of the original judgment, for an additional A$756,880. On January 20, 2005, my attorney sent the claim to the investigators so that it could be placed, in compliance with the law, directly into the hands of James Montgomery.

The process server went to James' home on February 1, 2005, at 12:54 p.m. He was told there was no James Montgomery at that address—there was a Janna Montgomery, who was a six-year-old girl. The agent left, called his boss, and was advised to return the documents to the office. They e-mailed a report to Leon, my solicitor, and he forwarded it to me.

What a bunch of idiots!

I quickly banged out a reply. They were the ones who found James Montgomery's address! Of course there's a six-year-old named Janna Montgomery living there—I told them that! Didn't they give the agent the information I provided? Didn't they give the agent their own report?

The answer was no—one part of the company didn't know what the other part was doing. Leon blasted them, and told them to get the papers served.

Two days later, we heard from the company again. The agent called Charles Sturt University, and the university confirmed that James Montgomery was employed there, but would not reveal exactly where he worked without a formal written request from my solicitor. Could he please draft a letter?

By this time I felt like we were dealing with the Keystone Kops. James was the manager of the National Radio News Network—he posted it on the Internet! Once again, it appeared, the company had not conveyed all the information to the agent. Leon sent another nastygram—no, we weren't going to write a letter, and if the company didn't get the claim served we would sue them.

Finally, on February 7, 2005, we got the good news—the agent went to Charles Sturt University and served James personally with my statement of claim. He had 28 days to respond. There was nothing for me to do, except get married.

The Seaview Resort exuded an air of stately elegance. Founded as the Seaview Country Club in 1914, the building looked like a turn-of-the-century mansion in brilliant white. It featured classic, symmetrical Georgian architecture—a two-story main building with a central porte cochere, flanked at each end by large oval rooms with walls of windows. In one of them, called, appropriately, the Oval Room, Terry and I would get married.

On our wedding day, February 12, 2005, bright sunlight warmed the cold winter air. Terry and I arrived at Seaview together at 10:30 a.m. for photos before the ceremony. My husband-to-be looked handsome in his black tux; white shirt; black vest with small, shimmering white dots; and a solid red tie. His boutonniere was a red rose.

My wedding dress was a sleeveless, tea-length white silk shift, accented by subtle white appliquéd flowers, tiny crystal beads and white sequins. It featured a V-neckline in both the front and back, and a long, loose ruffle created an asymmetrical hemline that fluttered as I walked. I carried a small, natural-style bouquet of red roses, pink carnations, white alstroemeria and purple heather.

Our photographer, Bill Horin, positioned us at windows, in front of drapes, next to flowers, even reclining on a classic wicker chaise, capturing our happiness with his camera. We posed for an hour of photos, then I was hustled off to a side room, stocked with drinks and fruit, while Terry greeted our arriving guests. Shortly after noon, they were all seated, and Terry and I stood together at the French doors leading into the Oval Room. The pianist played the sweetly melodic *Air on the G String,* by J. S. Bach, as we slowly walked down the aisle between our seated guests.

Sunlight streamed through the big wall of windows, creating a warm glow that filled the room. In front of the windows, between two massive arrangements of roses and other flowers, our minister awaited us. When we met with the minister before our wedding, she asked us to write secret love letters to each other. She started our ceremony by reading our love letters.

Dear Terry,

How do I describe what I feel for you? I'm a writer, I should be able to do this—but I cannot put words to the love. I can only put words to the effects: a spontaneous smile, as I think of how you make me laugh. An urge to reach out and hold your hand, for no particular reason. An overload of joy and happiness, so that my heart feels like it is about to burst.

Six years ago, on February 12, 1999, I left a sham of a marriage. That was a different life. Today my life is so full of love that I call everyone "sweetheart"—you, family and friends, our pets, even my customers. Everyone will just have to get used to it. The love spills out, unbidden, because of the love I feel for you, and from you. You're my sweetheart, and today, you'll be my husband.

My Precious Donna,

My love for you is always present. It is there wherever I go or whatever I do. Ever since we met, time has disappeared. Our love is beyond time. It is beyond the limits of the universe. It is timeless. It is eternal.

Your love for me is the most precious gift that I have ever been given. Moments shared with you are like priceless gems that can never be replaced and never be forgotten. Our love for each other is a sanctuary in this world of uncertainty. Donna, it is my honor to marry you, to be closer to you and to forever love you.

I was deeply touched by Terry's words. Standing next to him, I squeezed his hand, and smiled into his eyes. The man who was about to become my husband was honestly romantic and poetic. I was so full of love, real love, that I could barely contain it.

The minister addressed our small assembly, reminding everyone that love was what gave precious meaning to life. Marriage was the union created by love, a union of privilege and responsibility that should be entered into thoughtfully, with an understanding of its true commitment.

This time, I knew, the commitment was real.

I tried to soak in every word and emotion. I wanted to be fully in the moment, experiencing everything that happened deeply, turning the day into a precious memory that I could recall at any time.

After more prayers, the actual marriage ceremony began. The minister handed me a flute of champagne—we'd upgraded from wine—which I sipped. I then gave it to Terry, so he could sip from the same cup, symbolizing how we would go forward and experience life as one.

Then it was time for our vows. As Terry placed the wedding ring on my finger, he repeated after the minister:

"I, Terry, give you, Donna, this ring to wear upon your hand as a symbol of our unity and of my everlasting love for you. You are my beloved and my best friend. I choose you now, Donna, to be my wife, my partner in life and my one true love."

Placing Terry's wedding ring on his finger, I repeated the same vows. I wasn't a bit nervous or hesitant, which surprised me. I felt happy and confident that my life was moving toward more love, support and connectedness than I had ever known.

The minister offered more prayers for holy union and finally made her pronouncement. "I declare you, Donna and Terry, to be life partners and husband and wife," she said, "married in accordance with the laws of the State of New Jersey. You may now kiss the bride!"

Terry and I kissed joyfully, then turned to accept the congratulations and applause of our guests. We stepped back down the aisle, between our families and close friends, while our duo played the *Wedding March*. I was beaming—the bliss in my heart apparent on my face. Oh, I was happy during and after my two weddings with James. But then I was happy because I thought I'd finally met society's expectations of me as a woman. This wedding was far different. When I married Terry, it was the natural expression of the wonderful love that flowed, and overflowed, between us. Our marriage was a proclamation that we made to each other. Society's expectations were irrelevant.

After the ceremony, Terry and I laughed and chatted with our guests over drinks and hors d'oeuvres in the lobby lounge, just outside the French doors, while the Seaview staff prepared the Oval Room for our luncheon. An hour later, with our guests at their tables, the pianist introduced the new "Mr. and Mrs. Terry Kelly!" We made our entrance and danced our first dance as a married couple to *Can't Help Falling in Love with You,* by Elvis Presley. We selected the song because Terry always said to me, "I love you. I can't help it."

Halfway through, the pianist invited our guests to join us on the dance floor. Everyone did—our families and friends were thrilled to celebrate with us. The music continued, and Terry and I danced again. Then I danced with Dad to *What a Wonderful World,* by Louis Armstrong. He, of course, showcased his talent by dancing to practically every song; almost every lady in the room had a whirl.

After a champagne toast, we sat down to a lunch of field greens salad, pastry wrapped salmon and oven-poached prawns. Everything was delicious. As the reception drew to a close, Terry and I cut our three-layer wedding cake. The entire top layer was untouched—we took it home to freeze and enjoy later, a luscious reminder of our lovely wedding day.

As we left Seaview, it was only 3:30 p.m., so we suggested moving the party to the Quarter, the new Cuban-themed dining and retail wing at the Tropicana Casino in Atlantic City. Terry and I, along with half of our guests, went there for more cocktails, snacks, conversation and laughs.

The day was wonderful, but by early evening, my husband and I were exhausted. We went home and soon fell asleep. The next morning, though, after our typical Sunday breakfast of turkey bacon and eggs, we had much more energy. It was finally time for our wedding night. Just as we were getting romantic in bed, we heard footsteps coming up the porch stairs and the front door opening.

"Hello, are you decent?"

It was my sister, Tracy, and her date, stopping by to say hello.

"Well, not really," I called down from the bedroom. Laughing, Terry and I found some clothes.

"Sorry to interrupt your sex life," she joked. "We thought we gave you enough time."

They visited for 20 minutes, then got up to leave. "Carry on," Tracy said as she was going out the door.

We did—passionately and joyfully.

St. John had no airport. Sixty percent of St. John, in the U.S. Virgin Islands, was preserved in its natural state as a national park. To get to the island, we flew into neighboring St. Thomas on February 15, 2005, and took a ferry to Cruz Bay. We were met at the dock by the rental agent for our cottage, or "villa" as it was called, who escorted us to the car rental office, about two blocks away. Our vehicle for the week was a Suzuki Vitara SUV with four-wheel drive, which, I soon learned, was absolutely essential.

Our villa was right in the middle of the island, near the Center Line Road. The property owner arrived; we were to follow her to the house. But first I wanted to stop at a food store to pick up some essentials. She took us to a small market, where we bought orange juice, eggs, tofu, red peppers, bread, milk and coffee, along with beer, wine and rum, all at amazingly high prices.

The villa was five miles from Cruz Bay. The entire trip was a white-knuckle ride.

The island of St. John was volcanic in origin, and the terrain was rocky and mountainous. The two-lane road to our villa on Bordeaux Mountain, the highest point of the island, never went in a straight line for more than 30 yards. We drove up steep grades, through hairpin turns and switchbacks, and near the edge of cliffs with no guardrails. Plus we were driving on the left side of the road, although the car was left-hand drive, so when oncoming cars raced around a bend, not quite staying in their lane, they were headed right for me in the passenger seat.

At one point, while trying to keep up with our landlady, who was probably driving a little more than 25 mph, we had to completely stop to let a pig cross the road. As we reached the interior of the island, there were no more houses or animals, but thousands of trees. Our landlady waited for us on Center Line Road at the beginning of the driveway to our villa. Terry pulled up behind her. "Put your jeep in four-wheel drive," she said, and then led us down the driveway, which was a dirt road between the trees, rutted and full of rocks, descending at a steep angle that seemed to be nearly 40 degrees. We reached a small dirt ledge, where we made a three-point turn to go sharply to the right, and continued down another incline to the house.

I was truly terrified.

Terry parked the SUV, and I emerged, shaking. "I never would have booked this house if I knew about the driveway," I complained to the owner. "This place should have a warning label on it."

She felt badly, and asked if we wanted to go someplace else. I knew that the chances of finding another villa were slim—we were in St. John at the highest of the high season, and had been lucky to reserve anything at all. If I were going to enjoy my honeymoon—which I wanted to do—I needed an attitude adjustment.

The villa itself was charming and secluded. We had no neighbors around us, only trees. The small, West Indian-style home was one story, with yellow walls and a red metal roof. Inside, the diminutive kitchen had half-size appliances, a small table and a wicker loveseat. Beyond it was the bathroom with a large, Caribbean-style shower—no door or curtain, but a window open to the outside. The bedroom, which was the last room in the house, featured an antique Jamaican four-poster bed covered with colorful green and yellow linens. The bed was so high that I had to hoist myself onto it.

The property's best and most endearing feature, however, was the view. Clinging to the edge of Bordeaux Mountain, the villa offered a breathtaking vista to the east of Coral Bay, the sea, and in the distance, the British Virgin Islands. To capitalize on the view, a porch extended along the entire front of the house, and both the bedroom and kitchen had large windows facing the sunrise.

The sun, however, was behind us—it was early evening. I was thankful that we stopped at the market, but wished we'd bought more substantial food, because I was too scared to venture out again and look for a restaurant, especially in the dark. Terry, my sweetheart, humored me, and for the first dinner of our honeymoon, we ate eggs.

Sunrise was spectacular. The sky began to brighten around 5:30 a.m. Lying in bed, Terry and I could see the outline of clouds low on the horizon. Gradually, the sky melted from gray to yellow and gold, silhouetting the distant islands. Around 6:15, beams of sunlight began to pierce the clouds. Nature's show was so beautiful, and so romantic, that Terry and I were inspired to romance as well.

This was paradise.

We ate breakfast on the porch, which, by 8 a.m., started to get hot. It was time for us to begin the day's excursions, which meant backing the SUV up the driveway. I wasn't ready for that adventure, so I walked up the driveway to the point where it made a right angle.

Terry started the SUV, put it in reverse, stepped on the gas—and went nowhere. Wheels spun, dirt and pebbles flew, but he made no progress. While I watched anxiously from above, my husband rocked the vehicle back and forth. Finally, he figured out the problem—the four-wheel drive needed to be set to low, not high, in order to get enough traction to make it up the mountain.

Whew! We got on the road and drove to Cruz Bay—with a population of about 2,700, it was the biggest town on the island. Our objective was to find out where to go snorkeling. The beaches along the North Shore of St. John were among the most popular in the Caribbean, but on that day, we learned at the National Park Service headquarters, even though it was clear and sunny, the water on the North Shore was too rough for snorkeling. The ranger recommended that we go to Salt Pond Bay on the South Shore.

We drove along the North Shore to get there. Periodically, the roadway widened to form scenic overlooks, and we stopped at every one of them. Each view was like a post card: Deep blue or turquoise water dotted with white boats at anchor. Narrow, curving strips of sandy beaches along the water's edge. Hills covered with trees. Blue sky with fluffy white clouds. Yes, indeed, it was paradise.

At Salt Pond Bay, we found an underwater paradise. Snorkeling was easy— we just walked into the water from the beach, put on our masks and immediately saw tropical fish. We swam along a coral reef, and then swam out past a few boats that were moored in the bay.

After a lovely afternoon, we walked back to the parking lot, which was a quarter mile from the beach. As we loaded our SUV, a middle-aged couple approached us. They'd missed the island's bus, and asked if we could give them a ride to Skinny Legs, which was a bar. We hadn't heard of it. The couple visited St. John often, and Skinny Legs, they said, had the best hamburgers on the island.

"Why don't we go there and get hamburgers?" I suggested to Terry. Although my fear of St. John's roads was diminishing, I still wasn't ready to search for a restaurant at night.

Skinny Legs was in Coral Bay, St. John's other town, and was more of a local haunt than a tourist attraction. Although called a "complex," the place was a series of adjoining shacks, with the bar at its center. A large, L-shaped wooden bench defined the edge of the room; approximately 10 tables filled the space between the bench and the actual bar. One wall was open to the elements, and the roof was actually an old sail.

The patrons must have come from central casting. Several weathered old guys in hats and shorts looked like they'd been leaning against the bar for decades. A heavyset young girl had long dark blond hair, about the color of mine, which she wore in Rastafarian braids. One guy literally looked like a pirate—he was slight and wiry, with a serious tan, a long gray beard and a red bandana on his head.

We ordered the world-famous Skinny Legs hamburgers, and they were, indeed, delicious. Then we walked around and looked at the shops that occupied the shacks. One of them was a booking agent for snorkeling trips to the British Virgin Islands, and Terry signed us up for an excursion the next day.

At 8:30 a.m. on February 17, 2005, we were at the dock next to the National Forest Service headquarters in Cruz Bay, waiting for our boat. The *Limnos V* pulled up—a 53-foot powerboat with twin hulls and two decks. I sat on the top deck, with my hair blowing in the wind, as we cruised along the North Shore of St. John, past Tortola and other islands, to Virgin Gorda in the British Virgin Islands.

We docked at the Spanish Town Harbor, and a "safari taxi" transported us to the Baths of Virgin Gorda at the southern tip of the island. This was a geological formation from the island's volcanic past—massive granite boulders were deposited on the beach in an ancient explosion and eroded over time. The boulders created numerous grottoes, arches, caves and tidal pools, all linked together like a maze. Terry and I, along with hundreds of other tourists, made our way through the maze, squatting and crawling through tight places, holding onto rope handrails attached to the boulders, climbing up and down ladders. Finally we reached Devil's Bay Beach, where we swam in turquoise water.

We returned to our boat, where the crew served us lunch. Afterwards, we set off for Norman Island, which was believed to be the inspiration for the classic book by Robert Lewis Stevenson, *Treasure Island*. The captain threw bread into the water, and an entire school of silver fish leapt to the surface. All 27 passengers on our boat, plus several crewmembers, jumped into the water for snorkeling; the fish had no fear. Sergeant major fish—silver with black stripes and a touch of yellow—approached to check us out. We swam by caves carved into the bluffs, and saw black spiny sea urchins attached to the rocks. Our tour allowed an hour for snorkeling, and Terry and I were the last ones out of the water.

Archeologists determined that St. John was first settled around 300 A.D. by indigenous people who migrated from coastal South America. Sometime before Christopher Columbus sailed to the New World, these people carved dozens of petroglyphs into the rock around a freshwater pool on the island. The only way to see the petroglyphs was to hike there, which we decided to do on February 18, 2005.

One of the trails to the petroglyphs started at Lameshur Bay on the south coast. We were told we could drive there, but once we got past Salt Pond Bay, the pavement ended and the road became a track of rutted dirt embedded with sharp rocks. It was astonishingly rough—I expected us to blow a tire, or bust the shock absorbers, at any moment.

We made it to the bay and parked, then started our hike to the petroglyphs, which was also rough. Footing was precarious on the two-mile trail; I had to pay close attention to where I stepped. We hiked up a hill, passing tall cacti and massive century plants, foliage typical of dry climates. Dark brown, solid masses, about the size of five-gallon buckets, hung in some trees. They turned out to be termite nests.

On the downward slope of the hill, the climate was noticeably more moist, and when we reached the petroglyphs, it was downright lush. Although our destination was called a waterfall, when we were there, the water was a thin trickle dripping down the rocks into a pool, and eventually into a second, lower pool. On the boulders between the pools, we could make out the petroglyphs, although they were faint from the passage of time. The predominant symbol that the ancient people carved into the rock resembled a smile that curled in upon itself at both ends. I wondered what it meant, and imagined the people who lived on St. John 1,000 years earlier attributing mystical qualities to the lovely waterfall in the cool, quiet woods.

After a pleasant rest, we hiked back to Lameshur Bay for more snorkeling. The fish we saw were exquisite. A few hours later, we stopped once again for dinner at Skinny Legs. My theory that it was a local haunt was confirmed—the people we saw a few days earlier where there again. Or still.

The next day, we went back into Cruz Bay. At a dive shop, I bought new fins and reef walker shoes. Then Terry pulled me into a jewelry store—a sign in the window said, "Petroglyph Jewelry." The jewelry designer said that the symbols had spiritual significance, and according to legend, they were tattooed on women's breasts. He showed us a bracelet—a simple, narrow gold band with a petroglyph symbol as the clasp. It was beautiful, and Terry bought it for me as a wedding gift.

The place to be on Sundays, we heard, was Miss Lucy's Jazz Brunch on Friis Bay. Miss Lucy's did not accept reservations, so it was important to get there early. Terry and I arrived before 10 a.m., and plenty of people were already there, seated outside at plastic tables, waiting. We scored one of the tables on the patio, under a tree.

While Terry was off taking photographs, I noticed a couple searching for seats. By this time, still before the restaurant opened, there were no more empty tables, so I invited them to join us. Terry and I ordered half a bottle of champagne, and our new friends ordered the other half. Over our meals—I selected salmon; Terry had crab eggs Benedict—we told the couple we were on our honeymoon, and they generously bought our champagne for us.

This got us on the topic of weddings, and the man told us that his daughter had married someone who turned out to have a hidden drug addiction.

"My first marriage was also a disaster," I said. "I married a sociopath."

"What's a sociopath?" the woman asked.

"It's someone with no conscience," I explained, and gave a few examples of my ex-husband's outrageous behavior. I'd soon be launching a website called Lovefraud.com, I told her, to educate people about the dangers of sociopaths. The couple listened intently, confirming my belief that there was a tremendous need for the information that Lovefraud would provide.

After brunch, Terry and I checked out another snorkeling spot, Leinster Bay on the North Shore. As we waded into the water, the skies clouded up and it started to drizzle. We were wet anyway, so it wasn't a big deal, until I got cold. We left, and were home and showered by mid-afternoon. With nothing else to do, we put our high Jamaican bed to good use again. After all, that's what honeymoons were for.

The next day, February 21, 2005, was the last full day of our honeymoon. We planned to go to Trunk Bay, considered the most spectacular snorkeling location on St. John, but again, the water was too rough. So we drove the rugged road back to Lameshur Bay, near the petroglyph trail, put down our towels in the shade under a tree, and started our last snorkeling adventure.

The rocks and coral beds of Lameshur Bay teemed with fish—we saw tangs, sergeant majors, butterfly fish and other species that I couldn't name. Tiny specks in the water, I realized, were babies—thousands of them, or perhaps millions. In one location, adult fish were obviously guarding juveniles as they munched on algae attached to the rocks. They must have been guarding the young ones from predators like squid and barracuda, because they certainly weren't afraid of humans.

After a lovely, relaxing day, we left to shower and dress for dinner. For only the second time, we were going to a nice restaurant—a few days earlier, on Saturday night, we ate at Chateau Bordeaux, which was close to our villa. This time, we had reservations at Asolare in Cruz Bay. We heard it was excellent.

During our entire week in St. John, we saw spectacular sunrises. Asolare faced west, overlooking Cruz Bay, so on our final night, we enjoyed an equally dramatic sunset, accompanied by a nice bottle of champagne. We both ordered the special—sea bass topped with scallops. Terry said it was the best sea bass he ever ate. To top off our exquisite dinner, we shared a dessert—a fruit-filled spring roll with a scoop of ice cream.

Terry and I talked about how much we enjoyed our honeymoon, and how much in love we were. We both felt so lucky, so blessed, to have finally found each other. When we finished our delightful meal, it was after 8 p.m. Terry drove us home over St. John's twisting, turning roads in the dark, and I was no longer afraid.

Chapter 34

James retained a Bathurst lawyer to defend himself from my legal action against him. I could picture my ex-husband, full of righteous outrage, spinning his own, creative version of our divorce. It must have been a good story, because the letter from his lawyer, dated February 18, 2005, was ludicrous.

My judgment against James, the lawyer wrote, "may have been obtained in breach of due process and the principles of natural justice." On the breakdown of the marriage, the lawyer said, James had already left New Jersey for China with nothing but the clothes on his back, and was not properly notified of my claims against him, nor of the court's orders. Yeah, right.

"Presently," the lawyer wrote, "our client is a university lecturer on a disproportionately small salary for a man of his credentials and experience. He has a wife and child to support, and lives from paycheque to paycheque." I laughed about the reference to credentials and experience, but living hand-to-mouth—that was probably true.

The size of my claim—A\$2,411,220—was absurd, the lawyer wrote, because James never had that kind of money. My ex-husband had no way to pay any part of my claim, and if I obtained a judgment against him, he would file for bankruptcy. Then, the lawyer made a settlement offer: I should drop my claim, pay James' legal fees and no other money would exchange hands.

What a deal! How could I possibly turn it down?

I did. In my letter back to my Australian solicitor, Leon Davis, I reiterated that James was in Florida, not China, when he was served with divorce papers. He originally retained a lawyer but refused to comply with any court order. Then he dismissed the attorney, represented himself and defaulted. He was found guilty of fraud, ordered to repay all the money that he took from me, plus US\$1million in punitive damages. I had documentation to prove all of it. I wanted to move forward. If James declared bankruptcy because of the case, that was fine with me.

My solicitor demanded a declaration of James's assets. He had a 1995 Holden Statesman—a 10-year-old luxury car with 143,000 miles on it, valued at A\$8,500. He had a 1984 Ford Falcon station wagon with 186,000 miles, valued at A$1,000. His furniture was worth A$400.

On the liabilities side, James had a loan for A$19,500 secured by the Holden, two unsecured loans totaling A$22,750, and he owed A$3,500 for rented appliances. Obviously, his bad behavior with credit had not changed.

James said he earned A$3,150 per month after taxes, which was all the money he had to service the debts and support himself, his wife and child. His wife wasn't contributing financially because, James said, she was not permitted to work in Australia.

Yep, the man was broke, and I hoped to make him more broke. I instructed my solicitor to proceed with my claim.

The pictures from our wedding day captured the happiness and joy Terry and I felt, and when I went for a session with Elaine Anderson on April 5, 2005, I showed them to her.

"I'm so happy for you and Terry," Elaine said as she turned the pages of our album. "You really could have shut down with all that happened to you. I was worried about that for awhile."

I told Elaine what transpired since I last saw her in October. Terry proposed. I found James on the Internet. My lawyers finally served him with my claim. I rejected his offer to settle, and was waiting for his next move. "It feels like the momentum is really gathering," I said.

"Yes, it does," she agreed.

I lay on the table, and Elaine barely got the music on before she started talking. No opening ceremony, no "we invite Guidance."

"I'm feeling like there are two different parts of you," she said. "There's a part of you that doesn't want to face James, doesn't want to get involved with him again. It doesn't feel like there's anything wrong, but I'd like you to acknowledge it."

I couldn't sense what she was talking about right away, but then I got a twinge in my stomach. "It feels like nausea," I said. "Disgust."

I noticed energy trapped in the back of my body—the back of my head, my neck, my shoulders and my legs. All those muscles were compressing. Then my head started twitching to the right.

"What are you looking at?" Elaine asked. "What do you want to see?"

"I'm looking over my shoulder, watching my back."

Every time I dealt with James, in all those lifetimes, I got stabbed in the back. I never knew what he was doing behind my back. He was deceitful behind my back. So that's where the energy was trapped—in my back. As it slowly drained off, my right hand started moving of its own accord.

"Important messages are coming through your right hand," Elaine said. "What does the movement mean?" She was sitting on my left side and couldn't see my hand.

"Writing," I said. "Taking action. Getting things done. Working on the project."

The motion continued for awhile, then changed. My hand started going up and down, tapping the table rapidly. "Now what is the message?" Elaine asked.

"Clapping," I said. "Also running fast, keeping the pace up, like in a marathon."

My hand seemed to be controlled by an unseen force, and the movements were fast and repetitive. "This is really weird," I said. Elaine didn't say anything—nothing was weird to her.

The tapping went on, and then the motion changed again. I started scratching the tabletop, like I was digging a hole.

"What does it mean?" Elaine asked.

"Digging," I said. "Like planting."

"Planting seeds."

"I think I'm planting the whole farm."

"Yes. A lot of people are going to be touched by what you do."

Then the hand changed again. It turned open, palm up and drifted out to the right, so it was no longer on the table. Again, Elaine asked me what it meant.

"It's about receiving support," I said. My hand, floating in mid-air with fingers and palm outstretched, signified accepting invisible support. The energy of having to watch my back was released. This time, I was going to confront James head on, with clear knowledge of what he was.

In his Australian Service History document, James claimed he was part of the Australian Army Training Team Vietnam (AATTV). This was a small, specialized unit of the Australian army that provided training and assistance to South Vietnamese forces during the war. The team saw a lot of combat, and was believed to be the most decorated Australian unit to serve in Vietnam. I was certain James was lying about his involvement, but I had no proof.

While reviewing Australian military websites, I came across one called Australian and New Zealand Military Impostors, with the stated mission of exposing people who falsely claimed to be veterans. On April 20, 2005, I contacted the organization: James Montgomery claimed that he did two tours of Vietnam and earned the Victoria Cross for valor. He was active in U.S. veterans' organizations. But he was a con man, and I suspected that he fabricated his service history. Were they interested in investigating?

The next morning, I had a reply—yes, they were interested. Could I send documents and photos?

I certainly could, although, following my lawyers' advice related to Lovefraud.com, I wanted to wait until after my court case was finished. Then, perhaps, this organization could prove, once and for all, that James Montgomery was never in the military.

But I had second thoughts about my plan. I'd been reading *The Sociopath Next Door,* by Martha Stout, Ph.D. Fairly early in the book, she described the prime motivation of a sociopath: To win. These people did not feel normal human connections. They did not feel love, in fact, they felt no concern about other human beings at all. To them, the game was everything, and their only desire was to come out on top.

What did this mean regarding my court case against James?

As Terry and I finished dinner on May 7, 2005, I asked his advice. My original plan was to wait until the court case was over, then stir up more trouble for James with the Australian military organization. I'd also tell Robert Palmer, the man who was involved with James' school in New Zealand, about finding my ex-husband at Charles Sturt University. But maybe it was better not to wait. Maybe it would be best to make James fight on several fronts at once.

Terry agreed. "Hit him with everything you've got," he said. "This is war. That's how battles are lost—the enemy isn't hit hard enough." He then broke into a smile and did a little chair dance at the dining room table. "Go get him!"

We talked about it further, and could see no downside to sending the military documents and tipping off Robert Palmer right away. I would pursue James with my court case and push him into bankruptcy. Then let the real Vietnam veterans go after him as a military fraud. Then let Robert Palmer, with his stellar education connections, get him fired from his job.

I started to smile.

"I know that smile," Terry said. "It's the vengeance smile. Montgomery won't know what hit him—and it was the doormat. But a doormat going at 60 miles per hour hits pretty hard."

An investigator from the Australian and New Zealand Military Impostors (ANZMI) e-mailed me, requesting more information about James. His screen name was "Curtains," which made me laugh. I hoped it was a good omen, as in "Curtains for my ex-husband and his lying, cheating ways."

According to Curtains, Australia's Vietnam Veterans Nominal Roll—the list of soldiers who served in Vietnam—included a James Henry Montgomery and a Robert James Montgomery. Was either of them my husband? The answer was no.

I scanned the documents that Curtains wanted: James' Australian Service History, which listed his alleged tours of duty. His Mention in Dispatches, purportedly detailing how James earned the United States Silver Cross for bravery under fire. His notice from the Department of the Navy, supposedly recalling him, as a retired officer, to active duty. His Special Forces and Delta Force photo ID cards.

I also sent a package of documents to Robert Palmer. It turned out that Robert had already done his own investigation of James' military claims. He'd checked with Veterans Affairs authorities—no James A. Montgomery ever served in Vietnam; James had usurped the identity of a genuine war hero.

Curtains forwarded the ID card scans to other fraud busters in the United States. The Delta Force ID was preposterous, they said. No such unit officially existed—it certainly didn't issue ID cards. And James' photo on the Special Forces ID was identical. They surmised that James got two standard passport photos and fabricated the IDs himself.

This made perfect sense to Robert Palmer, because he'd already seen James award himself fake credentials. "He went from 'James Montgomery' to 'James Montgomery TPTC' - Trained Primary Teacher's Certificate - to 'Professor Montgomery' to 'Doctor Montgomery' in the space of six months, while in China," Robert wrote in an e-mail to Curtains and me.

The Australians, of course, were in a time zone 14 hours ahead of me, so they did their work while I slept. Every morning, the first thing I did was check my e-mail. I was sitting at my desk early in the morning on May 18, 2005, when Terry appeared at the door of my office.

"Any news from our guys in Australia?" he asked.

"I got an e-mail from Leon," I replied. "He hasn't heard from Montgomery, so he's filing a default judgment."

Terry did a little dance. "Pressure," he said, and swung his fist into his palm like he was squashing a bug.

"Then I got an e-mail from Robert Palmer. He and Curtains have been in communication."

Terry did another little dance. He pantomimed shooting someone with a rifle.

"Robert gave Curtains the name of the guy he spoke to who confirmed Montgomery was never in Vietnam."

This time Terry pantomimed lobbing a hand grenade, with sound effects— KER-POW! "This is just too good," he chortled.

Actually, it was exhilarating—I opened the e-mails from my Australian comrades-in-arms with glee. Two days later I heard from Curtains again. "We are receiving information from our friends in the U.S. daily," he wrote, "and none of it looks good for James."

Curtains was putting the finishing touches on his analysis of my ex-husband's military fraud. I told him about Lovefraud.com—it was ready to go live as soon as my lawyers gave the okay, and the first of my *True Lovefraud Stories* was entitled, *James Montgomery—using the Internet to meet and defraud women*. We agreed that we'd expose James at the same time—Curtains would post his story on the ANZMI website, and I'd launch Lovefraud.com.

My old house had been neglected for many years. A previous owner covered cracks in the master bedroom ceiling with acoustical tiles; they were falling down. Burgundy carpet on the stairs and in the hallway had faded to a sickly shade of orange. The kitchen sorely lacked cabinet storage and counter space.

Terry and I had been planning renovations for months. In fact, we'd already selected kitchen cabinets from Lowe's Home Improvement, and requested Lowe's gift cards as wedding presents. But we wouldn't be able to do all the work on gift cards—we needed to refinance the house.

I was nervous. I still had a bankruptcy on my credit record, and I'd been turned down for refinancing two years earlier. But I always kept up with the mortgage, and now there were two of us applying for the loan. On June 3, 2005, I called my mortgage company, Chase. When I told the representative that I wanted to refinance, I also told him he'd see a bankruptcy on my credit report because my ex-husband defrauded me. The representative said he'd call me back.

Thirty minutes later, he did. We were approved.

I was shocked. I was relieved. I was grateful. My financial credibility was returning. I felt like big, heavy chains were disintegrating and I was finally moving forward.

Two weeks later, the evidence of forward motion was even stronger. I returned from a garden-party fundraiser to important phone and e-mail messages, which I relayed to Terry, who was sitting at his desk.

"Chase called to schedule our settlement," I said.

"All right," he replied, and did his little chair dance.

"And I heard from Leon. We don't have to wait 28 days. As soon as the court confirms that the affidavit of debt is filed, we can launch Lovefraud."

On my birthday, July 19, 2005, Lovefraud went live. The home page proclaimed:

Beware the sociopath
No heart, no conscience, no remorse

I married a con man—a man who I now consider to be a sociopath. I didn't know anything about sociopaths when I said, "I do." I learned about sociopaths (also called psychopaths) the hard way.

I thought I was marrying a successful businessman, James Montgomery. It turned out I was his business. He took all my money and left me seriously in debt.

Think it couldn't happen to you? Think again.

I found out, far too late, that my husband had a history of defrauding women. I also found out he's not alone.

Experts estimate that 1 percent to 4 percent of the population are sociopaths, depending upon whom you ask. That means there may be 3 million to 12 million sociopaths in the United States, and 68 million to 272 million sociopaths worldwide. What's worse, as adults, sociopathic men and women cannot be rehabilitated. Once a sociopath, always a sociopath.

Sociopaths have no heart, no conscience and no remorse. They don't worry about paying bills. They think nothing of lying, cheating and stealing. In extreme cases, sociopaths can be serial rapists and serial killers.

Think you can spot a sociopath? Think again. Sociopaths often blend easily into society. They're entertaining and fun at parties. They appear to be intelligent, charming, well-adjusted and likable. The key word is "appear." Because for sociopaths it's all an illusion, designed to convince you to give them what they want.

Sociopaths are masters of manipulation. So before you give away your love, your money or your life, read this website.

Lovefraud was packed with information to help readers figure out if they were involved with a sociopath. A section called *What's a sociopath?* listed the key symptoms of the condition, explained the terms "psychopath" and "sociopath," and pointed out that these people were disordered, but not insane. Sociopaths knew exactly what they were doing when they exploited people, they just didn't care.

I wrote a section called *Internet threat,* which detailed why the Internet was rife with predators. Another section, entitled *Legal system failures,* explained why society's legal and financial systems were impotent when dealing with sociopaths: The systems were based on people following the rules. Sociopaths didn't follow the rules, so the systems were practically useless.

Upon launch, Lovefraud had four case studies—my *True Lovefraud Stories.* Right at the top of the list was the story of my ex-husband, James Montgomery. I described how I met James on the Internet, how he swept me off my feet with his larger-than-life personality, and how he kept coming up with moneymaking schemes that he wanted me to finance. After more than two years of stress and anxiety caused by his lies and my dwindling funds, I discovered his infidelity. Then I discovered that he had targeted me strictly as a revenue source—as he had done with many women before me and after me. In my divorce, I proved that he committed fraud and was awarded a judgment of more than $1.25 million. I collected a grand total of $517.

At the end of the article, I included a link to the James Montgomery case on the Australian and New Zealand Military Impostors website, ANZMI.net, which was posted the same day. ANZMI skewered him.

Curtains, whose real name was Curt Ainsworth, wrote the analysis. After reproducing James' fraudulent account of his combat heroism (see page 87), Curtains erupted:

> The US Silver Cross? There's a lot more wrong with that "citation" as there is a lot more wrong with the fool who wrote it.
>
> This blatant liar, poseur and forger claims to have been a 5th Special Forces Group Captain attached to the Australian Army Training Team Vietnam, or an AATTV Captain attached to the 5th SFG? He's not sure which one he should be posing as.
>
> Was he either?
>
> No, nor was he a US Marine, a US Navy SEAL, a SAS Captain or Major, a Commando, a RAN Reserve Captain or a recipient of the Victoria Cross and lesser awards.
>
> He is an Australian and a major fraud who, amongst other things, liked to make public speeches in the US about Vietnam while dressed in his Special Forces outfit complete with green beret.
>
> He did go to China, in pursuit of a get-rich-quick scheme, but Beijing in '99 was a long way from the mountains, jungles, rice paddies and swamps of what was South Vietnam during the war.
>
> We hold copies of documents that indicate he has been constructing his false history over many years and we have never before run across such an obviously labour intensive project. One other wannabe

on our Cases page comes close, but Montgomery gets the award for the
wannabe who tried the hardest to perpetuate his fraud while also being
the most incredibly stupid.

Curtains reproduced James' Delta Force and Special Forces ID cards, and
showed why they were fakes. He dissected all of James' claims, meticulously
proving each one false. Official seals were wrong. Names were wrong. Letters
weren't signed. Some of James' military analysis papers appeared to be plagia-
rized, others were factually impossible. All of the medals James claimed were
denied—two of them didn't even exist.

The exposé ended with:

> Because you never dragged on a boot in any branch of any country's
> Military Forces, you will appear on this page for life. Perennial civilians
> like you don't rate a letter from us asking for an explanation of your foul
> deeds, nor do they rate an opportunity to apologise to those who they
> pretended to be as honourable.
>
> Mongrel dogs like you who even dream of being able to walk in the
> shadow or boot prints of brave men deserve no less. You weren't there
> in Kontum with them then, and you're not going to be with them now.
>
> You "dared to win" and "persevered" from the business end of a
> typewriter only.

Netcraft.com, a company that did research and data analysis about the
Internet, announced on August 1, 2005 that more than 70 million websites populated the web. The month before, 2.7 million new sites were launched, the
biggest increase in the 10-year history of Netcraft's survey. One of them was
Lovefraud.com.

With 70 million websites out there, how would anyone find mine? For my
first rudimentary marketing, I e-mailed a link to Lovefraud.com to everybody I
knew. Two of my friends wrote back immediately—after reading the key symptoms of a sociopath on my website, they realized that they'd been involved with
disordered individuals.

To help people beyond my mailing list find Lovefraud, I developed the content, and selected keywords, to boost rankings on search engines like Google. It
soon started working. Within 10 days of the launch, I received an e-mail from a
man in Alabama who told me his story of marriage to a sociopathic woman. More
stories, from people around the United States and the world, began to trickle in.

Then came the bombshell.

The morning of August 3, 2005, I received an e-mail from a member of the
Rotary Club in Bathurst, Australia. "James is a member of our Rotary Club," he
wrote. "If all that I read in a Sydney paper and on your website is true and correct
about James, then we will have to address the situation." He asked me to call him.

What was in the newspaper?

Soon, I was talking to the Rotarian on the phone. He read an article about James in the Daily Telegraph—a tabloid newspaper that had the largest circulation in Sydney—and then read what I wrote about him on Lovefraud.com.

"If 10 percent of what you wrote on Lovefraud.com about him is true, we have a problem," he said.

"Well, 100 percent of what I wrote on Lovefraud is true," I replied, "and it's only 10 percent of the story."

"The Rotary Club has a creed of service and high ethical standards," the man said. "I invited James to speak about ethics in his business. He's supposed to give his presentation next week."

I burst out laughing. My ex-husband, con artist extraordinaire, giving a presentation on ethics in business? "You might want to rethink that," I said.

As soon as I got off the phone, I sent e-mails to Robert Palmer and Curtains—had they seen the article? What did it say? Curtains came through with a scan of it the next morning.

At the top of the story was a big picture of James, in a suit and tie, presenting a certificate to a smiling Chinese student. It was one of the photos on his "James Montgomery—New man at the helm" web page for Charles Sturt University. Superimposed upon the photo were his Special Forces and Delta Force ID cards, with his mean-looking mug shot.

The headline of the story was *Meet Major Fraud.*

James Montgomery, the newspaper ridiculed, was a bored advertising executive who reinvented himself as a secret agent and Vietnam war hero, claiming to have won Australia's highest military honor, the Victoria Cross. He kept the charade going for more than 20 years, forging military ID cards to support his elaborate lies. But now he was busted.

It was priceless, and got even better. James actually admitted to the reporter that he forged the documents, but said he was working on a "secret project" to show how easy it was to impersonate an authentic war hero. The documents were never supposed to be made public, James said, and accused me of stealing them from a safety deposit box. He also denied that he owed me any money—I was setting him up.

Terry and I were practically rolling on the floor, laughing about the article. Finally, deliciously, James was exposed. The next day, however, we laughed even harder. My new best friend at the Bathurst Rotary Club sent an e-mail telling me that James had resigned, "much to our relief." He also sent a copy of another article that appeared in The Daily Telegraph entitled *Parading Fake Medals.* It was accompanied by a photo of James marching in an Anzac Day parade.

Anzac Day paid tribute to military veterans of Australia and New Zealand, like Veterans Day and Memorial Day in the United States. James marched in Bathurst's most recent Anzac Day parade on April 25, 2005—despite stating in the newspaper that he never impersonated a returned soldier in Australia. The local newspaper, the Western Advocate, had photographed James marching in the parade. Local veterans were outraged, and one reported James to the Australian Federal Police—impersonating a military veteran was a crime.

The next day, August 5, 2005, Charles Sturt University accepted the resignation of James Montgomery. "The misrepresentation of military service is, in the University's view, a serious allegation," the school stated in a press release. "We hope that the Defence Department will investigate this matter further."

One last article about James' resignation appeared in The Daily Telegraph. The headline was: *March Order for Major Fraud.*

I rowed, by myself, to the starting line of the Kings Head Regatta in King of Prussia, Pennsylvania for the women's senior masters singles event. My rowing partner in the double had accepted a new job with more responsibility; she was no longer available to train like we had in the past. I loved the strenuous physical exercise of rowing and wanted to stay with the sport, so I learned how to row in a single scull.

At first, I felt wobbly. Single sculls are much narrower and lower in the water than doubles and quads. The oars in all racing sculls acted like outriggers—when they were flat on the water, they prevented the boat from tipping over. With only one set of oars in a single—mine—it was much easier to flip, and once, when the wind kicked up during a springtime training row, I did. But oars were not meant to lay still. Rowing was about movement, and I learned to balance my body and hold the oars so that as I rolled up the slide, they sliced through the air a few inches above the water, until I dropped the blades in for the stroke. Gradually, my technique, strength and stamina improved, and in the King's Head Regatta, I put myself to the test.

The race official summoned me to the starting chute. "Twenty meters to start," he called through his bullhorn. "Ten meters to start. You're on the course."

Roll to the top of the slide, drop the oars in the water, push with the legs, pull with the arms. Again. Again. Again. In a single scull, I was responsible for everything that happened. I kept the balance. I steered the course. I set the pace. Whether I won, lost or placed somewhere in the middle was totally up to me.

For nearly three miles, I pushed hard, glancing over my shoulder frequently to stay on course. Two bridges crossed the river near the finish line; when I saw them, I started my sprint. Fifty meters past the second bridge, the air horn sounded—I crossed the line. The race was over.

On that day, I won. I proudly wore my gold medal—recognition that all my effort paid off.

Through pouring rain on October 25, 2005, I drove my new Honda—I finally got rid of the Thunderbird that I leased for James—to my session with Elaine Anderson. I had a lot to tell her—Lovefraud.com had launched; James was exposed as a fraud in Australia; he got sacked from his job. People from all over the world were finding Lovefraud and contacting me—they were entangled with sociopaths, and desperate for information on how they got snared and how to get out.

"I feel a lot of satisfaction when I'm able to help someone," I said.

"That's because when you do it, you're aligned with your true purpose."

When I lay on the table, however, Elaine could feel a pain around my heart. "Breathe into it," she said. "Try to find out what it is."

I felt the pain, and slowly identified it—the embarrassment of getting involved with James in the first place, of making such a stupid mistake. "That's how they do it," I said, referring to the sociopaths. "They make us so embarrassed that we don't do anything about it."

"It's a powerless place," Elaine agreed.

Then I felt something else—deep pain and sorrow piercing my heart. Painful energy moved up to my throat. It was so intense that I couldn't speak. Finally, I got the words out. "It's more than that," I said. "It's the embarrassment of the original fall from grace."

"You're on to something," Elaine said. "Go with it."

My heart was breaking. The pain was so deep, so old. It was the embarrassment of the original mistake, the mistake of separating from the One. "We make this huge mistake, and then we spend all these lifetimes trying to make up for it," I said. "The pain of the mistake, the fall from grace, it's just heartbreaking. We're so embarrassed. We separated from God; it was so stupid. But God doesn't care."

I paused, continuing to process the ancient trauma in silence.

"This is really deep," Elaine said. "You're right—God doesn't care. We have this image of a vengeful god, but God is not that way."

The pain moved from my heart into my throat and face. Then both of my hands shook violently under the blanket, above the crystals. An insight came to me: Here on Earth, we got involved with nasty people like sociopaths to re-experience the pain and embarrassment of doing something stupid. Hopefully, in the process, we would gain access to that original pain and embarrassment—the separation from God—and release it.

I didn't want to think that we chose involvement with these predators to help our own healing—why would anyone intentionally take on such horror?—but that was how it appeared.

My hands slowed down, and then, right between my shoulder blades, I felt twinges. "My back is twitching," I said. "I feel like I'm growing angel wings."

The twitching kept up for quite awhile. Then my back involuntarily arched, and my chest expanded. Exposing my shoulders, back and chest had always bothered me—I tended to hunch over, protecting my heart. But my back wanted to arch; my chest wanted to be exposed. My heart wanted to be seen and felt.

This was recovery. This was reunion.

I lay quietly, integrating the experience. The session came to a close.

"So it is," Elaine said. "We give thanks."

Bankruptcy in Australia was much more unpleasant than it was in the United States. In the U.S., the main consequence of bankruptcy was an inability to get credit. In Australia, the bankrupt person faced many more restrictions on keeping assets, earning income and even travel. I imagined that was why pissed-off creditors forced debtors into bankruptcy—exactly what I was trying to do to James.

My efforts stalled. Apparently the court wouldn't allow us to demand five years' worth of interest, going back to the date of my original judgment in 2000, but all summer long, no one bothered to inform my solicitor of the problem. So we refiled the paperwork, and on October 11, 2005, finally received a sealed copy of the judgment. Two weeks later, James was served with the bankruptcy notice. It was the first step in my final legal battle against my ex-husband.

Surprisingly, James saved me the trouble and expense of fighting him in court by filing his own bankruptcy petition. On November 22, 2005, I received a letter from the Insolvency and Trustee Service Australia—James was declared bankrupt.

A trustee was appointed to investigate James' financial affairs and administer his bankruptcy estate. By law, James was required to notify the trustee if he changed his address, earned new income, inherited property or won money. If he earned income above a certain amount, he had to pay the trustee half of it toward his debt. Any tax refunds were also applied toward the debt.

James was prohibited from being a company manager or director, and could not continue in any business partnership. If he wanted to borrow money over a certain amount, he had to disclose that he was bankrupt.

James could not travel overseas without the permission of the trustee—my personal favorite in the new rules of his life.

Bankruptcy typically lasted three years, but could be extended if the trustee objected to discharge for reasons such as failing to disclose income. After the bankruptcy ended, James could still be liable for debts incurred by fraud, and he had defrauded me. Furthermore, the name James Alwyn Montgomery would appear on Australia's National Personal Insolvency Index forever.

Chapter 35

Slowly, people started finding Lovefraud.com on the Internet. On my *Contact Lovefraud* page, I invited readers to tell me their stories of entanglements with sociopaths, and they did. Even after the treachery I experienced with James Montgomery, some of the stories I heard were truly shocking—seven-figure fraud, legal shenanigans, corruption, child custody battles, physical abuse, child molestation, murder.

Listening to these stories, I realized that the incomprehensible behavior I saw from James—lies great and small, wanton spending, senseless rages, perpetual cheating—was typical of a sociopath. I also learned that when sociopaths troll for victims, they operate from the same playbook. At first, they are charming, helpful, flattering and romantic. If the target responds, the sociopath quickly moves to "love bombing:" He proclaims that the target is the woman he's been waiting for all his life. He wants to be with the target constantly—even 24 hours a day. He quickly starts talking about love at first sight, finding his soul mate, and dreams of being together forever. (I said "he," but female sociopaths employ the same techniques.)

It is a "whirlwind romance," and it is enough to disarm almost anyone—especially if the target is feeling an emotional void. I certainly fell for it.

If the sociopath is looking for benefits such as money or a place to live, again, he moves quickly. The sociopath may tell the target that he "can't stand to be apart," when the real problem is that he is being evicted. He may tell the target that by helping him financially, she is investing in their future together, although the sociopath probably spends her money seducing his next victim.

At some point—and it could take years—the whole charade falls apart. The sociopath then reacts in one of two ways—either he leaves the target in the dust without a care, as James Montgomery left me, or he continues to grip the target. Some sociopaths hold on just to torment the victim—they find it entertaining. Others hold on so they can bleed the victim again, as James did to Jody McClure—the woman who joined him in Florida, even though he took all her money in California.

Why would anyone put up with that? Why would a victim, who knew a sociopath ripped her life apart, allow the predator back in? The answer, I learned, involves human psychology.

Healthy human beings bond with each other, especially in romantic relationships. A love bond is first created through pleasure—the happiness and excitement of a new romance—and is reinforced through sex. In the beginning, of course, a sociopath is on his best behavior, and becomes the source of pleasure for the target. This creates a psychological love bond, and the target feels an internal compulsion to be with the object of her desire.

Then life gets rocky—the sociopath may be taking the target's money, or threatening to leave the relationship. James did both of these things to me. This creates anxiety and fear in the target. But instead of driving the target away from the sociopath, *anxiety and fear strengthen the psychological love bond*. For relief from the anxiety and fear, the target turns to the sociopath. The sociopath reassures the target, which leads to sex, which further strengthens the love bond.

Life may become downright miserable for the target, yet she still doesn't leave the sociopath. Why? Because even though pleasure is required to establish a psychological bond, addiction research has shown that pleasure is not required to maintain it. The target still feels the love bond—the internal compulsion to be with the sociopath—even though the relationship is no longer pleasurable.

So here's how it works: The sociopath seduces the target with what appears to be love and romance. The target forms a psychological love bond with the sociopath. The sociopath causes anxiety and fear, which strengthens the love bond. The target turns to the sociopath for relief, which leads to sex. Sex alleviates the anxiety and makes the target feel even more bonded. The relationship, therefore, becomes a vicious cycle of bonding, anxiety, fear, relief, sex and further bonding. The longer it goes on, the harder it is for the target to escape.

Sociopaths, however, do not feel love bonds for anyone, so the cycle doesn't affect them. But they instinctively know how to manipulate the natural human bonding process so they can get what they want from their victims.

Lovefraud readers started asking me for advice on handling their situations with sociopaths. The information on Lovefraud was critical, I realized, so it was important to boost the website's visibility. One way to do that was with a blog, which I added in January 2006. The Lovefraud Blog enabled me to present new information quickly and easily. It also gave my readers an opportunity to interact with me, and with each other.

The blog was where I editorialized. One of my first posts, on February 5, 2006, was entitled *Psycho movies add to the confusion*. I complained that movies like *The Silence of the Lambs* and the classic Alfred Hitchcock thriller, *Psycho*, left people with the impression that all psychopaths were deranged serial killers, when they were far more likely to be a philandering spouse, abusive boss or shady lawyer. In another post, *Sociopaths troll for victims with online ads,* I explained why Internet dating was so seductive, and so dangerous.

Sociopaths specialized in targeting lonely people, and everybody who posted a personal ad online was, by definition, advertising the fact that they were lonely.

Lovefraud's reach spread, with surprising results. On April 17, 2006, I heard from an Australian woman, Roberta Laidley,* who dated James Montgomery back in 1985:

From: Roberta Laidley
Subj: James A Montgomery

Dear Donna

I just found your website. Wow! I am—hopefully—one of quite a few who got away.

I met James Alwyn Montgomery in early 1985 when I lived in Sydney. He lived in Melbourne and told me he was working on a WWII military miniseries for a Sydney TV station. It seemed genuine; he had a meeting with the recordkeeper and took me along. I also went with him to the home of the man who was writing the miniseries plus I met his cameraman and soundman at the home base of his (supposedly) old Commando unit one day.

He went overseas soon after I met him and I got strange phone calls from him every day, strange because they almost all ended very abruptly but he always phoned back a little while later with a plausible excuse, the most notable being the day he phoned from somewhere in Japan saying he was in the Police Commissioner's office. When he phoned back he told me there had been a power failure.

Shortly after he returned to Australia James came to Sydney because his father was getting married again. I remember it was at the Registry Office, and afterwards we drove to his father's apartment for the "reception." The newlyweds were going overseas for their honeymoon and James gave them a card (which I had to buy) plus a large cheque—he wrote, "Have a country or two on me" on the card.

I knew something didn't add up with James. He avoided giving me his home address and telephone number in Melbourne. The only number I had was his mobile (cell) phone in his car. When he was in Melbourne he called me every day on his way home and asked me to ring back.

I tested James out the next time he came to Sydney. We went to the country for the day and, on arrival, I took a shower. A few seconds later James put my makeup bag on the basin, so I peeked through the door and saw him speaking to an obviously important female on the phone. Back in Sydney, the following day was my birthday and James committed the final faux pas that broke this camel's back. He said he didn't have any wrapping paper for my present and asked me to go and buy some. It was MY birthday but nothing I said could dissuade him, so I drove straight to a phone box and called my home. Surprise, surprise, the phone was engaged!

He went back to Melbourne and then on another overseas trip.

Soon after my quarterly telephone bill arrived. It was horrendous, so I photocopied it, highlighted all the calls I felt belonged to him and sent it to his home address (which I had gotten from the label on the inside of one of his large suitcases, while he was in the shower). I eventually received a cranky call from him at my place of work, but insisted he send me a cheque or I would contact my lawyer. I now realise how fortunate I was to actually get the full amount back from him.

By the way, I got rid of him by telling him I was getting married!! A couple of years later I saw him from a distance when I was coming home from the theatre one night. He was standing beside a white Mercedes sports car with personalised JAM-000 numberplates outside a well-known "pick up" hotel in Sydney. Enough said.

I can't help wondering how many other women he messed with in Australia before he went to the US?? I found out later he was living with (or married to) someone in Melbourne when I knew him. And yes, there were stories of his military service, his planes and his brother, Dr. Bob Montgomery, a well-known Australian psychologist.

Donna, it was serendipity that I found your website. A military historian friend, a genuine Vietnam Vet, called me yesterday and said he was investigating someone posing as a former SAS veteran. I mentioned James and my friend looked him up and said he wasn't on any of the official lists. Today I picked up a magazine which had an article on Dr. Bob Montgomery. I figured someone was trying to tell me something, so I Googled and found your website!!

James gave Roberta a record album produced in the early 1980s as a promotional piece by an advertising agency where he once worked—Arnold Lester and Associates Pty., Ltd. Surprisingly, Roberta still had the album cover, and she sent me a copy of it. It featured a group photo of the staff, including James—so he did, back then, have a job. His bio said he was director of media and research, and president of the Advertising Club.

During the three months that Roberta had contact with James, he spent seven weeks overseas, and when he was in Australia, lived 750 miles away. Luckily, Roberta quickly figured out that he was talking to other women and dumped him. Roberta's e-mail proved to me that James had been a cheater all his life.

The next woman who contacted me in reference to James was his wife, Kim Goodson. She sent me an e-mail on February 19, 2007—a total surprise. Although Kim Goodson was central to my divorce, because of the child and James' bigamy, I never had any direct communication with her.

She wanted me to remove her name from the Lovefraud story about James. I was reluctant to do this—her marriage to my ex-husband was a matter of public record. But I did want to speak to her. "Are you still with Montgomery?" I replied. "Please feel free to call me."

Kim didn't call, but two days later, she sent a link to a diabetes blog that James wrote.

"Thank you for sending the link," I replied. "As I suspect you can understand, my involvement with Montgomery ripped my life apart. Besides wiping me out financially, eventually forcing me into bankruptcy, he destroyed my trust and my self-esteem."

I told Kim that I was writing a book, and I'd like to know about her experience with James. She wasn't ready to talk to me, but started telling me her story via e-mail. She also started forwarding the Lovefraud story about James Montgomery when her friends asked how she was doing. It was easier than trying to explain the soap opera she was living.

Kim Goodson, who was from Florida, met James via an Internet personal ad in January 1992. He lived in Tampa, and told her the same story he told all the women—he was single (although living with Jody McClure at the time), writing movie scripts (with Colleen Jessick actually doing the work) and was an ex-Green Beret. James was attentive—communicating prolifically via Prodigy and phone, and taking Kim out to nice places. At one point he even gave her a ring set with a large topaz—the same ring that he gave to Colleen, Gale and me.

James asked Kim to invest in one of his projects, but she refused; in fact, she never gave him any money. He also asked her multiple times to marry him, but she refused that as well. She'd discovered his propensity for lying—about his age, his ownership of cars, his status as military active reserve. Although James frequently alluded to his military missions, he didn't have clearance to enter MacDill Air Force Base in Tampa—he only got in with Kim, who, as a member of the Civil Air Patrol, had base privileges. She attributed the lies to James wanting to show off.

Kim just didn't take James seriously. He traveled frequently, so when he was around, they had a good time together and she enjoyed the sex. When he wasn't around, he wasn't. The relationship, in her mind, was casual, and she lost interest in James for months at a time, ignoring his attempts to contact her.

In 1995, when James moved into Gale Lewis' townhouse in Mays Landing, New Jersey, he stayed in touch with Kim. He never bothered to tell Kim that he married Gale until after his wife died. Apparently James left the day after the funeral in Sumter, South Carolina and went directly to Florida. He visited Kim from May 25 to 28, 1996. (Kim had learned to keep written records of when she saw James—it avoided arguments later.) Crying, James told Kim about Gale's death—although without much detail—and then said he only married Gale because he felt sorry for her, and because Kim had shut him out. He also said Gale's parents accused him of murder, but they were grief-stricken and incoherent.

Kim saw James in June and again in July 1996—after he proposed to me. The next time James visited her was right before Thanksgiving, when he and I were married, which he also didn't tell her. James left Florida—giving some excuse about a military assignment—so he could spend the Thanksgiving holiday with me. Kim then went with him to the Bahamas for three days in April 1997. That was when James told me he went to the Nassau Film Festival, which didn't exist. Obviously, he forged the letter from Walt Disney Pictures in which we were supposedly invited to return to the festival as presenters.

During one of the trysts, Kim became pregnant, and her daughter was born on April 17, 1998. For the first 10 months, Kim said, James had no interest in the child. When James and I moved from Atlantic City to Orlando in December 1998—only 100 miles from Kim's home—he didn't even tell her.

But while we lived in Orlando, James was out of town every Friday night, telling me that he was pulling shifts at MacDill Air Force Base. Only two of the weekends were spent with Kim—one in a motel in Kissimmee, near Disney World. The other weekends that he went missing were apparently spent with Sharon Decamp, his new business partner in the IICE venture.

Suddenly, on Valentine's Day 1999, James proposed to Kim again—probably right after the phone call in which he begged me to come home, saying that his baby's mother meant nothing to him, and he got her pregnant as a favor. James told Kim he'd relocate her and her daughter to Australia. "It was an easy out for me," Kim wrote. "I wanted to have time out of work to raise my daughter and Australia seemed as good a place as anywhere else." They married on February 22, 1999, she became Kim Montgomery and James moved into her home. James also used Kim's car—he drove it the day after the wedding when he picked up Sylvia Banning at the Orlando airport. The pearl-colored Ford Thunderbird had been stolen from the airport, he said. Or the car was in New Jersey. Or it was a rental that was returned. For reasons that remained murky, James no longer had transportation.

Four months later, at 10 p.m., a process server banged on their door with my divorce papers. James self-righteously explained the intrusion by saying he was being sued, personally and professionally, by a psychotic former business partner over a failed deal. James and I were involved in an Atlantic City gambling consortium that was opening a casino, he said, and he used my office and stayed in my basement. Now I was insanely accusing him of misdeeds.

Every time legal papers arrived from my attorney, James quickly made them vanish.

Kim Goodson and her daughter moved to Australia in August 1999, staying temporarily in the home of Archie Turner, James' partner, who was the best man when James and I got married. Three months later, James relocated the family to New Zealand, where he attempted to run the ESL school for Chinese students. The school failed and closed, owing many people money. Leaving Kim in New Zealand, James went to China with Sharon Decamp, the woman from Florida who was funding IICE, and another woman, Rachel Lenox,* who lived near Melbourne, Australia. In January 2001, Kim joined James in Beijing. She worked at international schools while James tried to get his IICE business going.

In James' office in China, Kim found a packet of photos of naked women. The photos included herself, Sharon, Rachel, me and other women whom Kim didn't recognize. She shredded them. Sharon, Kim learned, was passionately in love with James. James told Sharon that he married Kim to help take care of her daughter, although he didn't know if the child was really his. James told Kim that Sharon was nothing but a business partner who he happened to sleep with.

James was awarded an honorary doctorate of humane letters when he was the commencement speaker for Schiller International University's London campus in 2003, supposedly for his ESL services to China. From that point on, he referred to himself as Dr. James Montgomery. But by December of that year, James' ventures in China failed. He returned to Australia, where he took a job and lived with Rachel in Melbourne. Kim was left in China.

Then James got the job at Charles Sturt University, and in June 2004, Kim joined him in Bathurst. James worked at the radio network, joined the local Rotary and Lions Clubs, and volunteered at the Australian Fossil and Mineral Museum. Kim also became part of the community—working as a substitute teacher, attending church, involving her daughter with music and Girl Guides.

Although Kim wasn't present, James was served with my judgment on February 7, 2005. She described his reaction:

> He stuck to his story of a disgruntled business partner who was chasing him. It wasn't until the newspaper story and looking at the website that I started to doubt his veracity. Even then, I believed him that he was divorced before he married me. I was, however, on guard for any future lies and they did eventuate. His tactic of using enough truth along with more lies to cover his lies is very surface effective.

The story of James Montgomery's military fraud took up the entire front page of the tabloid-sized Western Advocate, the local Bathurst newspaper, on August 8, 2005. Beside a massive photo of James wearing his Special Forces beret and fake medals in the Anzac Day parade, the headline read, *Montgomery hands in resignation: Claims service record is false.*

For Kim and her daughter, the story was devastating. Kim let her daughter see the newspaper. "I explained that people thought her dad lied," she wrote to me. "That daddy said it was not true. That we knew already that sometimes daddy lied. That she loved daddy even if he did lie but we couldn't always trust him."

Both Kim and her daughter went to school that day. Other teachers didn't connect Kim Montgomery, the American substitute teacher, with James Montgomery, the Australian fraud, and started talking about the story at lunch. Kim excused herself.

James raged to Kim that the newspaper articles and my website were nothing but lies, the fantasies of unstable people who were out to destroy him. He insisted that Lovefraud.com and the Australian and New Zealand Military Impostors website would be gone. In fact, he tried to find hackers to take them down. He failed.

For Kim, subsequent events flowed together into one long flood of embarrassment. Charles Sturt University, the Rotary Club and the Lions Club all asked for James' resignation. The Bathurst Regional Council asked that James no longer volunteer at the museum or for any other purpose. James was irate, but he was never embarrassed.

"The lasting impact on James has been nil," Kim wrote. "The impact on me was to demand that he lie to me never again and that if he did, I would leave."

Having lost his job, James was now a pensioner, although his pension was quite small. To supplement his income, and have a reason to exercise, Kim found a paper route for him, delivering junk mail. In September 2006, James slipped on gravel in a driveway, fell and broke his leg. The break required a plate and 14 pins.

While James was in the hospital, Kim opened the mail and discovered that her husband hadn't been reporting his or Kim's income properly to the Australian Tax Authority (ATO), or to Centrelink, the agency that administered pensions, child credits and other social welfare programs. He'd even put his paper route in Kim's name. She wrote:

> I confronted James on these lies. He glossed over them saying that he had to hide his income from the bankruptcy court and that everyone cheated Centrelink and ATO. I told him it was flatly a lie and thus I would be leaving him. He manipulated his injury into being something that made that impossible. I fell for it. Though for all intents and purposes, our relationship as "married" ended there.

After making arrangements for James' daily care—he was still incapacitated with the broken leg, which hadn't healed properly due to his diabetes and a golden staph infection—Kim returned to the United States to visit her family shortly after Christmas 2006. From Florida, she did something that she was unable to do from Australia—she ordered a copy of my divorce decree. The documents proved that James had, indeed, committed bigamy in marrying her. Kim returned to Australia on February 15, 2007 to undo the lie that James had made of her life.

James had cautioned Kim not to speak to me. He said I was insanely jealous and hated her, not because they were together, but because they had a child and I did not. All of James' problems, he said, were because of me and my actions.

Kim contacted me anyway.

She was still living in the same house as James in Bathurst. She and her daughter were upstairs, and James, who suffered setbacks with his broken leg, was downstairs.

James proposed a solution to the bigamy problem—they'd get married again. Kim wasn't interested. She considered herself to be a faithful person, which was why she remained with James for so long. But now she just wanted to escape the charade and protect her daughter.

Kim decided to move out. But before the day she planned to tell James, he asked her why she had so many boxes upstairs. She answered his question honestly—she was leaving. Here's how Kim described the scene:

> He kept on about how my daughter and I couldn't make it on our own, how we needed him, how he loved me, how his actions (lies) were

> always to help us and proof of his love for us. He asked for help with the
> bills, to know who I was going to be living with, what my address was
> going to be, how to contact me, how I would get around as he owned
> both of the cars. He told me it was his right to know, I couldn't take any-
> thing from the house, couldn't leave town, couldn't move out. I stood
> there and listened. I told him I was sorry for him, but it wasn't my prob-
> lem. I told him to contact me through his lawyer or sister. I told him my
> living arrangements were none of his business. I told him I did not wish
> to speak, see or e-mail to/from him. I didn't say anything else!!!!! He
> backed down and said I could borrow his 1984 Ford station wagon with-
> out power steering; I could take our personal belongings!!!!! I don't want
> to say how much I was shaking after this. But I felt great!

James supervised Kim's packing, insisting that she not take anything he considered to be his, like the food mixer, which he never touched. Kim moved out
on March 17, 2007, leaving with only her and her daughter's personal items.
Friends helped, and while James sat at his computer, they were out of the house
in an hour. Her new place was furnished through donations from her church.

Kim retained a solicitor to have her marriage nullified.

James, in the meantime, did computer-based work, without reporting his
income to the authorities. Kim, however, did report him to Centrelink, the tax
authorities and the landlord—with her and her income gone, James would no
longer be able to pay the rent.

"Did you empty a storage unit in Florida?" Kim asked me on April 2, 2007.

I'd been wondering how to broach the subject of the storage unit. For years
I thought that Kim was James' accomplice, but through my correspondence with
her, I'd come to believe that she was just another of his victims. I'd taken, sold
and disposed of her property. At the time it was necessary. But seven years later,
I felt badly about it, and I wrote an e-mail to tell her the truth.

Yes, I emptied it. Desperately trying to avoid bankruptcy, I was searching for
information so I could serve my judgment on James. I did find some information, although the only money I got was from selling Kim's things. Anything that
wasn't sold was donated to the Salvation Army. Then I apologized:

> I am not particularly proud of this incident, but I did what I had to
> do. Through my divorce, I learned that authorities and law enforcement
> are practically useless when it comes to dealing with sociopaths, so I
> took actions that were totally contrary to my nature in order to survive.
> James' papers and other materials were helpful. The funds from the sale
> of the items did keep me going for awhile.
>
> I did save some of your items that appeared to be of sentimental
> value—mostly photos. Perhaps I had an inkling that we would one day be
> in touch. I would be happy to return them to you. I am sorry about the

rest of it. I hope you can understand and forgive me.

I pressed the send button and held my breath.

"There is justice in the world," Kim wrote in her reply the next day. "The toys I had as a child went to the Salvation Army, and a similar organization has provided me with a home, furnishings, food and sustenance."

I was grateful for Kim's understanding. Much of what she stored was memorabilia—her Girl Scout sash, her great-grandmother's diary, black and white photos. With the thorough purge of my house, all that remained of Kim's possessions were items that fit into a file drawer. I packed them up and shipped them to Kim's family in Florida.

A few days later, Kim asked for my assistance—her solicitor needed a copy of my certificate of marriage to James Montgomery, and the authorities would only release it with my permission. The solicitor also needed an affidavit from me, attesting to when James and I were married, how long we lived together, and when we were legally divorced. I gladly provided everything that Kim needed.

Kim's legal proceedings dragged on. Because her case was so complicated, the Bathurst court wouldn't hear it—the case was moved to Sydney. On July 30, 2007, Kim told me that James said he would not attend court nor contest her actions. Kim's nullification was granted on August 8, 2007.

Although James kept telling people that Kim would return to care for him, she and her daughter immediately left Australia to live permanently in the United States.

As his marriage to Kim Goodson disintegrated, James was once again on the Internet prowling for women—although Kim believed he never stopped. On June 7, 2007, I heard from a woman named Patricia Barnes, who met James on RSVP.com.au, which claimed to be Australia's largest online dating site. She was e-mailing him and talking to him on the phone when, on a whim, she Googled his name and found Lovefraud. Without telling James what she had discovered, Patricia dumped him and notified RSVP of his past.

More than a year later, on September 6, 2008, I heard from another woman named Kerrie Lay. James contacted her through aboutmyage.com, an Australian social networking community for people over 50, saying that he was a retired Ph.D. Kerrie checked out his story by Googling his name—he was now going by "Jim Montgomery," although he insisted on being called James when married to me. Kerrie found no Ph.D., but she did find Lovefraud, and sent me a copy of James' profile on aboutmyage.com. "Retired academic – screenwriter," he wrote. "Returned to Oz after 25 years in USA and Asia – last stop Beijing. Left when SARS hit and did two years at CSU retiring at the end of 2005. Still live in Bathurst." His photo on the profile was taken more than 10 years earlier, when he lived with me—and he no longer resembled the picture. Kerrie contacted the website to advise them of James' history. Management replied that they could do nothing about him until he broke the site's rules.

Another Australian woman e-mailed me on February 13, 2009. "I came across Jim Montgomery on a website," she wrote. "I was nearly taken in until the kids did a Google search on him. He claims to be on a disability pension, but also claims to be a screenwriter and film writer and other things. I stopped all communication with him, but he has my phone number. I'm a little scared."

Five months later I heard from yet another Australian woman, Andrea Baldwinson.* "I have just had Jim visiting in my home for five days and am now very concerned," she wrote on July 8, 2009. "I had Googled him prior to his visit, but because there were hundreds of listings for James Montgomery, I got bored by page 30 and found nothing. I Googled him the day after he left under 'Jim Montgomery Bathurst Australia' and your site appeared. What a nightmare!"

Andrea Baldwinson, of Queensland, Australia, had been widowed for three years. Her husband was a sea captain and a genuine war hero, but he lost a long battle with lung cancer. Andrea had retired from her job as a coordinator of the local women's domestic violence refuge to care for him. For the last two years of his life, she hardly ever left the house.

Andrea was 62, and although no longer the stunning beauty of her youth, she was still a handsome woman. She was a statuesque 5 feet 9 inches tall, with strawberry blond hair that framed her face and drew attention to her clear blue eyes. Andrea's life was full of family, friends and clubs, but at times she felt lonely and bored. She wanted to add some excitement to her days.

Ignoring warnings about the perils of Internet dating, she joined the social networking site, Tagged.com. Tagged offered a game called "Pets," in which members "bought" and "sold" each other, all in fun. On March 15, 2009, Andrea invited a man named Jim Montgomery to join her circle of friends in the Pets game.

Jim first made sure none of Andrea's friends came from Nigeria or the Philippines—he didn't want to be involved with any scammers. Andrea assured him that all of her friends were legitimate. Jim joined, then invited Andrea to e-mail him at his private e-mail address. They started sending chatty notes to each other. Andrea liked Jim. He wasn't smutty like the other men on Tagged; he was sweet and respectful.

Before long, Jim was telling Andrea that he wanted to get close to her. He could tell from her personality, as expressed in her e-mails, that she was the woman he'd been waiting for all his life. Andrea thought Jim was moving too fast—after all, they were just corresponding over the Internet. Still, it was exciting. Maybe she wasn't too old. Maybe she would have another chance at love.

At the end of May, Jim asked Andrea to call him on the phone, and they really hit it off. Jim was interesting, charming and a terrific conversationalist. Andrea quickly fell into a pattern of calling him every night at 7 p.m., when she had free minutes on her phone. Their conversations lasted an hour or more.

Between the calls and their continued e-mail correspondence, Jim told Andrea all about himself. He started his rich and varied career in advertising—in fact, many years ago he and another man founded Grey Advertising in Australia. He lived all over the world—he especially enjoyed Portofino, Italy, where he'd love to take Andrea one day. He also floated around Paris in a hot-air balloon; he sent her a link to his online photo album, which included a picture of him in the balloon's gondola. (I took that photo on our second trip to Paris—the balloon never left the ground.)

Eventually, Jim said, he became a Hollywood scriptwriter. He claimed that he worked on *Star Trek,* and was directly responsible for the fact that, in the *Star Trek Voyager* series, the ship's captain was a woman. Jim was still writing scripts—one had recently been accepted in Hollywood, and he was awaiting payment. When it arrived, he'd be back on his feet financially.

Jim readily admitted that he was broke. He'd transitioned into education, he said, which was why he was Dr. Jim Montgomery. He was a millionaire when he was in China operating schools for students to learn English. But then the SARS (Severe Acute Respiratory Syndrome) epidemic struck, which, within a few weeks in early 2003, spread from Guangdong province in China to infect people around the world. To protect the health of his wife and daughter, Jim said, he immediately returned to Australia—losing most of the money he made in the schools. (He left China, but Kim and Janna remained.)

Jim secured a position at Charles Sturt University in Bathurst, where he was head of the literature department. After two years, he retired. Then, while jogging, he fell and broke his leg. Later he contracted the sometimes-fatal staph infection, MRSA (multidrug-resistant *Staphylococcus aureus*). While Jim was flat on his back, his wife, Kim Goodson, left him. She was angry that he brought her to China, so when she returned to America, she stole the rest of his money.

Andrea was horrified. How could any woman be so mean?

In one phone conversation, Jim mentioned his second wife. "How many wives have you had?" Andrea asked in surprise.

"Ah, I wish you hadn't asked me that," Jim replied.

"What, six?"

"No, five."

"Oh, my heavens."

Jim then launched into his marital history. He was married to his first wife, Pat, when he lived in London. (He was actually in Australia.) She had five children from her first marriage and decided to return to her former husband. His second wife, Kathleen Maloney, was a blond trophy wife. His third wife, Gale Lewis, was the only woman he ever really loved, and she died in his arms.

He married his fourth wife, me, on the rebound from Gale, when he was out of his mind with grief. I agreed to marry him because I wanted to have a child, and we tried, but I had fertility problems. I was stressed during the marriage and obsessed with having a baby, so our relationship quickly went downhill. Then, when I found out that he had succeeded in having a child with Kim Goodson, I became stark raving mad and hell bent on revenge.

Finally Jim married Kim, but only because of the child—there was no love between them at all. She left him without a thought while he lay dying of MRSA. Andrea, however, would be different. By mid-June 2009, Jim told Andrea that he wanted to spend the rest of his life with her.

"You have a history of marrying in haste and repenting at leisure," Andrea replied, dumbfounded. "So why make a sixth mistake?"

"I'm a very good judge of character," Jim assured her. "Even though I haven't yet met you, I know you are the one I've been looking for all my life."

"This is not real, Jim. This is just on the phone."

But Jim started sending her quotations that said to really know someone, it was important to know their minds. "That's what we've been doing," he said. "We've been getting to know each others' minds."

Jim also promised that they'd get to know each other physically. He hadn't had sex in four years, but was an accomplished lover, and hadn't forgotten how to please a woman. Once Jim asked Andrea if she'd ever been in a threesome. She hadn't, so Jim sent her an erotic bedtime story. The first line was: "Do you think he wants to fuck me?"

Called *The Bet,* the story had three characters—Jim, Andrea and Burton. Andrea was Jim's lover, and would only have an orgasm for him, no matter what Burton did. Once she got over the shock, Andrea had to admit the story was clever, although she doubted that Jim wrote it in one hour as he claimed. Still, she expressed her concerns that he was more sexually experienced than she was. Jim didn't send any more stories, but assured her that she would enjoy their lovemaking.

Andrea was intrigued enough to see what developed. Jim soon started talking about her coming to live with him in Bathurst. Andrea wasn't opposed to the idea, if their relationship worked out—it would bring her closer to her daughters, who lived in Sydney. But Andrea told him to slow down. Jim apologized, saying that he didn't want to lose her, but continued to make plans.

First, she'd come to live in his two-bedroom flat in Bathurst, although it sounded like it was already so crowded that Andrea wondered if there was room for her. Andrea wouldn't have to cook all the time, Jim said, because he was eligible for Meals on Wheels. He said the food was nice, cheap and nutritious. They'd stay there together until October, when his lease was up, and then they'd rent a place somewhere else.

"Why would I want to rent when I've got my own four-bedroom house?" Andrea asked.

"Well, between us, we could rent someplace really nice," James replied.

"I'd rather sell this place and buy another one."

"You don't want to buy. You're just buying trouble. You have to maintain a house. You have to worry about taxes. It's much easier to rent."

Well, no decisions needed to be made right away—the economy was bad, so it was a terrible time to put a house on the market. The only decision they made was that Jim would visit her.

Bathurst was more than 600 miles from Andrea's home, and Jim did not have a car or money. Andrea agreed to pay for a flight—she could afford it, and was willing to exchange a bit of cash for fun. Before she actually bought the ticket—in the name of Dr. Jim Montgomery—she researched him on Google, but found no references that appeared to match.

They excitedly talked on the phone about his upcoming visit. Jim would show her how to make proper Chinese food—did Andrea have a wok? She didn't, but went out and bought one, along with a steaming basket. Then Jim was afraid that, because of his computer equipment, his luggage would go over the weight limit. Could she buy him some Neutrogena T/Gel Daily Control Shampoo? Shaving gel for sensitive skin? And could they share toothpaste?

Wanting to be agreeable, and make her guest comfortable, Andrea bought everything that Jim asked for.

On a beautiful, cloudless day, June 27, 2009, Andrea waited, with a mixture of anticipation and nervousness, for Jim's flight to arrive. She was meeting him at the Hervey Bay Airport in Queensland. Hervey Bay was a lovely place to start his visit—a seaside resort with a subtropical climate, known for beaches, boating and whale watching.

Andrea recognized Jim from his photo—bald head, white moustache and beard—although he looked like he weighed 20 stone (280 pounds), which was a lot heavier than he said he was. Well, Jim wanted to lose weight, and they talked about going on the Low GI (Glycemic Index) Diet together. From their phone conversations, Andrea knew Jim was a dynamic and fun-loving man; she wasn't going to let a few extra pounds crush their good time.

"I'm so happy that you're here," she welcomed him.

"I told you I'd come," Jim replied. "This is just a continuation of what we already had."

They held hands at the baggage carousel while waiting for his luggage. Then Andrea drove to the Hervey Bay Boat Club for lunch. They sat in the warm sunshine on a deck, overlooking the marina, and Andrea gazed lovingly at the man who might become her beau. Jim, however, wouldn't look Andrea in the eye. His expression was not soft—it was cold and serious. He must be nervous, Andrea thought.

In the midst of this romantic setting, Jim took her right hand, and brought her pointer finger to his lips. Andrea thought he was going to kiss her fingertip. Instead, Jim stuck her finger in his mouth and moved it from side to side, so she could feel where his four front teeth were missing.

This was totally inappropriate. In fact, it was gross.

After lunch, which Andrea bought because Jim made no offer to pay, she drove them to the Palace Backpackers Memorial Museum in Childers. In 2000, the original Palace Hotel was burned by an arsonist and 15 backpackers died. A friend of Andrea's had been commissioned to paint a large painting to memorialize the deaths, and on the phone, Jim expressed an interest in seeing it. But when they got there, he could care less. He did, however, grab Andrea when they were alone in the elevator and stick his tongue into her mouth. It was not pleasant. His lips were hard and taut—he reminded Andrea of a lizard drinking.

"How bloody disappointing," she thought. Plus, his stomach was so large that she had to lean way forward to kiss him. A shorter woman would have no chance.

Andrea brought Jim home, where he soon was asleep on the couch in front of the television. Well, he'd been up since 4 a.m. to catch his flight; she could understand if he was tired. She planned to cook a nice dinner—a seafood stir-fry, using the prawns Jim asked her to buy that cost A\$26 per kilo. She'd serve the meal in her exquisite dining room, with wine, perhaps even candles. But as she was cooking the stir-fry in the wok, she heard Jim sing out from the lounge room:

"I hate vegetables. Just give me the prawns with some dip on a plate, and I'll eat it here in front of the TV."

Andrea gave Jim his prawns, and ate by herself in the kitchen.

Perhaps Jim would wake up refreshed the next morning—he was, after all, going to be 68 years old in two weeks. It didn't happen. The next day, Jim had no desire to get up and do anything. The only place he wanted to be was in front of Andrea's computer.

In the afternoon, Andrea dragged Jim away—one of her friends invited them to a barbecue lunch. They weren't there long when Andrea's friend looked at her quizzically—what was she doing with this overweight clod? Andrea made a face—she knew already that she wasn't interested in Jim Montgomery.

Andrea was terribly disappointed. In his e-mails and phone conversations, Jim was delightful, clever, interesting. What happened to that man? The person she met was nothing like the person she imagined from the telephone. He was not exciting. He was not dynamic. He was not attentive.

Noticing the collection of books in the home of Andrea's friend—many of them rare and expensive—Jim started talking about how his whole life was built on his ability with words. He became an advertising executive because of his ability with words, and then became a movie scriptwriter and producer because of his ability with words. He earned a lot of money because of his ability with words, and they took him all over the world. He knew a lot about books. He knew a lot about movies. And because of his scripts, everyone in Hollywood knew about him.

Andrea's friend had heard enough. "Oh, get over yourself, will you Jim?" she said. "Stop living in the past. We're not interested in what your past has been or what might have been. We're interested in what you are now."

What he was now, Andrea realized, was a boring old fart.

It was a long five days.

Andrea was horrified to find that Jim had set up his computer on her antique Queen Ann mahogany dining room table. He may have reasoned the table wasn't being used anyway—Jim ate every meal in front of the television, while Andrea ate alone in the kitchen. Andrea asked him to teach her Chinese cooking like he promised, but Jim couldn't be bothered. When they went out for meals, Andrea paid—not once did Jim offer to buy so much as a cup of coffee. He even asked Andrea to buy him cream donuts. She was horrified at that, too—a man with diabetes should not be eating cream donuts. But Jim pouted until she gave in and bought three of them, which he quickly consumed. And although Jim told Andrea he didn't drink, he became quite familiar with her liquor cabinet.

The visit wasn't totally one-sided. Jim gave Andrea a tie-died silk scarf and some laminated placemats, which he said he made at the Seymour Centre in Bathurst, a senior citizen home. The bus picked him up and brought him to the center on Tuesdays and Fridays. The placemats were decorated with pictures of Jim and a copy of a menu from the Titanic. They reminded Andrea of crafts a child would make in primary school.

They barely spoke. Not that they argued—Jim simply had no interest in anything Andrea had to say. One emotionless expression occupied his face. The man had no personality.

Sex was another disappointment. Despite all of Jim's bragging about his sexual prowess, he had a bad back and could hardly move in bed. And with his diabetes, his back wasn't the only thing that didn't work.

On the last full day of Jim's visit, Andrea went to see her mother, who suffered from dementia, in a nursing home. When she returned, Andrea and Jim sat on her sun deck—which Jim observed was bigger than his entire flat—eating the lunch he prepared. The next morning, Andrea would be driving Jim back to the airport. She couldn't wait.

Jim said he called his sister, Robin, who lived between Andrea's home and the airport. "We're going to meet her tomorrow morning. We'll leave early, and have coffee with her for half an hour."

"Oh, that's nice," Andrea replied.

"Also, I told her that I was up here on business, and I met you at a business meeting. So just go along with that, will you?"

Something snapped in Andrea—she was tired of his crap. "What did you tell her that for, Jim?"

"I didn't want her to know that I met you on the Internet. I was trying to protect you. I don't want you to be embarrassed about that."

"I'm not embarrassed. I don't care who knows how we met. You're not protecting me; you're protecting yourself." Andrea paused, and then continued. "You know, Jim, I don't like telling people lies. If lies come so easily to you when you're talking to your sister, I have to wonder how many lies you've told me."

Jim changed the subject, and eventually got around to what he really wanted to discuss. He was determined to get Andrea's commitment to live with him in Bathurst, and told her so.

"No," Andrea said. "I can't give you an answer at this stage."

"Why? Why can't you?"

Andrea chose her words carefully. Jim was beginning to remind her of the cases she dealt with in domestic violence. She didn't want to give him a reason to belt her. "Well, you sound too good to be true, Jim," she replied. "And things that sound too good to be true usually are."

Jim's demeanor changed dramatically. His face turned white, and he got very quiet. "What makes you think I'm too good to be true?" he demanded.

"Well, Jim, you do brag a lot, and you sound like a big nothing bullshit artist. I'm not saying you are one, but you're sailing pretty close to the wind."

"Tell me one thing that you don't believe. I'll prove it's true."

"No, I'm not saying any one of your things is untrue. I just said that's the feeling I get overall."

Jim's eyes glassed over. "Well you lied to me too," he countered. "You made out that you were a widow who was struggling financially, but it is obvious that you are not."

"Well I don't tell people on the Internet what my bank balance is. Anyway, what does it matter how much money I have? You aren't getting any of it."

Jim pushed his chair back from the table. The chair fell over, but he didn't pick it up. "If you loved me," he sulked, "you wouldn't say those sorts of things to me."

"Maybe I love you in spite of them."

Jim huffed into the house, and did not speak to Andrea for the rest of the day. That night, in bed, he turned his back on her.

The next morning, they did not see Jim's sister. "It's more important for us to get us sorted out," he said. For Andrea, there was nothing to sort out. She dropped Jim off at the airport, and couldn't get home fast enough.

As soon as Jim got home, he started romancing Andrea by phone and e-mail again, as if none of their confrontations over the past five days had occurred. Jim pretended that he was in love with Andrea, and Andrea was in love with him.

Andrea did not answer his calls and did not reply to his e-mails. For a few days, she agonized about how to break off the relationship—a relationship that she now knew was imaginary. Wondering what Jim's real story was, she tried Googling him once more, this time using the search term "Jim Montgomery Bathurst Australia."

Up popped Lovefraud: "James Montgomery of Australia claimed to be a Hollywood scriptwriter, a Special Forces commando, a successful entrepreneur. In reality, he was a con artist."

Reading my Lovefraud story, all Andrea could feel was deep, petrified shock. She left Jim alone in her house when she visited her mother! He got up at 4 a.m. while she slept! She feared that he rifled through her drawers and cabinets, looking for her bank statements and stock certificates. Andrea immediately called the banks and cancelled her passwords. But what about her stock shares? All Jim had to do was forge her signature and he could steal them. She visited the fraud squad at the police station, but they could do nothing until he tried to defraud her in some way.

Jim, in the meantime, deluged her with calls, text messages and e-mails, which Andrea continued to ignore:

From: ceoiice
Subject: Bad night

But I suspect we are both hurting.
What we both had was special for different reasons. I don't under-

stand how whatever you think I did was so bad you couldn't at least talk
to me about it.

Andy, please talk to me ... I am not whatever you now think I
am ... Our relationship is some 55 days long — for some 53 days I had
no idea that you had more money than an average person ... I have not
made love to anyone except my ex some four plus years ago ... I have
no idea what I could have done ... If it is something involving my ex-wife
#4 - she is stark raving mad.

Andy, please talk to me.

Earlier that same day, Andrea first contacted me by e-mail. I replied immediately. "Yes, get rid of him," I wrote. "Since at least 1989, Montgomery's main source of income has been women who he convinced to 'invest' in his projects. You are the fifth woman from Australia to contact me after having found my website."

Andrea and I continued to correspond, and the more she told me about her experience with James Montgomery, the more I howled with laughter. He was living from week to week on his pension! He didn't have a car! He fell while jogging so he wasn't able to exercise—James probably hadn't jogged since high school! He was estranged from his family! He was a boring old fart and didn't have any go in him at all! He had no teeth! He couldn't get it together in bed! He was making tie-dyed scarves at the senior citizen center! He got his food from Meals on Wheels!

I wanted to be sensitive to Andrea's emotions—I knew first-hand how upsetting it was to learn that everything I once believed was a lie. But after a few days, I just had to tell her that I was laughing my ass off. "He's a toothless old fart with no friends, no relatives and no one to swindle," I wrote. "How the mighty have fallen!"

"I am so pleased to know that what I am passing on to you about Jim is giving you a laugh," Andrea replied. "You deserve it, lady!!" Then she printed out the line—"He's a toothless old fart ..."—and stuck it on her computer screen to remind her not to respond when Jim sent his pleading e-mails.

Andrea warned all of Jim's friends on Tagged.com, and sent them links to Lovefraud. They all deleted him as a friend, and put scammer alerts on his profile. Then Tagged closed his account.

Finally, on July 21, 2009, Andrea sent a short message to the four e-mail addresses she had for Jim Montgomery, requesting that he never contact her again. If he did, the police would charge him with stalking.

Jim Montgomery replied:

At least I now know that "we" are to be victims of Donna's
attempts to bring me down. Surely if I had committed a fraction of what
she claimed I would have been charged; my record anywhere in the
world is clean except for a couple of speeding tickets in the sixties.

Andy - I never scammed you - what grew out of months of telephone calls was real - I never asked you for anything other than to consider a life where we shared the basics and to really care for each other.

Again, Andrea ignored him. Finally, Jim left her alone.

One way or another, the women I came to know because of James Montgomery moved on with their lives. Sylvia Banning finally did get her divorce, and her two children went to college, with much of their tuition paid by scholarships. Kathleen Maloney kept her home, and gradually chipped away at the debt James left her. Jody McClure was happily married for a few years, then she died peacefully in her sleep. Colleen Jessick became executive story consultant for a sci-fi television show, which earned her enough money to buy a home and focus on writing a fantasy trilogy, and a book about her pug.

The Internet was the tool that James used to snag me, Sylvia and many other women; the Internet was how I found him; and in the end, the Internet brought him down. It also kept him down. Nearly five years after he was exposed in Australia, James moved from Bathurst to Katoomba, New South Wales, about 50 miles away. He tried to pass himself off as a war hero and join the Katoomba Returned and Services League. An authentic vet became suspicious, checked ANZMI.net, and James was in the new again: *Alleged military fraud reappears in NSW* proclaimed the Sydney Morning Herald on April 29, 2010.

Lovefraud.com exposed James Montgomery as a con artist, and prevented at least four women from becoming new victims. But this turned out to be a minor accomplishment.

In the five years since my website went live, the number of visits to Lovefraud climbed to 3,000 per day. I received hundreds of e-mails and phone calls thanking me for the information that I provided. The people who wrote to me thought they were going crazy—how could someone proclaim their love, yet lie continuously, cheat prolifically, steal their money, abuse them physically and emotionally, and then accuse the recipient of all this "love" of being insane, untrusting and paranoid? I heard from people who turned themselves inside out, often for decades, trying to understand and accommodate the perpetrator. Then they found Lovefraud, and suddenly there was an explanation for all the torment they suffered: They were involved with a sociopath.

Lovefraud turned on the lights—making sense of the nonsensical, offering suggestions for escaping the impossible drama. Then, to my surprise, Lovefraud grew into something more. It became a healing community.

It happened because of the Lovefraud Blog. In addition to my weekly articles, I invited other people who knew the devastation of a sociopath to become regular contributors. Sometimes I published letters that readers sent in about their experiences. Other readers responded with comments, posed questions and told their own stories. People began commenting on the comments, having online conversations with each other to offer encouragement and advice. The blog evolved into an online support group of people from all over the world who understood exactly what each other had gone through, because they'd gone through the same trauma.

I was amazed and gratified at the good that Lovefraud was doing, as evidenced by the hundreds of e-mails I received, like this one:

When I first found your site two-and-a-half years ago, I was at the lowest point in my life. I had no one to talk to, or no one that understood what had happened to me. At that time, I had pretty much decided that life was just not worth living anymore. I had all my affairs in order, and had given up. None of my kids realize just how close they came to not having a parent. My church saved me spiritually. Your site has saved me mentally and emotionally. It is the first thing I read in the morning, and the last thing I read at night. I have gained so much from reading here. You literally saved my life. I am forever thankful to you and this site for all the help you give to all of us victims. God bless you for all you do.

None of this would have been possible without my husband, Terry Kelly. He believed in me, and provided the financial backing to transform Lovefraud.com from an idea to reality. He became my biggest cheerleader and my foremost source of encouragement.

Terry was my pal, my confidante and my lover. Unlike when I was with James, it was easy to buy Valentines, birthday and anniversary cards for him, because I truly felt the mushy sentiments those Hallmark writers crafted—and so did he. We enjoyed being with each other, whether we were riding on a jet ski, painting our new kitchen, vacationing in Florida or California, or simply having another terrific dinner at home. I continued to feed him straight lines, and he continued to make me laugh. Our physical passion kept burning. Our love was real, and it was easy.

I wrote about our relationship in a Lovefraud Blog article:

Lessons after the sociopath: Real love is easy

In posts to this blog, and in e-mails that I receive, many Lovefraud readers wonder, after the devastation of a sociopath, if they can love again.

Yes, you can.

I am living proof. In February 2000, I was divorced from James Montgomery, who took a quarter of a million dollars from me, cheated throughout our brief two-and-a-half year relationship, had a child with another woman while married to me, and then married that woman 10 days after I left him, committing bigamy. I was devastated.

After I left Montgomery, I had one nice relationship with a man, although it didn't turn out to be permanent. He was normal, not disordered, and supportive of me. I was sad when the relationship ended, but it was a step along my path toward healing.

Then, in April 2001, I met Terry Kelly. We married in 2005. We are totally happy and in love. Here is something that I've learned from my new marriage: Real love is easy.

Signs of real love

In real love, there are no mind games. There is no manipulation. There are no guilt-producing accusations like, "Don't you trust me?" or "Who are you sleeping with?" There is no pleading to be forgiven, no promises to never do it again, because there are no violations of trust that require forgiveness.

I do not wonder if my husband really loves me, because I know he does. I can feel it.

Here's what you get in a true, loving relationship: Enjoyment of each other's company. Honest caring for each other. Consideration of each other's feelings. Real partnership—not a one-sided deal, with you as the giver and the other as the taker.

Sure, there are problems that need to be solved. Guess what? Issues are resolved and life goes on. There is no drama.

I will say this—after the disaster of a marriage to a sociopath, I am highly appreciative of my new husband. He, too, was previously married, and although his ex wasn't malicious, the relationship had become empty. So we both appreciate each other. In fact, we find joy in each other.

Making the transition

So how does this happen? How do you make the transition from wounded victim to a whole person ready for love?

As I've written before, I believe your emotional pain needs to be processed. When my heart was broken, it allowed all the trauma from my bad marriage, and all the pent-up pain from other disappointments in my life, to be released. Slowly, over time, it came flowing out, through tears, yelling, screaming and punching pillows.

You don't want to inflict this display on other people—my releases were witnessed only by my therapist and my dog. And they really upset the dog.

The emotional release takes time, because we all have many layers of pain. But as the negative energy dissipates, there is room in your being for something else. That something else is love.

So if you're in recovery after a run-in with a sociopath, give yourself time and permission to heal. Trust that you've learned the red flags of personality disorders, and by listening to your instincts, you won't be deceived again. Believe that love is possible, and someday, it will find you.

While writing this book, I reviewed my years and years of journal entries, the majority of which lamented my inability to get a date. Back on August 5, 1992, as I was just beginning the journey, I wrote a description of the man I wanted: Youthful, six feet or taller, good physical condition, great lover, good career, wide range of interests, ethical, spiritual, fun, calm, self-confident, likes the beach and loves me (page 51). In Terry Kelly, the universe gave me gave me exactly what I asked for.

When I told my husband that he'd be in the book, he was totally surprised. "Why am I in the book?" he asked.

"Because, Terry," I said, smiling and giving him a kiss, "you're the happy ending."

Epilogue

In December 1990, long before I ever met James Montgomery, a psychic told me that I would embark on a spiritual journey. She was right.

Wondering why my life was so empty, I sought answers in the self-help and New Age sections of bookstores, through positive thinking tapes and from spiritual counselors. By the time James Montgomery showed up in my life, I was somewhat in touch with my higher self, and aware of metaphysical concepts such as reincarnation and the support available to us from unseen beings.

Then came the lies, fraud and betrayal—and the acceleration of my spiritual journey. I resisted it. As my life fell apart, the last thing that I wanted to hear was that the trauma was for my own good. But living through the devastation of my marriage to the sociopath, and the assistance I received from those unseen beings, whom I called "Guidance," eventually brought me the clarity, peace and love that I wanted all along.

So what did I learn?

1. We are all one, we are all one with God, and God is love.

All life in the universe is interconnected: All human souls, including those on Earth and on the Other Side. All animals and plants, like my dog, Beau, and the orchid that bloomed when he passed. All angels and spirit guides. All aspects of God and love, because God is love.

Anytime we feel love, we feel the magnificence of God.

Unfortunately, most of us have forgotten that we are all one, and that we are one with God. Our objective on Earth is to remember, find our way back to God and feel the love of the universe.

God loves and trusts us all, and knows that we will each return to wholeness in our own time. That's why God does not interfere with the choices we make using our free will, even when the choices damage ourselves and others.

2. We come into life with a plan for what we want to learn.

Each of us is responsible for our own journey back to God. Before we are born, we draw up a plan of what we want to experience in this life to enhance our spiritual growth.

My soul wanted to be free of James Montgomery.

I'd been tangling with his soul during multiple lifetimes over 2,000 years. All the lifetimes that I glimpsed were traumatic—at his hand, I was beaten, raped, injured and killed. My soul wanted to end it.

Guidance knew this, although in my human incarnation, I'd forgotten. So the unseen beings helped me follow my spiritual plan. We all have free will, and can make life choices that will either abide by our plans or diverge from them. When I suspected James was lying to me and cheating on me, and pleaded for advice on what to do, Guidance told me to stay with my husband and continue to love him. They even gave those same messages to Elaine Anderson, my spiritual counselor, to relay to me. Why? Because I had not yet reached the point where I could spiritually break free of him.

And how was I to break free? By giving up the struggle.

During all those lifetimes, I kept trying to reform James, or beat him at his own game, or regain what he had taken from me. When he defrauded me in this lifetime, I relentlessly pursued him, first in divorce court, then with my judgment. I wanted him to make me whole.

I failed. Eventually, I had no choice but to give up, let go and viscerally understand that none of it mattered. With that, I achieved my spiritual objective.

My marriage to James Montgomery looks like a terribly stupid mistake in human terms, but it was the learning opportunity that my soul craved.

3. Our internal energy creates our life experiences.

Many people in New Age and positive thinking circles talk about the "Law of Attraction"—the idea that we create our experience with our thoughts. If we believe it, we can have it. Like attracts like; what we are within is what we manifest in our lives.

This is all true. However, it is important to recognize that the process is not limited to the thoughts upon which we consciously focus. The process also reflects the condition of our energy fields.

We are all composed of energy, called the auric field. Researchers in human auras identify seven layers of energy that incorporate and extend beyond our physical bodies. These energy fields stay with us over multiple lifetimes. Therefore, traumatic experiences in our past lives create disturbances that may be stuck in our energy fields and follow us into our current lives. We all have them—human history is filled with pain, suffering, deceit, treachery and tragedy.

These disturbances, even when we are not aware of them, affect our life experiences. In fact, they may overwhelm our efforts to engage in positive thinking—especially if our souls have selected difficult lessons to learn. That's one reason why psychics kept telling me that I would find James' money. The lesson that I'd chosen was much harder on Earth than it looked from the Other Side. The psychics were conveying messages of hope just so I could keep going through the trials. Perhaps, if I were better able to focus on the positive, I could have created more of the experiences that were predicted. Or maybe not—my soul had its own agenda.

Clearing away the negative energy enables us to feel, and employ, the power of the universe. Then we can create the lives we truly want. Guidance can nudge us and show us opportunities, but we actually determine what happens to us through our energy. We are the creators.

4. Through pain comes healing.

I had many past life traumas related to James Montgomery that were calcified in my energetic field. My soul wanted to be rid of them. Breaking down these energetic structures, however, is difficult. The key tool for doing it, in my case, was emotional pain.

Take, for example, the disappointment I felt over not being able to make a romantic connection. Relationship after relationship failed. Then came James Montgomery, who promised me the great love I pined for. But his words of love were lies; his objective in marrying me was to take my money. When I was forced to accept the vileness of his intentions, my disappointment expanded and compounded until it was so big and unbearable that it finally burst and poured out of me. I cracked open, released the pain, and was then able to bring true love into my life.

Pain is our indication of energetic disturbances that need to be released. And the pain usually comes from mistaken beliefs that we are isolated, poor, unlovable or unworthy.

5. Healing our hearts is always the answer.

When our hearts are numb or broken—both of which I experienced—it is difficult to bring circumstances of joy and love into our lives. At these times, our most important task is to heal our hearts so we can feel the love of the universe.

To do this, we need to release our internal burdens. We must stop worrying about how things will turn out, and trust that the universe will support us. We must let go of the hatred for having been wronged, because hatred impedes our own progress. We must give up our expectations, because expectations actually limit our options, preventing us from seeing opportunities when they arise.

Then we must find joy in our lives wherever we can. Any moment of joy—no matter how small—draws opportunities and miracles. When something good does happen, we need to be grateful. Gratitude enables us to receive even more gifts from the universe.

6. Sociopaths are predators.

In the midst of pursuing my judgment against James Montgomery, as fear of bankruptcy consumed me, I suddenly felt, grudgingly, gratitude toward my ex-husband. I was still outraged at his actions. But I recognized that his betrayal enabled me to bring my deeply buried pain to the surface.

Many Lovefraud readers have noticed the same phenomenon—as devastated as they are over the actions of sociopaths in their lives, they emerged on the other side of the experience stronger and wiser.

So should we thank sociopaths? Let them off the hook?

No. They are predators and they should be punished for their actions.

Sociopaths have blackened their hearts, extinguished all love, and forgotten their connections to God. They believe they are superior, and cling to the belief, no matter how much damage it causes themselves and the people they exploit.

But sociopaths cannot survive without victims. As more people become enlightened, sociopaths will entice fewer and fewer takers for their games. Faced with less success, they will need to find another way, which may be the opening for divine grace to enter their lives. Eventually, after many lifetimes, they may find their way back to God.

Although I learned about sociopaths the hard way, we don't all have to be crushed in order to grow. Awareness of the predators, and of our vulnerabilities, can help us avoid them. For protection against the deceit of the sociopaths, we should examine ourselves, discovering our own weaknesses. The very act of examination can start the healing process. It enables us to work on healing our trust, and realize where we have forgotten our relationship with God.

7. God's plan is messy, but it works.

Each soul must find its own way back to God. God does not care how long it takes. God does not care how many mistakes a soul makes. The only requirement is that the soul freely chooses to return to the unified whole. We all have access to God. We can all have a personal relationship with God at any time.

So how does a soul return to God? There are billions of answers to the question, because there are billions of souls. Each has its individual journey. Life is messy, but the love of God, and the unity of the universe, can absorb it all.

Sometimes we don't believe this, and we righteously think that we know a better way. I quarreled with God—why were there sociopaths? Why were they allowed to continue to hurt and destroy people?

The answer was that individual souls had lessons to learn.

The purpose of everything that happens on Earth is individual growth. If we want speed up our return to wholeness, we just need to stop worrying, release our fears and trust the plan.

When I finally did exactly that, I found peace, contentment and love.

To see photos and video related to this story,
and for discussion of the ideas in this book,
please visit:
www.lovefraud.com/book